AN INTRODUCTION TO ARISTOTLE'S ETHICS

AN INTRODUCTION TO ARISTOTLE'S ETHICS

BOOKS I-IV

WITH A CONTINUOUS ANALYSIS AND NOTES

Intended for the use of Beginners and junior Students

EDWARD MOORE, D.D.

GYAN

Published by

Gyan Publishing House
5, Ansari Road
Daryaganj, New Delhi-110002
Phone: 011-47034999, 9811692060
E-mail: books@gyanbooks.com

Distribution Network
gyanbooks.com
India, USA, Canada, UK, Australia, France

ISBN: 978-81-212-8983-2 (PB)
First Published, 1871

2nd Impression 2023

Printed at: Gyan Press, Delhi.

AN INTRODUCTION TO ARISTOTLE'S ETHICS

AUTHOR: EDWARD MOORE

AN INTRODUCTION TO

ARISTOTLE'S ETHICS

AN INTRODUCTION TO

ARISTOTLE'S ETHICS

BOOKS I—IV.

(BOOK X. CH. VI—IX. IN AN APPENDIX)

WITH A CONTINUOUS ANALYSIS AND NOTES

Intended for the use of Beginners and Junior Students

BY THE

REV. EDWARD MOORE, D.D.

PRINCIPAL OF S. EDMUND HALL, OXFORD, AND LATE FELLOW AND TUTOR OF QUEEN'S COLLEGE

FOURTH EDITION, REVISED

RIVINGTONS

WATERLOO PLACE, LONDON

MDCCCXC

CONTENTS.

BOOK IV.

APPENDIX.--BOOK X.

PREFACE.

The object of this work is to provide a simple introduction to the subject of the Ethics for beginners generally, and especially for those who are commencing it with a view to the Oxford Final Examination. It may also perhaps be found useful in the Upper Forms of Public Schools. The chief aim throughout has been clearness and simplicity, even at the risk of occasional repetition and diffuseness. Technical phraseology has been as far as possible avoided, and the principal technical terms occurring are explained in a Glossary.

The author hopes that this specific object of the work will be borne in mind throughout the whole of it.

Thus the Introductory Sketch, which simply aims at giving a beginner an intelligent notion of the subject upon which he is entering, makes no pretence to be exhaustive. Several important systems and writers are omitted altogether. The object has been to select systems which have a distinct (perhaps one-sided) character: such as are typical of some well-defined bias or direction of thought. In fact names and references have been added in the notes almost as an afterthought, to give the clue to further inquiry to those who may desire it.

In the Glossary likewise, the explanations given of some of the more important technical terms of Aristotle's philosophy are altogether popular and rudimentary. To have attempted anything like an adequate account of such difficult words as ἀρχή, φύσις, ψυχή, δύναμις, etc., would have defeated the purpose of the work altogether, and repelled those for whose benefit it is intended.

The same considerations must serve as an apology for language sometimes consciously loose and unphilosophical in the Analysis and Notes. The attempt to put such a treatise as that of Aristotle into such a 'modern' light as may be intelligible to a reader *ex hyp.* unacquainted with philosophical phraseology, seems necessarily to involve the sacrifice of technical accuracy. This desire to appeal as far as possible to modern sympathies has occasioned a certain amount of diffuseness in parallel quotations from recent popular writers.

The best thanks of the author are due to several friends who have kindly assisted him by their advice in various parts of the work: and he will feel grateful for any further criticisms or suggestions that may be offered to him.

ıe difficulty of the task has become more apparent on ɜr acquaintance with it, and this experiment is now made c not without hesitation and a full consciousness of its tive execution.

ƐDMUND HALL, OXFORD,
June 1871.

PREFACE TO SECOND EDITION.

NEW edition of this work being now called for, I take opportunity of introducing several corrections, and ng considerable additions to the Glossary and Notes.

The additional matter (except in the case of actual corrections or obvious improvements of detail) has been for the most part either embodied in the Glossary or collected in 'Supplementary Notes and Illustrations.'

The reasons for adopting this method have been (1) to disturb as little as possible the existing arrangement of Text, Analysis, and Footnotes; (2) to admit of the occasional introduction of discussions and references, which may make the Book (as I venture to hope) more useful to a higher class of Students, especially in the earlier stages of their acquaintance with so difficult an author as Aristotle; (3) to allow of a considerable enlargement of the illustrations from modern authors. This kind of illustration, while interesting to all students, is, I believe, especially valuable for Passmen, because calculated to impart something of a living interest to what they are apt to consider as empty formulæ, and mere 'dry bones' of speculation. Most of these illustrations are from Shakespeare, as it seems to me that the numerous and striking coincidences between these two of the greatest observers of human nature and life are especially instructive from the certainty of their complete independence. I have also allowed myself some liberty in introducing illustrations from Dante for the opposite reason, that his phraseology and theories are, so to speak, saturated with Aristotelian language and lore. We can thus trace the influence on one of the greatest minds, intellectual and imaginative, that the world has yet seen, of one whom he regarded as his master and guide both in Speculative and Practical Philosophy, of one who was to him not only '*il Maestro di color che sanno*,' but also '*il Maestro di nostra vita.*'

I am indebted to several friends for kindly suggesting corrections and improvements. My especial thanks are due to the Rev. J. R. Magrath, Senior Fellow and Tutor of Queen's College, for much valuable advice and assistance throughout the work.

E. M.

S. Edmund Hall, Oxford,
October 1877.

INTRODUCTION.

Much difficulty is sometimes felt, especially by beginners, in distinguishing the spheres of Ethical and Religious teaching. A dilemma like that which traditionally proved fatal to the Alexandrian library represents not inaptly the feeling with which the Science of Ethics is regarded in its relations to Religion. It is thought that if its conclusions agree with those of Religion they are superfluous, if they differ from them they are wicked. We will first then endeavour to gain a clear conception of the purpose and limits of the Science of Ethics, as contrasted with those of Religion.

We may consider this and kindred sciences to have their origin somewhat as follows.

Man is obviously compounded of two distinct natures, which may be roughly described as Body and Soul. He desires to know more of each of these natures. The nature of his Body is investigated by the Science of Physiology, which reveals to him that it is composed of Bones, Nerves, Muscles, etc. His Soul (using the word broadly for the immaterial side of man's nature) is similarly discovered by the Science of Psychology to contain Reasoning, Imaginative (or Artistic), Moral, and other powers. Further inquiries in each of these last-named departments give rise to the practical Sciences of

Logic, Æsthetics, Ethics, etc., which are *Sciences* because their main object is to ascertain the laws and facts of these several portions of our compound nature; *practical* because the enunciation of these laws and facts, when discovered, constitutes *ipso facto* practical rules for the direction of the faculties to which the investigation refers. In each case notice that the process is one of a careful but simple observation of *facts*, followed by a judicious enunciation of the laws which bind those facts together. In a word the method is what logicians call Inductive. This cannot be too clearly insisted upon. Let us therefore explain it a little more fully in each of the cases mentioned. The primary object of Logic is to ascertain under what laws, principles, limits, men do, *as a matter of fact*, reason and think. The statement of these laws becomes the groundwork of practical rules for reasoning. The primary object of Æsthetics is to ascertain what constitutes, *as a matter of fact*, good and bad taste in art of all kinds according to the decision of those competent to judge. The enunciations of these principles become the practical rules to which the Sculptor, Artist, Poet must conform. So, lastly, the primary object of Ethics is to ascertain *as a matter of fact*, what are the principles, feelings, or motives which regulate men's conduct as *moral* agents, what *is* the distinction which men do actually draw between Right and Wrong? by what faculty or faculties are they enabled to draw such a distinction? on what sanction do such distinctions rest? The answers to such questions, when formulated, become *ipso facto* practical rules for the conduct of life. But in all these cases the practical rules are as it were adjuncts to the science strictly so called. The main object of the science is to discover, and group under general laws, the *facts* in each department of human nature, by the ordinary powers of accurate observation. It is due to the nature of the subject-matter in each case that the facts when formulated become practical rules. Now we see how the spheres of Ethics and Religion do not interfere. The object of Ethics is to ascertain the facts of a certain department of human nature so far as they are matters of observation. Practical rules of conduct are secondary, and in a manner accidental. On the other hand the main object of Religion is generally thought to be to provide us with practical rules of conduct and an adequate sanction for obeying them. The discovery of facts of, or theories about, our moral nature is in this case what is secondary and accidental. Again, if Science (whether Ethics or any other Science) accepts a proposition as true which does not rest upon observation but on authority, it ceases so far to be Science. On the other hand Religion, or at least revealed Religion (and it is about this only that we are now speaking), often claims our obedience on the grounds of the authority to which it can appeal. Consequently the aim, the purpose, the fundamental principles, of Religion and Ethics are perfectly distinct. One does not supersede or clash with the other. It is now a trite saying that Revelation is not meant to teach us Physical Science; it is equally true that it is not designed to teach us Ethical or Moral Science.

Let us now suppose the Science of Ethics started on its independent career. What will be the main question or questions which it will seek to answer? It finds mankind, as a matter of fact, approving, and, as it would seem, instinctively approving, certain actions, and condemning others. Not, be it observed, the same actions universally. Very far from it. But it finds the same sentiment of approbation and disapprobation however variously applied in detail; a sentiment which is reflected in language by the words Right and Wrong.

And (to recur for a moment to the question above discussed) these phenomena are just as conspicuous when revealed religion is unknown: they are indeed in that case more important, scientifically speaking. They arise independently of religion, and therefore call for a solution independent of it. What then are these notions of Right and Wrong, asks the Science of Ethics, which, apart from external aid and instruction, the human mind spontaneously and universally recognises? What is the exact meaning of the distinction? What precisely constitutes the difference between Right and Wrong in actions? Further, by what faculty or faculties do we recognise it? Again, by what motive are we impelled to regulate our practice by these notions? What is the nature and sanction of the Feeling of Duty? Or once more, as Aristotle himself puts the question, What is the Chief Good for man? What is the ultimate aim of all his efforts and aspirations? What is he living for? What is he hoping to attain to?

Such are the main problems which present themselves for solution to the Science of Ethics, and they arise (let it be noticed) from observation of the actual facts and phenomena of that department of human nature with which the

Science in question is concerned. We will reduce them to these four questions:

1. What constitutes the difference between Right and Wrong *in actions?*
2. What is the faculty *in ourselves* which is able to recognise that difference?
3. What is the nature of the feeling of Duty or Moral Obligation?
4. What is the 'Chief Good,' or ultimate aim of human action?

A brief account of the answers that have been given to each of these questions by the best known systems of Moral Philosophy will serve as a general introduction to the subject before us.

I. The various answers given to this question reduce themselves to two types. One is that Right and Wrong may be resolved into manifestations of some other familiar notions, such as (*e.g.*) Advantageous and Disadvantageous. The other is that they cannot be resolved at all, but are ultimate ideas which are incapable of analysis. The former systems may be called Utilitarian[1] systems of Morality, because they consider the

[1] *Note.*—Owing to the difficulty of finding one word to include all systems non-Intuitive, I use Utilitarian here and elsewhere in this Introduction in its widest sense, to include all Systems which reduce Virtue to a question of Utility or Advantage whether it be of one's-self only, or of others only, or of one's-self and others conjointly. These are sometimes distinguished as Selfish, Benevolent, and Utilitarian Systems respectively.

recognition of Right and Wrong to depend upon a calculation of Utility or Advantage. The latter are called Intuitive Systems because they refer the perception of Right and Wrong to a special faculty which simply approves and disapproves without being able always, or even usually, to assign its reasons: in other words to an *Intuitive* Faculty. But we must not encroach upon our second question. We will now therefore illustrate these two divergent theories as to the nature of Right and Wrong in themselves.

(A) Utilitarian Systems.

(α) Some assert that all Morality is a thinly-disguised selfishness, that man has and can have, no motive for action but self-interest[1], and that even benevolence, gratitude, and love are but forms of the desire of power, the wish to exhibit our superiority, the appreciation of possible advantages to be derived from the goodwill of others. (β) Others again that virtuous actions are simply the observance of the varying enactments of law, framed at first by the rulers in their own

[1] Hobbes, Mandeville, La Rochefoucauld, etc. Take as a specimen Hobbes's account of Love—'a conception a man hath of his need of the person desired.' Or Mandeville's statement that 'men do not really admire such actions as those of Regulus or Decius, but only observe that men of such dispositions are very useful for the defence of any state, and therefore by panegyrics, etc., encourage such tempers in others.' Or La Rochefoucauld (Maxime 264): 'Pity is a clever foresight of ills into which we may ourselves fall. We assist others in order to secure their services for ourselves under similar circumstances: and the services we render are strictly speaking conferred upon ourselves in advance'!

interest[1], and observed afterwards by others from fear of civil punishments or hope of rewards, *i.e.* from a calculation of self-interest. (γ) Others[2], that 'honesty is found by experience to be the best policy,' that virtue conduces to health of body, and peace of mind, that it secures the honour and goodwill of society, and, as some add[3], above all the friendship and goodwill of Heaven. Hence taking a far-sighted view of their best interests in this world, and still more, regarding the overwhelming balance in favour of virtue in the probable arrangements of the next, men prudently choose virtue and avoid vice. (δ) A more refined system[4] teaches us that human nature is by its very constitution endowed with so strong a feeling of sympathy that it cannot but experience pleasure and pain at the happiness and misery of others, and that it is thus impelled to strive after what makes for the general welfare, to dislike whatever has a contrary tendency; and that this

[1] The ancient Sophists, Hobbes, Mandeville, etc. *e.g.* Hobbes says, 'The notions of right and wrong, justice and injustice, have there (*i.e.* in a state of nature) no place. Where there is no common power, there is no law, where no law, no injustice.'

[2] Butler to some extent—See especially *Anal.* pt. I. c. iii.—though his Utilitarianism is qualified by the frequent assertion that 'duty' and 'conscience' are really supreme, yet 'Conscience and self-love, if we understand our true happiness, always lead us the same way. Duty and interest are perfectly coincident,' etc. See Summary at the close of Sermon iii.

[3] Especially Paley.

[4] Hume and Hutcheson maintain that Right is what conduces to Utility in general, as contrasted with mere personal and selfish Utility, as Hobbes would say. Hume, Adam Smith, and Bentham in different ways connected these opposing theories through the medium of the feeling of Sympathy.

instinct of sympathy overrides the instinct of self-interest: in a word, that Right is that which tends to produce the greatest aggregate amount of happiness, 'the greatest happiness of the greatest number;' Wrong, the reverse of this. (ε) Finally we ought to notice a theory[1] which serves as a sort of connecting link between the Utilitarian and Intuitive systems—viz., that originally Virtue was chosen for its advantages, but that soon it came to be sought without a conscious sense of the advantage to be derived from it. It had been found from the first so uniformly to be advantageous that the calculation whether it was so in any special case was omitted, and virtue as such, and so apparently for its own sake, was chosen. Just in the same way that money is sought after, first with a view to its use, and then, as the habit of hoarding grows, for its own sake, and without any thought of using it.

Such are some of the answers given by various systems of Ethics, which resolve Right and Wrong into some form of Utility or the reverse. We pass on now to the

(B) Intuitive Systems.

The following will serve as specimens of this type of solutions. It is said that Right and Wrong are distinctions *sui generis.* They cannot be further analysed or explained. They differ from any other notion as much, for example, as Light differs from Sound. All we can do is to recognise them and accept them simply as we do the phenomena of Light, Sound, etc. Thus Right is something which commends itself necessarily and naturally to us. To explain this (α) some

[1] Hartley, Mackintosh.

maintain that it exhibits a certain propriety, and an accordance with 'the fitness of things'[1] which we cannot choose but recognise, though we cannot analyse the feeling, or explain the grounds of our approbation. The distinction between Right and Wrong would thus be eternal and invariable. (β) Or if 'accordance with the fitness of things' be thought vague and beyond the reach of verification, at least it is said there is in Right and Wrong a conformity or suitableness (and the reverse) to the *nature of Man*[2] in the truest sense and highest development of that nature; very much in the way that fresh and bracing air is naturally wholesome to our bodily constitutions provided they are in a sound and healthy state, or that certain tastes and smells are agreeable *to us*, whatever they may be to other animals or organisms, from some suitableness to our organs of sense which we are unable to explain.

Thus these and similar systems regard the distinction between Right and Wrong as a specific and essential difference in the nature of things, which we must simply recognise *as a fact*, just as for instance we recognise the contrast between Hot and Cold, Black and White, Bitter and Sweet.

It is no part of our purpose to criticise the merits of these several systems, but only to state them in outline: we will therefore now proceed to our second question, viz. :—

II. By what faculty in ourselves is the distinction between Right and Wrong recognised?

The answers given to this question fall under two general

[1] Cudworth, Clarke. Plato's 'Ideal' System. [*e.g.* Plato in the *Euthyphron* contends that a quality or act is not holy because it is loved by the gods, but is loved by the gods because it is holy.]

[2] Butler.

types, as is pointed out by Hume. The one, that the recognition of Right and Wrong is derived from Reason; the other, that it is derived from Sentiment. To these may be added the view which Hume himself maintains, that 'Reason and Sentiment concur in almost all moral determinations and conclusions.' To illustrate these types:—

Those who (as we have seen) maintain that Right and Wrong consist in an immutable 'conformity to the nature of things' hold further that Reason in general (*i.e.* Intuitive Reason), or a special department of Reason (*i.e.* Practical Reason), is the faculty by which such distinctions become known to us[1].

Those who refer the origin of the notions of Right and Wrong to Sentiment in some form or another may again be divided into two classes, (1) those who trace it to some already recognised Sentiment, such as Self-Love or the Desire of Utility; and (2) those who assert that the notions of Right and Wrong, being primary and fundamental notions, require a special sense or faculty for their recognition. The latter class, with whom we are chiefly concerned, argue somewhat as follows. Looking at the case of our bodily senses we observe that differences of Colour, Sound, Taste, Smell, Touch, can only be appreciated each by a special sense. If any of those senses be wanting the distinction of objects corresponding to it is lost. One sense cannot do the work of another, except perhaps in a very slight degree and by artificial training. Thus each sense has a special and appropriate object of its own. Another characteristic of the Senses is

[1] Cudworth, Clarke, Whewell, etc.

that they are 'Intuitive,' *i.e.* they tell us *as a fact* that one object is green, another red, that one sound is loud, another soft, and so on; but they cannot say *why* the rose is red or the leaf green, much less inform us as to the essential distinction in the nature of things between red and green. Here then we have an exact parallel (it is argued) to the recognition of the distinction between Right and Wrong. That distinction we feel to be *sui generis*, and whether the feeling be, as the Utilitarian would say, a deception or no, at any rate we do feel that we mean by it something different from the distinction between Advantageous and Disadvantageous or any other such antithesis that might be suggested; just as the difference between a good and bad Smell is distinct from the difference between a good and bad Taste. If this be so, then, on the analogy just explained of the bodily senses, it will require a special faculty for its recognition, just as much as Taste and Smell require different faculties; and further, that faculty must be Intuitive, because it is clear that we continually apply the terms Right and Wrong instinctively, and without being able to say exactly *why* we apply them, much less to explain what constitutes the precise difference implied by the words. Hence this faculty is not inaptly described as the Moral Sense[1]. But, it is said by

[1] Shaftesbury, Hutcheson, etc. The latter insists on the fundamental distinction between 'Natural' Good (*e.g.* Riches, Health, etc.) which we pursue from a view of Interest or from Self-Love, and 'Moral' Good (*e.g.* Honesty, Generosity, etc.) in reference to which he sums up his theory as follows:—

(i.) 'That some actions have to men an immediate goodness; or that by a superior sense, which I call a Moral one, we

others, this Moral faculty not only affirms Right and Wrong of certain acts, but it also involves a sentiment of approbation and disapprobation of them. The Senses in fact suggest here a further analogy. To recognise the distinction between Harmony and Discord so as to derive satisfaction or the reverse from sounds, it is necessary not only that we have the sense of hearing, but also that we have to some extent what is called 'a musical ear.' To appreciate harmonious and inharmonious combinations of colour it is necessary not only to possess the sense of sight, but also to have what is called 'an eye for colour.' Hence, it is urged, the recognition of Right and Wrong, involving as it does also the approbation and disapprobation of them, is analogous to the operation of the cultivated ear and eye rather than to that of the simple Senses of hearing and seeing. In a word the element of Taste is so conspicuous in the operations of this moral faculty that some have preferred to describe it as a Moral[1] *Taste* rather than a Moral *Sense.* Others observing

perceive pleasure in the contemplation of such actions in others, and are determined to love the agent (and much more do we perceive pleasure in being conscious of having done such actions ourselves) without any view of further *natural* advantage from them.

(ii.) That what excites us to these actions, which we call virtuous, is not an intention to obtain even this sensible pleasure, much less the future rewards from sanctions of laws, or any other *natural* good, which may be the consequence of the virtuous action, but an entirely different principle of action from Interest or Self-Love.'

An Inquiry concerning Moral Good and Evil—Introduction.—See further § I. viii.

[1] *e.g.* Hume: 'As virtue is an end and is desirable on its own account, without fee or reward,

that this perception together with approbation (or the reverse) of Right and Wrong is further accompanied by a feeling of Duty, or of Obligation to regulate our own actions accordingly, lay stress upon *this* portion of the complex phenomenon and describe the moral faculty as Conscience[1].

Thus the complex phenomenon is threefold. It involves (1) The *recognition* of Right and Wrong; (2) *Approbation or disapprobation* based upon that recognition; (3) A *Sense of obligation* to regulate our own actions accordingly. As each of these functions respectively is considered the most important the Moral Faculty is described as Moral Sense, Moral Taste, or Conscience.

III. This brings us naturally to our third question, What is the Motive for Moral Action? or in other words, the nature of Moral Obligation?

The distinction which we have met with before reappears in this part of our subject. Some regard the Motive to Moral Action as something *sui generis;* others as a particular application of some other already recognised Motives. Among the latter we may class those who view it as merely a natural

merely for the immediate satisfaction it conveys, it is requisite that there should be some sentiment which it touches, some internal *taste* or *feeling*, or whatever you please to call it, which distinguishes moral good and evil, and which embraces the one and rejects the other.'—(*Inquiry concerning Morals*, App. I. p. 331, Ed. 1825.) 'Morality is determined by *sentiment*. We define Virtue to be whatever mental action or quality gives to a spectator the *pleasing sentiment* of approbation.'—(*Ib.* p. 326.) Compare also *Ethics*, II. iii. 7 (καὶ γὰρ τὸ καλὸν καὶ τὸ συμφέρον ἡδὺ φαίνεται), and the argument in III. ix. 2-5.

[1] *e.g.* Butler.

prudential regard for our own interest, or as an instinctive benevolent desire for the good of our fellow-men, or as a combination of both these impulses. Those also who adhere to the theory of a Moral Taste give a somewhat similar answer to the question, viz., that the *pleasure* derived from the gratification of that Taste disposes us to act so as to secure it, as naturally as a musician would seek for the enjoyment of good music. So far then the answer given would deny the existence of Duty or Moral Obligation in any distinctive sense. It is merely a phase, or a special application, of some other familiar instinct.

Many Intuitive Moralists however claim for this feeling of Duty a character perfectly distinct and independent. They affirm it to be different from a sense of approbation, or of gratification; from a desire of self-interest, or of general expediency. It is declared to be a primary fact of our nature[1], and as primary, to some extent inexplicable, just as is the case with the axioms of Mathematics or the fundamental Laws of Thought. That it is so is evidenced by an appeal to the various languages of men[2] which provide a distinct word for the idea of 'Duty,' 'Ought,' 'Obligation,'—distinct that is from Self-

[1] *e.g.* Kant.

[2] Compare the following argument of Hume for the reality of our conceptions of Moral distinctions:—'Had Nature made no such distinction founded on the original constitution of the mind, the words "honourable" and "shameful," "lovely" and "odious," "noble" and "despicable," had never had place in any language; nor could politicians, had they invented these terms, ever have been able to render them intelligible, or make them convey any idea to the audience.'—*Inquiry concerning Principles of Morals*, § 5.)

Interest, Benevolence, Utility, Approbation, or any other motive that can be assigned—while each and all indicate it by a metaphor, the imperfect applicability of which bears witness to the difficulty of expressing the thing signified. Two metaphors generally occur—that of a *debt due*, or that of a *binding* or *compelling* force. Of the former, χρεία, χρὴ, 'debeo,' due,' 'duty,' 'ought' (owed), are examples: of the latter, δεῖ, 'religio,' 'obligation,' 'bound.' Imperfect metaphors they are, because a *debt* implies a creditor, as well as some service received from him which is to be repaid: *obligation* implies a superior power by which the compulsion is exercised. But in the case before us, though we feel that there is a 'due' or 'debt,' we have no distinct conception of the accessory circumstances just enumerated, or at least not necessarily so: and the 'obligation' is one which is not strictly binding or compulsory. The debt is one which we are free to repudiate, the obligation one which we are free to neglect. These metaphors thus indicate efforts on the part of the mind to express a feeling which it cannot adequately explain to itself or others because it is *sui generis*, the effort to do so however evidencing the real existence of some such feeling.

Thus we see the same broad twofold division runs through the various answers given to the three questions we have now discussed, a division depending on the consideration whether (1) the distinction of Right and Wrong in themselves, (2) the faculty by which it is appreciated, (3) the motive by which it is acted upon, *are, or are not, sui generis.* It is not however the case that systems which adopt either of these opposed lines in answer to any one of the questions necessarily adopt the same line in regard to the others.

IV. Whatever be the character of the motive power of our moral nature, whether it be a calculation of self-interest, or a desire for the good of others, or the instinctive gratification of a Taste, or a Sense of Duty generically distinct from other motives, the question still remains open, What is the ultimate end to which our moral nature tends? What is it, by the conduct which it adopts, struggling or hoping to reach at last as its ideal consummation? or, as Aristotle phrases it, 'What is the Chief Good for man?' This is a question scarcely, if at all, inferior in importance, and certainly not so in practical interest, to the three already considered. Aristotle, as we have seen, regards it as *the* main question of Ethical Science.

We cannot then do better than answer this question in his own words. That final end and aim is Happiness, *i.e.* a state in which there shall be no deferred hopes, no unsatisfied desires. All are agreed upon this, high and low, learned and unlearned, but the conceptions of the conditions constituting such a state are as various as the varieties of human aims and human characters. Each selects his own favourite desire or pursuit, and considers the state of Happiness to depend mainly upon *its* gratification. (It will be remembered that we are now speaking of Man apart from the influence of revealed Religion on his aspirations or his conduct.) Still in the midst of this variety certain leading types may be noticed, which are generally speaking characteristic of different stages of growth in Society or in the Individual. (See Ethics, I. v.)

1. The whole occupation of savage life (where society means little more than local proximity of habitation), is to secure by hunting and fishing the precarious support of daily life. The highest happiness conceivable is the abundant supply of the best food without toil, trouble, or anxiety. Heaven is a perpetual banquet. The full and free gratification of Bodily pleasure (ἡδονὴ) constitutes Happiness.

2. When the growth of civilisation (by organization of labour, mechanical improvements, etc.) is able to secure the supply of these simple wants of the community, then the desire for power over others and social distinction (τιμὴ) becomes the ruling passion. Successful kings, rulers, generals, are the ideals which command the admiration of mankind at large. Nobler spirits however regard these distinctions as deriving their value from Active Virtue and Goodness of Character (ἀρετὴ), and endeavour to persuade themselves and others that the desires of human nature would all be satisfied if this type of Character were fully attained.

3. In a state of still more advanced cultivation and refinement, this divergence between higher and lower natures, the one pursuing ἀρετὴ, the others τιμὴ, becomes yet more marked. The former—experience having shown the practical attainment of their ideal standard (ἀρετὴ), at least on any large scale, to be hopeless—take refuge in literature, philosophy, intellectual cultivation (θεωρητικὸς βίος). The latter, and the majority, —finding out of the pursuit of distinction and power that 'the quest is not for them,'—betake themselves to the accumulation

of wealth (χρηματιστικὸς βίος). Hence the familiar remark that both high literary cultivation, and also wealth with its natural accompaniment of luxury, are signs in societies of full maturity verging towards decay.

In the life of the Individual we may trace a somewhat similar progress in his various conceptions of Happiness. Pleasure is the sole thought of youth; Ambition to excel, in its lower or its higher forms, is the characteristic of manhood; and the closing scene is marked either by 'years that bring the philosophic mind,' or by 'avarice, the prevailing passion of old age.'

Such are the chief types of that aim or end of life which men are found, as a mere observation of fact (see p. xiv.), to place before themselves as the Chief Good, the attainment of which they think would wholly satisfy the desires of their nature. In this last, as in the case of the other three questions, it becomes the office of the Science of Ethics to judge of the merits of these conflicting theories, and if all must be pronounced imperfect, to point out if possible 'a more excellent way.'

[1] We are now in a position to explain the broad features of Aristotle's system of Ethics in particular, as delineated in the following Treatise. We may perhaps notice these three distinctive characteristics:—

(1) His attention is directed to the *external* rather than to the *internal* aspect of morals[2]. The central question of this

[1] The student may omit pp. xxx. to xxxv. until he has acquired a certain familiarity with the text of the Ethics.

[2] This idea will be found clearly worked out in Grant's *Ethics*, vol. i. Essay vii.)

system is, What is the Chief Good for Man? What is the Final End of action, the End-in-itself? So again it will be seen that a large portion of Books II. III. and IV. is occupied with the distinction between Virtues and Vices as manifested in outward actions, while we hear little or nothing of the faculty in ourselves by which that distinction is apprehended further than that it is 'right reason' (ὀρθὸς λόγος); and the sense of Duty or Obligation is scarcely touched upon (Cf. perhaps III. i. 24 ὧν δεῖ ὀρέγεσθαι). So again we find a full discussion of Voluntary and Involuntary actions (B. III. chaps. i.—v.), but not of the Nature of the Will in itself or of its relation to the other parts of our moral constitution.

It must be clearly understood that this is no depreciation of Aristotle's system. It simply amounts to a statement of the totally different standpoint of ancient and modern times. The accumulated experience of more than two thousand years, together with the influence of Christianity pervading, even when not explicitly recognised, all modern thought, has given us an utterly different position *at starting* in Ethical Science, just as in Natural Science now-a-days a schoolboy starts with appliances and discoveries at his disposal which enable him to leave the wisest of the ancients far behind before he has mastered the very alphabet of his subject.

(2) The *political* or rather *social* character of Aristotle's system of Morals will also attract our notice. The science of Ethics is regarded at the outset as a branch of Political or Social Science (πολιτική τις I. ii. 9), while at the close of B. X. it is said absolutely to require the sanction and compelling powers of Civil Government to enforce its precepts in

practice. Throughout the treatise the discussion of various moral questions is justified by the argument that Statesmen have employed or might employ such knowledge (*e.g.* ἀρετὴ in I. xiii. 2-4; ψυχὴ *ib.* § 8; add I. ix. 8, II. i. 5, and III. v. 7, etc.). This characteristic again is due to the circumstances of the writer's age and country. If we consider (1) the absence, comparatively speaking, of domestic life among the Greeks; (2) the fact that in the ancient Greek states, which were *cities* and not *countries*, representative government was comparatively unnecessary, and practically regarded with disfavour[1]; (3) the practical disabilities and general contempt visited upon trading and commerce; we can see how, under all these circumstances, a man's social and political life acquired an importance which it is difficult for us, with our domestic habits, our vast empires, and our commercial pursuits, at all to realize. It was in fact the only avenue to distinction. Poets, philosophers, artists, were almost always statesmen or soldiers. The wealthy did not merely pay a larger sum to the aggregate of national taxation. A rich man raised and equipped so many horsemen, or he fitted out a vessel of war (which was usually commanded by himself), or he undertook the expenses of an embassy, or of a public festival. Hence the prominence of civic virtues in Aristotle's[2] and other

[1] Aristotle says in the *Politics* that one who does not himself share in political life might as well be a resident alien (ὥσπερ μέτοικος γάρ ἐστιν ὁ τῶν τιμῶν μὴ μετέχων).

[2] *e.g.* The primary importance of Courage, which is, in Aristotle's conception, almost restricted to military Courage. With the Spartans this Virtue was so pre-eminent that others were entirely subordinate to it: *e.g.* Theft was encouraged because of the cour-

ancient systems of morality. Hence too the tendency to regard virtues generally from their social or political side[1]. The relative badness of different vices is frequently estimated by Aristotle in reference not to the depravity of character which they either imply or tend to generate, but to their effect on society[2]. With many ancient moralists, and notably with Plato, the consideration that 'public benefits' may result from 'private vices' is so strong as to obscure the sense of wrong in such cases altogether, *e.g.* when community of wives, the practice of abortion, the destruction of weakly children, pious frauds, etc., are not only sanctioned, but advocated, on the ground of advantages that may be secured thereby to the State[3]. That Aristotle's Ethical System

age cultivated by its execution. That the Greeks in earlier times generally displayed an excessive regard to this Virtue is noticed by Gladstone, *Juventus Mundi*, p. 380. It was not the treachery nor the adultery but the effeminate cowardice of Paris which chiefly moved their indignation. The very name for Courage is ἀνδρεία, Manliness. Also the distinction drawn between μεγαλοπρέπεια and ἐλευθερία (II. vii. 6, IV. ii. 1), and we may perhaps add that between μεγαλοψυχία and φιλοτιμία (in its good sense) (II. vii. 8, IV. vi. 1) are socially rather than morally important.

[1] The limitations imposed upon the sphere for the exercise of Courage in III. vi. may be so explained. (Plato's Definition of Courage exhibits still more strongly this tendency, which in fact distorts his whole Ethical system. See *Rep.* p. 429, B. Courage is 'such a power as will preserve under all circumstances that precise estimate of things to be feared which the legislator has imparted in education.')

[2] *e.g.* ἀσωτία is preferred on this ground, among others, to ἀνελευθερία, IV. i. 32, 44. Compare IV. v. 12, in reference to Anger.

[3] We even find a moralist (Archytas) quoted in Cic. *de*

should have a 'political' hue is almost as much a necessity of his age and country as that the language in which he wrote should be Greek[1]; that this colouring but seldom disguises important moral questions is a merit peculiarly his own.

(3) Thirdly, the attentive student will be struck by a tendency in Aristotle to regard Virtue very much on its *intellectual* side. This again was an inheritance from the times in which he lived[2], and with his master Plato it is found in a vastly greater degree. With Plato Virtue *is* Knowledge and Vice *is* Ignorance. No man, according to his system, can deliberately act *against* knowledge. When any man chooses the Wrong he must do so with the conviction, at least for the moment, that it is preferable to secure the forbidden pleasure and risk the future consequences than to undergo the present pain of the self-denial. This is simply a miscalculation, and Vice is due therefore to an error of

Senect. xii. § 40, denouncing sensuality on the main ground that it leads to actions politically dangerous.

[1] 'Every nation, from its peculiar circumstances and position, tends to some particular type, both of beauty and of virtue, and it naturally extols its national type beyond all others.'—(Lecky, *Hist. Eur. Morals*, vol. i. p. 82.)

[2] 'If we compare the different virtues that have flourished among Pagans and Christians, we invariably find that the prevailing type of excellence among the former is that in which the will and judgment, and among the latter, that in which the emotions are most prominent. Friendship rather than love, hospitality rather than charity, magnanimity rather than tenderness, clemency rather than sympathy, are the characteristics of ancient goodness.'—(Lecky, *Eur. Mor.* vol. i. p. 200.)

judgment, a mistake, an intellectual blunder, and is consequently with Plato, at least in theory, involuntary. We find no such exaggeration of the intellectual portion of moral action in Aristotle, but on the contrary frequent protests against it. But we do find, as compared with our modern ideas, little account taken of the emotional or impulsive side of Virtue. Though Aristotle insists in III. ii. at much length on the compound character of Moral Choice (προαίρεσις) —which is an essential condition of all Moral Action (see II. iv. 3)—as involving an element of Impulse (ὄρεξις) as well as of Judgment (δόξα), yet in his detailed account of the Virtues it often strikes us that he makes the Moral Agent too self-conscious[1]; there is a sort of cold and studied propriety, an absence of impulse and enthusiasm, even in virtues which seem to involve a large element of impulse in actual practice, such as Courage, Liberality, Benevolence, and High-Mindedness.[2] No doubt it might be said that this unruffled philosophic self-control is his ideal of Moral perfection. We are not now discussing the merits of such an ideal. We are simply noting that Aristotle's conception of Moral Virtue does in a marked way, compared with our modern habits of thought, fall under this type.

Finally, the beginner should be warned of the difficulties

[1] The often-noted absence of humility in Aristotle's ideal character, the High-Minded Man (IV. iii.), is an instance of this. Humility viewed on its *intellectual* side (as a Greek would view it) becomes a low estimate of one's-self and especially of one's moral character, which, if undeserved, is mere folly; if deserved, implies the reverse of a Virtuous condition.

[2] See notes on IV. i. 27, ii. 10, iii. 24.

which lie before him in the way of (i.) literal translation, (ii.) analysis and distinction of argument, in this Book.

i. It is difficult, or rather in many cases impossible, to translate the technical language of Aristotle by any precisely equivalent terms in English. It is very rare to find two technical words in different languages precisely agreeing in their significance, in their extent, and still more in their associations. The words of different nations, like their coinage or their weights and measures, are often incommensurable. We cannot exactly translate francs into shillings or kilomètres into miles. Hence we must not be startled if we read that it is absurd to 'praise' (ἐπαινεῖν) the gods (I. xii.), or if we find physical functions such as nutriment and growth attributed to the 'soul' (ψυχή) (I. xiii.), or if we are told that moral science is a branch of 'political' science (πολιτική) (I. ii.). The explanation is that our words 'praise,' 'soul,' 'political,' have different meanings and associations from those of the most nearly corresponding Greek terms. Still more impossible is it to translate passages the force of which depends on the double meaning of a Greek word or phrase (*e.g.* ἀκόλαστος in III. xii., λόγον ἔχειν in I. xiii., τέλειος 'final' and 'perfect,' I. vii. 4), or upon the etymology of a technical term (*e.g.* ἠθική in II. i. 1).

In all such cases as we have mentioned, we must either (1) paraphrase, *i.e. describe* rather than *translate* the words in the text (*e.g.* this will be found recommended in I. ii. for πολιτική), or (2) adopt different English words at different times for the same Greek word according to the particular side of the complex idea which is for the time prominent, *e.g.*

we may sometimes translate ψυχὴ 'soul,' sometimes 'mind,' sometimes perhaps 'vital principle.' It must always be borne in mind that the object of translation is not 'verbum verbo reddere,' but to convey to a modern hearer as far as possible the same ideas and impressions as the original would have produced in a contemporary.

ii. It would be an error to regard this work in the light of a modern treatise carefully written and revised by its author, put forth as the formal result of his labours in one special field of knowledge, and intended by him to occupy a definite position among his collected works. So far is this from being the case that the Nicomachean Ethics as they have come to us are generally thought to consist of fragments of two or more distinct treatises which were never intended to form parts of one whole. And more than this, they have sometimes been regarded as merely notes of different courses of oral lectures, taken down by one or more pupils, perhaps, and perhaps not, revised by Aristotle himself. We find (1) promises of subsequent discussion unfulfilled, or announced arrangements departed from[1]; (2) inconsistent theories or statements in different Books[2]; (3) confusion in the grouping of arguments or in the statement of single arguments[3]; (4) sometimes a series of arguments appears in a sort of skeleton form, as if they were merely heads or memoranda[4]; (5) sometimes arguments in support of a point from which the discussion has passed on, seem to be added like after-thoughts, just

[1] See II. vii. 16.

[2] This applies chiefly to other Books than I.-IV.

[3] As perhaps in I. viii. 10 etc., I. ix. 4.

[4] See II. iii., v.; III. ii.

as they occurred to the author, instead of being placed in their natural position[1]; (6) misquotations occur from well-known authors, which have evidently been cited from memory and not verified[2]; (7) perhaps the note-theory might explain occasional instances of confusion, such as that in respect of φθόνος and ἐπιχαιρεκακία (II. vii. 15); or the sudden collapse of an unfinished discussion, as in IV. ix.[3] These blemishes, and especially the last four, are just such as might be expected in oral lectures, or notes from such lectures, but not in a revised or finished treatise. Hence the student must not expect to be always able to analyse satisfactorily, or distinguish quite clearly, the several arguments in the text, as it stands; nor to develop a finished plan of treatment for each subject under discussion.

[1] *e.g.* I. viii. 12, etc.; II. iii. 7; III. iii. 14, etc.

[2] *e.g.* Calypso for Circe, II. ix. 3; and perhaps the illustration from Homer about Thetis, IV. iii. 25; but see *Suppl. Notes.*

[3] To the arguments given above might be added two considerations derived from the diction: (i.) the frequent use of ἀκροαταὶ, ἀκούειν, etc. Shilleto (note on Thuc. i. 90) remarks on this: 'If the Nic. Ethics and some other works of Aristotle were not syllabuses of lectures, what is the meaning of more than once calling ὁ πεπαιδευμένος (the pupil) ἀκροατής, and of the expression ματαίως ἀκούσεται καὶ ἀνωφελῶς?' He proceeds to defend the reading πρῴην for πρότερον in Eth. II. iii. 5 = 'as we said in our lecture the other day,' and suggests that the frequent use of ἀλλὰ νὴ Δία in the Politics [*i.e.* the Ethics *continued*] points in the same direction. (ii.) The use of *accusative* and *infinitive* without any strict grammatical construction; which quasi-reminiscence of *Or. Obl.* is suggestive of the process of jotting down notes. This is very common in the *Politics*, and in the *Ethics* we may cite as examples, IV. iii. 25 (διὸ καὶ κ.τ.λ.), *ib.* § 28 (εἴρωνα δὲ κ.τ.λ.), etc.

GLOSSARY.

ABBREVIATIONS USED IN THESE NOTES.

cf. '*confer*,' 'compare.'

q.v. '*quod vide*,' 'to which refer.'

sc. '*scilicet*,' 'namely.'

s.v. '*sub voce*' (*e.g.* 'see Glossary s.v. τέλος' means 'see the Glossary under the word τέλος').

l.c. '*loco citato*,' 'in the passage quoted.'

h.l. '*hoc loco*,' 'in this passage.'

ib. '*ibidem*,' 'in the same place or passage.'

κ.τ.λ. 'καὶ τὰ λοιπά,' 'et cetera.'

The references to Books, Chapters, and Sections are made in different figures, thus: II. iii. 5 means Book II., Chapter iii., Section 5.

LIST OF TERMS EXPLAINED IN THE GLOSSARY.

πρᾶξις—ποίησις.

Πρᾶξις (1) has the general sense of outward action, in contrast with inward and mental activity (θεωρία, for which see below). (2) It is applied to a particular kind of outward actions, viz., such as have no tangible result distinct from the action itself; where our aim is not at *making* something but at *doing* something. *e.g.* The practice of the Art of Navigation, or the Art of Healing: for the safety of the ship or the health of the body is not a result of a distinct and tangible character. (3) Since the most important cases of such actions are Moral Actions, where either the action itself is the result in view, or the character which it tends to form, πρᾶξις acquires the still more limited sense of Moral Action.

Ποίησις is applied to actions which leave some definite and tangible result, actions which aim at *making* something; as is the case in most of the Arts: *e.g.* in house-building or ship-building the house or the ship is such a result, in composing poetry (ποίησις), the poem (ποίημα); in sculpture or painting, the statue or the picture.

The adjectives πρακτική, ποιητική, θεωρητική, naturally follow the same distinction. See in illustration, X. viii. 7. So in *Pol.* I. iv. 4, Aristotle describes a Shuttle as ὄργανον ποιητικόν, its value consisting in its *productions*, but a Bed or Clothing as ὄργανα πρακτικά, their value consisting in their *use.*

θεωρία.

Θεωρία is grouped with ποίησις and πρᾶξις by Aristotle, and he regards these three as the only possible forms which intelligent activity can take. Observe they are all forms of *activity* (ἐνέργεια). Activity of the productive or artistic powers is ποίησις. Activity of the powers of action, and especially moral action, is πρᾶξις. Activity of the powers of intellect or contemplation is θεωρία. In the first, there is outward action and a tangible result; in the second, there is outward action but no tangible result; in the last, there is neither outward action nor tangible result; still it is not a passive state, but one of internal, mental activity, 'the depth, and not the tumult of the soul' (Wordsworth). (See *Pol.* IV. (VII.) iii. *sub. fin.*) As Pope writes (*Essay on Man*, ii. 106), the 'strength of mind is exercise, not rest.' But further, it must be distinguished from the mental activity displayed in the pursuit or acquisition of knowledge. It is the active fruition of knowledge already possessed. (See X. vii. 5, *οὐδὲν ἀπ' αὐτῆς γίγνεται πλὴν τὸ θεωρῆσαι.*) It is, to use a homely illustration, like 'chewing the cud' of knowledge, dwelling upon it, assimilating it. Persuasion, or discovery, of a truth leads to belief or knowledge of it; if it be a matter of personal interest, faith in it follows; finally it may become as it were a part of our very selves, our intellectual food, the thought upon which our minds for ever dwell and meditate. This last condition would constitute *θεωρία* of it. These stages are admirably expressed by Wordsworth:

> One in whom persuasion and belief
> Had ripened into faith, and faith become
> A *passionate intuition.*

This 'passionate intuition' is *θεωρία.* It is this intellectual energy in repose, this active yet tranquil contemplation and enjoyment of Truth and Knowledge already possessed, that, under the name of *θεωρία* (in B. X.), Aristotle considers to be perfect and ideal Happiness, as realized only in the life of the gods.

Art—Science.

Science is knowledge for its own sake (*scire ut sciamus*). Art is knowledge for some practical end (*scire ut operemur*). It is objectionable to say that Art is 'Science turned to account,' because an Art is generally prior in time to its related Science. In fact the existence of an Art in a rude state is generally the stimulating cause of the study of the related Science. *e.g.* The Science of Astronomy was originally cultivated with a view to the Art of Navigation, or the Art (or practical Science) of Astrology: the Science of Anatomy with a view to the Art of Surgery: the Science of Chemistry with a view to the Art of Alchemy.

So much for the general distinction of the terms. There is however an ambiguity about the word 'practical,' which causes some difficulty in the application of the words Art and Science (*e.g.* Logic, Grammar, Rhetoric, Astrology, Navigation, etc., are called by either title). This makes it desirable to have an intermediate term, 'practical Science.' Let the reader refer to the difference already explained (p. xli.) between *πρᾶξις* and *ποίησις*, and he will then understand the following distinction: 'Art' is strictly applicable to cases of *ποίησις*, 'Practical Science' to cases of *πρᾶξις*, 'Science' (as above explained), to knowledge for its own sake. Hence Logic, Grammar, Rhetoric, Ethics, and Politics are 'practical Sciences.' (See further, Introduction, p. xiii.)

Speaking broadly, ἐπιστήμη corresponds with Science, and τέχνη with Art. We find however ἐπιστήμη used in reference to practical applications of knowledge (*e.g.* I. i. 5, vi. 15, II. vi. 9, III. iii. 8) and τέχνη, at least by implication, referred to Moral action, *i.e.* πρᾶξις, not ποίησις (II. i. 4, vi. 9, etc.). We must not therefore press the correspondence too closely.

Also it must be observed that τέχνη and ἐπιστήμη with Aristotle more usually refer, not to Art and Science regarded as external results of man's genius (*i.e.* a body of practical rules, or a system of abstract knowledge), but rather to the *mental states* by which we stand related to the objects of practical or theoretic knowledge respectively.

a priori—a posteriori.

These terms refer to what is prior, or posterior, to observation and experience.

An *a priori* argument means one which starts from principles which are (or were thought to be by those who invented these terms) prior to, and independent of, experience. Such for instance are Mathematical and other Axioms. These have been held to be prior to experience, either as being 'innate ideas,' or as not depending *for proof* on experience. Without entering into this controversy further, we may assert that the phraseology *a priori*, having arisen in this manner, is now used to describe arguments starting from general principles.

An *a posteriori* argument, on the other hand, is one that derives its whole force from experience and observation of facts. Its premisses are not general principles or obvious truths, but statements of facts of experience.

Consequently the Mathematical Sciences are purely *a priori* Sciences. They start from general principles such (*e.g.*) as Euclid's Axioms, and end in particular, or at any rate less general, statements, such as Euclid's Propositions. They proceed, as Aristotle would say, ἀπὸ τῶν ἀρχῶν.

On the other hand the Physical Sciences are purely *a posteriori* Sciences. They assume no general principles, but start from observed facts, and end in the discovery of general laws, *e.g.* that of gravitation. They proceed ἐπὶ τὰς ἀρχάς.

As to the Science of Ethics, or Morals, both methods have at different times been advocated and adopted. See note on I. iv. 5.

δύναμις—ἐνέργεια.

We first explain the principal meanings of *δύναμις*, which may be connected thus:—*δύναμις* is (1) power or capacity, in a literal or general sense; (2) power *merely*, *i.e.* power existent, but not exercised; dormant, not in operation (see below); (3) power regarded as the source and spring of practical results, such as is given us by Arts in contradistinction to Sciences (see p. xliv). Hence *δύναμις* is sometimes used as a sort of equivalent term for *τέχνη*, *e.g.* *τίνος τῶν ἐπιστημῶν ἢ δυνάμεων*, I. ii. 3; and again *ib.* §§ 5 and 6. See also V. i. 4.

The most important of the usages of the word is (2). In this sense it stands in contrast with *ἐνέργεια*, somewhat as 'potential' and 'actual,' 'latent' and 'developed,' are contrasted in English. Take these illustrations. The flower exists potentially but not actually (*δυνάμει* but not *ἐνεργείᾳ*) in the bud, or in the seed; the ear of corn in the 'bare-grain'; the oak in the acorn. So the photographic picture, which exists *potentially* on the collodion film, becomes *actual* when brought out by the developing fluid. Again, an infant has not actually the power of speaking or reading any more than a horse or a dog. Still there is an important difference between the two cases, because experience tells us that there is that in the infant which may be developed into these powers, whereas no amount of training would develop anything of the sort in the lower animals, any more than cultivation could produce an oak from an imitation acorn though undistinguishable to the eye from a real one. It is convenient therefore to say that these powers exist in the infant potentially (*δυνάμει*), in distinction to cases where they do not exist at all. So again if we have information given us in cipher, or in sympathetic ink, or in a sealed document, we have the information *δυνάμει* but not *ἐνεργείᾳ*. This distinction is also sometimes indicated by the antithesis of *ἕξις* and *ἐνέργεια*, or of *κτῆσις* and *χρῆσις*. Passages in illustration will be found in I. viii. 8, II. i. 4. See also the use of *δύναμις* in contrast with *πάθος* and *ἕξις* in II. v. 2.

Again, the distinction may be applied both to *existence* and *action*. As regards the former, *δύναμις* is applied to that which *can be, but is not*: as regards the latter to that which *can do, but does not*. See especially the use of *δύναμις* in I. xii.

τέλος, τέλειος.

Τέλος = our word 'End' (1) in its literal sense of a 'termination'; and (2) in its other sense of a 'motive' or 'aim': of which the latter use is much more common in Aristotle. (3) It is also used in reference to his doctrine of the 'end-in-itself,' or 'final end' of all human action, described in other words as 'the Chief Good.' Often however these meanings are combined in a manner which it is all but impossible to represent in translation, *e.g.* I. ix. 3, *τὸ τῆς ἀρετῆς ἆθλον καὶ τέλος*. Similarly *τέλειος* means 'complete,' 'perfect,' and also 'final': *e.g.* in I. vii. it is difficult to retain this double signification in translation.

Aristotle's doctrine of the 'end-in-itself' may be thus explained:—There must be an end or purpose (in sense (2)) for which man exists in the world, as there is for everything else (see I. vii. 11). There must also be an end or limit (in sense (1)) to man's desires and efforts, else they would be in vain and useless (see I. ii. 1). That end once attained, man would 'rest and be satisfied.' There could be nothing further to look to or to wish for. Hence it is called the 'absolute end,' or the 'end-in-itself.' To discover this in theory, and to secure the attainment of it in practice, is regarded by Aristotle as the main object of Ethics. This is spoken of as *τὸ τέλος*, *e.g.* III. ix. 5. Also as to *τὸ τῶν πρακτῶν τέλος*, I. vii. 8, and *τὸ τῶν ἀνθρωπίνων τέλος*, X. vi. 1.

ἀρχή.

'Αρχὴ means literally a 'starting-point' or 'beginning,' or, as Aristotle himself explains it, *ᾗ ἐστὶν ἢ γίγνεται ἢ γιγνώσκεται τὸ πρᾶγμα*, 'that by which anything exists, or is produced, or is known.' Thus it is a very general term.

As a cause of *existence* or *production*. In this sense it may be used for any of the Four Causes (explained p. li); see *Metaph.* I. iii. We find it in the *Ethics* for Efficient Cause, as when man is said to be the *ἀρχὴ* of his own actions (III. v. 5); and when Volition is described as the *ἀρχὴ* of the movement of the limbs (III. i. 6); for Final Cause, as when Happiness is said to be the *ἀρχὴ* of our actions (I. xii. 8).

As a cause of *knowledge*. At either end of the scale of knowledge there must be a starting-point (*ἀρχὴ*), which is taken for granted without demonstrative proof, otherwise πρόεισιν οὕτω γ' εἰς ἄπειρον. Hence the general principles or axioms, at the top of the scale, and the particular facts of perception or observation, at the bottom, must be *assumed* to start with, and hence both are sometimes called ἀρχαί. Hence (says Aristotle) νοῦς τῶν ἀρχῶν ἐπ' ἀμφότερα, 'There is an intuitive faculty for the truths we start with in both directions.' An example of one kind would be, 'Two straight lines cannot enclose a space.' An example of the other, 'This is a straight line, a triangle,' 'This magnet attracts iron,' etc. See the following passages in illustration: I. vii. 20, τῶν ἀρχῶν αἱ μὲν θεωροῦνται κ.τ.λ., 'Of the truths we start from some are *apprehended*, etc.; the last word, purposely vague, expresses at any rate an *immediate* apprehension, independent of proof. Again, τὸ δ' ὅτι πρῶτον καὶ ἀρχὴ (*ib.* and I. iv. 7), 'The fact is a beginning and a point to start from.'

In the quotation, I. vii. 21, ἀρχὴ . . . πλεῖον ἢ ἥμισυ παντὸς, we have ἀρχὴ in its literal meaning, but the *dictum* is applied by Aristotle to the technical sense of the word also.

Since the Greeks seldom employed any other than the *a priori* method (see p. xlv) in the pursuit of knowledge, ἀρχὴ comes to stand often for 'general principle,' 'first principle,' or 'axiom.' This will explain its use in I. iv., where λόγοι ἀπὸ τῶν ἀρχῶν = 'arguments starting from general principles'; λόγοι ἐπὶ τὰς ἀρχὰς = 'arguments leading up to general principles.'

ψυχή.

This word, generally translated 'Soul,' has no precise English equivalent. It stands for all that is immaterial in man, including Mind, Desires, Will, and even Life. On the one hand, 'Soul' includes too much. It is impossible to disconnect theological and religious ideas from the word 'Soul,' which are quite foreign to the conception of Aristotle: *e.g.* To employ such expressions in translation as 'the life of the Soul,' 'the good of the Soul,' would be misleading. On the other hand, 'Soul' includes too little, as it does not reach to mere physical life, such as Animals and even Plants possess (see I. xiii. 11). Again, the word 'Life,' or Vital Principle, is too narrow, excluding Reason, Moral action, etc. So also is 'Mind,' excluding all else beside Reason.

The following passages will serve to show how impersonal, and how widely different from our notion of 'Soul' is Aristotle's conception of ψυχή. 'If the eye were a living creature, sight would be its ψυχή'

(*De An.* II. i. 9). So again the Soul is said to bear a relation to the Body like that of Form to Matter. Again (and this throws light on the abbreviated discussion in *Eth.* I. xiii.—note especially the expression in § 15, ἄλλη τις φύσις τῆς ψυχῆς), in *De. An.* II. ii. Aristotle explains that there are different kinds of Life (cf. *Eth.* I. vii. 12, etc.), such as Motive, Nutritive, Sentient, Intelligent, and that to each of them, ἡ ψυχή ἐστιν ἀρχὴ καὶ τούτοις ὥρισται, each kind of Life corresponding either to a different *kind* of ψυχή, or to a different *part* of the ψυχὴ (*De An.* II. ii. 8; cf. *Eth.* I. xiii. 10), but in either case the higher kinds or parts possess all the qualities of the lower, as well as their own (*De An.* II. iii. 5). The Nutritive ψυχὴ belongs to Plants; the Sentient (+ Nutritive) to Animals; the Intelligent (+ Sentient + Nutritive) to Man.

Compare Dryden (*Knight's Tale*)—

> 'First vegetive, then feels, and reasons last;
> Rich of three souls.'

In reference to the two important controversies as to (1) the Origin; (2) the Immortality of the Soul, we may note—(1) Aristotle considers that Man derives the θρεπτικὴ ψυχὴ from the Female (hence the state of the embryo at first is that of mere vegetative life), the αἰσθητικὴ ψυχὴ from the Male; while of the διανοητικὴ he says, λείπεται τὸν νοῦν μόνον θύραθεν ἐπεισιέναι καὶ θεῖον εἶναι μόνον (*De Gen. Anim.* II. iii. 4, 7, 10). Thus it would seem that Aristotle (like Dante, *Purg.* xxv. 77, etc.) combines in some sense the Traducianist and Creationist theories of the Origin of the Soul. (2) As to its future existence, Aristotle never explicitly pronounces himself, not even in *Eth.* I. x. and xi. It would appear, however, even from the above very imperfect sketch, that a personal immortality could not attach to ψυχὴ as understood by Aristotle; and it is clear, throughout the present and other treatises, that such a notion did not at any rate enter into his Ethical theories. (See further Grant's *Aristotle*, Essay V.)

On the whole, we may perhaps best translate ψυχὴ conventionally by 'Soul' as a general rule, adopting the words 'Life' or 'Mind' occasionally, when the passage refers especially to those parts of the complex idea.

ἀρετή.

Ἀρετὴ means 'excellence' in all its various senses and applications. (It is obviously connected with the same root as ἄριστος, Ἄρης, etc. Compare the connexion of *virtus* in Latin with *vir*.) Hence we find it applied to the eye, and to the horse, in II. vi. 2; to a musician (by implication) in I. vi. 14; and by Plato to the dog, to a pruning-knife, etc. etc. · in short, to anything that has any work or function to perform; the ἀρετή in each case consisting in the good performance of that work. We cannot describe this general sense of the term better than in Aristotle's own words in II. vi. 2: 'Every excellence (ἀρετή) perfects that of which it is the excellence, and causes its work to be well performed.'

There are however two special kinds of excellence to which the word ἀρετή is most frequently applied:—(1) Excellence of our *intellectual* or *rational* nature. Instances of such excellences are, prudence, wisdom, intelligence, argumentative power, retentive memory, acuteness, etc. etc. (2) Excellence of our *moral* nature; *i.e.* a well-regulated condition of the appetites, passions, and desires. Instances of such excellences are, temperance, courage, gentleness, high-mindedness, etc. etc., in other words, the *moral virtues*. It is in this restricted sense of the term that we translate it by 'Virtue.' These two kinds of excellence will be found in I. xiii. 20.

In this case, as in others that have been mentioned, the meanings are often so blended in Greek that we cannot translate by one word in English.

προαίρεσις.

In any deliberate action the following steps or processes may be traced:—

(1) Desire or *wish* for some *end* to be attained (βούλησις).

(2) Reflection or *deliberation* upon the several *means* by which the end may be reached (βούλευσις).

(3) *Deliberate Choice* of some one means or series of means as the most eligible (προαίρεσις). This choice once made, the *action* follows accordingly.

Thus the distinction between βούλησις, βούλευσις, and προαίρεσις resembles that with which we are familiar between 'holy *desires*, good *counsels*, and just *works*' (or at least *resolutions* to act).

προαίρεσις sometimes corresponds nearly with 'purpose,' or 'resolution,' or even 'will,' but as these translations, and especially the last, would often be misleading, it seems best to adopt 'deliberate choice.' This translation has the further advantage of displaying the composite nature of the process, which Aristotle constantly insists upon, it being not merely 'choice' or 'purpose,' nor merely 'deliberation,' but a choice succeeding upon deliberation.

The following passages from the *Ethics* may be referred to in illustration. For a general account of προαίρεσις, especially in its compound character, and its relation to processes or faculties more or less similar to it, see III. ii. and III. iii. 17, 18. (Compare also VI. ii. 5, where προαίρεσις is described as ἢ ὀρεκτικὸς νοῦς ἢ ὄρεξις διανοητική.) It has to do with the Means, not (like βούλησις) with the End in action, III. ii. 9. It is coupled with πρᾶξις in I. i. 1 and I. vii. 1. It occurs in the sense of 'purpose,' or a 'particular state of the Will,' in contrast with 'action' or 'performance,' in II. iv. 3, VIII. xiii. 11, X. viii. 5; and similarly in IV. vii. 12 (on which see *Suppl. Note*). It is an essential condition of a Virtuous Act, see II. iv. 3, and the Definition of Virtue as ἕξις προαιρετική κ.τ.λ., in II. vi. 15. It can only be good under the guidance of φρόνησις, VI. xiii. 7. Finally, in two passages it seems to waver between the ordinary sense of 'purpose' or 'intention,' and 'the design or plan purposed' ('id quod disputatione propositum est,'—*Bonitz*); viz., I. xiii. 4, κατὰ τὴν ἐξ ἀρχῆς προαίρεσιν; X. ix. 1, τέλος ἔχειν τὴν προαίρεσιν.

The Four Causes.

A complete knowledge of any Being or Object implies an acquaintance with Four different Causes to which its Existence is in different senses due.

(1) The *Matter* of which it is composed. The *Material* Cause.

(2) The *Form* by which it is distinguished. The *Formal* Cause.

(3) The *Force* which has brought about the particular combination of Matter and Form which constitute the Being or Object under consideration. The *Efficient* Cause.

(4) The *Purpose* or *Object in View* in such a combination. The *Final* Cause.

(2) and (4) require further explanation.

(2) 'Form' is to be taken not merely for external shape, but for whatever is characteristic or essential. The same *Matter* may be made into a hundred different objects, but the same *Form* (within certain limits) belongs to one class of objects only, and hence 'formal' came to mean 'essential'; and the 'formal cause' = 'the essential nature'; *i.e.* the group of such qualities or characteristics as are essential to the existence of anything in its barest form, or to the simplest conception we can have of it; which qualities are therefore always present in all different types

or developments of it.[1] Thus the 'formal cause,' when described in words, becomes the *Definition* of the object.

In Aristotle's phraseology, 'Formal Cause' is identical with οὐσία (when = essence), and with τὸ τί ἦν εἶναι, which will be found explained in note on II. vi. 17. See *Metaph.* I. iii. 1.

Hence to take a single example—a Statue :—

The Material Cause is the marble or metal of which it is made.

Its Formal Cause is in one sense the shape by which we recognise it as a statue, and in another, the qualities which would constitute the scientific definition of 'Statue.'

Its Efficient Cause is in one sense the Artist, in another the Chisel, or the Furnace.

Its Final Cause the purpose with which it was made, *e.g.* the gain of the artist, the decoration of some public place, honour to be paid to some great man, etc. etc. Again, the Final Cause of a clock is to mark time. As soon as a certain combination of wood, brass, etc., fulfils this condition, we call it a clock, and thus 'marking time' may be said to be the *cause* of its being a clock rather than anything else.

(4) The Final Cause (an expression familiar to us from the theological 'Argument from Final Causes,' or 'Argument from Design'), is the Purpose, End, or Object-in-View of anything. In all cases however we may trace (as Aristotle shows, B. I. c. i. and c. ii. *init.*) both proximate and ultimate purposes. All purposes if traced far enough resolve themselves into this one, that there is some *good* to be gained by the action; or, in more technical language, all ends ultimately converge to the Chief Good or τὸ ἀγαθόν. Thus, strictly speaking, there is only one really Final Cause. The term however is applied to any subordinate end or inducement to act. (See further *s.v.* τέλος, τέλειος.)

It will further follow that the Efficient Cause must be *prior to*, but need not be *simultaneous with*, its Effect; the Formal Cause must be *simultaneous* but need not be *prior;* the Material Cause must be *both.* (Cf. *Post. Anal.* II. xi.)

θεὸς—φύσις.

It may be worth while to explain very briefly once for all Aristotle's conception of God and Nature in relation to the world, as several passages

[1] In this sense Bacon speaks of the *Form* of Light and of Heat. Compare Wordsworth's use of the word in the passage :—

For the Man
Who in this spirit communes with the *Forms*
Of Nature,

i.e. the great essential types of Nature's varied operations.

in the Ethics would mislead those who adopted without some precaution the two English words in question.

Aristotle's philosophical conception of God excludes the ideas of the Creation, the Moral Government, and even the Providential Government, of the world. *Creation* and *providential government* are excluded, since Aristotle maintains that the world is eternal, and distinctly asserts (in X. viii. 7) that ποίησις (creative energy) of any kind is unworthy of God, and also in B. X. and elsewhere, that God is absolutely unmoved, unchangeable, unaffected by anything external to himself; his existence consisting in thought thinking upon itself (νόησις νοήσεως νόησις), or in a conscious fruition of perfect knowledge (see above *s.v.* θεωρία). *Moral government* is excluded, partly for the same reasons; and also because πρᾶξις (or moral action) is likewise in the same passage of B. X. distinctly stated to be unworthy of the divine nature. Also in VII. i. 2, it is asserted that the condition of excellence in θεὸς is τιμιώτερον ἀρετῆς. (Cf. the distinctions made in I. xiii.)

In short, any kind of *agency* was held by Aristotle to be unworthy of the Divine perfection. Such action would be ἀναγκαῖος, βίαιός τις (see note on I. v. 8). This was the main point of the much misunderstood theory of Epicurus as to the gods. (See Grote's *Aristotle*, ii. p. 436.)

Yet Aristotle maintains that God, though unmoved, is the cause and source (αἴτιον καὶ ἀρχή) of all motion. This paradox is thus explained: God is not the *efficient* but the *final* cause of all motion (see above, *s.v.* 'The Four Causes'). In other words, the universe moves under the attraction of, and by striving after, the supreme Good, which is God: in its endeavours thereafter, it for ever, so to speak, circles and revolves about God as a centre, who thus, himself unmoved, becomes

> The one far-off divine Event
> To which the whole Creation moves.

So Dante :—

> (*Dio*) Solo ed Eterno che tutto il cielo move
> Non moto, con amore e con disio.
>
> (*Parad.* xxiv. 131.)

Still it should be noted that Aristotle often speaks popularly of Divine agency, feelings, etc., in a manner quite inconsistent with his formal theories, *e.g. Eth.* I. ix.; X. viii. 13; ix. 6. Cf. *Rhet.* II. ix. 2, τοῖς θεοῖς ἀποδίδομεν τὸ νεμεσᾶν. It should be added also that Aristotle (like Plato), following the popular usage, speaks indifferently of 'God' and 'Gods' (*e.g.* I. xii. 3; X. viii., etc.), yet his conception of the nature of God, taken strictly, excludes altogether the idea of plurality of Gods.

The precise meaning of *φύσις*, and its relation to *θεὸς*, in Aristotle, is perhaps as difficult to define as it would be to formulate accurately our own conception of Nature. Aristotle doubtless would not, in strict speaking, regard Nature as a personal or rational agent (see *Eth.* III. iii. 7, note), though he often (as we do) uses language which would imply it. Confining our attention chiefly to such passages as occur in the Ethics, or obvious illustrations of them, we may note :—

(1) Optimism in Nature. See *Eth.* I. ix. 5, *εἴπερ τὰ κατὰ φύσιν, ὡς οἷόν τε κάλλιστα ἔχειν, οὕτω πέφυκεν.* [Compare *De Caelo*, I. iv. fin., *ὁ θεὸς καὶ ἡ φύσις οὐδὲν μάτην ποιοῦσιν.* Also *Pol.* I. ii. 8-10. Again, in various passages cited by Bonitz, *s.v.*, *ἡ φύσις οὐδὲν μάτην ποιεῖ, οὐδὲ περίεργον οὐδὲ ἐλλεῖπον, οὐδὲ ἀτελὲς, ἀλλὰ πάντα πρὸς τὸ ἄριστον ἀποβλέπουσα.*]

In regard to this Optimism we may observe :—

(*α*) It is assigned to a conscious and intelligent purpose in Nature in such passages as *De An.* II. iv. 5, *ὥσπερ γὰρ ὁ νοῦς ἕνεκά του ποιεῖ, τὸν αὐτὸν τρόπον καὶ ἡ φύσις*, etc. etc. Also such expressions as *δημιουργεῖ, βούλεται, ἀποδίδωσιν*, and many others, are frequently applied to *φύσις*.

(*β*) Nature, like Art, often falls short of its aim, being thwarted by Necessity, or Chance, or the Matter it has to work upon. Hence the limitation *ὡς οἷόν τε κάλλιστα ἔχειν* above. Cf. *De Caelo*, II. v. 3, *ἐκ τῶν ἐνδεχομένων τὸ βέλτιστον*, and see *Pol.* I. vi. 8, *ἡ φύσις βούλεται μὲν τοῦτο ποιεῖν πολλάκις οὐ μέντοι δύναται.* With this we may compare the exquisite simile of Dante—

> 'La natura . . .
> Similmente operando all' artista,
> C'ha l'abito dell' arte e man che trema.'—(*Par.* xiii. 75.)
>
> 'Nature . . .
> Resembling thus the Artist in her work,
> Whose faltering hand is faithless to his skill.

(2) *φύσις* is the source of order, fixity, and regularity in the Universe (*e.g.* seeds and animals reproducing their like), being intermediate to Necessity on the one side (implying the impossibility of any variation), and Chance on the other (implying the absence of any law). Cf. *De Caelo*, III. ii. 8, *ἡ τάξις ἡ οἰκεία τῶν αἰσθητῶν φύσις ἐστίν.*

Hence we may perhaps explain *τὰ φύσει ἡδέα*, I. viii. 11, and *φύσει βουλητὸν*, III. iv., as contrasted with the irregular tastes of individuals. [Comp. *Rhet.* I. xi. 3, where *ἡδέα φύσει*, and *ἡδέα ἔθει* are contrasted, especially, *ἔστιν ἡ μὲν φύσις τοῦ ἀεὶ τὸ δὲ ἔθος τοῦ πολλάκις.*] So *Eth.* I. iii. 2, *καλὰ καὶ δίκαια φύσει* as opposed to *νόμῳ*. (Cf. *φύσει* opposed to *κατὰ* συμβεβηκὸς, *De An.* I. iii. 3.) See also the distinction between φυσικὸν and νομικὸν δίκαιον, as explained in *Eth.* V. vii. 1; the former, however, not being rigidly invariable (as though due to ἀνάγκη; see note on III. iii. 7), though exceptions are so comparatively rare as 'to prove the rule'; just as (Aristotle adds) the right hand is φύσει stronger than the left in spite of the existence of ἀμφιδέξιοι. So again, γνώριμα τῇ φύσει elsewhere occurs as synonymous with γνώριμα ἁπλῶς in *Eth.* I. iv. 5. Under this head also compare *Eth.* II. i. 2, οὐθὲν τῶν φύσει ὄντων ἄλλως ἐθίζεται.

(3) φύσις and θεὸς seem sometimes almost identified, as our own usage might lead us to expect; *e.g.* in *Eth.* X. ix. 6, that which belongs to us φύσει is said διά τινας θείας αἰτίας ὑπάρχειν. Many passages occur elsewhere in which direct creative and providential functions are attributed to φύσις.

(4) φύσις is often used in reference to the operations of Nature in a limited sphere, such as the constitution of Man, or of some other Animal, or class of Objects. Though it is difficult to discriminate such a usage precisely, yet something like 'human nature' seems to be the prominent idea in the following:—*Eth.* II. i. 3, etc., ἠθικὴ ἀρετὴ neither φύσει nor παρὰ φύσιν; III. v. 18, 19, whether our end and aim in action φύσει ἢ ὁπωσδήποτε φαίνεται καὶ κεῖται. See X. ix. 14, in reference to πατρικοὶ λόγοι, children προϋπάρχουσι στέργοντες καὶ εὐπειθεῖς τῇ φύσει. Compare further with this usage the sense in which some moralists have held that Human Virtue consists in 'following Nature.'

(5) φύσις and τέχνη are frequently put into relation and comparison, *e.g.* *Eth.* I. ix. 6; II. vi. 9. These passages may be illustrated by others in which it is more definitely laid down that Art *follows* and *supplements* Nature; and also that the mode of their operations is similar, *e.g* πᾶσα τέχνη . . . τὸ προσλεῖπον τῆς φύσεως βούλεται ἀναπληροῦν (*Pol.* IV. (VII.) xvii. 15); ἡ τέχνη τὰ μὲν ἐπιτελεῖ ἃ ἡ φύσις ἀδυνατεῖ ἀπεργάσασθαι, τὰ δὲ μιμεῖται (*Phys.* II. viii. 8). Dante, referring to the *Physics* by name (*Inf.* xi. 101), amplifies this Aristotelian idea by making Nature the child of God, and Art the child of Nature (sì che vostr' arte a Dio quasi è *nipote*), and therefore includes in the same punishment those who have offered violence to God, or Nature, or Art.

BOOKS I. II.

ΗΘΙΚΩΝ ΝΙΚΟΜΑΧΕΙΩΝ

I.

[N.B.—*The marginal figures on the left-hand side denote Sections, and on the right the lines in the page. See the first page of the Glossary for an explanation of the references to Books, Chapters, and Sections occurring in the Notes.*]

1 I. ΠΑΣΑ τέχνη καὶ πᾶσα μέθοδος, ὁμοίως δὲ πρᾶξίς τε καὶ προαίρεσις, ἀγαθοῦ τινὸς ἐφίεσθαι δοκεῖ· διὸ

CHAP. I.—*Explanation of Terms, 'End,' 'Good,' 'Chief Good'—Different kinds of Ends, and their degrees of finality.*

1 ALL human action, of whatsoever kind, implies an end or purpose, *i.e.* the attainment of some good. The Chief The *su bonum* be des as th mate all o tions.

The main purpose of the Science of Ethics is, in Aristotle's conception, the discovery of the Chief Good, or Final End of all man's actions and aspirations, the attainment of which would leave him nothing to desire. He commences, therefore, in this chapter with first laying down broadly the conception of the Chief Good, and points out the *primâ facie* difficulty in accepting such a conception of it. Next (in ch. ii. and iii.), having asserted that it is a reality notwithstanding (*i.e.*, that there *is* a Chief Good or Final End), he settles some preliminary points as to the utility, scope, method, etc., of its investigation. Then, in ch. iv., he passes on to the question, *What* is the Chief Good? and finding that the general agreement that it is Happiness vanishes as soon as we further ask, In what does Happiness consist? he usually puts the main question thenceforth in the modified form, What is Happiness?

1. *μέθοδος* is strictly a method or process of science, and is therefore contrasted with *τέχνη*, which stands for a process of art. (See Glossary, *s. v.* Art and Science). *πρᾶξις* = action, and especially moral action. *προαίρεσις* = purpose or resolve which

2 καλῶς ἀπεφήναντο τἀγαθὸν, οὗ πάντ' ἐφίεται. Διαφορὰ δέ τις φαίνεται τῶν τελῶν· τὰ μὲν γάρ εἰσιν ἐνέργειαι, τὰ δὲ παρ' αὐτὰς ἔργα τινά. Ὧν δ' εἰσὶ τέλη τινὰ

Good is well described as the ultimate end of *all* our
But it appears that there is a vast difference of ends; 2 actions and desires. Ends differ from one another in a

precedes action. The opening sentence then amounts to this:—Whether we are working to *produce* anything (τέχνη), or to *know* anything (μέθοδος), or to *do* anything (πρᾶξις), or even are forming *resolutions* to act (προαίρεσις), in all these cases we must have an end or purpose (in other words, some *good*), in view.

1. τἀγαθὸν, literally '*the* good,' *i.e.* the chief good, or '*summum bonum*.' 'End' and 'good' are nearly synonymous. The 'end' of an action is the 'good' we hope to secure by the action; it being obvious that every end must at least *appear* good or desirable, at the time it is chosen, to the person choosing it. ''Tis real good or seeming moves us all.'—*Pope*. See III. iv. and III. v. 17. The first words of the next chapter assert the identity of the Final End (the conception of which is developed in this chapter) and the Chief Good, the definition of which is the main object of the whole treatise.

1. Διαφορὰ δέ τις φαίνεται κ.τ.λ.] Though the general conception of a Chief Good can be readily explained, as has just been done in the words οὗ πάντ' ἐφίεται, yet the variety of our ends and aims (διαφορὰ τῶν τελῶν) is such that we cannot assume that all things *do* converge to any one such end; in other words, that there *is* a Chief Good, much less say *what* it is. The former point is established in ii. 1; the solution of the latter is the subject, more or less, of the whole treatise. See especially, however, iv. 1 and vii. 1.

2. If we take a walk simply for the sake of walking, or to 'kill time,' the action (ἐνέργεια) of walking is itself so far the end that we look for no *ulterior* result (ἔργον). If we walk to get an appetite, or for the sake of health, then the appetite or health is a further end beyond the action of walking, and is therefore, as Aristotle proceeds to point out, an end of higher value to us than the act of walking. In this passage, however, Aristotle is thinking chiefly of acts of ποίησις, which are distinguished from acts of πρᾶξις by having definite and tangible products resulting from the action. (See Glossary.)

3. τέλη obviously correspond with ἔργα, and πράξεις with ἐνέργειαι, in the previous sentence.

παρὰ τὰς πράξεις, ἐν τούτοις βελτίω πέφυκε τῶν ἐνερ-
3 γειῶν τὰ ἔργα. Πολλῶν δὲ πράξεων οὐσῶν καὶ τεχνῶν
καὶ ἐπιστημῶν πολλὰ γίνεται καὶ τὰ τέλη· ἰατρικῆς
μὲν γὰρ ὑγίεια, ναυπηγικῆς δὲ πλοῖον, στρατηγικῆς δὲ
4 νίκη, οἰκονομικῆς δὲ πλοῦτος. Ὅσαι δ' εἰσὶ τῶν τοιούτων
ὑπὸ μίαν τινὰ δύναμιν, καθάπερ ὑπὸ τὴν ἱππικὴν ἡ
χαλινοποιϊκὴ καὶ ὅσαι ἄλλαι τῶν ἱππικῶν ὀργάνων
εἰσίν· αὕτη δὲ καὶ πᾶσα πολεμικὴ πρᾶξις ὑπὸ τὴν
στρατηγικήν· τὸν αὐτὸν δὴ τρόπον ἄλλαι ὑφ' ἑτέρας·
ἐν ἁπάσαις δὲ τὰ τῶν ἀρχιτεκτονικῶν τέλη πάντων ἐστὶν
αἱρετώτερα τῶν ὑπ' αὐτά· τούτων γὰρ χάριν κἀκεῖνα

(a) In kind.

variety of ways. (α) They differ in kind: sometimes the action is itself the end; sometimes a definite result beyond the action. And notice that when there is such an end beyond the action it is obviously something better than the
3 action itself, which is subordinate to it. (β) But further, the character of ends is as various as the character of the actions of which they are ends: *e.g.* health, victory, wealth, a boat, a house, the equipments of a horse, etc. etc., are all ends of different actions, and differ *inter se* accordingly.
4 (γ) In the midst of this variety, however, we may trace a relation of subordination, or degrees of finality, in ends. One art often embraces a variety of others, and their ends being subservient to the production of its end are of inferior value; for the ends of the higher and more comprehensive arts are

(β) in general character;

(γ) but many of these are connected in the way of subordination.

6. δύναμις is here equivalent to τέχνη. Art, differing from Science in that it supplies the *power* to produce practical results, is not unfrequently described as δύναμις. See in next ch. § 3. τίνος τῶν ἐπιστημῶν ἢ δυνάμεων, *i.e.* 'of which of the sciences or arts.' (See Glossary under δύναμις, and also under Art and Science.)

10. ἀρχιτεκτονικὴ] *i.e.* master-science, or arch-science, if we allowed such a compound. ἀρχιτέκτων is literally a ruler or director of workmen. (See next chapter, § 4, and esp. the expression αὕτη διατάσσει in § 5.)

5 διώκεται. Διαφέρει δ' οὐδὲν τὰς ἐνεργείας αὐτὰς εἶναι τὰ τέλη τῶν πράξεων ἢ παρὰ ταύτας ἄλλο τι, καθάπερ ἐπὶ τῶν λεχθεισῶν ἐπιστημῶν.

1 II. Εἰ δή τι τέλος ἐστὶ τῶν πρακτῶν ὃ δι' αὑτὸ βουλόμεθα, τἆλλα δὲ διὰ τοῦτο, καὶ μὴ πάντα δι' ἕτερον αἱρούμεθα (πρόεισι γὰρ οὕτω γ' εἰς ἄπειρον, ὥστ' εἶναι κενὴν καὶ ματαίαν τὴν ὄρεξιν), δῆλον ὡς τοῦτ' ἂν εἴη

5 obviously more final than those of the subordinated arts. In regard to this relation of subordination, it will make no difference whether the ends compared together are actions themselves or the results of actions.

CHAPS. II. AND III.—*There is such a thing as a* final *end of action*, i.e. *a Chief Good. If so,*

(α) *It will be practically useful to define it.*

(β) *The Political* (*or Social*) *Science is the Science which treats of it.*

(γ) *This is not an exact Science.*

(δ) *Its study requires special training and conditions.*

However, this subordination must stop somewhere; *i.e.* there must be some Final End.

1 Now we may safely infer that this subordination of ends cannot go on *ad infinitum*, because we should in that case be endued with a desire (viz. of finality) which would be objectless and useless: in other words, we may infer that there *is*

3. τῶν λεχθεισῶν ἐπιστημῶν] ἐπιστήμη appears to be used here, as elsewhere sometimes, for τέχνη. (See Glossary.)

7. κενή, empty, *i.e.* objectless. ματαία, vain and useless. This passage resembles what is called the argument from design. The major premiss is (as Aristotle elsewhere phrases it) οὐδὲν μάτην ἡ φύσις ποιεῖ, 'Nature does nothing in vain;' or, as we read in ix. 5, τὰ κατὰ φύσιν, ὡς οἷόν τε κάλλιστα ἔχειν, οὕτω πέφυκε, 'All things are by nature ordered in the best possible way.' The fact that human nature is created with a desire for some final good proves that such a good must exist. That it should not exist is as inconceivable as that nature should have created an animal re-

2 τἀγαθὸν καὶ τὸ ἄριστον. Ἆρ' οὖν καὶ πρὸς τὸν βίον ἡ
γνῶσις αὐτοῦ μεγάλην ἔχει ῥοπήν, καὶ καθάπερ τοξόται
3 σκοπὸν ἔχοντες, μᾶλλον ἂν τυγχάνοιμεν τοῦ δέοντος; εἰ
δ' οὕτω, πειρατέον τύπῳ γε περιλαβεῖν αὐτὸ τί ποτ'
4 ἐστὶ καὶ τίνος τῶν ἐπιστημῶν ἢ δυνάμεων. Δόξειε δ'
5 ἂν τῆς κυριωτάτης καὶ μάλιστα ἀρχιτεκτονικῆς. Τοι-
αύτη δ' ἡ πολιτικὴ φαίνεται. Τίνας γὰρ εἶναι χρεὼν

one supreme and Final End, to which all other ends converge; If so
2, 3 and that is, in fact, the Chief Good. (*α*) If this be so, it know of it w
must be useful to define it, because we shall be more likely to be pr
4 hit the mark when we have a distinct view of it. (*β*) The cally u
science to which pertains the knowledge of the Chief Good is It is Scienc
naturally the supreme of sciences, and this is the Science of Social
5 Social Life. We argue this supremacy on two grounds—(1) which t of it,

quiring a particular sort of food, and then have placed it where that sort of food could not be procured. Take as another illustration the precisely similar argument for a future state (which is still often regarded as the strongest, apart from revelation) based upon the aspirations of mankind for immortality, and for a higher ideal than can be reached in this life. 'It is not at all probable (says Dr. Clarke) that God should have given men appetites which were never to be satisfied, desires which had no objects to answer them, and unavoidable apprehensions of what was never really to come to pass.'

1. *καὶ πρὸς τὸν βίον*] 'even upon life.' These words are emphatic. The knowledge of the Chief Good might perhaps be thought to be theoretically interesting, but not practically important—just as Optics and Acoustics increase our knowledge, but do not help us to see and hear better. The objection here implied may be compared with that sometimes made to the utility of the study of Logic, viz., that men do reason correctly without it. The answer would be similar to that given in the text.

5. *δυνάμεων*] See note on i. 4.

6. *κύριος* = authoritative or supreme—as explained by the first argument in § 5.

ἀρχιτεκτονική] (see note on i. 4). This epithet is justified by the second argument in § 6. § 7 merely sums up the two preceding arguments, inverting their order.

7. *πολιτική* is difficult to translate, because both 'Politics' and

τῶν ἐπιστημῶν ἐν ταῖς πόλεσι, καὶ ποίας ἑκάστους
6 μανθάνειν καὶ μέχρι τίνος, αὕτη διατάσσει. Ὁρῶμεν δὲ
καὶ τὰς ἐντιμοτάτας τῶν δυναμεων ὑπὸ ταύτην οὔσας,
7 οἷον στρατηγικὴν οἰκονομικὴν ῥητορικήν. Χρωμένης δὲ
ταύτης ταῖς λοιπαῖς πρακτικαῖς τῶν ἐπιστημῶν, ἔτι δὲ
νομοθετούσης τί δεῖ πράττειν καὶ τίνων ἀπέχεσθαι, τὸ
ταύτης τέλος περιέχοι ἂν τὰ τῶν ἄλλων, ὥστε τοῦτ᾽
8 ἂν εἴη τἀνθρώπινον ἀγαθόν. Εἰ τὸ καὶ ταὐτόν ἐστιν
ἑνὶ καὶ πόλει, μεῖζόν γε καὶ τελεώτερον τὸ τῆς πόλεως
φαίνεται καὶ λαβεῖν και σώζειν· ἀγαπητὸν μὲν γὰρ καὶ
ἑνὶ μόνῳ, κάλλιον δὲ καὶ θειότερον ἔθνει καὶ πόλεσιν.)
9 Ἡ μὲν οὖν μέθοδος τούτων ἐφίεται, πολιτική τις
οὖσα.

this y be own be the preme ience:

this science regulates the study of all the other sciences in a
6, 7 community; and (2.) it employs their results, even in the
case of the most esteemed of them, in its own service, and
8 thus their ends are subordinated to its end. (If it be argued
that the good of society, which is the end of this science, is
only another name for the good of the individual men who
constitute society, we reply that the science which secures
9 this good on a large scale is still the supreme science.) Hence
the Science of Ethics is a branch of the Science of Social
Life.

'Social Science' have acquired a technical and inappropriate meaning. Paraphrased, it means the science which investigates the conditions of the perfection of social life, or of man living as a member of a well-ordered community. Aristotle remarks elsewhere, Man is created by nature a social animal, and therefore unless he lives in a society a portion of his nature is undeveloped. We cannot therefore treat of the well-being of man without considering him as a member of a society, nor therefore without also considering the conditions of the well-being of society. See further note on vii. 6.

1 III. *Λέγοιτο δ' ἂν ἱκανῶς, εἰ κατὰ τὴν ὑποκειμένην ὕλην διασαφηθείη· τὸ γὰρ ἀκριβὲς οὐχ ὁμοίως ἐν ἅπασι τοῖς λόγοις ἐπιζητητέον, ὥσπερ οὐδ' ἐν τοῖς δημιουρ-*
2 *γουμένοις. Τὰ δὲ καλὰ καὶ τὰ δίκαια, περὶ ὧν ἡ πολιτικὴ σκοπεῖται, τοσαύτην ἔχει διαφορὰν καὶ πλάνην*
3 *ὥστε δοκεῖν νόμῳ μόνον εἶναι, φύσει δὲ μή. (Τοιαύτην δέ τινα πλάνην ἔχει καὶ τἀγαθὰ διὰ τὸ πολλοῖς συμβαίνειν βλάβας ἀπ' αὐτῶν· ἤδη γάρ τινες ἀπώλοντο*
4 *διὰ πλοῦτον, ἕτεροι δὲ δι' ἀνδρείαν.) Ἀγαπητὸν οὖν περὶ τοιούτων καὶ ἐκ τοιούτων λέγοντας παχυλῶς καὶ*

1 CHAP. III.—(γ) In this subject we must be content with general and approximate conclusions. Ethics is not an
2 exact science. Exactness in a science must always be proportionate to the nature of its subject-matter. Now the ideas of 'right' and 'wrong,' 'just' and 'unjust,' are so fluctuating that some have been led to deny the reality of
3 such distinctions altogether. (We may just note in passing that this is due to a confusion of thought between 'wrong' and 'harmful,' or 'injurious.' Many things in them-
4 selves good and desirable are on occasions a source of mischief.) Such then being our subject-matter and such

This is a Scien which e ness is tainabl re consequently, our conclusions will be genera and approximate only.

1. ὕλη and ὑποκειμένη are philosophical terms. The former = 'matter' or 'material,' and the latter (as is seen from its etymology) = 'underlying' or 'subject.' Hence the words together = 'subject-matter.'

3. δημιουργουμένοις] δημιουργὸς is a workman. Hence δημιουργούμενα are 'products of art.' See note on vii. 18. As we do not expect a model in cork or wood to be as well finished as one in ivory, so we ought not to expect an argument in a subject variable and fluctuating to be as rigid as one in mathematics.

6. We may notice, once for all, that δοκεῖ in Aristotle's phraseology does not necessarily imply (like our expression 'it seems') that what follows is the writer's own opinion. Here, for instance, he proceeds to argue against the statement introduced by δοκεῖ in § 3. It would generally be better to translate, 'it has been thought.'

τύπῳ τἀληθὲς ἐνδείκνυσθαι, καὶ περὶ τῶν ὡς ἐπὶ τὸ πολὺ καὶ ἐκ τοιούτων λέγοντας τοιαῦτα καὶ συμπεραίνεσθαι.

Τὸν αὐτὸν δὲ τρόπον καὶ ἀποδέχεσθαι χρεὼν ἕκαστον τῶν λεγομένων· πεπαιδευμένου γάρ ἐστιν ἐπὶ τοσοῦτον τἀκριβὲς ἐπιζητεῖν καθ' ἕκαστον γένος, ἐφ' ὅσον ἡ τοῦ πράγματος φύσις ἐπιδέχεται· παραπλήσιον γὰρ φαίνεται μαθηματικοῦ τε πιθανολογοῦντος ἀποδέχεσθαι καὶ ῥητορικὸν ἀποδείξεις ἀπαιτεῖν. Ἕκαστος δὲ κρίνει

our premisses, such must also be our conclusions, in respect of exactness.

...ica- requi- in the ...nt of Science

(δ) The aims of the teacher being thus qualified, so also must be the demands of the learner. He must neither require too rigid accuracy, nor be content with any needless generality. Such exactness as is admitted by the subject-matter, neither more nor less, should he demand. But this discrimination

1. ὡς-ἐπὶ-τὸ-πολὺ is equivalent to one word, and means 'general' or 'variable.' τὰ ὡς-ἐπὶ-τὸ-πολὺ γιγνόμενα are things which happen as a general rule in such and such a way; 'generalities' as opposed to 'certainties.'

3. ἀποδέχεσθαι means 'to allow,' in the old English sense of 'to approve' (*e.g.* 'The Lord *alloweth* the righteous'); hence *h. l.* 'to accept as satisfactory,' 'to acquiesce in.' See IV. vi. 3, where ἀποδέξεται, 'he will allow,' stands in opposition to δυσχερανεῖ, 'he will disapprove.'

6. παραπλήσιον γὰρ φαίνεται κ.τ.λ.] It would be equally absurd to be satisfied with plausible arguments from a mathematician, as to insist upon rigid demonstration from an orator. Mathematics being an exact science, no considerations of the probability of a theorem being true, however great, are of the slightest use. Rhetoric being the 'art of persuasion,' the logical value of its arguments is entirely subordinate to their persuasiveness.

8. ἕκαστος δὲ κρίνει κ.τ.λ.] '*Cuique perito credendum est in suâ arte.*' The right of criticism in any subject depends on special training in that subject. We bow to the dictum of the painter in painting, to that of the musician in music. In general matters we look, in like manner, to the man of general knowledge and cultivation. This is evidently the sense re-

καλῶς ἃ γινώσκει, καὶ τούτων ἐστὶν ἀγαθὸς κριτής.
Καθ' ἕκαστον ἄρα ὁ πεπαιδευμένος, ἁπλῶς δ' ὁ περὶ
πᾶν πεπαιδευμένος. Διὸ τῆς πολιτικῆς οὐκ ἔστιν οἰκεῖος
ἀκροατὴς ὁ νέος· ἄπειρος γὰρ τῶν κατὰ τὸν βίον
6 πράξεων, οἱ λόγοι δ' ἐκ τούτων καὶ περὶ τούτων. Ἔτι
δὲ τοῖς πάθεσιν ἀκολουθητικὸς ὢν ματαίως ἀκούσεται
καὶ ἀνωφελῶς, ἐπειδὴ τὸ τέλος ἐστὶν οὐ γνῶσις ἀλλὰ
7 πρᾶξις. Διαφέρει δ' οὐθὲν νέος τὴν ἡλικίαν ἢ τὸ ἦθος
νεαρός· οὐ γὰρ παρὰ τὸν χρόνον ἡ ἔλλειψις, ἀλλὰ διὰ
τὸ κατὰ πάθος ζῆν καὶ διώκειν ἕκαστα. Τοῖς γὰρ τοιού-
τοις ἀνόνητος ἡ γνῶσις γίνεται, καθάπερ τοῖς ἀκρατέσιν·

implies special education and special qualities in the learner,
else he will have neither the right nor the power of exercising
such a judgment. The young therefore are not fit students of (1.) mature age;
6 Ethical Science, partly from their ignorance of life and its ex-
periences, and partly from the strength of their passions, which
7 they have not yet learned to master. And we must further (2.) well-regulated passions.
exclude all who, however old in years, are but children in

quired; and so the following passage would certainly be clearer if it read thus:—Καθ' ἕκαστον ἄρα ὁ [καθ' ἕκαστον] πεπαιδευμένος, ἁπλῶς δὲ κ.τ.λ., the words in brackets being supplied. Some critics suppose this to have been the original reading.

3. The young should be taught the *practice* of morals before they attempt the *theory*. Their duty is to obey, without asking questions, without criticising the principles of what they have to obey, until the habit of obedience is gained. Then they may be trusted to look into the theory and principles of conduct, and indeed, unless they would always be children, they ought to do so. '*Oportet discentem credere, edoctum judicare*' (Bacon). For the latter point see the end of § 7, where εἰδέναι is emphatic; for the former see X. x., where Aristotle maintains that moral teaching will be lost labour unless either parental authority or State laws can be relied on to enforce this preliminary work of training and discipline.

11. ἀκρατέσιν] The following explanation of terms may be useful:-

τοῖς δὲ κατὰ λόγον τὰς ὀρέξεις ποιουμένοις καὶ πράτ-
8 τουσι πολυωφελὲς ἂν εἴη τὸ περὶ τούτων εἰδέναι. Καὶ
περὶ μὲν ἀκροατοῦ, καὶ πῶς ἀποδεκτέον, καὶ τί προτιθέμεθα, πεφροιμιάσθω τοσαῦτα.

I IV. *Λέγωμεν δ' ἀναλαβόντες, ἐπειδὴ πᾶσα γνῶσις καὶ προαίρεσις ἀγαθοῦ τινὸς ὀρέγεται, τί ἐστιν οὗ λέγομεν*

8 character; all, that is, who live under the sway of passion and not reason. For Ethics is a science in which right knowledge profits nothing unless it is accompanied by right practice; while right practice will ever derive the greatest advantage if supplemented by right knowledge.

CHAP. IV.—*What is the Chief Good?—Conflicting opinions—Determination of the method to be adopted.*

All allow that 'Happiness' is the Chief Good.

I After these preliminary explanations we recur to the question, What is the aim of this Science of Social Life? or,

ἀκρατὴς is a man who acts wrongly after a struggle between good and bad desires.

ἐγκρατὴς is a man who acts rightly in a similar case.

ἀκόλαστος is one in whom vice has become a habit, and the desire of good is eradicated; he does wrong without a struggle.

σώφρων is one in whom virtue has become a habit; bad desires are conquered; he does right without an effort; or, as Bishop Butler expresses it, 'particular affections become absolutely coincident with the moral principle.' *Anal.* p. 101 (Angus's edit.).

See, in illustration, I. xiii. 15; III. ii. 4. Hence the *ἀκρατὴς* is precisely in the case described in the text: he *knows* right but *does* wrong.

IV. Compare Pope, *Essay on Man*, iv. 1:—

Oh Happiness! our being's end and aim!
Good, Pleasure, Ease, Content, whate'er thy name—
That something still which prompts the eternal sigh,
For which we bear to live, or dare to die.

Or again, line 21, etc.

Some place the bliss in action, some in ease,
Those call it Pleasure, and Contentment these;
Some, sunk to beasts, find pleasure end in pain;
Some, swelled to gods, confess ev'n virtue vain:

τὴν πολιτικὴν ἐφίεσθαι καὶ τί τὸ πάντων ἀκρότατον τῶν
2 πρακτῶν ἀγαθῶν. Ὀνόματι μὲν οὖν σχεδὸν ὑπὸ τῶν
πλείστων ὁμολογεῖται· τὴν γὰρ εὐδαιμονίαν καὶ οἱ πολλοὶ
καὶ οἱ χαρίεντες λέγουσιν, τὸ δ' εὖ ζῆν καὶ τὸ εὖ πράττειν
ταὐτὸν ὑπολαμβάνουσι τῷ εὐδαιμονεῖν. Περὶ δὲ τῆς
εὐδαιμονίας, τί ἐστιν, ἀμφισβητοῦσι καὶ οὐχ ὁμοίως οἱ
3 πολλοὶ τοῖς σοφοῖς ἀποδιδόασιν. Οἱ μὲν γὰρ τῶν
ἐναργῶν τι καὶ φανερῶν, οἷον ἡδονὴν ἢ πλοῦτον ἢ τιμήν,
ἄλλοι δ' ἄλλο, πολλάκις δὲ καὶ ὁ αὐτὸς ἕτερον· νοσήσας
μὲν γὰρ ὑγίειαν, πενόμενος δὲ πλοῦτον· συνειδότες δ'
ἑαυτοῖς ἄγνοιαν τοὺς μέγα τι καὶ ὑπὲρ αὐτοὺς λέγοντας
θαυμάζουσιν. Ἔνιοι δ' ᾤοντο παρὰ τὰ πολλὰ ταῦτα
ἀγαθὰ ἄλλο τι καθ' αὑτὸ εἶναι, ὃ καὶ τοῖσδε πᾶσιν

2 as we put it at first, What is the Chief Good? In name all
alike agree that it is Happiness: but when we further ask
3 What is Happiness? one says one thing, and one another,
and even the same person says differently at different times.
Pleasure, wealth, honour, health, some abstract ideal of good,

But there is endless variety of opinions as to what Happiness consists in.

Or indolent, to each extreme they fall,
To trust in everything, or doubt of all.
Who thus define it, say they more or less
Than this, that Happiness is Happiness?

2. πρακτῶν is emphatic. See note below on line 13.

4. χαρίεντες] 'men of culture.'

6. This divergence of opinion may be illustrated by the fact that an ingenious writer (Varro) claimed to have counted 285 different theories on this subject.

10. συνειδότες κ.τ.λ.] We always value that most which for the time we want. In sickness we think no good can compare with health; in poverty we think nothing would make us so happy as money; when conscious of ignorance ourselves we are dazzled by a display of knowledge which is beyond us.

13. This is Plato's theory of the 'Idea' of Good, criticised by Aristotle at length in chapter vi. The Chief Good, according to Plato, is the Quality or Condition invariably present in everything Good, the possession of which causes the same term 'Good' to be applicable in each case. We speak of a good man, or horse, or poem, or poison, or antidote, etc. etc. We should not apply the same term 'Good,'

4 αἴτιόν ἐστι τοῦ εἶναι ἀγαθά. Ἁπάσας μὲν οὖν ἐξετάζειν
τὰς δόξας ματαιότερον ἴσως ἐστίν, ἱκανὸν δὲ τὰς μάλιστα
5 ἐπιπολαζούσας ἢ δοκούσας ἔχειν τινὰ λόγον. Μὴ λανθανέτω δ' ἡμᾶς ὅτι διαφέρουσιν οἱ ἀπὸ τῶν ἀρχῶν λόγοι καὶ οἱ ἐπὶ τὰς ἀρχάς. Εὖ γὰρ καὶ Πλάτων ἠπόρει τοῦτο καὶ ἐζήτει, πότερον ἀπὸ τῶν ἀρχῶν ἢ ἐπὶ τὰς ἀρχάς ἐστιν ἡ ὁδός, ὥσπερ ἐν τῷ σταδίῳ ἀπὸ τῶν ἀθλοθετῶν ἐπὶ τὸ πέρας ἢ ἀνάπαλιν. Ἀρκτέον μὲν οὖν ἀπὸ τῶν γνωρίμων, ταῦτα δὲ διττῶς· τὰ μὲν γὰρ ἡμῖν τὰ

All s that ' piness the ' Good.

We determine the *method* of our inquiry to be *from* facts of observation *to* general principles, and not *vice versâ.*

4 are some of these various answers. We shall not attempt to
do more than investigate the more obvious or more reason-
5 able of these conflicting views. At the very outset we must determine the *method* of our inquiry. Shall we start *a priori* from general principles, or shall we start *a posteriori* from observed facts? One thing is clear: we must argue from the known to the unknown; and that in reference to our human knowledge, not in reference to any abstract or ideal system of knowledge. Now, in the order of *our* knowledge, facts come

unless the same idea were present in all these various cases. Whatever that be which is thus the one cause of Goodness, wherever it is found, is itself the Chief Good of all. This Plato termed the Ἰδέα of Good. Notice the contrast between the search for this 'Idea' of Good, and Aristotle's carefully limited inquiry for the Chief Good *for man*, the Chief Good of *human action*, etc.

3. ἐπιπολή is a 'surface' or 'superficies'; ἐπιπολάζω is 'to lie on the surface; hence *h.l.* either 'obvious' (the reverse of 'recondite'), or 'widely-spread.' (See *Suppl. Note.*)

4. See the Glossary on the terms *a priori* and *a posteriori*, and also *s.v.* ἀρχή.

9. γνωρίμων . . . . . διττῶς] Aristotle elsewhere explains that general laws are better known than particular facts in the *perfect* or *ideal* order of knowledge (γνωριμώτερα φύσει or ἁπλῶς), but particular facts are better known than general laws in the order of *human* knowledge (γνωριμώτερα ἡμῖν). *We* are more familiar with the fall of an apple, or the motion of a particular star than with the law of gravitation. A being with more perfect knowledge would be more familiar with the general

δ' ἁπλῶς. Ἴσως οὖν ἡμῖν γε ἀρκτέον ἀπὸ τῶν ἡμῖν
6 γνωρίμων. Διὸ δεῖ τοῖς ἔθεσιν ἦχθαι καλῶς τὸν περὶ

before general laws. We must therefore start from facts.
6 But seeing that the very facts of moral science are unintel-

laws governing the universe, than with particular instances of their application. As we ascend in the scale of intelligence 'the individual withers and the world is more and more.' Hence, practically, γνώριμα φύσει come to be Laws, Principles, Universals; γνώριμα ἡμῖν, Facts, Particulars.

1. Observe the emphasis on ἡμῖν γε. 'Perhaps then *we* at any rate must begin from what is known *to us*.' Aristotle does not assert that there may not be a more ideally perfect way of approaching the subject. Compare the two methods of ethical teaching explained by Bishop Butler (Introd. to Sermons): 'There are two ways in which the subject of Morals may be treated. One begins from inquiring into the abstract relations of things (ἀπὸ τῶν ἀρχῶν), the other from a matter of fact, namely, what the particular nature of man is, its several parts, etc. (ἐπὶ τὰς ἀρχὰς). . . . The first seems the most direct *formal* proof: . . . the latter is, in a peculiar manner, adapted to satisfy a fair mind, and is more easily applicable to the several particular relations and circumstances in life.' So also Hume (*General Principles of Morals*, p. 221, ed. 1800): 'As this is a question of fact, not of abstract science, we can only expect success by following the experimental method, and deducing general maxims from a comparison of particular instances (λόγοι ἐπὶ τὰς ἀρχάς). The other scientific method, where a general abstract principle is first established (λόγοι ἀπὸ τῶν ἀρχῶν), and is afterwards branched out into a variety of inferences and conclusions, may be more perfect in itself, but suits less the imperfection of human nature' (ἡμῖν γε ἀρκτέον ἀπὸ τῶν ἡμῖν γνωρίμων). To begin with γνώριμα ἡμῖν is, of course, to proceed ἐπὶ τὰς ἀρχάς, and not ἀπὸ τῶν ἀρχῶν.

2. Διο δεῖ τοῖς ἔθεσιν ἦχθαι] The *facts* of morals (in the sense of this passage) are the notions (in their most simple and rudimentary form) of right, wrong, just, unjust, duty, etc. The study presupposes that these notions are, at least to some degree, intelligible to us; that when the terms are used they convey some sort of meaning to us (τὸ ὅτι), though we may not be able to define them accurately, or to say *what constitutes* rightness, wrongness, etc. (τὸ διότι), or even to prove that there are any real distinctions in the

καλῶν καὶ δικαίων καὶ ὅλως τῶν πολιτικῶν ἀκουσόμενον ἱκανῶς. Ἀρχὴ γὰρ τὸ ὅτι· καὶ εἰ τοῦτο φαίνοιτο ἀρ-

ligible without some preliminary training in good habits, we must further presuppose such a training. Nor is it necessary

nature of things corresponding to the notions expressed by these and similar words. Still, even such a dim appreciation as this implies some training in good habits, and it would scarcely be found in a perfectly untutored savage. Nay more, even in civilized life it is only experience of a virtue (*τοῖς ἔθεσιν ἦχθαι*) which can make it intelligible to us individually. Hence the idea of 'humility' was unintelligible to the Greeks; it was never practised, and so their language had no word for it. Missionaries find it impossible to explain or express to savages some of the fundamental ideas of the Christian religion for the same reason. The condition '*τοῖς ἔθεσιν ἦχθαι*' has not been fulfilled.

2. Ἀρχὴ γὰρ τὸ ὅτι] 'For the *fact* is a starting point;' or, 'the assumption of moral *facts* (without their reason or theory) will enable us to make a start.' All that we need presuppose, and that much we must presuppose, is the *primâ facie* fact of moral distinctions, and a capacity for their recognition in the learner, though he may not at first know how to apply them to the details of action. Without this much, Ethics would have no *raison d'être* (see Introd. p. xvi); there would be no subject-matter for the science to treat of, or faculties to which it could appeal. This will appear plainly if we look at the case of one or two other sciences. The Science of Painting (1) assumes, or does not question, the existence of colours; and (2) presupposes that the learner is able to distinguish colours—that he is not blind. The Science of Music (1) assumes the existence of harmonious and discordant sounds; and (2) presupposes that the learner can appreciate the difference—that he is not deaf. That would be the meaning of *ἀρχὴ τὸ ὅτι* as applied in these two cases. Similarly the Science of Morals assumes (1) a distinction between Right and Wrong; and (2) a capacity in the learner to recognise that distinction (hence *δεῖ τοῖς ἔθεσιν ἦχθαι*). The grounds in Nature which constitute differences of colours, or harmony and discord of sounds, or the essential distinction between Right and Wrong,—these lie not at the threshold, but in the inmost shrine of the respective sciences. These questions would correspond with *τὸ διότι*, with which, as Aristotle says, we have nothing to do at the commencement.

κούντως, οὐδὲν προσδεήσει τοῦ διότι. Ὁ δὲ τοιοῦτος ἢ ἔχει ἢ λάβοι ἂν ἀρχὰς ῥᾳδίως. ᾯ δὲ μηδέτερον ὑπάρχει, τούτων, ἀκουσάτω τῶν Ἡσιόδου·

Οὗτος μὲν πανάριστος ὃς αὐτὸς πάντα νοήσῃ,
Ἐσθλὸς δ' αὖ κἀκεῖνος ὃς εὖ εἰπόντι πίθηται.
Ὃς δέ κε μήτ' αὐτὸς νοέῃ μήτ' ἄλλου ἀκούων
Ἐν θυμῷ βάλληται, ὁ δ' αὖτ' ἀχρήϊος ἀνήρ.

1 V. Ἡμεῖς δὲ λέγωμεν ὅθεν παρεξέβημεν. Τὸ γὰρ ἀγαθὸν καὶ τὴν εὐδαιμονίαν οὐκ ἀλόγως ἐοίκασιν ἐκ τῶν βίων ὑπολαμβάνειν οἱ μὲν πολλοὶ καὶ φορτικώτατοι τὴν ἡδονήν, διὸ καὶ τὸν βίον ἀγαπῶσι τὸν ἀπολαυστικόν.
2 Τρεῖς γάρ εἰσι μάλιστα οἱ προὔχοντες, ὅ τε νῦν εἰρη-

at the outset that the learner should be able to explain the principles and reasons of the facts from which we start. To the learner who is worth anything these will come in due time, if he have them not already.

CHAP. V.—*Criticism of the chief typical theories as to the nature of Happiness.*

1 Returning from this digression, let us consider some typical
2 views as to the nature of Happiness. Some say that it consists in bodily pleasure, others in honour, others in philosophic

We next consider some of the chief theories about Happiness, such that it consists in (a) Pleasure.

CHAP. V.—Three main theories about Happiness, which may at least be inferred from the actual lives of men, are suggested for examination in this chapter; two more come in incidentally. That they are justly selected as typical and progressive views of the nature of Happiness is shown at length in the Introduction, p. xxix.

8. ὅθεν παρεξέβημεν] viz., the promise in § 4 of the last chapter.

9. 'They are not unreasonably inferred from their manner of life to suppose happiness to consist in pleasure.' Most men have no conscious theory about Happiness and the Chief Good, but what they really think may be inferred from their practice.

10. φορτικὸς = 'troublesome,' 'burdensome;' and then (like βάναυσος) 'coarse,' 'vulgar.' It is applied to buffoons in IV. viii. 3. See also X. viii. 7.

3 μένος καὶ ὁ πολιτικὸς καὶ τρίτος ὁ θεωρητικός. Οἱ μὲν
οὖν πολλοὶ παντελῶς ἀνδραποδώδεις φαίνονται βοσκη-
μάτων βίον προαιρούμενοι, τυγχάνουσι δὲ λόγου διὰ τὸ
πολλοὺς τῶν ἐν ταῖς ἐξουσίαις ὁμοιοπαθεῖν Σαρδανα-
4 πάλλῳ. Οἱ δὲ χαρίεντες καὶ πρακτικοὶ τιμήν· τοῦ γὰρ
πολιτικοῦ βίου σχεδὸν τοῦτο τέλος. Φαίνεται δ' ἐπι-
πολαιότερον εἶναι τοῦ ζητουμένου· δοκεῖ γὰρ ἐν τοῖς
τιμῶσι μᾶλλον εἶναι ἢ ἐν τῷ τιμωμένῳ, τἀγαθὸν δὲ
5 οἰκεῖόν τι καὶ δυσαφαίρετον εἶναι μαντευόμεθα. Ἔτι δ'
ἐοίκασι τὴν τιμὴν διώκειν, ἵνα πιστεύωσιν ἑαυτοὺς ἀγα-
θοὺς εἶναι· ζητοῦσι γοῦν ὑπὸ τῶν φρονίμων τιμᾶσθαι,
καὶ παρ' οἷς γιγνώσκονται, καὶ ἐπ' ἀρετῇ· δῆλον οὖν ὅτι

3 contemplation. As to the *first*, it is the life of mere animals,
though the ignorant have the example of the great and
4 powerful to justify their choice. As to the *second*, we object:
β) Honour; —(1) Honour is precarious, being dependent upon others,
5 who may refuse it however well it be deserved; and (2)
Honour is only sought as a kind of recognition of merit, and
on the ground of virtue. And if so, Virtue is, according to
the principles already laid down, a more final end than

4. Sardanapalus was the last king of Nineveh, whose name became proverbial for luxury and effeminacy.

5. πρακτικοὶ] 'of an active turn.'

6. ἐπιπολαιότερον] 'too superficial.' See note on iv. 4.

7. ἐν τοῖς τιμῶσι] Compare Pope—

What's fame? A fancied life in others' breath,
A thing beyond us, e'en before our death.

And with the next clause compare—

All fame is foreign, but of true desert.

9. οἰκεῖόν τι] 'something peculiarly one's own.'

10. Compare Bacon's *Essay on Praise*, which commences,—'Praise is the reflection of Virtue (ἵνα πιστεύωσιν ἑαυτοὺς ἀγαθοὺς εἶναι), but it is as the glass or body which giveth the reflection. If it be from the common people it is commonly false and naught, and rather followeth vain persons than virtuous' (ζητοῦσι γοῦν ὑπὸ τῶν φρονιμῶν τιμᾶσθαι κ.τ.λ.)

12. ἐπ' ἀρετῇ] 'on grounds of merit.' We do not care to be held in honour by worthless

6 κατά γε τούτους ἡ ἀρετὴ κρείττων. Τάχα δὲ καὶ μᾶλλον
ἂν τις τέλος τοῦ πολιτικοῦ βίου ταύτην ὑπολάβοι. Φαί-
νεται δὲ ἀτελεστέρα καὶ αὕτη· δοκεῖ γὰρ ἐνδέχεσθαι καὶ
καθεύδειν ἔχοντα τὴν ἀρετήν, ἢ ἀπρακτεῖν διὰ βίου, καὶ
πρὸς τούτοις κακοπαθεῖν καὶ ἀτυχεῖν τὰ μέγιστα· τὸν δ'
οὕτω ζῶντα οὐδεὶς ἂν εὐδαιμονίσειεν, εἰ μὴ θέσιν δια-
7 φυλάττων. Καὶ περὶ μὲν τούτων ἅλις· ἱκανῶς γὰρ καὶ
ἐν τοῖς ἐγκυκλίοις εἴρηται περὶ αὐτῶν· τρίτος δ' ἐστὶν
ὁ θεωρητικός, περὶ οὗ τὴν ἐπίσκεψιν ἐν τοῖς ἑπομένοις
8 ποιησόμεθα. Ὁ δὲ χρηματιστὴς βίαιός τις ἐστίν, καὶ ὁ
πλοῦτος δῆλον ὅτι οὐ τὸ ζητούμενον ἀγαθόν· χρήσιμον

6 Honour, which cannot therefore be the Chief Good. If it be
further asked, Is Virtue itself the Chief Good? we reply, No: (γ) Virtue;
because a man may be virtuous and yet through various
accidents lead a life of forced inactivity or of positive suffer-
ing, and this could not without paradox be called a happy
7 life. As to the *third*, we reserve what we have to say for the (δ) Philosophical contemplation:
8 present. We ought perhaps to add that wealth cannot be (ε) Riches.
the Chief Good, because wealth is obviously a means and not

men, or upon trivial or discreditable grounds. Cf. IV. iii. 17.

6. *θέσιν διαφυλάττων* refers to the discussions in the rhetorical schools, where, a subject or thesis (*θέσις*) being proposed, the pupils took different sides of the question to defend (*διαφυλάττειν*) as an exercise, irrespective of their own views on the subject.

8. *ἐγκυκλίοις*] *sc.* *λόγοις*. *i.e.* 'Popular treatises,'—such as might be met with in the ordinary round of life.

9. *ἐπίσκεψις*] 'a thorough investigation.' This will be found in B. X.

10. *βίαιός τις* may be explained either (1) 'under a sort of constraint,' opposed to *ἑκούσιος* (as in III. i., etc.), because no one would toil for wealth if he could secure the luxuries etc. which wealth procures without this toil; (*ἀναγκαῖος* is used to express the same idea in X. vi. 2); or (2) 'unnatural' (= *παρὰ φύσιν*), because it is a perversion of the nature of things to make an end of wealth, which is essentially a means, as much as it would be (*e.g.*) to accumulate railway-tickets without any intention of travelling.

γὰρ καὶ ἄλλου χάριν. Διὸ μᾶλλον τὰ πρότερον λεχθέντα τέλη τις ἂν ὑπολάβοι· δι' αὑτὰ γὰρ ἀγαπᾶται. Φαίνεται δ' οὐδ' ἐκεῖνα· καίτοι πολλοὶ λόγοι πρὸς αὐτὰ καταβέβληνται.

1 VI. Ταῦτα μὲν οὖν ἀφείσθω· τὸ δὲ καθόλου βέλτιον ἴσως ἐπισκέψασθαι καὶ διαπορῆσαι πῶς λέγεται, καίπερ προσάντους τῆς τοιαύτης ζητήσεως γινομένης διὰ τὸ φίλους ἄνδρας εἰσαγαγεῖν τὰ εἴδη. Δόξειε δ' ἂν ἴσως βέλτιον εἶναι καὶ δεῖν ἐπὶ σωτηρίᾳ γε τῆς ἀληθείας καὶ τὰ οἰκεῖα ἀναιρεῖν, ἄλλως τε καὶ φιλοσόφους ὄντας·

an end, and, as such, men seek it of compulsion and not of free choice, in order to secure the results to which it leads.

CHAP. VI.—*Criticism of the Platonic Theory that the Chief Good is the abstract 'Idea' of Good.*

Finally, the Chief Good has been held to consist in a 'transcendental Idea' of Good.

1 We proceed to the last of the important theories as to the nature of the Chief Good above mentioned (iv. 3), viz., that it is some one abstract ideal entering into each several manifestation of 'good.' Respect for the authors of this theory makes the discussion unwelcome, but the love of truth renders

4. καταβέβληνται] 'have been constructed.' The metaphor is probably from καταβάλλειν θεμέλια, 'to lay down the foundations of a building.'

CHAP. VI.—This chapter simply continues the proposed examination of the theories of the Chief Good selected in ch. iv. as being the most important and worthy of notice. See note on iv. 3 for a brief explanation of the theory criticised in this chapter.

5. τὸ καθόλου] literally 'the Universal,' *i.e.* the theory of one abstract and universal Good present in all particular manifestations of Good, and yet separable from them. This was called by Plato the 'Idea' of Good.

8. τὰ εἴδη] much the same as τὰς ἰδέας, *i.e.* the theory of 'Ideas.'

φίλους ἄνδρας] Especially Aristotle's own master and teacher, Plato.

ἀμφοῖν γὰρ ὄντοιν φίλοιν ὅσιον προτιμᾶν τὴν ἀλήθειαν.
2 Οἱ δὲ κομίσαντες τὴν δόξαν ταύτην οὐκ ἐποίουν ἰδέας ἐν
οἷς τὸ πρότερον καὶ τὸ ὕστερον ἔλεγον, διόπερ οὐδὲ τῶν
ἀριθμῶν ἰδέαν κατεσκεύαζον· τὸ δ' ἀγαθὸν λέγεται καὶ
ἐν τῷ τί ἐστι καὶ ἐν τῷ ποιῷ καὶ ἐν τῷ πρός τι, τὸ δὲ
καθ' αὑτὸ καὶ ἡ οὐσία πρότερον τῇ φύσει τοῦ πρός τι·
παραφυάδι γὰρ τοῦτ' ἔοικε καὶ συμβεβηκότι τοῦ ὄντος,
3 ὥστ' οὐκ ἂν εἴη κοινή τις ἐπὶ τούτων ἰδέα. Ἔτι ἐπεὶ

2 it necessary. We argue against it as follows:—(i) There
can be no one abstract 'Idea' of several objects of which
some are necessarily prior or posterior to others. (This is
allowed by the authors of the theory, who on this account
denied its application to *numbers*.) Now this is evidently the
case with the numerous objects called 'Good,' since we have
Good in Substance and Good in Relation, etc. Therefore
3 there cannot be one abstract Idea of 'Good.' (ii) If all Good

We object to this—That Good is predicated (1) of objects prior and posterior to one another in nature; (2) of objects falling under various Categories;

1. Hence the well-known saying, 'Amicus Plato, sed magis amica veritas.'

6. πρότερον τῇ φύσει.] Aristotle (Categ. xii. 1, 2) distinguishes πρότερον κατὰ χρόνον and πρότερον in the following sense (which practically amounts to πρότερον τῇ φύσει): When two things, A and B, are so related that the existence of B necessarily implies the existence of A, but not *vice versâ*, then A is πρότερον 'in the order of Being' as compared with B. He gives as an instance the numbers 1 and 2, which stand in this relation to one another. On this ground (he argues in the text) the Platonists made no 'Idea' of Numbers, such an interdependence in respect of essential priority and posteriority being out of the question among phenomena partaking of one 'Idea' (see further note on § 6). Thus the major premiss would be granted by his opponents. In the minor premiss Aristotle contends that such an essential priority (πρότερον τῇ φύσει) belongs to Substance as compared with Accident or Relation, and as Good is predicated of each, there cannot be a common Idea of Good in these cases.

8. This second argument is little more than a repetition of the first, clothed in more technical Aristotelian phraseology, and worked out into more detail.

ταγαθὸν ἰσαχῶς λέγεται τῷ ὄντι (καὶ γὰρ ἐν τῷ τί λέ-
γεται, οἷον ὁ θεὸς καὶ ὁ νοῦς, καὶ ἐν τῷ ποιῷ αἱ ἀρεταί,
καὶ ἐν τῷ ποσῷ τὸ μέτριον, καὶ ἐν τῷ πρός τι τὸ χρή-
σιμον, καὶ ἐν χρόνῳ καιρὸς, καὶ ἐν τόπῳ δίαιτα καὶ
ἕτερα τοιαῦτα), δῆλον ὡς οὐκ ἂν εἴη κοινόν τι καθόλου
καὶ ἕν· οὐ γὰρ ἂν ἐλέγετ' ἐν πάσαις ταῖς κατηγορίαις,
4 ἀλλ' ἐν μιᾷ μόνῃ. Ἔτι δ' ἐπεὶ τῶν κατὰ μίαν ἰδέαν μία
καὶ ἐπιστήμη, καὶ τῶν ἀγαθῶν ἁπάντων ἦν ἂν μία τις
ἐπιστήμη· νῦν δ' εἰσὶ πολλαὶ καὶ τῶν ὑπὸ μίαν κατηγο-
ρίαν, οἷον καιροῦ ἐν πολέμῳ μὲν στρατηγικὴ ἐν νόσῳ δ'

were included under one 'Idea,' it ought to be predicated under one Category only: but it can be predicated under all and each of the Categories. Hence again it cannot be reduced
4 to one 'Idea.' (iii) The knowledge of things reducible to one Idea must be one and indivisible, whereas of things Good there are many divisions of knowledge, and that even of Goods

(3) of objects treated of by various divisions of knowledge.

1. ἰσαχῶς λέγεται τῷ ὄντι] 'can be predicated in as many ways as Being itself.' The expressions which follow are taken from the phraseology of Aristotle's Categories. Only the first six out of the ten usually given are mentioned in the text. They have been variously held to be a classification of things, words, or thoughts. For a clear and succinct account of Aristotle's Categories, and the controversy respecting their nature, the student is referred to Dean Mansel's edition of Aldrich's Logic. Note B. in the Appendix (Ed. iii.) The argument in the text is, that as 'good' may be predicated of each and all of the several modes of existence classified in the Categories, such variety cannot be reduced under one 'Idea.'

7. Ἔτι δ' ἐπεὶ] Aristotle now argues that the divisions of Knowledge relating to the various manifestations of Good indicate a still further subdivision even than the distinction of Categories. It should be remembered that ἐπιστήμη in Aristotle refers rather to a mental state (see VI. ii., and Glossary, *s.v.* Art, Science) than to a concrete body of knowledge. He argues therefore that if the various manifestations of Good were reducible to one 'Idea,' the knowledge of one would be the knowledge of all.

ἰατρική, καὶ τοῦ μετρίου ἐν τροφῇ μὲν ἰατρικὴ ἐν πόνοις
5 δὲ γυμναστική. Ἀπορήσειε δ' ἄν τις τί ποτε καὶ βού-
λονται λέγειν αὐτοέκαστον, εἴπερ ἔν τε αὐτοανθρώπῳ
καὶ ἀνθρώπῳ εἷς καὶ ὁ αὐτὸς λόγος ἐστὶν ὁ τοῦ ἀνθρώ-
που· ᾗ γὰρ ἄνθρωπος, οὐδὲν διοίσουσιν· εἰ δ' οὕτως,
6 οὐδ' ᾗ ἀγαθόν. Ἀλλὰ μὴν οὐδὲ τῷ ἀίδιον εἶναι μᾶλλον
ἀγαθὸν ἔσται, εἴπερ μηδὲ λευκότερον τὸ πολυχρόνιον
7 τοῦ ἐφημέρου. Πιθανώτερον δ' ἐοίκασιν οἱ Πυθαγόρειοι

5 which can be brought under one Category. (iv) Again,
What *is* this abstract 'Idea' of anything? and how does its
definition differ from that of any object in which it is em-
bodied? and if there is no difference how can the 'Idea' lay
6 claim to a separate existence? We cannot admit the answer
that the 'Idea' is eternal, while the objects in which it is
embodied exist only in time, for mere length of duration does
7 not alter the intrinsic nature of anything. In short we pre-

Further we object (4) That this 'Idea' is indistinguishable from the phenomena which embody it.

2. Ἀπορήσειε δ' ἄν τις] Aristotle now argues, 'There is no difference between the Definition of anything and the Definition of its 'Idea,' and conceptions with one and the same definition are not to be distinguished.

3. αὐτοέκαστον] 'the ideal of anything,' or more literally, 'the abstract-anything.'

6. τῷ ἀίδιον εἶναι] Aristotle here assumes that 'duration of time' and 'eternity' are identical. This at any rate would be repudiated at once by Plato, who held that time and eternity were different in kind, and that time was created, so to speak, when the material world was created. Moreover, he held the Abstract Ideas to be eternal and uncreated, and therefore prior to and independent of all relations of time. They existed independently of the Deity himself, and were voluntarily adopted by Him as the types which the created world should embody. Another, but later, view of the Platonists was, that they existed only in the Divine Mind, as His ideas (in the modern sense) of what creation should be. In either case, however, they would be independent of relation to Time.

8. Πιθανώτερον κ.τ.λ.] There is not exactly a logical opposition between the theory of the Pythagoreans and that of Plato. They deal with the question of the relation between Unity and Goodness from somewhat differ-

λέγειν περὶ αὐτοῦ, τιθέντες ἐν τῇ τῶν ἀγαθῶν συστοιχίᾳ τὸ ἕν· οἷς δὴ καὶ Σπεύσιππος ἐπακολουθῆσαι δοκεῖ.
8 Ἀλλὰ περὶ μὲν τούτων ἄλλος ἔστω λόγος, τοῖς δὲ λεχθεῖσιν ἀμφισβήτησίς τις ὑποφαίνεται διὰ τὸ μὴ περὶ παντὸς ἀγαθοῦ τοὺς λόγους εἰρῆσθαι, λέγεσθαι δὲ καθ' ἓν εἶδος τὰ καθ' αὑτὰ διωκόμενα καὶ ἀγαπώμενα, τὰ δὲ ποιητικὰ τούτων ἢ φυλακτικά πως ἢ τῶν ἐναντίων κωλυ-

fer the Pythagorean formula (apparently adopted even by Speusippus) that 'All Unity is Good,' rather than that of
8 Plato, that 'All Good is one.' (v) If our opponents take the ground of distinguishing 'Goods' into two classes, according as they are (1) desired for their own sake, (2)

(5) If the theory be limited to Goods desired *per se* only, we deny that even they can be reduced to one Definition.

ent, though not hostile, points of view. Aristotle merely says that if he had to choose one of them, he would rather adopt the Pythagorean formula.

1. ἐν τῇ τῶν ἀγαθῶν συστοιχίᾳ] συστοιχία is literally 'a standing together in a row' (στοῖχος), then a 'co-ordinate arrangement,' a 'series' (L. and S.) Some Pythagoreans held that all the variety of Existence in the Universe might be divided into two antithetical or opposed classes, and that in ten different ways, the one set being the συστοιχία of Good, the other set the συστοιχία of Evil: in other words, they held that the Universe exhibits everywhere a conflict or opposition between Good and Evil, and that ten various forms of each may be distinguished. Among the manifestations of Good (ἐν τῇ συστοιχίᾳ τῶν ἀγαθῶν) is found Unity (ἕν); among those of Evil is found Multiplicity (πλῆθος). All that is One is Good; all that is multiplex, that lacks unity, is Evil. The former involves the idea of order, the latter of confusion.

2. Speusippus was Plato's nephew, and his successor as head of the Academy, and yet even he (καὶ Σπευσιππος) abandoned the theory; which is a strong point against it.

3. τοῖς δὲ λεχθεῖσιν] Aristotle now deals with an objection that might be taken to his previous arguments, that they assume an extension of the Ideal theory to *relative* Goods, whereas it was meant by its author to apply only to *absolute* Goods.

5. τοὺς λόγους apparently refers to Plato's language or arguments. καθ' ἓν εἶδος means 'in one class or species' (*Grant*).

9 τικὰ διὰ ταῦτα λέγεσθαι καὶ τρόπον ἄλλον. Δῆλον οὖν ὅτι διττῶς λέγοιτ' ἂν τἀγαθὰ, καὶ τὰ μὲν καθ' αὑτὰ, θάτερα δὲ διὰ ταῦτα. Χωρίσαντες οὖν ἀπὸ τῶν ὠφελίμων τὰ καθ' αὑτὰ σκεψώμεθα εἰ λέγεται κατὰ μίαν
10 ἰδέαν. Καθ' αὑτὰ δὲ ποῖα θείη τις ἄν; ἢ ὅσα καὶ μονούμενα διώκεται, οἷον τὸ φρονεῖν καὶ ὁρᾶν καὶ ἡδοναί τινες καὶ τιμαί; ταῦτα γὰρ εἰ καὶ δι' ἄλλο τι διώκομεν, ὅμως τῶν καθ' αὑτὰ ἀγαθῶν θείη τις ἄν. Ἢ οὐδ' ἄλλο οὐδὲν πλὴν τῆς ἰδέας; ὥστε μάταιον ἔσται τὸ εἶδος.
11 Εἰ δὲ καὶ ταῦτ' ἐστὶ τῶν καθ' αὑτὰ, τὸν τἀγαθοῦ λόγον ἐν ἅπασιν αὐτοῖς τὸν αὐτὸν ἐμφαίνεσθαι δεήσει, καθάπερ ἐν χιόνι καὶ ψιμμυθίῳ τὸν τῆς λευκότητος. Τιμῆς δὲ καὶ φρονήσεως καὶ ἡδονῆς ἕτεροι καὶ διαφέροντες οἱ

9 desired for their results, and then should limit the application of the theory under consideration to the first of these classes,
10 we should ask for some instances of this class. Probably intellect, sight, certain pleasures and honours, would be admitted as Goods desired for their own sake. (α) *If they are not*, and if in short nothing but the 'Idea' of Good is admitted to be desired for its own sake, then the first of these classes
11 is useless, having no objects included under it. (β) *If they are*, then supposing them to have one 'Idea' in common, they must have one Definition; but as this is obviously not

3. ὠφελίμων is used as equivalent to τῶν διὰ ταῦτα ἀγαθῶν.

→ 9. μάταιον ἔσται τὸ εἶδος] 'The class (viz. that of *absolute*, as opposed to *relative* Goods) will come to nothing.' If the Platonist maintains that only absolute Goods have one Idea, and then refuses to admit that there are any absolute Goods, except the one 'Idea' of Good, then the supposed class of absolute Goods to which the 'Idea' refers has no contents, and is therefore useless. εἶδος (as in § 8) is not here to be taken in the technical sense of ἰδέα.

13. ἕτεροι καὶ διαφέροντες κ.τ.λ.] This, if not a direct *petitio principii*, is an off-hand and dogmatic way of disposing of the very kernel of the whole question, to which the opponents would doubtless at once demur.

λόγοι ταύτῃ ᾗ ἀγαθά. Οὐκ ἔστιν ἄρα τὸ ἀγαθὸν κοινόν
12 τι κατὰ μίαν ἰδέαν. Ἀλλὰ πῶς δὴ λέγεται; οὐ γὰρ
ἔοικε τοῖς γε ἀπὸ τύχης ὁμωνύμοις. Ἀλλ' ἆρά γε τῷ
ἀφ' ἑνὸς εἶναι, ἢ πρὸς ἓν ἅπαντα συντελεῖν, ἢ μᾶλλον
κατ' ἀναλογίαν; ὡς γὰρ ἐν σώματι ὄψις, ἐν ψυχῇ νοῦς,
13 καὶ ἄλλο δὴ ἐν ἄλλῳ. Ἀλλ' ἴσως ταῦτα μὲν ἀφετέον
τὸ νῦν· ἐξακριβοῦν γὰρ ὑπὲρ αὐτῶν ἄλλης ἂν εἴη φιλο-
σοφίας οἰκειότερον. Ὁμοίως δὲ καὶ περὶ τῆς ἰδέας· εἰ

(6) If asked for a theory ourselves, we prefer to say that Goods are called by a common name, by analogy.

the case, we conclude that there cannot be one 'Idea' even
12 of this limited class of Goods. (vi) If asked ourselves to
account for the application of the one term 'Good' to such a
variety of objects (which of course cannot be a mere coinci-
dence), we should suggest that it is in virtue of a certain
13 analogy between them, though we cannot now pause to fully
investigate or justify such a theory. (vii) Finally, such a

2. πῶς δὴ λέγεται;] These words represent a supposed attempt on the part of the Platonist to shift the burden of establishing a theory on his opponent. 'If you reject my theory, how do you account yourself for the acknowledged fact of a unity of name for the diverse manifestations of Good?'

3. ὁμωνύμοις] When the same word was applied to different objects in more than one sense, they were termed ὁμώνυμα. The following classification of ὁμώνυμα is implied in the text:

ὁμώνυμα:
- ἀπὸ τύχης, accidental — *i.e.* equivocal words, *e.g.* νέω; Gallus; page, etc.
- ἐκ διανοίας, intentional:
  - ἀφ' ἑνὸς coming from one source.
  - πρὸς ἓν tending to one result.
  - κατ' ἀναλογίαν by virtue of resemblance or analogy.

The last-named abound in every language as a means (*inter alia*) of economizing the number of words—*e.g.* 'foot' of an animal and of a mountain, 'hand' of a man and of a clock, etc. etc. Aristotle here asserts his preference for some such explanation as this in reference to the various applications of the word 'Good.'

8. ὁμοίως δὲ καὶ περὶ τῆς ἰδέας] In short, a theory respecting an abstract Ideal of good belongs to Metaphysics (ἄλλης φιλοσοφίας), and its truth or falsehood is indifferent to Ethics, which deals with the *practical* well-being of Man. We may therefore dismiss the subject as far as this treatise is concerned.

γὰρ καὶ ἔστιν ἕν τι τὸ κοινῇ κατηγορούμενον ἀγαθὸν ἢ
χωριστόν τι αὐτὸ καθ' αὑτό, δῆλον ὡς οὐκ ἂν εἴη
πρακτὸν οὐδὲ κτητὸν ἀνθρώπῳ· νῦν δὲ τοιοῦτόν τι ζητεῖ-
14 ται. Τάχα δέ τῳ δόξειεν ἂν βέλτιον εἶναι γνωρίζειν
αὐτὸ πρὸς τὰ κτητὰ καὶ πρακτὰ τῶν ἀγαθῶν· οἷον γὰρ
παράδειγμα τοῦτ' ἔχοντες μᾶλλον εἰσόμεθα καὶ τὰ ἡμῖν
15 ἀγαθά, κἂν εἰδῶμεν, ἐπιτευξόμεθα αὐτῶν. Πιθανότητα
μὲν οὖν ἔχει τινὰ ὁ λόγος, ἔοικε δὲ ταῖς ἐπιστήμαις
διαφωνεῖν· πᾶσαι γὰρ ἀγαθοῦ τινὸς ἐφιέμεναι καὶ τὸ
ἐνδεὲς ἐπιζητοῦσαι παραλείπουσι τὴν γνῶσιν αὐτοῦ.
Καίτοι βοήθημα τηλικοῦτον ἅπαντας τοὺς τεχνίτας ἀγ-
16 νοεῖν καὶ μηδ' ἐπιζητεῖν οὐκ εὔλογον. Ἄπορον δὲ καὶ τί
ὠφεληθήσεται ὑφάντης ἢ τέκτων πρὸς τὴν αὑτοῦ τέχνην

(7) In any case this 'Ideal' theory, if true, is not of any *practical* use.

theory as this, whether true or false, may be dismissed from
further consideration in a treatise which is rigidly limited to
the inquiry into that which is *practically* useful to and attain-
14 able by man. And if it be argued that the knowledge of the
abstract Idea of Good will advance us towards the knowledge
15 of human good, we reply that this argument though plausible
is unsupported by experience. The Sciences, pursuing each
the knowledge of some special good for man, know nothing of
16 this abstract 'Idea' of Good. Still more striking is it that

3. τοιοῦτόν τι ζητεῖται] See ii. 1 note.

6. παράδειγμα] 'model,' or 'exemplar.' Compare Aristotle's own argument in ii. 2. Plato frequently maintains the practical utility of the 'Idea' as a παράδειγμα—*e.g. Rep.* p. 484 C, p. 501 B, etc. etc. As a question of *fact*, Plato and Aristotle would of course admit that men *do not* avail themselves of these abstract Ideals in practice. As to whether they *might* do it, Aristotle asserts that it would be impossible, but Plato maintains the reverse, and declares that all real progress is hopeless until this shall be the case.

10. τὸ ἐνδεὲς ἐπιζητοῦσαι] 'seeking to supply that which is lacking.' Science is ever seeking to supply defects of knowledge, Art defects of practical power. (See Glossary, *s.v.* Art, Science.)

εἰδὼς αὐτὸ τἀγαθὸν, ἢ πῶς ἰατρικώτερος ἢ στρατηγικώτερος ἔσται ὁ τὴν ἰδέαν αὐτὴν τεθεαμένος. Φαίνεται μὲν γὰρ οὐδὲ τὴν ὑγίειαν οὕτως ἐπισκοπεῖν ὁ ἰατρὸς, ἀλλὰ τὴν ἀνθρώπου, μᾶλλον δ' ἴσως τὴν τοῦδε· καθ' ἕκαστον γὰρ ἰατρεύει.

1 VII. Καὶ περὶ μὲν τούτων ἐπὶ τοσοῦτον εἰρήσθω· πάλιν δ' ἐπανέλθωμεν ἐπὶ τὸ ζητούμενον ἀγαθὸν, τί ποτ'

the Arts, with their practical aims, derive no help from it, nor, as far as we can see, could they ever do so.

CHAP. VII.—*Construction of the Definition of the Chief Good.*

§§ 1-8.—*Certain positive characteristics of the Chief Good stated with a view to its Definition.*

§§ 9-16.—*A Definition constructed out of another such characteristic.*

§§ 17-21.—*The Definition not to be treated as mathematically exact.*

In seeking now to build up a Definition of the Chief Good we observe—(1) That it is τελειότατον.

1 After these refutations of others we must now endeavour ourselves to answer the question, What is the Chief Good?

3. οὐδὲ τὴν ὑγίειαν] Not only does the physician disregard the abstract 'Idea' of health, but he does not aim at producing even health in any general sense, but the health of the one particular individual whom he has in hand. This, it must be admitted, is captious. Indeed, here and elsewhere in the Chapter, in spite of the profession of § 1, Aristotle shows little sympathy with, scarcely even fairness to, the theory he is criticising. This argument, if it proved anything, would be a defence of empiricism against scientific knowledge.

CHAP. VII.—Here commences the *constructive* part of the treatise. Ch. iv. having set forth the conflicting theories on the subject before us, and chapters v. and vi. having been destructive, *i.e.* having shown which of these theories are *not* true, or in other words, What the Chief Good is *not*, we now proceed to inquire What the Chief Good *is*. The chapter naturally falls into three divisions—(1) §§ 1-8, (2) §§ 9-16,

ἂν εἴη. Φαίνεται μὲν γὰρ ἄλλο ἐν ἄλλῃ πράξει καὶ τέχνῃ· ἄλλο γὰρ ἐν ἰατρικῇ καὶ στρατηγικῇ καὶ ταῖς λοιπαῖς ὁμοίως. Τί οὖν ἑκάστης τἀγαθόν; ἢ οὗ χάριν τὰ λοιπὰ πράττεται; τοῦτο δ' ἐν ἰατρικῇ μὲν ὑγίεια, ἐν στρατηγικῇ δὲ νίκη, ἐν οἰκοδομικῇ δ' οἰκία, ἐν ἄλλῳ δ' ἄλλο, ἐν ἁπάσῃ δὲ πράξει καὶ προαιρέσει τὸ τέλος· τούτου γὰρ ἕνεκα τὰ λοιπὰ πράττουσι πάντες. Ὥστ' εἴ τι τῶν πρακτῶν ἁπάντων ἐστὶ τέλος, τοῦτ' ἂν εἴη
2 τὸ πρακτὸν ἀγαθόν, εἰ δὲ πλείω, ταῦτα. Μεταβαίνων

One characteristic of it is this: The *good* of any art, science, action, or purpose, is always the *end* in each several case, however many other points of difference there may be between them. So that the *Chief* Good of action will also be the *Final*
2 End of action. This however is the same conception as that

(3) §§ 17-21. [§§ 1-8]—In this part Aristotle enumerates certain positive characteristics, or conspicuous qualities, of the Chief Good, which any Definition must embody, in order, if possible, to construct a Definition upon them. Three such characteristics are suggested, which however prove too vague for this purpose.

In the 2d Division [§§ 9-16] another more specific characteristic is found, upon which Aristotle then builds his own Definition of Happiness or the Chief Good.

In the 3d Division [§§ 17-21] he renews the protest of ch. iii. against demanding mathematical exactness in such a Definition.

This chapter, and especially the 2d portion of it, is one of the most important in the treatise. It contains, in fact, the answer to the main question with which the Book opened. All that follows is simply the confirmation and defence of the Definition here given.

9. Μεταβαίνων κ.τ.λ.] 'By a different course then the argument has come round to the same point,' viz. the same point as in ch. i. The conclusion in each case is the identity of the Chief Good and the Final End. The slightly *different courses* are as follows:—In this passage we argue, The 'good' and the 'end' are identical in all *individual* cases, and therefore the *Chief* Good and the *Final* End will be identical also. Thus ἑκάστης in l. 3 and ἁπάντων in l. 8 are the emphatic words. In ch. i. we argued, Every action, etc., aims at some Good, and therefore the

δὴ ὁ λόγος εἰς ταὐτὸν ἀφῖκται. Τοῦτο δ' ἔτι μᾶλλον
3 διασαφῆσαι πειρατέον. Ἐπεὶ δὲ πλείω φαίνεται τὰ τέλη,
τούτων δ' αἱρούμεθά τινα δι' ἕτερα, οἷον πλοῦτον
αὐλοὺς καὶ ὅλως τὰ ὄργανα, δῆλον ὡς οὐκ ἔστι πάντα
τέλεια· τὸ δ' ἄριστον τέλειόν τι φαίνεται. Ὥστ' εἰ μέν
ἐστιν ἕν τι μόνον τέλειον, τοῦτ' ἂν εἴη τὸ ζητούμενον,
4 εἰ δὲ πλείω, τὸ τελειότατον τούτων. Τελειότερον δὲ
λέγομεν τὸ καθ' αὑτὸ διωκτὸν τοῦ δι' ἕτερον, καὶ τὸ
μηδέποτε δι' ἄλλο αἱρετὸν τῶν καὶ καθ' αὑτὰ καὶ διὰ
τοῦθ' αἱρετῶν, καὶ ἁπλῶς δὴ τέλειον τὸ καθ' αὑτὸ
5 αἱρετὸν ἀεὶ καὶ μηδέποτε δι' ἄλλο. Τοιοῦτον δ' ἡ εὐδαι-
μονία μάλιστ' εἶναι δοκεῖ· ταύτην γὰρ αἱρούμεθα ἀεὶ
δι' αὐτὴν καὶ οὐδέποτε δι' ἄλλο, τιμὴν δὲ καὶ ἡδονὴν
καὶ νοῦν καὶ πᾶσαν ἀρετὴν αἱρούμεθα μὲν καὶ δι' αὐτά
(μηδενὸς γὰρ ἀποβαίνοντος ἑλοίμεθ' ἂν ἕκαστον αὐτῶν),

with which we started. We may however further explain
3 this idea of Finality. Any End which is itself but a means
to a further End, or indeed which ever can be such a means,
4 cannot be final. And hence we obtain this conception of the
Chief Good, that it is something always desired for its own
5 sake, and never with a view to anything beyond it. Obviously,
Happiness fulfils this condition, and we can think of nothing

Chief Good is what all things aim at, *i.e.* it is the ultimate aim or Final End of all things; and hence again the Chief Good and the Final End are identical.

5. We cannot adequately translate τέλειον, which combines the meanings of 'perfect' and 'final.' (See Glossary *s. v.* τέλειος.) That the Chief Good fulfils this positive condition follows from the primary conception of it given in the opening words of the Book, and in the beginning of ch. ii.

11. τοιοῦτον δὲ κ.τ.λ.] Thus the steps of the argument are:— The Chief Good is τελειότατον: then (after the notion of τελειότης has been expounded) Happiness is shewn to fulfil this condition: the result of which is, that Happiness, as before, is found to constitute the Chief

αἱρούμεθα δὲ καὶ τῆς εὐδαιμονίας χάριν, διὰ τούτων ὑπολαμβάνοντες εὐδαιμονήσειν. Τὴν δ' εὐδαιμονίαν οὐ-
6 δεὶς αἱρεῖται τούτων χάριν, οὐδ' ὅλως δι' ἄλλο. Φαί-
νεται δὲ καὶ ἐκ τῆς αὐταρκείας τὸ αὐτὸ συμβαίνειν· τὸ γὰρ τέλειον ἀγαθὸν αὔταρκες εἶναι δοκεῖ. Τὸ δ' αὔταρκες λέγομεν οὐκ αὐτῷ μόνῳ τῷ ζῶντι βίον μονώτην, ἀλλὰ καὶ γονεῦσι καὶ τέκνοις καὶ γυναικὶ καὶ ὅλως τοῖς φίλοις καὶ πολίταις, ἐπειδὴ φύσει πολιτικὸς ἄνθρωπος.
7 Τούτων δὲ ληπτέος ὅρος τις· ἐπεκτείνοντι γὰρ ἐπὶ τοὺς
γονεῖς καὶ τοὺς ἀπογόνους καὶ τῶν φίλων τοὺς φίλους

else which does. This however will not help us to a clearer
6 Definition of the Chief Good. The same may be said of (2) It is αὐταρκέστατον.
another characteristic of the Chief Good, viz. that it is entirely *Self-sufficient*, by which we mean that it needs nothing besides itself to make life all that we could desire. (We must not however understand this to mean that it would enable a man to be independent of his fellow-men and live happily in isola-
7 tion. That would be a spurious self-sufficiency, being a
mutilation, not an elevation, of human nature.) Happiness

Good, but we are not as yet any nearer to a Definition of it. In §§ 7, 8 similar steps occur.

4. ἐκ τῆς αὐταρκείας] That the Chief Good fulfils this condition as it is defined in § 7 *fin.*, follows again from ii. 1. For if we desire everything else only for the sake of Happiness, the possession of it would render all such minor desires superfluous: we should be 'μηδενὸς ἐνδεεῖς.'

5. τὸ δ' αὔταρκες λέγομεν κ.τ.λ.] 'When we use the term "αὐταρκὲς," we do so not in reference to a man's self alone, in the case of one living a life of isolation, but also in reference to his parents, etc.'

8. φύσει πολιτικὸς ἄνθρωπος] 'Man is by nature a social animal.' Nature intended man for society as much as she intended him to use two hands or to walk on two feet. A man who should accustom himself to live out of all relation to his fellow-creatures would not have gained in real independence any more than one who should go always on one leg, or should use only one hand. The error thus protested against by Aristotle was conspicuous in the teaching of the Cynics.

εἰς ἄπειρον πρόεισιν. Ἀλλὰ τοῦτο μὲν εἰσαῦθις ἐπισκεπτέον, τὸ δ' αὔταρκες τίθεμεν ὃ μονούμενον | αἱρετὸν ποιεῖ τὸν βίον καὶ μηδενὸς ἐνδεᾶ· τοιοῦτον δὲ τὴν εὐδαι-
8 μονίαν οἰόμεθα εἶναι. Ἔτι δὲ πάντων αἱρετωτάτην, μὴ συναριθμουμένην, συναριθμουμένην δὲ δῆλον ὡς αἱρετωτέραν μετὰ τοῦ ἐλαχίστου τῶν ἀγαθῶν· ὑπεροχὴ γὰρ ἀγαθῶν γίνεται τὸ προστιθέμενον, ἀγαθῶν δὲ τὸ μεῖζον αἱρετώτερον ἀεί. Τέλειον δή τι φαίνεται καὶ αὔταρκες ἡ εὐδαιμονία, τῶν πρακτῶν οὖσα τέλος.

9 Ἀλλ' ἴσως τὴν μὲν εὐδαιμονίαν τὸ ἄριστον λέγειν ὁμολογούμενόν τι φαίνεται, ποθεῖται δ' ἐναργέστερον
10 τί ἐστιν ἔτι λεχθῆναι. Τάχα δὴ γένοιτ' ἂν τοῦτ', εἰ

again fulfils this condition of Self-sufficiency, but we cannot yet advance to a Definition of the Chief Good. Once more,

(3) It is *sui generis.*

8 the Chief Good is *sui generis.* If it were only the chief good of a class, the addition to it of any other good in the class, however small, would make it better, which is inconsistent with the supposition that it is itself the Chief Good. Happiness is then perfectly Final and Self-sufficient, and is the end of all human action.

(4) But more particularly, it consists in the fulfilment of Man's proper function.

9 All this, however true, is too vague to construct a definition upon. Another consideration may perhaps serve this
10 purpose. Could we ascertain the proper function of man

5. μὴ συναριθμουμένην κ.τ.λ.] 'provided it be not counted in the same class with other Goods; but if it be so counted in,' etc. The expression 'Chief Good,' by which we are obliged to translate the simple τὸ ἀγαθὸν is misleading. τἀγαθὸν must be held to *include in itself* all other Goods, such as health, wealth, honour, etc., in the most perfect degree, *i.e.* the utmost amount of them really desirable. Clearly if A be only the principal Good of a class made up of the Goods A, B, C, D, etc., then A + B, or even A + Z, is a greater good than A alone. Therefore no single member of the Class can ever be the Chief Good. It must be something *sui generis*, in a class by itself.

12. The conception now started, that Happiness consists in the fulfilment of man's proper function (or as we might say, the

ληφθείη τὸ ἔργον τοῦ ἀνθρώπου. Ὥσπερ γὰρ αὐλητῇ
καὶ ἀγαλματοποιῷ καὶ παντὶ τεχνίτῃ, καὶ ὅλως ὧν ἐστὶν
ἔργον τι καὶ πρᾶξις, ἐν τῷ ἔργῳ δοκεῖ τἀγαθὸν εἶναι
καὶ τὸ εὖ, οὕτω δόξειεν ἂν καὶ ἀνθρώπῳ, εἴπερ ἔστι τι
11 ἔργον αὐτοῦ. Πότερον οὖν τέκτονος μὲν καὶ σκυτέως
ἔστιν ἔργα τινὰ καὶ πράξεις, ἀνθρώπου δ' οὐδέν ἐστιν,
ἀλλ' ἀργὸν πέφυκεν; ἢ καθάπερ ὀφθαλμοῦ καὶ χειρὸς
καὶ ποδὸς καὶ ὅλως ἑκάστου τῶν μορίων φαίνεταί τι
ἔργον, οὕτω καὶ ἀνθρώπου παρὰ πάντα ταῦτα θείη τις
12 ἂν ἔργον τι; τί οὖν δὴ τοῦτ' ἂν εἴη ποτέ; τὸ μὲν γὰρ
ζῆν κοινὸν εἶναι φαίνεται καὶ τοῖς φυτοῖς, ζητεῖται δὲ

as man, his Chief Good would surely consist (as in all
similar cases) in the perfect fulfilment of that function; and
this is a more definite conception of it than those already
suggested. We ought perhaps first to show that man, as man,
11 has such a proper function, and this we should argue (1) from
the fact that man in every individual character and relation
of life (*e.g.* as an artist or any other sort of workman) has a
definite function, and therefore man *simply as man* cannot
be purposeless; and (2) from the consideration that every
part of man, the eye, the hand, the foot, etc., has its proper
12 function, and therefore man as a whole has one also. Now,
granting this, it is clear that this function must be something

purpose of his being, the object for which he was created and sent into the world), is found sufficiently fruitful to form the basis of a Definition.

7. ἀργὸν has precisely its etymological force (ἀ-ἔργον) 'without any work.' Translate 'has no work assigned to him by nature.'

11. ζητεῖται δὲ τὸ ἴδιον] 'We are seeking for that which is peculiar to himself.' This would be explained by Plato's definition of the ἔργον of anything, viz. 'that which it either alone, or better than anything else, is able to perform.' Hence he says, though we might prune a vine with a sword, a chisel, or a pruning-knife, the operation would be so much better performed with the last instrument that we say that it is its ἔργον. It is ἴδιόν τι, something peculiarly appropriate to it.

τὸ ἴδιον. Ἀφοριστέον ἄρα τὴν θρεπτικὴν καὶ αὐξητικὴν
ζωήν. Ἑπομένη δὲ αἰσθητική τις ἂν εἴη, φαίνεται δὲ
13 καὶ αὐτὴ κοινὴ καὶ ἵππῳ καὶ βοῒ καὶ παντὶ ζῴῳ. Λείπε-
ται δὴ πρακτική τις τοῦ λόγον ἔχοντος. (Τούτου δὲ τὸ
μὲν ὡς ἐπιπειθὲς λόγῳ, τὸ δ' ὡς ἔχον καὶ διανοούμενον.)
Διττῶς δὲ καὶ ταύτης λεγομένης τὴν κατ' ἐνέργειαν
14 θετέον· κυριώτερον γὰρ αὕτη δοκεῖ λέγεσθαι. Εἰ δ'
ἐστὶν ἔργον ἀνθρώπου ψυχῆς ἐνέργεια κατὰ λόγον ἢ

peculiar to, and characteristic of, man. This excludes that mere existence which he shares with the animal and vegetable world, and also that conscious life (or life endued with sensa-
13 tion) which is common to the brute creation. There remains then what we may call a life of action belonging to the rational part of our nature; including by the term 'rational' that which recognises the sway of Reason as well as that which exerts Reason. This being the function of man, we now seek the perfection of that function. First it must be in active operation. Hence the Chief Good from this point of view will be 'An active condition of the soul guided by, or not
14 opposed to, Reason.' But further, such an active condition

From this point of view we may now define it as

ψυχῆς ἐνέργεια,

4. πρακτική is easier to explain than translate; 'moral,' 'active,' 'practical,' being in different ways misleading. Man is sometimes said to be the only animal that can form a conception of *actions* as distinguished from *events*. πρακτική is co-extensive with 'action' in the sense here indicated. 'Τις' implies that the expression in the Greek is felt to be not quite satisfactory.

Τούτου δὲ κ.τ.λ.] This distinction is more fully explained in ch. xiii. Its relevancy here has been thought so questionable, that some Editors have treated the sentence as an interpolation, though against MS. evidence.

6. κατ' ἐνέργειαν] as opposed to κατὰ δύναμιν or καθ' ἕξιν. See Glossary, p. xlvi., also viii. 9. The various steps by which each term of the Definition is gained should be carefully noted.

7. εἰ δ' ἐστὶν] The apodosis to this εἰ is found in § 15 *init.*, τὸ ἀνθρώπινον ἀγαθὸν κ.τ.λ. We are reminded that the sentence is still unfinished by the twice repeated εἰ δ' οὕτω in l. 6 and l. 9 of the next page.

8. ψυχῆς is translated 'soul'

μὴ ἄνευ λόγου, τὸ δ' αὐτό φαμεν ἔργον εἶναι τῷ γένει τοῦδε καὶ τοῦδε σπουδαίου, ὥσπερ κιθαριστοῦ καὶ σπουδαίου κιθαριστοῦ, καὶ ἁπλῶς δὴ τοῦτ' ἐπὶ πάντων, προστιθεμένης τῆς κατ' ἀρετὴν ὑπεροχῆς πρὸς τὸ ἔργον· (κιθαριστοῦ μὲν γὰρ τὸ κιθαρίζειν, σπουδαίου δὲ τὸ εὖ·) —εἰ δ' οὕτως, ἀνθρώπου δὲ τίθεμεν ἔργον ζωήν τινα, ταύτην δὲ ψυχῆς ἐνέργειαν καὶ πράξεις μετὰ λόγου, σπουδαίου δ' ἀνδρὸς εὖ ταῦτα καὶ καλῶς, ἕκαστον δ' εὖ κατὰ τὴν οἰκείαν ἀρετὴν ἀποτελεῖται—εἰ δ' οὕτω, τὸ ἀν-

admits of various degrees of excellence. The function of a good or of an ordinary artist is *generically* the same, only by one it is well performed, and by the other not necessarily so. We must therefore include this condition of excellence in our κατ' ἀρετὴν

in the Analysis for want of a better word (see Glossary *s. v.* ψυχή). It seems to stand here as a sort of substitute for πρακτικὴ above, because πρακτικὴ ζωὴ must belong to this part of man (as Aristotle plainly states in viii. 3), in contrast with θρεπτικὴ and αἰσθητικὴ ζωὴ, which belong to the body. Similarly κατὰ λόγον corresponds to τοῦ λόγου ἔχοντος above.

1. τῷ γένει] This is the emphatic idea in the sentence. 'The work of anyone and of a good anyone are the same *in kind.*' . . . the superiority in respect of excellence being (in the latter case) added to the description of the work. *e.g.* If the 'anyone' be a musician, 'to play' in the former case, 'to play *well*' in the latter case, would describe the work of each. 'Well' is the ὑπεροχὴ κατ' ἀρετὴν which is added.

3. δὴ = as it obviously is. Supply εἰ again before ἁπλῶς.

9. οἰκεία ἀρετή] 'appropriate excellence.' It should be remembered that ἀρετὴ is simply 'excellence,' though it is most frequently applied to a particular sort of excellence, viz. moral excellence, and so is translated Virtue: just as πρᾶξις and πρακτικὴ come to be similarly restricted in meaning (see Glossary under ἀρετὴ and πρᾶξις). This general meaning of ἀρετὴ is explained by Plato's Definition, that the appropriate excellence (οἰκεία ἀρετή) of anything is that quality by which it is able to perform its own function well. Aristotle's account of ἀρετὴ in II. vi. 2 should also be referred to.

θρώπινον ἀγαθὸν ψυχῆς ἐνέργεια γίνεται κατ' ἀρετήν,
εἰ δὲ πλείους αἱ ἀρεταί, κατὰ τὴν ἀρίστην καὶ τελειο-
16 τάτην. Ἔτι δ' ἐν βίῳ τελείῳ. Μία γὰρ χελιδὼν ἔαρ
οὐ ποιεῖ, οὐδὲ μία ἡμέρα· οὕτω δὲ οὐδὲ μακάριον καὶ
εὐδαίμονα μία ἡμέρα οὐδ' ὀλίγος χρόνος.
17 Περιγεγράφθω μὲν οὖν τἀγαθὸν ταύτῃ· δεῖ γὰρ ἴσως
ὑποτυπῶσαι πρῶτον, εἶθ' ὕστερον ἀναγράψαι. Δόξειε
δ' ἂν παντὸς εἶναι προαγαγεῖν καὶ διαρθρῶσαι τὰ καλῶς

Definition; and as there are various kinds and degrees of
ἀρίστην excellence, we must also specify the highest excellence. And
so the Chief Good becomes 'An active condition of the soul in
16 accordance with its highest excellence.' One other condition:
it must be a permanent settled state, the habit of a life, not
the accident of a moment. We add then the words 'in a
ἐν βίῳ τελείῳ. complete life,' and so our Definition stands thus: Happiness
is 'An active condition of the soul in accordance with its
Too much precision is not to be expected in such a Definition. 17 highest excellence in a complete life.' Let this serve as an
outline sketch at any rate of our conception of the Chief Good

3. *βίος τέλειος*] 'a *complete* life,' not necessarily 'a *completed* life;' or 'life as a whole,' though not necessarily 'a whole life;' else we get into the difficulty raised at the beginning of ch. x. 'Can we not call a man happy till his life is completed?' We should not describe a man as having good spirits, or excellent health, unless we had known him for a certain time, and had had opportunities for observing him under various circumstances; in fact, till we can judge of his life *as a whole*. Sometimes even a few observations enable us to form such a judgment, and for practical purposes these represent *βίος τέλειος*. So it is in the case of Happiness. All we need is a sufficiently complete period of duration to be sure that it is a settled habit of life, and not a momentary or transient gleam of joy. It is a well-known point of distinction between 'pleasure' and 'happiness,' that pleasure is perfect at any moment, whereas happiness implies duration and permanence.

7. *ὑποτυπῶσαι* is a metaphor from sculpture, *ἀναγράψαι* from painting: but it should be remembered that ancient statues were frequently painted.

8. *παντὸς* is emphatic here and in l. 3, next page. In Morals, as in

ἔχοντα τῇ περιγραφῇ, καὶ ὁ χρόνος τῶν τοιούτων εὑρετὴς ἢ συνεργὸς ἀγαθὸς εἶναι. Ὅθεν καὶ τῶν τεχνῶν γεγόνασιν αἱ ἐπιδόσεις· παντὸς γὰρ προσθεῖναι τὸ ἐλ-
18 λεῖπον. Μεμνῆσθαι δὲ καὶ τῶν προειρημένων χρὴ, καὶ τὴν ἀκρίβειαν μὴ ὁμοίως ἐν ἅπασιν ἐπιζητεῖν, ἀλλ' ἐν ἑκάστοις κατὰ τὴν ὑποκειμένην ὕλην καὶ ἐπὶ τοσοῦτον
19 ἐφ' ὅσον οἰκεῖον τῇ μεθόδῳ. Καὶ γὰρ τέκτων καὶ γεω-

or Happiness. Time and individual experience will fill in further details in a subject like this, just as they advance our
18 knowledge of the Arts. We make however two provisos: 1. Exactness of treatment (as we have already said) must not be indiscriminately demanded. 2. The reason, as well as the fact, must not in all cases be required. As to the first, let us not forget that two considerations limit the amount of precision to be required in any case. (1) The nature of the subject-matter, of which we have spoken already (iii. 2); and
19 (2) our immediate object in handling it: as for instance a car-

the Arts (both being [1] *practical*, and [2] *not*, like Mathematics, *exact*), every one's experience may contribute something to their progress, and every additional fact adds something in confirmation of their very principles; and moreover, every one is interested in their progress, and in the subjects of which they treat. In the exact science of Mathematics, on the other hand, though progress in the knowledge of facts and the efficiency of methods is continually being made, nothing can ever add to the clearness and certainty of its fundamental Definitions and Axioms. Besides, it is not every one (παντος) who can understand or feel interest in such a subject.

6. κατὰ τὴν ὑποκειμένην ὕλην] 'dependent on the subject-matter;' *e.g.* a model in cork or deal could never be finished like one in ivory.

7. οἰκεῖον τῇ μεθόδῳ] 'suitable to the process in hand;' *e.g.* it would be possible perhaps to make the corner of a deal table precisely 90°, but there would be no object gained by such exactness. It would not be οἰκεῖον τῇ μεθόδῳ. Cf. restrictions on discussion of ψυχὴ in c. xiii. §§ 8, 10, 16.

Both these considerations apply to the case of morals. The subject-matter does not admit of exactness, and the practical purpose in view does not require it.

μέτρης διαφερόντως ἐπιζητοῦσι τὴν ὀρθήν· ὁ μὲν (γὰρ) ἐφ' ὅσον χρησίμη πρὸς τὸ ἔργον, ὁ δὲ τί ἐστιν ἢ ποῖόν τι· θεατὴς γὰρ τἀληθοῦς. Τὸν αὐτὸν δὴ τρόπον καὶ ἐν τοῖς ἄλλοις ποιητέον, ὅπως μὴ τὰ πάρεργα τῶν ἔργων πλείω γίγνηται. Οὐκ ἀπαιτητέον δ' οὐδὲ τὴν αἰτίαν ἐν ἅπασιν ὁμοίως, ἀλλ' ἱκανὸν ἔν τισι τὸ ὅτι δειχθῆναι καλῶς, οἷον καὶ περὶ τὰς ἀρχάς· τὸ δ' ὅτι πρῶτον καὶ

penter does not always make the most perfect square even that the wood admits of, if he is engaged on rough work. As to our second proviso, some propositions, *e.g.* certainly first principles, are exempt fro the necessity of demonstrative

As to the former, we may compare Bp. Butler, *Analogy*, p. 105 (ed. Angus): 'Observations of this kind cannot be supposed to hold universally in every case. It is enough that they hold in general.'

1. ὀρθήν] Understand γωνίαν, *i.e.* a right angle.

6. τὸ ὅτι (the *fact* that a thing is so and so) is constantly opposed to τὸ διότι (the *reason* why it is so); *e.g.* In Euclid's Axioms and Definitions the fact alone is stated (τὸ ὅτι); in his Propositions the reasons for asserting the fact are given (τὸ διότι).

τὸ δ' ὅτι πρῶτον καὶ ἀρχή] 'The fact is something primary and a starting-point.' It is so at any rate in Morals, where the *fact* that we feel sentiments of approbation or disapprobation on certain occasions forms the starting-point of the inquiry. See note on iv. 7 ('Ἀρχὴ γὰρ τὸ ὅτι), and Introduction, p. xiv. Translation fails to preserve the full meaning of ἀρχή, including not only 'first principle,' but also 'beginning' or 'starting-point' (see Glossary). Indeed all sciences require to make assumptions independent of demonstrative proof (as Aristotle points out elsewhere), at *both* the higher and the lower ends of the scale of knowledge. General principles rise above, and facts of observation fall below, the limits of such proof; and both are sometimes called ἀρχαί. *e.g.* the Mathematician assumes the Axioms on the one hand, and on the other assumes the existence of triangles, circles, and other figures, the properties of which he investigates. In the latter case, τὸ ὅτι πρῶτον καὶ ἀρχὴ applies.

7. Axioms or first principles rest upon such grounds as the *universality* of their belief, the *necessity* of their belief, and the *greater certainty* attaching to

καλῶς· τῶν ἀρχῶν δ' αἱ μὲν ἐπαγωγῇ θεωροῦνται, αἱ δ' αἰσθήσει, αἱ δ' ἐθισμῷ τινὶ καὶ ἄλλαι δ' ἄλλως. Μετιέναι δὲ πειρατέον ἑκάστας ᾗ πεφύκασιν, καὶ σπουδαστέον ὅπως ὁρισθῶσι καλῶς· μεγάλην γὰρ ἔχουσι ῥοπὴν πρὸς τὰ ἑπόμενα. Δοκεῖ γὰρ πλεῖον ἢ ἥμισυ παντὸς εἶναι ἡ ἀρχή, καὶ πολλὰ συμφανῆ γίνεσθαι δι' αὐτῆς τῶν ζητουμένων.

proof, and the primary facts themselves of any science are in some sense first principles. Now first principles rest upon evidence of different kinds in different cases; and though never *demonstratively* proved, they must be, each in its own appropriate way, fully established and clearly defined. This is of the utmost importance, and it is just an instance in which 'well begun is half done.'

them than to any other principles that could be alleged in their support (Sir W. Hamilton). If any higher principles could be found (the necessary condition of demonstrative proof), the others would *ipso facto* cease to be *first* principles.

1. ἐπαγωγῇ] *h.l.* probably = 'by appeal to experience': *i.e.* (as VI. iii. 3 seems to show) 'that amount of experience which is the *condition*, not the *cause*, of necessary truths' (Grant's note *l.c.*): *e.g.* in Mathematics we need *some* experience to comprehend what is meant by straight lines, right angles, etc.; but the ἀρχαὶ, or Axioms relating to them, are not (like Physical Laws) *proved* by such experience.

2. αἰσθήσει] 'by perception'; probably referring to the *facts* of Physics, which are 'the truths we start from' (ἀρχαὶ) in such subjects.

ἐθισμῷ τινὶ] 'by a kind of habituation.' We become so familiar by frequent repetition with some truths, that by a sort of 'unconscious induction' (Grant *h. l.*) we come to believe them as axioms. This is especially common in the case of principles of conduct. 'Numberless little rules of action and conduct, which we could not live without, . . . are learned so insensibly and so perfectly as to be mistaken perhaps for instinct, though they are the effect of long experience and exercise' (ἐθισμὸς) Butler, *Anal.* pt. i. ch. v. p. 95 (ed. Angus). In all these three cases, it will be observed, there is no *demonstrative* proof.

3. Μετιέναι δὲ πειρατέον ἑκασ-

1 VIII. Σκεπτέον δὴ περὶ αὐτῆς οὐ μόνον ἐκ τοῦ συμπεράσματος καὶ ἐξ ὧν ὁ λόγος, ἀλλὰ καὶ ἐκ τῶν λεγομένων περὶ αὐτῆς· τῷ μὲν γὰρ ἀληθεῖ πάντα συνᾴδει τὰ ὑπάρχοντα, τῷ δὲ ψευδεῖ ταχὺ διαφωνεῖ τἀληθές.
2 Νενεμημένων δὴ τῶν ἀγαθῶν τριχῇ, καὶ τῶν μὲν ἐκτὸς

CHAP. VIII.—*Other views, popular and philosophical, on the subject of Happiness compared with the above Definition.*

Certain familiar *general beliefs* about Happiness fall in with our Definition; *e.g.*

1 We will now compare our Definition with the views held by
2 others, and test it by the facts of experience. (α) It is a

τας ᾗ πεφύκασι] 'We must endeavour to investigate them, each in its natural way.'

Chapters viii.-xii. form a sort of parenthetical section, in which Aristotle compares his Definition just found with various received opinions on the subject, and considers its bearing upon certain popular difficulties and questions of the day (esp. ch. ix. x. and xi.). His object throughout is to show how much there is in common between his own theory and others, while he asserts the superiority of his own. The latter consideration justifies a new treatment of the subject; the former not only conciliates opposition, but is itself an argument in favour of any new theory on the ground explained in § 7. This is a truth generally forgotten in controversy. The following are the contents of the five chapters:—ch. viii. Sundry popular and philosophical notions about Happiness compared with Aristotle's Definition; ch. ix. Common views as to the acquisition of Happiness, on what it depends; ch. x. xi. The popular difficulty whether a man cannot be called happy (as Solon said) while still living, with questions arising therefrom, considered from the point of view of Aristotle's Definition; ch. xii. The relation of Happiness, upon Aristotle's theory, to another familiar classification of Goods.

1. ἐκ τοῦ συμπεράσματος καὶ ἐξ ὧν ὁ λόγος] 'We must not only consider this question from the point of view of our conclusion and of our premisses.' We had similar expressions in ch. iii. § 4.

4. τὰ ὑπάρχοντα] *h.l.* 'all facts' from ὑπάρχειν in the sense of 'to exist.' If a general theory is true, all the facts of experience in detail must be consistent with it.

5. The words Νενεμημένων . . . ἀγαθά state the popular opinion which is to be compared with Aristotle's Definition given

λεγομένων τῶν δὲ περὶ ψυχὴν καὶ σῶμα, τὰ περὶ ψυχὴν κυριώτατα λέγομεν καὶ μάλιστα ἀγαθά. Τὰς δὲ πράξεις καὶ τὰς ἐνεργείας τὰς ψυχικὰς περὶ ψυχὴν τίθεμεν. Ὥστε καλῶς ἂν λέγοιτο κατά γε ταύτην τὴν δόξαν παλαιὰν οὖσαν καὶ ὁμολογουμένην ὑπὸ τῶν φιλοσοφούν-
3 των. Ὀρθῶς δὲ καὶ ὅτι πράξεις τινὲς λέγονται καὶ
ἐνέργειαι τὸ τέλος· οὕτω γὰρ τῶν περὶ ψυχὴν ἀγαθῶν γίνεται, καὶ οὐ τῶν ἐκτός. Συνᾴδει δὲ τῷ λόγῳ καὶ τὸ εὖ ζῆν καὶ τὸ εὖ πράττειν τὸν εὐδαίμονα· σχεδὸν γὰρ εὐζωία τις εἴρηται καὶ εὐπραξία.

5 Φαίνεται δὲ καὶ τὰ ἐπιζητούμενα περὶ τὴν εὐδαι-

time-honoured saying of philosophers that all goods are either of mind, body, or estate, and that those of the mind are the highest. On two grounds our Definition may be said to imply this: (1) because it describes Happiness as an active con-
3 dition of the soul or mind; (2) because 'activity' or 'moral
4 action' itself is not an external but an internal good. (β)
Others say that Happiness is living well and doing well. This again may be considered to be embodied in our Definition.
5 To these general theories succeed others which enter more into detail as to the precise character of Happiness, such that

(α) That Goods belonging to the Mind are the highest:

(β) That living well and doing well is implied by Happiness.

Several of the popular *theories in detail* about Happiness are also,

in ch. vii. Τὰς δὲ πράξεις . . . οὐ τῶν ἐκτός state the grounds for asserting the Definition to be in accordance with that opinion, viz. on the strength of the two words ψυχή and ἐνέργεια forming parts of it.

8. τῷ λόγῳ] the definition in the last Chapter, to which also εἴρηται in the next line refers. The concurrence of Aristotle's Definition with *this* popular opinion would rest chiefly on the expressions κατ' ἀρετὴν ἀρίστην and ἐν βίῳ τελείῳ, which form part of it.

11. ἐπιζητούμενα] 'quæ requiruntur ad beatitudinem' (Bonitz); 'the conditions demanded as necessary to constitute Happiness.' To say that Virtue or Pleasure, etc., constitute Happiness, as contrasted with the two vague and general theories already spoken of, answers to this description. The former view is discussed in §§ 8 and 9, the latter in §§ 10-14.

6 μονίαν ἅπανθ' ὑπάρχειν τῷ λεχθέντι. Τοῖς μὲν γὰρ
ἀρετή, τοῖς δὲ φρόνησις, ἄλλοις δὲ σοφία τις εἶναι δο-
κεῖ, τοῖς δὲ ταῦτα ἢ τούτων τι μεθ' ἡδονῆς ἢ οὐκ ἄνευ
ἡδονῆς· ἕτεροι δὲ καὶ τὴν ἐκτὸς εὐετηρίαν συμπαραλαμ-
7 βάνουσιν. Τούτων δὲ τὰ μὲν πολλοὶ καὶ παλαιοὶ λέγου-
σιν, τὰ δὲ ὀλίγοι καὶ ἔνδοξοι ἄνδρες· οὐδετέρους δὲ
τούτων εὔλογον διαμαρτάνειν τοῖς ὅλοις, ἀλλ' ἕν γέ τι ἢ
8 καὶ τὰ πλεῖστα κατορθοῦν. Τοῖς μὲν οὖν λέγουσι τὴν
ἀρετὴν ἢ ἀρετήν τινα συνῳδός ἐστιν ὁ λόγος· ταύτης
9 γάρ ἐστιν ἡ κατ' αὐτὴν ἐνέργεια. Διαφέρει δὲ ἴσως οὐ
μικρὸν ἐν κτήσει ἢ χρήσει τὸ ἄριστον ὑπολαμβάνειν,
καὶ ἐν ἕξει ἢ ἐνεργείᾳ. Τὴν μὲν γὰρ ἕξιν ἐνδέχεται
μηδὲν ἀγαθὸν ἀποτελεῖν ὑπάρχουσαν, οἷον τῷ καθεύδοντι
ἢ καὶ ἄλλως πως ἐξηργηκότι, τὴν δ' ἐνέργειαν οὐχ οἷόν

under limitations, in accordance with our Definition: such as

(a) That Happiness consists in Virtue:

6 it is Virtue, Prudence, Wisdom, Pleasure, or that it cannot
7 exist without external prosperity. Now all these views,
whether popular or philosophical, are likely to have *some*
element of truth in them. We will therefore consider some
8 of them. (*a*) That Happiness consists in Virtue. Without
going so far as this, our Definition asserts that it *implies*
9 Virtue, and it adds the important condition that that Virtue

2. φρόνησις is practical, and σοφία speculative, wisdom. σοφία is in fact nearly = philosophy. The distinction is fully explained by Aristotle in B. VI. These two theories are not referred to again in the discussion which follows here.

6. οὐδετέρους] 'neither of them (the many or the philosophers) are likely to be entirely at fault, but rather to be right in some one point at least, or even in most points.' There is no error but it contains some germ of truth, however distorted or obscured.

11. κτήσει ἢ χρήσει . . . ἕξει ἢ ἐνεργείᾳ] See Glossary, p. xlvi. Though at the Olympian games there may be better men among the spectators than among the combatants, yet they are not crowned, because their prowess is not proved or exhibited. It is latent, it exists δυνάμει and not ἐνεργείᾳ.

τε· πράξει γὰρ ἐξ ἀνάγκης, καὶ εὖ πράξει. Ὥσπερ δ'
Ὀλυμπίασιν οὐχ οἱ κάλλιστοι καὶ ἰσχυρότατοι στεφα-
νοῦνται ἀλλ' οἱ ἀγωνιζόμενοι (τούτων γάρ τινες νικῶσιν),
οὕτω καὶ τῶν ἐν τῷ βίῳ καλῶν κἀγαθῶν οἱ πράττοντες
10 ὀρθῶς ἐπήβολοι γίγνονται. Ἔστι δὲ καὶ ὁ βίος αὐτῶν
καθ' αὑτὸν ἡδύς. Τὸ μὲν γὰρ ἥδεσθαι τῶν ψυχικῶν,
ἑκάστῳ δ' ἐστὶν ἡδὺ πρὸς ὃ λέγεται φιλοτοιοῦτος, οἷον
ἵππος μὲν τῷ φιλίππῳ, θέαμα δὲ τῷ φιλοθεώρῳ· τὸν
αὐτὸν δὲ τρόπον καὶ τὰ δίκαια τῷ φιλοδικαίῳ, καὶ ὅλως
11 τὰ κατ' ἀρετὴν τῷ φιλαρέτῳ. Τοῖς μὲν οὖν πολλοῖς
τὰ ἡδέα μάχεται διὰ τὸ μὴ <u>φύσει</u> τοιαῦτ' εἶναι, τοῖς δὲ

(β) That it implies Pleasure:

10 must be not dormant, but in active exercise. (*b*) That Hap-
piness implies Pleasure. This we agree to, and moreover
claim that our Definition asserts it in a far higher and more
real sense than that usually intended. (1) Because a virtu-
ous life (ἐνέργεια κατ' ἀρετὴν in our Definition) is necessarily
one of pleasure, seeing that every one who is really virtuous
takes pleasure in acting virtuously, and so the pleasure is
11 inherent in the very actions themselves. (2) Because the

5. §§ 10-12] The emphatic words are καθ' αὑτὸν (l. 6) and φύσει (l. 11). The superiority of the pleasures derived from Virtue to other pleasures is argued, because (1) the former are intrinsic or inherent in the acts themselves (l. 5-10), and (2) they are natural and not artificial (l. 10, to l. 3, on next page). But in the statement of his conclusion in p. 42, l. 3—5, having repeated the words καθ' αὑτάς and ἐν ἑαυτῷ, Aristotle recurs to his former argument, stating it, however, more strongly, and then again summing up in p. 43, l. 4.

5. ἐπήβολοι] See x. 14 (note).

6. Τὸ μὲν γὰρ ἥδεσθαι τῶν ψυχικῶν] 'For the feeling of pleasure is something internal,' *i.e.* it is not separable from the occasion which causes it, as two external objects might be separated. The pleasure and the act which is its source are separable in thought but not in fact (λόγῳ δύο ἀχώριστα πεφυκότα, as Ar. says in xiii. 10). Hence the pleasure of Virtuous acts is inherent in, and inseparable from, the acts themselves. ψυχικῶν (cf. ψυχικὰς, § 2) clearly refers to ψυχῆς ἐνέργεια in the Def. of Happiness.

φιλοκάλοις ἐστὶν ἡδέα τὰ φύσει ἡδέα. Τοιαῦτα δ' αἱ
κατ' ἀρετὴν πράξεις, ὥστε καὶ τούτοις εἰσὶν ἡδεῖαι καὶ
12 καθ' αὑτάς. Οὐδὲν δὴ προσδεῖται τῆς ἡδονῆς ὁ βίος
αὐτῶν ὥσπερ περιάπτου τινός, ἀλλ' ἔχει τὴν ἡδονὴν ἐν
ἑαυτῷ. Πρὸς τοῖς εἰρημένοις γὰρ οὐδ' ἐστὶν ἀγαθὸς

pleasures of Virtue, being natural pleasures, never clash or
interfere with one another, as our artificial pleasures do; and
further, being both natural, and also, as we just now said,
12 inherent in the very actions themselves, there is no need of
any adventitious pleasure besides (as the theory we are con-

4. περιάπτου] literally 'something fastened round'; so an appendage, a charm, or amulet. It here indicates an arbitrary reward (which Hegel irreverently described as a 'Trinkgeld') for Virtue.

ἔχει τὴν ἡδονὴν ἐν ἑαυτῷ] This touches upon a very important question in Morals, the relation of Virtue to the Pleasure or Satisfaction which its practice involves. The view in the text is admirably expressed by Seneca: 'We do not love Virtue because it gives us pleasure, but it gives us pleasure because we love it' (Non quia delectat placet, sed quia placet delectat); and again, 'Pleasure is not the motive, but the accompaniment of virtuous action' (Non dux sed comes voluptas). Again, 'Honesty is the best policy, but he who is governed by that maxim is not an honest man' (Whately). We must carefully distinguish between the *conscious aim* and the *actual tendency* of actions. Happiness (according to Aristotle) *must* be the actual tendency of Virtue, but it *cannot* be its conscious aim. In fact, when it is the conscious aim, we run the risk not only of destroying the Virtue of the act, but even of losing the Happiness. The pleasure of Virtue is one which can only be obtained on the express condition of its not being the object sought. There are many other things which exhibit the same phenomenon (see some good remarks on this in *Ecce Homo*, ch. x. p. 113, 3d ed.) Just as in speculation, 'Wisdom is ofttimes nearer when we stoop than when we soar,' so in practice, Happiness is best secured by those who least consciously aim at it. Aristotle discusses at length in III. ix. an apparent exception to the statement of the text which occurs in the case of Courage, the exercise of which is accompanied by pain and loss.

5. Πρὸς τοῖς εἰρημένοις] The addition to the former statement

ὁ μὴ χαίρων ταῖς καλαῖς πράξεσιν· οὔτε γὰρ δίκαιον οὐδεὶς ἂν εἴποι τὸν μὴ χαίροντα τῷ δικαιοπραγεῖν, οὔτ' ἐλευθέριον τὸν μὴ χαίροντα ταῖς ἐλευθερίοις πράξεσιν·
13 ὁμοίως δὲ καὶ ἐπὶ τῶν ἄλλων. Εἰ δ' οὕτω, καθ' αὑτὰς ἂν εἶεν αἱ κατ' ἀρετὴν πράξεις ἡδεῖαι. Ἀλλὰ μὴν καὶ ἀγαθαί γε καὶ καλαί, καὶ μάλιστα τούτων ἕκαστον, εἴπερ καλῶς κρίνει περὶ αὐτῶν ὁ σπουδαῖος· κρίνει δ'

sidering would imply) to make a virtuous life happy; nor need the word therefore be *explicitly* included in the Definition.
13 (3) Nor, lastly, must it be forgotten that our conception of Happiness, as dependent on Virtue, is such as to include, *besides* the highest kind of Pleasure, also the highest degree both of Goodness and Nobleness; all these being united in one, and not separated as the opinion under examination would imply. That this union is real is testified

of the argument in § 10 consists in this: Aristotle said before that the Virtuous man loves Virtue, and therefore finds pleasure in it. He now goes further and says that unless a man feels pleasure in it he is *ipso facto* proved not to be virtuous at all. This would be further illustrated by the contrast between σώφρων and ἐγκρατής (explained above in iii. 7); for the conduct of the latter fails of being strictly Virtue, because it is accompanied with pain and difficulty. See also II. iii., where it is maintained that pleasure accompanying actions is the test of the formation of the *habit* of doing them.

5. Ἀλλὰ μὴν καὶ] 'But moreover they are also.' This formula, as usual, introduces the answer to a supposed objection, or possible misunderstanding. It might be thought that pleasure is the exclusive, or at least distinctive, characteristic of such acts, but this is not the case. Thus we have three points of superiority claimed for Aristotle's theory of the connexion of Pleasure with Happiness over the common view which we are considering. (1) Pleasure is present in a higher *manner*,—it is *inherent*: (2) It is of a higher *sort*,—it is *natural*, not artificial: (3) It is more *comprehensive*, as it includes also τὸ καλὸν and τὸ ἀγαθὸν as fully as τὸ ἡδύ.

7. σπουδαῖος] lit. 'serious' or 'in earnest,' just as φαῦλος is 'light' or 'trifling.' Then the two words come to be used respectively for morally good and bad. Aristotle

14 ὡς εἴπομεν. Ἄριστον ἄρα καὶ κάλλιστον καὶ ἥδιστον ἡ εὐδαιμονία, καὶ οὐ διώρισται ταῦτα κατὰ τὸ Δηλιακὸν ἐπίγραμμα·

Κάλλιστον τὸ δικαιότατον, λῷστον δ' ὑγιαίνειν·
Ἥδιστον δὲ πέφυχ' οὗ τις ἐρᾷ τὸ τυχεῖν.

ἅπαντα γὰρ ὑπάρχει ταῦτα ταῖς ἀρίσταις ἐνεργείαις· ταύτας δέ, ἢ μίαν τούτων τὴν ἀρίστην, φαμὲν εἶναι τὴν
15 εὐδαιμονίαν. Φαίνεται δ' ὅμως καὶ τῶν ἐκτὸς ἀγαθῶν προσδεομένη, καθάπερ εἴπομεν· ἀδύνατον γὰρ ἢ οὐ ῥᾴ-
16 διον τὰ καλὰ πράττειν ἀχορήγητον ὄντα. Πολλὰ μὲν γὰρ πράττεται, καθάπερ δι' ὀργάνων, διὰ φίλων καὶ πλούτου καὶ πολιτικῆς δυνάμεως· ἐνίων δὲ τητώμενοι ῥυπαίνουσι τὸ μακάριον, οἷον εὐγενείας εὐτεκνίας καλ-

14 by the judgment of the best among men, and also that in Happiness this combination is found. The last opinion we shall
15 consider is this:—(*c*) That external prosperity is a condition of Happiness. This we are also disposed to agree to, up to
16 a certain point, partly because many noble actions cannot be performed without means or appliances; and partly because (as we have already admitted) the absence of certain con-

(γ) That it cannot dispense with external prosperity.

appeals in a similar way to the decision of the σπουδαῖος as final in III. iv. 5, and still more emphatically in X. vi. 5, and to the decision of the φρόνιμος in his Definition of Virtue, II. vi. 15. (See note in each case.)

7. μίαν τὴν ἀρίστην] Though they are all inseparably united in Happiness, yet if one be more prominent or characteristic than the rest we might select it alone for the purpose of Definition.

9. εἴπομεν] viz. v. 6 (τὸν δ' οὕτω κ.τ.λ.).

10. ἀχορήγητον] lit. 'unfurnished with a chorus,'—and so generally 'without appliances.' The state provided the chorus for dramatic performances. This duty (called χορηγία) was one of the λειτουργίαι at Athens. (See note on IV. ii. 11.) Cf. conversely κεχορηγημένος in x. 15. The same statement is more fully illustrated in X. vii. 4.

14. εὐδαιμονικὸς] Observe the force of the termination—'adapted for happiness.' Compare πρακτικὸς, 'apt to do,' in ix. 8.

λους· οὐ πάνυ γὰρ εὐδαιμονικὸς ὁ τὴν ἰδέαν παναίσχης
ἢ δυσγενὴς ἢ μονώτης καὶ ἄτεκνος, ἔτι δ' ἴσως ἧττον,
εἴ τῳ πάγκακοι παῖδες εἶεν ἢ φίλοι, ἢ ἀγαθοὶ ὄντες
17 τεθνᾶσιν. Καθάπερ οὖν εἴπομεν, ἔοικε προσδεῖσθαι καὶ
τῆς τοιαύτης εὐημερίας· ὅθεν εἰς ταὐτὸ τάττουσιν ἔνιοι
τὴν εὐτυχίαν τῇ εὐδαιμονίᾳ, ἕτεροι δὲ τὴν ἀρετήν.

1 IX. Ὅθεν καὶ ἀπορεῖται πότερόν ἐστι μαθητὸν ἢ

17 ditions of prosperity is enough to mar Happiness. Some have even identified Happiness with external prosperity just as others have identified it with Virtue. It will be seen that we cannot go so far as this in either case.

CHAP. IX.—*On what does the acquisition of Happiness depend?*

Various causes have been suggested for the acquisition of Happiness

1 Such being our views as to the *connexion* of Happiness with external circumstances and internal conditions of character,

4. Some degree then of external prosperity is demanded on two grounds, (1) because it assists towards the active exercise of Virtue. From this point of view too much of it is almost as great a hindrance as too little, and indeed always it is more or less a source of danger (as Aristotle explains elsewhere, *e.g.* X. viii. 6). Compare Bacon on Riches: 'As the Baggage is to an Army, so is Riches to Virtue: it cannot be spared or left behind, but it hindereth the March.' (2) The other ground is, that the total absence of it in important particulars is obviously enough to interfere with Happiness. See x. 12, where the same two reasons are repeated (λύπας τε γὰρ ἐπιφέρει κ.τ.λ.). Also ix. 7 (Τῶν δὲ λοιπῶν κ.τ.λ.).

7. Ὅθεν καὶ κ.τ.λ.] As Happiness has just been shown to imply both Virtue and also external prosperity in some degree, the former consideration would imply that its acquisition was in our own power (*μαθητὸν, ἐθιστὸν, ἀσκητὸν*), the latter that it was independent of ourselves (*κατὰ θείαν μοῖραν, διὰ τύχην*). Taking the latter first, Aristotle indicates somewhat hesitatingly that *θεία μοῖρα* cannot be the immediate cause of human Happiness, apart from all effort or conduct of our own. He then excludes *τύχη* at once, on the

ἐθιστὸν ἢ ἄλλως πως ἀσκητὸν, ἢ κατά τινα θείαν μοῖ-
2 ραν ἢ καὶ διὰ τύχην παραγίνεται. Εἰ μὲν οὖν καὶ
ἄλλο τι ἐστὶ θεῶν δώρημα ἀνθρώποις, εὔλογον καὶ τὴν
εὐδαιμονίαν θεόσδοτον εἶναι, καὶ μάλιστα τῶν ἀνθρω-
3 πίνων ὅσῳ βέλτιστον. Ἀλλὰ τοῦτο μὲν ἴσως ἄλλης
ἂν εἴη σκέψεως οἰκειότερον, φαίνεται δὲ κἂν εἰ μὴ θεόπεμπτός ἐστιν ἀλλὰ δι' ἀρετὴν καί τινα μάθησιν ἢ ἄσκησιν παραγίνεται, τῶν θειοτάτων εἶναι· τὸ γὰρ τῆς ἀρετῆς ἆθλον καὶ τέλος ἄριστον εἶναι φαίνεται καὶ θεῖόν

it is natural to inquire upon what its *acquisition* depends:—whether it be on learning; on moral, or other, training; on
Relation of Happiness to Divine Providence.
2 Divine dispensation; or on chance. The best of all human goods is certainly the most likely of all to be the gift of
3 Heaven; and whether thus given directly, or through the medium of instruction or discipline, to be of all human things

ground that it is clearly better that the Chief Good should not depend on chance. Arguments are then adduced in favour of considering Virtuous action as the main cause, or at least as an indispensable condition, of Happiness.

1. μαθητὸν refers to intellectual teaching; ἐθιστὸν to moral training; ἀσκητὸν to any sort of training or practice.

5. ἄλλης σκέψεως] i.e. it is a question rather for Theology than Ethics. The Science of Ethics only notes the observed *fact* that Happiness depends in different degrees both on our own efforts and on external circumstances. It leaves to Theology the question whether *theories* of 'Natural Laws' or 'Special Providence' will best explain the facts.

6. εἰ μὴ θεόπεμπτος . . τῶν θειοτάτων] The interventi n of natural laws does not exclude Divine agency, which, having first established the laws, works through them as means. 'If He thunder by Law, the thunder is yet His Voice' (Tennyson).

This paragraph seems added to conciliate religious prejudices, which might be shocked by the bare statement that Happiness is secured by our own efforts, to the apparent exclusion of Divine help. It need be none the less a gift of God, though He wills only to 'help those who help themselves.'

4 τι καὶ μακάριον. Εἴη δ' ἂν καὶ πολύκοινον· δυνατὸν
γὰρ ὑπάρξαι πᾶσι τοῖς μὴ πεπηρωμένοις πρὸς ἀρετὴν
5 διά τινος μαθήσεως καὶ ἐπιμελείας. Εἰ δ' ἐστὶν οὕτω
βέλτιον ἢ διὰ τύχην εὐδαιμονεῖν, εὔλογον ἔχειν οὕτως,
εἴπερ τὰ κατὰ φύσιν, ὡς οἷόν τε κάλλιστα ἔχειν, οὕτω
6 πέφυκεν. Ὁμοίως δὲ καὶ τὰ κατὰ τέχνην καὶ πᾶσαν
αἰτίαν, καὶ μάλιστα κατὰ τὴν ἀρίστην. Τὸ δὲ μέγιστον
καὶ κάλλιστον ἐπιτρέψαι τύχῃ λίαν πλημμελὲς ἂν εἴη.
7 Συμφανὲς δ' ἐστὶ καὶ ἐκ τοῦ λόγου τὸ ζητούμενον·
εἴρηται γὰρ ψυχῆς ἐνέργεια κατ' ἀρετὴν ποιά τις. Τῶν

4 the most divine. It is moreover something within the reach
of all, if it be sought after, or at least of all who are not in-
5 capacitated for Virtue. Chance at any rate we may exclude
from the inquiry at once, if it is better, as it most clearly
6 is, that this greatest prize should depend on our own efforts
rather than on chance. We argue for some such view as this,
because (1) our Definition implies something of this sort,
7 when it describes Happiness as an active condition in accord-

Happiness cannot depend on Chance, for it is obviously better that it have relation to our own efforts. That this is so is already virtually implied (1) in our Definition:

1. Εἴη δ' ἂν καὶ πολύκοινον] 'It would also be within common reach,'—a consideration in favour of supposing Happiness to be in some degree at least the result of our own exertions (which Aristotle has rather hinted at than stated directly as yet, in the words εἰ μὴ θεόπεμπτος κ.τ.λ.),—'for every one can obtain it except those incapacitated, etc.'

7. αἰτία in this context refers to any sort of conscious or intentional causation as contrasted with τυχή.

ἀρίστη αἰτία seems to be Nature (φύσις l. 5), which would convey to a Greek a notion similar to that of Providence with us. See Glossary on θεὸς and φύσις, and compare a similar argument to this in ii. 1, and *note* there. The argument in this passage appears to be: Nature does all for the best; for indeed in like manner (ὁμοίως) every art and every intelligent cause does its best, whatever that may be; and therefore *a fortiori* Nature, the First of Causes, above all others, does what is best; *its* best being of course the absolutely best.

10. κατ' ἀρετὴν] It is taken for granted here and elsewhere that Virtue depends on our own efforts.

τῶν δὲ λοιπῶν ἀγαθῶν τὰ μὲν ὑπάρχειν ἀναγκαῖον, τὰ δὲ
8 συνεργὰ καὶ χρήσιμα πέφυκεν ὀργανικῶς. Ὁμολογούμενα δὲ ταῦτ' ἂν εἴη καὶ τοῖς ἐν ἀρχῇ· τὸ γὰρ τῆς πολιτικῆς τέλος ἄριστον ἐτίθεμεν, αὕτη δὲ πλείστην ἐπιμέλειαν ποιεῖται τοῦ ποιούς τινας καὶ ἀγαθοὺς τοὺς
9 πολίτας ποιῆσαι καὶ πρακτικοὺς τῶν καλῶν. Εἰκότως οὖν οὔτε βοῦν οὔτε ἵππον οὔτε ἄλλο τῶν ζώων οὐδὲν εὔδαιμον λέγομεν· οὐδὲν γὰρ αὐτῶν οἷόν τε κοινωνῆσαι τοιαύτης ἐνεργείας. Διὰ ταύτην δὲ τὴν αἰτίαν οὐδὲ παῖς

ance with Excellence or Virtue, though we do not deny the necessity of other goods as aids and instruments even towards
8 that excellence. (2) Our original conception of the Chief Good as the End of the Science of Social Life points in the same direction, the primary object of that Science being to secure the virtuous life of all the members of society. (3)
9 Lastly, we derive an argument from the use of language, which does not apply the term Happiness (in its full and proper sense) either to the lower animals or to children, both being

(2) in our original conception of Ethical Science:

(3) and in the common language of men.

1. λοιπῶν] *i.e.* Goods other than Virtue just mentioned. These it is true are not wholly under our control. Observe the same two grounds as before (viii. 15, 16) for the need of some measure of external Goods.

3. τοῖς ἐν ἀρχῇ] viz. ii. 5.

4. Hence πολιτική has a wider sense than the 'science of government,' because it aims at making good *men*, as well as good *citizens*. See note on xiii. 3. The point of the argument here is that πολιτική aims at securing Happiness through the means of Virtuous conduct and character, and this implies that the acquisition of Happiness depends mainly on ourselves.

7. If it sound strange to say that neither the lower animals nor children can be called happy, we must remember the full meaning attached to the term in the Definition of ch. vii., and not be misled by the popular application of the word 'happy' in English. See further, X. vi. 8 (note).

9. τοιαύτης] viz. πρακτικῆς τῶν καλῶν from l. 6.

οὐδὲ παῖς] 'not even a child.' This is a stronger case than that of the lower animals just cited, because a child has Happiness ἐν

εὐδαίμων ἐστίν· οὔπω γὰρ πρακτικὸς τῶν τοιούτων διὰ τὴν ἡλικίαν· οἱ δὲ λεγόμενοι διὰ τὴν ἐλπίδα μακαρίζονται. Δεῖ γάρ, ὥσπερ εἴπομεν, καὶ ἀρετῆς τελείας καὶ
11 βίου τελείου. Πολλαὶ γὰρ μεταβολαὶ γίνονται καὶ παντοῖαι τύχαι κατὰ τὸν βίον, καὶ ἐνδέχεται τὸν μάλιστ' εὐθηνοῦντα μεγάλαις συμφοραῖς περιπεσεῖν ἐπὶ γήρως, καθάπερ ἐν τοῖς ἡρωικοῖς περὶ Πριάμου μυθεύεται· τὸν δὲ τοιαύταις χρησάμενον τύχαις καὶ τελευτήσαντα ἀθλίως οὐδεὶς εὐδαιμονίζει.

1 X. Πότερον οὖν οὐδ' ἄλλον οὐδένα ἀνθρώπων εὐδαι-

characterized by incapacity for Virtuous practice,—the former absolutely, the latter temporarily: for both Virtue and Happi-
11 ness are imperfect unless exhibited in 'a complete life'; the changes and chances to which life is exposed being so many and so various.

CHAPS. X. XI.—*What is the relation of Happiness to the varying fortunes of life, especially in reference to a well-known dictum of Solon's.*

1 Hence arises the question, Must we (as Solon used to say) wait till we see the end of a man's life before we can call him

Solon's dictum stated.

δυνάμει though not *ἐν ἐνεργείᾳ* (See Glossary, p. xliv.), and hence *διὰ τὴν ἐλπίδα μακαρίζονται*, whereas a brute has it not in any sense, either *δυνάμει* or *ἐνεργείᾳ*.

CHAPS. X. and XI.—The mention of *βίος τέλειος* at the end of the last Chapter, and the statement made in reference to it, suggests the popular question said to have been first raised by Solon, 'Can we not call a man happy till his life is completed?' In §§ 1-5 Aristotle points out the difficulties involved in every solution or interpretation of this question, especially as it cannot be separated from the wider question of the condition of the departed. In § 6 he returns to the consideration of the dictum of Solon, proposing afterwards to apply its solution (gained by the help of his own theory of Happiness) to that of the wider question just mentioned. It is so applied in ch. xi.

10. *οὐδ' ἄλλον οὐδένα*] i.e. even

μονιστέον ἕως ἂν ζῇ, κατὰ Σόλωνα δὲ χρεὼν τέλος ὁρᾶν;
2 *Εἰ δὲ δὴ καὶ θετέον οὕτως, ἆρά γε καὶ ἔστιν εὐδαίμων*
τότε ἐπειδὰν ἀποθάνῃ; ἢ τοῦτό γε παντελῶς ἄτοπον,
ἄλλως τε καὶ τοῖς λέγουσιν ἡμῖν ἐνέργειάν τινα τὴν
3 *εὐδαιμονίαν; εἰ δὲ μὴ λέγομεν τὸν τεθνεῶτα εὐδαίμονα,*
μηδὲ Σόλων τοῦτο βούλεται, ἀλλ' ὅτι τηνικαῦτα ἄν τις
ἀσφαλῶς μακαρίσειεν ἄνθρωπον ὡς ἐκτὸς ἤδη τῶν κακῶν
ὄντα καὶ τῶν δυστυχημάτων, ἔχει μὲν καὶ τοῦτ' ἀμφισ-
βήτησίν τινα· δοκεῖ γὰρ εἶναί τι τῷ τεθνεῶτι καὶ κακὸν
καὶ ἀγαθόν, εἴπερ καὶ τῷ ζῶντι μὴ αἰσθανομένῳ δέ, οἷον
τιμαὶ καὶ ἀτιμίαι καὶ τέκνων καὶ ὅλως ἀπογόνων εὐ-
4 *πραξίαι τε καὶ δυστυχίαι. Ἀπορίαν δὲ καὶ ταῦτα*

2 happy? Those who say this mean, *either* that he is happy when
dead—which is absurd, especially if happiness consists in ac-
tivity (ἐνέργεια) as our Definition asserts, and indeed Solon pro-
3 bably never meant this;—*or* that we can then safely apply the
term 'happy' to him, as being now beyond the reach of trouble.
But are we so sure that he is beyond its reach? Do not the for-
tunes of the family or friends that he has left behind affect him
4 still? But this again opens another difficulty. If we suppose

It involves the further question of the condition of the dead in reference to the living, which is full of difficulties.

any other than ὁ Πριαμικαῖς ξυμφοραῖς περιπεσών. This might be thought an exceptional case, and so the question is put, 'Can we not then call even any ordinary man happy while he lives, by reason of the changes and chances of life?'

9. δοκεῖ] 'It is supposed,' see note on iii. 2.

δοκεῖ γὰρ κ.τ.λ.] 'It is thought that both good and evil may occur to the dead, if indeed they can to the living without his being conscious of it.' Œdipus for instance would not have been considered a happy man even if he had never discovered his incestuous marriage, but had gone on till death in 'happy' ignorance of it. His 'ignorance' would not have been 'bliss' from the Greek point of view. This at least is assumed in the text, and the argument drawn from it is, that it is equally natural to suppose that the happiness of a dead man, even though he be unconscious, is marred by misfortunes occurring to his family on earth. Aristotle however is only stating a popular belief.

παρέχει· τῷ γὰρ μακαρίως βεβιωκότι μέχρι γήρως καὶ τελευτήσαντι κατὰ λόγον ἐνδέχεται πολλὰς μεταβολὰς συμβαίνειν περὶ τοὺς ἐκγόνους, καὶ τοὺς μὲν αὐτῶν ἀγαθοὺς εἶναι καὶ τυχεῖν βίου τοῦ κατ' ἀξίαν, τοὺς δ' ἐξ ἐναντίας. Δῆλον δ' ὅτι καὶ τοῖς ἀποστήμασι πρὸς τοὺς
5 γονεῖς παντοδαπῶς ἔχειν αὐτοὺς ἐνδέχεται. Ἄτοπον δὴ γίνοιτ' ἄν, εἰ συμμεταβάλλοι καὶ ὁ τεθνεὼς καὶ γίνοιτο ὁτὲ μὲν εὐδαίμων πάλιν δ' ἄθλιος. Ἄτοπον δὲ καὶ τὸ μηδὲν μηδ' ἐπί τινα χρόνον συνικνεῖσθαι τὰ τῶν ἐκγόνων
6 τοῖς γονεῦσιν. Ἀλλ' ἐπανιτέον ἐπὶ τὸ πρότερον ἀπορηθέν· τάχα γὰρ ἂν θεωρηθείη καὶ τὸ νῦν ἐπιζητούμενον

that they *do* affect him, then it would seem that the happiness of a complete life may be marred after death, and that even
5 the dead may change from happiness to misery and *vice versâ* with the fluctuating fortunes of their descendants on earth. And yet on the other hand, it is very hard to suppose that these *do not* affect the dead at all. How then are we to escape
6 from this concourse of difficulties? Perhaps this large question concerning the condition of the dead, into which we have wandered, may best be solved by first giving an answer to the simpler one,—Was Solon right in saying we must never call a

Solon's question however should be solved first.

2. κατὰ λόγον] 'accordingly.' A quasi-mathematical expression = 'in proportion.'

5. καὶ τοῖς ἀποστήμασι κ.τ.λ.] 'also in their several degrees of removal (*i.e.* in their several generations) it is possible for them to be related in every variety of way to their progenitors,' *i.e.* some giving them pleasure and others pain.

6. ἄτοπον] This is 'out of place,' because even the dead (καὶ ὁ τεθνεὼς) would not at this rate be exempt from the difficulty felt by Solon.

8. ἄτοπον] Why this is 'out of place' is more fully explained in xi. 1. It would be λίαν ἄφιλον καὶ ταῖς δόξαις ἐναντίον. Notice here and elsewhere Aristotle's respect for popular feelings and beliefs.

10. The πρότερον ἀπορηθὲν is the dictum of Solon, χρὴ τὸ τέλος ὁρᾶν. The τὸ νῦν ἐπιζητούμενον is the relation of the dead to the fortunes of their friends,

7 ἐξ ἐκείνου. Εἰ δὴ τὸ τέλος ὁρᾶν δεῖ καὶ τότε μακαρίζειν
ἕκαστον οὐχ ὡς ὄντα μακάριον ἀλλ' ὅτι πρότερον ἦν, πῶς
οὐκ ἄτοπον, εἰ ὅτ' ἔστιν εὐδαίμων, μὴ ἀληθεύσεται κατ'
αὐτοῦ τὸ ὑπάρχον, διὰ τὸ μὴ βούλεσθαι τοὺς ζῶντας
εὐδαιμονίζειν διὰ τὰς μεταβολάς, καὶ διὰ τὸ μόνιμόν τι
τὴν εὐδαιμονίαν ὑπειληφέναι καὶ μηδαμῶς εὐμετάβολον,
τὰς δὲ τύχας πολλάκις ἀνακυκλεῖσθαι περὶ τοὺς αὐτούς;
8 δῆλον γὰρ ὡς εἰ συνακολουθοίημεν ταῖς τύχαις, τὸν
αὐτὸν εὐδαίμονα καὶ πάλιν ἄθλιον ἐροῦμεν πολλάκις,
χαμαιλέοντά τινα τὸν εὐδαίμονα ἀποφαίνοντες καὶ σα-
9 θρῶς ἱδρυμένον. Ἢ τὸ μὲν ταῖς τύχαις ἐπακολουθεῖν
οὐδαμῶς ὀρθόν; οὐ γὰρ ἐν ταύταις τὸ εὖ ἢ κακῶς, ἀλλὰ
προσδεῖται τούτων ὁ ἀνθρώπινος βίος, καθάπερ εἴπαμεν,
κύριαι δ' εἰσὶν αἱ κατ' ἀρετὴν ἐνέργειαι τῆς εὐδαιμονίας,

The difficulty is due to making changing circumstances the test of Happiness which is most stable,

7 man happy while still *living?* Now surely if we can ever
say with truth that a man *has been* happy, it must have been
possible at some time or another to say that he *is* happy.
8 The supposed difficulty in doing so is that Happiness is most
9 stable, and the chances of Fortune most variable. The solu-
tion is obvious. These chances ought never to be made the test of Happiness at all. The fact is that external prosperity, however necessary a *condition* of Happiness (and this we have amply admitted before), cannot be its *cause.* We say again, as we said in our Definition, that Virtuous Actions are the true cause of Happiness, as Vicious actions are of misery.

which question arose out of attempts to explain that dictum.

4, 5. διὰ three times repeated is somewhat awkward. It will be seen that the first διὰ explains μὴ ἀληθεύσεται: the second and third explain τὸ μὴ βούλεσθαι εὐδαιμονίζειν.

13, 14. Observe the contrast between προσδεῖται = 'has further need of' (*i.e.* this is not a *primary* condition of Happiness) and κύριαι εἰσὶ = they 'test' or 'determine.' Compare προσδεομένη, viii. 15, and προσδεῖσθαι in viii. 17 and iv. 7.

10 αἱ δ' ἐναντίαι τοῦ ἐναντίου. Μαρτυρεῖ δὲ τῷ λόγῳ καὶ τὸ νῦν διαπορηθέν. Περὶ οὐδὲν γὰρ οὕτως ὑπάρχει τῶν ἀνθρωπίνων ἔργων βεβαιότης ὡς περὶ τὰς ἐνεργείας τὰς κατ' ἀρετήν· μονιμώτεραι γὰρ καὶ τῶν ἐπιστημῶν αὗται δοκοῦσιν εἶναι. Τούτων δ' αὐτῶν αἱ τιμιώταται μονιμώταται διὰ τὸ μάλιστα καὶ συνεχέστατα καταζῆν ἐν αὐταῖς τοὺς μακαρίους· τοῦτο γὰρ ἔοικεν αἰτίῳ τοῦ μὴ
11 γίγνεσθαι περὶ αὐτὰ λήθην. Ὑπάρξει δὴ τὸ ζητούμενον τῷ εὐδαίμονι, καὶ ἔσται διὰ βίου τοιοῦτος· ἀεὶ γὰρ ἢ μάλιστα πάντων πράξει καὶ θεωρήσει τὰ κατ' ἀρετήν, καὶ τὰς τύχας οἴσει κάλλιστα καὶ πάντῃ πάντως ἐμ-

whereas Virtue is the real test; and Virtue is in fact more stable than anything else.

10 To the truth of that Definition in this respect, the very difficulty that has now arisen bears witness. It is the recognised stability of Happiness that makes us so cautious in our application of the term. But what is there so stable as Virtuous action? Not intellectual knowledge. This may be forgotten. But active Virtue *vi nominis* must be in continual practice, and is thus necessarily permanent and stable, and the more so
11 as it exists in its noblest forms and highest degree in perfect Happiness. How then will a man who thus lives stand in

1. τῷ λόγῳ] 'our Definition,' which asserts Happiness to be κατ' ἀρέτην. The present difficulty (τὸ νῦν διαπορηθὲν) turns upon the universally believed stability of Happiness, which makes us reluctant to apply the name where change may come. But this stability is intelligible if Happiness depends on Virtue, as our Definition asserts, because Virtuous practice is more stable than anything else, as the reasons now to be adduced sufficiently prove. Thus the difficulty itself is a support to the Definition.

4-8. This may suggest one reason among others why 'Knowledge (ἐπιστῆμαι) shall vanish away, but charity (ἐνέργειαι κατ' ἀρετὴν) never faileth.'

5. Τούτων δὲ αὐτῶν] is 'of Virtues in active exercise,' ἐνεργειῶν κατ' ἀρετήν.

8. τὸ ζητούμενον] 'the quality we are seeking for,' viz. stability.

10. Happiness being according to the Definition κατ' ἀρετὴν ἀρίστην.

μελῶς ὅ γ' ὡς ἀληθῶς ἀγαθὸς καὶ τετράγωνος ἄνευ
12 *ψόγου. Πολλῶν δὲ γινομένων κατὰ τύχην καὶ διαφερόντων μεγέθει καὶ μικρότητι, τὰ μὲν μικρὰ τῶν εὐτυχημάτων, ὁμοίως δὲ καὶ τῶν ἀντικειμένων, δῆλον ὡς οὐ ποιεῖ ῥοπὴν τῆς ζωῆς, τὰ δὲ μεγάλα καὶ πολλὰ, γιγνόμενα μὲν εὖ, μακαριώτερον τὸν βίον ποιήσει (καὶ γὰρ αὐτὰ συνεπικοσμεῖν πέφυκεν, καὶ ἡ χρῆσις αὐτῶν καλὴ καὶ σπουδαία γίγνεται), ἀνάπαλιν δὲ συμβαίνοντα θλίβει καὶ λυμαίνεται τὸ μακάριον· λύπας τε γὰρ ἐπιφέρει καὶ ἐμποδίζει πολλαῖς ἐνεργείαις. Ὅμως δὲ καὶ ἐν τούτοις διαλάμπει τὸ καλὸν, ἐπειδὰν φέρῃ τις εὐκόλως πολλὰς καὶ μεγάλας ἀτυχίας, μὴ δι' ἀναλγησίαν,*
13 *ἀλλὰ γεννάδας ὢν καὶ μεγαλόψυχος. Εἰ δ' εἰσὶν αἱ ἐνέργειαι κύριαι τῆς ζωῆς, καθάπερ εἴπομεν, οὐδεὶς ἂν*

How then does the virtuous man stand related to the changes of fortune?

12 relation to the gifts of Fortune? If they be *small*, whether good or bad, they will not affect the balance of his life. If they be *great*, and also good, they will naturally add a lustre to his happiness; but if evil, they will mar it, inflict on him pain, and impede his activity in virtue. Still the very greatness of such troubles affords scope for nobleness of character, when they are keenly felt and yet complacently endured.
13 Hence we conclude that if (as we have said) Virtue and Vice

1. *τετράγωνος ἄνευ ψόγου*] 'a cube without flaw,'—a mathematical metaphor to express perfection. Squares, cubes, circles, spheres (*i.e.* 'regular' figures and solids), are familiar metaphors to express perfection in various languages.

7. *αὐτὰ*] 'of themselves.' This parenthesis is explained by viii. 15. For the converse statement in l. 8 [*ἀνάπαλιν δὲ συμβαίνοντα θλίβει καὶ λυμαίνεται κ.τ.λ.*] see viii. 16.

9. *λύπας τε γὰρ κ.τ.λ.*] See these two reasons expounded in viii. 15, 16 (note).

11. *εὐκόλως*] Contrast *δύσκολος* in IV. vi. 9.

12. *δι' ἀναλγησίαν*] Such was the view of the Stoics. Aristotle on the contrary maintains that natural feelings, though under control, are not to be crushed or eradicated.

γένοιτο τῶν μακαρίων ἄθλιος· οὐδέποτε γὰρ πράξει τὰ μισητὰ καὶ φαῦλα. Τὸν γὰρ ὡς ἀληθῶς ἀγαθὸν καὶ ἔμφρονα πάσας οἰόμεθα τὰς τύχας εὐσχημόνως φέρειν, καὶ ἐκ τῶν ὑπαρχόντων ἀεὶ τὰ κάλλιστα πράττειν, καθάπερ καὶ στρατηγὸν ἀγαθὸν τῷ παρόντι στρατοπέδῳ χρῆσθαι πολεμικώτατα, καὶ σκυτοτόμον ἐκ τῶν δοθέντων σκυτῶν κάλλιστον ὑπόδημα ποιεῖν· τὸν αὐτὸν δὲ τρόπον
14 καὶ τοὺς ἄλλους τεχνίτας ἅπαντας. Εἰ δ' οὕτως, ἄθλιος μὲν οὐδέποτε γένοιτ' ἂν ὁ εὐδαίμων, οὐ μὴν μακάριός γε, ἂν Πριαμικαῖς τύχαις περιπέσῃ. Οὐδὲ δὴ ποικίλος γε καὶ εὐμετάβολος· οὔτε γὰρ ἐκ τῆς εὐδαιμονίας κινηθήσεται ῥᾳδίως, οὐδ' ὑπὸ τῶν τυχόντων ἀτυχημάτων ἀλλ' ὑπὸ μεγάλων καὶ πολλῶν, ἔκ τε τῶν τοιούτων οὐκ

alone *determine* the happiness or misery of life, external circumstances (which in all cases the virtuous man will make the
14 best of, like a good general) can never altogether destroy Happiness and change it into misery, though we do not pretend that they will not in some degree affect it. We conclude further (and this was another of the difficulties raised at the beginning of the chapter), that the happy man is not easily

In no case is he easily moved or changed by them.

9. Notice the contrast between εὐδαίμων and μακάριος, the latter being the higher state; though the distinction is by no means always maintained. The words 'happiness' and 'felicity' respectively are the best English equivalents, and in Latin 'felix' and 'beatus.' 'The happy man could never become wretched, though he would not be in a state of perfect felicity if he fell into troubles like those of Priam.' The Stoics would say that he could be. They maintained that the virtuous man would be perfectly happy even while being broken on the wheel. Aristotle says that external circumstances however great or various can never *constitute* either happiness or misery, but they can make the difference of greater or less degrees of either one or the other. Virtue and Vice alone have power to *constitute* these states. To regard external goods as the *cause* of Happiness would be like giving the lyre the credit of a brilliant musical performance. (See *Pol.* IV. (VII.) xiii. 8.)

ἂν γένοιτο πάλιν εὐδαίμων ἐν ὀλίγῳ χρόνῳ, ἀλλ' εἴπερ, ἐν πολλῷ τινὶ καὶ τελείῳ, μεγάλων καὶ καλῶν ἐν αὐτῷ
15 γενόμενος ἐπήβολος. Τί οὖν κωλύει λέγειν εὐδαίμονα τὸν κατ' ἀρετὴν τελείαν ἐνεργοῦντα καὶ τοῖς ἐκτὸς ἀγαθοῖς ἱκανῶς κεχορηγημένον, μὴ τὸν τυχόντα χρόνον ἀλλὰ τέλειον βίον; ἢ προσθετέον καὶ βιωσόμενον οὕτω καὶ τελευτήσοντα κατὰ λόγον, ἐπειδὴ τὸ μέλλον ἀφανὲς ἡμῖν, τὴν εὐδαιμονίαν δὲ τέλος καὶ τέλειον τίθεμεν
16 πάντῃ πάντως; Εἰ δ' οὕτω, μακαρίους ἐροῦμεν τῶν ζώντων οἷς ὑπάρχει καὶ ὑπάρξει τὰ λεχθέντα, μακαρίους δ' ἀνθρώπους.

1 XI. Καὶ περὶ μὲν τούτων ἐπὶ τοσοῦτον διωρίσθω· τὰς

moved; and that as it will take a great deal to mar happiness, so it will take a great deal to restore it if once disturbed.

Solon's question may now be answered. We can call a man still living 'happy.'

15 Finally then we ask, granted the conditions of perfect virtue, a sufficient supply of external goods, and both these for an adequate duration of time, why may we not call a man happy while he still lives? Some may desire that in view of the uncertainty of the future, and the perfect finality of happiness, we should add, provided such a life be crowned by a fitting
16 death. Still it must be remembered that in calling men happy, we of course mean only happy as mortal men can be.

How far then is the condition of the dead affected by the fortunes of the living?

1 CHAP. XI.—Now we can return to the solution of the other

3. ἐπήβολος] (ἐπί, βάλλω) 'having hit upon.' ἐν αὐτῷ, viz. χρόνῳ.

9. Thus then the question raised by Solon is answered. We *can* call men happy while still alive, but happy as men, and not as gods; being as men still liable to the dangers incident to humanity; and *this being understood*, we need not explicitly add 'καὶ βιωσόμενον οὕτω κ.τ.λ.' (l. 6), when we apply the term 'happy,' any more than when we apply the terms 'healthy,' 'rich,' 'wise,' etc.; any of which conditions are similarly liable to the possibility of disturbance. τὰ λεχθέντα are the three conditions specified at the beginning of § 15, viz. Virtue, External Goods in sufficiency, and Stability.

CHAP. XI.—In this Chapter

δὲ τῶν ἀπογόνων τύχας καὶ τῶν φίλων ἁπάντων τὸ μὲν
μηδοτιοῦν συμβάλλεσθαι λίαν ἄφιλον φαίνεται καὶ ταῖς
2 δόξαις ἐναντίον· πολλῶν δὲ καὶ παντοίας ἐχόντων δια-
φορὰς τῶν συμβαινόντων, καὶ τῶν μὲν μᾶλλον συνικ-
νουμένων, τῶν δ' ἧττον, καθ' ἕκαστον μὲν διαιρεῖν μακ-
ρὸν καὶ ἀπέραντον φαίνεται, καθόλου δὲ λεχθὲν καὶ
3 τύπῳ τάχ' ἂν ἱκανῶς ἔχοι. Εἰ δή, καθάπερ καὶ τῶν περὶ
αὑτὸν ἀτυχημάτων τὰ μὲν ἔχει τι βρῖθος καὶ ῥοπὴν

difficulty, viz. whether the happiness of the dead can be altered
by the fortunes of the living. To suppose the dead *wholly*
untouched by these fortunes seems cold, and runs counter to
2 received beliefs. To estimate accurately the various *degrees*
of influence exercised by such occurrences great and small
would be endless. This then may serve as a general solution.
3 —*In life itself*, different circumstances affect us in very different

Aristotle returns to the question of the condition of the dead in relation to the fortunes of the living. He applies to its solution (as he promised in x. 6) the results arrived at in reference to Solon's problem thus:—if the fortunes of life are no obstacle to our calling a man happy while still alive and still exposed to their full force, *a fortiori* they cannot seriously interfere with the happiness of the dead who are removed from their immediate influence.

7, to l. 8 next page. Εἰ δή . . . ἀντικειμένων] The sentence is somewhat complicated. Two conditions are stated:—(1) If misfortunes even in this life differ in degree when they concern ourselves, and similarly when they concern our friends (εἰ δὴ . . . ἁπάντας); (2) If absence from the actual scene of their occurrence in this world, and *a fortiori* if removal to another world altogether, dull their effect upon us (διαφέρει . . . πράττεσθαι); then the result (the apodosis of the sentence) is,—These points, and especially the latter (ταύτην τὴν διαφορὰν), must be taken into consideration (συλλογιστέον δὴ) in determining the question before us. Unless indeed we go further still, and make the question not one of degree but of fact, i.e. not *How far* are the dead affected? but Are they affected even *at all?* (μᾶλλον δὲ ἴσως τὸ διαπορεῖσθαι κ.τ.λ.). τὸ διαπορεῖσθαι = 'the utter doubt and uncertainty.'

πρὸς τὸν βίον, τὰ δ' ἐλαφροτέροις ἔοικεν, οὕτω καὶ τὰ
4 περὶ τοὺς φίλους ὁμοίως ἅπαντας, διαφέρει δὲ τῶν
παθῶν ἕκαστον περὶ ζῶντας ἢ τελευτήσαντας συμβαί-
νειν πολὺ μᾶλλον ἢ τὰ παράνομα καὶ δεινὰ προϋπάρχειν
5 ἐν ταῖς τραγῳδίαις ἢ πράττεσθαι, συλλογιστέον δὴ καὶ
ταύτην τὴν διαφοράν, μᾶλλον δ' ἴσως τὸ διαπορεῖσθαι
περὶ τοὺς κεκμηκότας εἴ τινος ἀγαθοῦ κοινωνοῦσιν ἢ τῶν
ἀντικειμένων· ἔοικε γὰρ ἐκ τούτων εἰ καὶ διϊκνεῖται πρὸς
αὐτοὺς ὁτιοῦν, εἴτ' ἀγαθὸν εἴτε τοὐναντίον, ἀφαυρόν τι
καὶ μικρὸν ἢ ἁπλῶς ἢ ἐκείνοις εἶναι, εἰ δὲ μή, τοσοῦτόν
γε καὶ τοιοῦτον ὥστε μὴ ποιεῖν εὐδαίμονας τοὺς μὴ ὄντας
6 μηδὲ τοὺς ὄντας ἀφαιρεῖσθαι τὸ μακάριον. Συμβάλλεσ-
θαι μὲν οὖν τι φαίνονται τοῖς κεκμηκόσιν αἱ εὐπραξίαι
τῶν φίλων, ὁμοίως δὲ καὶ αἱ δυσπραξίαι, τοιαῦτα δὲ
καὶ τηλικαῦτα ὥστε μήτε τοὺς εὐδαίμονας μὴ εὐδαίμονας
ποιεῖν μήτ' ἄλλο τῶν τοιούτων μηδέν.

degrees, when they concern ourselves, and naturally also when
4 they concern our friends. *After our death*, such circumstances,
being acted on another stage, must affect us infinitely less.
5 We must then make full allowance for this difference, even
supposing we grant the general question that they do affect us
6 somewhat. Hence we conclude that the dead are influenced
by such occurrences, if at all, only slightly, and certainly not
to such a degree as to change Happiness into Misery, or
vice versâ.

5. The lines in Hor. *A. P.* 180-2 will occur to every one:—

Segnius irritant animos demissa per aures
Quam quae sunt oculis subjecta fidelibus, et quae
Ipse sibi tradit spectator.

(See *Supplementary Notes.*)

10. ἢ ἁπλῶς ἢ ἐκείνοις] 'Either in itself, or to them.' Referring to the two conditions respectively in §§ 3 and 4. The influence of these occurrences, if they do reach the dead, must be trifling anyhow, either in itself (as explained in § 3), or at least trifling in the effect produced upon the dead (as explained in § 4).

1 XII. *Διωρισμένων δὲ τούτων ἐπισκεψώμεθα περὶ τῆς εὐδαιμονίας πότερα τῶν ἐπαινετῶν ἐστὶν ἢ μᾶλλον τῶν τιμίων· δῆλον γὰρ ὅτι τῶν γε δυνάμεων οὐκ ἔστιν.*
2 *Φαίνεται δὴ πᾶν τὸ ἐπαινετὸν τῷ ποιόν τι εἶναι καὶ πρός τι πῶς ἔχειν ἐπαινεῖσθαι· τὸν γὰρ δίκαιον καὶ τὸν ἀνδρεῖον καὶ ὅλως τὸν ἀγαθὸν καὶ τὴν ἀρετὴν ἐπαινοῦμεν διὰ τὰς πράξεις καὶ τὰ ἔργα, καὶ τὸν ἰσχυρὸν καὶ τὸν δρομικὸν καὶ τῶν ἄλλων ἕκαστον τῷ ποιόν τινα πε-*

CHAP. XII.—*Comparison of another popular theory with Aristotle's Definition.*

Goods are sometimes said to be either potential, or praiseworthy, or admirable.

1 One more popular division of Goods calls for comparison with our theory, before we proceed. It is commonly said that Goods are *potential* or *actual*; the former *may* be good, the latter *must* be. Further, 'actual' Goods are said to be either objects of praise, or objects of admiration, as being beyond praise. It may be asked then under which of these three classes does our conception of the Chief Good or Happiness
2 fall. Obviously not under the first. Nor yet under the second, viz. objects of praise. Praise is only applied to things

Our conception of Happiness would bring it under the last of these.

CHAP. XII. contains the last of the popular opinions and questions to which Aristotle adjusts his theory (see note at beginning of ch. viii.). This opinion is, that Good things may be divided into *δυνάμεις*, *ἐπαινετά*, and *τίμια*. The question is, To which class does the Chief Good in Aristotle's conception of it belong?

3. *τιμίων*] things on which we bestow *τιμή*, a much higher tribute than *ἔπαινος*, as is explained by IV. iii. 10.

δυνάμεων] *i.e.* things which are potentially but not necessarily good, their character depending on the use made of them. Aristotle gives as instances elsewhere, power, riches, beauty, strength. Compare what was said in iii. 3. That Happiness is not of this class needs no proof.

4. *τῷ ποιόν τι κ.τ.λ.*] literally 'from possessing a certain character and bearing a certain relation to something else.' In other words, all praise is *relative* (*δι' ἀναφορᾶς*) as Aristotle says in § 3.

φυκέναι καὶ ἔχειν πως πρὸς ἀγαθόν τι καὶ σπουδαῖον.
3 Δῆλον δὲ τοῦτο καὶ ἐκ τῶν περὶ τοὺς θεοὺς ἐπαίνων·
γελοῖοι γὰρ φαίνονται πρὸς ἡμᾶς ἀναφερόμενοι, τοῦτο
δὲ συμβαίνει διὰ τὸ γίνεσθαι τοὺς ἐπαίνους δι' ἀναφο-
4 ρᾶς, ὥσπερ εἴπαμεν. Εἰ δ' ἐστὶν ὁ ἔπαινος τῶν τοιού-
των, δῆλον ὅτι τῶν ἀρίστων οὐκ ἔστιν ἔπαινος, ἀλλὰ
μεῖζόν τι καὶ βέλτιον, καθάπερ καὶ φαίνεται· τούς τε γὰρ
θεοὺς μακαρίζομεν καὶ εὐδαιμονίζομεν, καὶ τῶν ἀνδρῶν
τοὺς θειοτάτους μακαρίζομεν. Ὁμοίως δὲ καὶ τῶν ἀγα-
θῶν· οὐδεὶς γὰρ τὴν εὐδαιμονίαν ἐπαινεῖ καθάπερ τὸ
δίκαιον, ἀλλ' ὡς θειότερόν τι καὶ βέλτιον μακαρίζει.
5 Δοκεῖ δὲ καὶ Εὔδοξος καλῶς συνηγορῆσαι περὶ τῶν ἀρισ-

in reference to their results, and because they are well adapted
3 to produce these results. Hence it is applied to justice,
courage, strength, etc. Hence also we cannot employ the
term 'praise,' involving this notion of commendation, to the
4 Gods, nor is it applicable to the highest goods, which are not
desired for their results, but for themselves; nor consequently
5 can it be applied to Happiness. When Eudoxus claimed that

2. *ἔπαινος* involves the idea of commendation. In this sense it is clear we cannot 'praise' the Deity.

6. *δῆλον ὅτι κ.τ.λ.*] If praise is always applied with a view to results, and if results are necessarily higher than the actions or means which lead to them (see i. 2), then there must be something better than praise to apply to the results themselves. For we must suppose some results to be final (otherwise *πρόεισιν οὕτω γε εἰς ἄπειρον* ii. 1), and these at any rate cannot *ex hyp.* be subjects for praise.

8. Observe the distinction between *μακαρία* and *εὐδαιμονία*, 'felicity' and 'happiness.' See x. 14 (note). Both belong to the Gods, the former only in rare instances to men.

9. *Ὁμοίως δὲ κ.τ.λ.*] The same remark applies to the best among good things. *Ἀγαθῶν* is in the gen. after some superl. understood from *τοὺς θειοτάτους*, perhaps the word *θειότατα* itself, as it is so applied in ix. 3.

12. *καλῶς συνηγορῆσαι*] 'to have put in a good claim for the first place.' He was *right* in supposing that the fact of praise

τείων τῇ ἡδονῇ· τὸ γὰρ μὴ ἐπαινεῖσθαι τῶν ἀγαθῶν
οὖσαν μηνύειν ᾤετο ὅτι κρεῖττόν ἐστι τῶν ἐπαινετῶν,
τοιοῦτον δ' εἶναι τὸν θεὸν καὶ τἀγαθόν· πρὸς ταῦτα γὰρ
6 καὶ τἆλλα ἀναφέρεσθαι. Ὁ μὲν γὰρ ἔπαινος τῆς ἀρετῆς·
πρακτικοὶ γὰρ τῶν καλῶν ἀπὸ ταύτης· τὰ δ' ἐγκώμια τῶν
ἔργων ὁμοίως καὶ τῶν σωματικῶν καὶ τῶν ψυχικῶν.
7 Ἀλλὰ ταῦτα μὲν ἴσως οἰκειότερον ἐξακριβοῦν τοῖς
περὶ τὰ ἐγκώμια πεπονημένοις, ἡμῖν δὲ δῆλον ἐκ τῶν
εἰρημένων ὅτι ἐστὶν ἡ εὐδαιμονία τῶν τιμίων καὶ τε-
8 λείων. Ἔοικε δ' οὕτως ἔχειν καὶ διὰ τὸ εἶναι ἀρχή·
ταύτης γὰρ χάριν τὰ λοιπὰ πάντα πάντες πράττομεν,

Pleasure was the Chief Good because though good it was not
praised, as being above praise, the principle at least of his ar-
6 gument was sound. 'Praise' then is peculiarly appropriate to
virtuous *habits*, in consideration of the results to which they
lead, just as 'panegyric' is appropriate to great *deeds*. But these
7 refinements of language are carrying us too far. We decide
then that Happiness belongs to the third class mentioned
8 above, viz. things admirable, and this we might have at once

not being applied to some acknowledged good indicated a high degree of excellence: but *wrong* in supposing that only God and the Chief Good (l. 3) corresponded to that description.

5. Thus ἐγκώμιον belongs to noble *acts*; ἔπαινος to virtuous *habits*, which result from, and tend to reproduce, such acts; μακαρισμὸς to Happiness, which results again from those virtuous habits.

5. πρακτικοὶ γὰρ] This reason is explained by the first words of § 2.

10. ἀρχὴ] This sense of the word is a little unusual. It is here almost the same as τέλος, just as in English we can speak indifferently of a *primary* or an *ultimate* principle in the same sense. The ultimate motive is also the primary motive of an action. If we desire money with a view to obtain a certain luxury, that luxury is the ultimate, and also the primary, motive for the effort to procure money. (See Glossary, *s.v.* ἀρχή). Ἀρχὴ is in fact here equivalent to 'final cause.' (See Glossary, *s.v.* The Four Causes.)

τὴν ἀρχὴν δὲ καὶ τὸ αἴτιον τῶν ἀγαθῶν τίμιόν τι καὶ θεῖον τίθεμεν.

1 XIII. Ἐπεὶ δ' ἐστὶν ἡ εὐδαιμονία ψυχῆς ἐνέργειά τις κατ' ἀρετὴν τελείαν, περὶ ἀρετῆς ἐπισκεπτέον· τάχα γὰρ οὕτως ἂν βέλτιον καὶ περὶ τῆς εὐδαιμονίας θεωρήσαιμεν.

inferred from the consideration of its being an ultimate principle of action, not chosen for its results, but itself the motive and result for which all else is chosen.

CHAP. XIII.—*Commencement of the elucidation of the several terms in the Definition of Happiness, and especially of the word Soul* (ψυχή).

The Definition of Happiness implies the knowledge (1) of the nature of Virtue,

1 We now proceed to a detailed analysis of our Definition of Happiness. Happiness was said to involve the highest degree of Virtue. We cannot therefore fully understand Happiness without a complete investigation of Virtue. We premise one

CHAP. XIII.—It is worth while now to review the position we have reached. Chaps. i—iii were introductory; ch. iv—vi criticised the principal existing theories about Happiness; ch. vii. constructed a new Definition of Happiness, which, if accepted, would close the treatise at once with a Q.E.D. All that follows now is the defence of that Definition. Ch. viii—xii contrast it with the principal received opinions on the same subject, in order to claim as much accordance with them as possible. Ch. xiii. commences a more formal analysis of the Definition itself. Two words in that Definition require special elucidation, ἀρετὴ and ψυχή. ψυχὴ is explained, as far as is practically necessary, in this chapter. It is found to contain two parts at any rate which are capable of degrees of excellence (ἀρετή), viz. an *appetitive* and a *rational* part. The excellence of the former is Moral (ἠθικὴ ἀρετή). The excellence of the latter is Intellectual (διανοητικὴ ἀρετή). These two kinds of excellence are discussed at length, the former in Bks. II—V., the latter in Bk. VI.

3. ἐστὶν ἡ εὐδαιμονία . . . τελείαν] This is simply a recapitulation of the Definition in ch. vii. omitting only 'ἐν βίῳ τελείῳ.'

2 Δοκεῖ δὲ καὶ ὁ κατ᾽ ἀλήθειαν πολιτικὸς περὶ ταύτην
μάλιστα πεπονῆσθαι· βούλεται γὰρ τοὺς πολίτας ἀγα-
3 θοὺς ποιεῖν καὶ τῶν νόμων ὑπηκόους. Παράδειγμα δὲ
τούτων ἔχομεν τοὺς Κρητῶν καὶ Λακεδαιμονίων νομο-
4 θέτας, καὶ εἴ τινες ἕτεροι τοιοῦτοι γεγένηνται. Εἰ δὲ τῆς
πολιτικῆς ἐστὶν ἡ σκέψις αὕτη, δῆλον ὅτι γένοιτ᾽ ἂν ἡ
5 ζήτησις κατὰ τὴν ἐξ ἀρχῆς προαίρεσιν. Περὶ ἀρετῆς
δὲ ἐπισκεπτέον ἀνθρωπίνης δῆλον ὅτι· καὶ γὰρ τἀγαθὸν
Δοκεῖ δὲ καὶ ὁ κατ᾽ ἀλήθειαν πολιτικὸς περὶ ταύτην
6 μάλιστα πεπονῆσθαι· βούλεται γὰρ τοὺς πολίτας ἀγα-
θοὺς ποιεῖν καὶ τῶν νόμων ὑπηκόους. Παράδειγμα δὲ
7 τούτων ἔχομεν τοὺς Κρητῶν καὶ Λακεδαιμονίων νομο-
θέτας, καὶ εἴ τινες ἕτεροι τοιοῦτοι γεγένηνται. Εἰ δὲ τῆς

2 or two remarks. (1) As both the true theory and highest
3 practice of the Science of Social Life aims at the attainment
4 of Virtue, we are strictly within the limits laid down at the
5 outset of this inquiry (2) It is *human* not *ideal* Virtue and
6 Happiness which we are investigating, and as these both belong
not to the Body but to the Soul, the nature of the Soul must
7 also be expounded. And this also comes within the scope of

and consequently (2) of the nature of the Soul (ψυχή).

4. Κρητῶν καὶ Λακεδαιμονίων] These political systems are selected for praise here and elsewhere, because beyond all others they attempted to regulate by legislation all the details of the private morality, the domestic life, the personal expenses, etc., of the citizens; regarding their character not only as citizens, but as men, see I. ix. 8, II. i. 5, etc. Contrast with this the tendency of modern legislation, which is not to interfere with private morality except so far as the interests of society are compromised by it. *e.g.* No modern state punishes drunkenness, unless it be public and disorderly. 'Good government' (says Buckle) 'is often inversely to its "carnestness" and the amount of its interference.'

7. κατὰ τὴν ἐξ ἀρχῆς προαίρεσιν] viz. I. ii. 9, ἡ μεθόδος τοιούτων ἐφίεται πολιτική τις οὖσα.

9. ἀνθρώπινον] On this limitation see note on ii. 1. Cf. also vi. 13.

τὸν ὀφθαλμοὺς θεραπεύσοντα καὶ πᾶν σῶμα, καὶ μᾶλλον
ὅσῳ τιμιωτέρα καὶ βελτίων ἡ πολιτικὴ τῆς ἰατρικῆς.
Τῶν δ' ἰατρῶν οἱ χαρίεντες πολλὰ πραγματεύονται περὶ
8 τὴν τοῦ σώματος γνῶσιν. Θεωρητέον δὴ καὶ τῷ πολι-
τικῷ περὶ ψυχῆς, θεωρητέον δὲ τούτων χάριν, καὶ ἐφ'
ὅσον ἱκανῶς ἔχει πρὸς τὰ ζητούμενα· τὸ γὰρ ἐπὶ πλεῖον
ἐξακριβοῦν ἐργωδέστερον ἴσως ἐστὶ τῶν προκειμένων.
9 Λέγεται δὲ περὶ αὐτῆς καὶ ἐν τοῖς ἐξωτερικοῖς λόγοις
ἀρκούντως ἔνια, καὶ χρηστέον αὐτοῖς. Οἷον τὸ μὲν
10 ἄλογον αὐτῆς εἶναι, τὸ δὲ λόγον ἔχον. Ταῦτα δὲ πότε-
ρον διώρισται καθάπερ τὰ τοῦ σώματος μόρια καὶ πᾶν
τὸ μεριστόν, ἢ τῷ λόγῳ δύο ἐστὶν ἀχώριστα πεφυκότα,
καθάπερ ἐν τῇ περιφερείᾳ τὸ κυρτὸν καὶ τὸ κοῖλον,

both however within the practical limits which we have already imposed on ourselves. The Soul is commonly divided into a Rational and an Irrational part.

8 the Science of Social Life, provided the inquiry be confined
within the limits of what is practically necessary to throw
9 light upon the subject of Virtue. For our present object the
ordinary popular treatises will suffice. We there find it stated
that the Soul consists of two parts, a rational part and an
10 irrational part. Whether these parts be literally separate, like
the limbs of the body, or separate in thought only, like the
concave and convex sides of a curve, is indifferent for our

1. After *πᾶν σῶμα* understand again the words '*δεῖ εἰδέναι πως*.' As the Oculist must study also to some extent the conditions of health of the whole body, so must the social philosopher acquaint himself in some degree with the whole *ψυχή*, though his own practice is limited to a portion of it.

3. *χαρίεντες*] 'accomplished.' Opp. to *οἱ πολλοὶ* in iv. 2, and somewhat similarly in v. 4.

8. *ἐξωτερικὸς* means what is adapted for the world outside (*ἔξω*), *ἐσωτερικὸς* what is adapted for the inner (*ἔσω*) circle of philosophic students. Hence 'exoteric' 'esoteric' refer to 'popular' and 'scientific' methods respectively. Some have supposed *οἱ ἐξωτερικοὶ λόγοι* to refer to a division of Aristotle's own works. It is more probable, however, that they denote ordinary popular treatises.

11 οὐθὲν διαφέρει πρὸς τὸ παρόν. Τοῦ ἀλόγου δὲ τὸ μὲν
ἔοικε κοινῷ καὶ φυτικῷ, λέγω δὲ τὸ αἴτιον τοῦ τρέφεσ-
θαι καὶ αὔξεσθαι· τὴν τοιαύτην γὰρ δύναμιν τῆς
ψυχῆς ἐν ἅπασι τοῖς τρεφομένοις θείη τις ἂν καὶ ἐν
τοῖς ἐμβρύοις, τὴν αὐτὴν δὲ ταύτην καὶ ἐν τοῖς τελείοις·
12 εὐλογώτερον γὰρ ἢ ἄλλην τινά. Ταύτης μὲν οὖν κοινή
τις ἀρετὴ καὶ οὐκ ἀνθρωπίνη φαίνεται· δοκεῖ γὰρ ἐν
τοῖς ὕπνοις ἐνεργεῖν μάλιστα τὸ μόριον τοῦτο καὶ ἡ
δύναμις αὕτη, ὁ δ' ἀγαθὸς καὶ κακὸς ἥκιστα διάδηλοι
καθ' ὕπνον, ὅθεν φασὶν οὐδὲν διαφέρειν τὸ ἥμισυ τοῦ
13 βίου τοὺς εὐδαίμονας τῶν ἀθλίων. Συμβαίνει δὲ τοῦτο
εἰκότως· ἀργία γάρ ἐστιν ὁ ὕπνος τῆς ψυχῆς ᾗ λέγεται
σπουδαία καὶ φαύλη, πλὴν εἴ πῃ κατὰ μικρὸν διϊκνοῦν-
ταί τινες τῶν κινήσεων, καὶ ταύτῃ βελτίω γίνεται τὰ
14 φαντάσματα τῶν ἐπιεικῶν ἢ τῶν τυχόντων. Ἀλλὰ
περὶ μὲν τούτων ἅλις, καὶ τὸ θρεπτικὸν ἐατέον, ἐπειδὴ

11 present purpose. 1. Let us first consider the *irrational* part.—
(*a*) One portion of this is the source of nutriment and growth
which is found wherever there is life, in all creatures, and
even in plants, in the fœtus as well as in the full-grown animal.
12 There can be no specially human Virtue in this part. In fact
13 it acts with most vigour in sleep, when good and bad men
14 differ not at all, or else in a manner which is of no conse-

(1) The irrational part is also twofold, including—(*a*) the source of nutrition and growth;

4. ψυχῆς] Observe the wide use of ψυχή, which makes it so difficult a word to translate. We should scarcely regard the 'soul' as the seat of physical life, growth, and nutriment. (See Glossary on ψυχή.)

5. There is no difference in that which is the source of growth and nutrition in the embryo and in the full-grown animal. If there were, *when* did the change occur? Aristotle insists upon this identity in order to show that this part of our nature is out of all relation to Virtue, Moral or Intellectual (see § 14), as there can of course be nothing of the kind in the embryo. This absence of change or progress cannot be asserted of the other two parts of the ψυχὴ, the Appetitive and the Rational.

15 τῆς ἀνθρωπικῆς ἀρετῆς ἄμοιρον πέφυκεν. Ἔοικε δὲ καὶ ἄλλη τις φύσις τῆς ψυχῆς ἄλογος εἶναι, μετέχουσα μέντοι πῃ λόγου. Τοῦ γὰρ ἐγκρατοῦς καὶ ἀκρατοῦς τὸν λόγον καὶ τῆς ψυχῆς τὸ λόγον ἔχον ἐπαινοῦμεν· ὀρθῶς γὰρ καὶ ἐπὶ τὰ βέλτιστα παρακαλεῖ· φαίνεται δ' ἐν αὐτοῖς καὶ ἄλλο τι παρὰ τὸν λόγον πεφυκός, ὃ μάχεταί
16 τε καὶ ἀντιτείνει τῷ λόγῳ. Ἀτεχνῶς γὰρ καθάπερ τὰ παραλελυμένα τοῦ σώματος μόρια εἰς τὰ δεξιὰ προαιρουμένων κινῆσαι τοὐναντίον εἰς τὰ ἀριστερὰ παραφέρεται, καὶ ἐπὶ τῆς ψυχῆς οὕτως· ἐπὶ τἀναντία γὰρ αἱ ὁρμαὶ τῶν ἀκρατῶν. Ἀλλ' ἐν τοῖς σώμασι μὲν ὁρῶμεν τὸ παραφερόμενον, ἐπὶ δὲ τῆς ψυχῆς οὐχ ὁρῶμεν. Ἴσως δ' οὐδὲν ἧττον καὶ ἐν τῇ ψυχῇ νομιστέον εἶναί τι παρὰ τὸν λόγον, ἐναντιούμενον τούτῳ καὶ ἀντιβαῖνον.
17 Πῶς δ' ἕτερον, οὐδὲν διαφέρει. Λόγου δὲ καὶ τοῦτο

the petites [illegible] desires, [illegible]ich are [illegible]tly and [illegible]some [illegible]se [illegible]ional.

15 quence to our present inquiry. (β) There is however another division of the irrational part, which seems to partake of reason in some degree. This is evidenced by the phenomena of Continence and Incontinence, terms which we technically apply to cases where either right or wrong is done *after a conscious inward struggle.* This struggle occurs between Reason and something opposed to Reason. In the continent man we applaud the triumph of Reason. In the incontinent man, though Reason directs one course, there is something in
16 him which causes him to do the reverse, just as a paralysed limb refuses to obey the control of the Will. We conclude therefore from this that there is something in the Soul distinct
17 from Reason (though in what precise way distinct we need

1. ἀνθρωπικῆς ἀρετῆς] to throw light upon *that* being the sole object of this inquiry about ψυχή. See § 8.

3. ἐγκρατοῦς καὶ ἀκρατοῦς] See the precise meaning of these terms explained in note on iii. 7.

6. ἄλλο τι κ.τ.λ.] 'We find another law in our members, warring against the law of our mind' (Rom. vii. 23).

15. Λόγου δὲ καὶ τοῦτο κ.τ.λ.] Otherwise it could not even oppose Reason, as it does in the case

φαίνεται μετέχειν, ὥσπερ εἴπομεν· πειθαρχεῖ γοῦν τῷ λόγῳ τὸ τοῦ ἐγκρατοῦς. Ἔτι δ' ἴσως εὐηκοώτερόν ἐστι τὸ τοῦ σώφρονος καὶ ἀνδρείου· πάντα γὰρ ὁμοφωνεῖ τῷ
18 λόγῳ. Φαίνεται δὴ καὶ τὸ ἄλογον διττόν. Τὸ μὲν γὰρ φυτικὸν οὐδαμῶς κοινωνεῖ λόγου, τὸ δ' ἐπιθυμητικὸν καὶ ὅλως ὀρεκτικὸν μετέχει πως, ᾗ κατήκοόν ἐστιν αὐτοῦ καὶ πειθαρχικόν. Οὕτω δὴ καὶ τοῦ πατρὸς καὶ

not determine) which is thus able to oppose Reason. Yet since in the case of Continence, and still more in that of perfect Self-control, it harmonizes with Reason, it might be thought
18 itself to share in Reason and so to belong to the Rational part of the Soul. However the *irrational* part (which we are still considering) is at any rate twofold, viz.—(1) The source of physical life, nutriment, and growth. (2) The appetitive part, the passions and the desires. The former division is

of the ἀκρατής, much less could it side with Reason as it does in the ἐγκρατής (l. 2), or become as it were merged in Reason, as it is in the σώφρων (l. 3). If then the Appetitive part were purely Irrational it *could* not oppose Reason; if it were purely Rational it *would* not do so.

5. οὐδαμῶς κοινωνεῖ] The nutritive portion has no relation whatever to Reason. It can neither oppose it, nor obey it. 'No man by taking thought can add a cubit to his stature.' The appetitive part, however, has some relation to Reason, because it can 'by taking thought' be checked and regulated.

7. οὕτω δὴ κ.τ.λ.] The explanation seems to be this: The words λόγον ἔχειν have two different senses in Greek:—

(1) To possess reason; or, to have understanding of (as, *e.g.* of Mathematics);

(2) To pay regard to (as we do to admonitions of parents or friends).

If we confine ourselves to the strict sense of (1), then the Appetitive part belongs clearly to the irrational division (ἄλογον μέρος) of the Soul.

If we use the term loosely so as to include (2), then we may regard the Appetitive part as λόγον ἔχον, because it can 'pay regard to' Reason, and so in some sense shares in it. But the expression λόγον ἔχειν must be employed in a different sense in the case of the Appetites, and in that of the Reason. Compare what Aristotle says of a Slave (*Pol.* I. v. 9) κοινωνεῖ λόγου το-

τῶν φίλων φαμὲν ἔχειν λόγον, καὶ οὐχ ὥσπερ τῶν μαθηματικῶν. Ὅτι δὲ πείθεταί πως ὑπὸ λόγου τὸ ἄλογον, μηνύει καὶ ἡ νουθέτησις καὶ πᾶσα ἐπιτίμησίς
19 τε καὶ παράκλησις. Εἰ δὲ χρὴ καὶ τοῦτο φάναι λόγον
ἔχειν, διττὸν ἔσται καὶ τὸ λόγον ἔχον, τὸ μὲν κυρίως καὶ ἐν αὐτῷ, τὸ δ' ὥσπερ τοῦ πατρὸς ἀκουστικόν τι.
20 Διορίζεται δὲ καὶ ἡ ἀρετὴ κατὰ τὴν διαφορὰν ταύτην·
λέγομεν γὰρ αὐτῶν τὰς μὲν διανοητικάς, τὰς δὲ ἠθικάς,

wholly irrational, the latter only partially so, because it is at any rate amenable to Reason.

Hence (2) the Rational part also may be regarded as twofold if the Appetites should be rather referred to it.

19 2. Let us now consider the *rational* part.—Here we have simply to determine the degree of strictness with which we will use the word 'rational.' If we use it so as to include the partially-rational *appetites*, then this part of the Soul may be considered as twofold, viz.—(α) The Reason itself; (β) The appetitive part. Thus the assignment of the appetitive part to the Rational or to the Irrational division of the Soul is a question of words, or of arrangement merely.

Corresponding to the division of the Soul into Rational and Appetitive is the twofold division of Virtue into Intellectual and Moral.

20 Now to apply this to the question it was intended to elucidate,

σοῦτον ὥστε αἰσθάνεσθαι ἀλλὰ μὴ ἔχειν. He adds that the lower animals (like τὸ φυτικὸν in the text here) οὐδὲ λόγου αἰσθάνεται.

The result is, that it becomes to some extent a question of words to which of the two divisions of the Soul, Rational or Irrational, we assign the Appetites. The main point is that, in either case, we recognise the three distinct parts φυτικόν, ἐπιθυμητικόν, λογιστικόν. The following scheme will exhibit the two methods of arrangement by which this result may be reached:—

I.

ψυχὴ
- ἄλογον μέρος
  - (i) wholly ἄλογον . . . . . τὸ φυτικόν.
  - (ii) τὸ ἀντιτεῖνον τῷ λόγῳ (which τὸ φυτικὸν is *not*) . . τὸ ἐπιθυμητικόν.
- λόγον ἔχον μέρος . . . . τὸ λογιστικόν.

II

ψυχὴ
- ἄλογον μέρος . . . . τὸ φυτικόν.
- λόγον ἔχον μέρος
  - (i) a part amenable to reason, and so λόγον ἔχον in sense (2) . τὸ ἐπιθυμητικόν.
  - (ii) a part in full possession of reason, λόγον ἔχον in sense (1) τὸ λογιστικόν.

3. We speak of Intellectual *Excellences* and Moral *Virtues*. In Greek ἀρετή could be used equally for both. (See Glossary, *s.v.* ἀρετή.)

σοφίαν μὲν καὶ σύνεσιν καὶ φρόνησιν διανοητικὰς, ἐλευθεριότητα δὲ καὶ σωφροσύνην ἠθικάς. Λέγοντες γὰρ περὶ τοῦ ἤθους οὐ λέγομεν ὅτι σοφὸς ἢ συνετὸς ἀλλ' ὅτι πρᾶος ἢ σώφρων, ἐπαινοῦμεν δὲ καὶ τὸν σοφὸν κατὰ τὴν ἕξιν· τῶν ἕξεων δὲ τὰς ἐπαινετὰς ἀρετὰς λέγομεν.

viz. the nature of Virtue. The part of the Soul relating to nutriment, etc., has nothing to do with Virtue, as we have already seen. The perfection of the purely Rational part gives rise to Intellectual Virtues or Excellences, *e.g.* Wisdom, Prudence, Intelligence. The perfection of the Appetitive part gives rise to Moral Virtues, such as Gentleness, Liberality, Self-restraint. The term 'Virtue' we apply to any permanent state or habit which is praiseworthy.

1. *φρόνησις* is inadequately translated by 'Prudence,' which indicates more or less a *Moral* Virtue. It is explained in B. VI. to be the intellectual element of right judgment which is essential to all moral virtue: 'essential,' because mere blind 'earnestness' without a reasonable exercise of judgment is not Virtue: or (as Dr. Johnson phrased it) 'intellectual imbecility is no excuse for moral perversity.' Aristotle thinks that we are bound to have 'a right judgment in all things,' and would have no sympathy with 'imbecile virtue.' In B. IV. he frequently insists on the necessity of applying intellectual judgment to the details of moral action (*e.g.* esp. in *μεγαλοπρέπεια*, *εὐτραπελία*, etc.). For proof that *φρόνησις* itself is an Intellectual and not a Moral quality, see *Supplementary Notes, h.l.*

5. *κατὰ τὴν ἕξιν*] 'in reference to his state,' *i.e.* if his wisdom is a settled state or habit.

Thus the *essential* or *fundamental* difference between Intellectual and Moral excellence is, that they belong to different parts of the Soul; the former being the perfection of the Rational, and the latter of the Appetitive, part. Upon this follows a *practical* difference in the manner of their acquisition or cultivation, which is pointed out in the beginning of the next Book.

II.

1 1. *Διττῆς δὲ τῆς ἀρετῆς οὔσης, τῆς μὲν διανοητικῆς τῆς δὲ ἠθικῆς, ἡ μὲν διανοητικὴ τὸ πλεῖον ἐκ διδασκαλίας ἔχει καὶ τὴν γένεσιν καὶ τὴν αὔξησιν, διόπερ ἐμπειρίας δεῖται καὶ χρόνου, ἡ δ' ἠθικὴ ἐξ ἔθους περιγίνεται, ὅθεν καὶ τοὔνομα ἔσχηκε μικρὸν παρεκκλῖνον ἀπὸ τοῦ ἔθους.*

CHAP. I.—*Moral Virtue is not implanted in us by Nature.*

Moral Virtue differs from Intellectual Excellence, in that it is not innate: because—

1 IT is an essential difference between Intellectual Excellence and Moral Virtue, that the former is acquired and developed mainly by *instruction*, and the latter (as its name in Greek indicates) by *practice*. Dismissing the former, we proceed

1. See note at the beginning of I. xiii. for the connexion of the argument. The divisions of ψυχὴ led us to a corresponding division of ἀρετὴ into Moral and Intellectual (I. xiii. 20). These further exhibit an essential difference in the mode of their acquisition, which is first positively stated, and after this statement, the subject of Intellectual Excellence is tacitly dropped (to be resumed in B. VI.), and the discussion proceeds to establish the assertion just made so far as it relates to Moral Virtue, viz. that it is not implanted in us by nature.

2. τὸ πλεῖον] 'for the most part.' This qualification is meant to allow for the exceptional case of great natural genius.

5. This etymological argument is of course untranslatable. ἔθος (Lat. *mos*) is a habit or custom. ἦθος (Lat. *mores*) is character which is the result of habits. The value of this and similar arguments, such as that derived from the practice of men in legislation in § 5 and III. v. 7, is simply this:—They show the general belief of mankind as reflected in language, but they do not prove that the belief in

2 Ἐξ οὗ καὶ δῆλον ὅτι οὐδεμία τῶν ἠθικῶν ἀρετῶν φύσει
ἡμῖν ἐγγίνεται· οὐθὲν γὰρ τῶν φύσει ὄντων ἄλλως
ἐθίζεται, οἷον ὁ λίθος φύσει κάτω φερόμενος οὐκ ἂν
ἐθισθειη ανω φέρεσθαι, οὐδ' ἂν μυριάκις αὐτὸν ἐθίζῃ
τις ἄνω ῥίπτων, οὐδὲ τὸ πῦρ κάτω, οὐδ' ἄλλο οὐδὲν τῶν
3 ἄλλως πεφυκότων ἄλλως ἂν ἐθισθείη. Οὔτ' ἄρα φύσει
οὔτε παρὰ φύσιν ἐγγίνονται αἱ ἀρεταί, ἀλλὰ πεφυκόσι
μὲν ἡμῖν δέξασθαι αὐτὰς, τελειουμένοις δὲ διὰ τοῦ

2 to prove the important point involved in the latter, that
no Moral Virtue is implanted by Nature. (1) Nothing
fixed by Nature can be altered by practice. No amount
of practice will make a stone rise, or fire burn downwards.
But our moral habits can be so altered, and therefore
3 they are not implanted by Nature. The same argument
proves that as they are not formed *by* Nature, so they
are not formed *against* Nature. Nature gives us moral
capacities; we ourselves by practice develope moral *habits.*

(1) It can be altered by habit.

question is necessarily true; though, as we read in I. viii. 7, such consensus is not likely to be altogether at fault. Other instances will be found in v. 4 (the distinction between *κινεῖσθαι* and *διακεῖσθαι*), III. ii. 17 (*προαίρεσις*), III. xii. 5 and 6 (*ἀκολασία*), IV. ii. 1 (*μεγαλοπρέπεια*).

1. This point is essential, because if Moral Virtue be implanted by nature, and not acquired by practice, the Science of Ethics has no *raison d'être* as a practical Science. See § 7, *οὐδὲν ἂν ἔδει τοῦ διδάξοντος, ἀλλὰ πάντες ἂν ἐγίγνοντο ἀγαθοὶ ἢ κακοί*, and the Appetitive part of the ψυχή (*ἐπιθυμητικὸν μέρος*) would be as much out of our control as the Nutritive and vital functions (*θρεπτικὸν καὶ αὐξητικὸν*), see I. xiii.

6. *ἄρα* implies an inference from the preceding. It is clear that this same argument proves Virtue not to be contrary to nature; because if nature had decided the question positively or negatively, it would be equally out of our power to alter her decision. Thus we are neither 'predestined' to Virtue, nor 'reprobated' to vice, according to Aristotle. At the same time he would not of course deny that some have more tendency to virtue or to vice than others.

7. *πεφυκόσι* and *τελειουμένοις* both agree with *ἡμῖν*, which is dat. after *ἐγγίνονται*. Cf. Pope, 'Nature its mother, habit is its nurse.'

4 ἔθους. Ἔτι ὅσα μὲν φύσει ἡμῖν παραγίνεται, τὰς δυνάμεις τούτων πρότερον κομιζόμεθα, ὕστερον δὲ τὰς ἐνεργείας ἀποδίδομεν. Ὅπερ ἐπὶ τῶν αἰσθήσεων δῆλον· οὐ γὰρ ἐκ τοῦ πολλάκις ἰδεῖν ἢ πολλάκις ἀκοῦσαι τὰς αἰσθήσεις ἐλάβομεν, ἀλλ' ἀνάπαλιν ἔχοντες ἐχρησάμεθα, οὐ χρησάμενοι ἔσχομεν. Τὰς δ' ἀρετὰς λαμβάνομεν ἐνεργήσαντες πρότερον, ὥσπερ καὶ ἐπὶ τῶν ἄλλων τεχνῶν· ἃ γὰρ δεῖ μαθόντας ποιεῖν, ταῦτα ποιοῦντες μανθάνομεν, οἷον οἰκοδομοῦντες οἰκοδόμοι γίνονται καὶ κιθαρίζοντες κιθαρισταί. Οὕτω δὲ καὶ τὰ μὲν δίκαια πράττοντες δίκαιοι γινόμεθα, τὰ δὲ σώφρονα σώφρονες,
5 τὰ δ' ἀνδρεῖα ἀνδρεῖοι. Μαρτυρεῖ δὲ καὶ τὸ γινόμενον ἐν ταῖς πόλεσιν· οἱ γὰρ νομοθέται τοὺς πολίτας ἐθίζοντες ποιοῦσιν ἀγαθούς, καὶ τὸ μὲν βούλημα παντὸς νομοθέτου τοῦτ' ἐστίν, ὅσοι δὲ μὴ εὖ αὐτὸ ποιοῦσιν ἁμαρτάνουσιν, καὶ διαφέρει τούτῳ πολιτεία πολιτείας
6 ἀγαθὴ φαύλης. Ἔτι ἐκ τῶν αὐτῶν καὶ διὰ τῶν αὐτῶν

(2) Its existence does not precede its exercise in practice.

4 (2) In the case of natural faculties (*e.g.* the senses), we have them before we use them. In the case of Moral Virtues (as in artistic skill), we develope them by use, *i.e.* by trying to practise them: *e.g.* Temperance is acquired by acting tempe-
5 rately, Courage by acting bravely and so on. (3) The action of legislators bears witness to the general belief of mankind
6 that Moral Virtue is to be acquired by practice. (4) While

(3) Practical legislation proceeds on the assumption that Moral Virtue is not innate.

7. τῶν ἄλλων τεχνῶν] Virtue is often regarded by Plato and Aristotle as a kind of Art (*e.g.* iii. 10, iv. 3, vi. 9).

14. τὸ βούλημα κ.τ.λ.] See note on I. xiii. 3.

17. ἐκ τῶν αὐτῶν καὶ διὰ τῶν αὐτῶν] 'from the same causes and by the same means.' The argument is, that *Natural* phenomena differ from *Moral* phenomena in that, in the former case, the antecedents being the same, the consequents are always the same, whereas in Moral phenomena, from the same antecedents, so far as outward circumstances go, *opposite* results follow. This difference then must arise from something contributed by the moral agent himself.

καὶ γίνεται πᾶσα ἀρετὴ καὶ φθείρεται, ὁμοίως δὲ καὶ
τέχνη· ἐκ γὰρ τοῦ κιθαρίζειν καὶ οἱ ἀγαθοὶ καὶ οἱ κακοὶ
γίνονται κιθαρισταί. Ἀνάλογον δὲ καὶ οἱ οἰκοδόμοι καὶ
οἱ λοιποὶ πάντες· ἐκ μὲν γὰρ τοῦ εὖ οἰκοδομεῖν ἀγαθοὶ
7 οἰκοδόμοι ἔσονται, ἐκ δὲ τοῦ κακῶς κακοί. Εἰ γὰρ μὴ
οὕτως εἶχεν, οὐδὲν ἂν ἔδει τοῦ διδάξοντος, ἀλλὰ πάντες
ἂν ἐγίνοντο ἀγαθοὶ ἢ κακοί. Οὕτω δὴ καὶ ἐπὶ τῶν
ἀρετῶν ἔχει· πράττοντες γὰρ τὰ ἐν τοῖς συναλλάγμασι
τοῖς πρὸς τοὺς ἀνθρώπους γινόμεθα οἱ μὲν δίκαιοι οἱ δὲ
ἄδικοι, πράττοντες δὲ τὰ ἐν τοῖς δεινοῖς καὶ ἐθιζόμενοι
φοβεῖσθαι ἢ θαρρεῖν οἱ μὲν ἀνδρεῖοι οἱ δὲ δειλοί.
Ὁμοίως δὲ καὶ τὰ περὶ τὰς ἐπιθυμίας ἔχει καὶ τὰ περὶ
τὰς ὀργάς· οἱ μὲν γὰρ σώφρονες καὶ πρᾶοι γίνονται, οἱ
δ' ἀκόλαστοι καὶ ὀργίλοι, οἱ μὲν ἐκ τοῦ οὑτωσὶ ἐν αὐ-
τοῖς ἀναστρέφεσθαι, οἱ δὲ ἐκ τοῦ οὑτωσί. Καὶ ἑνὶ δὴ
8 λόγῳ ἐκ τῶν ὁμοίων ἐνεργειῶν αἱ ἕξεις γίνονται. Διὸ

in nature the same causes invariably produce the same results, in the case of Moral Habits, as in the Arts, the same circumstances and courses of action produce opposite results; *i.e.* they produce both good artists and bad, just men and unjust,
7 brave men and cowards. This difference of results then must be due to a difference *in ourselves*, in fact to the different ways in which different people act under the same circumstances. In short, as are our *acts*, so are the *habits* which
8 spring from them. Hence it is important what sort of acts

(4) Out of the same circumstances are developed opposite results in respect of Moral Virtue and Vice.

7. ἐγίνοντο is emphatic 'every one would have been born a good or bad craftsman,' and so all apprenticeship and practice would have been useless.

16. 'All habits have their origin in courses of action similar to themselves.' Habits are simply the result of repeated acts. *Why* acts from repetition should become easier we cannot say. *What* is the precise change that has taken place in us when (*e.g.*) the laborious acts of spelling out each word have grown into the easy habit of reading we cannot explain. We really know little more of the phenomena of the formation of habits than Aristotle here states; as a

δεῖ τὰς ἐνεργείας ποιὰς ἀποδιδόναι· κατὰ γὰρ τὰς τούτων διαφορὰς ἀκολουθοῦσιν αἱ ἕξεις. Οὐ μικρὸν οὖν διαφέρει τὸ οὕτως ἢ οὕτως εὐθὺς ἐκ νέων ἐθίζεσθαι, ἀλλὰ πάμπολυ, μᾶλλον δὲ τὸ πᾶν.

1 II. Ἐπεὶ οὖν ἡ παροῦσα πραγματεία οὐ θεωρίας ἕνεκά ἐστιν ὥσπερ αἱ ἄλλαι (οὐ γὰρ ἵν' εἰδῶμεν τί ἐστιν ἡ

we become familiar with from earliest youth; for to the character of the resulting habits it makes simply all the difference in the world.

CHAP. II.—*Some general characteristics of such Habits as are Virtuous.*

Virtuous habits differ from others in being in accordance with Right Reason:

1 In a practical treatise like ours we at once follow up what has now been proved by asking, What is the definite character

fact, all habits grow from the repetition of acts similar to themselves.

ὁμοίων] There is no contradiction between this and the statement in § 6 *init.*, viz. That similar acts produce opposite results. Acts and circumstances may be externally the same and yet very different to different people. And it is on the latter consideration, viz. their relation to the individual doing them, that their influence on resulting habits depends. *e.g.* A subscription of precisely the same amount would be liberal in one man and mean in another. Thus the same act has a tendency to form a *habit* of liberality in the one case, and of stinginess in the other.

CHAP. II.—This Chapter holds a somewhat similar position in the investigation of a Definition of Virtue to that of I. vii. 1-8, in the investigation of the Definition of Happiness. Aristotle feels his way towards a Definition in each case by first laying down certain broad and general characteristics of the thing to be defined. Two such are arrived at in this Chapter. Next, Chapters iii. and iv. consider questions arising out of the statements here made. Then Chapters v. and vi. contain the systematic construction of the Definition of ἀρετή, and so far may be compared with the formal construction of the Definition of Happiness in I. vii. 9-16.

6. αἱ ἄλλαι] Either 'the rest of treatises on this subject,'—it being a complaint of Aristotle's elsewhere that this is a general fault of the systems of his time (τῶν χρησιμῶν διαμαρτάνουσι,

ἀρετὴ σκεπτόμεθα, ἀλλ' ἵν' ἀγαθοὶ γενώμεθα, ἐπεὶ οὐδὲν
ἂν ἦν ὄφελος αὐτῆς, ἀναγκαῖόν ἐστι σκέψασθαι τὰ περὶ
τὰς πράξεις, πῶς πρακτέον αὐτάς· αὗται γάρ εἰσι κύριαι
καὶ τοῦ ποιὰς γενέσθαι τὰς ἕξεις, καθάπερ εἰρήκαμεν.
2 Τὸ μὲν οὖν κατὰ τὸν ὀρθὸν λόγον πράττειν κοινὸν καὶ
ὑποκείσθω, ῥηθήσεται δ' ὕστερον περὶ αὐτοῦ, καὶ τί
ἐστιν ὁ ὀρθὸς λόγος, καὶ πῶς ἔχει πρὸς τὰς ἄλλας
3 ἀρετάς. Ἐκεῖνο δὲ προδιομολογείσθω, ὅτι πᾶς ὁ περὶ
τῶν πρακτῶν λόγος τύπῳ καὶ οὐκ ἀκριβῶς ὀφείλει λέ-
γεσθαι, ὥσπερ καὶ κατ' ἀρχὰς εἴπομεν ὅτι κατὰ τὴν
ὕλην οἱ λόγοι ἀπαιτητέοι· τὰ δ' ἐν ταῖς πράξεσι καὶ τὰ
συμφέροντα οὐδὲν ἑστηκὸς ἔχει, ὥσπερ οὐδὲ τὰ ὑγιεινά.
4 Τοιούτου δ' ὄντος τοῦ καθόλου λόγου, ἔτι μᾶλλον ὁ περὶ

of actions, and, by consequence, of habits, which determine
2 them as Virtuous? We can at once say that they must be in
accordance with right reason, but that is vague, and we must
hereafter explain what right reason is, and what is its relation to
3 the Moral Virtues. But though we admit this to be too vague we
must at the same time renew our protest against demanding any-
4 thing like mathematical precision in such a subject as this, espe-

'they fail of being practical')—or else, 'treatises on other subjects' than morals, which may perhaps have a right to be theoretical and independent of practice.

2. αὐτῆς prob. σκέψεως understood from σκεπτόμεθα, or πραγματείας, or possibly ἀρετῆς in the sense of Virtue in theory, severed from practice.

4. καθάπερ εἰρήκαμεν] see esp. § 7 (*fin.*) of last Chapter (ἑνὶ δὴ λόγῳ κ.τ.λ.), πράξεις here being equivalent to ἐνεργεῖαι in the passage quoted. Thus πῶς in l. 3 is emphatic, *how* we are to do the *acts*, so that the *habits* desired may follow.

6. ὑποκείσθω] 'Let it be taken for granted.' Compare the somewhat similar way in which τελειότης and αὐτάρκεια are put aside in I. vii. as vague, though real, characteristics of Happiness.

ὕστερον κ.τ.λ.] This will be found in B. VI., but the subject is touched upon in ch. vi. of this Book, where see the Definition of Virtue, and see also note on I. xiii. 20.

10. κατ' ἀρχὰς εἴπομεν κ.τ.λ.] For explanations of this see I.

τῶν καθ' ἕκαστα λόγος οὐκ ἔχει τἀκριβές· οὔτε γὰρ ὑπὸ τέχνην οὔθ' ὑπὸ παραγγελίαν οὐδεμίαν πίπτει, δεῖ δ' αὐτοὺς ἀεὶ τοὺς πράττοντας τὰ πρὸς τὸν καιρὸν σκοπεῖν, ὥσπερ καὶ ἐπὶ τῆς ἰατρικῆς ἔχει καὶ τῆς κυβερνητικῆς.
5 Ἀλλὰ καίπερ ὄντος τοιούτου τοῦ παρόντος λόγου πει-
6 ρατέον βοηθεῖν. Πρῶτον οὖν τοῦτο θεωρητέον, ὅτι τὰ τοιαῦτα πέφυκεν ὑπὸ ἐνδείας καὶ ὑπερβολῆς φθείρεσθαι, (δεῖ γὰρ ὑπὲρ τῶν ἀφανῶν τοῖς φανεροῖς μαρτυρίοις χρῆσθαι) ὥσπερ ἐπὶ τῆς ἰσχύος καὶ τῆς ὑγιείας ὁρῶμεν· τά τε γὰρ ὑπερβάλλοντα γυμνάσια καὶ τὰ ἐλλείποντα

5 cially in matters of detail. With this proviso we may now make two general statements which hold good of Virtuous Habits.
6 Both are suggested by the analogy of bodily habits, such as health and strength. (i) The first is:—*Excess and defect are injurious, moderation is beneficial, to the formation of such habits.* This is true of bodily health in reference to the amount of

but, more definitely, like good bodily habits, (1) *in their formation*, they involve an avoidance of excess and defect, and aim at moderation:

vii. 17, etc., also (and esp. in reference to the words of I. 10, p. 75) see I. iii. 2-4.

2. παραγγελία] 'body of rules.' αὐτοὺς in the next line is of course emphatic.

8. δεῖ γὰρ κ.τ.λ.] This is the clue to the line of thought pursued in this Chapter. It is *the analogy existing between the Body and Soul* in respect of their habits or acquired capacities. In ch. vi., where the formal Definition of Virtue is investigated, the argument proceeds from another analogy, viz. that existing between Virtue and Art. The words in the parenthesis express very well the principle of what is generally called 'the Argument from Analogy.' *e.g.* In Butler's 'Analogy' the 'φανερὰ' are the obvious arrangements of the *Natural* world, the 'ἀφανῆ' the arrangements of the *Moral* world, as indicated to us by Religion, Natural or Revealed. The point of similarity is that the arrangements in both cases proceed from the same Author, and the 'Argument from Analogy' is, that they are therefore likely to resemble one another. So in the present passage the φανερὰ are bodily habits, the ἀφανῆ habits of the Soul: the point of similarity that they are parts of the same complex Being: and the 'Argument from Analogy' is that they are likely to resemble one another in their nature and growth.

φθείρει τὴν ἰσχύν, ὁμοίως δὲ καὶ τὰ ποτὰ καὶ τὰ σιτία πλείω καὶ ἐλάττω γινόμενα φθείρει τὴν ὑγίειαν, τὰ δὲ
7 σύμμετρα καὶ ποιεῖ καὶ αὔξει καὶ σώζει. Οὕτως οὖν καὶ ἐπὶ σωφροσύνης καὶ ἀνδρείας ἔχει καὶ τῶν ἄλλων ἀρετῶν· ὅ τε γὰρ πάντα φεύγων καὶ φοβούμενος καὶ μηδὲν ὑπομένων δειλὸς γίνεται, ὅ τε μηδὲν ὅλως φοβούμενος ἀλλὰ πρὸς πάντα βαδίζων, θρασύς. Ὁμοίως δὲ καὶ ὁ μὲν πάσης ἡδονῆς ἀπολαύων καὶ μηδεμιᾶς ἀπεχόμενος ἀκόλαστος, ὁ δὲ πάσας φεύγων, ὥσπερ οἱ ἀγροῖκοι, ἀναίσθητός τις· φθείρεται γὰρ ἡ σωφροσύνη καὶ ἡ ἀνδρεία ὑπὸ τῆς ὑπερβολῆς καὶ τῆς ἐλλείψεως, ὑπὸ δὲ
8 τῆς μεσότητος σώζεται. Ἀλλ' οὐ μόνον αἱ γενέσεις καὶ αἱ αὐξήσεις καὶ αἱ φθοραὶ ἐκ τῶν αὐτῶν καὶ ὑπὸ τῶν αὐτῶν γίνονται, ἀλλὰ καὶ αἱ ἐνέργειαι ἐν τοῖς αὐτοῖς ἔσονται· καὶ γὰρ ἐπὶ τῶν ἄλλων τῶν φανερωτέρων οὕτως ἔχει, οἷον ἐπὶ τῆς ἰσχύος· γίνεται γὰρ ἐκ τοῦ πολλὴν τροφὴν λαμβάνειν καὶ πολλοὺς πόνους ὑπομέ-

7 food, drink, and exercise; and so it is of Temperance in respect of pleasure, and of Courage in respect of fear, and similarly of other Virtues, in respect of the subject-matter
8 with which each is concerned. (ii) Our second point is:— *Virtuous habits when formed reproduce the acts by which they were formed.* Bodily habits suggest this law also: *e.g.* Strength is gained by taking food and exercise, and when

(2) *when formed,* they reproduce the acts which form them.

9. ἀγροῖκοι] perhaps 'ascetics,' or 'boors,' with probable ref. to the Cynics. ἀναίσθητός τις, 'A sort of insensible man.' Τις is a kind of apology for the term 'insensible,' because, as stated elsewhere, such phenomenon scarcely exists. See vii. 3 and III. xi. 7.

12. οὐ μόνον αἱ γενέσεις κ.τ.λ.] Observe that the former characteristic of Virtuous Habits had reference to their formation and growth (γενέσεις καὶ αὐξήσεις), the present characteristic has reference to their operation (ἐνέργειαι) when formed.

14. φανερωτέρων] is explained by the parenthesis in § 6 above.

9 νειν, καὶ μάλιστα δύναται ταῦτα ποιεῖν ὁ ἰσχυρός. Οὕτω δ' ἔχει καὶ ἐπὶ τῶν ἀρετῶν· ἔκ τε γὰρ τοῦ ἀπέχεσθαι τῶν ἡδονῶν γινόμεθα σώφρονες, καὶ γενόμενοι μάλιστα δυνάμεθα ἀπέχεσθαι αὐτῶν. Ὁμοίως δὲ καὶ ἐπὶ τῆς ἀνδρείας· ἐθιζόμενοι γὰρ καταφρονεῖν τῶν φοβερῶν καὶ ὑπομένειν αὐτὰ γινόμεθα ἀνδρεῖοι, καὶ γενόμενοι μάλιστα δυνησόμεθα ὑπομένειν τὰ φοβερά.

1 III. Σημεῖον δὲ δεῖ ποιεῖσθαι τῶν ἕξεων τὴν ἐπι-

9 gained enables us to take more food and exercise. So Temperance is acquired by resisting pleasure, and when acquired exhibits itself in the resistance of pleasure. Similarly of Courage and other Virtues.

CHAP. III.—*The test of the formation of Habits is the pleasure or pain by which acts are accompanied.*

A habit is formed whenever we do the *acts* related to it with pleasure.

I We can judge at once whether a *habit* is already formed or is only in process of formation, by the pleasure or pain

CHAP. III.—If the statement at the end of the last Chapter be true, how can we tell *when* a habit is formed? If we become brave by doing brave acts, and when we have become brave we still do brave acts, how are we to know whether our brave acts are tending to form the habit, or are results of the formed habit? Are they in the relation of cause or effect to the habit of bravery, and when do they pass the line from cause to effect? The answer is simple. If the acts are done with pain and difficulty the habit is not yet formed. If they are done with pleasure and ease they are the result of a habit already formed. When then we feel pleasure in doing any act, if it be a right act we have formed a habit of Virtue, if a wrong act we have formed a habit of Vice. When we do any act, right or wrong, with pain or without pleasure, we have not yet formed a habit either Virtuous or Vicious in that respect. It would thus appear that Moral Virtue is an affair of pleasure and pain: that Virtue and Vice may be resolved into a question of feeling pleasure and pain when we ought. And so after § 1 the discussion proceeds upon this text as it were, the immediate question with which the Chapter opened having been sufficiently answered.

8. ποιεῖσθαι] the middle voice

γινομένην ἡδονὴν ἢ λύπην τοῖς ἔργοις· ὁ μὲν γὰρ ἀπεχόμενος τῶν σωματικῶν ἡδονῶν καὶ αὐτῷ τούτῳ χαίρων σώφρων, ὁ δ' ἀχθόμενος ἀκόλαστος, καὶ ὁ μὲν ὑπομένων τὰ δεινὰ καὶ χαίρων ἢ μὴ λυπούμενός γε ἀνδρεῖος, ὁ δὲ λυπούμενος δειλός. Περὶ ἡδονὰς γὰρ καὶ λύπας ἐστὶν ἡ ἠθικὴ ἀρετή· διὰ μὲν γὰρ τὴν ἡδονὴν τὰ φαῦλα πράττομεν, διὰ δὲ τὴν λύπην τῶν
2 καλῶν ἀπεχόμεθα. Διὸ δεῖ ἦχθαί πως εὐθὺς ἐκ νέων,
ὡς ὁ Πλάτων φησίν, ὥστε χαίρειν τε καὶ λυπεῖσθαι οἷς
3 δεῖ· ἡ γὰρ ὀρθὴ παιδεία αὕτη ἐστίν. Ἔτι δ' εἰ ἀρεταί
εἰσι περὶ πράξεις καὶ πάθη, παντὶ δὲ πάθει καὶ πάσῃ πράξει ἕπεται ἡδονὴ καὶ λύπη, καὶ διὰ τοῦτ' ἂν εἴη ἡ

Thus Virtue and Vice depend on our relation to Pleasure and Pain, as may be shown by a variety of arguments.

respectively by which the *acts* related to the habit are accompanied. From this it would seem that Moral Virtue may be described as feeling pleasure and pain when we ought. That this is so we now proceed to prove at length.—(i) It is pleasure which tempts us to wrong, and pain which deters us from what
2 is right. Hence moral education consists in the due regula-
3 tion of the feelings of pleasure and pain. (ii) All virtue is
concerned with the management of our actions and feelings, and every action and every feeling is necessarily accompanied

means 'to consider,' *i.e.* to make in one's own mind.

3. ἀκόλαστος and δειλὸς are rather loosely used here in contrast with σώφρων and ἀνδρεῖος. They imply strictly speaking the formation of a habit of the opposite kind, *i.e.* a state in which acts of intemperance or cowardice are done with ease and pleasure. The ἀκόλαστος (see note on I. iii. 7) does not restrain himself even ἀχθόμενος. Perhaps, however, ἀκολαστος is here used from the point of view of III. xi. 5, 6, where Aristotle states that the ἀκόλαστος is pained by the mere absence of pleasure.

11. παντὶ δὲ πάθει κ.τ.λ.] For this statement as far as πάθη are concerned see the Definition of πάθη in ch. v. ὅλως οἷς ἕπεται ἡδονὴ ἢ λύπη, 'whatever is followed by pleasure or pain.'

4 ἀρετὴ περὶ ἡδονὰς καὶ λύπας. Μηνύουσι δὲ καὶ αἱ κο-
λάσεις γινόμεναι διὰ τούτων· ἰατρεῖαι γάρ τινές εἰσιν,
αἱ δὲ ἰατρεῖαι διὰ τῶν ἐναντίων πεφύκασι γίνεσθαι.
5 Ἔτι, ὡς καὶ πρότερον εἴπομεν, πᾶσα ψυχῆς ἕξις, ὑφ'
οἵων πέφυκε γίνεσθαι χείρων καὶ βελτίων, πρὸς ταῦτα
καὶ περὶ ταῦτα τὴν φύσιν ἔχει· δι' ἡδονὰς δὲ καὶ λύπας
φαῦλαι γίνονται, τῷ διώκειν ταύτας καὶ φεύγειν, ἢ ἃς
μὴ δεῖ ἢ ὅτε οὐ δεῖ ἢ ὡς οὐ δεῖ ἢ ὁσαχῶς ἄλλως ὑπὸ
τοῦ λόγου διορίζεται τὰ τοιαῦτα. Διὸ καὶ ὁρίζονται τὰς
ἀρετὰς ἀπαθείας τινὰς καὶ ἠρεμίας· οὐκ εὖ δέ, ὅτι ἁπλῶς
λέγουσιν, ἀλλ' οὐχ ὡς δεῖ καὶ ὡς οὐ δεῖ, καὶ ὅτε, καὶ
6 ὅσα ἄλλα προστίθεται. Ὑπόκειται ἄρα ἡ ἀρετὴ εἶναι ἡ

4 by pleasure or pain. (iii) The infliction of punishment by
means of pain (all remedies being through the medium of
contraries) proves that it is intended to remedy an excess of
pleasure: in other words, that vice consists in pleasure out of
5, 6 place. (iv) As we saw in ch. ii., whatever promotes or hinders
the *formation* of a Virtuous habit is the sphere of its operation
when formed. Now Moral habits are *formed* (not, as some
suppose, by indifference to pleasure and pain, but) by feeling

2. διὰ τούτων] 'by means of these,' viz. pleasure and pain, though the latter only is strictly speaking referred to. The use of διὰ with the accus. = 'because of' must not be confused with this. It occurs just below in l. 6.

On κόλασις see note III. v. 7.

4. πρότερον] viz. in c. ii. § 8.

10. ἀπαθείας τινὰς καὶ ἠρεμίας] The Cynics and Stoics held this view. Cf. Pope, *Essay on Man*, ii. 101:—

In lazy apathy let Stoics boast
Their virtue fix'd: 'tis fix'd as in a frost.

12. ὑπόκειται ἄρα κ.τ.λ.] 'Virtue therefore is established to be,' etc. This seems to close the discussion, but Aristotle adds three supplementary arguments.

ἡ ἀρετὴ ἡ τοιαύτη] This collocation of article, adjective, and substantive always denotes an epithet added emphatically, or by way of limitation, to the substantive. Transl. 'Virtue, at least Virtue of this kind,' *i.e.* Moral Virtue (ἠθικὴ ἀρετή), for the statement here made would not be true of διανοητικὴ ἀρετή. Compare a similar limitation in vi. 10.

τοιαύτη περὶ ἡδονὰς καὶ λύπας τῶν βελτίστων πρακτική,
7 ἡ δὲ κακία τοὐναντίον. Γένοιτο δ' ἂν ἡμῖν καὶ ἐκ τούτων
φανερὸν ἔτι περὶ τῶν αὐτῶν. Τριῶν γὰρ ὄντων τῶν
εἰς τὰς αἱρέσεις καὶ τριῶν τῶν εἰς τὰς φυγάς, καλοῦ
συμφέροντος ἡδέος, καὶ τριῶν τῶν ἐναντίων, αἰσχροῦ
βλαβεροῦ λυπηροῦ, περὶ πάντα μὲν ταῦτα ὁ ἀγαθὸς
κατορθωτικός ἐστιν, ὁ δὲ κακὸς ἁμαρτητικός, μάλιστα δὲ
περὶ τὴν ἡδονήν· κοινή τε γὰρ αὕτη τοῖς ζῴοις, καὶ
πᾶσι τοῖς ὑπὸ τὴν αἵρεσιν παρακολουθεῖ· καὶ γὰρ τὸ
8 καλὸν καὶ τὸ συμφέρον ἡδὺ φαίνεται. Ἔτι δ' ἐκ νηπίου
πᾶσιν ἡμῖν συντέθραπται· διὸ χαλεπὸν ἀποτρίψασθαι
τοῦτο τὸ πάθος ἐγκεχρωσμένον τῷ βίῳ. Κανονίζομεν

pleasure and pain when we ought. Hence the *exercise* of
Moral habits when formed (*i.e.* of Moral Virtue) will be ex-
hibited in feeling pleasure and pain when we ought. In the
case of Vicious habits this just relation to pleasure and pain
7 is reversed. We may further add the following arguments:
—(v) We choose things because they are either good, useful,
or pleasant. We avoid things because they are either bad,
harmful, or painful. Now though Virtue goes right and Vice
goes wrong in all these motives, yet this is pre-eminently the
case in regard to pleasure and pain, which in some sense in-
8 clude all the other motives. (vi) Regarded as *feelings* pleasure

3. Observe the position of the articles, making τριῶν the predicate. 'The inducements for choosing being three in number, and the inducements for avoiding also three.'

9. πᾶσι τοῖς ὑπὸ κ.τ.λ.] 'accompanies all the motives which come under the head of choice.' For both the 'good' and the 'useful' are also 'pleasant.' In III. ix. 2-5, the argument implies that τὸ καλὸν is a kind, and indeed a most exalted kind, of ἡδύ.

12. Observe the antithesis between τοῦτο τὸ πάθος and καὶ τὰς πράξεις,—πάθη and πράξεις being, as we were reminded in § 3, the sphere of the operation of Moral Virtue. Also καὶ τὰς πράξεις = 'even our actions,' or 'our actions also,' the continual presence of pleasure and pain as regulating *action*, being at first

δὲ καὶ τὰς πράξεις, οἱ μὲν μᾶλλον οἱ δ' ἧττον, ἡδονῇ
9 καὶ λύπῃ. Διὰ τοῦτ' οὖν ἀναγκαῖον εἶναι περὶ ταῦτα
τὴν πᾶσαν πραγματείαν· οὐ γὰρ μικρὸν εἰς τὰς πράξεις
10 εὖ ἢ κακῶς χαίρειν καὶ λυπεῖσθαι. Ἔτι δὲ χαλεπώτερον
ἡδονῇ μάχεσθαι ἢ θυμῷ, καθάπερ φησὶν Ἡράκλειτος,
περὶ δὲ τὸ χαλεπώτερον ἀεὶ καὶ τέχνη γίνεται καὶ ἀρετή·
καὶ γὰρ τὸ εὖ βέλτιον ἐν τούτῳ. Ὥστε καὶ διὰ τοῦτο
περὶ ἡδονὰς καὶ λύπας πᾶσα ἡ πραγματεία καὶ τῇ ἀρετῇ
καὶ τῇ πολιτικῇ· ὁ μὲν γὰρ εὖ τούτοις χρώμενος ἀγαθὸς
ἔσται, ὁ δὲ κακῶς κακός.

11 Ὅτι μὲν οὖν ἐστὶν ἡ ἀρετὴ περὶ ἡδονὰς καὶ λύπας, καὶ ὅτι ἐξ ὧν γίνεται, ὑπὸ τούτων καὶ αὔξεται καὶ φθείρεται (μὴ ὡσαύτως γινομένων) καὶ ὅτι ἐξ ὧν ἐγένετο περὶ ταῦτα καὶ ἐνεργεῖ, εἰρήσθω.

and pain have been more ingrained into our lives, so to speak,
by familiarity than any others; and regarded as *motives for*
action also they are constantly present, though in varying
9 degrees, with all of us. With them therefore our whole
10 treatise must be concerned. (vii) Finally, nothing is so hard
to contend with as pleasure; nothing is therefore more meritorious, and consequently more virtuous, than to bring pleasure and pain under due control.

11 On all these grounds therefore we argue that Moral Virtue consists in the proper regulation of the feelings of pleasure and pain.

sight less obvious than the fact of our constant susceptibility to them as mere *feelings*.

5. Heraclitus was an Ionian philosopher who flourished at Ephesus about 150 years before Aristotle.

6. περὶ δὲ τὸ χαλεπώτερον] This principle is again applied by Aristotle in III. ix. 2, IV. i. 8, 9.

1 IV. Ἀπορήσειε δ' ἄν τις πῶς λέγομεν ὅτι δεῖ τὰ μὲν
δίκαια πράττοντας δικαίους γίνεσθαι, τὰ δὲ σώφρονα
σώφρονας· εἰ γὰρ πράττουσι τὰ δίκαια καὶ τὰ σώφρονα,
ἤδη εἰσὶ δίκαιοι καὶ σώφρονες, ὥσπερ εἰ τὰ γραμματικὰ
2 καὶ τὰ μουσικά, γραμματικοὶ καὶ μουσικοί. Ἢ οὐδ' ἐπὶ
τῶν τεχνῶν οὕτως ἔχει; ἐνδέχεται γὰρ γραμματικόν τι
ποιῆσαι καὶ ἀπὸ τύχης καὶ ἄλλου ὑποθεμένου. Τότε
οὖν ἔσται γραμματικός, ἐὰν καὶ γραμματικόν τι ποιήσῃ
καὶ γραμματικῶς· τοῦτο δ' ἐστὶ τὸ κατὰ τὴν ἐν αὑτῷ
3 γραμματικήν. Ἔτι οὐδ' ὅμοιόν ἐστιν ἐπὶ τῶν τεχνῶν
καὶ τῶν ἀρετῶν· τὰ μὲν γὰρ ὑπὸ τῶν τεχνῶν γινόμενα
τὸ εὖ ἔχει ἐν αὑτοῖς, αρκει ουν ταῦτά πως ἔχοντα γενέ-

CHAP. IV.—*Explanation of the apparent paradox that we become just by doing just actions.*

1 Another difficulty is suggested by the last statement made
in ch. ii. How can we become just by doing just acts? Are
we not just already if we do them, as (*mutatis mutandis*) is
the case in the practice of the Arts? To this we answer—
2 (1) This is not so in the case of the Arts: (2) Even if it
were, the Arts are not a parallel case. (1) It is not so in the
Arts.—Unless an artist understands the principles of his art
3 *for himself*, he is not properly speaking an artist. (2) The
Arts are not a parallel case.—The Artistic Excellence of any
work depends simply on the quality of the thing produced.

It may be asked, If we do just acts are we not therefore just men, even as we are artists if we produce artistic works? We reply—(1) It is not so in the Arts. (2) The Arts are not a strictly parallel case.

CHAP. IV.—This Chapter discusses another difficulty arising out of the statement at the end of ch. ii. 'that virtuous habits when formed reproduce the acts by which they were formed.'

6. In the Arts a beginner may go right by chance, or by following mechanically the directions of his master. In either case he is not yet an artist. Or again, one may argue logically and yet not be a logician.

12. τὸ εὖ ἔχει ἐν αὑτοῖς] A work of art as such must be judged by its own merits. It is not affected by the circumstances, disadvantages, etc., of the artist.

σθαι· τὰ δὲ κατὰ τὰς ἀρετὰς γινόμενα οὐκ ἐὰν αὐτά πως ἔχῃ, δικαίως ἢ σωφρόνως πράττεται, ἀλλὰ καὶ ἐὰν ὁ πράττων πως ἔχων πράττῃ, πρῶτον μὲν ἐὰν εἰδώς, ἔπειτ' ἐὰν προαιρούμενος, καὶ προαιρούμενος δι' αὐτά, τὸ δὲ τρίτον καὶ ἐὰν βεβαίως καὶ ἀμετακινήτως ἔχων πράττῃ. Ταῦτα δὲ πρὸς μὲν τὸ τὰς ‹πρὸς› τέχνας ἔχειν οὐ συναριθμεῖται, πλὴν αὐτὸ τὸ εἰδέναι· πρὸς δὲ τὸ τὰς ἀρετὰς τὸ μὲν εἰδέναι μικρὸν ἢ οὐδὲν ἰσχύει, τὰ δ' ἄλλα οὐ μικρὸν ἀλλὰ τὸ πᾶν δύναται, ἅπερ ἐκ τοῦ πολλάκις
4 πράττειν τὰ δίκαια καὶ σώφρονα περιγίνεται. Τὰ μὲν οὖν πράγματα δίκαια καὶ σώφρονα λέγεται, ὅταν ᾖ τοι-

Special conditions are required to constitute an act as moral.

But in Moral Excellence we further require in the agent himself, (α) Knowledge of what he is doing. (β) Deliberate choice so to act, and moreover a pure and disinterested choice. (γ) Resolute and unflinching purpose. Of these conditions knowledge is of the least weight, while it is the first and only requisite in the case of the Arts. The two latter conditions, on the other hand, are everything, and they can only be secured
4 by often *doing* acts of justice, temperance, etc. Hence neither to actions nor to individuals can the terms 'just,' etc., be

1. So Pope (*Moral Essays*):—
Not always actions show the man: we find
Who does a kindness is not therefore kind.

6. Ταῦτα δὲ κ.τ.λ.] The artistic or technical merit of a work of art is not affected by the motive of the artist, whether good or bad, *e.g.* whether his work may have been done with a religious or charitable purpose, or from jealousy or spite. In judging of a moral act, such considerations would be all-important.

7. With πρὸς δὲ τὸ τὰς ἀρετὰς supply ἔχειν from l. 6.

8. Knowledge, though an essential requisite, of itself advances us but little in the way of virtuous character. This is explained by §§ 5 and 6 below. See also ii. 1.

τὰ δ' ἄλλα] *i.e.* the other conditions mentioned, viz. deliberate choice and unflinching purpose.

10. πράττειν is the emphatic word. See § 1, above. Also πράγματα μὲν δίκαια (just *acts*) in the next line stand in contrast with δίκαιος δὲ (just *character*) in the following clause.

*αὐτὰ οἷα ἂν ὁ δίκαιος ἢ ὁ σώφρων πράξειεν· δίκαιος δὲ
καὶ σώφρων ἐστὶν οὐχ ὁ ταῦτα πράττων, ἀλλὰ καὶ ὁ
οὕτω πράττων ὡς οἱ δίκαιοι καὶ οἱ σώφρονες πράττουσιν.
5 Εὖ οὖν λέγεται ὅτι ἐκ τοῦ δίκαια πράττειν ὁ δίκαιος
γίνεται καὶ ἐκ τοῦ τὰ σώφρονα ὁ σώφρων· ἐκ δὲ τοῦ
μὴ πράττειν ταῦτα οὐδεὶς ἂν οὐδὲ μελλήσειε γενέσθαι
6 ἀγαθός. Ἀλλ' οἱ πολλοὶ ταῦτα μὲν οὐ πράττουσιν,
ἐπὶ δὲ τὸν λόγον καταφεύγοντες οἴονται φιλοσοφεῖν
καὶ οὕτως ἔσεσθαι σπουδαῖοι, ὅμοιόν τι ποιοῦντες τοῖς
κάμνουσιν, οἳ τῶν ἰατρῶν ἀκούουσι μὲν ἐπιμελῶς, ποιοῦσι δ' οὐθὲν τῶν προσταττομένων. Ὥσπερ οὖν οὐδ'
ἐκεῖνοι εὖ ἕξουσι τὸ σῶμα οὕτω θεραπευόμενοι, οὐδ'
οὗτοι τὴν ψυχὴν οὕτω φιλοσοφοῦντες.*

strictly applied, unless there be, beside the outward act, the inward spirit and purpose of the formed habit in the doing of it. We were right then in saying that only by *doing* just acts can we become just. Mere theories of Virtue without practice can no more form virtuous habits, than physicians' prescriptions if not followed can restore health. And yet this truth is very commonly forgotten.

Above all, knowledge without practice is, in Morals, useless.

7. This is well expressed by Bp. Butler, *Anal.* ch. v. (p. 91 Angus's ed.), 'Habits of the mind seem to be produced by repeated acts, as well as habits of the body. And in like manner as habits belonging to the body are produced by external acts, so habits of the mind are produced by the exertion of inward practical principles, *i.e.* by carrying them into act, or acting upon them. . . . . . But going over the theory of virtue in one's thoughts, talking well, and drawing fine pictures of it; this is so far from necessarily or certainly conducing to form a habit of it in him who thus employs himself, that it may harden the mind in a contrary course, and render it gradually more insensible to all moral considerations.'

8. *τὸν λόγον* (in contrast with *οὐ πράττουσι*) means theory as opposed to practice.

13. *φιλοσοφοῦντες*] The word *φιλοσοφία* in Greek has a much wider significance than that

1 V. Μετὰ δὲ ταῦτα τί ἐστιν ἡ ἀρετὴ σκεπτέον. Ἐπεὶ οὖν τὰ ἐν τῇ ψυχῇ γινόμενα τρία ἐστὶ, πάθη, δυνάμεις,

CHAP. V.—*The Genus of Virtue determined.*

All attributes of the Soul (including therefore Virtue) are either πάθη, δυνάμεις, or ἕξεις.

1 We have now to investigate the formal Definition of Virtue, and first, in natural order, to determine its Genus. It is evidently connected with the soul and not with the body.

which 'Philosophy' would convey to us. In the absence of any revealed Religion, and the admitted inadequacy of the popularly received system of Religion, Philosophy would to a thinking Greek supply to some extent the place of Religion. To it alone he could look not only for theories of morality, but for practical rules for the guidance of life. Thus when Plato speaks of men ἔθει ἄνευ φιλοσοφίας ἀρετῆς μετειληφότες (*Rep.* p. 619), he would convey nearly the same notion, as if we should say 'men who have lived a life of morality without religion.'

CHAP. V.—We now commence the formal construction of the Definition of Virtue. And as all Logical Definition consists in assigning the Genus and the Differentia, we first ascertain the Genus of Virtue (τί ἐστιν) in ch. v., and then its Differentia (ποῖόν τι) in ch. vi. Now there are two ways in which we may hunt (θηρεύειν) for a Definition, according to Aristotle. (1) We may take a wide Genus or class which is sure to include the object to be defined besides a good deal more, and then narrow that class by adding qualities or conditions till it becomes co-extensive with the thing to be defined; or we may exclude one by one such members of the class as are obviously beside our purpose. *e.g.* In this Chapter to define Virtue Aristotle takes the wide Genus τὰ ἐν τῇ ψυχῇ—and since all attributes of the soul may be divided into πάθη, δυνάμεις, and ἕξεις, and as Virtue cannot (for reasons assigned) be either πάθος or δύναμις, we thus obtain ἕξις as the proper Genus of Virtue. (2) The other method of 'hunting' for a Definition is to take a number of concrete instances in which the quality to be defined is found, and then ascertain what it is which they have in common. *e.g.* On this plan Aristotle's course would have been to take the several virtues and find what they have in common in the midst of their various distinctions and individual peculiarities, and that common element would account for their being called by the common name Virtue, and would in fact constitute the Definition of Virtue.

2 ἕξεις, τούτων ἄν τι εἴη ἡ ἀρετή. Λέγω δὲ πάθη μὲν
ἐπιθυμίαν, ὀργήν, φόβον, θράσος, φθόνον, χαράν, φι-
λίαν, μῖσος, πόθον, ζῆλον, ἔλεον, ὅλως οἷς ἕπεται ἡδονὴ
ἢ λύπη, δυνάμεις δὲ καθ' ἃς παθητικοὶ τούτων λεγόμεθα,
οἷον καθ' ἃς δυνατοὶ ὀργισθῆναι ἢ λυπηθῆναι ἢ ἐλεῆσαι,
ἕξεις δὲ καθ' ἃς πρὸς τὰ πάθη ἔχομεν εὖ ἢ κακῶς, οἷον
πρὸς τὸ ὀργισθῆναι, εἰ μὲν σφοδρῶς ἢ ἀνειμένως,
κακῶς ἔχομεν, εἰ δὲ μέσως, εὖ. Ὁμοίως δὲ καὶ πρὸς
3 τἆλλα. Πάθη μὲν οὖν οὐκ εἰσὶν οὔθ' αἱ ἀρεταὶ οὔθ'
αἱ κακίαι, ὅτι οὐ λεγόμεθα κατὰ τὰ πάθη σπουδαῖοι ἢ
φαῦλοι, κατὰ δὲ τὰς ἀρετὰς ἢ τὰς κακίας λεγόμεθα, καὶ
ὅτι κατὰ μὲν τὰ πάθη οὔτ' ἐπαινούμεθα, οὔτε ψεγόμεθα
(οὐ γὰρ ἐπαινεῖται ὁ φοβούμενος οὐδὲ ὁ ὀργιζόμενος,
οὐδὲ ψέγεται ὁ ἁπλῶς ὀργιζόμενος ἀλλ' ὁ πῶς), κατὰ
δὲ τὰς ἀρετὰς καὶ τὰς κακίας ἐπαινούμεθα ἢ ψεγόμεθα.

Having defined πάθη, δυνάμεις, ἕξεις, we can show that

Now all attributes of the soul are either emotions, capabilities,
2 or habits. 'Emotions' are any affections of the soul accompanied by pleasure or pain. 'Capabilities' simply render us 'capable' of being so affected. 'Habits' are the permanent relations in which we stand to such affections, which may be either good or bad relations, depending on the manner or degree in which we allow ourselves to be affected by them.

Virtue is not πάθος,

3 i. Virtue is not an Emotion, because—(*a*) We do not apply the terms right, wrong, praise, blame, to Emotions *per se*, as

6. ἕξις is not exactly equivalent to 'habit,' by which it is conventionally translated. It is rather 'state' or 'settled condition.' ἔχειν meant originally to 'hold on' or 'keep on' (hence such phrases as ἀτιμάσας ἔχει, ἔχεσθαί τινος), and so ἕξις was 'a holding on.' *e.g.* ἕξις τῶν ὅπλων 'an armed state or condition.' Hence Aristotle's Definition ἕξεις καθ' ἃς ἔχομεν κ.τ.λ.

7. ἀνειμένως] 'remissly,' *i.e.* in defect, opp. to σφοδρῶς, in excess. This fault in respect of anger is criticised in IV. v. 5, 6. It is possible to take ἀνειμένως as in III. v. 10 = 'dissolutely,' but this would repeat, rather than oppose, σφοδρῶς.

4 Ἔτι ὀργιζόμεθα μὲν καὶ φοβούμεθα ἀπροαιρέτως, αἱ δ' ἀρεταὶ προαιρέσεις τινὲς ἢ οὐκ ἄνευ προαιρέσεως. Πρὸς δὲ τούτοις κατὰ μὲν τὰ πάθη κινεῖσθαι λεγόμεθα, κατὰ δὲ τὰς ἀρετὰς καὶ τὰς κακίας οὐ κινεῖσθαι ἀλλὰ διακεῖ-
5 σθαί πως. Διὰ ταῦτα δὲ οὐδὲ δυνάμεις εἰσίν· οὔτε γὰρ ἀγαθοὶ λεγόμεθα τῷ δύνασθαι πάσχειν ἁπλῶς οὔτε κακοί, οὔτ' ἐπαινούμεθα οὔτε ψεγόμεθα. Καὶ ἔτι δυνατοὶ μέν ἐσμεν φύσει, ἀγαθοὶ δὲ ἢ κακοὶ οὐ γινόμεθα φύσει· εἴ-

4 we obviously do apply them to virtue and vice. (β) There is no deliberate choice in Emotions, as we have already stated (ch. iv.) that there is in Virtue. (γ) We are said to be 'moved' by our Emotions, but 'disposed' by virtue and vice, and this difference of language implies a difference of fact.
ιτ δύναμις. 5 ii. Virtue is not a mere 'Capability,' because—(α) The argument above as to the application of praise, blame, etc., applies to Capabilities as well as to Emotions. (β) Capabilities come

1. ἀπροαιρέτως] = 'without purpose,' 'spontaneously.' The objects corresponding to particular passions or emotions being present, the emotion must be *felt* (though not necessarily encouraged or indulged), as necessarily as heat must be felt on approaching a fire. No reason or deliberation can prevent this.

Compare Butler's *Analogy*, pt. i. ch. v. (p. 98, ed. Angus). 'The principle of Virtue can neither excite them (viz. such affections) nor prevent their being excited. On the contrary, they are naturally felt when the objects of them are present to the mind, not only before all consideration whether they can be obtained by lawful means, but after it is found they cannot. For the natural objects of affection continue so.' . . And again, 'Particular propensions (by which name Butler describes such affections) from their very nature must be felt, the objects of them being present' (p. 100).

2. προαιρέσεις] The authority for this statement at present is iv. 3. It is afterwards embodied in the formal Definition of Virtue in vi. 15.

4. οὐ κινεῖσθαι ἀλλὰ διακεῖσθαι] Not 'moved' but 'disposed.' The latter word implying a more permanent affection. The distinction being made in language is a proof that such a distinction is commonly believed to exist. See note on i. 1.

6 πομεν δὲ περὶ τούτου πρότερον. Εἰ οὖν μήτε πάθη εἰσὶν αἱ ἀρεταὶ μήτε δυνάμεις, λείπεται ἕξεις αὐτὰς εἶναι.

1 VI. Ὅ τι μὲν οὖν ἐστὶ τῷ γένει ἡ ἀρετή, εἴρηται· δεῖ δὲ μὴ μόνον οὕτως εἰπεῖν, ὅτι ἕξις, ἀλλὰ καὶ ποία τις.
2 Ῥητέον οὖν ὅτι πᾶσα ἀρετή, οὗ ἂν ᾖ ἀρετή, αὐτό τε εὖ ἔχον ἀποτελεῖ, καὶ τὸ ἔργον αὐτοῦ εὖ ἀποδίδωσιν, οἷον ἡ τοῦ ὀφθαλμοῦ ἀρετὴ τόν τε ὀφθαλμὸν σπουδαῖον ποιεῖ καὶ τὸ ἔργον αὐτοῦ· τῇ γὰρ τοῦ ὀφθαλμοῦ ἀρετῇ εὖ

by nature, Virtue does not, as we have fully proved in ch. i.
6 iii. Hence we argue that if Virtue is neither an Emotion nor a Capability it must be a Habit.

Therefore Virtue is a ἕξις.

CHAP. VI.—*The differentia of Virtue determined, and thus its full Definition arrived at.*

1 The next point will be to show *what sort* of a Habit Virtue
2 is. Now speaking generally Excellence (ἀρετὴ) of whatever kind perfects that of which it is the excellence, and causes

We next ask, What sort of a habit is Virtue? We conceive of Excellence generally as perfecting any work.

CHAP. VI.—In this Chapter Aristotle discovers what sort of a Habit Virtue is, as follows. First he lays down the broad general conception that Excellence (ἀρετή) of any kind perfects the work of that of which it is the Excellence (§§ 1-3). Next he asks, In what then consists the perfection of *Man's* works? (§ 4). Having noted that all things capable of division at all can be taken in excess, defect, or moderation, he states that the perfecting of all human work, scientific, artistic, and therefore still more, moral, consists in securing the mean or moderate amount (neither too much nor too little) of that with which it has to deal (§§ 5-9). He then explains that this is true only of Moral and not of Intellectual Excellence (§§ 10-13). After another argument pointing to the same conclusion derived from there being in all cases only one right and many wrong courses (§ 14), the formal Definition of Virtue is enunciated (§ 15), and the Chapter concludes with removing two possible misconceptions of, or objections to, the theory that all Virtue is a 'mean' state (§§ 16, etc.).

ὁρῶμεν. Ὁμοίως ἡ τοῦ ἵππου ἀρετὴ ἵππον τε σπουδαῖον ποιεῖ καὶ ἀγαθὸν δραμεῖν καὶ ἐνεγκεῖν τὸν ἐπι-
3 βάτην καὶ μεῖναι τοὺς πολεμίους. Εἰ δὴ τοῦτ' ἐπὶ πάντων οὕτως ἔχει, καὶ ἡ τοῦ ἀνθρώπου ἀρετὴ εἴη ἂν ἕξις ἀφ' ἧς ἀγαθὸς ἄνθρωπος γίνεται καὶ ἀφ' ἧς εὖ τὸ
4 ἑαυτοῦ ἔργον ἀποδώσει. Πῶς δὲ τοῦτ' ἔσται, ἤδη μὲν εἰρήκαμεν, ἔτι δὲ καὶ ὧδ' ἔσται φανερὸν, ἐὰν θεωρήσωμεν ποία τις ἐστὶν ἡ φύσις αὐτῆς. Ἐν παντὶ δὴ συνεχεῖ καὶ διαιρετῷ ἔστι λαβεῖν τὸ μὲν πλεῖον, τὸ δ' ἔλαττον, τὸ δ' ἴσον, καὶ ταῦτα ἢ κατ' αὐτὸ τὸ πρᾶγμα, ἢ πρὸς ἡμᾶς· τὸ δ' ἴσον μέσον τι ὑπερβολῆς καὶ ἐλλεί-
5 ψεως. Λέγω δὲ τοῦ μὲν πράγματος μέσον τὸ ἴσον

3 its peculiar function to be well performed. Hence Moral Virtue (*i.e. human* Excellence) will perfect human nature and cause the proper function of human nature to be well
4 performed. How this will be has been already hinted at (in ch. ii.) from the analogy existing between the functions of the body of man and of his soul and of their respective Excellences, but we now proceed to discuss the question on more general principles. In everything which is capable of division at all, whatever be the nature of the connexion of its parts, we can have an excessive, a defective, and a just amount. These amounts may be taken either absolutely or relatively, and the just amount is always a *mean* in respect of the excess and defect, *i.e.* it lies somewhere between them. An
5 'absolute' mean then is that which is precisely half-way

Whenever different degrees of a thing are possible, Excellence consists in securing a mean or moderate amount, and that judged in relation to circumstances.

4. καὶ marks the conclusion of the argument.

9. ξυνεχὴς is applied to that whose parts are continuous or in close connexion, *e.g.* a stick or stone; διαιρετὸς to that whose parts are not so connected, *e.g.* a heap of stones, a handful of sand or gravel. In either case it is possible to take varying amounts of the things in question. Another interpretation explains ξυνεχὴς of geometrical magnitudes, line, figure, etc.; διαιρετὸς of arithmetical numbers.

ἀπέχον(ἀφ' ἑκατέρου τῶν ακρων, οπερ ἐστὶν ἓν καὶ
ταὐτὸν πᾶσιν, πρὸς ἡμᾶς δὲ ὃ μήτε πλεονάζει μήτε
6 ἐλλείπει. Τοῦτο δ' οὐχ ἓν, οὐδὲ ταὐτὸν πᾶσιν, οἷον εἰ
τὰ δέκα πολλὰ τὰ δὲ δύο ὀλίγα, τὰ ἓξ μέσα λαμβάνουσι
κατὰ τὸ πρᾶγμα· ἴσῳ γὰρ ὑπερέχει τε καὶ ὑπερέχεται,
τοῦτο δὲ μέσον ἐστὶ κατὰ τὴν ἀριθμητικὴν ἀναλογίαν.
7 Τὸ δὲ πρὸς ἡμᾶς οὐχ οὕτω ληπτέον· οὐ γὰρ εἴ τῳ δέκα
μναῖ φαγεῖν πολὺ δύο δὲ ὀλίγον, ὁ ἀλείπτης ἓξ μνᾶς
προστάξει· ἔστι γὰρ ἴσως καὶ τοῦτο πολὺ τῷ ληψομένῳ
ἢ ὀλίγον· Μίλωνι μὲν γὰρ ὀλίγον, τῷ δὲ ἀρχομένῳ τῶν
8 γυμνασίων πολύ. Ὁμοίως ἐπὶ δρόμου καὶ πάλης. Οὕτω
δὴ πᾶς ἐπιστήμων τὴν ὑπερβολὴν μὲν καὶ τὴν ἔλλειψιν
φεύγει, τὸ δὲ μέσον ζητεῖ καὶ τοῦθ' αἱρεῖται, μέσον δὲ
9 οὐ τὸ τοῦ πράγματος ἀλλὰ τὸ πρὸς ἡμᾶς. Εἰ δὴ πᾶσα

between a given excess and a given defect, and is therefore
6, 7 always the same and easily found in every case. By a
'relative mean' we indicate that intermediate amount between
excess and defect which is *best for us*; *i.e.* the mean *relative*
to our interest and advantage. This is of course sometimes
more and sometimes less than the 'absolute mean,' and is
8, 9 different for different persons. Now when we say that every
practical science places the perfection of its work in its being

This is obviously the case in artistic or scientific work.

6. ἀριθμητικὴν ἀναλογίαν] Arithmetic progression or proportion: *i.e.* when each term differs from the preceding by a constant quantity. Consequently the absolute or arithmetic mean between two quantities is found by adding them together and dividing by 2.

10. Milo was a celebrated athlete of Crotona, a sort of Greek Samson, of whose marvellous strength many traditions were preserved.

14. Εἰ δὴ πᾶσα κ.τ.λ.] Observe that the argument now depends on the analogy between Virtue and the Arts or practical Sciences, *i.e.* between the work of man as a Moral agent, and the work of man as an Artistic or Scientific agent: and the inference is that what constitutes excellence in one sort of work (Artistic) will also consti-

ἐπιστήμη οὕτω τὸ ἔργον εὖ ἐπιτελεῖ, πρὸς τὸ μέσον βλέπουσα καὶ εἰς τοῦτο ἄγουσα τὰ ἔργα (ὅθεν εἰώθασιν ἐπιλέγειν τοῖς εὖ ἔχουσιν ἔργοις ὅτι οὔτ' ἀφελεῖν ἔστιν οὔτε προσθεῖναι, ὡς τῆς μὲν ὑπερβολῆς καὶ τῆς ἐλλείψεως φθειρούσης τὸ εὖ, τῆς δὲ μεσότητος σωζούσης), οἱ δ' ἀγαθοὶ τεχνῖται, ὡς λέγομεν, πρὸς τοῦτο βλέποντες ἐργάζονται, ἡ δ' ἀρετὴ πάσης τέχνης ἀκριβεστέρα καὶ ἀμείνων ἐστὶν, ὥσπερ καὶ ἡ φύσις, τοῦ μέσου ἂν εἴη στοχαστική. Λέγω δὲ τὴν ἠθικήν· αὕτη γάρ ἐστι περὶ πάθη καὶ πράξεις, ἐν δὲ τούτοις ἔστιν ὑπερβολὴ καὶ ἔλλειψις καὶ τὸ μέσον. Οἷον καὶ φοβηθῆναι καὶ θαρ-

Ience it is o with Ioral Excellence or Virtue.

neither excessive nor defective, but in due moderation, it is this *relative mean* that is always intended. And since then to attain to this relative mean is the end of every art or practical science, much more will it be so in the pre-eminent practical science of morals. Therefore it will be the characteristic feature of Moral Virtue that it perfects the work of man by aiming at a relative mean (in other words, at moderation) in all that it is concerned with. *Moral* Vmora, be it observed (for all this does not apply to *Intellectual ora* ullonce),

'his applies o Moral Excellence only, not to ntellectual.

tute excellence in the other sort of work (Moral). This analogy must be carefully distinguished from that between the body and the soul of man in ii. 5-7.

8. ὥσπερ καὶ ἡ φύσις] i.e. Virtue is better than Art, just as Nature also is better than Art. Virtue is often regarded by Plato and Aristotle as a species of art, as has been noticed before, and indeed as its most perfect exemplification.

9. The argument only applies to ἠθικὴ ἀρετή, because it alone comes within the general case upon which the whole argument is based (see § 4, ἐν παντὶ κ.τ.λ.), as being concerned with something (viz. πάθη and πράξεις) admitting of excess, mean, and defect. Such is clearly not the case in regard to Intellectual Excellence. That this is so with πάθη is proved in §§ 10 and 11, and similarly (ὁμοίως) it is asserted of πράξεις in § 12. πάθη and πράξεις are again thus united as forming the groundwork of Virtue in § 16 and also in iii. 3.

ρῆσαι καὶ ἐπιθυμῆσαι καὶ ὀργισθῆναι καὶ ἐλεῆσαι καὶ
ὅλως ἡσθῆναι καὶ λυπηθῆναι ἔστι καὶ μᾶλλον καὶ ἧττον,
11 καὶ ἀμφότερα οὐκ εὖ· τὸ δ' ὅτε δεῖ καὶ ἐφ' οἷς καὶ πρὸς
οὓς καὶ οὗ ἕνεκα καὶ ὡς δεῖ, μέσον τε καὶ ἄριστον, ὅπερ
12 ἐστὶ τῆς ἀρετῆς. Ὁμοίως δὲ καὶ περὶ τὰς πράξεις ἔστιν
ὑπερβολὴ καὶ ἔλλειψις καὶ τὸ μέσον. Ἡ δ' ἀρετὴ περὶ
πάθη καὶ πράξεις ἐστίν, ἐν οἷς ἡ μὲν ὑπερβολὴ ἁμαρτά-
νεται καὶ ἡ ἔλλειψις ψέγεται, τὸ δὲ μέσον ἐπαινεῖται
13 καὶ κατορθοῦται· ταῦτα δ' ἄμφω τῆς ἀρετῆς. Μεσότης
τις ἄρα ἐστὶν ἡ ἀρετή, στοχαστική γε οὖσα τοῦ μέσου.
14 Ἔτι τὸ μὲν ἁμαρτάνειν πολλαχῶς ἔστιν (τὸ γὰρ κακὸν
τοῦ ἀπείρου, ὡς οἱ Πυθαγόρειοι εἴκαζον, τὸ δ' ἀγαθὸν
τοῦ πεπερασμένου), τὸ δὲ κατορθοῦν μοναχῶς· διὸ καὶ

for Moral Virtue has for its object emotions and actions, both
12 of which admit of excess, defect, and moderation. This
moderation will consist in a due regulation of time, occasions,
objects, motives, manner, etc., in regard to emotions and
actions; and such regulation of emotions and actions is con-
14 fessedly a characteristic of Virtue. Once more, it is possible
to go wrong in many ways, right in one way only: just as we
may miss a mark in any and every direction and can hit it

That Wrong is manifold, Right is one, points to the same conclusion.

9. ταῦτα ἄμφω] viz. both praise and success (ἐπαινεῖται καὶ κατορθοῦται) are characteristics of Virtue, as they have just been shown to be of moderation (μέσον). Compare ὅπερ ἐστὶ τῆς ἀρετῆς above in l. 4, where ὅπερ similarly refers to excellence (ἄριστον) as being a characteristic of virtue.

12. The Pythagoreans expressed their teaching on Moral and other subjects by mathematical metaphors, which however have been often taken literally. The doctrine quoted in the text is a specimen. All that is infinite (involving the notion of indefinite) is bad; the finite is good. Aristotle's inference from this, that right lies intermediate to the various courses of wrong, somewhat resembles the argument which is called the 'Principle of Sufficient Reason' in Mathematics, as it is applied, *e.g.* to establish what is called the first Law of Motion. See further, note on I. vi. 7.

προσποιούμενος μηθενὸς ἕνεκα φαύλῳ μὲν ἔοικεν (οὐ γὰρ ἂν ἔχαιρε τῷ ψεύδει), μάταιος δὲ φαίνεται μᾶλλον ἢ
11 κακός. Εἰ δ' ἕνεκά τινος, ὁ μὲν δόξης ἢ τιμῆς οὐ λίαν ψεκτὸς, ὡς ὁ ἀλαζὼν, ὁ δὲ ἀργυρίου, ἢ ὅσα εἰς ἀργύ-
12 ριον, ἀσχημονέστερος. Οὐκ ἐν τῇ δυνάμει δ' ἐστὶν ὁ

coming naturally as it were to a man. In that case it is
11 rather foolish than actually vicious. (β) It may be assumed with a view to secure honour, or with a view to make gain;
12 the latter being the worse form. And observe that Boastfulness is a moral state, the character of which is determined mainly by its motive or purpose. For the force of

1. φαύλῳ μὲν ἔοικε] 'is a bad man in some sense.' This is in natural contrast with the statement in § 8, δόξειε δ' ἂν κ.τ.λ.

4. ὡς ὁ ἀλαζὼν] As the ἀλαζὼν is the character whose different types Aristotle is now distinguishing, it seems out of place to give as an example of *one* of them 'ὁ ἀλαζών.' Two other readings are proposed (α) ὡς ἀλαζὼν (omitting ὁ), *i.e.* 'he is not very much to be blamed, for a braggart' (=considering that he is a braggart): (β) ὁ ἀλαζὼν (omitting ὡς), *i.e.* 'He who does it for the sake of honour is not very much to be blamed—he who boasts, I mean.' Thus the words supply the place of the participle προσποιούμενος which must be understood with ὁ, and if the sentence were written in full would follow τιμῆς. It is most probable however that the words ὡς ὁ ἀλαζὼν represent a marginal gloss that has crept into the text.

5. Οὐκ ἐν τῇ δυνάμει κ.τ.λ.] Boastfulness as a reprehensible habit consists not so much in the mere capacity (δύναμις) or propensity to boast. That may arise in a manner from natural constitution (τῷ τοιόσδε εἶναι—with which compare a similar statement as regards Friendliness, vi. 5, τῷ τοιοῦτος εἶναι κ.τ.λ.), or from force of habit (κατὰ τὴν ἕξιν—with which again compare τῷ τὴν ἕξιν τοιοῦτος εἶναι in § 7 above). The moral depravity of Boastfulness depends rather upon the motives for which it is adopted (προαίρεσις), the distinction between some of which motives has just been pointed out. The distinction is in fact the same as that which discriminates ἄρεσκος and κόλαξ in the last Chapter.

The remark is introduced in the text to show that the classification just made of boasters according to their motive indicates a real moral difference.

ὑπακουσομένων τῶν ἐπιεικῶς τοῖς ἔθεσι προηγμένων, ἀπειθοῦσι δὲ καὶ ἀφυεστέροις οὖσι κολάσεις τε καὶ τιμωρίας ἐπιτιθέναι, τοὺς δ' ἀνιάτους ὅλως ἐξορίζειν· τὸν μὲν γὰρ ἐπιεικῆ καὶ πρὸς τὸ καλὸν ζῶντα τῷ λόγῳ πειθαρχήσειν, τὸν δὲ φαῦλον ἡδονῆς ὀρεγόμενον λύπῃ κολάζεσθαι ὥσπερ ὑποζύγιον. Διὸ καί φασι δεῖν τοιαύτας γίνεσθαι τὰς λύπας αἳ μάλιστ' ἐναντιοῦνται ταῖς ἀγαπωμέναις ἡδοναῖς.
11 Εἰ δ' οὖν, καθάπερ εἴρηται, τὸν ἐσόμενον ἀγαθὸν τραφῆναι καλῶς δεῖ καὶ ἐθισθῆναι, εἶθ' οὕτως ἐν ἐπιτηδεύμασιν ἐπιεικέσι ζῆν καὶ μήτ' ἄκοντα μήθ' ἑκόντα πράττειν τὰ φαῦλα, ταῦτα δὲ γίγνοιτ' ἂν βιουμένοις κατά τινα νοῦν
12 καὶ τάξιν ὀρθήν, ἔχουσαν ἰσχύν. Ἡ μὲν οὖν πατρικὴ πρόσταξις οὐκ ἔχει τὸ ἰσχυρὸν οὐδὲ τὸ ἀναγκαῖον, οὐδὲ δὴ ὅλως ἡ ἑνὸς ἀνδρός, μὴ βασιλέως ὄντος ἤ τινος τοιούτου· ὁ δὲ νόμος ἀναγκαστικὴν ἔχει δύναμιν, λόγος ὢν

appeal to the nobler instincts of those in whom nature or good training has implanted such instincts, but to compel obedience from all others by pains and penalties, and, speaking generally, by inflicting such pains as are most opposed to the
11 offending pleasures. All this implies a guiding Intellect, with power to enforce its decrees. Where then is this to be
12 found? Parental authority, and indeed that of any single individual, except he be an absolute monarch, lacks that

Parental authority cannot adequately enforce it.

ρεύει, *i.e.* 'quod lex non jubet vetat.'

2. *κολάσεις τε καὶ τιμωρίας*] For this distinction see note on III. v. 7.

7. *αἳ μάλιστ' ἐναντιοῦνται κ.τ.λ.*] Compare the argument in II. iii. 4, *αἱ δὲ ἰατρεῖαι διὰ τῶν ἐναντίων πεφύκασι γίνεσθαι.*

11. *ταῦτα δὲ γίγνοιτ' ἂν*] *δὲ* marks the apodosis or conclusion of the sentence.

15. *λόγος ὢν κ.τ.λ.*] 'being a declaration proceeding as it were from wisdom and intelligence.' *i.e.* Law expresses in an impersonal form the conclusions of human wisdom. As expressing such conclusions, it commands our obedience, as doing so impersonally and in the abstract, it does not excite our resentment. Aristotle in the *Politics* describes Law as *νοῦς ἄνευ ὀρέξεως.*

18 *ἀρετή, κατὰ δὲ τὸ ἄριστον καὶ τὸ εὖ ἀκρότης. Οὐ πᾶσα δ' ἐπιδέχεται πρᾶξις οὐδὲ πᾶν πάθος τὴν μεσότητα· ἔνια γὰρ εὐθὺς ὠνόμασται συνειλημμένα μετὰ τῆς φαυλότητος, οἷον ἐπιχαιρεκακία, ἀναισχυντία, φθόνος, καὶ ἐπὶ τῶν πράξεων μοιχεία, κλοπή, ἀνδροφονία· πάντα γὰρ ταῦτα καὶ τὰ τοιαῦτα ψέγεται τῷ αὐτὰ φαῦλα εἶναι, ἀλλ' οὐχ αἱ ὑπερβολαὶ αὐτῶν οὐδ' αἱ ἐλλείψεις. Οὐκ ἔστιν οὖν οὐδέποτε περὶ αὐτὰ κατορθοῦν, ἀλλ' ἀεὶ ἁμαρτάνειν· οὐδ' ἔστι τὸ εὖ ἢ μὴ εὖ περὶ τὰ τοιαῦτα ἐν τῷ*

itself and in the abstract that Virtue is a 'mean.' Considered in a special aspect and in reference to a special standard, viz. that of Excellence or Goodness, it is no longer a mean but extreme, *i.e.* it includes not a moderate, but the greatest

(2) Not all moderation is Virtue.

18 possible, amount of good. (2) Conversely it must not be thought that because Virtue consists in modemuion that a mean or moderate amount of *anything* is good muply because it is moderate. In respect of things essentiallmuad the right

means the 'essence' (*i.e.* the simplest form, or notion, of the existence) of anything.

(2) τί ἦν εἶναι = 'what was the essence of anything?'

(3) τὸ τί-ἦν-εἶναι = 'the what the essence [of anything] was'; or 'that which the essence was'; or in other words again, 'the essence' [of anything].

(4) τὸν λόγον τὸν τί-ἦν-εἶναι λέγοντα, 'the definition stating the essence'; *i.e.* the 'essential' or 'logical' Definition of anything: *quite literally* 'the Definition which says what [the] essence [of a thing] was.' Thus the whole expression is nearly equivalent to οὐσία occurring just before, which also means the 'being' or 'essence' of anything, '*essentia*' being the exact Latin equivalent of οὐσία.

It remains to explain ἦν and not ἐστι being used. This is done to indicate that the Essence of a thing is *prior to* the existence of the thing itself. *e.g.* Before any individual man existed the essence of man, *i.e.* humanity, or the ideas constituting humanity, existed as the type after which man was created, just as the idea of a house exists on paper or in the architect's mind before the house itself is built.

3. εὐθὺς ὠνόμασται συνειλημμένα κ.τ.λ.] 'involve the notion of badness the moment they are named.'

ἣν δεῖ καὶ ὅτε καὶ ὡς μοιχεύειν, ἀλλ' ἁπλῶς τὸ ποιεῖν
19 ὁτιοῦν τούτων ἁμαρτάνειν ἐστίν. Ὅμοιον οὖν τὸ ἀξιοῦν
καὶ περὶ τὸ ἀδικεῖν καὶ δειλαίνειν καὶ ἀκολασταίνειν
εἶναι μεσότητα καὶ ὑπερβολὴν καὶ ἔλλειψιν· ἔσται γὰρ
οὕτω γε ὑπερβολῆς καὶ ἐλλείψεως μεσότης καὶ ὑπερ-
20 βολῆς ὑπερβολὴ καὶ ἔλλειψις ἐλλείψεως. Ὥσπερ δὲ
σωφροσύνης καὶ ἀνδρείας οὐκ ἔστιν ὑπερβολὴ καὶ
ἔλλειψις διὰ τὸ μέσον εἶναί πως ἄκρον, οὕτως οὐδὲ
ἐκείνων μεσότης οὐδὲ ὑπερβολὴ καὶ ἔλλειψις, ἀλλ' ὡς
ἂν πράττηται ἁμαρτάνεται· ὅλως γὰρ οὔθ' ὑπερβολῆς
καὶ ἐλλείψεως μεσότης ἔστιν, οὔτε μεσότητος ὑπερβολὴ
καὶ ἔλλειψις./

1 VII. Δεῖ δὲ τοῦτο μὴ μόνον καθόλου λέγεσθαι, ἀλλὰ
καὶ τοῖς καθ' ἕκαστα ἐφαρμόττειν· ἐν γὰρ τοῖς περὶ τὰς

amount is no longer a mean or moderate amount, but the least
19 possible amount or rather none at all. If a thing is in itself
bad, it is *already*, according to our theory, in excess or in
defect, and therefore we cannot again have excess mean and
20 defect of it. If it is itself good, it is, according to our theory,
already a mean, and therefore we cannot again have excess
mean and defect of it.

CHAP. VII.—*A Table or Catalogue of Virtues with their related Vices.*

List of Virtues and Vices in detail.

1 In order to prove that our Definition holds good of all the Virtues in detail, we proceed to classify them, shewing the

8. πως] 'in some sense,' *i.e.* as is explained in § 17 *fin.*, Virtue if regarded in its special relation to the standard of excellence is an extreme and not a mean.

CHAP. VII.—Aristotle's plan now is to prove the correctness of this Definition of Virtue, by showing it to apply in the case of every individual Virtue in detail. This is clearly expressed again in § 11, ῥητέον οὖν κ.τ.λ. With a view to this it is necessary to have an exhaustive Cata-

πράξεις λόγοις οἱ μὲν καθόλου κενώτεροί εἰσιν, οἱ δ' ἐπὶ μέρους ἀληθινώτεροι· περὶ γὰρ τὰ καθ' ἕκαστα αἱ πράξεις, δέον δ' ἐπὶ τούτων συμφωνεῖν. Ληπτέον οὖν
2 ταῦτα ἐκ τῆς διαγραφῆς. Περὶ μὲν οὖν φόβους καὶ θάρρη ἀνδρεία μεσότης· τῶν δ' ὑπερβαλλόντων ὁ μὲν τῇ ἀφοβίᾳ ἀνώνυμος (πολλὰ δ' ἐστὶν ἀνώνυμα), ὁ δ' ἐν

subject-matter in reference to which each Virtue is a mean state, together with its related Vices of excess and defect. Arranging them in the order of—1. Excess, 2. Mean, 3.
i. Courage. 2 Defect, we have—i. In reference to Confidence and Fear

logue of the Virtues. This is therefore given in the present Chapter, and it forms a sort of 'Table of Contents' for the discussion which follows to the end of Bk. IV.; though the actual order here indicated is not always observed.

2. ἀληθινώτεροι = 'more real,' not to be confused with ἀληθέστεραι = 'more true.'

4. διαγραφῆς] the table or catalogue. This will be found in an Appendix at the end of this Book, together with a note on the probable principle of classification upon which it is constructed.

Περὶ φόβους καὶ θάρρη] Observe that in each case Aristotle first lays down the morally-indifferent (*i.e.* neither good nor bad in itself, see note on vi. 17) subject-matter, upon the excess, defect, or mean amount, of which the related Virtue and Vices in each case depend. Observe further that this subject-matter is in several cases described by a pair of words converse to one another, *e.g.* Confidence and Fear, Pleasure and Pain, Giving and Receiving, etc. Now of either member of these pairs we may have excess, mean, or defect, and therefore theoretically there would be *two* Virtues, *each* with two related Vices, belonging to each pair. But as excess of confidence is much the same as defect of fear, and *vice-versâ*, (and similarly in the case of the other pairs), the subdivision in each case is a needless refinement, like the distinction between D♯ and E♭ commonly in Music. Hence it is only carried out in two cases, viz. Courage and Liberality, and no stress is laid upon it in the fuller discussion of Bks. III. and IV.

6. πολλὰ δ' ἐστὶν ἀνώνυμα] It must often be the case that refinements of theory are not of sufficient practical importance to be represented by distinct words in common language, *e.g.* though in *theory* excess of confidence (ἐν τῷ θαρρεῖν ὑπερβάλλειν) and

τῷ θαρρεῖν ὑπερβάλλων θρασύς, ὁ δὲ τῷ μὲν φοβεῖσθαι
3 ὑπερβάλλων τῷ δὲ θαρρεῖν ἐλλείπων δειλός. Περὶ
ἡδονὰς δὲ καὶ λύπας οὐ πάσας, ἧττον δὲ καὶ περὶ τὰς
λύπας, μεσότης μὲν σωφροσύνη, ὑπερβολὴ δὲ ἀκολασία.
Ἐλλείποντες δὲ περὶ τὰς ἡδονὰς οὐ πάνυ γίνονται·
διόπερ οὐδ᾽ ὀνόματος τετυχήκασιν οὐδ᾽ οἱ τοιοῦτοι,
4 ἔστωσαν δὲ ἀναίσθητοι. Περὶ δὲ δόσιν χρημάτων καὶ
λῆψιν μεσότης μὲν ἐλευθεριότης, ὑπερβολὴ δὲ καὶ ἔλ-
λειψις ἀσωτία καὶ ἀνελευθερία. Ἐναντίως δ᾽ ἑαυταῖς
ὑπερβάλλουσι καὶ ἐλλείπουσιν· ὁ μὲν γὰρ ἄσωτος ἐν
μὲν προέσει ὑπερβάλλει, ἐν δὲ λήψει ἐλλείπει, ὁ δ᾽
ἀνελεύθερος ἐν μὲν λήψει ὑπερβάλλει, ἐν δὲ προέσει
5 ἐλλείπει. Νῦν μὲν οὖν τύπῳ καὶ ἐπὶ κεφαλαίῳ λέγο-
μεν, ἀρκούμενοι αὐτῷ τούτῳ· ὕστερον δὲ ἀκριβέστερον
6 περὶ αὐτῶν διορισθήσεται. Περὶ δὲ τὰ χρήματα καὶ

(especially the former)—(1) Rashness, (2) Courage, (3) Cowar-
3 dice. ii. In reference to Pleasure and Pain (especially the ii. Temperance.
former)—(1) Intemperance, (2) Temperance, (3) Insensi-
4, 5 tiveness, if indeed such a state exists. iii. In reference to iii. Liberality.
giving and receiving Money (especially the former)—(1) Pro-
6 digality, (2) Liberality, (3) Sordidness. iv. In reference to iv. Magnificence.

deficiency of fear (ἐν τῷ φοβεῖσθαι ἐλλείπειν) are distinct, yet *practically* the result of both is the same, viz. rashness, and so this one word serves for both cases. It should also be noticed that some languages possess refinements of this kind which others have not; and indeed it is seldom that any one word (in such cases as we are considering) in one language has its precise equivalent, meaning neither more nor less, in another language. (See Introd. p. xxxvi.).

3. οὐ πάσας] This limitation is fully explained in III. x.

ἧττον δὲ καὶ περὶ τὰς λύπας] This is explained by III. xi. 5.

7. ἀναίσθητοι] 'insensible,' or perhaps 'insensitive,' the latter reproducing not only the meaning of the Greek word, but also the somewhat unfamiliar character which Aristotle admits it to have.

δόσιν καὶ λῆψιν] That the former however is much more important is shown in IV. i. 6-11.

ἄλλαι διαθέσεις εἰσὶ, μεσότης μὲν μεγαλοπρέπεια (ὁ
γὰρ μεγαλοπρεπὴς διαφέρει ἐλευθερίου· ὁ μὲν γὰρ περὶ
μεγάλα, ὁ δὲ περὶ μικρὰ), ὑπερβολὴ δὲ ἀπειροκαλία καὶ
βαναυσία, ἔλλειψις δὲ μικροπρέπεια· διαφέρουσι δ᾽
αὗται τῶν περὶ τὴν ἐλευθεριότητα, πῇ δὲ διαφέρουσιν,
7 ὕστερον ῥηθήσεται. Περὶ δὲ τιμὴν καὶ ἀτιμίαν μεσότης
μὲν μεγαλοψυχία, ὑπερβολὴ δὲ χαυνότης τις λεγομένη,
8 ἔλλειψις δὲ μικροψυχία· ὡς δ᾽ ἐλέγομεν ἔχειν πρὸς
τὴν μεγαλοπρέπειαν τὴν ἐλευθεριότητα, περὶ μικρὰ δια-
φέρουσαν, οὕτως ἔχει τις καὶ πρὸς τὴν μεγαλοψυχίαν,

Wealth on a large scale—(1) Vulgar Display, (2) Magnifi-
v. Highmindedness. 7 cence, (3) Paltriness. v. In reference to honour and dis-
honour on a grand scale—(1) Vaingloriousness, (2) High-
vi. Laudable Ambition. 8, 9 mindedness, (3) Littlemindedness. vi. In reference to the
same in ordinary matters language supplies us only with the terms 'Ambition' and 'Ambitious' on the one hand, and 'Want of Ambition' and 'Unambitious' on the other. As

1. ἄλλαι διαθέσεις] The distinction between Liberality and Magnificence, and between Highmindedness and Laudable Ambition respectively, derives its value partly from the political or social aspect in which the Virtues were regarded by Greek philosophers. Socially the difference is considerable; morally (in the proper sense of the word, *i.e.* in reference to the character of the agent), the difference, though not perhaps wholly unreal, is less important. The term διάθεσις is here used as equivalent to ἕξις, though it is sometimes distinguished from it as indicating a disposition or tendency only, in contrast with a formed habit (ἕξις), *e.g.* ἐγκράτεια is a διάθεσις related to σωφροσύνη as a ἕξις (see note I. iii. 7).

3. ἀπειροκαλία] 'bad taste;' literally 'inexperience of what is beautiful.' βαναυσία = βαυναυσία (from βαῦνος a forge and αὔω to burn), 'the practice of a mechanical art,' and hence 'vulgarity' generally. (Liddell and Scott.)

7. Translate 'As we said that Liberality was related to Magnificence, differing from it in that it is on a small scale, so also there is a certain Virtue related to Highmindedness, the latter being concerned with great honours, while the Virtue in question deals with small honours.'

περὶ τιμὴν οὖσαν μεγάλην, αὐτὴ περὶ μικρὰν οὖσα· ἔστι
γὰρ ὡς δεῖ ὀρέγεσθαι τιμῆς καὶ μᾶλλον ἢ δεῖ καὶ ἧττον,
λέγεται δ' ὁ μὲν ὑπερβάλλων ταῖς ὀρέξεσι φιλότιμος, ὁ
δ' ἐλλείπων ἀφιλότιμος, ὁ δὲ μέσος ἀνώνυμος. Ἀνώνυ-
μοι δὲ καὶ αἱ διαθέσεις, πλὴν ἡ τοῦ φιλοτίμου φιλο-
τιμία. Ὅθεν ἐπιδικάζονται οἱ ἄκροι τῆς μέσης χώρας.
Καὶ ἡμεῖς δὲ ἔστι μὲν ὅτε τὸν μέσον φιλότιμον καλοῦμεν
ἔστι δ' ὅτε ἀφιλότιμον, καὶ ἔστιν ὅτε μὲν ἐπαινοῦμεν
9 τὸν φιλότιμον, ἔστι δ' ὅτε τὸν ἀφιλότιμον. Διὰ τίνα δ'
αἰτίαν τοῦτο ποιοῦμεν, ἐν τοῖς ἑξῆς ῥηθήσεται· νῦν δὲ
περὶ τῶν λοιπῶν λέγωμεν κατὰ τὸν ὑφηγημένον τρόπον.
10 Ἔστι δὲ καὶ περὶ ὀργὴν ὑπερβολὴ καὶ ἔλλειψις καὶ
μεσότης, σχεδὸν δὲ ἀνωνύμων ὄντων αὐτῶν, τὸν μέσον
πρᾶον λέγοντες τὴν μεσότητα πραότητα καλέσομεν· τῶν
δ' ἄκρων ὁ μὲν ὑπερβάλλων ὀργίλος ἔστω, ἡ δὲ κακία
ὀργιλότης, ὁ δ' ἐλλείπων ἀόργητός τις, ἡ δ' ἔλλειψις
11 ἀοργησία. Εἰσὶ δὲ καὶ ἄλλαι τρεῖς μεσότητες, ἔχουσαι

however excess and defect are thus recognised there must
clearly be a mean state, though, in the absence of a settled
name, either of the above pairs of terms are, according to
10 circumstances, applied to it. vii. In reference to the regula- vii. Meekness.
tion of the Temper—(1) Passionateness, (2) Meekness, (3)
Impassionateness (if there be such a word to describe a
11 state which rarely exists). Three Virtues follow relating to Three Social Virtues, viz.,

5. διαθέσεις] 'The habits as well as the individual characters corresponding are nameless; (or, the abstract as well as the concrete terms are nameless)—except the term "ambition," corresponding with "ambitious".' Similarly in English we have no word 'unambition,' to correspond with 'unambitious.'

6. ἐπὶ in Composition has a reciprocal force, *e.g.* ἐπαμοιβαδίς, ἐπιμαχία (offensive and defensive alliance) (see *Suppl. Note*), etc.

10. ἐν τοῖς ἑξῆς ῥηθήσεται] See IV. iv. 4.

16. ἀόργητός τις] A sort of 'impassionate' man. 'τις' as it were apologizes for the uncouthness of the term employed: as it

μέν τινα ὁμοιότητα πρὸς ἀλλήλας, διαφέρουσαι δ' ἀλλήλων· πᾶσαι μὲν γάρ εἰσι περὶ λόγων καὶ πράξεων κοινωνίαν, διαφέρουσι δὲ ὅτι ἡ μέν ἐστι περὶ τἀληθὲς τὸ ἐν αὐτοῖς, αἱ δὲ περὶ τὸ ἡδύ· τούτου δὲ τὸ μὲν ἐν παιδιᾷ, τὸ δ' ἐν πᾶσι τοῖς κατὰ τὸν βίον. Ῥητέον οὖν καὶ περὶ τούτων, ἵνα μᾶλλον κατίδωμεν ὅτι ἐν πᾶσιν ἡ μεσότης ἐπαινετόν, τὰ δ' ἄκρα οὔτ' ὀρθὰ οὔτ' ἐπαινετὰ ἀλλὰ ψεκτά. Ἔστι μὲν οὖν καὶ τούτων τὰ πλείω ἀνώνυμα, πειρατέον δ', ὥσπερ καὶ ἐπὶ τῶν ἄλλων, αὐτοὺς ὀνοματοποιεῖν σαφηνείας ἕνεκεν καὶ τοῦ εὐπαρακολουθήτου.

12 Περὶ μὲν οὖν τὸ ἀληθὲς ὁ μὲν μέσος ἀληθής τις, καὶ ἡ μεσότης ἀλήθεια λεγέσθω, ἡ δὲ προσποίησις ἡ μὲν ἐπὶ τὸ μεῖζον ἀλαζονεία καὶ ὁ ἔχων αὐτὴν ἀλαζών, ἡ δ' ἐπὶ τὸ ἔλαττον εἰρωνεία καὶ εἴρων.

13 Περὶ δὲ τὸ ἡδὺ τὸ μὲν ἐν παιδιᾷ ὁ μὲν μέσος εὐτράπελος καὶ ἡ διάθεσις εὐτραπελία, ἡ δ' ὑπερβολὴ βωμολοχία καὶ ὁ ἔχων αὐτὴν βωμολόχος, ὁ δ' ἐλλείπων ἀγροικός τις καὶ ἡ ἕξις ἀγροικία. Περὶ δὲ τὸ λοιπὸν ἡδὺ τὸ ἐν τῷ βίῳ ὁ μὲν ὡς δεῖ ἡδὺς ὤν, φίλος, καὶ ἡ μεσότης φιλία,

our conduct *in* and *towards* Society—and here we must apologize for having to employ somewhat inadequate names

viii. Truthfulness. 12 to describe our meaning. viii. As regards Truth—(1) Boast-

ix. Geniality. 13 fulness, (2) Truthfulness, (3) Self-Depreciation. ix. As regards pleasantness in times of relaxation—(1) Buffoonery,

x. Friendliness. (2) Geniality, (3) Boorishness. x. As regards general

does elsewhere for its inadequacy, when it does not express the precise shade of meaning desired: *e.g.* χαυνότης τις in § 7, ἀληθής τις in § 12, ἀγροῖκός τις in § 13, ἀναίσθητός τις in ii. 7.

4. ἐν αὐτοῖς] *i.e.* ἐν λόγοις καὶ πράξεσιν.

14. εἰρωνεία = *dissimulatio*, *i.e.* a concealment of what you are; ἀλαζονεία = *simulatio*, *i.e.* a pretension to what you are not. εἰρωνεία is a difficult word to translate; see further note on IV. vii. 3.

19. φίλος and φιλία are not to

ὁ δ' ὑπερβάλλων, εἰ μὲν οὐδενὸς ἕνεκα, ἄρεσκος, εἰ δ' ὠφελείας τῆς αὑτοῦ, κόλαξ, ὁ δ' ἐλλείπων καὶ ἐν πᾶσιν
14 ἀηδὴς δύσερίς τις καὶ δύσκολος. Εἰσὶ δὲ καὶ ἐν τοῖς πάθεσι καὶ ἐν τοῖς περὶ τὰ πάθη μεσότητες· ἡ γὰρ αἰδὼς ἀρετὴ μὲν οὐκ ἔστιν, ἐπαινεῖται δὲ καὶ ὁ αἰδήμων. Καὶ γὰρ ἐν τούτοις ὁ μὲν λέγεται μέσος, ὁ δ' ὑπερβάλλων, ὡς ὁ καταπλὴξ, ὁ πάντα αἰδούμενος· ὁ δ' ἐλλείπων

pleasantness of demeanour—(1) Obsequiousness, degenerating into Sycophancy if it be adopted to serve our own inter-
14 ests, (2) Friendliness, (3) Churlishness. We add two conditions, which, though not so much settled *habits* as occasionally aroused *feelings*, are yet virtuous and praiseworthy as com-

Two imperfectly Virtuous states, viz.,

be translated 'friend' and 'friendship,' but 'friendly' and 'friendliness.' The character described is that of a man who naturally 'gets on' with every one he comes into contact with; one who naturally attracts every one, just as the 'churl' mentioned presently is one who naturally repels every one.

1. οὐδενὸς ἕνεκα] 'Obsequiousness' is spontaneous and natural to the character in which it is displayed, and so may be in some sense sincere. 'Flattery' is put on, and is adopted to serve a man's own interests and advancement, and therefore is necessarily insincere.

4. Sense of Shame and Indignation are not in the fullest sense Virtues, for two reasons;—(1) They are themselves occasional Feelings (πάθη) rather than permanent States (ἕξεις) in relation to the Feelings. This is more fully expressed in IV. ix. 1. A permanent State, either of Shame for our own wrong doings or of Indignation at the success of others, would be in no sense desirable. (2) Because they cannot exist unless there has been previous wrong-doing on the part of ourselves or others. Hence they are only virtuous *on this condition*, ἐξ ὑποθέσεως, as Aristotle himself expresses it in IV. ix. 7.

On the other hand two reasons are given in the text why they *are* in some sense Virtues;—(1) They are objects of praise, and this is an indication of Virtue as we have seen in the concluding words of B. I., also in I. xii. 6 and II. vi. 12 (see note). (2) The phenomena of excess, mean, and defect, are exhibited in these two cases, as well as in those already considered (καὶ γὰρ ἐν τούτοις κ.τ.λ. l. 6).

ἢ ὁ μηδὲ ὅλως ἀναίσχυντος· ὁ δὲ μέσος αἰδήμων. Νέ-
15 μεσις δὲ μεσότης φθόνου καὶ ἐπιχαιρεκακίας. Εἰσὶ δὲ περὶ λύπην καὶ ἡδονὴν τὰς ἐπὶ τοῖς συμβαίνουσι τοῖς πέλας γινομένας· ὁ μὲν γὰρ νεμεσητικὸς λυπεῖται ἐπὶ τοῖς ἀναξίως εὖ πράττουσιν, ὁ δὲ φθονερὸς ὑπερβάλλων τοῦτον ἐπὶ πᾶσι λυπεῖται, ὁ δ' ἐπιχαιρέκακος τοσοῦτον
16 ἐλλείπει τοῦ λυπεῖσθαι ὥστε καὶ χαίρειν. Ἀλλὰ περὶ μὲν τούτων καὶ ἄλλοθι καιρὸς ἔσται· περὶ δὲ δικαιο-

xi. Sense of Shame.

pared with their opposites: viz. xi. In reference to shame felt at our own conduct—(1) Excessive Bashfulness, (2) Sense of

xii. Resentment.

15 Shame, (3) Shamelessness. xii. In reference to indignation felt at the success, deserved or undeserved, of others—(1)

Finally, xiii. Justice in its several types.

16 Envy, (2) Resentment, (3) Malevolence. xiii. Finally, Justice is a word of such various meanings that we must

6. τοῦτον] viz. τὸν νεμεσητικόν.

ὁ δὲ ἐπιχαιρέκακος κ.τ.λ.] This account of ἐπιχαιρεκακία is very confused. (1) There is no real, but only a verbal, opposition between grieving at the prosperity of others (φθόνος) and rejoicing at the misfortunes of others (ἐπιχαιρεκακία). These two habits are related like those which arise from excess of confidence or defect of fear, which are not really two but one, and are called by the common name θρασύτης, as was explained in § 2. (2) The mean (νέμεσις) consisting in grieving at the prosperity of others, when it is undeserved, and the excess (φθόνος) in grieving at the prosperity of others in *all* cases, whether deserved or undeserved, —the defect *ought* to consist in never grieving at the prosperity of others in any case, but in either rejoicing at it or being indifferent to it. But in order to make any sense of the words as they stand, we must understand with χαίρειν in l. 7 ἐπὶ τοῖς κακῶς πράττουσιν or some similar words, about which nothing has been said or implied. (See *Suppl. Notes.*)

8. ἄλλοθι καιρὸς ἔσται] On referring to the end of B. IV. it will be seen that the subject of νέμεσις is not referred to in the fuller discussions which follow. Otherwise the confusion of the present passage would probably have been corrected in some way.

δικαιοσύνη is a difficult word to translate. It not only means 'justice' in the limited sense (though even this, as Aristotle shows in Bk. V., is used in two or three distinct applications),

σύνης, ἐπεὶ οὐχ ἁπλῶς λέγεται, μετὰ ταῦτα διελόμενοι περὶ ἑκατέρας ἐροῦμεν πῶς μεσότητές εἰσιν· [ὁμοίως δὲ καὶ περὶ τῶν λογικῶν ἀρετῶν].

1 VIII. Τριῶν δὲ διαθέσεων οὐσῶν, δύο μὲν κακιῶν, τῆς
μὲν καθ' ὑπερβολὴν τῆς δὲ κατ' ἔλλειψιν, μιᾶς δ' ἀρετῆς
τῆς μεσότητος, πᾶσαι πάσαις ἀντίκεινταί πως· αἱ μὲν
γὰρ ἄκραι καὶ τῇ μέσῃ καὶ ἀλλήλαις ἐναντίαι εἰσὶν, ἡ
2 δὲ μέση ταῖς ἄκραις· ὥσπερ γὰρ τὸ ἴσον πρὸς μὲν τὸ

hereafter distinguish them, and then show of each kind separately how the law of the mean is applicable to it. The discussion on Intellectual Excellence will follow after that.

CHAP. VIII.—*The nature and degrees of the opposition existing between Virtues and the Vices related to them.*

1 Excess, mean, and defect are all opposed to one another in
2 various degrees. Compared with the excess, the mean appears

The opposition of the two extremes *inter se* is greater than that of either of them to the mean.

but it has also the general sense of 'uprightness' or 'righteousness,' divested of the religious or theological savour attaching to these words. In this application, Aristotle in Bk. V. describes it as συλλήβδην πᾶσα ἀρετή, *i.e.* Virtue in the aggregate. Bk. V. is occupied with distinguishing and defining these several senses of δικαιοσύνη, and, as is promised here, showing how to each of them separately the law of the 'mean' is applicable in different ways.

2. ὁμοίως κ.τ.λ.] The words in brackets are probably interpolated by some copyist who thought it might be well to give the contents of Bk. VI., as well as those of Bks. IV. and V. The objections to them are: (1) ὁμοίως is not true; for the Intellectual Excellences are in no sense 'mean' states, and Aristotle never suggests or attempts to prove anything of the kind (see note on vi. 10). (2) Aristotle never speaks of λογικαὶ ἀρεταὶ in this sense, but always of διανοητικαὶ ἀρεταὶ, *e.g.* see I. xiii. 20, II. i. 1, etc. If we retain the words we must attach a very loose sense to ὁμοίως and translate—'similarly we shall speak about the Intellectual Excellences also:' in fact understanding ἐροῦμεν only, and not ἐροῦμεν πῶς μεσότητές εἰσιν.

CHAP. VIII.—The fact that Virtue is a *relative* and not an *absolute* mean (*i.e.* not always

ἔλαττον μεῖζον, πρὸς δὲ τὸ μεῖζον ἔλαττον, οὕτως αἱ
μέσαι ἕξεις πρὸς μὲν τὰς ἐλλείψεις ὑπερβάλλουσι, πρὸς
δὲ τὰς ὑπερβολὰς ἐλλείπουσιν, ἔν τε τοῖς πάθεσι καὶ
ταῖς πράξεσιν. Ὁ γὰρ ἀνδρεῖος πρὸς μὲν τὸν δειλὸν
θρασὺς φαίνεται, πρὸς δὲ τὸν θρασὺν δειλός· ὁμοίως δὲ
καὶ ὁ σώφρων πρὸς μὲν τὸν ἀναίσθητον ἀκόλαστος,
πρὸς δὲ τὸν ἀκόλαστον ἀναίσθητος, ὁ δ' ἐλευθέριος πρὸς
μὲν τὸν ἀνελεύθερον ἄσωτος, πρὸς δὲ τὸν ἄσωτον ἀνε-
3 λεύθερος. Διὸ καὶ ἀπωθοῦνται τὸν μέσον οἱ ἄκροι
ἑκάτερος πρὸς ἑκάτερον, καὶ καλοῦσι τὸν ἀνδρεῖον ὁ μὲν
δειλὸς θρασύν, ὁ δὲ θρασὺς δειλόν, καὶ ἐπὶ τῶν ἄλλων
4 ἀνάλογον. Οὕτω δ' ἀντικειμένων ἀλλήλοις τούτων,
πλείων ἐναντιότης ἐστὶ τοῖς ἄκροις πρὸς ἄλληλα ἢ πρὸς
τὸ μέσον· πορρωτέρω γὰρ ταῦτα ἀφέστηκεν ἀλλήλων ἢ
τοῦ μέσου, ὥσπερ τὸ μέγα τοῦ μικροῦ καὶ τὸ μικρὸν τοῦ
5 μεγάλου ἢ ἄμφω τοῦ ἴσου. Ἔτι πρὸς μὲν τὸ μέσον ἐνίοις
ἄκροις ὁμοιότης τις φαίνεται, ὡς τῇ θρασύτητι πρὸς τὴν

in defect; compared with the defect, it appears in excess.
3 A man who is in either extreme, reserving to himself the title
of the mean, applies to the true mean the name of the ex-
4 treme opposite to his own. Obviously however the opposition
between the extremes (excess and defect) is greater than that
between the mean and either of them;—partly because the
interval between them is greater in actual distance, as we
5 might say; and partly because sometimes one extreme appears

The mean is nearer sometimes to the excess, sometimes to the defect.

half-way between the extremes to which it is related) implies that it will sometimes be nearer to one extreme than the other, and hence that the degrees of its opposition to them will differ in different cases. The main results of this chapter are;—(1) There is a greater opposition between the extremes *inter se* than between either of them and the mean. (2) Sometimes the excess and sometimes the defect is more opposed to the mean. (3) The degree of this divergence may depend either upon the nature of the case or upon our own dispositions in reference to it.

ἀνδρείαν, καὶ τῇ ἀσωτίᾳ πρὸς τὴν ἐλευθεριότητα· τοῖς δὲ
ἄκροις πρὸς ἄλληλα πλείστη ἀνομοιότης. Τὰ δὲ πλεῖστον
ἀπέχοντα ἀλλήλων ἐναντία ὁρίζονται, ὥστε καὶ μᾶλλον
6 ἐναντία τὰ πλεῖον ἀπέχοντα. Πρὸς δὲ τὸ μέσον ἀντίκειται
μᾶλλον ἐφ' ὧν μὲν ἡ ἔλλειψις, ἐφ' ὧν δὲ ἡ ὑπερβολή,
οἷον ἀνδρείᾳ μὲν οὐχ ἡ θρασύτης ὑπερβολὴ οὖσα, ἀλλ'
ἡ δειλία ἔλλειψις οὖσα, τῇ δὲ σωφροσύνῃ οὐχ ἡ ἀναι-
σθησία ἔνδεια οὖσα, ἀλλ' ἡ ἀκολασία ὑπερβολὴ οὖσα.
7 Διὰ δύο δ' αἰτίας τοῦτο συμβαίνει, μίαν μὲν τὴν ἐξ
αὐτοῦ τοῦ πράγματος· τῷ γὰρ ἐγγύτερον εἶναι καὶ
ὁμοιότερον τὸ ἕτερον ἄκρον τῷ μέσῳ, οὐ τοῦτο ἀλλὰ
τοὐναντίον ἀντιτίθεμεν μᾶλλον, οἷον ἐπεὶ ὁμοιότερον
εἶναι δοκεῖ τῇ ἀνδρείᾳ ἡ θρασύτης καὶ ἐγγύτερον, ἀνο-

to have a sort of affinity with the mean, whereas extremes *inter se* are radically opposed. Thus Rashness (excess) is more akin to Courage than Cowardice (defect) is, and so on.
6 This natural affinity to the mean of sometimes the excess and
7 sometimes the defect, depends on two causes:—i. *The nature of things.*—Some faults would be universally allowed to be

This may depend on two causes.

i. The nature of things.

2. τὰ δὲ πλεῖστον ἀπέχοντα κ.τ.λ.] 'Things which differ most widely are defined to be contraries.' It will be understood that we are speaking of things falling under the same class (*i.e.* πλεῖστον ἀπέχοντα ἐν τῷ αὐτῷ γένει as Aristotle elsewhere more fully expresses it). All opposition or contrariety implies some degree of similarity. Otherwise Rashness for example might be thought to differ more from (say) Meanness, than from Cowardice.

9. The twofold grounds of opposition between Extremes and the Mean explained in §§ 7 and 8 suggest the first two of the practical rules for attaining the mean given in the next Chapter.

10. Practical applications of this principle will be found in the discussion of Liberality (IV. i. 31, 44), Highmindedness (IV. iii. 37), and Meekness (IV. v. 12). In the first two cases, as in that of Courage, the defect is more opposed than the excess to the mean. In the case of Meekness, as in that of Temperance, it is the reverse. (See *Supplementary Note.*)

ἀνομοιότερον δ' ἡ δειλία, ταύτην μᾶλλον ἀντιτίθεμεν· τὰ γὰρ ἀπέχοντα πλεῖον τοῦ μέσου ἐναντιώτερα δοκεῖ εἶναι.
8 Μία μὲν οὖν αἰτία αὕτη, ἐξ αὐτοῦ τοῦ πράγματος, ἑτέρα δὲ ἐξ ἡμῶν αὐτῶν· πρὸς ἃ γὰρ αὐτοὶ μᾶλλον πεφύκαμέν πως, ταῦτα μᾶλλον ἐναντία τῷ μέσῳ φαίνεται. Οἷον αὐτοὶ μᾶλλον πεφύκαμεν πρὸς τὰς ἡδονάς, διὸ εὐκατάφοροί ἐσμεν μᾶλλον πρὸς ἀκολασίαν ἢ πρὸς κοσμιότητα. Ταῦτ' οὖν μᾶλλον ἐναντία λέγομεν, πρὸς ἃ ἡ ἐπίδοσις μᾶλλον γίνεται· καὶ διὰ τοῦτο ἡ ἀκολασία ὑπερβολὴ οὖσα ἐναντιωτέρα ἐστὶ τῇ σωφροσύνῃ.
1 IX. Ὅτι μὲν οὖν ἐστὶν ἡ ἀρετὴ ἡ ἠθικὴ μεσότης, καὶ

'errors on the right side,' and therefore nearer the mean.

ii. Our own dispositions and inclinations.

8 ii. *Our own dispositions.*—If our natural bent or inclination is to one extreme rather than the other, then that extreme appears more opposed to the mean than the other. Its indulgence would carry us further from the Virtuous mean than would the practice of the opposite extreme.

CHAP. IX.—*The difficulty of Virtue—Practical rules for attaining the Virtuous Mean—The liberty of private judgment in points of detail.*

Difficulty of Virtue.

1 The various points now established concerning Virtue

4. ἐξ ἡμῶν αὐτῶν] This follows because virtue is a relative mean (ἐν μεσότητι τῇ πρὸς ἡμᾶς). Theories of the most absolute morality (see Introd. p. xxi.) must allow some variation in its application to practical details. Within certain limits what is right for one man is not necessarily right for another. The fallacy of Casuistry is that it ignores the considerations pointed out in this section. Conversely it might be said that theories which make moral distinctions purely relative err in overlooking the considerations of § 7.

9. ἐπίδοσις] lit. 'increase' or 'addition,' hence, probably, 'bias' or 'inclination.'

CHAP. IX.—Another result from the mean in Virtue being relative and dependent on circumstances, and also from the

πῶς, καὶ ὅτι μεσότης δύο κακιῶν, τῆς μὲν καθ' ὑπερβο-
λὴν τῆς δὲ κατ' ἔλλειψιν, καὶ ὅτι τοιαύτη ἐστὶ διὰ τὸ
στοχαστικὴ τοῦ μέσου εἶναι τοῦ ἐν τοῖς πάθεσι καὶ ταῖς
2 πράξεσιν, ἱκανῶς εἴρηται. Διὸ καὶ ἔργον ἐστὶ σπου-
δαῖον εἶναι· ἐν ἑκάστῳ γὰρ τὸ μέσον λαβεῖν ἔργον, οἷον
κύκλου τὸ μέσον οὐ παντὸς ἀλλὰ τοῦ εἰδότος. Οὕτω δὲ
καὶ τὸ μὲν ὀργισθῆναι παντὸς καὶ ῥᾴδιον, καὶ τὸ δοῦναι
ἀργύριον καὶ δαπανῆσαι· τὸ δ' ᾧ καὶ ὅσον καὶ ὅτε καὶ
οὗ ἕνεκα καὶ ὥς, οὐκέτι παντὸς οὐδὲ ῥᾴδιον· διόπερ τὸ
3 εὖ καὶ σπάνιον καὶ ἐπαινετὸν καὶ καλόν. Διὸ δεῖ τὸν
στοχαζόμενον τοῦ μέσου πρῶτον μὲν ἀποχωρεῖν τοῦ
μᾶλλον ἐναντίου, καθάπερ καὶ ἡ Καλυψὼ παραινεῖ

> τούτου μὲν καπνοῦ καὶ κύματος ἐκτὸς ἔεργε
> νῆα·

τῶν γὰρ ἄκρων τὸ μέν ἐστιν ἁμαρτωλότερον, τὸ δ' ἧτ-
4 τον· ἐπεὶ οὖν τοῦ μέσου τυχεῖν ἄκρως χαλεπόν, κατὰ
τὸν δεύτερόν, φασι, πλοῦν τὰ ἐλάχιστα ληπτέον τῶν
κακῶν· τοῦτο δ' ἔσται μάλιστα τοῦτον τὸν τρόπον ὃν

2 plainly show that it is difficult to become Virtuous, and a
complicated matter to attain the accurate mean. Three
3 practical rules are obvious. i. *Avoid the extreme most*
4 *opposed to the mean in the nature of things.* If we must
err, it is at any rate best to choose the lesser of two evils.

Three Rules for attaining the mean. Rule i.

varying degrees of opposition between it and its related Vices explained in the last Chapter, is that it is hard to hit the exact mean in all cases. Hence (1) practical rules for this purpose are suggested, and (2) the right of individual liberty of action within certain moderate limits is maintained.

12. Καλυψὼ] There is a slip of memory here. Advice similar to this was given to Ulysses by Circe (*Od.* xii. 108). The actual words, however, occur in the subsequent admonition of Ulysses to his pilot (*Od.* xii. 219).

17. *δεύτερος πλοῦς* corresponds to our expression 'a second-best course,' or a '*pis-aller*.'

λέγομεν. Σκοπεῖν δὲ δεῖ πρὸς ἃ καὶ αὐτοὶ εὐκατάφοροί
5 ἐσμεν· ἄλλοι γὰρ πρὸς ἄλλα πεφύκαμεν. Τοῦτο δ'
ἔσται γνώριμον ἐκ τῆς ἡδονῆς καὶ τῆς λύπης τῆς γινο-
μένης περὶ ἡμᾶς. Εἰς τοὐναντίον δ' ἑαυτοὺς ἀφέλκειν
δεῖ· πολὺ γὰρ ἀπαγαγόντες τοῦ ἁμαρτάνειν εἰς τὸ μέσον
ἥξομεν, ὅπερ οἱ τὰ διεστραμμένα τῶν ξύλων ὀρθοῦντες
6 ποιοῦσιν. Ἐν παντὶ δὲ μάλιστα φυλακτέον τὸ ἡδὺ καὶ
τὴν ἡδονήν· οὐ γὰρ ἀδέκαστοι κρίνομεν αὐτήν. Ὅπερ
οὖν οἱ δημογέροντες ἔπαθον πρὸς τὴν Ἑλένην, τοῦτο
δεῖ παθεῖν καὶ ἡμᾶς πρὸς τὴν ἡδονήν, καὶ ἐν πᾶσι τὴν
ἐκείνων ἐπιλέγειν φωνήν· οὕτω γὰρ αὐτὴν ἀποπεμπό-

Rule ii. ii. *Avoid the extreme to which our natural inclination*
5 *tends.* The pleasure we derive from actions affords a simple
Rule iii. 6 test of this inclination. iii. *Beware above all of allowing the*
pleasure of actions to bias our judgment respecting them.

1. αὐτοὶ] Thus for example although as a general rule the Virtue of Courage would be gained rather by acts of Rashness than by acts of Cowardice, yet there may be fearless and hot-brained persons who would arrive at it best by acts of what would seem to them cowardice. Again, in order to arrive at the just mean in the way of spending money (ἐλευθεριότης) this rule would probably direct a Scotchman to aim at prodigality (ἀσωτία), but an Irishman to practise what he would consider sordidness (ἀνελευθερία).

6. διεστραμμένα κ.τ.λ.] Straightening a roll of paper by rolling it the opposite way would be another familiar illustration.

8. ἀδέκαστοι] from δεκάζω (and this from δεκὰς, a body of ten), =decuriare, to tamper with the 'decuriæ,' and so generally 'to bribe.' ἀδέκαστοι therefore = 'impartial,' literally 'unbribed.'

9. δημογέροντες] The reference is to *Il.* iii. 158:—

"On Ilion's towers
Sat the sage chiefs and councillors of Troy.
Helen they saw, as to the tower she came;
And, 'tis no marvel, one to other said,
The valiant Trojans and well-greavèd Greeks
For beauty such as this should long endure
The toils of war; for goddess-like she seems;
And yet, despite her beauty, let her go,
Nor bring on us and on our sons a curse."—*Lord Derby's Translation.*

Similarly, says Aristotle, we must dismiss pleasure from our consideration, while we are deliberating, else unbiassed judgment will be out of the question.

7 μενοι ἧττον ἁμαρτησόμεθα. Ταῦτ' οὖν ποιοῦντες, ὡς ἐν
κεφαλαίῳ εἰπεῖν, μάλιστα δυνησόμεθα τοῦ μέσου τυγ-
χάνειν. Χαλεπὸν δ' ἴσως τοῦτο, καὶ μάλιστ' ἐν τοῖς
καθ' ἕκαστον· οὐ γὰρ ῥᾴδιον διορίσαι πῶς καὶ τίσι καὶ
ἐπὶ ποίοις καὶ πόσον χρόνον ὀργιστέον· καὶ γὰρ ἡμεῖς
ὁτὲ μὲν τοὺς ἐλλείποντας ἐπαινοῦμεν καὶ πρᾴους φαμέν,
ὁτὲ δὲ τοὺς χαλεπαίνοντας ἀνδρώδεις ἀποκαλοῦμεν.
8 τοὺς ὁ μὲν μικρὸν (τοῦ εὖ) παρεκβαίνων οὐ ψέγεται,
οὔτ' ἐπὶ τὸ μᾶλλον οὔτ' τοὺς τὸ ἧττον· ὁ δὲ πλέον· οὗτος
γὰρ οὐ λανθάνει. Ὁ δὲ μεχρι τίνος καὶ ἐπὶ πόσον ψεκ-
τος οὐ ῥᾴδιον τῷ λόγῳ αφορισαι· οὐδὲ γὰρ ἄλλο οὐδὲν
τῶν αἰσθητῶν· τὰ δὲ τοιαῦτα ἐν τοῖς καθ' ἕκαστα, καὶ
ἐν τῇ αἰσθήσει ἡ κρίσις. Τὸ μὲν ἄρα τοσοῦτο δῆλον
9 ὅτι ἡ μέση ἕξις ἐν πᾶσιν ἐπαινετὴ, ἀποκλίνειν δὲ δεῖ
ὁτὲ μὲν ἐπὶ τὴν ὑπερβολὴν, ὁτὲ δ' ἐπὶ τὴν ἔλλειψιν·
οὕτω γὰρ ῥᾷστα τοῦ μέσου καὶ τοῦ εὖ τευξόμεθα.

Slight variations must still be left to individual judgment.

7 The observance of such practical rules will enable us, roughly
8 speaking, to attain the Virtuous mean. And, after all, small
deviations from the ideal mean are not important, nor is it
easy to say when they become so. In such matters of detail
much must be left to the decision of individual judgment.
9 Indeed the surest way of attaining the mean in practice is to
allow such liberty.

4. What follows is another illustration of the often repeated caution in Bk. I., that it is neither possible nor desirable to reduce Morals to a rigid or mathematical precision, for 'Virtue itself turns Vice, being *misapplied*' (Shakespeare). See esp. § 9 just below ἀποκλίνειν δὲ δεῖ κ.τ.λ.

13. *αἴσθησις* has no technical meaning here, such as Moral Sense. It resembles rather the popular use of the word in English, as when we say 'That must be left to each man's own "sense" to decide.' See further note on IV. v. 13.

14. Observe the word δεῖ. Though the mean is always in theory the best, yet in order to attain it practically, it sometimes becomes a duty (δεῖ) to aim at something in excess or defect of it. See viii. 8 (note), and § 5 of this Chapter.

THE CATALOGUE OF VIRTUES AND VICES REFERRED TO IN B. II. c. vii.

Indifferent subject-matter neither good nor bad in itself.	Excess. (Vice).	Mean. (Virtue).	Defect. (Vice).	Remarks.
i. περὶ θάῤῥη καὶ φόβους . .	θρασύτης	ἄνδρεια	δειλότης	In regard to θαῤῥη only.
	δειλότης	ἄνδρεια	(ἀνώνυμος)	In regard to φόβοι only.
ii. περὶ ἡδονὴν (καὶ λυπὴν) .	ἀκολασία	σωφροσύνη	ἀναισθησία	In regard to ἡδονὴ only.
iii. περὶ χρημάτων δόσιν καὶ λῆψιν	ἀσωτία	ἐλευθεριότης	ἀνελευθερία	In regard to δόσις only.
	ἀνελευθερία	ἐλευθεριότης	ἀσωτία	In regard to λῆψις only.
iv. περὶ χρήματα μεγάλα . .	ἀπειροκαλία καὶ βαναυσία	μεγαλοπρέπεια	μικροπρέπεια	In regard to δόσις only.
v. περὶ τιμὴν (καὶ ἀτιμίαν) .	χαυνότης	μεγαλοψυχία	μικροψυχία	In regard to τιμὴ only.
vi. περὶ τιμὴν μικρὰν . .	φιλοτιμία	(ἀνώνυμος)	ἀφιλοτιμία	Also in regard to τιμὴ only.
vii. περὶ ὀργὴν	ὀργιλότης	πραότης	ἀοργησία	
viii. περὶ τὸ αληθὲς . . .	ἀλαζονεία	ἀλήθεια	εἰρωνεία	viii. ix. x. are grouped as social virtues—περὶ λόγων καὶ πράξεων κοινωνίαν.
ix. περὶ τὸ ἡδὺ τὸ ἐν παιδίᾳ .	βωμολοχία	εὐτραπελία	ἀγροικία	
x. περὶ τὸ ἡδὺ τὸ ἐν τῷ βίῳ .	ἄρεσκος κόλαξ	φίλος (φιλία)	δύσερις καὶ δύσκολος	In the case of x. the names of the excess and defect are given only in the adjectival form. The former is ἄρεσκος, if his conduct be disinterested; κόλαξ, if it arise from interested motives.
(Supplementary.)				
xi.	κατάπληξ (ὁ πάντα αἰδούμενος)	αἰδήμων	ἀναίσχυντος	Occasional feelings rather than settled habits.
xii.	φθονερὸς	νεμεσητικὸς	ἐπιχαιρέκακος	

The principle of Classification in the Catalogue on the opposite page appears to be (for Aristotle never explicitly states it) the *degree of relationship to society* implied by the different Virtues : a natural principle in a treatise which regards Ethics as a branch of the Science of Social Life (πολιτική τις, I. ii. 8). From this point of view the Catalogue breaks up into five divisions :—

I. (i and ii) Courage and Temperance are Virtues bearing no *necessary* relation to society. They might be practised on a desert island. They belong to the lowest part of our nature, which we have in common with the brutes, who are incapable of Society. (In III. x. 1 Aristotle hints that this is his reason for treating of these two Virtues first.)

II. iii—vi) These four Virtues can only be exercised in a society of some kind, and yet they belong rather to ourselves and to our personal character than to our behaviour towards society. This is so especially from Aristotle's point of view, in which Benevolence and such feelings are scarcely, if at all, recognised. See notes on IV. i. 27, IV. iii. 24, etc. Hence the *personal* element still predominates.

III. (vii) The regulation of the Temper forms a sort of connecting link with the purely social virtues which follow. The personal and social elements in this case are nearly balanced.

IV. (viii—x) Three Social Virtues which derive their whole force and meaning from society, and relate simply to our conduct *in* and *towards* society. The *social* element now preponderates over the *personal.*

V. (xi—xii) Supplementary. Two virtuous states which (as is explained in the text) are not in the fullest sense Virtues, but yet under certain circumstances are commended.

III.

1 I. Τῆς ἀρετῆς δὴ περὶ πάθη τε καὶ πράξεις οὔσης, καὶ ἐπὶ μὲν τοῖς ἑκουσίοις ἐπαίνων καὶ ψόγων γινομένων,

CHAP. I.—*Voluntary, Involuntary, Mixed and Non-Voluntary Actions distinguished and discussed.*

1 The discussion of the difference between Voluntary and Involuntary actions is important (1) in reference to the

Recalling the Definition of Virtue in II. vi. 17 (*ἕξις προαιρετικὴ ἐν μεσότητι οὖσα τῇ πρὸς ἡμᾶς ὡρισμένῃ λόγῳ καὶ ὡς ἂν ὁ φρόνιμος ὁρίσειεν*), we shall obtain the clue to the plan of what follows to the end of Bk. VI., the whole of which portion of the treatise consists of the illustration of this Definition in detail.

(1) *ἕξις*—This was sufficiently explained in II. v.

(2) *προαιρετικὴ*—This has been rather assumed than proved as yet (see II. iv. 3 and v. 4, etc.). Consequently the nature of *προαίρεσις* is now discussed at length in its relation to Moral action, ch. i—v.

(3) *ἐν μεσότητι οὖσα τῇ πρὸς ἡμᾶς*—This point is next proved of each of the Virtues in the list given in II. vii. in detail, from III. vi. to end of IV., and of *δικαιοσύνη* in each of its various senses (for which see II. vii. 16) in Bk. V.

(4) *ὡρισμένῃ . . . ὁρίσειεν*—The intellectual powers by which the variable relative mean is to be determined form the subject of Bk. VI., and this completes the discussion of the various terms in the Definition of Virtue.

The discussion of *προαίρεσις* or Deliberate Choice is approached by determining first the more comprehensive notion of voluntariness; since all that is deliberately chosen must of course be Voluntary, though not *vice versâ* (see ii. 16). The contents of the

ἐπὶ δὲ τοῖς ἀκουσίοις συγγνώμης, ἐνίοτε δὲ καὶ ἐλέου,
τὸ ἑκούσιον καὶ ἀκούσιον ἀναγκαῖον ἴσως διορίσαι τοῖς
περὶ ἀρετῆς ἐπισκοποῦσι, χρήσιμον δὲ καὶ τοῖς νομο-
2 θετοῦσι πρός τε τὰς τιμὰς καὶ τὰς κολάσεις. Δοκεῖ δὲ
3 ἀκούσια εἶναι τὰ βίᾳ ἢ δι' ἄγνοιαν γινόμενα. Βίαιον δὲ
οὗ ἡ ἀρχὴ ἔξωθεν, τοιαύτη οὖσα ἐν ᾗ μηδὲν συμβάλ-
λεται ὁ πράττων ἢ ὁ πάσχων, οἷον εἰ πνεῦμα κομίσαι
4 ποι ἢ ἄνθρωποι κύριοι ὄντες. Ὅσα δὲ διὰ φόβον μει-
ζόνων κακῶν πράττεται ἢ διὰ καλόν τι, οἷον εἰ τύραννος

verdict we pronounce upon them, whether it be one of praise,
blame, pardon, or pity; and (2) from the social or political
2 point of view, to which we have often referred. Briefly then,
Involuntary acts are those done *under compulsion* or *through*
3 *ignorance*. We will speak of these in order.

Involuntary acts defined as acts due to compulsion or ignorance.

i. Compulsion occurs when our actions are entirely determined
by some external cause, such as a storm or the superior strength
5 of other men. There are also cases of *Moral* compulsion, *i.e.*
when we do something in itself undesirable under the fear of

i. Involuntary acts from compulsion. (§§ 3—12). This may be Physical or Moral. The latter gives rise to Mixed Acts.

first five Chapters are briefly as follows:—

i. A general distinction between Voluntary and Involuntary Actions, together with the intermediate classes of 'Mixed' (if the *compulsion* [βία] is incomplete), and 'Non-Voluntary' (if the *ignorance* [ἄγνοια] is incomplete).

ii. Deliberate Choice is compounded of an element of impulse and an element of judgment.

iii. The relation of Deliberate Choice to Deliberation (βούλευσις), *i.e.* to the element of *judgment* in ch. ii.

iv. Its relation to Desire or Wish (βούλησις), which it presupposes, *i.e.* to the element of *impulse* in ch. ii.

v. A digression to refute the view held by Plato and others that Vice is involuntary, while Virtue is voluntary.

3. Observe the frequent recurrence to the social point of view indicated at the commencement in I. ii. 8, μέθοδος πολιτική τις οὖσα, and see Introd. p. xxxi.

4. κόλασις is punishment with a view to reformation (see note on v. 7), and so is naturally put in contrast with τιμή, reward for the sake of encouragement.

6. ἀρχή] the originating or

προστάττοι αἰσχρόν τι πρᾶξαι κύριος ὢν γονέων καὶ
τέκνων, καὶ πράξαντος μὲν σώζοιντο, μὴ πράξαντος δ'
ἀποθνήσκοιεν, ἀμφισβήτησιν ἔχει πότερον ἀκούσιά ἐστιν
5 ἢ ἑκούσια. Τοιοῦτον δέ τι συμβαίνει καὶ περὶ τὰς ἐν
τοῖς χειμῶσιν ἐκβολάς· ἁπλῶς μὲν γὰρ οὐδεὶς ἀπο-
βάλλεται ἑκών, ἐπὶ σωτηρίᾳ ὁ αυτοῦ καὶ τῶν λοιπῶν
6 ἅπαντες οἱ νοῦν ἔχοντες. Μικταὶ μὲν οὖν εἰσὶν αἱ τοι-
αῦται πράξεις, ἐοίκασι δὲ μᾶλλον ἑκουσίοις· αἱρεταὶ
γάρ εἰσι τότε ὅτε πράττονται, τὸ δὲ τέλος τῆς πράξεως
κατὰ τὸν καιρόν ἐστιν· καὶ τὸ ἑκούσιον δὴ καὶ τὸ ἀκού-
σιον, ὅτε πράττει, λεκτέον. Πράττει δὲ ἑκών· καὶ γὰρ
ἡ ἀρχὴ τοῦ κινεῖν τὰ ὀργανικὰ μέρη ἐν ταῖς τοιαύταις
πράξεσιν ἐν αὐτῷ ἐστίν· ὧν δ' ἐν αὐτῷ ἡ ἀρχὴ, ἐπ'
αὐτῷ καὶ τὸ πράττειν καὶ μή. Ἑκούσια δὴ τὰ τοιαῦτα,
ἁπλῶς δ' ἴσως ἀκούσια· οὐδεὶς γὰρ ἂν ἕλοιτο καθ' αὑτὸ

6 some greater evil, or the hope of some greater good. But such actions are, so to speak, mixed, being neither purely voluntary nor purely involuntary. They are rather voluntary however, (1) because they are deliberately chosen *at the moment of performance;* and (2) because it is always physi-

Such mixed acts are rather voluntary than involuntary.

motive cause of the action: speaking technically, the Efficient Cause (see Glossary p. xlvii.).

9. τὸ δὲ τέλος κ.τ.λ.] The object or motive of an act is to be determined in reference to the time of its performance; so (δὴ) whether the action were voluntary or involuntary is to be determined in reference to the moment of action. If a conscious motive determined the action *then*, the action itself must have been voluntary, and that fact cannot be altered by regrets or afterthoughts when the danger is past. That such is the case in the actions we are considering is evident, because the movement of the limbs at least is perfectly free at the moment of action (see l. 12).

12. ὀργανικὰ μέρη] the limbs which are instrumental in the performance of the act.

15. ἁπλῶς] *i.e.* simply or abstractedly, *i.e.* considered apart from surrounding circumstances.

7 τῶν τοιούτων οὐδέν. Ἐπὶ ταῖς πράξεσι δὲ ταῖς τοιαύ-
ταις ἐνίοτε καὶ ἐπαινοῦνται, ὅταν αἰσχρόν τι ἢ λυπηρὸν
ὑπομένωσιν ἀντὶ μεγάλων καὶ καλῶν· ἂν δ᾽ ἀνάπαλιν,
ψέγονται· τὰ γὰρ αἴσχισθ᾽ ὑπομεῖναι ἐπὶ μηδενὶ καλῷ
ἢ μετρίῳ φαύλου. Ἐπ᾽ ἐνίοις δ᾽ ἔπαινος μὲν οὐ γίνεται,
συγγνώμη δ᾽, ὅταν διὰ τοιαῦτα πράξῃ τις ἃ μὴ δεῖ, ἃ
τὴν ἀνθρωπίνην φύσιν ὑπερτείνει καὶ μηδεὶς ἂν ὑπομεῖ-
8 ναι. Ἔνια δ᾽ ἴσως οὐκ ἔστιν ἀναγκασθῆναι, ἀλλὰ
μᾶλλον ἀποθανετέον παθόντι τὰ δεινότατα· καὶ γὰρ τὸν
Εὐριπίδου Ἀλκμαίωνα γελοῖα φαίνεται τὰ ἀναγκάσαντα
9 μητροκτονῆσαι. Ἔστι δὲ χαλεπὸν ἐνίοτε διακρῖναι ποῖον
ἀντὶ ποίου αἱρετέον καὶ τί ἀντὶ τίνος ὑπομενετέον, ἔτι
δὲ χαλεπώτερον ἐμμεῖναι τοῖς γνωσθεῖσιν· ὡς γὰρ ἐπὶ
τὸ πολύ ἐστι τὰ μὲν προσδοκωμενα λυπηρά, ἃ δ᾽ ἀναγ-
κάζονται αἰσχρά, ὅθεν ἔπαινοι καὶ ψόγοι γίνονται περὶ

7, 8 cally in our power to abstain from them. Their *moral*
character is various. We praise, blame, or make allowance
9 for them, according to circumstances; but it is impossible to

and their moral character varies with circumstances.

1. Regarded in their moral aspect these mixed actions fall into three classes. (Note, it is due to their *mixed* character, and so far as they have an element of *voluntariness* about them, that they admit of a moral aspect at all.)

(1) *Praise* is accorded, when something painful or humiliating (αἰσχρὸν) is endured from a noble motive, *e.g.* the case of martyrdom, and the legends of Scævola, Regulus, Lady Godiva, etc.

(2) *Blame*, when shame or disgrace is accepted without ade-

This is explained by ἔχουσαν ἰσχὺν in § 11 above.

13. νομοθετικὸς γενόμενος. Legislation is naturally the highest branch of πολιτική. See § 20, *fin.* of this chapter. At the very outset (in I. ii. 8) Aristotle described Ethics as πολιτική τις, and this concluding chapter brings out the connexion still more

aspect these mixed actions fall into three classes. (Note, it is due to their *mixed* character, and so far as they have an element of *voluntariness* about them, that they admit of a moral aspect at their *mixed* character.

10 τοὺς ἀναγκασθέντας ἢ μή. Τὰ δὴ ποῖα φατέον βίαια; Ἢ ἁπλῶς μέν, ὁπότ' ἂν ἡ αἰτία ἐν τοῖς ἐκτὸς ᾖ καὶ ὁ πράττων μηδὲν συμβάλληται; Ἃ δὲ καθ' αὑτὰ μὲν ἀκούσιά ἐστι, νῦν δὲ καὶ ἀντὶ τῶνδε αἱρετά, καὶ ἡ ἀρχὴ ἐν τῷ πράττοντι, καθ' αὑτὰ μὲν ἀκούσιά ἐστι, νῦν δὲ καὶ ἀντὶ τῶνδε ἑκούσια. Μᾶλλον δ' ἔοικεν ἑκουσίοις· αἱ γὰρ πράξεις ἐν τοῖς καθ' ἕκαστα, ταῦτα δ' ἑκούσια. Ποῖα δ' ἀντὶ ποίων αἱρετέον, οὐ ῥᾴδιον ἀποδοῦναι· πολ-
11 λαὶ γὰρ διαφοραί εἰσιν ἐν τοῖς καθ' ἕκαστα. Εἰ δέ τις τὰ ἡδέα καὶ τὰ καλὰ φαίη βίαια εἶναι (ἀναγκάζειν γὰρ ἔξω ὄντα), πάντα ἂν εἴη οὕτω βίαια· τούτων γὰρ χάριν πάντες πάντα πράττουσιν. Καὶ οἱ μὲν βίᾳ καὶ ἄκοντες λυπηρῶς, οἱ δὲ διὰ τὸ ἡδὺ καὶ καλὸν μεθ' ἡδονῆς. Γελοῖον δὴ τὸ αἰτιᾶσθαι τὰ ἐκτός, ἀλλὰ μὴ αὑτὸν εὐθή-

10 lay down any general rules on such a subject. We reserve then the term Involuntary for cases of physical compulsion.

The violent pleasure of actions is in no case to be considered as a source of compulsion which can excuse them.

11 Under no circumstances, however, must the violent desire for what is pleasurable or honourable be regarded as causing such compulsion as would make an act involuntary, for (1) This would make all our actions compulsory, and so would prove too much; (2) Such actions are pleasurable, while compulsion is painful. The fault really rests with those who allow themselves to be so easily 'compelled,' who wish to escape the responsibility of their bad actions and yet retain

10. No emphasis is to be laid on *τὰ καλὰ* here, because *practically*, no one does argue against the voluntariness of noble acts on the ground that the intense pleasure to be derived from them forces us on. (This is clear from the concluding words of this ch., and also from ch. v.) *Logically*, however, the higher pleasure of *τὸ καλὸν* and the lower pleasure of *τὸ ἡδὺ* stand on the same footing, so far as they affect the voluntariness or involuntariness of actions. Indeed, as Ar. argued in II. iii. 7 (fin.), *τὸ καλὸν* as a motive for action is in some sense included under *τὸ ἡδύ*. This reference also illustrates what follows, *τούτων γὰρ χάριν κ.τ.λ.*

ρατον ὄντα ὑπὸ τῶν τοιούτων, καὶ τῶν μὲν καλῶν ἑαυτὸν,
12 τῶν δ' αἰσχρῶν τὰ ἡδέα. Ἔοικε δὴ τὸ βίαιον εἶναι οὗ
ἔξωθεν ἡ ἀρχὴ, μηδὲν συμβαλλομένου τοῦ βιασθέντος.
13 Τὸ δὲ δι' ἄγνοιαν οὐχ ἑκούσιον μὲν ἅπαν ἐστὶν, ἀκου-
σιον δὲ τὸ ἐπίλυπον καὶ ἐν μεταμελείᾳ· ὁ γὰρ δι' ἄγνοιαν
πράξας ὁτιοῦν, μηδὲν δὲ δυσχεραίνων ἐπὶ τῇ πράξει,
ἑκὼν μὲν οὐ πέπραχεν, ὅ γε μὴ ᾔδει, οὐδ' αὖ ἄκων, μὴ
λυπούμενός γε. Τοῦ δὴ δι' ἄγνοιαν ὁ μὲν ἐν μεταμελείᾳ
ἄκων δοκεῖ, ὁ δὲ μὴ μεταμελόμενος, ἐπεὶ ἕτερος, ἔστω
οὐχ ἑκών· ἐπεὶ γὰρ διαφέρει, βέλτιον ὄνομα ἔχειν ἴδιον.
14 Ἕτερον δ' ἔοικε καὶ τὸ δι' ἄγνοιαν πράττειν τοῦ ἀγνο-

12 credit for their good ones. We therefore define a compulsory act to be one caused by some external force to which the agent himself contributes nothing.

ii. Involuntary acts through ignorance. (§§ 13–19). Two conditions are required. 1. Subsequent regret. 2. Ignorance must be of facts, not of principles.

13 ii. The other cause of involuntary actions was said to be *ignorance.* This statement must be guarded by two conditions:—(1) First there must be *subsequent sorrow* for the act done in ignorance: else it cannot be considered as really involuntary. Still as we cannot exactly say that it was voluntary, we shall for convenience sake describe such actions
14, 15 as *non-voluntary.* (2) Ignorance must not extend to the

5. ἐπίλυπον] Compare Jean Paul, 'Joyful remembrances of wrong actions are their half repetitions, as repentant remembrances of good ones are their half abolitions.'

10. As another illustration of the difference between involuntary and non-voluntary, Aristotle elsewhere states that the action of the heart is involuntary, that of respiration non-voluntary: the former is entirely beyond our control, the latter not so.

11. Observe that the expressions, ἄγνοια τοῦ συμφέροντος, ἡ καθόλου ἄγνοια, ἄγνοια ἐν τῇ προαιρέσει, ἀγνοοῦντα ποιεῖν, are all equivalent, and are opposed to ἡ καθ' ἕκαστα ἄγνοια and to δι' ἄγνοιαν ποιεῖν. The former is ignorance in the major premiss, or the general principle; the latter ignorance in the minor premiss, or the particular application of the general principle. The drift of the passage seems to be to show that ignorance does not make an action involuntary unless the ignorance itself is in-

οὕτω ποιεῖν· ὁ γὰρ μεθύων ἢ ὀργιζόμενος οὐ δοκεῖ δι' ἄγνοιαν πράττειν, ἀλλὰ διά τι τῶν εἰρημένων, οὐκ εἰδὼς δὲ ἀλλ' ἀγνοῶν. Ἀγνοεῖ μὲν οὖν πᾶς ὁ μοχθηρὸς ἃ δεῖ πράττειν καὶ ὧν ἀφεκτέον, καὶ διὰ τὴν τοιαύτην ἁμαρτίαν ἄδικοι καὶ ὅλως κακοὶ γίνονται. Τὸ δ' ἀκούσιον βούλεται λέγεσθαι οὐκ εἴ τις ἀγνοεῖ τὸ συμφέρον· οὐ γὰρ ἡ ἐν τῇ προαιρέσει ἄγνοια αἰτία τοῦ ἀκουσίου ἀλλὰ τῆς μοχθηρίας, οὐδ' ἡ καθόλου (ψέγονται γὰρ διά γε ταύτην) ἀλλ' ἡ καθ' ἕκαστα, ἐν οἷς καὶ περὶ ἃ ἡ πρᾶξις· ἐν τούτοις γὰρ καὶ ἔλεος καὶ συγγνώμη· ὁ γὰρ τούτων τι ἀγνοῶν
16 ἀκουσίως πράττει. Ἴσως οὖν οὐ χεῖρον διορίσαι αὐτά, τίνα καὶ πόσα ἐστί, τίς τε δὴ καὶ τί καὶ περὶ τί ἢ ἐν τίνι πράττει, ἐνίοτε δὲ καὶ τίνι, οἷον ὀργάνῳ, καὶ ἕνεκα τίνος,

principles of conduct, but only to the *details*, or *acts:* else a drunkard or a passionate man, or indeed any one who does wrong, might plead ignorance in some sense, and hence involuntariness. Therefore, for the sake of distinction again, we shall say that one who acts in ignorance of the general principles of conduct, or of what is befitting, or in ignorance affecting the deliberate choice of his actions, acts '*ignorantly*,'
16 but not '*through ignorance*,' nor involuntarily. But one who acts in ignorance of some of the details or circumstances accompanying his action, we shall say acts '*through ignorance*,' and involuntarily. *e.g.* Ignorance of 'fact' or of

voluntary. If the ignorance could have been avoided at the outset, the agent is fully responsible for it, and also for all and any consequences that it may lead to.

2. διά τι τῶν εἰρημένων] *i.e.* μέθη or ὀργὴ understood from μεθύων ἢ ὀργιζόμενος.

12. περὶ τί ἢ ἐν τίνι refers to the object upon which or whom the act takes place, *e.g.* a man slaying his son or his father in battle unwittingly. The murder of Laius in ignorance did not make Œdipus, morally speaking, a parricide.

13. ἕνεκα τίνος (like οὗ ἕνεκα in § 18) has not its usual meaning of 'motive' (of which ignorance would be out of the question), but that of 'tendency,' as the examples show.

17 οἷον σωτηρίας, καὶ πῶς, οἷον ἠρέμα ἢ σφόδρα. Ἅπαντα
μὲν οὖν ταῦτα οὐδεὶς ἂν ἀγνοήσειε μὴ μαινόμενος, δῆλον
δ' ὡς οὐδὲ τὸν πράττοντα· πῶς γὰρ ἑαυτόν γε; Ὃ δὲ
πράττει, ἀγνοήσειεν ἄν τις, οἷον λέγοντές φασιν ἐκ-
πεσεῖν αὐτούς, ἢ οὐκ εἰδέναι ὅτι ἀπόρρητα ἦν, ὥσπερ
Αἰσχύλος τὰ μυστικά, ἢ δεῖξαι βουλόμενος ἀφεῖναι, ὡς
ὁ τὸν καταπέλτην. Οἰηθείη δ' ἄν τις καὶ τὸν υἱὸν πολέ-
μιον εἶναι ὥσπερ ἡ Μερόπη, καὶ ἐσφαιρῶσθαι τὸ λελογ-
χωμένον δόρυ, ἢ τὸν λίθον κίσσηριν εἶναι· καὶ ἐπὶ
σωτηρίᾳ παίσας ἀποκτεῖναι ἄν· καὶ δεῖξαι βουλόμενος,
18 ὥσπερ οἱ ἀκροχειριζόμενοι, πατάξειεν ἄν. Περὶ πάντα
δὴ ταῦτα τῆς ἀγνοίας οὔσης ἐν οἷς ἡ πρᾶξις, ὁ τούτων
τι ἀγνοήσας ἄκων δοκεῖ πεπραχέναι, καὶ μάλιστα ἐν
τοῖς κυριωτάτοις· κυριώτατα δ' εἶναι δοκεῖ ἐν οἷς ἡ

'detail' may apply to the agent, the act itself, the object,
17 the instrument, the tendency, or the manner of the act. Of
all of these at once, and especially of the first, none but a
18 maniac could be ignorant. But ignorance of one or more of
such details, and especially of the object or of the tendency
of the act, may well occur, and cause the act to be an in-

4. οἷον κ.τ.λ.] 'as men in conversation say that they made a slip ('let the cat out of the bag'), or else that they did not know that it was any secret.' These are of course two different excuses, either of which would illustrate what is meant by ignorance of the act itself. So also would the other case mentioned, viz. when a gun goes off accidentally and kills some one.

8. *ἐσφαιρῶσθαι τὸ λελογχωμένον δόρυ*] 'believing the spear to be rounded at the end when it was actually pointed,' *i.e.* like a foil with a button for fencing.

9. *κίσσηριν*] pumice-stone, and therefore not likely to hurt any one. This illustrates ignorance of the instrument.

ἐπὶ σωτηρίᾳ] 'with a view to save;' *e.g.* if William Tell had hit his son, when aiming at the apple. (In ref. to *ἕνεκα τίνος* above.)

11. *ἀκροχειριζόμενοι*] 'sparring.' This example explains ignorance of the manner or degree of force of an act (*πῶς, οἷον ἠρέμα ἢ σφόδρα*, § 16).

19 πρᾶξις καὶ οὗ ἕνεκα. Τοῦ δὴ κατὰ τὴν τοιαύτην ἄγνοιαν
ἀκουσίου λεγομένου ἔτι δεῖ τὴν πρᾶξιν λυπηρὰν εἶναι
καὶ ἐν μεταμελείᾳ.
20 Ὄντος δ' ἀκουσίου τοῦ βίᾳ καὶ δι' ἄγνοιαν, τὸ ἑκού-
σιον δόξειεν ἂν εἶναι οὗ ἡ ἀρχὴ ἐν αὐτῷ εἰδότι τὰ καθ'
21 ἕκαστα ἐν οἷς ἡ πρᾶξις. Ἴσως γὰρ οὐ καλῶς λέγεται
22 ἀκούσια εἶναι τὰ διὰ θυμὸν ἢ δι' ἐπιθυμίαν. Πρῶτον
μὲν γὰρ οὐδὲν ἔτι τῶν ἄλλων ζῴων ἑκουσίως πράξει,
23 οὐδ' οἱ παῖδες· εἶτα πότερον οὐδὲν ἑκουσίως πράττομεν
τῶν δι' ἐπιθυμίαν καὶ θυμόν, ἢ τὰ καλὰ μὲν ἑκουσίως
τὰ δ' αἰσχρὰ ἀκουσίως; ἢ γελοῖον ἑνός γε αἰτίου ὄντος;
24 ἄτοπον δὲ ἴσως τὸ ἀκούσια φάναι ὧν δεῖ ὀρέγεσθαι·

19 voluntary one 'through ignorance'; provided always that subsequent sorrow attends the discovery of what has been thus done through ignorance.

Voluntary acts defined.

20 Having now explained the nature of both kinds of involuntary actions, we may define Voluntary acts conversely to be 'those originating from the agent himself, he having a full knowledge of the circumstances under which he is acting.'

Arguments to prove that acts done through anger or strong desire are Voluntary.

21 This definition must be defended against the false view (which it in fact condemns) that acts done from anger or desire are involuntary, though originating in the agent himself. (1) They
22 are not so, because all the acts of the lower animals and
23 even children would then be involuntary. (2) Take this dilemma:—*Either* it is meant that *all* acts of anger and desire are involuntary, *or* that the bad ones are involuntary and the good voluntary. The latter supposition is absurd, because the motive cause (anger and desire) is the same in both cases.
24 The former is absurd because there are occasions when we

6. Ἴσως γὰρ] The force of γὰρ is to indicate that the following class of actions (viz. τὰ διὰ θυμὸν ἢ δι' ἐπιθυμίαν), which are intentionally excluded by the Definition just given from involuntary actions, are rightly so excluded. (See *Suppl. Notes.*)

12. δεῖ is of course the emphatic word. The sense of 'duty excludes the notion of involuntariness. If we 'ought' to do.

δεῖ δὲ καὶ ὀργίζεσθαι ἐπί τισι καὶ ἐπιθυμεῖν τινῶν, οἷον
25 ὑγιείας καὶ μαθήσεως. Δοκεῖ δὲ τὰ μὲν ἀκούσια λυπηρὰ
26 εἶναι, τὰ δὲ κατ' ἐπιθυμίαν ἡδέα. Ἔτι δὲ τί διαφέρει
τῷ ἀκούσια εἶναι τὰ κατὰ λογισμὸν ἢ θυμὸν ἁμαρτη-
27 θέντα; φευκτὰ (μὲν γὰρ) ἄμφω, δοκεῖ δὲ οὐχ ἧττον
ἀνθρωπικὰ εἶναι τὰ ἄλογα πάθη. Αἱ δὲ πράξεις τοῦ
ἀνθρώπου ἀπὸ θυμοῦ καὶ ἐπιθυμίας. Ἄτοπον δὴ τὸ
τιθέναι ἀκούσια ταῦτα.

1 II. Διωρισμένων δὲ τοῦ τε ἑκουσίου καὶ τοῦ ἀκουσίου,

ought to feel anger and desire, and there can be no 'ought' in
5 the case if we are then involuntary agents. (3) The actions we are considering are done with pleasure, whereas involun-
6 tariness necessarily involves pain. (4) If wrong acts done deliberately are voluntary, and those done through anger and desire involuntary, how is it that, making no difference, we feel that we are to avoid the one as well as the other?
7 And passion and reason being equally essential parts of human nature, and springs of human action, it is absurd to attempt this distinction between the acts which result from them.

CHAP. II.—*Deliberate Choice* (προαίρεσις) *is compounded of an element of impulse and an element of judgment.*

1 This explanation of 'voluntary' and 'involuntary' clears Discussion of προαίρεσις introduced.
2 the way for the discussion of Deliberate Choice, which obvi-

anything it is clearly a voluntary act to do it.

3. τί διαφέρει κ.τ.λ.] The words τῷ ἀκούσια εἶναι belong in sense to 'τὰ κατὰ θυμὸν ἁμαρτηθέντα' only. What difference is there between deliberate errors and errors of passion from the fact of the latter being (as it is argued) involuntary, since we ought to avoid both kinds of error? If one class were voluntary and the other involuntary, we should not have the same feeling about avoiding them both.

6. τὰ ἄλογα πάθη] i.e. τὰ κατὰ θυμὸν ἢ ἐπιθυμίαν, as opposed to τὰ κατὰ λογισμόν.

CHAP. II.—The object of this

περὶ προαιρέσεως ἕπεται διελθεῖν· οἰκειότατον γὰρ εἶναι
δοκεῖ τῇ ἀρετῇ καὶ μᾶλλον τὰ ἤθη κρίνειν τῶν πράξεων.
2 *Ἡ προαίρεσις δὴ ἑκούσιον μὲν φαίνεται, οὐ ταὐτὸν δέ,*
ἀλλ' ἐπὶ πλέον τὸ ἑκούσιον· τοῦ μὲν γὰρ ἑκουσίου καὶ
παῖδες καὶ τἆλλα ζῷα κοινωνεῖ, προαιρέσεως δ' οὔ, καὶ
τὰ ἐξαίφνης ἑκούσια μὲν λέγομεν, κατὰ προαίρεσιν δ'
3 *οὔ. Οἱ δὲ λέγοντες αὐτὴν ἐπιθυμίαν ἢ θυμὸν ἢ βού-*
λησιν ἤ τινα δόξαν οὐκ ἐοίκασιν ὀρθῶς λέγειν. Οὐ γὰρ

i. It is not merely an *impulse*, because—

3 ously is a particular case of voluntary action. i. Some consider deliberate choice to be a matter of impulse. If so, it must be either Desire, Anger, or Wish, this being admitted as a complete list of our Impulses. (1) It is not the same as Desire, because—(*a*) Irrational animals have desires but do

(1) It is not the same as Desire.

chapter is to establish the *compound* character of *προαίρεσις* or deliberate choice, as consisting of an element of impulse and an element of judgment. This is done by proving that it is not identical with any sort of impulse singly, or of judgment singly. If it were identical with impulse, it must be either desire, spirit, or wish (these being assumed as an exhaustive classification of impulse (*ὄρεξις*), as Aristotle elsewhere (*De An.* II. iii. 2) explains). That it is not any of these, is shown in §§ 3—9. If it were identical with judgment (*δόξα*), or the expression of an opinion merely, it must be either judgment generally (*δόξα ἁπλῶς*), or judgment when exercised in a certain sphere, viz. matters of practical interest (*δόξα τις*). That this is not so is shewn in §§ 10—15. It is then affirmed to be a choice resulting from deliberation, thus combining both impulse and judgment.

1. *οἰκειότατον γὰρ*] 'It (viz. *προαίρεσις*) appears to be very closely connected with Virtue, and to be a better test of moral character than actions.' The question whether the intention or the outward act is more important in morals is again referred to, X. viii. 5.

6. *τὰ ἐξαίφνης*] Acts done 'on the spur of the moment.'

7. The principal difference between *ἐπιθυμία* (for which 'desire' is too wide, and 'appetite' too narrow) and *βούλησις*, or 'wish,' is that *ἐπιθυμία* is in connexion with a body, while *βούλησις* is not. A spirit could experience *βούλησις*, but not *ἐπιθυμία*.

κοινὸν ἡ προαίρεσις καὶ τῶν ἀλόγων, ἐπιθυμία δὲ καὶ
4 θυμός. Καὶ ὁ ἀκρατὴς ἐπιθυμῶν μὲν πράττει, προαι-
ρούμενος δ' οὔ· ὁ ἐγκρατὴς δ' ἀνάπαλιν προαιρούμενος
5 μέν, ἐπιθυμῶν δ' οὔ. Καὶ προαιρέσει μὲν ἐπιθυμία
ἐναντιοῦται, ἐπιθυμίᾳ δ' ἐπιθυμία οὔ. Καὶ ἡ μὲν ἐπι-
θυμία ἡδέος καὶ ἐπιλύπου, ἡ προαίρεσις δ' οὔτε λυπηροῦ
6 οὔθ' ἡδέος. Θυμὸς δ' ἔτι ἧττον· ἥκιστα γὰρ τὰ διὰ θυ-
7 μὸν κατὰ προαίρεσιν εἶναι δοκεῖ. Ἀλλὰ μὴν οὐδὲ
βούλησίς γε, καίπερ σύνεγγυς φαινόμενον· προαίρεσις
μὲν γὰρ οὐκ ἔστι τῶν ἀδυνάτων, καὶ εἴ τις φαίη προαι-
ρεῖσθαι, δοκοίη ἂν ἠλίθιος εἶναι· βούλησις δ' ἐστὶ τῶν

not act with deliberate choice. (This argument applies to
4 Anger also.) (*b*) The incontinent act in accordance with
their desires, but against their deliberate choice; the con-
5 tinent, *vice versâ*. (*c*) Desire is not opposed to desire, but
to something else, viz. deliberate choice, which checks or
resists it. (*d*) Desire is limited to what is pleasurable and
6 painful, but deliberate choice is not. (2) Still less can it be (2) nor Spirit;
Spirit, for impetuous actions are the very last we should
7 describe as done through deliberate choice. (3) It is not the (3) nor Wish.
same as Wish, though not very dissimilar to it. (*a*) We may
wish for impossibilities, but we cannot deliberately choose

4. The third argument seems to rest on the notion (found also in Plato) that conflict or opposition can only occur between two *different* parts of our constitution, *e.g.* between desire and reason, between impulse and resolution, etc., but that no department, whether that of reason or desire, or any other, can be 'divided against itself.' In fact, it follows from the 'law of contradiction' that nothing can do or suffer contraries at the same time in reference to the same part of itself, etc. A similar argument was employed in I. xiii. 15, etc., to show the distinctness of the appetitive and rational parts of the soul. Also it should be remembered that ἐπιθυμία (as was explained above), like 'appetite,' implies a physical or bodily affection, such as thirst, hunger, etc., of which the statement in the text is clearly true.

7. For θυμὸς see *Suppl. Note.*

8 ἀδυνάτων, οἷον ἀθανασίας. Καὶ ἡ μὲν βούλησίς ἐστι
καὶ περὶ τὰ μηδαμῶς δι' αὑτοῦ πραχθέντα ἄν, οἷον
ὑποκριτήν τινα νικᾶν ἢ ἀθλητήν· προαιρεῖται δὲ τὰ
τοιαῦτα οὐδείς, ἀλλ' ὅσα οἴεται γενέσθαι ἂν δι' αὑτοῦ.
9 Ἔτι δ' ἡ μὲν βούλησις τοῦ τέλους ἐστὶ μᾶλλον, ἡ δὲ
προαίρεσις τῶν πρὸς τὸ τέλος, οἷον ὑγιαίνειν βουλόμεθα,
προαιρούμεθα δὲ δι' ὧν ὑγιανοῦμεν, καὶ εὐδαιμονεῖν
βουλόμεθα μὲν καὶ φαμέν, προαιρούμεθα δὲ λέγειν οὐχ
ἁρμόζει· ὅλως γὰρ ἔοικεν ἡ προαίρεσις περὶ τὰ ἐφ' ἡμῖν
10 εἶναι. Οὐδὲ δὴ δόξα ἂν εἴη· ἡ μὲν γὰρ δόξα δοκεῖ περὶ
πάντα εἶναι, καὶ οὐδὲν ἧττον περὶ τὰ ἀΐδια καὶ τὰ ἀδύ-
νατα ἢ τὰ ἐφ' ἡμῖν· καὶ τῷ ψευδεῖ καὶ ἀληθεῖ διαιρεῖται,
οὐ τῷ κακῷ καὶ ἀγαθῷ, ἡ προαίρεσις δὲ τούτοις μᾶλλον.
11 Ὅλως μὲν οὖν δόξῃ ταὐτὸν ἴσως οὐδὲ λέγει οὐδείς. Ἀλλ'

8 them. (*b*) We may wish for things which, though not im-
9 possible, are out of our own power. (*c*) Wish refers to ends,
deliberate choice to means. Hence deliberate choice is no
10 sort of impulse singly. ii. Secondly, it is not judgment, or
expression of opinion, merely. (*a*) Judgment or opinion may
be on *all* subjects, whether in our power or out of it. (*b*) The
excellence, or the reverse, of judgment consists in its being
true or false to fact; that of deliberate choice in its being
11 morally good or bad. It might however be thought to be

ii. It is not merely a judgment or opinion, either generally,

or limited to the sphere of morals and practice.

1. ἀθανασίας] 'exemption from death.' This, like vi. 6 (see note), is an allusion of too passing a kind to bear on the question of Aristotle's belief in a future state.

8. καὶ φαμὲν] 'we use the expression wish to be happy;'—an appeal to common language.

10. δόξα here stands for an intellectual decision, the mere pronouncing of an opinion as to a fact, apart from any impulse or desire for action. Though it would be hardly supposed that προαίρεσις could be identical with this generally (§ 11), yet it might be thought identical with such an expression of opinion on practical or moral subjects. This is the δόξα τις or particular application of opinion referred to in §§ 11, etc.

οὐδέ τινι· τῷ γὰρ προαιρεῖσθαι τἀγαθὰ ἢ τὰ κακὰ ποιοί
12 τινές ἐσμεν, τῷ δὲ δοξάζειν οὔ. Καὶ προαιρούμεθα μὲν
λαβεῖν ἢ φυγεῖν ἤ τι τῶν τοιούτων, δοξάζομεν δὲ τί ἐστιν
ἢ τίνι συμφέρει ἢ πῶς· λαβεῖν δ' ἢ φυγεῖν οὐ πάνυ
13 δοξάζομεν. Καὶ ἡ μὲν προαίρεσις ἐπαινεῖται τῷ εἶναι οὗ
δεῖ μᾶλλον ἢ τῷ ὀρθῶς, ἡ δὲ δόξα τῷ ὡς ἀληθῶς. Καὶ
προαιρούμεθα μὲν ἃ μάλιστα ἴσμεν ἀγαθὰ ὄντα, δοξά-
14 ζομεν δὲ ἃ οὐ πάνυ ἴσμεν. Δοκοῦσί τε οὐχ οἱ αὐτοὶ
προαιρεῖσθαί τε ἄριστα καὶ δοξάζειν, ἀλλ' ἔνιοι δοξάζειν
15 μὲν ἄμεινον, διὰ κακίαν δ' αἱρεῖσθαι οὐχ ἃ δεῖ. Εἰ
δὲ προγίνεται δόξα τῆς προαιρέσεως ἢ παρακολουθεῖ,
οὐδὲν διαφέρει· οὐ τοῦτο γὰρ σκοποῦμεν, ἀλλ' εἰ ταὐτὸν

simply an expression of opinion *on subjects practical or moral.*
This is not the case, for (*a*) Character is formed by deliberate
choice of good and evil, not by opinions on such subjects.
12 (*b*) Deliberate Choice relates to pursuing or avoiding, opinion
13 relates to questions of fact. (*c*) The excellence of deliberate
choice depends on its direction to right objects; that of
opinion on its correctness in fact. (*d*) We deliberately choose
what we know or feel sure about; we form opinions irrespec-
14 tive of knowledge or certainty. (*e*) Excellence of deliberate
choice and of opinion are not always united in the same per-
15 sons, *e.g.* the incontinent. Whether correct opinion pre-
cedes or accompanies deliberate choice is unimportant, we

4. λαβεῖν ἢ φυγεῖν] another appeal to the usage of language. We do not speak of forming an opinion to pursue or avoid, but of forming a resolution or choice to do so.

6. ἢ is '*or*,' not '*than*,' as may be inferred from what was said in § 10, just above.

9. ἔνιοι] precisely the case of the incontinent (ἀκρατεῖς). See § 4 above.

11. Aristotle here notices, without discussing, the interesting question whether correct views (δόξα) precede good resolutions (προαίρεσις), or *vice versâ*; whether right knowledge usually leads to right practice, or right practice to right knowledge.

16 ἐστι δόξῃ τινί. Τί οὖν ἢ ποῖόν τι ἐστὶν, ἐπειδὴ τῶν
εἰρημένων οὐθέν; ἑκούσιον μὲν δὴ φαίνεται, τὸ δ' ἑκού-
17 σιον οὐ πᾶν προαιρετόν. Ἀλλ' ἆρά γε τὸ προβεβου-
λευμένον; ἡ γὰρ προαίρεσις μετὰ λόγου καὶ διανοίας.
Ὑποσημαίνειν δ' ἔοικε καὶ τοὔνομα ὡς ὂν πρὸ ἑτέρων
αἱρετόν.

1 III. Βουλεύονται δὲ πότερα περὶ πάντων, καὶ πᾶν βου-
2 λευτόν ἐστιν, ἢ περὶ ἐνίων οὐκ ἔστι βουλή; (λεκτέον δ'
ἴσως βουλευτὸν οὐχ ὑπὲρ οὗ βουλεύσαιτ' ἄν τις ἠλίθιος
3 ἢ μαινόμενος, ἀλλ' ὑπὲρ ὧν ὁ νοῦν ἔχων.) Περὶ δὲ τῶν
ἀϊδίων οὐδεὶς βουλεύεται, οἷον περὶ τοῦ κόσμου ἢ τῆς
4 διαμέτρου καὶ τῆς πλευρᾶς, ὅτι ἀσύμμετροι. Ἀλλ' οὐδὲ

16 only maintain that they are not identical. We have then advanced thus far. Deliberate choice is voluntary and some-
17 thing more. In fact, as the name indicates, it is 'a choice following upon deliberation.'

CHAP. III.—*The proper objects of Deliberation* (βούλευσις).

Proper objects of Deliberation determined. (§§ 1–11).

1, 2 We now inquire what are the proper objects for deliberation, which is, as we have seen, the first stage in deliberate choice.
3 (1) *Negatively*, we do *not* deliberate about (*a*) Things eternal
4 and immutable; (*b*) Things changeable, which change accord-

5. Thus the compound character of deliberate choice is established, *choice* implying an element of impulse, *deliberation* an element of intellect or judgment.

CHAP. III.—Deliberate Choice having been shown in the last chapter to consist in choice after deliberation, we now inquire (1) what are the proper objects and limits of deliberation, and (2) how its objects are related to, or distinguished from, those of the compound, deliberate choice?

12. διαμέτρου κ.τ.λ.] We do not deliberate about the incommensurability of the side and diameter of a square, because we cannot alter it. The diameter = the side $\times \sqrt{2}$, and as $\sqrt{2}$ cannot be exactly found, the diameter and side are incommensurable.

περὶ τῶν ἐν κινήσει, ἀεὶ δὲ κατὰ ταὐτὰ γινομένων, εἴτ'
ἐξ ἀνάγκης εἴτε καὶ φύσει ἢ διά τινα αἰτίαν ἄλλην, οἷον
5 τροπῶν καὶ ἀνατολῶν. Οὐδὲ περὶ τῶν ἄλλοτε ἄλλως,
οἷον αὐχμῶν καὶ ὄμβρων. Οὐδὲ περὶ τῶν ἀπὸ τύχης,
6 οἷον θησαυροῦ εὑρέσεως. Ἀλλ' οὐδὲ περὶ τῶν ἀνθρω-
πικῶν πάντων, οἷον πῶς ἂν Σκύθαι ἄριστα πολιτεύοιντο
οὐδεὶς Λακεδαιμονίων βουλεύεται. Οὐ γὰρ γένοιτ' ἂν
7 τούτων οὐθὲν δι' ἡμῶν. Βουλευόμεθα δὲ περὶ τῶν ἐφ'
ἡμῖν πρακτῶν· ταῦτα δὲ καὶ ἔστι λοιπά. Αἴτιαι γὰρ

5 ing to a fixed law; (*c*) Things changeable, which change
according to no discoverable law; (*d*) Things depending on
6 pure chance where there can be no law; (*e*) In short anything
whatever which is not in our own power. (2) *Positively*, we
7 *do* deliberate (*a*) about things in our own power; and each

3. τροπῶν] 'solstices.' The accent shows that it comes from τροπὴ, not τρόπος.

9. αἴτια γὰρ δοκοῦσι κ.τ.λ.] This must be considered as a popular classification of causes familiar to his hearers (such current opinions being often introduced, as we have seen, by the verb δοκεῖν—see note on I. iii. 2), rather than one for which Aristotle would hold himself responsible.

With this proviso, we may suppose the classification to have originated from the observation that causes naturally distinguished themselves as either irrational or rational. The former were further divided into φύσις, ἀνάγκη, τύχη, perhaps on some such notion as the following:—

i. Some phenomena, varying within fixed limits, seem to imply the existence of law, yet tempered, as it were, by some power behind it (φύσις), regulating and modifying its applications: *e.g.* The relations between seed and crop; the variations of hot, cold, wet or dry seasons, subject to the invariable distinction between the seasons themselves; the preservation of the species in the reproduction of animals, notwithstanding endless minor differences in the individuals. Such operations would probably be assigned to Nature (φύσις).

ii. Some events seem to recur under a law invariable and inviolable, as if it worked itself mechanically: *e.g.* The rising and setting of the sun, the succession of summer and winter, day and night. Such phenomena

δοκοῦσιν εἶναι φύσις καὶ ἀνάγκη καὶ τύχη, ἔτι δὲ νοῦς
καὶ πᾶν τὸ δι' ἀνθρώπου. Τῶν δ' ἀνθρώπων ἕκαστοι
8 βουλεύονται περὶ τῶν δι' αὑτῶν πρακτῶν. Καὶ περὶ
μὲν τὰς ἀκριβεῖς καὶ αὐτάρκεις τῶν ἐπιστημῶν οὐκ ἔστι
βουλή, οἷον περὶ γραμμάτων (οὐ γὰρ διστάζομεν πῶς
γραπτέον·) ἀλλ' ὅσα γίνεται δι' ἡμῶν, μὴ ὡσαύτως δ'
ἀεί, περὶ τούτων βουλευόμεθα, οἷον περὶ τῶν κατὰ ἰα-
τρικὴν καὶ χρηματιστικήν, καὶ περὶ κυβερνητικὴν μᾶλ-
9 λον ἢ γυμναστικήν, ὅσῳ ἧττον διηκρίβωται, καὶ ἔτι περὶ

man about what is in *his* own power; (*b*) about the practical
8 arts and about some sciences, though not all (the amount of
9 deliberation being in inverse proportion to their precision), and,

would appear to be caused by Necessity (ἀνάγκη).

iii. In other cases no law or reason or method can be traced by us in the sequence of events, *e.g.* a 'windfall,' or a 'godsend,' as we term it, or the production of 'monsters.' Such occurrences would be referred to Chance (τύχη). Anaxagoras in fact defined τύχη to be ἄδηλος αἰτία ἀνθρωπίνῳ λογισμῷ. Compare Pope, 'All chance (is) direction which thou canst not see.'

It is scarcely necessary to point out that such distinctions are unphilosophical, being liable to disturbance upon every addition to our physical knowledge. (For Aristotle's own view of φύσις see Glossary p. liv.)

The class of rational causes is subdivided into νοῦς and πᾶν τὸ δι' ἀνθρώπου. The former apparently refers to Intelligence or Design as displayed in the physical world, which in a modern system would be described as Providence, or, still more personally, as God. πᾶν τὸ δι' ἀνθρώπου includes all results brought about by human agency. This last group alone falls within the sphere of Deliberation.

4. ἐπιστημῶν] The word is used loosely for knowledge generally, including arts, for strictly speaking it would follow from what is said throughout the Chapter that Deliberation is only concerned with *practical* and not *theoretical* subjects, and therefore strictly speaking not with Sciences but Arts only (see Glossary, Art and Science). The instances given by Aristotle of such ἐπιστῆμαι as we do deliberate about, viz. ἰατρική, κυβερνητική, χρηματιστική, are evidently in the strict sense not ἐπιστῆμαι but τέχναι.

ἀκριβεῖς καὶ αὐταρκεῖς] ἀκριβής means 'accurate' or 'pre-

τῶν λοιπῶν ὁμοίως, μᾶλλον δὲ καὶ περὶ τὰς τέχνας ἢ
τὰς ἐπιστήμας· μᾶλλον γὰρ περὶ αὐτὰς διστάζομεν.
10 Τὸ βουλεύεσθαι δὲ ἐν τοῖς ὡς ἐπὶ τὸ πολὺ, ἀδήλοις δὲ
πῶς ἀποβήσεται, καὶ ἐν οἷς ἀδιόριστον. Συμβούλους δὲ
παραλαμβάνομεν εἰς τὰ μεγάλα, ἀπιστοῦντες ἡμῖν αὐ-
11 τοῖς ὡς οὐχ ἱκανοῖς διαγνῶναι. Βουλευόμεθα δ᾽ οὐ περὶ
τῶν τελῶν ἀλλὰ περὶ τῶν πρὸς τὰ τέλη. Οὔτε γὰρ
ἰατρὸς βουλεύεται εἰ ὑγιάσει, οὔτε ῥήτωρ εἰ πείσει,
οὔτε πολιτικὸς εἰ εὐνομίαν ποιήσει, οὐδὲ τῶν λοιπῶν
οὐδεὶς περὶ τοῦ τέλους· ἀλλὰ θέμενοι τέλος τι, πῶς
καὶ διὰ τίνων ἔσται σκοποῦσι, καὶ διὰ πλειόνων μὲν
φαινομένου γίνεσθαι διὰ τίνος ῥᾷστα καὶ κάλλιστα ἐπι-
σκοποῦσι, δι᾽ ἑνὸς δ᾽ ἐπιτελουμένου πῶς διὰ τούτου
ἔσται κἀκεῖνο διὰ τίνος, ἕως ἂν ἔλθωσιν ἐπὶ τὸ πρῶτον
αἴτιον, ὃ ἐν τῇ εὑρέσει ἔσχατόν ἐστιν· ὁ γὰρ βουλευό-
μενος ἔοικε ζητεῖν καὶ ἀναλύειν τὸν εἰρημένον τρόπον

10 speaking generally, more in reference to arts than sciences,
there being naturally more generalities and uncertainties in the
11 former; (*c*) about means and not about ends. In short the
process of deliberation is this:—Some end is set up which we
desire to attain to. We consider the means by which it can be
reached; and if there are several, which will be the easiest and
best means. Having by choice or necessity settled upon some
one means, we then consider how this means can be secured,

Analysis of the process of Deliberation.

cise,' 'not subject to variations or uncertainties;' *αὐταρκὴς* 'independent of external circumstances or conditions.' *e.g.* The sciences of Anatomy, Harmonics, Geology are not *αὐταρκεῖς* in this sense, because each implies some special object-matter as the very condition of its existence as a science. Geometry would be *αὐταρκὴς* as postulating nothing but the existence of space and figure; Arithmetic still more so as implying only the notions of succession and number.

14. *πρῶτον αἴτιον*] the first link in the chain of causation leading to the result desired.

12 ὥσπερ διάγραμμα. (Φαίνεται δ᾽ ἡ μὲν ζήτησις οὐ πᾶσα
εἶναι βούλευσις, οἷον αἱ μαθηματικαί, ἡ δὲ βούλευσις
πᾶσα ζήτησις, καὶ τὸ ἔσχατον ἐν τῇ ἀναλύσει πρῶτον
13 εἶναι ἐν τῇ γενέσει.) Κἂν μὲν ἀδυνάτῳ ἐντύχωσιν, ἀφί-
στανται, οἷον εἰ χρημάτων δεῖ, ταῦτα δὲ μὴ οἷόν τε
πορισθῆναι· ἐὰν δὲ δυνατὸν φαίνηται, ἐγχειροῦσι πράτ-
τειν. Δυνατὰ δὲ ἃ δι᾽ ἡμῶν γένοιτ᾽ ἄν· τὰ γὰρ διὰ τῶν

and so on as long as may be necessary, until we arrive at some
12 means in our own power. This last step in the deliberation
is the first in the practical effort of securing the end desired.
If some necessary means prove impossible to secure, the
13 deliberation ceases and the project is abandoned. If on the
other hand the means prove feasible, then too deliberation

1. ὥσπερ διάγραμμα] like a geometrical figure. We might take for an instance Eucl. i. 10. It is desired to draw a perpendicular to a given line from a given point in the line (θέμενοι τέλος τι).

(1) Asking ourselves what conditions will secure this (πῶς καὶ διὰ τίνων ἔσται), we observe that making the adjacent angles equal would do so.

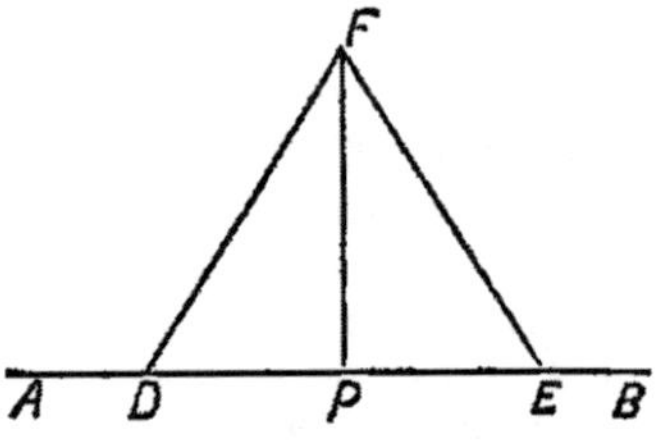

(2) Next, how can we make the adjacent angles equal (πῶς διὰ τούτων ἔσται)? By causing them to be parts of two triangles *either* with two sides and the included angles equal (Prop. 4), *or* with all three sides equal (Prop. 8).

(3) Choosing the latter as preferable (διὰ πλειόνων μὲν φαινομένου διὰ τίνος ῥᾷστα κ.τ.λ.), how can we secure a triangle with equal sides (κἀκεῖνο διὰ τίνος)? We see this to be in our power by taking any points in AB, viz. D and E, equidistant from P, erecting on DE an equilateral triangle DFE (by Prop. 1) and joining FP.

The problem being thus brought back to steps within our power (ἕως ἂν ἔλθωσιν ἐπὶ τὸ πρῶτον αἴτιον), our investigation is at an end (ἐν τῇ εὑρέσει ἔσχατόν ἐστι), and we at once proceed with the construction of the Proposition as given by Euclid, and thus 'ἔσχατον ἐν τῇ ἀναλύσει' becomes 'πρῶτον ἐν τῇ γενέσει.'

14 φίλων δι' ἡμῶν πως ἐστίν· ἡ γὰρ ἀρχὴ ἐν ἡμῖν. Ζητεῖ-
ται δ' ὁτὲ μὲν τὰ ὄργανα, ὁτὲ δ' ἡ χρεία αὐτῶν· ὁμοίως
δὲ καὶ ἐν τοῖς λοιποῖς ὁτὲ μὲν δι' οὗ, ὁτὲ δὲ πῶς ἢ διὰ
15 τίνος. Ἔοικε δή, καθάπερ εἴρηται, ἄνθρωπος εἶναι ἀρχὴ
τῶν πράξεων· ἡ δὲ βουλὴ περὶ τῶν αὑτῷ πρακτῶν, αἱ
16 δὲ πράξεις ἄλλων ἕνεκα. Οὐκ ἂν οὖν εἴη βουλευτὸν
τὸ τέλος ἀλλὰ τὰ πρὸς τὰ τέλη. Οὐδὲ δὴ τὰ καθ'
ἕκαστα, οἷον εἰ ἄρτος τοῦτο ἢ πέπεπται ὡς δεῖ· αἰσθή-
σεως γὰρ ταῦτα. Εἰ δὲ ἀεὶ βουλεύσεται, εἰς ἄπειρον
17 ἥξει. Βουλευτὸν δὲ καὶ προαιρετὸν τὸ αὐτό, πλὴν ἀφω-
ρισμένον ἤδη τὸ προαιρετόν· τὸ γὰρ ἐκ τῆς βουλῆς
προκριθὲν προαιρετόν ἐστιν. Παύεται γὰρ ἕκαστος ζη-
τῶν πῶς πράξει, ὅταν εἰς αὑτὸν ἀναγάγῃ τὴν ἀρχήν, καὶ
αὑτοῦ εἰς τὸ ἡγούμενον· τοῦτο γὰρ τὸ προαιρούμενον.
18 Δῆλον δὲ τοῦτο καὶ ἐκ τῶν ἀρχαίων πολιτειῶν, ἃς
Ὅμηρος ἐμιμεῖτο· οἱ γὰρ βασιλεῖς ἃ προέλοιντο ἀνήγ-

14 ceases and action begins. Sometimes deliberation seeks to
15 discover instruments, sometimes the way to employ them (in
all cases implying, as we have maintained before, that a man
is the originating cause of his actions about which he delibe-
16 rates), and it is concerned with means and not with ends; nor
finally does it deal with questions of fact, which are matters
of observation. Deliberation cannot of course be prolonged
indefinitely, but must be terminated by decision or choice of
7-19 means. The object of Deliberation and of Deliberate Choice

We can now distinguish Deliberation and Deliberate Choice.

4. ἔοικε δή] The process of deliberation affords another proof that man is the originating cause of his actions.

5. αἱ δὲ πράξεις ἄλλων ἕνεκα] Aristotle is of course speaking of such actions only as form subjects of deliberation.

14. προαιρούμενον is of course middle and not passive; 'that which chooses.'

16. The kings determine upon action, the people carry it out without further deliberation. So when προαίρεσις or τὸ προαιρούμενον which leads (τὸ ἡγούμενον)

19 γελλον τῷ δήμῳ. Ὄντος δὲ τοῦ προαιρετοῦ βουλευτοῦ ὀρεκτοῦ τῶν ἐφ' ἡμῖν, καὶ ἡ προαίρεσις ἂν εἴη βουλευτικὴ ὄρεξις τῶν ἐφ' ἡμῖν· ἐκ τοῦ βουλεύσασθαι γὰρ κρίναντες ὀρεγόμεθα κατὰ τὴν βούλευσιν.

20 Ἡ μὲν οὖν προαίρεσις τύπῳ εἰρήσθω, καὶ περὶ ποῖά ἐστι, καὶ ὅτι τῶν πρὸς τὰ τέλη·

1 IV. Ἡ δὲ βούλησις ὅτι μὲν τοῦ τέλους ἐστὶν εἴρηται, δοκεῖ δὲ τοῖς μὲν ἀγαθοῦ εἶναι, τοῖς δὲ τοῦ φαινομένου

are therefore the same, except that the latter is already resolved upon as the *result* of the deliberation. When the choice is made, the deliberation ceases.

20 Thus we define deliberate choice to be 'a choice following upon deliberation of something in our power.'

CHAP. IV.—*The proper objects of Wish* (βούλησις).

The proper objects of Wish (βούλησις) have been thought to be either what is really good or whatever *pro temp.* appears good.

1 As we should not deliberate about *means*, unless we had first conceived of some *end* as desirable, we next inquire into the nature of that faculty, viz. 'wish' or 'desire,' which sets

'in this little kingdom, man,' has made its decision, deliberation is over and action succeeds.

1. βουλευτοῦ ὀρεκτοῦ] This recalls the compound character of προαίρεσις described in ch. ii., βουλευτοῦ indicating the intellectual, and ὀρεκτοῦ the impulsive, element of the compound process.

CHAP. IV.—In this Chapter we inquire into the nature of the faculty which sets up the *end* in the first instance as desirable, with a view to which end deliberation (βούλευσις) discusses the *means*, and deliberate choice (προαίρεσις) decides upon them. In other words we ask what are the proper objects of wish (βούλησις)? Thus every deliberate act implies the three stages βούλησις, βούλευσις, and προαίρεσις. See Glossary, *s.v.* προαίρεσις.

This Chapter contains a criticism of the two extreme theories, (1) that the objects of wish are things really good, and so, ultimately, the Absolute or Chief Good (Plato); (2) that they are any things that appear at the time good (the Sophists), and also a solution of the question by Aristotle upon an intermediate ground, since the former theory contradicts facts, and the latter, feelings.

2 ἀγαθοῦ. Συμβαίνει δὲ τοῖς μὲν τὸ βουλητὸν τἀγαθὸν
λέγουσι μὴ εἶναι βουλητὸν ὃ βούλεται ὁ μὴ ὀρθῶς αἱ-
ρούμενος (εἰ γὰρ ἔσται βουλητὸν, καὶ ἀγαθόν· ἦν δ',
3 εἰ οὕτως ἔτυχε, κακὸν), τοῖς δ' αὖ τὸ φαινόμενον ἀγαθὸν
τὸ βουλητὸν λέγουσι μὴ εἶναι φύσει βουλητὸν, ἀλλ'
ἑκάστῳ τὸ δοκοῦν· ἄλλο δ' ἄλλῳ φαίνεται, καὶ εἰ οὕτως
4 ἔτυχε, τἀναντία. Εἰ δὲ δὴ ταῦτα μὴ ἀρέσκει, ἆρα φα-
τέον ἁπλῶς μὲν καὶ κατ' ἀλήθειαν βουλητὸν εἶναι τἀγα-
θὸν, ἑκάστῳ δὲ τὸ φαινόμενον; τῷ μὲν οὖν σπουδαίῳ
τὸ κατ' ἀλήθειαν εἶναι, τῷ δὲ φαύλῳ τὸ τυχὸν, ὥσπερ
καὶ ἐπὶ τῶν σωμάτων τοῖς μὲν εὖ διακειμένοις ὑγιεινά
ἐστι τὰ κατ' ἀλήθειαν τοιαῦτα ὄντα, τοῖς δ' ἐπινόσοις
ἕτερα. Ὁμοίως δὲ καὶ πικρὰ καὶ γλυκέα καὶ θερμὰ καὶ
βαρέα καὶ τῶν ἄλλων ἕκαστα· ὁ σπουδαῖος γὰρ ἕκαστα

2 such *ends* before us. Two views present themselves:—i. That
the objects of desire are really good. ii. That they are what-
ever may appear to each individual to be good. We object
to the first, that it contradicts facts, as men obviously do desire
3 what is bad; and to the second, that it seems to deny that
4 there are objects *per se* desirable, and *vice versâ*. The truth
seems to be that as when we speak of things being wholesome
and so on we mean wholesome to those whose *bodies* are in a
healthy state, so also when we speak of things being desirable,
we mean such things as are objects of desire to those whose
minds are well regulated. Thus we escape both the above objec-
tions: we maintain that there are things naturally and *per se*

Under certain limitations the former is true.

1. τἀγαθὸν] The Chief Good was, according to Plato, the ultimate object of all wish or desire, because all that was good in any lower objects was derived from, and limited to, their participation in the Chief Good. See note on I. iv. 3.

10. ὥσπερ καὶ κ.τ.λ.] Aristotle's argument is, that all relative terms whatsoever present the same difficulty, if we are to take account of individual exceptions and abnormal circumstances.

14. σπουδαῖος] See note on I. viii. 13.

κρίνει ὀρθῶς, καὶ ἐν ἑκάστοις τἀληθὲς αὐτῷ φαίνεται.
5 Καθ' ἑκάστην γὰρ ἕξιν ἴδιά ἐστι καλὰ καὶ ἡδέα, καὶ διαφέρει πλεῖστον ἴσως ὁ σπουδαῖος τῷ τἀληθὲς ἐν ἑκάστοις ὁρᾶν, ὥσπερ κανὼν καὶ μέτρον αὐτῶν ὤν. Τοῖς πολλοῖς δὲ ἡ ἀπάτη διὰ τὴν ἡδονὴν ἔοικε γίνεσθαι· οὐ
6 γὰρ οὖσα ἀγαθὸν φαίνεται. Αἱροῦνται οὖν τὸ ἡδὺ ὡς ἀγαθόν, τὴν δὲ λύπην ὡς κακὸν φεύγουσιν.
1 V. Ὄντος δὴ βουλητοῦ μὲν τοῦ τέλους, βουλευτῶν δὲ

5 desirable, and that in the midst of the aberrations and perversions of individual men, who simply follow pleasure and
6 avoid pain, the desires of the good man are an index to us of what is thus naturally and *per se* desirable.

CHAP. V.—*A refutation of the theory that Virtue is voluntary, but Vice involuntary.*

Virtue and Vice are equally voluntary.

1 Now we have seen that the choice of means to a given end is both voluntary and a matter of deliberate choice, conse-

1. τἀληθὲς αὐτῷ φαίνεται] Thus the real standard is an absolute and not a relative one. The σπουδαῖος does not fix the standard, but his known conformity to the standard enables us to use him as a substitute for it. Similarly it is not the barometer but the pressure of the atmosphere which regulates the weather; the barometer is only a convenient index of the phenomena which it does not itself influence. It is in this restricted sense, therefore, that the σπουδαῖος is said in l. 4 to be κανὼν καὶ μέτρον τοῦ ἀληθοῦς. Compare, 'He that is spiritual judgeth all things.'

CHAP. V.—Aristotle concludes this part of his subject with a sort of supplementary Chapter to refute a theory which, owing to Plato's advocacy, had obtained considerable prominence, viz. that Virtue is voluntary but Vice involuntary. The theory seems to have arisen thus:—In all cases of right or wrong action where a conscious struggle takes place, the two alternatives are presented to us, present pleasure involving future pain and regret, or present pain (of self-denial) with subsequent pleasure and satisfaction. Thus it becomes a matter for calculation, Is the present pleasure so great as to counterbalance the future pain? Is it so great as to make it worth

καὶ προαιρετῶν τῶν πρὸς τὸ τέλος, αἱ περὶ ταῦτα πράξεις κατὰ προαίρεσιν ἂν εἶεν καὶ ἑκούσιοι. Αἱ δὲ τῶν
2 ἀρετῶν ἐνέργειαι περὶ ταῦτα. Ἐφ' ἡμῖν δὲ καὶ ἡ ἀρετή, ὁμοίως δὲ καὶ ἡ κακία. Ἐν οἷς γὰρ ἐφ' ἡμῖν τὸ πράττειν, καὶ τὸ μὴ πράττειν, καὶ ἐν οἷς τὸ μή, καὶ τὸ ναί· ὥστ' εἰ τὸ πράττειν καλὸν ὂν ἐφ' ἡμῖν ἐστί, καὶ τὸ μὴ

quently the practice of Virtue involving (as we have seen) a
2 deliberate choice of means must be voluntary, and so likewise we maintain must Vice be voluntary. This latter point being

while to risk the consequences? If a man decides that it is, and does wrong accordingly, he has simply (it is argued) made a mistake in his calculation, he has committed an error of judgment merely, and all wrong-doing, since it arises out of such a mistake, is therefore involuntary. No one ever deliberately chooses anything but what *at the time* appears to him the better choice (τὸ δὲ τέλος τῆς πράξεως κατὰ τὸν καιρόν ἐστιν as we read in i. 6), and what is more, he cannot help its so appearing to him (see § 17 of this Chapter) any more than he can help an object's appearing red or green to him. Thus when a man chooses the right he chooses knowingly and voluntarily for the best: when he chooses the wrong he chooses it still under a mistaken impression that he is choosing for the best: he acts under an illusion and therefore involuntarily.

There seem to be four main arguments in the Chapter:—

(1) §§ 2—4. An *argumentum ad hominem* against the position of those half-necessitarians who maintain that though Vice is involuntary, Virtue is voluntary.

(2) §§ 5—16. Against the more logical and thorough-going necessitarians who argue that *all* our actions, virtuous as well as vicious, are merely the necessary result of causes and circumstances external to ourselves.

(3) §§ 17, 18. Against the principal argument by which the half-necessitarians supported their position.

(4) §§ 19, 20. Against a modified form of the same argument.

1. περὶ ταῦτα in l. 1 obviously refers to 'means' (τὰ πρὸς τὸ τέλος). περὶ ταῦτα in l. 3 must have the same reference, and the argument is, that as the exercise of Virtue involves the choice of means, it must be voluntary. This, however, is generally admitted, and the purpose of the Chapter is rather to show that the same inference applies to Vice.

πράττειν ἐφ' ἡμῖν ἔσται αἰσχρὸν ὄν, καὶ εἰ τὸ μὴ πράτ-
τειν καλὸν ὂν ἐφ' ἡμῖν, καὶ τὸ πράττειν αἰσχρὸν ὂν ἐφ'
3 ἡμῖν. Εἰ δ' ἐφ' ἡμῖν τὰ καλὰ πράττειν καὶ τὰ αἰσχρά,
ὁμοίως δὲ καὶ τὸ μὴ πράττειν, τοῦτο δ' ἦν τὸ ἀγαθοῖς
καὶ κακοῖς εἶναι, ἐφ' ἡμῖν ἄρα τὸ ἐπιεικέσι καὶ φαύλοις
4 εἶναι. Τὸ δὲ λέγειν ὡς

οὐδεὶς ἑκὼν πονηρὸς οὐδ' ἄκων μάκαρ,

ἔοικε τὸ μὲν ψευδεῖ τὸ δ' ἀληθεῖ· μακάριος μὲν γὰρ
5 οὐδεὶς ἄκων, ἡ δὲ μοχθηρία ἑκούσιον. Ἢ τοῖς γε νῦν
εἰρημένοις ἀμφισβητητέον, καὶ τὸν ἄνθρωπον οὐ φατέον

i. 'That Virtue is voluntary and Vice involuntary' refuted. (§§ 2—4).

disputed, we prove it as follows:—i. If it is in our own power to act, it must also be in our own power not to act (else our action was not really in our power but was compulsory), and *vice versâ*. Now if acting (or not acting) in any case be
3, 4 right, the reverse would be wrong. Consequently if to do right is in our power, so also is to do wrong: in a word, if
5 Virtue is voluntary, so is Vice. ii. If, in order to escape this conclusion, it be denied outright that man is himself the

ii. The more general position 'That our actions originate in causes beyond our control' refuted (§§ 5—16)

4. ἦν = 'this was admitted to constitute our being good or bad.' ἀγαθοῖς καὶ κακοῖς is in attraction with ἐφ' ἡμῖν. See another instance of ἦν thus used in viii. 14.

9. τοῖς γε νῦν εἰρημένοις refers to the previous conclusions about the voluntary nature of βούλευσις and προαίρεσις, with the assertion of which this Chapter opens.

Aristotle now turns to the more thorough-going and more logical position that *all* our actions, good and bad alike, are the *necessary* result of our condition and circumstances; in other words, that we are not free and responsible agents at all. His first argument against it consists in what is called 'shifting the burden of proof.' It is not for those who *accept*, but for those who *deny*, what is *prima facie* true, to bring arguments in support of their position. The *prima facie* truth in this case is that man himself originates his own acts, and until some other origin for them can be proved, we have a right, without further argument, to maintain that he does so originate them. Hence φαίνεται is emphatic.

ἀρχὴν εἶναι οὐδὲ γεννητὴν τῶν πράξεων ὥσπερ καὶ
6 τέκνων. Εἰ δὲ ταῦτα φαίνεται, καὶ μὴ ἔχομεν εἰς ἄλλας
ἀρχὰς ἀναγαγεῖν παρὰ τὰς ἐφ' ἡμῖν, ὧν καὶ αἱ ἀρχαὶ ἐν
7 ἡμῖν, καὶ αὐτὰ ἐφ' ἡμῖν καὶ ἑκούσια. Τούτοις δ' ἔοικε
μαρτυρεῖσθαι καὶ ἰδίᾳ ὑφ' ἑκάστων καὶ ὑπ' αὐτῶν τῶν
νομοθετῶν· κολάζουσι γὰρ καὶ τιμωροῦνται τοὺς δρῶντας
μοχθηρὰ, ὅσοι μὴ βίᾳ ἢ δι' ἄγνοιαν ἧς μὴ αὐτοὶ αἴτιοι,
τοὺς δὲ τὰ καλὰ πράττοντας τιμῶσιν, ὡς τοὺς μὲν προ-
τρέψοντες τοὺς δὲ κωλύσοντες. Καίτοι ὅσα μήτ' ἐφ'
ἡμῖν ἐστὶ, μήθ' ἑκούσια, οὐδεὶς προτρέπεται πράττειν,
ὡς οὐδὲν πρὸ ἔργου ὂν τὸ πεισθῆναι μὴ θερμαίνεσθαι ἢ
ἀλγεῖν ἢ πεινῆν ἢ ἄλλ' ὁτιοῦν τῶν τοιούτων· οὐθὲν γὰρ
8 ἧττον πεισόμεθα αὐτά. Καὶ γὰρ ἐπ' αὐτῷ τῷ ἀγνοεῖν

6 originating cause of his acts either good or bad, (1) we reply
that it rests with those who deny what is to all appearance the
case to suggest some other cause, and if they cannot, we infer
without further proof that a man does originate his acts, and
7 if so, that they are voluntary. (2) We appeal to the universal
practice of mankind in private and in public life, which by
rewards and punishments encourages to virtuous, and dis-
courages from vicious, acts. This proves at least that man-
kind generally consider both virtuous and vicious acts to be
8 in our power. (3) So far are mankind at large from regard-

(1) by throwing the burden of proof on the opponents.

(2) By appealing to the practice of mankind in rewarding Virtue and punishing Vice.

(3) By showing how they punish ignorance itself if avoidable

4. The second and third arguments consist in an appeal to the universal practice and belief of mankind. This further strengthens the assertion made by *φαίνεται* as explained in the last note, and serves to show that the opponents fly in the face not only of what is *prima facie* true, but also of what is universally believed and acted upon. (See *Supplementary Notes.*)

6. *κόλασις* and *τιμωρία* differ in that *κόλασις* is punishment for the sake of him who suffers it, that he may reform: *τιμωρία* is punishment for the sake of him who inflicts it, that he may be revenged. The idea of the former is 'chastisement,' that of the latter, 'vengeance.'

13. *καὶ γὰρ*] 'and what is more:' introducing a still more cogent proof.

κολάζουσιν, ἐὰν αἴτιος εἶναι δοκῇ τῆς ἀγνοίας, οἷον τοῖς
μεθύουσι διπλᾶ τὰ ἐπιτίμια· ἡ γὰρ ἀρχὴ ἐν αὐτῷ· κύ-
ριος γὰρ τοῦ μὴ μεθυσθῆναι, τοῦτο δ' αἴτιον τῆς ἀγ-
νοίας. Καὶ τοὺς ἀγνοοῦντάς τι τῶν ἐν τοῖς νόμοις, ἃ δεῖ
9 ἐπίστασθαι καὶ μὴ χαλεπά ἐστι, κολάζουσιν. Ὁμοίως
δὲ καὶ ἐν τοῖς ἄλλοις, ὅσα δι' ἀμέλειαν ἀγνοεῖν δοκοῦσιν,
ὡς ἐπ' αὐτοῖς ὂν τὸ μὴ ἀγνοεῖν· τοῦ γὰρ ἐπιμεληθῆναι
10 κύριοι. Ἀλλ' ἴσως τοιοῦτός ἐστιν ὥστε μὴ ἐπιμελη-
θῆναι. Ἀλλὰ τοῦ τοιούτους γενέσθαι αὐτοὶ αἴτιοι ζῶντες
ἀνειμένως, καὶ τοῦ ἀδίκους ἢ ἀκολάστους εἶναι, οἱ μὲν
κακουργοῦντες, οἱ δὲ ἐν πότοις καὶ τοῖς τοιούτοις διά-
γοντες· αἱ γὰρ περὶ ἕκαστα ἐνέργειαι τοιούτους ποιοῦ-
11 σιν. Τοῦτο δὲ δῆλον ἐκ τῶν μελετώντων πρὸς ἡντινοῦν
12 ἀγωνίαν ἢ πρᾶξιν· διατελοῦσι γὰρ ἐνεργοῦντες. Τὸ μὲν
οὖν ἀγνοεῖν ὅτι ἐκ τοῦ ἐνεργεῖν περὶ ἕκαστα αἱ ἕξεις
13 γίνονται, κομιδῇ ἀναισθήτου. Ἔτι δ' ἄλογον τὸν ἀδι-
κοῦντα μὴ βούλεσθαι ἄδικον εἶναι ἢ τὸν ἀκολασταίνοντα
14 ἀκόλαστον. Εἰ δὲ μὴ ἀγνοῶν τις πράττει ἐξ ὧν

ing ignorance as rendering Vice involuntary and therefore
excusable, that they even punish *for ignorance itself*, when-
ever it is such as could have been avoided. *e.g.* (*a*) Double
penalties for offences committed in drunkenness. (*b*) Punish-
ments for not knowing an offence to be forbidden by the law.
9, 10 (*c*) Or for any other sort of careless ignorance. (*d*) Or even
for ignorance through incapacity if the incapacity be the
result of previous Vice; for single acts repeated form perma-
11, 12 nent habits. Every one who is not a downright idiot *must* know
13 this much from daily experience, and it cannot avail to say
14 that he did not wish it to be so in his case: nor does it follow

1. τοῖς μεθύουσι κ.τ.λ.] a law of Pittacus of Mytilene.

4. Compare the maxim 'Ignoratio juris nocet, ignoratio facti non nocet.'

12. αἱ γὰρ περὶ κ.τ.λ.] 'Actions of any kind make us similar in character.' See II. ii. 8.

ἔσται ἄδικος, ἑκὼν ἄδικος ἂν εἴη, οὐ μὴν ἐάν γε βού-
ληται, ἄδικος ὢν παύσεται καὶ ἔσται δίκαιος· οὐδὲ γὰρ
ὁ νοσῶν ὑγιής. Καὶ εἰ οὕτως ἔτυχεν, ἑκὼν νοσεῖ, ἀκρα-
τῶς βιοτεύων καὶ ἀπειθῶν τοῖς ἰατροῖς. Τότε μὲν οὖν
ἐξῆν αὐτῷ μὴ νοσεῖν, προεμένῳ δ' οὐκέτι, ὥσπερ οὐδ'
ἀφέντι λίθον ἔτ' αὐτὸν δυνατὸν ἀναλαβεῖν· ἀλλ' ὅμως
ἐπ' αὐτῷ τὸ βαλεῖν καὶ ῥῖψαι· ἡ γὰρ ἀρχὴ ἐπ' αὐτῷ.
Οὕτω δὲ καὶ τῷ ἀδίκῳ καὶ τῷ ἀκολάστῳ ἐξ ἀρχῆς μὲν
ἐξῆν τοιούτοις μὴ γενέσθαι, διὸ ἑκόντες εἰσίν· γενομέ-
15 νοις δ' οὐκέτι ἔξεστι μὴ εἶναι. Οὐ μόνον δ' αἱ τῆς
ψυχῆς κακίαι ἑκούσιοί εἰσιν, ἀλλ' ἐνίοις καὶ αἱ τοῦ
σώματος, οἷς καὶ ἐπιτιμῶμεν· τοῖς μὲν γὰρ διὰ φύσιν
αἰσχροῖς οὐδεὶς ἐπιτιμᾷ, τοῖς δὲ δι' ἀγυμνασίαν καὶ
ἀμέλειαν. Ὁμοίως δὲ καὶ περὶ ἀσθένειαν καὶ πήρωσιν·
οὐθεὶς γὰρ ἂν ὀνειδίσειε τυφλῷ φύσει ἢ ἐκ νόσου ἢ ἐκ
πληγῆς, ἀλλὰ μᾶλλον ἐλεήσαι· τῷ δ' ἐξ οἰνοφλυγίας ἢ
16 ἄλλης ἀκολασίας πᾶς ἂν ἐπιτιμήσαι. Τῶν δὴ περὶ τὸ
σῶμα κακιῶν αἱ ἐφ' ἡμῖν ἐπιτιμῶνται, αἱ δὲ μὴ ἐφ' ἡμῖν

that he can arrest the formation of the habit at any step after
the first. The first steps of moral, as often of physical, disease
are voluntary, and though its progress soon passes out of our
power, yet as we are responsible for its beginning, we are also
15 answerable for all that it afterwards becomes. (*e*) The same
remarks apply to bodily defects, which we pity if of natural
or accidental growth, but visit with reproach if traceable to
16 neglect, excess, or any other avoidable causes, and we may
reasonably suppose that defects of body and of soul are blamed
on the same principle, viz. when men believe them to be

1. οὐ μὴν ἐάν γε κ.τ.λ.] 'It does not however follow that if,' etc.

5. προεμένῳ] 'When he has thrown away his health' (Grant). προιέσθαι is the word used for squandering money in IV. i, etc.

οὔ. Εἰ δ' οὕτω, καὶ ἐπὶ τῶν ἄλλων αἱ ἐπιτιμώμεναι τῶν
17 *κακιῶν ἐφ' ἡμῖν ἂν εἶεν. Εἰ δέ τις λέγοι ὅτι πάντες ἐφίενται τοῦ φαινομένου ἀγαθοῦ, τῆς δὲ φαντασίας οὐ κύριοι, ἀλλ' ὁποῖός ποθ' ἕκαστός ἐστι, τοιοῦτο καὶ τὸ τέλος φαίνεται αὐτῷ· [εἰ μὲν οὖν ἕκαστος ἑαυτῷ τῆς ἕξεώς ἐστί πως αἴτιος, καὶ τῆς φαντασίας ἔσται πως αὐτὸς αἴτιος·] εἰ δὲ μή, οὐθεὶς αὑτῷ αἴτιος τοῦ κακὰ ποιεῖν, ἀλλὰ δι' ἄγνοιαν τοῦ τέλους ταῦτα πράττει, διὰ τούτων οἰόμενος αὑτῷ τὸ ἄριστον ἔσεσθαι, ἡ δὲ τοῦ*

iii. The argument 'that we are not responsible for the *impressions* which external objects make upon us, nor therefore for acting accordingly,' is refuted (1) by denying its truth; (2) by showing that it proves too much, as it applies to Virtue as well as Vice.

17 voluntary. iii. It is sometimes argued, 'We all desire what *appears* to us good, and we are not responsible for the appearance presented, or impression made upon us, by external objects.' To this we reply (1) that if we are responsible for our general condition, we must be so in some sense for the impression which things make upon us, for this depends upon our condition to a great extent; (2) if we are not so responsible, then all that our opponents say is true: we are not

2. *εἰ δέ τις κ.τ.λ.*] The argument now returns to the first class of opponents who maintain that Virtue is voluntary and Vice involuntary, and it attacks the favourite argument on which they mainly relied. This was explained in the note at the commencement of this Chapter.

3. *φαντασία* here has its original signification of 'appearance,' and is little more than a repetition of *φαινομένου* just before.

5. Observe the alternatives *εἰ μὲν οὖν . . . εἰ δὲ μή*. The consequences following on the latter supposition are enumerated as far as the end of § 17, and the results of those consequences as bearing on the argument in hand are introduced by *εἰ δὴ ταῦτ' ἐστὶν ἀληθῆ* in § 18.

6. *ἕξις* has the simple meaning of 'state' or 'condition.' The impression which things make on us, morally as well as physically, depends very much on our condition, and for this we are in some degree (*πως*) responsible. Compare Butler: 'When we say that men are misled by external circumstances of temptation, it cannot but be understood that there is somewhat within themselves to render those circumstances temptations, or to render them *susceptible of impressions* from them' (*Anal.* p. 78, ed. Angus).

τέλους ἔφεσις οὐκ αὐθαίρετος, ἀλλὰ φῦναι δεῖ ὥσπερ
ὄψιν ἔχοντα, ᾗ κρινεῖ καλῶς καὶ τὸ κατ' ἀλήθειαν ἀγα-
θὸν αἱρήσεται· καὶ ἔστιν εὐφυὴς ᾧ τοῦτο καλῶς πέφυ-
κεν· τὸ γὰρ μέγιστον καὶ κάλλιστον, καὶ ὃ παρ' ἑτέρου
μὴ οἷόν τε λαβεῖν μηδὲ μαθεῖν, ἀλλ' οἷον ἔφυ, τοιοῦτον
ἕξει, καὶ τὸ εὖ καὶ τὸ καλῶς τοῦτο πεφυκέναι ἡ τελεία
18 καὶ ἀληθινὴ ἂν εἴη εὐφυΐα. Εἰ δὴ ταῦτ' ἐστὶν ἀληθῆ,
τί μᾶλλον ἡ ἀρετὴ τῆς κακίας ἔσται ἑκούσιον; ἀμφοῖν
γὰρ ὁμοίως, τῷ ἀγαθῷ καὶ τῷ κακῷ, τὸ τέλος φύσει ἢ
ὁπωσδήποτε φαίνεται καὶ κεῖται, τὰ δὲ λοιπὰ πρὸς τοῦτ'
19 ἀναφέροντες πράττουσιν ὁπωσδήποτε. Εἴτε δὴ τὸ τέλος
μὴ φύσει ἑκάστῳ φαίνεται οἱονδήποτε, ἀλλά τι καὶ παρ'

responsible if we do wrong; the choice of the ends at which we aim depends on our nature and constitution, not on ourselves; and a right tendency in this respect will constitute the
18 highest perfection of natural gifts. But all this applies just as much to the choice of good ends as of bad ones. It removes the credit of our good acts as well as the blame of our bad acts. In a word, it proves Virtue to be as involuntary as Vice.
19 iv. It is a slight modification of the last argument to maintain

iv. The argument that Virtue is

1. φῦναι is emphatic. 'One must be born with, as it were, a sense of sight by which,' etc. If a man is born colour-blind he cannot help seeing things differently from other people; he is not master of the appearance presented to him (τῆς φαντασίας οὐ κύριος). So, it is argued by the opponents, moral, like physical, impressions depend on purely natural causes beyond our control.

4. τὸ γὰρ μέγιστον κ.τ.λ.] Understand ἐστὶ. 'For it is that which is greatest and noblest, and that which none can (μή?) receive or learn from another, but as it is born with him so he will always have it.' We might also understand ἔχει or ἕξει before τὸ μέγιστον, and so avoid the change of nominative in the above rendering.

11. Εἴτε δὴ introduces Aristotle's own view; εἴτε τὸ μὲν (in l. 1, p. 144) that of the opponents, which he proceeds to refute; οὐθὲν ἧττον, the apodosis to both suppositions.

12. παρ' αὐτὸν] 'depending on himself.' Arnold (note on Thuc. i. 141. 9) compares the English

αὑτόν ἐστιν, εἴτε τὸ μὲν τέλος φυσικόν, τῷ δὲ τὰ λοιπὰ
πράττειν ἑκουσίως τὸν σπουδαῖον ἡ ἀρετὴ ἑκούσιόν
ἐστιν, οὐθὲν ἧττον καὶ ἡ κακία ἑκούσιον ἂν εἴη· ὁμοίως
γὰρ καὶ τῷ κακῷ ὑπάρχει τὸ δι' αὑτὸν ἐν ταῖς πράξεσι
20 καὶ εἰ μὴ ἐν τῷ τέλει. Εἰ οὖν, ὥσπερ λέγεται, ἑκού-
σιοί εἰσιν αἱ ἀρεταί (καὶ γὰρ τῶν ἕξεων συναίτιοί πως
αὐτοί ἐσμεν, καὶ τῷ ποιοί τινες εἶναι τὸ τέλος τοιόνδε
τιθέμεθα), καὶ αἱ κακίαι ἑκούσιοι ἂν εἶεν· ὁμοίως γάρ.
21 Κοινῇ μὲν οὖν περὶ τῶν ἀρετῶν εἴρηται ἡμῖν τό τε
γένος τύπῳ, ὅτι μεσότητές εἰσιν, καὶ ὅτι ἕξεις, ὑφ' ὧν
τε γίνονται, καὶ ὅτι τούτων πρακτικαὶ καθ' αὑτάς, καὶ
ὅτι ἐφ' ἡμῖν καὶ ἑκούσιοι, καὶ οὕτως ὡς ἂν ὁ ὀρθὸς
22 λόγος προστάξῃ. Οὐχ ὁμοίως δὲ αἱ πράξεις ἑκούσιοί

voluntary in the choice of means even if we are not responsible for the end, is shown to apply equally to Vice.

that while the *end* (or the appearance of things to us as desirable) is fixed for us by natural causes, whether it be good or bad, yet that there is scope for the voluntariness of Virtue in the right choice of the *means*. To this we reply at once that
20 the wrong choice of means, which would constitute Vice, is equally voluntary. Our position is now proved, that if Virtue is voluntary so also is Vice voluntary.

Recapitulation.

21 The point we have now reached is this:—We have asserted Virtues to be mean states; we have shown how they are formed, and that they are in our own power and voluntary,
22 and under the guidance of reason. The states or habits it is

vulgarism '*along of* himself.' Cf. vi. 11. παρὰ τὴν ἐμπειρίαν 'depending on their experience.'

1. φυσικὸν] 'fixed by nature.' τὰ λοιπὰ 'all the rest,' *i.e.* the means to the end.

6. συναίτιοι] 'partly responsible for.' Notice that Aristotle admits that our habits are to some extent the result of causes over which we have no control.

7. τῷ ποιοί τινες εἶναι κ.τ.λ.] 'The condition in which we are regulates the character of the end which we set before us.'

8. ὁμοίως γὰρ] *sc.* ἔχουσι, 'they are on the same footing.'

10. ὑφ' ὧν τε γίγνονται] This refers to such passages as II. i. 6, II. ii. 8, etc.

11. τούτων πρακτικαὶ καθ' αὑτὰς] Explained by II. ii. 8.

εἰσι καὶ αἱ ἕξεις· τῶν μὲν γὰρ πράξεων ἀπ' ἀρχῆς μέχρι τοῦ τέλους κύριοί ἐσμεν, εἰδότες τὰ καθ' ἕκαστα, τῶν ἕξεων δὲ τῆς ἀρχῆς, καθ' ἕκαστα δὲ ἡ πρόσθεσις οὐ γνώριμος, ὥσπερ ἐπὶ τῶν ἀρρωστιῶν· ἀλλ' ὅτι ἐφ' ἡμῖν ἦν οὕτως ἢ μὴ οὕτω χρήσασθαι, διὰ τοῦτο ἑκούσιοι.

1 VI. Ἀναλαβόντες δὴ περὶ ἑκάστης, εἴπωμεν τίνες εἰσὶ
καὶ περὶ ποῖα καὶ πῶς· ἅμα δ' ἔσται δῆλον καὶ πόσαι
2 εἰσίν. Καὶ πρῶτον περὶ ἀνδρείας. Ὅτι μὲν οὖν μεσότης
ἐστὶ περὶ φόβους καὶ θάρρη, ἤδη καὶ πρότερον εἴρηται·
φοβούμεθα δὴ δῆλον ὅτι τὰ φοβερά· ταῦτα δ' ἐστὶν ὡς
ἁπλῶς εἰπεῖν κακά· διὸ καὶ τὸν φόβον ὁρίζονται προσ-

true are not voluntary in the same sense as the single acts which form them. As however their beginnings, though not the subsequent stages of their growth, are in our own power, the habits themselves are really in our own power.

CHAP. VI.—*The proper sphere and objects of Courage.*

1 Proceeding now to the consideration of the Virtues in
2 detail, we commence with Courage. This we have already
described as a mean state in regard to Fear and Confidence.
Fear may be defined as the anticipation of Evil of any kind,

Courage, though it is, speaking generally, a due moderation of fear, does not relate to *all* objects of fear,

CHAP. VI.—We now return to a discussion of the Virtues in detail as given in the (presumed) exhaustive Catalogue of II. vii., in order to show how the law of the relative mean is applicable to every Virtue in detail, and so to justify its prominent position in our Definition of Virtue as a whole.

The discussion of Courage occupies four Chapters, of which the subjects are as follows:—

vi. The proper sphere and objects of Courage.

vii. Courage considered as a mean state, and in reference to its motive, together with the related Excess and Defect.

viii. The distinction between genuine and spurious Courage, of which latter five types are described.

ix. Courage, though involving pain and loss, is no exception to the rule that all Virtue has pleasure in itself.

3 δοκίαν κακοῦ. Φοβούμεθα μὲν οὖν πάντα τὰ κακά, οἷον
ἀδοξίαν, πενίαν, νόσον, ἀφιλίαν, θάνατον· ἀλλ' οὐ περὶ
πάντα δοκεῖ ὁ ἀνδρεῖος εἶναι· ἔνια γὰρ καὶ δεῖ φοβεῖ-
σθαι καὶ καλόν, τὸ δὲ μὴ αἰσχρόν, οἷον ἀδοξίαν· ὁ μὲν
γὰρ φοβούμενος ἐπιεικὴς καὶ αἰδήμων, ὁ δὲ μὴ φοβού-
4 μενος ἀναίσχυντος. Λέγεται δ' ὑπό τινων ἀνδρεῖος κατὰ
μεταφοράν· ἔχει γάρ τι ὅμοιον τῷ ἀνδρείῳ· ἄφοβος
γάρ τις καὶ ὁ ἀνδρεῖος. Πενίαν δ' ἴσως οὐ δεῖ φοβεῖ-
σθαι οὐδὲ νόσον, οὐδ' ὅλως ὅσα μὴ ἀπὸ κακίας μηδὲ δι'
αὑτόν. Ἀλλ' οὐδ' ὁ περὶ ταῦτα ἄφοβος ἀνδρεῖος. Λέ-
γομεν δὲ καὶ τοῦτον καθ' ὁμοιότητα· ἔνιοι γὰρ ἐν τοῖς
πολεμικοῖς κινδύνοις δειλοὶ ὄντες ἐλευθέριοί εἰσι καὶ
5 πρὸς χρημάτων ἀποβολὴν εὐθαρσῶς ἔχουσιν. Οὐδὲ δὴ
εἴ τις ὕβριν περὶ παῖδας καὶ γυναῖκα φοβεῖται ἢ φθόνον
ἤ τι τῶν τοιούτων, δειλός ἐστιν· οὐδ' εἰ θαρρεῖ μέλλων
6 μαστιγοῦσθαι, ἀνδρεῖος. Περὶ ποῖα οὖν τῶν φοβερῶν
ὁ ἀνδρεῖος; ἢ περὶ τὰ μέγιστα; οὐθεὶς γὰρ ὑπομενετι-
κώτερος τῶν δεινῶν. Φοβερώτατον δ' ὁ θάνατος· πέρας

3 but we speak of Courage in reference to *some* only of the
4 objects of fear. *e.g.* We do not call a man courageous for
5 having no fear of disgrace, poverty, sickness, insults to
himself or his friends, envy, or even bodily chastisement.
6 Though the term Courage may sometimes be applied to
these cases, yet, strictly speaking, it has reference only to the

5. ἐπιεικὴς] 'a man of proper feeling.'

16. μαστιγοῦσθαι] This is in allusion to the Spartan custom of whipping their youths to make them fearless of pain, and so brave soldiers.

17. After ὑπομενετικώτερος supply ἢ ὁ περὶ τὰ μέγιστα ἄφοβος.

18. πέρας γὰρ] This passage is sometimes quoted as a proof that Aristotle had no belief in any sort of life after death. He seems however here to be speaking popularly in reference to the circumstances and prospects of ordinary life, and therefore the passage cannot fairly be pressed into the above controversy.

γὰρ, καὶ οὐδὲν ἔτι τῷ τεθνεῶτι δοκεῖ οὔτ' ἀγαθὸν οὔτε
7 κακὸν εἶναι. Δόξειε δ' ἂν οὐδὲ περὶ θάνατον τὸν ἐν
παντὶ ὁ ἀνδρεῖος εἶναι, οἷον εἰ ἐν θαλάττῃ ἢ ἐν νόσοις.
8 Ἐν τίσιν οὖν; ἢ ἐν τοῖς καλλίστοις; τοιοῦτοι δὲ οἱ
ἐν πολέμῳ· ἐν μεγίστῳ γὰρ καὶ καλλίστῳ κινδύνῳ.
9 Ὁμόλογοι δὲ τούτοις εἰσὶ καὶ αἱ τιμαὶ αἱ ἐν ταῖς πόλεσι
10 καὶ παρὰ τοῖς μονάρχοις. Κυρίως δὴ λέγοιτ' ἂν ἀνδρεῖος
ὁ περὶ τὸν καλὸν θάνατον ἀδεής, καὶ ὅσα θάνατον ἐπι-
φέρει ὑπόγυια ὄντα· τοιαῦτα δὲ μάλιστα τὰ κατὰ πόλε-
11 μον. Οὐ μὴν ἀλλὰ καὶ ἐν θαλάττῃ καὶ ἐν νόσοις ἀδεὴς
ὁ ἀνδρεῖος, οὐχ οὕτω δὲ ὡς οἱ θαλάττιοι· οἱ μὲν γὰρ
ἀπεγνώκασι τὴν σωτηρίαν καὶ τὸν θάνατον τὸν τοιοῦτον
δυσχεραίνουσιν, οἱ δὲ εὐέλπιδές εἰσι παρὰ τὴν ἐμπειρίαν.
12 Ἅμα δὲ καὶ ἀνδρίζονται ἐν οἷς ἐστὶν ἀλκὴ ἢ καλὸν τὸ ἀπο-
θανεῖν· ἐν ταῖς τοιαύταις δὲ φθοραῖς οὐθέτερον ὑπάρχει.

greatest of dangers, and such, from its absolute finality, is
7 Death. But we limit Courage still further to death of a noble
8 kind (excluding, *e.g.* death in shipwreck or disease), in fact,
10 strictly speaking, to death (and circumstances which threaten
death) *in war*, for this is admitted to be the noblest of all
11 deaths. Of course the brave man will be brave in all the
other cases that we have mentioned, but in its strict application Courage is limited to death and danger in war, and cases where there is some service or some glory to be gained by death.

but only to the greatest viz. Death, and especially to death in battle.

9. ὑπόγυιος is literally 'under the hand' (γυῖον), and so 'handy,' or 'near at hand.' It is otherwise explained as = 'sudden.' In that case comp. viii. 15. (See *Suppl. Notes.*)

11. οἱ μὲν = οἱ ἀνδρεῖοι, οἱ δε = οἱ θαλάττιοι. The courage of sailors is often due to the familiarity of experience. On this kind of courage see further viii.

6, 9. The courage of the truly brave man is shown in that, though he despairs of safety and hates the notion of such an inglorious death, still he will meet it without flinching.

14. ἀνδρίζονται] 'they also play the man,' or 'actively display courage. On the force of the middle voice cf. note on ἀνθρωπεύεσθαι in X. viii. 6. There seems

1 VII. Τὸ δὲ φοβερὸν οὐ πᾶσι μὲν τὸ αὐτό, λέγομεν δέ τι καὶ ὑπὲρ ἄνθρωπον. Τοῦτο μὲν οὖν παντὶ φοβερὸν τῷ γε νοῦν ἔχοντι, τὰ δὲ κατ' ἄνθρωπον διαφέρει μεγέθει καὶ τῷ μᾶλλον καὶ ἧττον· ὁμοίως δὲ καὶ τὰ θαρραλέα.
2 Ὁ δὲ ἀνδρεῖος ἀνέκπληκτος ὡς ἄνθρωπος. Φοβήσεται μὲν οὖν καὶ τὰ τοιαῦτα, ὡς δεῖ δὲ καὶ ὡς ὁ λόγος ὑπομενεῖ, τοῦ καλοῦ ἕνεκα· τοῦτο γὰρ τέλος τῆς ἀρετῆς.
3 Ἔστι δὲ μᾶλλον καὶ ἧττον ταῦτα φοβεῖσθαι, καὶ ἔτι
4 τὰ μὴ φοβερὰ ὡς τοιαῦτα φοβεῖσθαι. Γίνεται δὲ τῶν ἁμαρτιῶν ἡ μὲν ὅτι οὐ δεῖ, ἡ δὲ ὅτι οὐχ ὡς δεῖ, ἡ δὲ ὅτι οὐχ ὅτε, ἤ τι τῶν τοιούτων· ὁμοίως δὲ καὶ περὶ τὰ
5 θαρραλέα. Ὁ μὲν οὖν ἃ δεῖ καὶ οὗ ἕνεκα ὑπομένων καὶ φοβούμενος, καὶ ὡς δεῖ καὶ ὅτε, ὁμοίως δὲ καὶ θαρρῶν,

CHAP. VII.—*Courage considered as a mean state, with its related excess and defect.*

Courage in its objects, degrees, and occasions is regulated by Reason and stimulated by desire for the ideally noble (τὸ καλόν). (§§ 1—6.)

1 The objects of terror and its degree differ with different indi-
viduals, though some things there are which no human being
2 in his right senses could regard without terror. Within these
limits of human endurance the truly brave man is unshaken;
3, 4 his confidence as well as his fears, in respect of their objects,
degrees, and occasions (in all of which points error is possible),
being regulated by Reason, and his motive being always (as in
5 all the other virtues) the ideally noble. Such are the charac-

to be a sort of *a fortiori* comparison of καὶ ἀνδρίζονται with the more passive condition ἀδεὴς ἐστι in the last section. Observe also that some force is due to the connexion both in etymology and thought between ἀνδρίζομαι and ἀνδρεία.

ἐν οἷς ἐστὶν ἀλκή] Either 'where there is opportunity for the display of prowess:' or (as in the analysis) 'some defence or security for others,' which is the case in war when a man dies to defend his country: in fact =βοήθεια, as elsewhere in Aristotle.

5. ὡς ἄνθρωπος] i.e. within human limits, as far as a man can be. Cf. μακαρίους δὲ ἀνθρώπους in I. x. 16, and the note on ὡς ἀλαζὼν in IV. vii. 11.

ἀνδρεῖος· κατ' ἀξίαν γάρ, καὶ ὡς ἂν ὁ λόγος, πάσχει
6 καὶ πράττει ὁ ἀνδρεῖος. Τέλος δὲ πάσης ἐνεργείας ἐστὶ
τὸ κατὰ τὴν ἕξιν. Καὶ τῷ ἀνδρείῳ δὲ ἡ ἀνδρεία καλόν.
Τοιοῦτον δὴ καὶ τὸ τέλος· (ὁρίζεται γὰρ ἕκαστον τῷ
τέλει). Καλοῦ δὴ ἕνεκα ὁ ἀνδρεῖος ὑπομένει καὶ πράττει
7 τὰ κατὰ τὴν ἀνδρείαν. Τῶν δ' ὑπερβαλλόντων ὁ μὲν τῇ
ἀφοβίᾳ ἀνώνυμος (εἴρηται δ' ἡμῖν ἐν τοῖς πρότερον ὅτι
πολλά ἐστιν ἀνώνυμα), εἴη δ' ἄν τις μαινόμενος ἢ ἀνάλ-
γητος, εἰ μηθὲν φοβοῖτο, μήτε σεισμὸν μήτε τὰ κύματα,

6 teristics of Courage. And not only the formed habit, but also each individual act of Courage, will be guided by this one motive, the attainment of the ideally noble.

7 Now both confidence and fear admit of excess. Excess of fearlessness (if we may so speak) *i.e.* a total absence of fear under

The Excess and Defect are Rashness and Cowardice. (§§ 7—12.)

2. The following points should be noticed in explaining this difficult section. (1) There is a marked opposition between ἐνέργεια (act) and ἕξις (habit) on which the argument turns. Compare IV. ii. 6 for a similar antithesis and somewhat similar argument. (2) ὁρίζεται γὰρ ἕκαστον τῷ τέλει is a parenthetical argument (or prosyllogism) supporting one of the premisses of the main syllogism. The main argument is:—

> The end of the formed habit (τὸ κατὰ τὴν ἕξιν (τέλος)) is also the end of each individual act (πάσης ἐνεργείας). τὸ καλὸν is the end of the formed habit of Courage (τοιοῦτον δὴ καὶ τὸ τέλος). Therefore it is the end of each act of Courage (καλοῦ δὴ ἕνεκα κ.τ.λ.).

The parenthesis supports the minor premiss thus:—

> That which characterizes anything is its end (ὁρίζεται ἕκαστον τῷ τέλει). τὸ καλὸν characterizes the habit of Courage (τῷ ἀνδρείῳ ἡ ἀνδρεία καλόν). Therefore τὸ καλὸν is the end of the habit of Courage (τοιοῦτον δὴ τὸ τέλος).

6. The complication of the extremes here is rather confusing. In *theory* four (viz. Excess of Confidence, Defect of Confidence, Excess of Timidity, Defect of Timidity), in *fact* they reduce to two. For Excess of Confidence and Defect of Timidity are the same, and constitute Rashness; while Defect of Confidence and Excess of Timidity are also identical, and constitute Cowardice. See further, note on II. vii. 2.

καθάπερ φασὶ τοὺς Κελτούς. Ὁ δὲ τῷ θαρρεῖν ὑπερ-
8 βάλλων περὶ τὰ φοβερὰ θρασύς. Δοκεῖ δὲ καὶ ἀλαζὼν
εἶναι ὁ θρασὺς καὶ προσποιητικὸς ἀνδρείας. Ὡς οὖν
ἐκεῖνος περὶ τὰ φοβερὰ ἔχει, οὕτως οὗτος βούλεται
9 φοβερὰ αι· ἐν οἷς οὖν δύναται, μιμεῖται. Διὸ καὶ εἰσὶν
οἱ πολλοὶ αὐτῶν θρασύδειλοι· ἐν τούτοις γὰρ θρασυνό-
10 μενοι τὰ φοβερὰ οὐχ ὑπομένουσιν. Ὁ δὲ τῷ φοβεῖσθαι
ὑπερβάλλων δειλός· καὶ γὰρ ἃ μὴ δεῖ καὶ ὡς οὐ δεῖ,
καὶ πάν τὰ τοιαῦτα ἀκολουθεῖ αὐτῷ. Ἐλλείπει δὲ
καὶ τῷ θαρρεῖν· ἀλλ' ἐν ταῖς λύπαις ὑπερβάλλων μᾶλ-
11 λον καταφανής ἐστιν. Δύσελπις δή τις ὁ δειλός· πάντα
γὰρ φοβεῖται. Ὁ δ' ἀνδρεῖος ἐναντίως· τὸ γὰρ θαρ-
12 ρεῖν εὐέλπιδος. Περὶ ταὐτὰ μὲν οὖν ἐστὶν ὅ τε δειλὸς
καὶ ὁ θρασὺς καὶ ὁ ἀνδρεῖος, διαφόρως δ' ἔχουσι πρὸς
αὐτά· οἱ μὲν γὰρ ὑπερβάλλουσι καὶ ἐλλείπουσιν, ὁ δὲ

all circumstances, exists rather in idea than in fact. Excess of
8 confidence gives rise to the extreme of Rashness. The Rash
man has also a tendency to swagger, and he makes an ostenta-
tion of Courage. To secure the reputation of Courage, for which
he is anxious, he imitates its external signs as far as he can.
9 In real danger however such characters are often found want-
10 ing. Excess of timidity (which implies defect of confidence)
gives rise to the other extreme of Cowardice, which is mani-
11 fested by over-sensitiveness to pain and by despondency.
12 Thus Rashness, Cowardice, and Courage relate to the same
objects and circumstances; but Rashness and Cowardice
manifest excess and defect, while Courage is a mean state,
respecting them. We might add that *before* the danger comes

4. ἐκεῖνος, *i.e.* ἀνδρεῖος. οὗτος, *i.e.* ὁ θρασύς.

6. θρασύδειλοι] Falstaff would be a familiar example. See especially *Henry IV.*, Part I. Act ii. Sc. 4; Act v. Sc. 4, etc.

ἐν τούτοις] *i.e.* ἐν οἷς δύνανται.

9. 'The coward is also deficient in confidence, but his character is more usually displayed by an excessive sensibility to pain.' Cf. x. 1 (fin.), xi. 5.

μέσως ἔχει καὶ ὡς δεῖ· καὶ οἱ μὲν θρασεῖς προπετεῖς, καὶ βουλόμενοι πρὸ τῶν κινδύνων, ἐν αὐτοῖς δ' ἀφίστανται, οἱ δ' ἀνδρεῖοι ἐν τοῖς ἔργοις ὀξεῖς, πρότερον δ' ἡσύχιοι.

13 Καθάπερ οὖν εἴρηται, ἡ ἀνδρεία μεσότης ἐστὶ περὶ θαρραλέα καὶ φοβερά, ἐν οἷς εἴρηται, καὶ ὅτι καλὸν αἱρεῖται καὶ ὑπομένει, ἢ ὅτι αἰσχρὸν τὸ μή. Τὸ δ' ἀποθνήσκειν

the Rash are eager, the Brave are calm; *in* the danger the Brave are full of energy, the Rash fall away altogether.

Suicide is rather a case of Cowardice than of Courage.

13 It will follow from what we have said that Suicthe is an act of Cowardice rather than of Courage. For the Suicide

1. Tacitus (*Hist.* i. 68) describes the Helvetii in very similar words as being 'ante discrimen feroces, in periculo pavidi,' and (in *Hist.* i. 84) he generalizes, as Aristotle does in this passage, 'Fortissimus in ipso discrimine exercitus qui ante discrimen quietissimus.' Compare the well-known description in Homer, *Il.* iii. 1-9, of the Greek host advancing in silence to the battle.

5. ἐν οἷς εἴρηται] in reference to the limitations introduced in ch. vi.

καὶ ὅτι καλὸν κ.τ.λ.] 'And it chooses and endures them (viz. φοβερά), because it is honourable to do so.' On this point see § 6.

6. The views of the ancients on Suicide (mixed up as the question must be with that of the nature of the Soul, Death, and a Future State) were very different from our own. It was allowed and even advocated by men of the highest moral character, and of great philosophical reputation, especially by the Stoics. Those who condemned it did so generally on one or other of these three grounds:—

(1) On political grounds. Suicide deprived the state of services which it had a right to claim. Aristotle urges this in V. xi. 1-3. The Stoics admitted that Suicide was wrong when this result could be shown to be involved in it. Hadrian regarded the suicide of a Roman soldier as equivalent to desertion.

(2) On the ground that it was an act of cowardice, as Aristotle argues in this passage. So Seneca, 'It is folly to die for fear of death,' and Ovid:—

Rebus in adversis facile est contemnere vitam;
Fortiter ille facit qui miser esse potest.

(3) Less seldom on the usual modern ground that it amounts to an abandonment of a post of duty in which God has placed us. This was the point of view of Plato (see *Phædo,* etc.) and his successors, also of Pythagoras (Cic. *de Senect.* xx. § 73), who

φεύγοντα πενίαν ἢ ἔρωτα ἤ τι λυπηρὸν οὐκ ἀνδρείου, ἀλλὰ μᾶλλον δειλοῦ· μαλακία γὰρ τὸ φεύγειν τὰ ἐπίπονα, καὶ οὐχ ὅτι καλὸν ὑπομένει, ἀλλὰ φεύγων κακόν.

1 VIII. Ἔστι μὲν οὖν ἡ ἀνδρεία τοιοῦτόν τι, λέγονται δὲ καὶ ἕτεραι κατὰ πέντε τρόπους, πρῶτον μὲν ἡ πολιτική· μάλιστα γὰρ ἔοικεν· δοκοῦσι γὰρ ὑπομένειν τοὺς κινδύνους οἱ πολῖται διὰ τὰ ἐκ τῶν νόμων ἐπιτίμια καὶ 2 τὰ ὀνείδη καὶ διὰ τὰς τιμάς. Καὶ διὰ τοῦτο ἀνδρειότατοι δοκοῦσιν εἶναι παρ' οἷς οἱ δειλοὶ ἄτιμοι καὶ οἱ ἀνδρεῖοι ἔντιμοι. Τοιούτους δὲ καὶ Ὅμηρος ποιεῖ, οἷον τὸν Διομήδην καὶ τὸν Ἕκτορα.

Πουλυδάμας μοι πρῶτος ἐλεγχείην ἀναθήσει·

καὶ Διομήδης,

Ἕκτωρ γάρ ποτε φήσει ἐνὶ Τρώεσσ' ἀγορεύων
"Τυδείδης ὑπ' ἐμεῖο."

faces death not because it is noble, but because he regards death as a less evil than that from which he seeks to escape.

CHAP. VIII.—*Spurious forms of Courage described.*

Five spurious forms of Courage arise severally from i. Fear of society. This may be due to either *moral* compulsion,

1 In contrast with genuine Courage now described, there are five spurious forms which must be distinguished from it. 1. *The courage of compulsion*, which may perhaps be called 2 'Social' courage, because it arises from fear of society. Its nobler type is that which is due to fear of loss of character, or of the good opinion of those among whom we live, or even 3 to the influence of the rewards and punishments by which

'forbids a man to desert his post without the order of his commander, who is God.'

(Several other quotations from ancient moralists will be found in Lecky, *Hist. Eur. Morals*, i. p. 223, etc.)

3. ὑπομένει] Understand *θάνατον* from the general sense of the context. See vi. 12.

15. The whole line runs, *Il.* viii. 149:

Τυδείδης ὑπ' ἐμεῖο φοβεύμενος ἵκετο νῆας.

Thus the Courage of Dio-

3 Ὡμοίωται δ' αὕτη μάλιστα τῇ πρότερον εἰρημένῃ, ὅτι
δι' ἀρετὴν γίνεται· δι' αἰδῶ γὰρ καὶ διὰ καλοῦ ὄρεξιν
4 (τιμῆς γὰρ) καὶ φυγὴν ὀνείδους, αἰσχροῦ ὄντος. Τάξαι
δ' ἄν τις καὶ τοὺς ὑπὸ τῶν ἀρχόντων ἀναγκαζομένους
εἰς ταὐτό· χείρους δ' ὅσῳ οὐ δι' αἰδῶ ἀλλὰ διὰ φόβον
αὐτὸ δρῶσι, καὶ φεύγοντες οὐ τὸ αἰσχρὸν ἀλλὰ τὸ λυ-
πηρόν· ἀναγκάζουσι γὰρ οἱ κύριοι, ὥσπερ ὁ Ἕκτωρ

> ὃν δέ κ' ἐγὼν ἀπάνευθε μάχης πτώσσοντα νοήσω,
> οὔ οἱ ἄρκιον ἐσσεῖται φυγέειν κύνας.

5 Καὶ οἱ προστάττοντες κἂν ἀναχωρῶσι τύπτοντες τὸ
αὐτὸ δρῶσι, καὶ οἱ πρὸ τῶν τάφρων καὶ τῶν τοιούτων
παρατάττοντες· πάντες γὰρ ἀναγκάζουσιν. Δεῖ δ' οὐ δι'
6 ἀνάγκην ἀνδρεῖον εἶναι, ἀλλ' ὅτι καλόν. Δοκεῖ δὲ καὶ

3 civil society encourages Bravery, and thus, the motive being
noble, in some cases this type approximates very nearly to
4 the genuine virtue. A baser form may be seen in the courage *or physical compulsion*
5 of troops who are driven to battle with the lash, or drawn up
6 in positions where retreat is impossible. 2. *The courage of* ii. Experience.

mede is represented as due to the fear that Hector would triumph over him, if defeated. Conversely to the case in the text it has been said, 'Perfect Courage is doing without witnesses all that one could do if the world were spectators' (La Rochefoucauld, *Max.* 216).

1. Aristotle here touches upon a question of the greatest interest in moral science, How far does a system of rewards and punishments destroy the character of Virtue by reducing it to a calculation of self-interest? It depends greatly on the character of the rewards and punishments themselves. If they consist in physical pleasure or pain, no true virtue can be developed by them. If however they be themselves moral (*e.g.* testimony of a good conscience, dread of shame or self-reproach, etc.), the stimulus to action which they afford is but a form of the love of Virtue and hatred of Vice in themselves. The case described in § 3 would illustrate the latter case, that in §§ 4 and 5 the former.

10. τύπτοντες] *e.g.* as Herodotus (vii. 223) says was the case with the Persian soldiers at the invasion of Greece.

ἡ ἐμπειρία ἡ περὶ ἕκαστα ἀνδρεία τις εἶναι· ὅθεν καὶ ὁ Σωκράτης ᾠήθη ἐπιστήμην εἶναι τὴν ἀνδρείαν. Τοιοῦτοι δὲ ἄλλοι μὲν ἐν ἄλλοις, ἐν τοῖς πολεμικοῖς δ' οἱ στρατιῶται· δοκεῖ γὰρ εἶναι πολλὰ κενὰ τοῦ πολέμου, ἃ μάλιστα συνεωράκασιν οὗτοι· φαίνονται δὴ ἀνδρεῖοι,
7 ὅτι οὐκ ἴσασιν οἱ ἄλλοι οἷά ἐστιν. Εἶτα ποιῆσαι καὶ μὴ παθεῖν μάλιστα δύνανται ἐκ τῆς ἐμπειρίας, δυνάμενοι

experience, which Socrates thought the truest type of Courage. Experience enables soldiers, for example, so to estimate the real danger that they are not alarmed by circumstances that
7, 8 would terrify the inexperienced. Thus experience as it were

1. ἡ ἐμπειρία ἡ περὶ ἕκαστα] 'Experience in any special subjects.' This is further explained by τοιοῦτοι (*i.e.* ἔμπειροι) ἄλλοι ἐν ἄλλοις in l. 3. Aristotle shows that experience cannot constitute courage—for if the danger be *unreal*, experience, which tells us that it is so, takes away the sphere for the exercise of courage (§§ 7, 8); while if the danger be *real*, experience, which reveals this, tends to make cowards of those who know it (§ 9).

2. Socrates defines Courage (in Plat. *Rep.* p. 429) as 'the power of preserving in danger the *right opinion* as to what is to be feared and what is not.' Or again in the *Protagoras*, 'Courage is the knowledge of what is terrible and what is not,' ἡ σοφία τῶν δεινῶν καὶ μὴ δεινῶν ἀνδρεία ἐστίν.

4. πολλὰ κενὰ τοῦ πολέμου] *i.e.* many dangers in war are unreal, *e.g.* the ferocious aspect and savage cries of barbarians, which are most alarming to the inexperienced, but which make no impression on the veteran. It was said that at the commencement of the war between France and Prussia, there were served out to the young German troops pictures of the Turcos and their mode of fighting, in order to give them that ἐμπειρία which would render them proof against such terrors. Another reading is καινὰ, *i.e.* there are many 'surprises' in war; but this evidently spoils the sense.

5. φαίνονται δὴ ἀνδρεῖοι κ.τ.λ.] This would be further illustrated by the example introduced in vi. 11. The indifference of sailors in an ordinary gale is regarded by a landsman as courage (ὅτι οὐκ ἴσασιν οἱ ἄλλοι οἷά ἐστιν), whereas in truth their ἐμπειρία reveals that there is no danger, and therefore no occasion for courage.

χρῆσθαι τοῖς ὅπλοις καὶ τοιαῦτα ἔχοντες ὁποῖα ἂν εἴη
καὶ πρὸς τὸ ποιῆσαι καὶ πρὸς τὸ μὴ παθεῖν κράτιστα.
8 Ὥσπερ οὖν ἀνόπλοις ὡπλισμένοι μάχονται καὶ ἀθληταὶ
ἰδιώταις· καὶ γὰρ ἐν τοῖς τοιούτοις ἀγῶσιν οὐχ οἱ ἀν-
δρειότατοι μαχιμώτατοί εἰσιν, ἀλλ' οἱ μάλιστα ἰσχύον-
9 τες καὶ τὰ σώματα ἄριστα ἔχοντες. Οἱ στρατιῶται δὲ
δειλοὶ γίνονται, ὅταν ὑπερτείνῃ ὁ κίνδυνος καὶ λείπωνται
τοῖς πλήθεσι καὶ ταῖς παρασκευαῖς· πρῶτοι γὰρ φεύ-
γουσι, τὰ δὲ πολιτικὰ μένοντα ἀποθνήσκει, ὅπερ κἀπὶ
τῷ Ἑρμαίῳ συνέβη. Τοῖς μὲν γὰρ αἰσχρὸν τὸ φεύγειν
καὶ ὁ θάνατος τῆς τοιαύτης σωτηρίας αἱρετώτερος· οἱ δὲ
καὶ ἐξ ἀρχῆς ἐκινδύνευον ὡς κρείττους ὄντες, γνόντες δὲ
φεύγουσι, τὸν θάνατον μᾶλλον τοῦ αἰσχροῦ φοβούμενοι·

puts a weapon into their hands which others have not, and hence their courage. There is however another aspect of
9 this. Experience sometimes points out the real magnitude of a danger which makes little impression on those who are inexperienced, and so sometimes veterans shrink back when raw levies press on. Thus courage which rests on the knowledge that the danger is small becomes cowardice when the danger is known to be great. This therefore is not true

9. *τὰ πολιτικὰ* nearly resembled our militia as distinguished from regular troops. It is not quite clear to what event reference is made in the text. It is easy, however, to suppose that veterans would be much more sensitive (say) to a flank movement on the part of the enemy, or to a threatening of their communications, than inexperienced troops would be, and would thus be more likely to be disorganized by it. It is experience which makes doctors proverbially the most desponding patients, because they understand what symptoms portend.

The following recent occurrence seems in point: 'The troops who behaved worst in this affair (a skirmish near Paris) were the regulars, Zouaves, who fled like deer. The Gardes Mobiles stood their ground' (Paris letter, *Sept.* 23, 1870).

10 ὁ δ' ἀνδρεῖος οὐ τοιοῦτος. Καὶ τὸν θυμὸν δ' ἐπὶ τὴν ἀνδρείαν ἐπιφέρουσιν· ἀνδρεῖοι γὰρ εἶναι δοκοῦσι καὶ οἱ διὰ θυμὸν ὥσπερ τὰ θηρία ἐπὶ τοὺς τρώσαντας φερόμενοι, ὅτι καὶ οἱ ἀνδρεῖοι θυμοειδεῖς· ἰτητικώτατον γὰρ ὁ θυμὸς πρὸς τοὺς κινδύνους, ὅθεν καὶ Ὅμηρος

σθένος ἔμβαλε θυμῷ

καὶ

μένος καὶ θυμὸν ἔγειρε

καὶ

δριμὺ δ' ἀνὰ ῥῖνας μένος

καὶ

ἔζεσεν αἷμα·

πάντα γὰρ τὰ τοιαῦτα ἔοικε σημαίνειν τὴν τοῦ θυμοῦ
11 ἔγερσιν καὶ ὁρμήν. Οἱ μὲν οὖν ἀνδρεῖοι διὰ τὸ καλὸν πράττουσιν, ὁ δὲ θυμὸς συνεργεῖ αὐτοῖς· τὰ θηρία δὲ διὰ λύπην· διὰ γὰρ τὸ πληγῆναι ἢ φοβεῖσθαι, ἐπεὶ ἐάν γε ἐν ὕλῃ ἢ ἐν ἕλει ᾖ, οὐ προσέρχονται. Οὐ δή ἐστιν ἀνδρεία διὰ τὸ ὑπ' ἀλγηδόνος καὶ θυμοῦ ἐξελαυνόμενα πρὸς τὸν κίνδυνον ὁρμᾶν, οὐθὲν τῶν δεινῶν προορῶντα, ἐπεὶ οὕτω γε κἂν οἱ ὄνοι ἀνδρεῖοι εἶεν πεινῶντες· τυπτόμενοι γὰρ οὐκ ἀφίστανται τῆς νομῆς· καὶ οἱ μοιχοὶ
12 δὲ διὰ τὴν ἐπιθυμίαν τολμηρὰ πολλὰ δρῶσιν. Οὐ δή ἐστιν ἀνδρεῖα τὰ δι' ἀλγηδόνος ἢ θυμοῦ ἐξελαυνόμενα πρὸς τὸν κίνδυνον. Φυσικωτάτη δ' ἔοικεν ἡ διὰ τὸν

iii. High Spirit.

10, 11 Courage. 3. *The courage of high spirit.*—It is true that the courageous are high-spirited, and that the outward signs of courage and high spirit are similar, and also that high spirit
12 is a stimulus to courage. But they are not identical, else

4. ἰτητικὸς] 'apt to advance,' connected with εἶμι (*ibo*) through the verbal ἰτέον.

24. φυσικωτάτη] 'more purely physical than other sorts of Courage.'

θυμὸν εἶναι, καὶ προσλαβοῦσα προαίρεσιν καὶ τὸ οὗ
ἕνεκα ἀνδρεία εἶναι. Καὶ οἱ ἄνθρωποι δὴ ὀργιζόμενοι
μὲν ἀλγοῦσι, τιμωρούμενοι δ' ἥδονται· οἱ δὲ διὰ ταῦτα
μαχόμενοι μάχιμοι μέν, οὐκ ἀνδρεῖοι δέ· οὐ γὰρ διὰ τὸ
καλὸν οὐδ' ὡς ὁ λόγος, ἀλλὰ διὰ τὸ πάθος· παραπλή-
13 σιον δ' ἔχουσί τι. Οὐδὲ δὴ οἱ εὐέλπιδες ὄντες ἀν-
δρεῖοι· διὰ γὰρ τὸ πολλάκις καὶ πολλοὺς νενικηκέναι
θαρροῦσιν ἐν τοῖς κινδύνοις. Παρόμοιοι δέ, ὅτι ἄμφω
θαρραλέοι· ἀλλ' οἱ μὲν ἀνδρεῖοι διὰ τὰ προειρημένα
θαρραλέοι, οἱ δὲ διὰ τὸ οἴεσθαι κρείττους εἶναι καὶ
14 μηθὲν ἀντιπαθεῖν. Τοιοῦτον δὲ ποιοῦσι καὶ οἱ μεθυσκό-
μενοι· εὐέλπιδες γὰρ γίνονται. Ὅταν δὲ αὐτοῖς μὴ
συμβῇ τοιαῦτα, φεύγουσιν· ἀνδρείου δ' ἦν τὰ φοβερὰ
ἀνθρώπῳ ὄντα καὶ φαινόμενα ὑπομένειν, ὅτι καλὸν καὶ
15 αἰσχρὸν τὸ μή. Διὸ καὶ ἀνδρειοτέρου δοκεῖ εἶναι τὸ
ἐν τοῖς αἰφνιδίοις φόβοις ἄφοβον καὶ ἀτάραχον εἶναι
ἢ ἐν τοῖς προδήλοις· ἀπὸ ἕξεως γὰρ μᾶλλον, ἢ καὶ ὅτι
ἧττον ἐκ παρασκευῆς· τὰ προφανῆ μὲν γὰρ κἂν ἐκ

some of the lower animals, or men of violent passions, would
afford the highest examples of courage. High spirit appears
to be the natural *substratum* of courage, and requires only
deliberate choice and a right motive to transform it from mere
13 pugnacity to true courage. 4. *The courage of a sanguine*
disposition.—This results from a confident belief in success;
in other words, from a belief that there is no serious danger
14 to fear. A drunken man exhibits this sort of courage. It
15 fails when danger appears contrary to expectation. Hence

iv. Sanguine disposition.

11. τοιοῦτον δὲ ποιοῦσι κ.τ.λ.] This would be an instance of what is sometimes called 'Dutch courage.' Falstaff's encomium on 'Sherris' as the source of Courage in *Henry IV.* Part II. Act iv. Sc. 3, may be quoted, under the influence of which 'the heart great and puffed up . . . doth any deed of courage; and this valour comes of sherris.'

λογισμοῦ καὶ λόγου τις προέλοιτο, τὰ δ' ἐξαίφνης κατὰ
16 τὴν ἕξιν. Ἀνδρεῖοι δὲ φαίνονται καὶ οἱ ἀγνοοῦντες, καὶ εἰσὶν οὐ πόρρω τῶν εὐελπίδων, χείρους δ' ὅσῳ ἀξίωμα οὐδὲν ἔχουσιν, ἐκεῖνοι δέ. Διὸ καὶ μένουσί τινα χρόνον· οἱ δ' ἠπατημένοι, ἐὰν γνῶσιν ὅτι ἕτερον ἢ ὑποπτεύσωσι, φεύγουσιν· ὅπερ οἱ Ἀργεῖοι ἔπαθον
17 περιπεσόντες τοῖς Λάκωσιν ὡς Σικυωνίοις. Οἵ τε δὴ ἀνδρεῖοι εἴρηνται ποῖοί τινες, καὶ οἱ δοκοῦντες ἀνδρεῖοι.

1 IX. Περὶ θάρρη δὲ καὶ φόβους ἡ ἀνδρεία οὖσα οὐχ ὁμοίως περὶ ἄμφω ἐστίν, ἀλλὰ μᾶλλον περὶ τὰ φοβερά· ὁ γὰρ ἐν τούτοις ἀτάραχος καὶ περὶ ταῦθ' ὡς δεῖ ἔχων ἀνδρεῖος μᾶλλον ἢ ὁ περὶ τὰ θαρραλέα. Τῷ δὴ τὰ λυπηρὰ ὑπομένειν, ὡς εἴρηται, ἀνδρεῖοι λέγονται.

sudden dangers are a better test of real courage than those which are foreseen. 5. *The courage of ignorance.*—This form, which results from ignorance of the existence of danger, is not unlike the last mentioned, but is inferior to it as not implying any self-reliance. Such courage vanishes at once if the ignorance on which it depends is dispelled.

v. Ignorance. 16, 17

CHAP. IX.—*How can the exercise of Courage, which involves pain and loss, have a 'pleasure in itself'?*

Courage relates to objects of

1 Thus Courage is a due regulation of confidence and fear, but more especially of the latter, because Courage implies

4. ἀξίωμα] 'self-reliance,' literally 'estimate of themselves.' The sanguine rely so strongly upon the estimate which they have formed of their own prowess or good fortune, that they can face danger in the strength which it gives them.

6. ὅπερ οἱ Ἀργεῖοι κ.τ.λ.] This incident is described by Xenophon (*Hell.* iv. 10). The Argives attacked with contemptuous boldness certain Spartans whom they mistook for Sicyonians owing to the Spartans having assumed some Sicyonian armour. The Argives fled at once on the discovery of their mistake.

2 Διὸ καὶ ἐπίλυπον ἡ ἀνδρεία, καὶ δικαίως ἐπαινεῖται·
χαλεπώτερον γὰρ τὰ λυπηρὰ ὑπομένειν, ἢ τῶν ἡδέων
ἀπέχεσθαι. Οὐ μὴν ἀλλὰ δόξειεν ἂν εἶναι τὸ κατα
τὴν ἀνδρείαν τελος ἡδὺ, ὑπὸ τῶν κύκλῳ δ' ἀφανίζεσθαι,
οἷον κἀν τοῖς γυμνικοῖς ἀγῶσι γίνεται· τοῖς γὰρ πύκταις
τὸ μὲν τέλος ἡδὺ, οὗ ἕνεκα, ὁ στέφανος καὶ αἱ τιμαὶ,
τὸ δὲ τύπτεσθαι ἀλγεινὸν, εἴπερ σάρκινοι, καὶ λυπηρὸν,
καὶ πᾶς ὁ πόνος· διὰ δὲ τὸ πολλὰ ταῦτ' εἶναι, μικρὸν ὂν
3 τὸ οὗ ἕνεκα οὐδὲν ἡδὺ φαίνεται ἔχειν. Εἰ δὴ τοιοῦτόν
ἐστι καὶ τὸ περὶ τὴν ἀνδρείαν, ὁ μὲν θάνατος καὶ τὰ
τραύματα λυπηρὰ τῷ ἀνδρείῳ καὶ ἄκοντι ἔσται, ὑπομένει
4 δὲ αὐτὰ, ὅτι καλὸν ἢ ὅτι αἰσχρὸν τὸ μή. Καὶ ὅσῳ ἂν
μᾶλλον τὴν ἀρετὴν ἔχῃ πᾶσαν καὶ εὐδαιμονέστερος

2 the endurance of things painful. Courage indeed cannot be
exercised without pain, and hence it is difficult and propor-
tionately praiseworthy. It may be asked, How is this recon-
cileable with our repeated assertion that the practice of any
virtue has pleasure in itself? We reply, As in training men
endure hardship and pain willingly for the sake of the superior
3 pleasure of the end they have in view, so the brave man
4 endures the loss of life (a greater loss to him by reason of its
superior happiness and virtue than it would be to any ordi-

fear rather than of confidence, and therefore cannot be exercised without pain and loss.

Still the joy of the noble end gained overbalances this pain.

2. χαλεπώτερον κ.τ.λ.] The regulation of fear implies enduring pain (λυπηρὰ ὑπομένειν), the regulation of confidence resembles checking pleasure (ἡδέων ἀπέχεσθαι), and the former is more difficult, and therefore more virtuous, as we have seen before (II. iii. 10, etc.).

8. μικρὸν ὂν] i.e. insignificant in comparison with the numerous and palpable circumstances of pain and terror. Comp. S. Paul in reference to the same γυμνικοὶ ἀγῶνες, 'they do it to obtain a corruptible crown,' etc.

11. ὑπομένει δὲ κ.τ.λ.] Though he loves life much, he loves honour more: and though the loss of life is painful, the loss of honour would be yet more painful, and therefore he chooses that course which after all secures for him the greatest and highest pleasure.

12. καὶ ὅσῳ ἂν μᾶλλον κ.τ.λ.]

ᾖ, μᾶλλον ἐπὶ τῷ θανάτῳ λυπηθήσεται· τῷ τοιούτῳ γὰρ μάλιστα ζῆν ἄξιον, καὶ οὗτος μεγίστων ἀγαθῶν ἀποστερεῖται εἰδώς· λυπηρὸν δὲ τοῦτο. Ἀλλ' οὐδὲν ἧττον ἀνδρεῖος, ἴσως δὲ καὶ μᾶλλον, ὅτι τὸ ἐν τῷ πολέμῳ καλὸν ἀντ' ἐκείνων αἱρεῖται. Οὐ δὴ ἐν ἁπάσαις ταῖς 5
ἀρεταῖς τὸ ἡδέως ἐνεργεῖν ὑπάρχει, πλὴν ἐφ' ὅσον τοῦ
6 τέλους ἐφάπτεται. Στρατιώτας δ' οὐδὲν ἴσως κωλύει μὴ

nary man), deliberately preferring to it the glory of death in
5 battle. In such cases then pleasure is possible only so far as the attainment of the end and ideal of his being is felt and
6 realized. Nor need we deny that a more reckless, though less brave, man might perhaps make a better rank-and-file soldier.

Jeremy Taylor says 'A great man is *naturally* a coward, as indeed most men are, knowing the value of life; but the power of reason enables him when required to conduct himself with uniform courage and hardihood.' This passage like that in the text would go far to excluding mere animal spirit (θυμὸς ch. viii.) from the highest form of courage. The recent successes of the civilian soldiers of Germany over the professional soldiers of France, with the further supposed advantage of natural *élan* on the part of the latter, would support Aristotle in assigning more importance than is popularly allowed to the rational or calculating element in true Courage.

4. μᾶλλον] *i.e.* because the sacrifice is greater and mor edifficult. See note on § 2. Grant quotes Wordsworth, whose 'Happy Warrior' is

'More brave for this, that he hath much to lose.'

6. τοῦ τέλους ἐφάπτεται] To understand this we must recall what was said in I. i. about the 'final end' of all human efforts and aspirations, and its identification with 'Happiness.' So far as the brave man secures for himself a result so ideally noble (compare vii. 6), he 'attains to something of the final end' (τοῦ τέλους ἐφάπτεται) of human existence, and therefore to Happiness; but *only* so far, because the accompanying circumstances of his actions are otherwise painful. He has what a modern religious writer would call 'a foretaste of heaven,' in this supreme act of self-sacrifice. We may even compare the language of the Apostle of a yet higher Ideal 'who *for the joy set before Him* endured the cross, despising the shame.'

7. Observe the emphatic position of στρατιώτας, 'As mere rank-and-file soldiers the most

τοὺς τοιούτους κρατίστους εἶναι, ἀλλὰ τοὺς ἧττον μὲν ἀνδρείους, ἄλλο δ' ἀγαθὸν μηδὲν ἔχοντας· ἕτοιμοι γὰρ οὗτοι πρὸς τοὺς κινδύνους, καὶ τὸν βίον πρὸς μικρὰ κέρδη καταλλάττονται.

7 Περὶ μὲν οὖν ἀνδρείας ἐπὶ τοσοῦτον εἰρήσθω· τί δ' ἐστίν, οὐ χαλεπὸν τύπῳ γε περιλαβεῖν ἐκ τῶν εἰρημένων.

1 X. Μετὰ δὲ ταύτην περὶ σωφροσύνης λέγωμεν· δοκοῦ-

CHAP. X.—*The proper objects of the Virtue of Temperance.*

1 The other Virtue of our lower and irrational nature is Temperance. Theoretically, it is a mean state in reference

Temperance consists in the due regulation of our pleasures.

truly brave may not be so good as those who have little or nothing to lose by death.' Mere recklessness of life is not courage. The savage Turcos may be the most serviceable soldiers in a bloody war, or for certain operations of war, but no one would say that they were therefore the bravest men.

CHAP. X.—The discussion of the Virtue of Temperance, with its related vices, occupies three Chapters (x—xii).

In ch. x. the proper objects of Temperance are determined by a method precisely similar to that employed in the case of Courage in ch. vi. It is first broadly stated that Temperance deals with Pleasures, and then by successive limitations we arrive at the precise class of Pleasures to which it properly refers.

In ch. xi. the excess and defect are described and contrasted with the mean state.

In ch. xii. the comparative voluntariness of Cowardice and Intemperance is discussed; and some supplementary remarks added concerning the nature of Intemperance as illustrated by its etymology.

7. *σωφροσύνη* is usually, though inadequately, translated by 'temperance.' 'Self-control' or 'self-mastery' would perhaps be nearer to it. The derivation of *σώφρων*, or *σαόφρων*, from *σῶς* (*σάος*) and *φρὴν*, shows that the original idea of the word was that of a man who never 'loses his head,' but keeps his mind clear and calm, however assaulted by pleasure or passion. Conversely the *ἀκόλαστος* is one subject to no restraint: *κόλασις* (see note on v. 7) being the technical word for chastisement, or punishment for the purpose of

σι γὰρ τῶν ἀλόγων μερῶν αὗται εἶναι αἱ ἀρεταί. Ὅτι
μὲν οὖν μεσότης ἐστὶ περὶ ἡδονὰς ἡ σωφροσύνη, εἴρηται
ἡμῖν· ἧττον γὰρ καὶ οὐχ ὁμοίως ἐστὶ περὶ τὰς λύπας·
2 ἐν τοῖς αὐτοῖς δὲ καὶ ἡ ἀκολασία φαίνεται. Περὶ
ποίας οὖν τῶν ἡδονῶν, νῦν ἀφορίσωμεν. Διῃρήσθωσαν
δὲ αἱ ψυχικαὶ καὶ αἱ σωματικαί, οἷον φιλοτιμία, φιλο-
μάθεια· ἑκάτερος γὰρ τούτων χαίρει, οὗ φιλητικός ἐστιν
οὐθὲν πάσχοντος τοῦ σώματος, ἀλλὰ μᾶλλον τῆς δια-
νοίας· οἱ δὲ περὶ τὰς τοιαύτας ἡδονὰς οὔτε σώφρονες
3 οὔτε ἀκόλαστοι λέγονται. Ὁμοίως δ' οὐδ' οἱ περὶ τὰς
ἄλλας ὅσαι μὴ σωματικαί εἰσιν· τοὺς γὰρ φιλομύθους
καὶ διηγητικοὺς καὶ περὶ τῶν τυχόντων κατατρίβοντας
τὰς ἡμέρας ἀδολέσχας, ἀκολάστους δ' οὐ λέγομεν, οὐδὲ
4 τοὺς λυπουμένους ἐπὶ χρήμασιν ἢ φίλοις. Περὶ δὲ τὰς
σωματικὰς εἴη ἂν ἡ σωφροσύνη, οὐ πάσας δὲ οὐδὲ
ταύτας· οἱ γὰρ χαίροντες τοῖς διὰ τῆς ὄψεως, οἷον

to pleasures and pains (as we have already said); but, practi-
2 cally, its operation is limited to pleasures. Next, we limit it
further to certain kinds of pleasures. First, pleasures being
either *mental* or *bodily*, we exclude the whole of the former
3 from the sphere of Temperance, as well as certain others, such
as love of gossip, idling, love of money or friends, which,
though not exactly mental, are not at any rate bodily pleasures.
4 Secondly, among bodily pleasures, it is not concerned with

Not however of *mental* pleasures.

Nor all *bodily* pleasures.

reformation. The derivation of the word ἀκολασία is discussed by Aristotle in xii. 5, etc.

1. τῶν ἀλόγων μερῶν] This (as was remarked in II. vii.) is almost the only hint as to the principle of arrangement in the Catalogue of Virtues.

3. ἧττον] This was noticed by Aristotle in passing in II. vii. 3. οὐχ ὁμοίως will be found explained in the next Chapter, § 5. Intemperance is shown not so much in avoiding pain, as in feeling pain at the loss of pleasure, or in excessive sensibility to pain.

7. ἑκάτερος γὰρ] i.e. both ὁ φιλότιμος and ὁ φιλομαθής.

χρώμασι καὶ σχήμασι καὶ γραφῇ, οὔτε σώφρονες οὔτε
ἀκόλαστοι λέγονται· καίτοι δόξειεν ἂν εἶναι καὶ ὡς
δεῖ χαίρειν καὶ τούτοις, καὶ καθ' ὑπερβολὴν καὶ ἔλ-
5 λειψιν. Ὁμοίως δὲ καὶ ἐν τοῖς περὶ τὴν ἀκοήν· τοὺς
γὰρ ὑπερβεβλημένως χαίροντας μέλεσιν ἢ ὑποκρίσει
οὐθεὶς ἀκολάστους λέγει, οὐδὲ τοὺς ὡς δεῖ σώφρονας.
6 Οὐδὲ τοὺς περὶ τὴν ὀσμήν, πλὴν κατὰ συμβεβηκός·
τοὺς γὰρ χαίροντας μήλων ἢ ῥόδων ἢ θυμιαμάτων
ὀσμαῖς οὐ λέγομεν ἀκολάστους, ἀλλὰ μᾶλλον τοὺς
μύρων καὶ ὄψων· χαίρουσι γὰρ τούτοις οἱ ἀκόλαστοι,
ὅτι διὰ τούτων ἀνάμνησις γίνεται αὐτοῖς τῶν ἐπιθυ-
7 μητῶν. Ἴδοι δ' ἄν τις καὶ τοὺς ἄλλους, ὅταν πει-
νῶσι, χαίροντας ταῖς τῶν βρωμάτων ὀσμαῖς. Τὸ δὲ
τοιούτοις χαίρειν ἀκολάστου· τούτῳ γὰρ ἐπιθυμητὰ
8 ταῦτα. Οὐκ ἔστι δὲ οὐδὲ τοῖς ἄλλοις ζῴοις κατὰ ταύτας
τὰς αἰσθήσεις ἡδονὴ πλὴν κατὰ συμβεβηκός· οὐδὲ γὰρ
ταῖς ὀσμαῖς τῶν λαγωῶν αἱ κύνες χαίρουσιν, ἀλλὰ τῇ
βρώσει· τὴν δ' αἴσθησιν ἡ ὀσμὴ ἐποίησεν. Οὐδ' ὁ λέων
τῇ φωνῇ τοῦ βοός, ἀλλὰ τῇ ἐδωδῇ· ὅτι δ' ἐγγύς ἐστι,
διὰ τῆς φωνῆς ᾔσθετο, καὶ χαίρειν δὴ ταύτῃ φαίνεται.

Nor those of Sight, or Hearing or Smell,

(α) pleasures of *sight*, such as love of painting, colour, etc.;
5 (β) nor pleasures of *hearing*, such as love of music; (γ) nor
6 pleasures of *smell*, except indirectly as they may suggest or
7, 8 recall gluttonous or luxurious desires, just as the scent of the
lower animals gives them pleasure only by its suggestion of

7. κατὰ συμβεβηκὸς] 'by a coincidence,' *i.e.* by the same occasion which excites the sense of taste exciting that of smell also.

14. τοιούτοις] *i.e.* such as μύρα καὶ ὄψα (l. 10) in contrast with the ordinary βρώματα last mentioned.

15. οὐκ ἔστι δὲ κ.τ.λ.] The truth of this assertion is made very doubtful by well-known facts, at least as regards smell and hearing.

Ὁμοίως δ' οὐδ' ἰδὼν ἢ εὑρὼν ἔλαφον ἢ ἄγριον αἶγα,
9 ἀλλ' ὅτι βορὰν ἕξει. Περὶ τὰς τοιαύτας δὴ ἡδονὰς ἡ σωφροσύνη καὶ ἡ ἀκολασία ἐστὶν ὧν καὶ τὰ λοιπὰ ζῷα κοινωνεῖ, ὅθεν ἀνδραποδώδεις καὶ θηριώδεις φαίνονται·
10 αὗται δ' εἰσὶν ἁφὴ καὶ γεῦσις. Φαίνονται δὴ καὶ τῇ γεύσει ἐπὶ μικρὸν ἢ οὐθὲν χρῆσθαι· τῆς γὰρ γεύσεώς ἐστιν ἡ κρίσις τῶν χυμῶν, ὅπερ ποιοῦσιν οἱ τοὺς οἴνους δοκιμάζοντες καὶ τὰ ὄψα ἀρτύοντες· οὐ πάνυ δὲ χαίρουσι τούτοις, ἢ οὐχ οἵ γε ἀκόλαστοι, ἀλλὰ τῇ ἀπολαύσει, ἣ γίνεται πᾶσα δι' ἁφῆς καὶ ἐν σιτίοις καὶ ἐν ποτοῖς καὶ τοῖς ἀφροδισίοις λεγομένοις. Διὸ καὶ ηὔξατό τις ὀψοφάγος ὢν τὸν φάρυγγα αὐτῷ μακρότερον
11 γεράνου γενέσθαι, ὡς ἡδόμενος τῇ ἁφῇ. Κοινοτάτη δὴ τῶν αἰσθήσεων καθ' ἣν ἡ ἀκολασία· καὶ δόξειεν ἂν δικαίως ἐπονείδιστος εἶναι, ὅτι οὐχ ᾗ ἄνθρωποί ἐσμεν ὑπάρχει, ἀλλ' ᾗ ζῷα. Τὸ δὴ τοιούτοις χαίρειν καὶ

or Taste (except slightly), but only those of Touch, and the lower types even of these.

9. 10 prey; (δ) nor pleasures of *taste*, except to a slight extent, viz. so far as by prolonged or artificially-stimulated contact of the food with the throat the sense of Touch is excited. (ε)
11 The sense of *touch* alone remains. We have thus limited Temperance to the regulation, and Intemperance to the indulgence, of the pleasures of the sense of Touch, and we must
12 further and finally limit it to the commonest and most ignoble

6. Aristotle regards the primary function of taste (as of the other senses) to be the discrimination of objects; the transmission of information to the mind concerning things external to it, rather than the communication of pleasure:—in a word, he looks at their powers of *perception* rather than their powers of *sensation.* Hence to judge of wine (as a trader), or of seasoned dishes (as a cook), would be the most proper function of the sense of taste as such; but it is not in such an exercise of it that pleasure is conveyed. That depends, according to Aristotle, upon the prolonged contact of the thing tasted with the throat; *i.e.* upon a particular application of the sense of Touch. It is of course true (though not quite in the sense intended by Aristotle) that

12 μάλιστα ἀγαπᾶν θηριῶδες. Καὶ γὰρ αἱ ἐλευθεριώταται τῶν διὰ τῆς ἁφῆς ἡδονῶν ἀφῄρηνται, οἷον αἱ ἐν τοῖς γυμνασίοις διὰ τρίψεως καὶ τῆς θερμασίας γινόμεναι· οὐ γὰρ περὶ πᾶν τὸ σῶμα ἡ τοῦ ἀκολάστου ἁφὴ, ἀλλὰ περί τινα μέρη.

1 XI. Τῶν δ' ἐπιθυμιῶν αἱ μὲν κοιναὶ δοκοῦσιν εἶναι, αἱ δ' ἴδιοι καὶ ἐπίθετοι· οἷον ἡ μὲν τῆς τροφῆς φυσική· πᾶς γὰρ ἐπιθυμεῖ ὁ ἐνδεὴς ξηρᾶς ἢ ὑγρᾶς τροφῆς, ὁτὲ δ' ἀμφοῖν, καὶ εὐνῆς, φησὶν Ὅμηρος, ὁ νέος καὶ ἀκμάζων· τὸ δὲ τοιᾶσδε ἢ τοιᾶσδε, οὐκέτι πᾶς, οὐδὲ
2 τῶν αὐτῶν. Διὸ φαίνεται ἡμέτερον εἶναι. Οὐ μὴν ἀλλ'

kinds of pleasures even of this, which is itself the lowest and most animal of all our senses.

CHAP. XI.—*The excess and defect related to the Virtue of Temperance.*

These pleasures are further divided into Natural and Acquired.

1 The pleasures spoken of in the last chapter admit of a further division into those which are common and natural, such as the desire of food generally; and those which are peculiar and acquired, such as the desire of some particular
2 kind of food; the latter depending (within certain broad

the sense of Taste depends upon Touch, but such is also the case with all the other senses.

1. ἐλευθεριώταται] 'the noblest pleasures,' a converse metaphor to ἀνδραποδώδεις in § 3 and elsewhere.

CHAP. XI.—This Chapter treats of (1) the Excess of Intemperance (*a*) in reference to natural and artificial Desires (§§ 1-4), (β) in reference to Pleasure and Pain generally (§§ 5, 6); (2) The Defect of Insensitiveness (§ 7); and (3) adds a few words on the Mean of Temperance in contrast with both.

6. τῶν μὲν ἐπιθυμιῶν] Plato (*Rep.* p. 558) makes a similar distinction of ἐπιθυμίαι, and adds that the gratification of the natural or necessary desires is always beneficial, that of the artificial desires not generally so.

7. ἐπίθετοι] 'acquired' or 'artificial.'

8. ξηρᾶς ἢ ὑγρᾶς τροφῆς] 'either solid or liquid food.'

ἔχει γέ τι καὶ φυσικόν· ἕτερα γὰρ ἑτέροις ἐστὶν ἡδέα,
3 καὶ ἔνια πᾶσιν ἡδίω τῶν τυχόντων. Ἐν μὲν οὖν ταῖς
φυσικαῖς ἐπιθυμίαις ὀλίγοι ἁμαρτάνουσι καὶ ἐφ' ἕν,
ἐπὶ τὸ πλεῖον· τὸ γὰρ ἐσθίειν τὰ τυχόντα ἢ πίνειν ἕως
ἂν ὑπερπλησθῇ, ὑπερβάλλειν ἐστὶ τὸ κατὰ φύσιν τῷ
πλήθει· ἀναπλήρωσις γὰρ τῆς ἐνδείας ἡ φυσικὴ ἐπι-
θυμία. Διὸ λέγονται οὗτοι γαστρίμαργοι, ὡς παρὰ τὸ
δέον πληροῦντες αὐτήν. Τοιοῦτοι δὲ γίνονται οἱ λίαν
4 ἀνδραποδώδεις. Περὶ δὲ τὰς ἰδίας τῶν ἡδονῶν πολλοὶ
καὶ πολλαχῶς ἁμαρτάνουσιν· τῶν γὰρ φιλοτοιούτων
λεγομένων ἢ τῷ χαίρειν οἷς μὴ δεῖ, ἢ τῷ μᾶλλον, ἢ ὡς
οἱ πολλοί, ἢ μὴ ὡς δεῖ, κατὰ πάντα δ' οἱ ἀκόλαστοι

Errors in the former are rare, and always in the direction of excess; in the latter, common and various in character.

3 natural limits) upon individual taste. Now in *natural* desires
error is rare, and must always take the form of supplying in
excess what is in itself a natural want; and this, when it is
4 found, indicates a degraded and almost brutish nature. In
the case of *acquired* desires, error is very common and multi-
form, extending to the object, manner, degree, etc., of the

2. ἔνια πᾶσιν] 'Some things there are which give every one more pleasure than things ordinary and indifferent.' *i.e.* However much individual tastes differ, there are still some things naturally more pleasant than others to every one.

3. ὀλίγοι κ.τ.λ.] *e.g.* Excessive eating is not likely to occur in regard to bread, or any simple food which is desired merely to supply a natural appetite, and not for any special pleasure to be derived from eating it, but rather in regard to some particular viand or favourite 'Gluttony on oatmeal porridge' οὐ πάνυ γίνεται.

9. ἀνδραποδώδεις] 'degraded,' a metaphor converse to ἐλευθέριος, both words having passed from a *social* to a *moral* signification. See last Ch. § 12, note.

11. ἢ ὡς οἱ πολλοὶ] In some editions ὡς is omitted, and if so, ἢ = 'than,' after the comparative μᾶλλον. If ὡς be retained, the sense may be explained by what is said in I. v. 3 about the excessive and exclusive devotion of οἱ πολλοὶ to Pleasure. See also the concluding words of this section.

ὑπερβάλλουσιν· καὶ γὰρ χαίρουσιν ἐνίοις οἷς οὐ δεῖ (μισητὰ γάρ), καὶ εἴ τισι δεῖ χαίρειν τῶν τοιούτων,
5 μᾶλλον ἢ δεῖ, καὶ ὡς οἱ πολλοὶ χαίρουσιν. Ἡ μὲν οὖν περὶ τὰς ἡδονὰς ὑπερβολὴ ὅτι ἀκολασία καὶ ψεκτὸν, δῆλον· περὶ δὲ τὰς λύπας οὐχ ὥσπερ ἐπὶ τῆς ἀνδρείας τῷ ὑπομένειν λέγεται σώφρων ἀκόλαστος δὲ τῷ μὴ, ἀλλ' ὁ μὲν ἀκόλαστος τῷ λυπεῖσθαι μᾶλλον ἢ δεῖ ὅτι τῶν ἡδέων οὐ τυγχάνει (καὶ τὴν λύπην δὲ ποιεῖ αὐτῷ ἡ ἡδονή), ὁ δὲ σώφρων τῷ μὴ λυπεῖσθαι τῇ ἀπουσίᾳ καὶ τῷ ἀπέχεσθαι τοῦ ἡδέος.

6 Ὁ μὲν οὖν ἀκόλαστος ἐπιθυμεῖ τῶν ἡδέων πάντων ἢ τῶν μάλιστα, καὶ ἄγεται ὑπὸ τῆς ἐπιθυμίας ὥστε ἀντὶ τῶν ἄλλων ταῦθ' αἱρεῖσθαι· διὸ καὶ λυπεῖται καὶ ἀποτυγχάνων καὶ ἐπιθυμῶν· μετὰ λύπης γὰρ ἡ ἐπιθυμία·
7 ἀτόπῳ δ' ἔοικε τὸ δι' ἡδονὴν λυπεῖσθαι. Ἐλλείποντες δὲ περὶ τὰς ἡδονὰς καὶ ἧττον ἢ δεῖ χαίροντες οὐ πάνυ γίνονται· οὐ γὰρ ἀνθρωπική ἐστιν ἡ τοιαύτη ἀναισθησία·

indulged desire. It is clear then that in this ill-regulated
5 pursuit of pleasure consists the Excess in reference to the Virtue of Temperance, viz., Intemperance. In its relation to pain, however, it does not consist (like cowardice) in shrinking from it, so much as in feeling pain at the absence of pleasure. This is not the case with
6 the temperate man. Thus the intemperate man in his excessive devotion to pleasure paradoxically makes it to
7 be a source of pain. The Defect, or absence of proper sensi-

The Excess has reference both to pleasure and pain, though in a different sense.

The Defect does not occur in fact.

15. Asceticism was evidently a conception wholly unintelligible to the Greek mind. In explanation of this we might quote the apology of Erasmus for Ecclus. xxv. 13 (where the wickedness of women is denounced as exceeding all other), 'Il faut remarquer qu'il n'y avait pas encore des moines.'

17. ἀναισθησία] 'insensitiveness,' the word being as unusual as the condition indicated by it. Indeed if it did occur, it would

καὶ γὰρ τὰ λοιπὰ ζῷα διακρίνει τὰ βρώματα, καὶ τοῖς μὲν χαίρει τοῖς δ' οὔ· εἰ δέ τῳ μηθέν ἐστιν ἡδὺ μηδὲ διαφέρει ἕτερον ἑτέρου, πόρρω ἂν εἴη τοῦ ἄνθρωπος εἶναι· οὐ τέτευχε δ' ὁ τοιοῦτος ὀνόματος διὰ τὸ μὴ
8 πάνυ γίνεσθαι. Ὁ δὲ σώφρων μέσως περὶ ταῦτ' ἔχει· οὔτε γὰρ ἥδεται οἷς μάλιστα ὁ ἀκόλαστος, ἀλλὰ μᾶλλον δυσχεραίνει, οὔθ' ὅλως οἷς μὴ δεῖ οὔτε σφόδρα τοιούτῳ οὐδενὶ, οὔτ' ἀπόντων λυπεῖται οὐδ' ἐπιθυμεῖ, ἢ μετρίως, οὐδὲ μᾶλλον ἢ δεῖ, οὐδ' ὅτε μὴ δεῖ, οὐδ' ὅλως τῶν τοιούτων οὐθέν· ὅσα δὲ πρὸς ὑγίειάν ἐστιν ἢ πρὸς εὐεξίαν ἡδέα ὄντα, τούτων ὀρέξεται μετρίως καὶ ὡς δεῖ, καὶ τῶν ἄλλων ἡδέων μὴ ἐμποδίων τούτοις ὄντων ἢ παρὰ τὸ καλὸν ἢ ὑπὲρ τὴν οὐσίαν. Ὁ γὰρ οὕτως ἔχων μᾶλλον ἀγαπᾷ τὰς τοιαύτας ἡδονὰς τῆς ἀξίας· ὁ δὲ σώφρων οὐ τοιοῦτος, ἀλλ' ὡς ὁ ὀρθὸς λόγος.

bility to pleasure, is only imaginary, for not only all men, but even all animals, must have *some* tastes and preferences.

The mean stands in contrast with both.

8 The Temperate man, as we have seen, holds a mean position between excessive devotion and utter insensibility to pleasures. He enjoys them in moderation, and with due regard to the various considerations as to objects, degree, occasions, and consequences which right reason suggests.

be rather a physical than a moral defect. The practical non-existence of ἀναισθησία and of ἀφοβία (see vii. 7) is a comment on the statement of x. 1, that the virtues of Courage and Temperance relate to feelings which are purely animal and instinctive (belonging to ἄλογον μέρος). In the case of all the other virtues of the catalogue (except perhaps to some extent ὀργή—see the similar difficulty about ἀοργησία in IV. v. 5), it is perhaps conceivable that a man might be without the feelings, or be altogether removed from the circumstances, in which the sphere of the exercise of the virtues lies. In sensibility to fear and to pleasure a man could hardly be wanting without ceasing to be human.

13. οὕτως] i.e. ἢ παρὰ τὸ καλὸν ἢ ὑπὲρ τὴν οὐσίαν.

1 XII. Ἑκουσίῳ δὲ μᾶλλον ἔοικεν ἡ ἀκολασία τῆς δει-
λίας. Ἡ μὲν γὰρ δι' ἡδονὴν, ἡ δὲ διὰ λύπην, ὧν τὸ μὲν
2 αἱρετὸν, τὸ δὲ φευκτὸν. Καὶ ἡ μὲν λύπη ἐξίστησι καὶ
φθείρει τὴν τοῦ ἔχοντος φύσιν, ἡ δὲ ἡδονὴ οὐδὲν τοι-
οῦτον ποιεῖ, μᾶλλον δ' ἑκούσιον· διὸ καὶ ἐπονειδιστό-
τερον. Καὶ γὰρ ἐθισθῆναι ῥᾷον πρὸς αὐτά· πολλὰ γὰρ
ἐν τῷ βίῳ τὰ τοιαῦτα, καὶ οἱ ἐθισμοὶ ἀκίνδυνοι. Ἐπὶ
3 δὲ τῶν φοβερῶν ἀνάπαλιν. Δόξειε δ' ἂν οὐχ ὁμοίως

CHAP. XII.—(*a*) *Is the external compulsion stronger in Cowardice or in Intemperance?*

(β) *The nature of* ἀκολασία *is illustrated by its etymology.*

1 The question may be asked, Which is more voluntary (and
therefore more blameable), Intemperance or Cowardice? We
reply, Intemperance:—(1) because the pressure arises from
2 pleasure, whereas in Cowardice it arises from pain; (2) be-
cause it is both easy and safe to practise resistance against
temptations to Intemperance; while the reverse is the case
3 with temptations to Cowardice. A distinction however must be

Intemperance is more voluntary than Cowardice, if we consider single acts, though perhaps the reverse is the case if we regard the settled habits.

CHAP. XII.—We have seen in ch. v. that no vice is really involuntary, still the degree of external pressure, though it never amounts to compulsion, varies in different cases. It is naturally greatest in regard to these two Virtues which relate to those feelings of our *animal* nature (x. 1) which are ever present, and *must* be excited under given external circumstances whenever they arise. The object of this Chapter is to determine in which of these two cases there is more external pressure, and, so far, less of voluntary action.

6. καὶ γὰρ] 'and what is more,' introducing, as usual, a fresh argument.

αὐτὰ from the context, though it has no grammatical antecedent, evidently refers to pleasurable objects, or temptations to Intemperance.

8. δόξειε δ' ἂν κ.τ.λ.] *e.g.* A man may resolve that he will give up his property, and offer himself as a prisoner, or indeed do anything, rather than face the enemy in fight. That would

ἑκούσιον ἡ δειλία εἶναι τοῖς καθ' ἕκαστον· αὐτὴ μὲν γὰρ ἄλυπος, ταῦτα δὲ διὰ λύπην ἐξίστησιν, ὥστε καὶ τὰ ὅπλα ῥίπτειν καὶ τἆλλα ἀσχημονεῖν· διὸ καὶ δοκεῖ
4 βίαια εἶναι. Τῷ δ' ἀκολάστῳ ἀνάπαλιν τὰ μὲν καθ' ἕκαστα ἑκούσια, ἐπιθυμοῦντι γὰρ καὶ ὀρεγομένῳ, τὸ δ' ὅλον ἧττον· οὐθεὶς γὰρ ἐπιθυμεῖ ἀκόλαστος εἶναι.

5 Τὸ δ' ὄνομα τῆς ἀκολασίας καὶ ἐπὶ τὰς παιδικὰς ἁμαρτίας φέρομεν· ἔχουσι γάρ τινα ὁμοιότητα. Πότερον δ' ἀπὸ ποτέρου καλεῖται, οὐθὲν πρὸς τὰ νῦν διαφέρει, δῆλον
6 δ' ὅτι τὸ ὕστερον ἀπὸ τοῦ προτέρου. Οὐ κακῶς δ' ἔοικε μετενηνέχθαι· κεκολάσθαι γὰρ δεῖ τὸ τῶν αἰσχρῶν ὀρε-

drawn according as we regard the *single acts*, or *general habits*. In the case of *acts* of Cowardice the violence of the present pain (of which there is none in Intemperance) is often such that a man hardly knows what he is doing. But looking at these Vices as *habits*, a man never de-
4 liberately resolves to be habitually intemperate, as he does sometimes to be an habitual coward. Thus in Cowardice the general habit is more voluntary than the single acts,
5 but in Intemperance the reverse is the case.

The etymology of the Greek word ἀκολασία throws light upon the nature of the vice.

The Greek term for Intemperance (ἀκολασία), or, as we might translate it, Wantonness, involves the idea of absence of restraint, and it is also familiarly applied to the errors of childhood. Without deciding which is the primary meaning of the term, we may assert that its application is in both cases appropriate.
6 No things need restraint more than desires of pleasure, and

imply a deliberate and voluntary *habit* of cowardice. Another may resolve to fight to the last, but when he sees actual bloodshed be overpowered with horror and throw down his arms. That would be the half-involuntary cowardice of *particular acts*. (See *Supplementary Notes*.)

1. αὐτή] i.e. δειλία 'Cowardice in itself.' ταῦτα δέ, i.e. τὰ καθ' ἕκαστον 'the surroundings.'

10. τὸ ὕστερον ἀπὸ τοῦ προτέρου] not 'the latter from the former,' but 'the later in conception from the earlier.'

11. Two conditions are noted as requiring κόλασις, viz. tendency to what is vicious, and capacity for rapid growth. Both

γόμενον καὶ πολλὴν αὔξησιν ἔχον, τοιοῦτον δὲ μάλιστα
ἡ ἐπιθυμία καὶ ὁ παῖς· κατ' ἐπιθυμίαν γὰρ ζῶσι καὶ τὰ
7 παιδία, καὶ μάλιστα ἐν τούτοις ἡ τοῦ ἡδέος ὄρεξις. Εἰ
οὖν μὴ ἔσται εὐπειθὲς καὶ ὑπὸ τὸ ἄρχον, ἐπὶ πολὺ ἥξει·
ἄπληστος γὰρ ἡ τοῦ ἡδέος ὄρεξις καὶ πανταχόθεν τῷ
ἀνοήτῳ, καὶ ἡ τῆς ἐπιθυμίας ἐνέργεια αὔξει τὸ συγγενές,
κἂν μεγάλαι καὶ σφοδραὶ ὦσι, καὶ τὸν λογισμὸν ἐκκρού-
ουσιν. Διὸ δεῖ μετρίας εἶναι αὐτὰς καὶ ὀλίγας, καὶ τῷ
8 λόγῳ μηθὲν ἐναντιοῦσθαι. Τὸ δὲ τοιοῦτον εὐπειθὲς λέ-
γομεν καὶ κεκολασμένον· ὥσπερ γὰρ τὸν παῖδα δεῖ κατὰ
τὸ πρόσταγμα τοῦ παιδαγωγοῦ ζῆν, οὕτω καὶ τὸ ἐπι-
9 θυμητικὸν κατὰ τὸν λόγον. Διὸ δεῖ τοῦ σώφρονος τὸ

children; and moreover in children desires of pleasure are in pre-
7 eminent force. Such desires grow prodigiously by indulgence,
are insatiable, and if unrestrained choke reason altogether.
8 They ought never therefore to be allowed to resist reason,
9 any more than a child to resist his master. When the habit

these conditions are found most strikingly in each of the two objects to which 'Wantonness' is attributed, viz. Desire of Pleasure, and Children.

5. πανταχόθεν τῷ ἀνοήτῳ] 'assails the weak man from every quarter.'

6. ἡ τῆς ἐπιθυμίας ἐνέργεια] 'the exercise (or gratification) of desire strengthens that which is kindred to it in our nature,' *i.e.* strengthens τὸ ἐπιθυμητικὸν until it altogether overpowers the rival part of our nature τὸ λογιστικόν. (See I. xiii.) This seems to be the idea of εὐπερίστατος ἁμαρτία in Heb. xii. 1, paraphrased by Chryst. 'παντόθεν ἱσταμένη'

11. It must be remembered that the παιδαγωγὸς was not the teacher, but the servant who conducted the boy to school, and was responsible for his conduct when *not* in the hands of the teacher. His office somewhat resembled that of the 'governor,' as contrasted with the 'tutor' of our royal princes. This adds point to the illustration, since moral and not intellectual discipline is in question in the text.

12. διὸ δεῖ κ.τ.λ.] This is illustrated by the often recurring distinction between σώφρων and ἐγκρατὴς (see notes on I. iii. 7 and I. xiii. 17). The σώφρων has no bad desires left to contend with.

ἐπιθυμητικὸν συμφωνεῖν τῷ λόγῳ· σκοπὸς γὰρ ἀμφοῖν τὸ καλὸν, καὶ ἐπιθυμεῖ ὁ σώφρων ὧν δεῖ καὶ ὡς δεῖ καὶ ὅτε· οὕτω δὲ τάττει καὶ ὁ λόγος. Ταῦτ' οὖν ἡμῖν εἰρήσθω περὶ σωφροσύνης.

of self-control is formed, reason and desire are in harmony, and both tend towards one goal, the ideally noble. So much then for the Virtue of Temperance or Self-control.

IV.

1 I. *Λέγωμεν δ' ἑξῆς περὶ ἐλευθεριότητος, δοκεῖ δ' εἶναι
ἡ περὶ χρήματα μεσότης· ἐπαινεῖται γὰρ ὁ ἐλευθέριος
οὐκ ἐν τοῖς πολεμικοῖς, οὐδ' ἐν οἷς ὁ σώφρων, οὐδ'
αὖ ἐν ταῖς κρίσεσιν, ἀλλὰ περὶ δόσιν χρημάτων καὶ
2 λῆψιν, μᾶλλον δ' ἐν τῇ δόσει. Χρήματα δὲ λέγομεν
3 πάντα ὅσων ἡ ἀξία νομίσματι μετρεῖται. Ἔστι δὲ καὶ
ἡ ἀσωτία καὶ ἡ ἀνελευθερία περὶ χρήματα ὑπερβολαὶ*

CHAP. I.—*On Liberality.*

Use of terms defined.

1 Our next subject is the Virtue of Liberality. Prodigality,
Liberality, and Sordidness relate simply to the giving and
2 taking of property, but chiefly the former. By 'property'
3 we understand whatever can be exchanged for money. The
term 'sordid' is generally restricted to the sense just indi-

CHAP. I.—The discussion of the Virtues in detail proceeds as in the order given in II. vii. Liberality occupies the next place. Refer to note on II. vii. for the principle of this arrangement.

This Chapter falls under three heads:—

1—5. Preliminary—The use of terms explained.

6—27. Liberality described in its various practical details.

28—45. Prodigality and Sordidness described.

4. *κρίσεσιν*] 'decisions,' in reference apparently to the Virtue of *δικαιοσύνη* discussed afterwards, as the words *ἐν τοῖς πολεμικοῖς* and *ἐν οἷς ὁ σώφρων* refer to the two Virtues already treated of in the last Book.

7. *ἀνελευθερία*] I have, after some hesitation, adopted 'Sordidness' rather than 'Illiberality' for *ἀνελευθερία*, as being more applicable to the various types of *ἀνελευθερία* distinguished in §§ 38-45.

*καὶ ἐλλείψεις· καὶ τὴν μὲν ἀνελευθερίαν προσάπτομεν
ἀεὶ τοῖς μᾶλλον ἢ δεῖ περὶ χρήματα σπουδάζουσι, τὴν
δ' ἀσωτίαν ἐπιφέρομεν ἐνίοτε συμπλέκοντες· τοὺς γὰρ
ἀκρατεῖς καὶ εἰς ἀκολασίαν δαπανηροὺς ἀσώτους καλοῦ-
4 μεν. Διὸ καὶ φαυλότατοι δοκοῦσιν εἶναι· πολλὰς γὰρ
5 ἅμα κακίας ἔχουσιν. Οὐ δὴ οἰκείως προσαγορεύονται·
βούλεται γὰρ ἄσωτος εἶναι ὁ ἕν τι κακὸν ἔχων, τὸ φθεί-
ρειν τὴν οὐσίαν· ἄσωτος γὰρ ὁ δι' αὑτὸν ἀπολλύμενος,
δοκεῖ δ' ἀπώλειά τις αὐτοῦ εἶναι καὶ ἡ τῆς οὐσίας φθορά,
ὡς τοῦ ζῆν διὰ τούτων ὄντος. Οὕτω δὴ τὴν ἀσωτίαν
6 ἐκδεχόμεθα. Ὧν δ' ἐστὶ χρεία, ἔστι τούτοις χρῆσθαι
καὶ εὖ καὶ κακῶς· ὁ πλοῦτος δ' ἐστὶ τῶν χρησίμων·*

cated; but 'prodigal' is often used in a wider sense, and
applied to the intemperate generally, who do in fact spend
4 money upon their lusts. Hence it is a comprehensive term
5 of reproach. We prefer however to use the word in its strict
6 and limited sense. Now whatever admits of being used may
be used well or ill, and a virtue related to any such object

Liberality has more to do with giving than taking.

4. 'Prodigal' is commonly so applied in English (*e.g.* The Prodigal Son), but scarcely the abstract term 'prodigality.' Reasons are given for this connexion between *ἀκολασία* and *ἀσωτία* in § 35 of this Chapter. 'Profligate' has a similar double meaning.

7. *βούλεται*] 'means'; like the French '*veut dire.*' Much of the force of this section depends on the etymological connexion of *ἄσωτος* and *ἀσωτία* with *σώζειν*, and is consequently difficult to reproduce in a translation.

12. 'The very essence of property is its use.' This would be explained by what is said in I. v. 8, or by Plato's remark in *Rep.* p. 333 B, that money laid by is as useless as a pilot on shore or a physician in health. Wealth is an instrument as much as a spade or any other tool, and in like manner, when not being used is for the time useless. The following passage from Bacon's Essay on Riches offers several points of comparison with this and the following Chapter: 'Riches are for spending, and spending for Honour and Good Actions (*τοῦ καλοῦ ἕνεκα*, § 12). Therefore extraordinary expense must be limited by the worth of the occasion (ii. 11, 15, etc.), but

ἑκάστῳ δ' ἄριστα χρῆται ὁ ἔχων τὴν περὶ τοῦτο ἀρετήν·
καὶ πλούτῳ δὴ χρήσεται ἄριστα ὁ ἔχων τὴν περὶ τὰ
7 χρήματα ἀρετήν. Οὗτος δ' ἐστὶν ὁ ἐλευθέριος. Χρῆσις
δ' εἶναι δοκεῖ χρημάτων δαπάνη καὶ δόσις· ἡ δὲ λῆψις
καὶ ἡ φυλακὴ κτῆσις μᾶλλον. Διὸ μᾶλλόν ἐστι τοῦ
ἐλευθερίου τὸ διδόναι οἷς δεῖ ἢ λαμβάνειν ὅθεν δεῖ καὶ
8 μὴ λαμβάνειν ὅθεν οὐ δεῖ. Τῆς γὰρ ἀρετῆς μᾶλλον
τὸ εὖ ποιεῖν ἢ τὸ εὖ πάσχειν, καὶ τὰ καλὰ πράττειν
μᾶλλον ἢ τὰ αἰσχρὰ μὴ πράττειν· οὐκ ἄδηλον δ' ὅτι τῇ
μὲν δόσει ἕπεται τὸ εὖ ποιεῖν καὶ τὸ καλὰ πράττειν,
τῇ δὲ λήψει τὸ εὖ πάσχειν ἢ μὴ αἰσχροπραγεῖν. Καὶ
ἡ χάρις τῷ διδόντι, οὐ τῷ μὴ λαμβάνοντι· καὶ ὁ ἔπαινος
9 δὲ μᾶλλον. Καὶ ῥᾷον δὲ τὸ μὴ λαβεῖν τοῦ δοῦναι· τὸ
γὰρ οἰκεῖον ἧττον προΐενται μᾶλλον ἢ οὐ λαμβάνουσι

is displayed in its being used well. Property is evidently a
thing to be used: Liberality therefore is that quality or virtue
which enables us to make the best possible use of property.
7 Again that use consists in spending and giving: taking and
keeping resemble acquisition rather than use. Hence, as we
have already hinted, liberality relates to giving more than to
8 taking. This appears also from the following considerations:
—(α) Virtue is always active and positive rather than passive
and negative. Giving is the former, taking is the latter.
9 (β) It is harder, and so more thankworthy, to give rightly

ordinary expense ought to be limited by a man's Estate, and governed by such regard that it be within his compass' (i. 19, ii. 12).

12. *χάρις*] Exactly in the sense found in 1 Pet. ii. 19, 20, *τοῦτο γὰρ χάρις*, 'for this is thankworthy'; and in Luke vi. 32, 'If ye love them which love you, what thank have ye?' *ποία ὑμῖν χάρις ἐστίν;*

13. *καὶ ῥᾷον δὲ*] Compare the dictum in II. iii. 10, *περὶ τὸ χαλεπώτερον ἀεὶ καὶ τέχνη γίγνεται καὶ ἀρετή.*

14. *ἧττον-μᾶλλον*] a redundant comparative, and = *ἧττον* simply. Cf. *μᾶλλον εὐτυχέστερον*, etc., and Shakespeare's 'most un-

10 τὸ ἀλλότριον. Καὶ ἐλευθέριοι δὲ λέγονται οἱ διδόντες·
οἱ δὲ μὴ λαμβάνοντες οὐκ εἰς ἐλευθεριότητα ἐπαινοῦν-
ται, ἀλλ' οὐχ ἧττον εἰς δικαιοσύνην· οἱ δὲ λαμβάνοντες
11 οὐδ' ἐπαινοῦνται πάνυ. Φιλοῦνται δὲ σχεδὸν μάλιστα
οἱ ἐλευθέριοι τῶν ἀπ' ἀρετῆς· ὠφέλιμοι γάρ, τοῦτο δ' ἐν
12 τῇ δόσει. Αἱ δὲ κατ' ἀρετὴν πράξεις καλαὶ καὶ τοῦ
καλοῦ ἕνεκα. Καὶ ὁ ἐλευθέριος οὖν δώσει τοῦ καλοῦ
ἕνεκα καὶ ὀρθῶς· οἷς γὰρ δεῖ καὶ ὅσα καὶ ὅτε, καὶ
13 τἆλλα ὅσα ἕπεται τῇ ὀρθῇ δόσει. Καὶ ταῦτα ἡδέως

10 than to decline to take wrongly. Those who give rightly are
called liberal; those who refrain from taking wrongly are
called honest and just, but not liberal: ~~while those~~ who merely
11 take or receive rightly are scarcely praised at all. (γ) Liber-
ality is one of the most popular of virtues, and that because
of its usefulness, and this consists in giving, not in taking.
12 However, as all virtue has a noble end in view, mere giving
freely is not enough to constitute Liberality. Regard must
be had to certain conditions, of which we specify three:—
1. A noble motive. 2. Due consideration of the recipients,
13 the amount, and the occasion of the gift. 3. Cheerfulness on

Yet liberal *giving* must fulfil certain conditions.

kindest cut of all.' Translate, 'Men are less inclined to spend their own money, than merely to refrain from taking that which belongs to others.' In other words, 'it is easier to be honest than to be generous.' Many men who are very reluctant to part with their money, and anxious to hoard, would yet scorn to gain anything by dishonest or suspicious means. Avarice is not necessarily accompanied by dishonesty.

4. οὐδ' ἐπαινοῦνται πάνυ] The virtue is in fact too common and easy to deserve commendation. Praise on such grounds would be almost derogatory (φορτικὸς ὁ ἔπαινος, as Aristotle says in X. viii. 7).

8. οἷς γὰρ δεῖ κ.τ.λ.] These words are explanatory of ὀρθῶς.

9. ἡδέως ἢ ἀλύπως] This condition is explained by such passages as I. viii. 10-12 (No one is virtuous unless he takes pleasure in virtuous actions); II. iii. 1 (The test of the formation of any habit (ἕξις) is that the actions to which it is related are done with pleasure); or by the

ἢ ἀλύπως· τὸ γὰρ κατ' ἀρετὴν ἡδὺ ἢ ἄλυπον, ἥκιστα
14 δὲ λυπηρόν. Ὁ δὲ διδοὺς οἷς μὴ δεῖ, ἢ μὴ τοῦ καλοῦ
ἕνεκα ἀλλὰ διά τιν' ἄλλην αἰτίαν, οὐκ ἐλευθέριος ἀλλ'
ἄλλος τις ῥηθήσεται. Οὐδ' ὁ λυπηρῶς· μᾶλλον γὰρ
ἕλοιτ' ἂν τὰ χρήματα τῆς καλῆς πράξεως, τοῦτο δ' οὐκ
15 ἐλευθερίου. Οὐδὲ λήψεται δὲ ὅθεν μὴ δεῖ· οὐδὲ γάρ
ἐστι τοῦ μὴ τιμῶντος τὰ χρήματα ἡ τοιαύτη λῆψις.
16 Οὐκ ἂν εἴη δὲ οὐδ' αἰτητικός· οὐ γάρ ἐστι τοῦ εὖ
17 ποιοῦντος εὐχερῶς εὐεργετεῖσθαι. Ὅθεν δὲ δεῖ, λήψε-
ται, οἷον ἀπὸ τῶν ἰδίων κτημάτων, οὐχ ὡς καλὸν ἀλλ'
ὡς ἀναγκαῖον, ὅπως ἔχῃ διδόναι. Οὐδ' ἀμελήσει τῶν
ἰδίων, βουλόμενός γε διὰ τούτων τισὶν ἐπαρκεῖν. Οὐδὲ
τοῖς τυχοῦσι δώσει, ἵνα ἔχῃ διδόναι οἷς δεῖ καὶ ὅτε καὶ

the part of the giver. There is no grudging or hesitation in
14 true liberality. The absence of any of these conditions would
15 destroy the liberality of the act. *Taking* however as well as
giving is subject to certain conditions: for—(1) The truly
liberal man does not care so much for money as to be indif-
16 ferent to the *source* from which it comes. (2) He will
17 be *reluctant to ask* for this as for other favours. (3) His *mo-
tive* in taking is to secure not the money itself but the
means of giving. Hence he will *not neglect his own affairs*,

So also must be liberal *taking* of money.

distinction regularly drawn between ἐγκράτεια and σωφροσύνη, the outward acts of which are the same; for this see note on I. iii. 7.

4. ὁ λυπηρῶς] Understand διδούς.

8. οὐ γάρ ἐστι κ.τ.λ.] See ch. iii. 24-26 for this trait in the character of the μεγαλόψυχος.

10. οὐχ ὡς καλὸν κ.τ.λ.] Cf. § 20 just below. There is nothing noble in taking or receiving, but it is none the less necessary with a view to giving; for liberality is one of those virtues which cannot be exercised without appliances, 'ἀχορήγητον ὄντα,' as we read in I. viii. 15. (See further on this point X. viii. 4.) With the statement in the text compare, 'It is more blessed to give than to receive.'

18 οὗ καλόν. Ἐλευθερίου δ' ἐστὶ σφόδρα καὶ τὸ ὑπερ-
βάλλειν ἐν τῇ δόσει, ὥστε καταλείπειν ἑαυτῷ ἐλάττω·
19 τὸ γὰρ μὴ ἐπιβλέπειν ἐφ' ἑαυτὸν ἐλευθερίου. Κατὰ
τὴν οὐσίαν δ' ἡ ἐλευθεριότης λέγεται· οὐ γὰρ ἐν τῷ
πλήθει τῶν διδομένων τὸ ἐλευθέριον, ἀλλ' ἐν τῇ τοῦ
διδόντος ἕξει, αὕτη δὲ κατὰ τὴν οὐσίαν δίδωσιν. Οὐθὲν
δὴ κωλύει ἐλευθεριώτερον εἶναι τὸν τὰ ἐλάττω διδόντα,
20 ἐὰν ἀπ' ἐλαττόνων διδῷ. Ἐλευθεριώτεροι δὲ εἶναι
δοκοῦσιν οἱ μὴ κτησάμενοι ἀλλὰ παραλαβόντες τὴν
οὐσίαν· ἄπειροί τε γὰρ τῆς ἐνδείας, καὶ πάντες ἀγαπῶσι
μᾶλλον τὰ αὑτῶν ἔργα, ὥσπερ οἱ γονεῖς καὶ οἱ ποιηταί.
Πλουτεῖν δ' οὐ ῥᾴδιον τὸν ἐλευθέριον, μήτε ληπτικὸν
ὄντα μήτε φυλακτικόν, προετικὸν δὲ καὶ μὴ τιμῶντα δι'

18 nor scatter his gifts indiscriminately (though his *tendency* would be rather in this direction than the opposite), for thus he would cut himself off from the power of giving on proper

The *relative* not the *absolute* amount given is to be considered.

19 occasions. Liberality is always to be measured, not by the absolute amount given, but by the proportion which it bears to the means of the giver. We conclude this part of our subject with some general considerations upon Liberality.

Sundry practical points of detail about Liberality (§§ 20—27). Liberality is more common with inherited than with acquired wealth.

20 Liberality is more often found in those who have inherited, than in those who have made, their money. This is partly because the former do not know what it is to want money, and partly because they have not that sort of parental love to it which men feel for anything which they have themselves

3. κατὰ τὴν οὐσίαν] 'in proportion to one's means.'

6. ἕξει] 'the disposition of the giver.' Cf. 'Non donum sed dantis animum.'

οὐθὲν δὴ κωλύει κ.τ.λ.] The 'widow's mite' affords a familiar illustration of this.

11. ἔργα is used in the sense of 'productions.' So Bacon speaks of the children of men who have first founded a family, as being 'both Children and *Creatures* (ἔργα), a continuation not only of their kind, but of their *work*.'

21 αὐτὰ τὰ χρήματα ἀλλ' ἕνεκα τῆς δόσεως. Διὸ καὶ ἐγκα-
λεῖται τῇ τύχῃ ὅτι οἱ μάλιστα ἄξιοι ὄντες ἥκιστα
πλουτοῦσιν. Συμβαίνει δ' οὐκ ἀλόγως τοῦτο· οὐ γὰρ
οἷόν τε χρήματ' ἔχειν μὴ ἐπιμελούμενον ὅπως ἔχῃ
22 ὥσπερ οὐδ' ἐπὶ τῶν ἄλλων. Οὐ μὴν δώσει γε οἷς οὐ
δεῖ οὐδ' ὅτε μὴ δεῖ, οὐδ' ὅσα ἄλλα τοιαῦτα· οὐ γὰρ
ἂν ἔτι πράττοι κατὰ τὴν ἐλευθεριότητα, καὶ εἰς ταῦτα
23 ἀναλώσας οὐκ ἂν ἔχοι εἰς ἃ δεῖ ἀναλίσκειν. Ὥσπερ
γὰρ εἴρηται, ἐλευθέριός ἐστιν ὁ κατὰ τὴν οὐσίαν δα-
πανῶν καὶ εἰς ἃ δεῖ· ὁ δ' ὑπερβάλλων ἄσωτος. Διὸ
τοὺς τυράννους οὐ λέγομεν ἀσώτους· τὸ γὰρ πλῆθος
τῆς κτήσεως οὐ δοκεῖ ῥᾴδιον εἶναι ταῖς δόσεσι καὶ ταῖς
24 δαπάναις ὑπερβάλλειν. Τῆς ἐλευθεριότητος δὴ μεσό-

The liberal seldom grow rich.

21 produced. Again the liberal seldom grow rich, and it is
unreasonable to complain of this, for no one can expect to
22 have what he takes no pains to obtain or to keep. This
tendency to spend however will always be checked (as we
have said already) by careful consideration of the objects
23 and occasions of expenditure, and also of the amount out of
which it is taken. (Hence, we may note in passing, princes,
whose wealth is all but boundless, can scarcely be called
24 prodigal for disregard of this last point at least.) Moreover

Liberality is regulated by various considerations of propriety,

1. *ἕνεκα τῆς δόσεως*] see note above on § 17.

2. *ἐγκαλεῖται τῇ τύχῃ*] This is like the familiar reproach against Providence: Why do the unworthy prosper in the world? The answer to this (as Aristotle says) is obvious; 'a man reaps what he sows.' The harvest of success which such men reap is not that which worthier men spend any pains upon, and therefore, naturally, do not obtain it. So in the case before us, the liberal do not devote themselves to making money, and naturally therefore do not make it.

5. *οὐ μὴν* guards against a misinterpretation of what precedes. Though the liberal man does not care about keeping his money, it does not follow that he is indifferent how it goes. For similar use of *οὐ μὴν* cf. I. x. 14, III. vi. 11, etc.

τητος οὔσης περὶ χρημάτων δόσιν καὶ λῆψιν, ἐλευθέ-
ριος καὶ δώσει καὶ δαπανήσει εἰς ἃ δεῖ καὶ ὅσα δεῖ,
ὁμοίως ἐν μικροῖς καὶ μεγάλοις, καὶ ταῦτα ἡδέως· καὶ
λήψεται δ' ὅθεν δεῖ καὶ ὅσα δεῖ. Τῆς ἀρετῆς γὰρ περὶ
ἄμφω οὔσης μεσότητος, ποιήσει ἀμφότερα ὡς δεῖ· ἕπε-
ται γὰρ τῇ ἐπιεικεῖ δόσει ἡ τοιαύτη λῆψις, ἡ δὲ μὴ
τοιαύτη ἐναντία ἐστίν. Αἱ μὲν οὖν ἑπόμεναι γίγνονται
25 ἅμα ἐν τῷ αὐτῷ, αἱ δ' ἐναντίαι δῆλον ὡς οὔ. Ἐὰν δὲ
παρὰ τὸ δέον καὶ τὸ καλῶς ἔχον συμβαίνῃ αὐτῷ ἀνα-
λίσκειν, λυπήσεται, μετρίως δὲ καὶ ὡς δεῖ· τῆς ἀρετῆς
γὰρ καὶ ἥδεσθαι καὶ λυπεῖσθαι ἐφ' οἷς δεῖ καὶ ὡς δεῖ.
26 Καὶ εὐκοινώνητος δ' ἐστὶν ὁ ἐλευθέριος εἰς χρήματα·
27 δύναται γὰρ ἀδικεῖσθαι, μὴ τιμῶν γε τὰ χρήματα, καὶ
μᾶλλον ἀχθόμενος εἴ τι δέον μὴ ἀνάλωσεν ἢ λυπού-

and that both in giving and taking.

such proprieties must not be disregarded either in giving or
taking, in great matters or in small: and though we have
admitted propriety in giving to be the more important, yet
25 the two habits will naturally be found together. If the liberal
man should have made a mistake in any of these points, he
will feel regret in due measure and moderation. And such
26 mistakes may occur, for the liberal man will not be hard to
27 deal with in money matters, nor is he by any means proof
against fraud, partly on account of his low esteem for money,
and partly because he will always regret more keenly having

The liberal man may make occasional mistakes, especially as he is not keen in driving a bargain or in measuring the precise amount he spends.

5. ἕπεται γὰρ κ.τ.λ.] Liberality, though mainly concerned with giving, cannot exist combined with dishonesty in taking. If money were gained unfairly, it would not be liberality to spend a part, or even the whole of it, in charity.

7. ἑπόμεναι] sc. ἕξεις or ἀρεταί.

11. καὶ ἥδεσθαι καὶ λυπεῖσθαι] For this see II. iii.

12. εὐκοινώνητος] 'an easy man to have dealings with.'

14. μᾶλλον ἀχθόμενος κ.τ.λ.] Hence he will rather cheat himself than cheat others even involuntarily. Or again, he would rather find that he has given money to an impostor than that he has turned a deaf ear to a case of real distress. This of course might arise from a true

μενος εἰ μὴ δέον τι ἀνάλωσε, καὶ τῷ Σιμωνίδῃ οὐκ
28 ἀρεσκόμενος. Ὁ δ' ἄσωτος καὶ ἐν τούτοις διαμαρτάνει·
οὔτε γὰρ ἥδεται ἐφ' οἷς δεῖ, οὐδὲ ὡς δεῖ, οὔτε λυπεῖται·
29 ἔσται δὲ προϊοῦσι φανερώτερον. Εἴρηται δ' ἡμῖν ὅτι
ὑπερβολαὶ καὶ ἐλλείψεις εἰσὶν ἡ ἀσωτία καὶ ἡ ἀνελευ-
θερία, καὶ ἐν δυσίν, ἐν δόσει καὶ λήψει· καὶ τὴν δαπά-
νην γὰρ εἰς τὴν δόσιν τίθεμεν. Ἡ μὲν οὖν ἀσωτία τῷ

Prodigality under two types (§§ 28-36).

28 spent too little than having spent too much. This and other
characteristics of the liberal man are wanting in the prodigal.
29 Both in giving and in taking he will err, and so will the
sordid man. Strictly speaking, the former exceeds in spend-

The first type unites excess in spending with defect in taking (§§ 29—32).

feeling of benevolence, but the assertion in the text probably has reference to the same sort of feeling which makes the magnanimous man prefer giving to accepting benefits (iii. 24). The error on the side spoken of has more of τὸ καλὸν in it. It accords better with that self-esteem, not to say pride, which forms so large an element in an ideal Greek character. Benevolence occupies a very subordinate place in the character of Aristotle's liberal man. There is a strong vein of self-consciousness running through all the manifestations of this strictly speaking unselfish virtue.

1. Simonides was the type of a courtly poet, a sort of embodiment of common-sense worldly wisdom. He figures thus in the introduction to Plato's *Republic.* Among his recorded sayings we find one that 'it is better to be rich than to be wise, because philosophers are dependent upon the patronage of the rich, and not *vice versâ.*'

7. Two types of prodigals are described. One exceeds in giving and falls short in taking; the other exceeds both in giving and in taking. The former perhaps may be styled the liberal prodigal, and the latter the mean prodigal. The former is an indolent *laisser-faire* sort of character, who spends freely, but is either too careless or thoughtless to trouble himself about replenishing his wasting resources: *e.g.* the typical Irish landlord of the close of the last century. The latter is a selfish and unprincipled man who cares not how or whence the money comes so long as he has it to spend. This is said in § 33 to be the commoner type, because indiscriminate giving soon necessitates unscrupulous receiving.

διδόναι καὶ μὴ λαμβάνειν ὑπερβάλλει, τῷ δὲ λαμβάνειν ἐλλείπει, ἡ δ' ἀνελευθερία τῷ διδόναι μὲν ἐλλείπει, τῷ
30 *λαμβάνειν δ' ὑπερβάλλει, πλὴν ἐπὶ μικροῖς. Τὰ μὲν οὖν τῆς ἀσωτίας οὐ πάνυ συνδυάζεται· (οὐ γὰρ ῥᾴδιον μηδαμόθεν λαμβάνοντα πᾶσι διδόναι· ταχέως γὰρ ἐπιλείπει ἡ οὐσία τοὺς ἰδιώτας διδόντας, οἵπερ καὶ δοκοῦσιν ἄσωτοι εἶναι)· ἐπεὶ ὅ γε τοιοῦτος δόξειεν ἂν οὐ μικρῷ*
31 *βελτίων εἶναι τοῦ ἀνελευθέρου. Εὐίατός τε γάρ ἐστι καὶ ὑπὸ τῆς ἡλικίας καὶ ὑπὸ τῆς ἀπορίας, καὶ ἐπὶ τὸ μέσον δύναται ἐλθεῖν. Ἔχει γὰρ τὰ τοῦ ἐλευθερίου· καὶ γὰρ δίδωσι καὶ οὐ λαμβάνει, οὐδέτερον δ' ὡς δεῖ οὐδ' εὖ. Εἰ δὴ τοῦτο ἐθισθείη, ἢ πως ἄλλως μεταβάλοι,*

ing (*i.e.* giving) and falls short in taking, the latter exceeds
30 in taking and falls short in spending. True, both these conditions are not generally united in prodigality. Should they be so, prodigality under this type becomes vastly superior to sor-
31 didness, for (1) it tends to work its own cure as life advances and means fail; and (2) its outward actions resemble those of liberality, and judicious training may complete the resem-

3. *πλὴν ἐπὶ μικροῖς*] 'only in reference to small matters.' Similar conduct on a large scale is otherwise characterized; see § 42.

4. The first *γὰρ* explains *οὐ πάνυ συνδυάζεται*, the second *γὰρ* (in line 5) explains *οὐ ῥᾴδιον*. *ἐπεί γε* (l. 7) appeals to the consideration that such prodigality as should unite both characteristics would be vastly superior to the opposite vice of sordidness, and that it would be a very little way removed from liberality itself. This, however, is not usually the case in actual life. See § 33, etc. Consequently the statement *οὐ πάνυ συνδυάζεται κ.τ.λ.* holds good of prodigality generally speaking.

6. *οἵπερ καὶ κ.τ.λ.*] 'who (*i.e.* *ἰδιῶται*) are in point of fact prodigal.' This is explained by the exclusion of *τύραννοι* from the class, for which see § 23.

9. *ἡλικίας*] It is a matter of common observation that avarice (*i.e.* the reverse of prodigality) is the characteristic vice (or as Simonides is said to have called it, 'the proper pleasure') of old age.

εἴη ἂν ἐλευθέριος· δώσει γὰρ οἷς δεῖ, καὶ οὐ λήψεται
ὅθεν οὐ δεῖ. Διὸ καὶ δοκεῖ οὐκ εἶναι φαῦλος τὸ ἦθος·
οὐ γὰρ μοχθηροῦ οὐδ' ἀγεννοῦς τὸ ὑπερβάλλειν διδόντα
32 καὶ μὴ λαμβάνοντα, ἠλιθίου δέ. Ὁ δὲ τοῦτον τὸν τρό-
πον ἄσωτος πολὺ δοκεῖ βελτίων τοῦ ἀνελευθέρου εἶναι
διά τε τὰ εἰρημένα, καὶ ὅτι ὁ μὲν ὠφελεῖ πολλούς, ὁ δὲ
33 οὐθένα, ἀλλ' οὐδ' αὑτόν. Ἀλλ' οἱ πολλοὶ τῶν ἀσώτων,
καθάπερ εἴρηται, καὶ λαμβάνουσιν ὅθεν μὴ δεῖ, καὶ εἰσὶ
34 κατὰ τοῦτο ἀνελεύθεροι. Ληπτικοὶ δὲ γίνονται διὰ τὸ
βούλεσθαι μὲν ἀναλίσκειν, εὐχερῶς δὲ τοῦτο ποιεῖν μὴ
δύνασθαι· ταχὺ γὰρ ἐπιλείπει αὐτοὺς τὰ ὑπάρχοντα.
Ἀναγκάζονται οὖν ἑτέρωθεν πορίζειν. Ἅμα δὲ καὶ διὰ

blance by supplying the proper motive and consideration as
32 to the circumstances of the expenditure. Again (3) a prodigal
of this type, a weak rather than a vicious man, benefits others,
33 the sordid no one, not even himself. Most prodigals however
err more actively on the side of taking. They take whence they
34 ought not. They must take in order to keep going, and they

The second type is marked by excess both in giving and in taking (§§ 33—36).

6. ὁ μὲν ὠφελεῖ πολλούς] This unqualified statement would not be universally accepted. *e.g.* Lecky (*Eur. Morals*, i. p. 38) maintains the direct contrary. 'The selfish interest which leads men to accumulate confers ultimately more advantage upon the world than the generous instinct which leads men to give.' Indeed it is generally acknowledged now that indiscriminate spending, even if it be with a directly *benevolent* intention, is most mischievous to society. Though it is true that 'the folly of one man may be the fortune of another' (as Bacon says), yet before we infer therefrom that 'private vices are public benefits,' we ought to strike a balance between the advantages and disadvantages resulting from each vice: *e.g.* in this particular case we must not forget that both hoarding and squandering have some good and some bad effects. Each is a perversion or exaggeration of a good tendency. Hence both good and bad results may be traced in each case. Aristotle excludes from his comparison (a passing one it is true) the favourable aspect of the former and the unfavourable aspect of the latter.

τὸ μηθὲν τοῦ καλοῦ φροντίζειν ὀλιγώρως καὶ πάντοθεν
λαμβάνουσιν· διδόναι γὰρ ἐπιθυμοῦσι, τὸ δὲ πῶς ἢ
35 πόθεν οὐθὲν αὐτοῖς διαφέρει. Διόπερ οὐδ' ἐλευθέριοι
αἱ δόσεις αὐτῶν εἰσίν· οὐ γὰρ καλαί, οὐδὲ τούτου αὐ-
τοῦ ἕνεκα, οὐδὲ ὡς δεῖ· ἀλλ' ἐνίοτε οὓς δεῖ πένεσθαι,
τούτους πλουσίους ποιοῦσι, καὶ τοῖς μὲν μετρίοις τὰ ἤθη
οὐδὲν ἂν δοῖεν, τοῖς δὲ κόλαξιν ἤ τιν' ἄλλην ἡδονὴν πο-
ρίζουσι πολλά. Διὸ καὶ ἀκόλαστοι αὐτῶν εἰσὶν οἱ πολ-
λοί· εὐχερῶς γὰρ ἀναλίσκοντες καὶ εἰς τὰς ἀκολασίας
δαπανηροί εἰσι, καὶ διὰ τὸ μὴ πρὸς τὸ καλὸν ζῆν πρὸς
36 τὰς ἡδονὰς ἀποκλίνουσιν. Ὁ μὲν οὖν ἄσωτος ἀπαιδα-
γώγητος γενόμενος εἰς ταῦτα μεταβαίνει, τυχὼν δ' ἐπι-
37 μελείας εἰς τὸ μέσον καὶ τὸ δέον ἀφίκοιτ' ἄν. Ἡ δ'
ἀνελευθερία ἀνίατός ἐστιν· δοκεῖ γὰρ τὸ γῆρας καὶ πᾶσα
ἀδυναμία ἀνελευθέρους ποιεῖν. Καὶ συμφυέστερον τοῖς

concern themselves as little where the money comes from as
35 they do where it goes to. They are neither honest nor gene-
rous; for money spent at hazard or squandered on pleasures,
flatterers, and other unworthy objects, may be spent lavishly,
but not liberally. Hence it is not difficult to see how a pro-
digal in the proper and limited sense of the word becomes a
prodigal in the wider sense noted at the beginning of the
36 chapter. This in fact is what prodigality comes to if it runs
its course unchecked, though, as we have pointed out, it is a
37 condition admitting of remedy and guidance. The condition
of Sordidness however is incurable: for—(1) Age and want
of means, so far from curing the habit, tend to produce it;
(2) It seems in some way a more natural vice among men

Sordidness under three types (§§ 37—45).

1. ὀλιγώρως] thoughtlessly, indifferently, unscrupulously.

6. τοῖς μετρίοις τὰ ἤθη] this being opposed to κόλαξιν apparently means 'persons of a fair disposition.'

15. ἀδυναμία corresponds to ἀπορία in the converse case of the prodigal (see § 31).

ἀνθρώποις τῆς ἀσωτίας· οἱ γὰρ πολλοὶ φιλοχρήματοι
38 μᾶλλον ἢ δοτικοί. Καὶ διατείνει δ' ἐπὶ πολὺ, καὶ πο-
λυειδές ἐστιν· πολλοὶ γὰρ τρόποι δοκοῦσι τῆς ἀνελευ-
θερίας εἶναι. Ἐν δυσὶ γὰρ οὖσα, τῇ τ' ἐλλείψει τῆς
δόσεως καὶ τῇ ὑπερβολῇ τῆς λήψεως, οὐ πᾶσιν ὁλό-
κληρος παραγίνεται, ἀλλ' ἐνίοτε χωρίζεται, καὶ οἱ μὲν
τῇ λήψει ὑπερβάλλουσιν, οἱ δὲ τῇ δόσει ἐλλείπουσιν.
39 Οἱ μὲν γὰρ ἐν ταῖς τοιαύταις προσηγορίαις οἷον φειδω-
λοὶ, γλίσχροι, κίμβικες, πάντες τῇ δόσει ἐλλείπουσι,
τῶν δ' ἀλλοτρίων οὐκ ἐφίενται οὐδὲ βούλονται λαμ-

38 than prodigality; (3) It is also widespread, and has many
forms. (*a*) Its complete development implies (as in the case
of prodigality) error both in giving and taking. In taking it
39 exceeds, in giving it falls short. But besides this perfect
growth of the vice, we have two other forms of it. (*b*) We
find Sordid men who are niggardly in spending, without being

(*a*) Excess in taking and defect in giving both combined.

(*b*) Defect in giving only.

5. ὁλόκληρος] 'in completeness.' The same expression occurs in v. 7 in reference to various types of Anger. Cf. James i. 4, τέλειοι καὶ ὁλόκληροι 'perfect and complete.' Add 1 Thess. v. 23.

8. Οἱ μὲν corresponds to οἱ δὲ in the first line of § 40. The class introduced by this οἱ μὲν is subdivided (and the subdivision marked by another οἱ μὲν and οἱ δὲ in l. 1 and l. 6, p. 186) before we come to the οἱ δὲ belonging to it. The sentence is further complicated by an explanatory parenthesis attached to the first of these subdivisions, Δοκοῦσι . . ἂν δοῦναι. The following analysis may be found useful:—

Full-blown Sordidness (ὁλόκληρος) implies both (*a*) falling short in giving and (*β*) excess in taking. There are two imperfectly developed types:

(*a*) only is found in	φειδωλοὶ γλίσχροι κίμβικες κυμινοπρίσται	who do not necessarily err in respect of (*β*)	some from natural shame, others from fear of reprisals, § 39.
(*β*) only is found in	πορνοβοσκοὶ τοκισταὶ, etc. add also λησταὶ κυβευταὶ λωποδύται	who do not necessarily err in respect of (*a*). Such people are in fact often extravagant, and their 'ill-gotten gains fly apace.'	

βάνειν, οἱ μὲν διά τινα ἐπιείκειαν καὶ εὐλάβειαν τῶν αἰσχρῶν· (δοκοῦσι γὰρ ἔνιοι ἤ φασί γε διὰ τοῦτο φυλάττειν, ἵνα μή ποτ' ἀναγκασθῶσιν αἰσχρόν τι πρᾶξαι. Τούτων δὲ καὶ ὁ κυμινοπρίστης καὶ πᾶς ὁ τοιοῦτος· ὠνόμασται δ' ἀπὸ τῆς ὑπερβολῆς τοῦ μηθενὶ ἂν δοῦναι). οἱ δ' αὖ διὰ φόβον ἀπέχονται τῶν ἀλλοτρίων, ὡς οὐ ῥᾴδιον τὸ αὐτὸν μὲν τὰ ἑτέρων λαμβάνειν, τὰ δ' αὑτοῦ ἑτέρους μή· ἀρέσκει οὖν αὐτοῖς τὸ μήτε λαμβάνειν μήτε
40 διδόναι. Οἱ δ' αὖ κατὰ τὴν λῆψιν ὑπερβάλλουσι τῷ πάντοθεν λαμβάνειν καὶ πᾶν, οἷον οἱ τὰς ἀνελευθέρους ἐργασίας ἐργαζόμενοι, πορνοβοσκοὶ καὶ πάντες οἱ τοιοῦτοι, καὶ τοκισταὶ κατὰ μικρὸν ἐπὶ πολλῷ. Πάντες γὰρ
41 οὗτοι ὅθεν οὐ δεῖ λαμβάνουσι, καὶ ὁπόσον οὐ δεῖ. Κοινὸν δ' ἐπ' αὐτοῖς ἡ αἰσχροκέρδεια φαίνεται· πάντες γὰρ ἕνεκα κέρδους, καὶ τούτου μικροῦ, ὀνείδη ὑπομένουσιν.

unprincipled in taking, money:—some from a natural sense of shame, others from fear of reprisals. This class we characterize as stingy, close, niggards, cheeseparers, and by other
40, 41 similar appellations. (*c*) We have again another class of
(*c*) Excess in taking only. sordid men, utterly unprincipled in the source from which

1. διά τινα ἐπιείκειαν κ.τ.λ.] A sort of honesty may accompany meanness and excessive devotion to money. See note on § 9.

4. κυμινοπρίστης] *i.e.* a man so stingy that he would split a cummin seed. Compare our metaphors 'skinflint,' 'cheeseparer,' and Juvenal's 'one who counts the fibres of a leek' (*Sat.* xiv. 133).

6. διὰ φόβον κ.τ.λ.] This according to the Sophists was the sole ground and principle of Justice between man and man, and the cause of the very existence of society. See Plato, *Rep.* p. 358, πλέονι κακῷ ὑπερβάλλειν τὸ ἀδικεῖσθαι ἢ ἀγαθῷ τὸ ἀδικεῖν.

12. τοκισταὶ κατὰ μικρὸν ἐπὶ πολλῷ] 'Money-lenders in small sums at a large rate'; ἐπὶ with dative expressing the conditions of the act.

15. μικροῦ is no contradiction to ἐπὶ πολλῷ above, for though the rate of interest is very large, yet the absolute amount is small.

42 Τοὺς γὰρ τὰ μεγάλα μὴ ὅθεν δὲ δεῖ λαμβάνοντας, μηδὲ
ἃ δεῖ, οὐ λέγομεν ἀνελευθέρους, οἷον τοὺς τυράννους
πόλεις πορθοῦντας καὶ ἱερὰ συλῶντας, ἀλλὰ πονηροὺς
43 μᾶλλον καὶ ἀσεβεῖς καὶ ἀδίκους. Ὁ μέντοι κυβευτὴς
καὶ ὁ λωποδύτης καὶ ὁ λῃστὴς τῶν ἀνελευθέρων εἰσίν·
αἰσχροκερδεῖς γάρ. Κέρδους γὰρ ἕνεκεν ἀμφότεροι πραγ-
ματεύονται καὶ ὀνείδη ὑπομένουσιν, καὶ οἱ μὲν κινδύνους
τοὺς μεγίστους ἕνεκα τοῦ λήμματος, οἱ δ' ἀπὸ τῶν φίλων
κερδαίνουσιν, οἷς δεῖ διδόναι. Ἀμφότεροι δὴ ὅθεν οὐ δεῖ
κερδαίνειν βουλόμενοι αἰσχροκερδεῖς, καὶ πᾶσαι δὴ αἱ
44 τοιαῦται λήψεις ἀνελεύθεροι. Εἰκότως δὲ τῇ ἐλευθεριό-
τητι ἀνελευθερία ἐναντίον λέγεται· μεῖζόν τε γάρ ἐστι

they take money, and at the same time open-handed in spend-
ing it; *e.g.* panders, usurers, and those who follow any such
42 base and illegal traffic. Still, as before, we are speaking of
gain on a small scale; we reserve other and stronger terms
43 for those who plunder wholesale. We ought however to add
to our list gamblers, pickpockets, and thieves, who all agree
in their indifference as to the source from which they take,
and are therefore described as sordid, no matter what subse-
44 quent use they make of the money thus unfairly taken. We
conclude by remarking that Sordidness is more opposed to

Sordidness is the worse extreme of the two.

4. μέντοι (='however') implies that those following are to be included among the sordid, though the somewhat similar characters just mentioned are excluded on account of the large scale on which their villanies are practised.

6. ἀμφότεροι] *i.e.* κυβευτὴς in one class, and λωποδύτης and λῃστὴς together in the other. The distinction between the latter corresponds nearly with that between 'picking and stealing' respectively. λωποδύτης is literally one who slips into other people's clothes, a clothes-stealer, and hence a thief on a small scale. The words οἱ μὲν obviously refer to λωποδύται and λῃσταὶ, and οἱ δὲ to κυβευταί.

12. ἐναντίον] 'the opposite to'—explained by II. viii. 7.

μεῖζον κακὸν] The reasons for this have been given in §§ 32, 37, 38.

κακὸν τῆς ἀσωτίας, καὶ μᾶλλον ἐπὶ ταύτην ἁμαρτάνουσιν ἢ κατὰ τὴν λεχθεῖσαν ἀσωτίαν.

45 *Περὶ μὲν οὖν ἐλευθεριότητος καὶ τῶν ἀντικειμένων κακιῶν τοσαῦτ' εἰρήσθω.*

1 II. *Δόξειε δ' ἂν ἀκόλουθον εἶναι καὶ περὶ μεγαλοπρεπείας διελθεῖν· δοκεῖ γὰρ καὶ αὐτὴ περὶ χρήματά τις ἀρετὴ εἶναι. Οὐχ ὥσπερ δ' ἡ ἐλευθεριότης διατείνει περὶ πάσας τὰς ἐν χρήμασι πράξεις, ἀλλὰ περὶ τὰς δαπανηρὰς μόνον· ἐν τούτοις δ' ὑπερέχει τῆς ἐλευθεριότητος μεγέθει. Καθάπερ γὰρ τοὔνομα αὐτὸ ὑποσημαίνει,*
2 *ἐν μεγέθει πρέπουσα δαπάνη ἐστίν. Τὸ δὲ μέγεθος πρός τι· οὐ γὰρ τὸ αὐτὸ δαπάνημα τριηράρχῳ καὶ ἀρχιθεωρῷ.*
3 *Τὸ πρέπον δὴ πρὸς αὐτὸν, καὶ ἐν ᾧ καὶ περὶ ἅ. Ὁ δ'*

Liberality than Prodigality is, as being both more mischievous
45 and more common. So much then for the Virtue of Liberality.

CHAP. II.—*On the Virtue of Magnificence.*

Use of terms explained (§§ 1—4).

1 Magnificence, as the name implies, differs from Liberality
2 in the largeness of the sums with which it deals. Its general
3 characteristic is magnitude, but this must be in relation

1. *μᾶλλον ἐπὶ ταύτην*] Obviously men in general are more ready to take than to give.

8. *τὰς δαπανηρὰς μόνον*] 'only the expensive ones,' *i.e.* those in which the expenditure is *grand:* this being the point of difference between *μεγαλοπρέπεια* and *ἐλευθεριότης*. Here and elsewhere throughout the Chapter the argument turns upon the etymology of the word *μεγαλοπρέπεια*, which implies a combination of greatness and propriety. (See *Supplementary Note.*)

12. *τριηράρχῳ*] The duty of equipping a trireme, and (as was usual) commanding it in person, was the most important of the *λειτουργίαι* at Athens. Cf. note on § 11 below.

ἀρχιθεωρῷ] *θεωρία* was a state embassy or deputation to a festival or public games. *ἀρχιθεωρὸς* was the head of such an embassy, who defrayed its expenses. This duty was one of the *lesser* *λειτουργίαι*. See further § 16.

13. *ἐν ᾧ* perhaps refers to the oc-

ἐν μικροῖς ἢ ἐν μετρίοις κατ' ἀξίαν δαπανῶν οὐ λέγεται
μεγαλοπρεπής, οἷον τὸ "πολλάκι δόσκον ἀλήτῃ" ἀλλ'
ὁ ἐν μεγάλοις οὕτως. Ὁ μὲν γὰρ μεγαλοπρεπὴς ἐλευ-
θέριος, ὁ δ' ἐλευθέριος οὐθὲν μᾶλλον μεγαλοπρεπής.
4 Τῆς τοιαύτης δ' ἕξεως ἡ μὲν ἔλλειψις μικροπρέπεια
καλεῖται, ἡ δ' ὑπερβολὴ βαναυσία καὶ ἀπειροκαλία καὶ
ὅσαι τοιαῦται, οὐχ ὑπερβάλλουσαι τῷ μεγέθει περὶ ἃ
δεῖ, ἀλλ' ἐν οἷς οὐ δεῖ καὶ ὡς οὐ δεῖ λαμπρυνόμεναι·
5 ὕστερον δὲ περὶ αὐτῶν ἐροῦμεν. Ὁ δὲ μεγαλοπρεπὴς
ἐπιστήμονι ἔοικεν· τὸ πρέπον γὰρ δύναται θεωρῆσαι καὶ
6 δαπανῆσαι μεγάλα ἐμμελῶς. Ὥσπερ γὰρ ἐν ἀρχῇ εἴ-
πομεν, ἡ ἕξις ταῖς ἐνεργείαις ὁρίζεται, καὶ ὧν ἐστίν.

to three things:—the person who gives, the circumstances of
the gift, and its object. Hence every magnificent man is
4 liberal, but not every liberal man is magnificent. The vice
of defect is Paltriness. The vice of excess, which we describe
as Bad Taste and Vulgarity, errs not in the greatness of the
amount spent, but in the inappropriateness in different ways
5 of the expenditure. But of these hereafter. There is a sort
of scientific skill implied in Magnificence. This is needed to
6 decide under what various circumstances, as they actually

Conditions required for the exercise of Magnificence (§§ 5–9).

casion and accompanying circumstances, περὶ ἃ the objects; but the distinction is not very marked in itself, nor carefully retained in the text. Another reading is ἃ instead of περὶ ἅ, i.e. the amount spent.

1. The widow's mite was an act of liberality but not of magnificence, Mr. Peabody's donations an example of both. The Viceroy of Egypt's gift of a doll, with dress, jewels, etc., valued at £2000, to the Sultan's child, was neither one nor the other, for the reasons explained in § 11, etc.

6. βαναυσία καὶ ἀπειροκαλία] see note on II. vii. 6.

11. ἐμμελῶς] 'harmoniously,' literally 'in tune' (ἐν, μέλος), just as πλημμελὲς (πλὴν, μέλος) is what is out of tune (cf. I. ix. 6, etc.).

12. ἡ ἕξις ταῖς ἐνεργείαις ὁρίζεται] 'The habit is determined by its outward acts, and by the objects on which it is exercised.'

*Αἱ δὴ τοῦ μεγαλοπρεποῦς δαπάναι μεγάλαι καὶ πρέ-
πουσαι. Τοιαῦτα δὴ καὶ τὰ ἔργα· οὕτω γὰρ ἔσται μέγα
δαπάνημα καὶ πρέπον τῷ ἔργῳ. Ὥστε τὸ μὲν ἔργον τῆς
δαπάνης ἄξιον δεῖ εἶναι, τὴν δὲ δαπάνην τοῦ ἔργου, ἢ
7 καὶ ὑπερβάλλειν. Δαπανήσει δὲ τὰ τοιαῦτα ὁ μεγαλο-
πρεπὴς τοῦ καλοῦ ἕνεκα· κοινὸν γὰρ τοῦτο ταῖς ἀρεταῖς.
8 Καὶ ἔτι ἡδέως καὶ προετικῶς· ἡ γὰρ ἀκριβολογία μι-
9 κροπρεπές. Καὶ πῶς κάλλιστον καὶ πρεπωδέστατον,*

There must be a scientific appreciation of the just relation between expense and its object; the motive must be noble; and the action ready and cheerful.

occur (for action is the only real test of disposition in this as in other Virtues), great expenditure is befitting and appropriate. The occasion must be worthy of the expenditure, and
7 the expenditure of the occasion. There must also be the same motive as in all the other virtues, viz. the desire for
8 what is noble. Again the magnificent act must be done cheerfully and ungrudgingly: there must be no close calculations;
9 no considerations of 'How much, or how little, will it cost?'

In the following sentence the *δαπάναι* correspond to the *ἐνέργειαι*, and the *ἔργα* to the *ὧν ἐστί* (which = *περὶ ἃ* of § 2) in the particular case under consideration, viz. Magnificence. Compare a similar passage in III. vii. 6 (and note there); and in explanation of the necessity of action (*ἐνέργεια*) for the perfect determination of a moral habit (*ἕξις*) see further X. viii. 4, 5. The *δὴ* in l. 1 and l. 2 marks the application of the general principle to the particular case. Divested of technical language the passage in §§ 5 and 6 means: 'Magnificence, to be determined and recognised as such, must be actually put in practice on certain definite occasions. It consists, as we have seen, in large expenditure on a befitting occasion. Hence there must actually occur both the expenditure and the occasion: and to form a correct judgment of these in practice implies a sort of scientific skill.'

2. *ἔργα*] the 'works' or 'results.'

5. We had similar conditions insisted on in the case of liberality, i. 12-14.

6. Here, as in the case of liberality, we miss any recognition of benevolence or the desire to do good. See note on i. 27.

7. *ἀκριβολογία μικροπρεπές*] as is explained in § 21. *σκοπῶν πῶς ἂν ἐλάχιστον κ.τ.λ.*

σκέψαιτ' ἂν μᾶλλον ἢ πόσου καὶ πῶς ἐλαχίστου. Ἀναγκαῖον δὴ καὶ ἐλευθέριον τὸν μεγαλοπρεπῆ εἶναι· καὶ γὰρ ὁ ἐλευθέριος δαπανήσει ἃ δεῖ καὶ ὡς δεῖ. Ἐν τούτοις δὲ τὸ μέγα τοῦ μεγαλοπρεποῦς (οἷον μέγεθος),

but rather, 'What will be the grandest and the most appropriate way of doing it?' And hence the magnificent man will necessarily be liberal also: but besides the mere grandeur of the amount spent, there is a grandeur of manner which im-

Magnificence differs in kind as well as in degree from Liberality. It always makes the most of what it spends.

3. *ἐν τούτοις . . . μεγαλοπρεπέστερον*] The object of this passage is to explain that magnificence differs from liberality not in degree only (which it commonly does, *οἷον μέγεθος*), but in kind also. It involves a sort of scientific instinct (so to speak, see § 5), which, even without adding to the cost, disposes of it to the best advantage. Whatever it spends it makes the very most of.

As to the translation:—*οἷον μέγεθος* is parenthetical and explains that *τὸ μέγα* may be, and commonly is, literal greatness of amount (*μέγεθος*). Translate, 'which may take the form of greatness of amount.' *ἐν τούτοις δέ*, literally 'but in these things,' and so nearly = 'still,' 'notwithstanding.' *καὶ* (l. 1, p. 192) is 'even.'

In illustration of the parenthesis *οἷον μέγεθος*, cf. §§ 17, 18 (*καὶ ἐπὶ τῶν δαπανημάτων κ.τ.λ.*), where we have an instance of *μέγα*, which is not *μέγεθος*, *i.e.* of appropriate greatness which is not greatness of bulk. With the statement involved in *καὶ ἀπὸ τῆς ἴσης δαπάνης κ.τ.λ.*, compare Bacon's *Essays* (on Expense), 'Ordinary Expense . . . should be so ordered that the bills be less than the estimation abroad.' Tacitus (*Hist.* ii. 80) attributes a gift of this kind to Mucianus, 'Omnium quae diceret atque ageret arte quâdam (cf. *ἐπιστήμονι* § 5) ostentator.' It is a familiar fact that some people spend profusely and yet 'have nothing to show for it,' while others contrive to do a surprising amount with slender means. The former lack, and the latter on a small scale possess, that peculiar skill which Aristotle in the text ascribes to the *μεγαλοπρέπης*, of making the most display from a given expenditure. Speaking generally, the French have this gift much more than ourselves. We notice again how the scientific or intellectual rather than the moral side of Magnificence is insisted on (See Introduction p. xxxiv.).

It should be added that the passage is also sometimes written with a parenthesis enclosing the

περὶ ταὐτὰ τῆς ἐλευθεριότητος οὔσης, καὶ ἀπὸ τῆς ἴσης δαπάνης τὸ ἔργον ποιήσει μεγαλοπρεπέστερον. Οὐ γὰρ ἡ αὐτὴ ἀρετὴ κτήματος καὶ ἔργου· κτῆμα μὲν γὰρ τὸ πλείστου ἄξιον τιμιώτατον, οἷον χρυσὸς, ἔργον δὲ τὸ μέγα καὶ καλόν. Τοῦ γὰρ τοιούτου ἡ θεωρία θαυμαστὴ, τὸ δὲ μεγαλοπρεπὲς θαυμαστόν. Καὶ ἔστιν ἔργου ἀρετὴ μεγαλοπρέπεια ἐν μεγέθει. ∠

11 Ἔστι δὲ τῶν δαπανημάτων οἷα λέγομεν τὰ τίμια, οἷον τὰ περὶ θεοὺς ἀναθήματα καὶ κατασκευαὶ καὶ θυσίαι, ὁμοίως δὲ καὶ ὅσα περὶ πᾶν το δαιμόνιον, καὶ ὅσα πρὸς

parts a special lustre to the acts of a magnificent man beyond what would be achieved by mere liberality even with the same expenditure. For a work and a possession are not to be estimated in the same way. In the latter case there is only a question of intrinsic value; in the former we must take into consideration the grandeur and the moral effect produced on the beholders. The perfection of any work or action is its magnificence, and that must be exhibited on a grand scale.

11 We pass on now to the occasions which are fitting for the display of Magnificence. We notice first, the service of re-

words οἷον μέγεθος . . . οὔσης. The sense will then be, 'The greatness of the magnificent man, being a sort of greatness of Liberality (or Liberality on a large scale),—Liberality having reference to the same objects,—even from an equal expenditure,' etc.

This however seems rather to mar the force of καὶ ἀπὸ τῆς ἴσης δαπάνης. It is probable that there is some corruption in the text. οἷον μέγεθος looks like a gloss.

7. μεγαλοπρέπεια combines the ideas of 'magnificence' indicated in its etymology, and 'munificence' implied by its technical limitation to money matters in this Chapter. As we have no one word exactly co-extensive with this, we may adopt 'munificence' or 'magnificence,' according to the idea most prominent in the context, but see Suppl. Notes, p. 289.

9. κατασκευαὶ] probably refers to the adornment and permanent furniture of the temples. κατασκευη denotes permanent, and παρασκευὴ temporary and moveable, decorations. Compare κατασκευάσασθαι just below, § 16.

τὸ κοινὸν εὐφιλοτίμητά ἐστιν, οἷον εἴ που χορηγεῖν οἴονται δεῖν λαμπρῶς ἢ τριηραρχεῖν ἢ καὶ ἑστιᾶν τὴν
12 πόλιν. Ἐν ἅπασι δ' ὥσπερ εἴρηται καὶ πρὸς τὸν πράττοντα ἀναφέρεται τὸ τίς ὢν καὶ τίνων ὑπαρχόντων· ἄξια γὰρ δεῖ τούτων εἶναι, καὶ μὴ μόνον τῷ ἔργῳ ἀλλὰ καὶ
13 τῷ ποιοῦντι πρέπειν. Διὸ πένης μὲν οὐκ ἂν εἴη μεγαλοπρεπής· οὐ γάρ ἐστιν ἀφ' ὧν πολλὰ δαπανήσει πρεπόντως· ὁ δ' ἐπιχειρῶν ἠλίθιος· παρὰ τὴν ἀξίαν γὰρ καὶ
14 τὸ δέον· κατ' ἀρετὴν δὲ τὸ ὀρθῶς. Πρέπει δὲ καὶ οἷς τὰ τοιαῦτα προϋπάρχει δι' αὐτῶν ἢ διὰ τῶν προγόνων ἢ ὧν αὐτοῖς μέτεστιν, καὶ τοῖς εὐγενέσι καὶ τοῖς ἐνδόξοις καὶ ὅσα τοιαῦτα· πάντα γὰρ ταῦτα μέγεθος ἔχει καὶ
15 ἀξίωμα. Μάλιστα μὲν οὖν τοιοῦτος ὁ μεγαλοπρεπής, καὶ ἐν τοῖς τοιούτοις δαπανήμασιν ἡ μεγαλοπρέπεια,

12 ligion, and next, great public or patriotic services. In all these cases however regard must be had to the social position, and to the means, of the doer, as well as to the work done.
13 It would be out of place for a man of small or moderate means
14 to aspire to be magnificent. It is a virtue reserved for those of great wealth, inherited or acquired, good birth, high station,
15 and so forth. To these cases we may add great and rare

Occasions appropriate for Magnificence (§§ 11—19) are chiefly *public*, such as the service of Religion or of the State:

1. εὐφιλοτίμητα] 'objects of laudable ambition.'

χορηγεῖν . . . τριηραρχεῖν . . . ἑστιᾶν] These λειτουργίαι at Athens resembled High Sheriffs' duties among ourselves, being imposed without remuneration on the rich citizens. καὶ joined with ἑστιᾶν implies that this office of providing a feast for the citizens was less costly than the others. See § 2 for other references to these offices, and note there.

4. τὸ groups the words that follow into one idea forming grammatically a sort of nominative to ἀναφέρεται. (Compare τὸ τί-ἦν-εἶναι in II. vi., etc.) 'There is also a reference made to the agent, viz. who he is, and what are his means.'

11. ὧν αὐτοῖς μέτεστιν] 'their relations or connexions.'

12. μέγεθος καὶ ἀξίωμα] 'grandeur and dignity.'

14. τοιούτοις] i.e. the two classes of objects already men-

ὥσπερ εἴρηται· μέγιστα γὰρ καὶ ἐντιμότατα· τῶν δὲ
ἰδίων ὅσα εἰσάπαξ γίνεται, οἷον γάμος καὶ εἴ τι τοιοῦτον,
καὶ εἰ περί τι πᾶσα ἡ πόλις σπουδάζει ἢ οἱ ἐν ἀξιώματι,
καὶ περὶ ξένων δὲ ὑποδοχὰς καὶ ἀποστολάς, καὶ δωρεὰς
καὶ ἀντιδωρεάς· οὐ γὰρ εἰς ἑαυτὸν δαπανηρὸς ὁ μεγαλο-
πρεπής, ἀλλ' εἰς τὰ κοινά· τὰ δὲ δῶρα τοῖς ἀναθήμασιν
16 ἔχει τι ὅμοιον. Μεγαλοπρεποῦς δὲ καὶ οἶκον κατα-
σκευάσασθαι πρεπόντως τῷ πλούτῳ· κόσμος γάρ τις καὶ
οὗτος. Καὶ περὶ ταῦτα μᾶλλον δαπανᾶν ὅσα πολυχρόνια
17 τῶν ἔργων· κάλλιστα γὰρ ταῦτα. Καὶ ἐν ἑκάστοις
τὸ πρέπον· οὐ γὰρ ταὐτὰ ἁρμόζει θεοῖς καὶ ἀνθρώποις,
οὐδ' ἐν ἱερῷ καὶ τάφῳ· καὶ ἐπὶ τῶν δαπανημάτων
ἕκαστον μέγα ἐν τῷ γένει, καὶ μεγαλοπρεπέστατον μὲν
τὸ ἐν μεγάλῳ μέγα, ἐνταῦθα δὲ τὸ ἐν τούτοις μέγα.

but also some occur in *private* life.

occasions in private life, such as a wedding, works of public
or general interest, entertaining strangers, making and return-
16 ing presents, and so on: or again, the furnishing and orna-
ments of one's house, and generally, permanent, rather than
17 perishable, objects. In all cases however the expenditure
must be fitting to the occasion, whatever it be. There is a
greatness in any work when it is perfect of its kind, even in

tioned, viz. the service of Religion and the service of the State, as contrasted with the less striking cases which follow, viz. great and rare occasions in private life.

2. ὅσα εἰσάπαξ] Compare 'A man ought warily to begin charges, which, once begun, will continue; but in matters that return not he may be more magnificent' (Bacon).

3. εἰ δὲ περί τι πᾶσα ἡ πόλις] The entertainment of the Viceroy of Egypt by Lord Dudley in 1867 would be an instance in point.

οἱ ἐν ἀξιώματι] 'the leading men in it.'

6. τὰ δὲ δῶρα] 'presents have something of the nature of offerings,' which have been specified already in § 11 as occasions fitting for Magnificence.

14. ἐνταῦθα δὲ κ.τ.λ.] 'It is possible to do a thing handsomely though it be no great matter in itself: but the handsomest actions are naturally those

18 Καὶ διαφέρει τὸ ἐν τῷ ἔργῳ μέγα τοῦ ἐν τῷ δαπανήματι·
σφαῖρα μὲν γὰρ ἢ λήκυθος ἡ καλλίστη ἔχει μεγαλοπρέ-
πειαν παιδικοῦ δώρου, ἡ δὲ τούτου τιμὴ μικρὸν καὶ ἀνε-
19 λεύθερον. Διὰ τοῦτό ἐστι τοῦ μεγαλοπρεποῦς, ἐν ᾧ ἂν
ποιῇ γένει, μεγαλοπρεπῶς ποιεῖν· τὸ γὰρ τοιοῦτον οὐκ
εὐυπέρβλητον, καὶ ἔχον κατ' ἀξίαν τοῦ δαπανήματος.
20 Τοιοῦτος μὲν οὖν ὁ μεγαλοπρεπὴς, ὁ δ' ὑπερβάλλων καὶ
βάναυσος τῷ παρὰ τὸ δέον ἀναλίσκειν ὑπερβάλλει ὥσπερ
εἴρηται. Ἐν γὰρ τοῖς μικροῖς τῶν δαπανημάτων πολλὰ
ἀναλίσκει καὶ λαμπρύνεται παρὰ μέλος, οἷον ἐρανιστὰς
γαμικῶς ἑστιῶν, καὶ κωμῳδοῖς χορηγῶν ἐν τῇ παρόδῳ

18 toy-presents to children, but not such greatness as to constitute magnificence in its proper sense. This is strictly speaking
19 a grand outlay on a grand occasion. Still even in the smallest matters the Magnificent man will act magnificently, and strive
20 if possible never to be outdone. In contrast with all this note the character of the Vulgar man. On small occasions he will spend large sums, and make a vulgar show, and that not from any noble motive, but simply to display his riches, and to draw

The Excess is Vulgar display.

which are on the largest scale, and next come those which are handsome in matters of smaller degree.' This seems from the context to be the meaning of ἐν τούτοις.

3. τιμὴ μικρὸν καὶ ἀνελεύθερον] 'The cost is small and not a matter for liberality.' Thus the condition ἐν ἑκάστοις τὸ πρέπον (§ 17) would be violated.

4. διὰ τοῦτο] *i.e.* because there is a 'great' even in small matters.

10. παρὰ μέλος] 'in bad taste.' Contrast ἐμμελῶς in § 5. ἐρανισταὶ are persons associated for festive purposes on condition of each bearing his share of the expense, or of each entertaining the rest in turn, as is here supposed. It would be vulgar display and not magnificence for any one, when his turn came, to furnish the club dinner with the splendour of a marriage feast.

11. πάροδος] literally 'a coming forward' or 'appearance;' technically applied to the first *entrance* of the Chorus in a Greek play (the Chorus usually not being on the stage from the commencement), and then to the *song* which accompanied that

πορφύραν εἰσφέρων, ὥσπερ οἱ Μεγαρεῖς. Καὶ πάντα τὰ τοιαῦτα ποιήσει οὐ τοῦ καλοῦ ἕνεκα, ἀλλὰ τὸν πλοῦτον ἐπιδεικνύμενος, καὶ διὰ ταῦτα οἰόμενος θαυμάζεσθαι, καὶ οὗ μὲν δεῖ πολλὰ ἀναλῶσαι, ὀλίγα δαπανῶν, οὗ δ'
21 ὀλίγα, πολλά. Ὁ δὲ μικροπρεπὴς περὶ πάντα ἐλλείψει, καὶ τὰ μέγιστα ἀναλώσας ἐν μικρῷ τὸ καλὸν ἀπολεῖ, καὶ ὅ τι ἂν ποιῇ μέλλων, καὶ σκοπῶν πῶς ἂν ἐλάχιστον ἀναλῶσαι, καὶ ταῦτ' ὀδυρόμενος, καὶ πάντ' οἰόμενος

attention to himself. When he ought to spend much, he will spend little; and when he ought to spend little, he will spend
The Defect, Paltriness. 21 much. On the other hand, the Paltry man always spends too little. If ever he does spend largely, he will spoil everything by some petty economy. He will be always hesitating and calculating how cheaply he can get off, and will be continually

entrance. The emphatic word here is κωμῳδοῖς, comedy naturally requiring less splendour than tragedy.

4. οὗ μὲν δεῖ κ.τ.λ.] This follows naturally, because his only object being to display *himself* and his riches, he pays no regard to the proprieties of circumstances and expense, which it needs a careful scientific discernment (§ 5) to observe properly. Consequently if a proper occasion for great expense happens to be one for little personal display, the βάναυσος holds aloof.

6. τὰ μέγιστα ἀναλώσας] This is a point of difference between ἀνελευθερία and μικροπρέπεια. The latter being the defect where great expenditure is in question, the Paltry man is one who tries to combine cheapness and display. He wishes to make a show and yet hates to part with his money. The Sordid (ἀνελεύθερος) cares only for keeping his money on any terms.

ἐν μικρῷ τὸ καλὸν ἀπολεῖ] *e.g.* If a man should make a handsome donation to a Charity and send in the bill for the carriage and packing. Or, as Theophrastus says, 'He will give a grand feast and stint the supply of wine, and the dishes will hardly go round; or 'when he is celebrating a marriage feast, he will hire the waiters on condition that they find their own food,' and so on. He is the sort of man who cannot feel that in reference to such cases it is better 'to do the thing well, or not at all.'

7. μέλλων] 'with hesitation or reluctance.'

22 μείζω ποιεῖν ἢ δεῖ. Εἰσὶ μὲν οὖν αἱ ἕξεις αὗται κακίαι,
οὐ μὴν ὀνείδη γ' ἐπιφέρουσι διὰ τὸ μήτε βλαβεραὶ τῷ
πέλας εἶναι, μήτε λίαν ἀσχήμονες.
1 III. Ἡ δὲ μεγαλοψυχία περὶ μεγάλα μὲν καὶ ἐκ τοῦ
ὀνόματος ἔοικεν εἶναι, περὶ ποῖα δ' ἐστὶ πρῶτον λά-
2 βωμεν. Διαφέρει δ' οὐθὲν τὴν ἕξιν ἢ τὸν κατὰ τὴν
3 ἕξιν σκοπεῖν. Δοκεῖ δὲ μεγαλόψυχος εἶναι ὁ μεγάλων

22 grumbling that whatever he does spend is excessive. Still, vices as these are, they are not of the worst dye, for they are neither very injurious, nor very offensive, to society.

CHAP. III.—*On the Virtue of Highmindedness or Self-Esteem.*

High-mindedness Vaingloriousness, and Little-mindedness are concerned with the relation between a man's merits and his own estimate of them:

1 The very name Highmindedness, which we give to the
virtue of well-grounded Self-esteem, implies that there is
2 something great about it—(whether we consider the habit in
the abstract or portray an individual character in the concrete
3 is indifferent)—and that greatness may be described as great

CHAP. III.—*μεγαλοψυχία* is another very difficult word to translate. The exact etymological equivalent 'Magnanimity' has by the usage of language acquired too restricted a sense. Perhaps we must content ourselves with the awkward compound, 'Highmindedness.' On the inadequacy of this and the related terms see further the Supplementary Note at the end of this Book.

The groundwork of this and the related types of character described in this Chapter is the amount of, and the relation between, a man's merits and his own estimate of them. A more tangible and practically applicable test is substituted in § 10, viz. his relation to Honour (*τιμή*).

The Chapter falls under the following divisions:—

§§ 1—8. Terminology explained.

§§ 9—17. Highmindedness described generally as the desire to deserve, and to secure, Honour.

§§ 18—34. The characteristics of Highmindedness in reference to sundry practical details of life.

§§ 35—37. The related vices of Excess and Defect.

6. *διαφέρει δὲ κ.τ.λ.*] In this case the latter method is con-

αὐτὸν ἀξιῶν ἄξιος ὤν· ὁ γὰρ μὴ κατ' ἀξίαν αὐτὸ ποιῶν
ἠλίθιος, τῶν δὲ κατ' ἀρετὴν οὐδεὶς ἠλίθιος οὐδ' ἀνόητος.
4 Μεγαλόψυχος μὲν οὖν ὁ εἰρημένος. Ὁ γὰρ μικρῶν
ἄξιος καὶ τούτων ἀξιῶν ἑαυτὸν σώφρων, μεγαλόψυχος
5 δ' οὔ· ἐν μεγέθει γὰρ ἡ μεγαλοψυχία, ὥσπερ καὶ τὸ
κάλλος ἐν μεγάλῳ σώματι, οἱ μικροὶ δ' ἀστεῖοι καὶ
6 σύμμετροι, καλοὶ δ' οὔ. Ὁ δὲ μεγάλων ἑαυτὸν ἀξιῶν
ἀνάξιος ὢν χαῦνος· ὁ δὲ μειζόνων ἢ ἄξιος οὐ πᾶς
7 χαῦνος. Ὁ δ' ἐλαττόνων ἢ ἄξιος μικρόψυχος, ἐάν
τε μεγάλων ἐάν τε μετρίων, ἐάν τε καὶ μικρῶν
ἄξιος ὢν ἔτι ἐλαττόνων αὐτὸν ἀξιοῖ. Καὶ μάλιστα
ἂν δόξειεν ὁ μεγάλων ἄξιος· τί γὰρ ἂν ἐποίει, εἰ

self-esteem based upon great merits. In the absence of great
4, 5 merits such self-esteem would be mere folly: and in such a
case an adequate estimate of ourself, being necessarily a low
6 one, is not Highmindedness, but rather sober judgment. A
too high estimate of self is Vaingloriousness, provided it be
7 not only too high but also high absolutely. Conversely a
lower estimate than facts would warrant, be it small or great
in itself, is Littlemindedness, and above all when a man's
merits are really great, because then the contrast is more

spicuously adopted. We have almost an individual portraiture of a μεγαλόψυχος in this Chapter. Pericles has even been suggested as the original.

6. According to the Greek estimate beauty implied bulk. Perhaps our word 'handsome,' as used in contrast with 'beautiful,' conveys the same idea. Comp. *Pol.* IV. iv. 8, τὸ καλὸν ἐν πλήθει καὶ μεγέθει εἴωθε γίνεσθαι.

8. ὁ δὲ μειζόνων κ.τ.λ.] A man may estimate himself at a low rate and yet more highly than he deserves, in which case he would hardly be called 'vain.' *e.g.* Whately says of his tutor at College that 'he would be generally described as an eminently modest man. He never rated himself high either in abilities or attainments, and yet he overrated himself to a great degree, else he never would have undertaken the office of a College tutor.' This is just the case described in the text. See

8 μὴ τοσούτων ἦν ἄξιος; ἔστι δὴ ὁ μεγαλόψυχος
τῷ μὲν μεγέθει ἄκρος, τῷ δὲ ὡς δεῖ μέσος· τοῦ γὰρ
κατ' ἀξίαν αὑτὸν ἀξιοῖ. Οἱ δ' ὑπερβάλλουσι καὶ ἐλ-
9 λείπουσιν. Εἰ δὲ δὴ μεγάλων ἑαυτὸν ἀξιοῖ ἄξιος ὤν,
καὶ μάλιστα τῶν μεγίστων, περὶ ἓν μάλιστα ἂν εἴη.
10 Ἡ δ' ἀξία λέγεται πρὸς τὰ ἐκτὸς ἀγαθά. Μέγιστον δὲ
τοῦτ' ἂν θείημεν ὃ τοῖς θεοῖς ἀπονέμομεν, καὶ οὗ μάλιστ'
ἐφίενται οἱ ἐν ἀξιώματι, καὶ τὸ ἐπὶ τοῖς καλλίστοις
ἆθλον. Τοιοῦτον δ' ἡ τιμή· μέγιστον γὰρ δὴ τοῦτο τῶν
ἐκτὸς ἀγαθῶν. Περὶ τιμὰς δὴ καὶ ἀτιμίας ὁ μεγα-
11 λόψυχός ἐστιν ὡς δεῖ. Καὶ ἄνευ δὲ λόγου φαίνονται
οἱ μεγαλόψυχοι περὶ τιμὴν εἶναι· τιμῆς γὰρ μάλισθ'
12 οἱ μεγάλοι ἀξιοῦσιν ἑαυτούς, κατ' ἀξίαν δέ. Ὁ δὲ

8 striking. In perfect Highmindedness self-esteem is in a sense extreme, because it is always in proportion to merit, which is in that case extreme. It is in the observance of that *proportion* that the familiar law of the mean is exhibited; while its violation gives rise to the related Vices of Vaingloriousness and Littlemindedness. So much for the phraseology which
9, 10 we propose to employ. Now how is merit estimated or recompensed by men? Chiefly by Honour. Honour therefore
11 is the aim of the Highminded; to obtain Honour on condition
12 of deserving it. The Little-minded man falls short in his

and the three characters may be judged by the amount of Honour they deem to be their due.

further note at the end of this Book.

1. He is *extreme* in the *greatness* of his self-estimate, *moderate* in the *propriety* of it. A similar paradox was explained in regard to Virtue generally in II. vi. 17.

6. Ἡ δ' ἀξία] i.e. the expression, 'worth' or 'worthy of,' has reference to some external good as the standard by which it is measured. The index of merit, in other words, is something external; it is in fact the honour or estimation of others (τιμή). Hence, practically, we may describe this as the object and aim of Highmindedness, and the related excess and defect. See further I. v. 5 and note. Hence in the Catalogue of Virtues in II. vii. τιμή and ἀτιμία were taken at once as the groundwork of μεγαλοψυχία with its related Vices.

μικρόψυχος ἐλλείπει καὶ πρὸς ἑαυτὸν καὶ πρὸς τὸ τοῦ
13 *μεγαλοψύχου ἀξίωμα. Ὁ δὲ χαῦνος πρὸς ἑαυτὸν μὲν*
14 *ὑπερβάλλει, οὐ μὴν τόν γε μεγαλόψυχον. Ὁ δὲ μεγαλόψυχος, εἴπερ τῶν μεγίστων ἄξιος, ἄριστος ἂν εἴη· μείζονος γὰρ ἀεὶ ὁ βελτίων ἄξιος, καὶ μεγίστων ὁ ἄριστος. Τὸν ὡς ἀληθῶς ἄρα μεγαλόψυχον δεῖ ἀγαθὸν εἶναι. Καὶ δόξειε δ' ἂν εἶναι μεγαλοψύχου τὸ ἐν ἑκάστῃ*
15 *ἀρετῇ μέγα. Οὐδαμῶς τ' ἂν ἁρμόζοι μεγαλοψύχῳ φεύγειν παρασείσαντι, οὐδ' ἀδικεῖν· τίνος γὰρ ἕνεκα πράξει αἰσχρά, ᾧ οὐθὲν μέγα; καθ' ἕκαστα δ' ἐπισκοποῦντι πάμπαν γελοῖος φαίνοιτ' ἂν ὁ μεγαλόψυχος μὴ ἀγαθὸς ὤν. Οὐκ εἴη δ' ἂν οὐδὲ τιμῆς ἄξιος φαῦλος ὤν· τῆς ἀρετῆς γὰρ ἆθλον ἡ τιμή, καὶ ἀπονέμεται τοῖς*
16 *ἀγαθοῖς. Ἔοικε μὲν οὖν ἡ μεγαλοψυχία οἷον κόσμος*

estimate of himself both in reference to his own merits and
13 also in reference to the standard of the Highminded. In reference to that standard the Vainglorious man on the other hand cannot exceed, but in reference to his own merits he
14 does so. Highmindedness, being based upon merit, implies the possession of the other virtues, and that in the highest
15 degree. Undignified flight, for example, or injustice of any kind, would be utterly incompatible with a well-merited self-
16 respect. True Highmindedness is, as it were, 'the head and

High-mindedness implies all other virtues in the highest degree.

2. *ἀξίωμα*] The vainglorious man's estimate of himself cannot of course exceed the highminded man's estimate of himself, but it does exceed the estimate which his own merits warrant.

7. *Καὶ δόξειε κ.τ.λ.*] He not only possesses every Virtue, but every one on a grand scale, just as the *μεγαλοπρεπής* was explained (in ii. 10) to possess the particular virtue of Liberality on a grand scale.

9. *παρασείσαντι*] understand *τὰς χεῖρας*, *i.e.* 'swinging the hands in precipitate flight.'

οὐδ' ἀδικεῖν κ.τ.λ.] His high sense of the dignity of his moral nature is such (*πάμπαν γελοῖος φαίνεται μὴ ἀγαθὸς ὤν*) that he scorns to do an unjust or base action. This has sometimes been censured as if it was mere pride, but we should not forget that *mutatis mutandis* Christianity

τις εἶναι τῶν ἀρετῶν· μείζους γὰρ αὐτὰς ποιεῖ, καὶ οὐ
γίνεται ἄνευ ἐκείνων. Διὰ τοῦτο χαλεπὸν τῇ ἀληθείᾳ
μεγαλόψυχον εἶναι· οὐ γὰρ οἷόν τε ἄνευ καλοκαγαθίας.
17 Μάλιστα μὲν οὖν περὶ τιμὰς καὶ ἀτιμίας ὁ μεγαλόψυχός
ἐστι, καὶ ἐπὶ μὲν ταῖς μεγάλαις καὶ ὑπὸ τῶν σπουδαίων
μετρίως ἡσθήσεται, ὡς τῶν οἰκείων τυγχάνων ἢ καὶ
ἐλαττόνων· ἀρετῆς γὰρ παντελοῦς οὐκ ἂν γένοιτο ἀξία
τιμή· οὐ μὴν ἀλλ' ἀποδέξεταί γε τῷ μὴ ἔχειν αὐτοὺς
μείζω αὐτῷ ἀπονέμειν. Τῆς δὲ παρὰ τῶν τυχόντων καὶ
ἐπὶ μικροῖς πάμπαν ὀλιγωρήσει· οὐ γὰρ τούτων ἄξιος.
Ὁμοίως δὲ καὶ ἀτιμίας· οὐ γὰρ ἔσται δικαίως περὶ
18 αὐτόν. Μάλιστα μὲν οὖν ἐστίν, ὥσπερ εἴρηται, ὁ μεγα-
λόψυχος περὶ τιμάς, οὐ μὴν ἀλλὰ καὶ περὶ πλοῦτον

crown' of all the virtues. Need we wonder that it is rare and
17 difficult to attain to? The Highminded man, when he re-
ceives high honour from good men, will feel pleasure, though
in a moderate degree, for he knows that he is obtaining his
due, or rather, less than his due, but still the best it is in
their power to give, and as such he is willing to accept it.
The paltry homage of ordinary men he will despise as un-
worthy of him, and so he will also their contempt, which he
18 knows is undeserved. With the same dignified attitude will

The Highminded man is sober and discriminating in regard to the honour paid him by others.

Minor practical characteristics of

appeals to a somewhat similar motive, *e.g.* Rom. vi. 2, 11, 21, etc. etc. So Plat. *Rep.* p. 486 A.

1. *μείζους . . . ποιεῖ*] Highmindedness is not so much a separate virtue as a combination of all virtues in one perfect character, each and all being enhanced by the full consciousness of their possession, or (as a modern might phrase it) 'the testimony of a good conscience' in respect of them. (See *Suppl. Note.*)

3. *καλοκαγαθίας*] 'Nobility' seems to hit the double significance of this word. *καλοκάγαθος*, if it has not (like 'optimates' in Latin) passed from a moral to a social significance, yet implies the latter in combination with the former.

5. *ὑπὸ τῶν σπουδαίων*] He only cares 'laudari a laudatis viris.' Comp. I. v. 5.

10. *ἐπὶ μικροῖς*] 'on trivial grounds.'

καὶ δυναστείαν καὶ πᾶσαν εὐτυχίαν καὶ ἀτυχίαν μετρίως ἕξει, ὅπως ἂν γίνηται, καὶ οὔτ' εὐτυχῶν περιχαρὴς ἔσται, οὔτ' ἀτυχῶν περίλυπος. Οὐδὲ γὰρ περὶ τιμὴν οὕτως ἔχει ὡς μέγιστον ὄν. Αἱ γὰρ δυναστεῖαι καὶ ὁ πλοῦτος διὰ τὴν τιμήν ἐστιν αἱρετά· οἱ γοῦν ἔχοντες αὐτὰ τιμᾶσθαι δι' αὐτῶν βούλονται. ᾯι δὴ καὶ ἡ τιμή μικρόν ἐστι, τούτῳ καὶ τἆλλα. Διὸ ὑπερόπται δοκοῦσιν
19 εἶναι. Δοκεῖ δὲ καὶ τὰ εὐτυχήματα συμβάλλεσθαι πρὸς μεγαλοψυχίαν. Οἱ γὰρ εὐγενεῖς ἀξιοῦνται τιμῆς καὶ οἱ

the Highminded man (§§ 18—34). His estimate of riches, power, prosperity, etc. Conversely the influence of these on Highmindedness.

he regard riches, power, and prosperity and adversity generally. Riches and power are but means to honour, and he who estimates *it* so soberly will not be dazzled by *them*. Hence
19 men think him supercilious. Indeed these very advantages are thought to tend to Highmindedness because they secure

8. Men expect to receive, and do receive, honour in respect of riches, power, or good birth. Hence the possession of these advantages will in fact help the Highminded man to that honour which is his due, though he deserves it on higher grounds. Hence too, as honour intensifies self-respect, Highmindedness itself is thought to be fostered by any of those external advantages which in the opinion and practice of mankind entitle their possessor to honour. In strict truth, however, goodness, and goodness alone, is the proper ground for self-respect, or for the esteem of others. In § 21 it is added that superciliousness, which is an external accompaniment of Highmindedness, is also a result of the possession of such advantages as these.

It is interesting to notice that the Greek words for moral excellence are generally derived from those which express outward beauty, good birth, strength, ability, etc. The primitive import of such words is generally found in Homer, and their ethical meaning can scarcely be said to be fixed before Socrates. *e.g.* καλὸς and αἰσχρὸς (cf. ὁ τὴν ἰδέαν παναίσχης, I. viii. 16), γενναῖος, ἐσθλὸς (*i.e.* ἐθλὸς = '*edel*' 'noble') χρηστός. This bears witness to the confusion noticed in the text between material prosperity and moral worth. The other side of the picture appears in the dictum of Tennyson's Farmer, 'The poor in a loomp is bad.'

δυναστεύοντες ἢ οἱ πλουτοῦντες· ἐν ὑπεροχῇ γάρ, τὸ
δ' ἀγαθῷ ὑπερέχον πᾶν ἐντιμότερον. Διὸ καὶ τὰ
τοιαῦτα μεγαλοψυχοτέρους ποιεῖ· τιμῶνται γὰρ ὑπὸ
20 τινῶν. Κατ' ἀλήθειαν δ' ὁ ἀγαθὸς μόνος τιμητέος· ᾧ δ'
ἄμφω ὑπάρχει, μᾶλλον ἀξιοῦται τιμῆς. Οἱ δ' ἄνευ ἀρε-
τῆς τὰ τοιαῦτα ἀγαθὰ ἔχοντες, οὔτε δικαίως ἑαυτοὺς
μεγάλων ἀξιοῦσιν, οὔτε ὀρθῶς μεγαλόψυχοι λέγονται·
21 ἄνευ γὰρ ἀρετῆς παντελοῦς οὐκ ἔστι ταῦτα. Ὑπερόπται
δὲ καὶ ὑβρισταὶ καὶ οἱ τὰ τοιαῦτα ἔχοντες ἀγαθὰ γίγ-
νονται. Ἄνευ γὰρ ἀρετῆς οὐ ῥᾴδιον φέρειν ἐμμελῶς τὰ
εὐτυχήματα· οὐ δυνάμενοι δὲ φέρειν καὶ οἰόμενοι τῶν
ἄλλων ὑπερέχειν ἐκείνων μὲν καταφρονοῦσιν, αὐτοὶ δ' ὅ
τι ἂν τύχωσι πράττουσιν. Μιμοῦνται γὰρ τὸν μεγαλό-
ψυχον οὐχ ὅμοιοι ὄντες, τοῦτο δὲ δρῶσιν ἐν οἷς δύναν-
ται· τὰ μὲν οὖν κατ' ἀρετὴν οὐ πράττουσι, καταφρονοῦσι
22 δὲ τῶν ἄλλων. Ὁ δὲ μεγαλόψυχος δικαίως καταφρονεῖ
23 (δοξάζει γὰρ ἀληθῶς), οἱ δὲ πολλοὶ τυχόντως. Οὐκ

20 honour among men to their possessor. In truth, merit alone
deserves honour, but when merit and these advantages are
united, honour is accorded more freely. Without merit they
cannot form the ground of that self-esteem which constitutes
21 Highmindedness, nor again can they justify the supercilious-
22 ness in which their possessors ape the Highminded. Unlike
him, they have no superior merit to warrant that feeling, nor
23 discrimination in its exercise. The Highminded man will

His courage in danger.

1. ἐν ὑπεροχῇ γὰρ] 'For they are in a position of superiority.'

13. ὅ τι ἂν τύχωσι πράττουσιν] is explained by the words τὰ μὲν οὖν κατ' ἀρετὴν οὐ πράττουσι just below.

Μιμοῦνται γὰρ κ.τ.λ.] The μεγαλόψυχος is imitated by inferior characters,

'Who stand aloof from other men
In impotence of fancied power.'
(*Tennyson.*)

He stands aloof in a well-founded consciousness of superiority.

14. δικαίως καταφρονεῖ] 'A *due* contempt for inferiors' is not regarded by Aristotle as in itself objectionable. It is per-

ἔστι δὲ μικροκίνδυνος οὐδὲ φιλοκίνδυνος διὰ τὸ ὀλίγα τιμᾶν, μεγαλοκίνδυνος δέ, καὶ ὅταν κινδυνεύῃ, ἀφειδὴς
24 τοῦ βίου, ὡς οὐκ ἄξιον ὂν πάντως ζῆν. Καὶ οἷος εὖ ποιεῖν, εὐεργετούμενος δ' αἰσχύνεται. Τὸ μὲν γὰρ ὑπερέχοντος, τὸ δ' ὑπερεχομένου. Καὶ ἀντευεργετικὸς πλειόνων· οὕτω γὰρ προσοφλήσει ὁ ὑπάρξας καὶ ἔσται
25 εὖ πεπονθώς. Δοκοῦσι δὲ καὶ μνημονεύειν οὓς ἂν ποιή-

not court danger, but if it be great and worthy of him he will face it without regard to his life, which he does not think
24 worth preserving at the cost of honour. He loves to confer and is ashamed to receive benefits, and he hastens to requite
25 them with increase. In fact men are apt to remember those

His behaviour in respect of conferring or accepting benefits

haps a corollary to the somewhat over-conscious self-respect inculcated as the basis of the Virtue under consideration. The following passage from an Essay of Archbishop Whately on 'Generosity' perhaps exhibits this trait in the more favourable aspect in which it appeared to Aristotle:—'If a man who feels himself capable of generous and exalted conduct, measures others by his own standard, he must be first disappointed, and then dissatisfied' (from which 'contempt' would be an easy step) 'with almost all the world: for very few have even any conception of real heroic generosity. As a celebrated ancient once said, "As he never excused a fault in himself, he could not tolerate any in others."'

6. προσοφλήσει ὁ ὑπάρξας] 'the one who began it will be left in his debt besides'; and so debtor and creditor will change places.

7. Δοκοῦσι used thus impersonally seems to refer to mankind generally, not to the μεγαλόψυχος in particular, though he so far shares the feeling as to hasten to requite benefits received, and so to wipe out the feeling of obligation.

So remarks Thucydides, II. xl. § 7, 'He who has conferred a benefit is glad to keep alive the obligation by renewed acts of kindness: while he who has received one is less keen about it, knowing that any service he may render will be regarded as payment of a debt, and not as an act of favour.' The point is further worked out by Aristotle himself in IX. vii. In the same spirit remarks La Rochefoucauld (*Maximes* 238), 'It is not so dangerous to do harm to the majority of men, as to go too far in doing

σωσιν εὖ, ὧν δ' ἂν πάθωσιν οὔ· ἐλάττων γὰρ ὁ παθὼν εὖ τοῦ ποιήσαντος, βούλεται δ' ὑπερέχειν. Καὶ τὰ μὲν ἡδέως ἀκούει, τὰ δ' ἀηδῶς· διὸ καὶ τὴν Θέτιν οὐ λέγειν τὰς εὐεργεσίας τῷ Διί· οὐδ' οἱ Λάκωνες πρὸς τοὺς
26 Ἀθηναίους, ἀλλ' ἃ πεπόνθεσαν εὖ. Μεγαλοψύχου δὲ καὶ τὸ μηθενὸς δεῖσθαι ἢ μόγις, ὑπηρετεῖν δὲ προθύμως, καὶ πρὸς μὲν τοὺς ἐν ἀξιώματι καὶ εὐτυχίαις μέγαν εἶναι, πρὸς δὲ τοὺς μέσους μέτριον· τῶν μὲν γὰρ ὑπερ-

whom they have benefited, but when they have received a benefit they are glad to forget it, because such a position is
26 one of dependence and inferiority. He is reluctant to ask a favour, though ready to confer one. With great men he carries his head high, while with ordinary men he is unaffected,

His comportment towards others.

them good.' 'There is scarcely any one who is not ungrateful for great benefits' (*Max.* 299). An Eastern despot is said to have beheaded a man who had saved his life in order to avoid remaining under an obligation which nothing could ever repay.

Again notice the absence of the recognition of Benevolence, or any desire to benefit *others.* (See Introduction, p. xxxv.) Both Aristotle and Thucydides look mainly at the pleasurable sense of superiority on the part of one who confers a benefit.

3. διὸ καὶ τὴν Θέτιν] Passing illustrations of this sort are apparently introduced by Aristotle from memory, and are not unfrequently incorrect. This would not be unnatural if they occurred to the author during an extempore Lecture. (See Introduction, p. xxxvii.) Thetis (Homer, *Il.* i. 503) seems to do the reverse—

> Ζεῦ πάτερ, Εἴποτε δή σε μετ' ἀθανάτοισιν ὄνησα
> Ἢ ἔπει ἢ ἔργῳ.

(See *Supplementary Note.*)

The reference in the case of the Lacedæmonians is uncertain. A case is related by Xen. *Hell.* VI. v. 33, in which however benefits conferred as well as received by themselves are mentioned by the Spartans.

6. δεῖσθαι here means, 'to ask for,' not 'to stand in need of,' as we judge from the High-minded man being said to do so reluctantly (μόγις) and also from the natural contrast between seeking and conferring favours (ὑπηρετεῖν). Compare δεητικὸς in § 32.

7. τοὺς ἐν ἀξιώματι] 'men of repute.' See § 15 of the last Chapter.

ἔχειν χαλεπὸν καὶ σεμνόν, τῶν δὲ ῥᾴδιον, καὶ ἐν ἐκείνοις μὲν σεμνύνεσθαι οὐκ ἀγεννές, ἐν δὲ τοῖς ταπεινοῖς φορ-
27 τικόν, ὥσπερ εἰς τοὺς ἀσθενεῖς ἰσχυρίζεσθαι. Καὶ εἰς τὰ ἔντιμα μὴ ἰέναι, ἢ οὗ πρωτεύουσιν ἄλλοι· καὶ ἀργὸν εἶναι καὶ μελλητήν, ἀλλ' ἢ ὅπου τιμὴ μεγάλη ἢ ἔργον. Καὶ ὀλίγων μὲν πρακτικόν, μεγάλων δὲ καὶ ὀνομαστῶν.
28 Ἀναγκαῖον δὲ καὶ φανερόμισον εἶναι καὶ φανερόφιλον· τὸ γὰρ λανθάνειν φοβουμένου. Καὶ μέλειν τῆς ἀληθείας μᾶλλον ἢ τῆς δόξης, καὶ λέγειν καὶ πράττειν φανερῶς· παρρησιαστὴς γὰρ διὰ τὸ καταφρονεῖν. Διὸ καὶ ἀληθευτικός, πλὴν ὅσα μὴ δι' εἰρωνείαν· εἴρωνα δὲ πρὸς
29 τοὺς πολλούς. Καὶ πρὸς ἄλλον μὴ δύνασθαι ζῆν ἀλλ' ἢ πρὸς φίλον· δουλικὸν γάρ, διὸ καὶ πάντες οἱ κόλακες θητικοὶ καὶ οἱ ταπεινοὶ κόλακες. Οὐδὲ θαυμαστικός·

for there is nothing grand in giving one's-self airs before them.
27 He is not roused to exertion by any but the greatest objects of ambition, and is therefore generally in a state of dignified
28 inaction. He is open in his hatreds and his friendships, cares for truth more than the opinion of men, scorns concealment in words or actions, and speaks the plain truth except when he shrinks from asserting his full rights, as he does in fact
29 with the majority of people. He cannot *μισεῖν*, himself to

He is only roused to action on great occasions.

His plain-spokenness.

His independence, undemonstrativeness,

4. ἔντιμα] 'objects of common esteem.' ἀργὸν καὶ μελλητὴν='inactive and hesitating.'

11. εἰρώνεια is explained afterwards in ch. vii. to be a conscious depreciation of one's own merits or powers, and must not be mistaken here for 'irony.' A man of such pre-eminent dignity and merit as the μεγαλόψυχος must 'let himself down' with the majority of those he meets. He therefore consciously lowers his own pretensions on most occasions, and this would be εἰρώνεια. The word ἀληθευτικὸς is of course to be supplied again after ὅσα μή.

14. θητικοὶ] 'slavish' (θής), ταπεινοὶ='mean' or 'grovelling.' The word (as has been noted elsewhere) has a bad meaning in classical Greek, though no better word could be found by Christian writers to express the new idea of 'humility' as a virtue.

30 οὐθὲν γὰρ μέγα αὐτῷ ἐστίν. Οὐδὲ μνησίκακος· οὐ γὰρ
μεγαλοψύχου τὸ ἀπομνημονεύειν, ἄλλως τε καὶ κακά,
31 ἀλλὰ μᾶλλον παρορᾶν. Οὐδ' ἀνθρωπολόγος· οὔτε γὰρ
περὶ αὑτοῦ ἐρεῖ οὔτε περὶ ἑτέρου· οὔτε γὰρ ἵνα ἐπαινῆ-
ται μέλει αὐτῷ, οὔθ' ὅπως οἱ ἄλλοι ψέγωνται· οὐδ' αὖ
ἐπαινετικός ἐστιν· διόπερ οὐδὲ κακολόγος, οὐδὲ τῶν
32 ἐχθρῶν, εἰ μὴ δι' ὕβριν. Καὶ περὶ ἀναγκαίων ἢ μικρῶν
ἥκιστα ὀλοφυρτικὸς καὶ δεητικός· σπουδάζοντος γὰρ
33 οὕτως ἔχειν περὶ ταῦτα. Καὶ οἷος κεκτῆσθαι μᾶλλον τὰ
καλὰ καὶ ἄκαρπα τῶν καρπίμων καὶ ὠφελίμων· αὐτάρ-
34 κους γὰρ μᾶλλον. Καὶ κίνησις δὲ βραδεῖα τοῦ μεγαλο-
ψύχου δοκεῖ εἶναι, καὶ φωνὴ βαρεῖα, καὶ λέξις στάσι-
μος· οὐ γὰρ σπευστικὸς ὁ περὶ ὀλίγα σπουδάζων,
οὐδὲ σύντονος ὁ μηθὲν μέγα οἰόμενος· ἡ δ' ὀξυφωνία

another's mode of life though he will do so for a friend. He
30 is not apt to express astonishment, nor to remember injuries.
31 He is no gossip: he is a man of few words, sparing alike in
32 his praise and in his reproaches. He will not be anxious
33 about trifles: he will prefer to possess what is grand and
34 unproductive rather than what is merely useful. His gait,

forgetfulness of injury, and general reserve. His indifference to trifles, and general dignity of manner.

1. οὐ γὰρ . . . ἀπομνημονεύειν] He is not apt to bear anything long in mind, good or ill, but especially (ἄλλως τε καὶ) the latter. For the former see § 25.

7. δι' ὕβριν] He is not abusive except when he wishes to express his disdain. If he does speak ill of people, he will do it to their face, and in order deliberately to brand *them* with contempt, not because he cannot control his own feelings, and still less to gratify any personal impulse of malignity or revenge. Our Lord's withering denunciations of the Pharisees might come under this head. In fact νέμεσις (see II. vii. 15) would sometimes find expression in ὕβρις or Scorn. (See *Supplementary Note.*)

ἀναγκαίων] 'things which cannot be helped.'

8. ὀλοφυρτικὸς] 'querulous.'

12. στάσιμος] 'stately.' Compare La Rochefoucauld (*Max.* 142), 'C'est le caractère des grands esprits de faire entendre en peu de paroles, beaucoup de choses, les petits esprits au contraire ont le don de beaucoup parler et de rien dire.'

καὶ ἡ ταχυτὴς διὰ τούτων. Τοιοῦτος μὲν οὖν ὁ μεγαλόψυχος, ὁ δ' ἐλλείπων μικρόψυχος, ὁ δ' ὑπερβάλλων χαῦνος. Οὐ κακοὶ μὲν οὖν δοκοῦσιν εἶναι οὐδ' οὗτοι· οὐ γὰρ κακοποιοί εἰσιν· ἡμαρτημένοι δέ. Ὁ μὲν γὰρ μικρόψυχος, ἄξιος ὢν ἀγαθῶν, ἑαυτὸν ἀποστερεῖ ὧν ἄξιός ἐστι, καὶ ἔοικε κακὸν ἔχειν τι ἐκ τοῦ μὴ ἀξιοῦν ἑαυτὸν τῶν ἀγαθῶν, καὶ ἀγνοεῖν δ' ἑαυτόν· ὠρέγετο γὰρ ἂν ὧν ἄξιος ἦν, ἀγαθῶν γε ὄντων. Οὐ μὴν ἠλίθιοί γε οἱ τοιοῦτοι δοκοῦσιν εἶναι, ἀλλὰ μᾶλλον ὀκνηροί. Ἡ τοιαύτη δὲ δόξα δοκεῖ καὶ χείρους ποιεῖν· ἕκαστοι γὰρ

his voice, and his manner of speech will be grave, dignified, and deliberate. Such is the Highminded man. The related characters who are in excess and defect in the matter of self-estimation are, as we have seen, the Vainglorious and the Little-minded. They are misguided, rather than actively vicious.

The related Vices are— Little-mindedness,

4. There is an obvious contrast between κακοποιοί (actively vicious) and κακὸν ἔχειν τι (having something wrong about them). Aristotle means to say that men would hardly form so low an estimate of themselves unless there was something to partially justify it. 'There cannot be so much smoke without some fire.'

9. ὀκνηροὶ] 'wanting in energy,' 'diffident.'

10. ἡ τοιαύτη δόξα κ.τ.λ.] In other words, the absence of moral aspiration is most injurious. The moral influence of a man's estimate of himself is very important. Witness the elevating effect of a conscious feeling that a man has powers beyond the perhaps humble sphere in which he finds himself placed, and conversely the depressing effect of the feeling (whether due to constitutional indolence, despondency, etc.), that one will never accomplish the task in hand. Many thus fail, simply because they have made up their minds that they cannot succeed. It is remarked by Nassau Senior in his Notes on Turkey, that the general spread of corruption among Turkish officials seems to date from the time when an oath of office was first imposed, in which the strictest integrity was promised; and he accounts for this by the supposition that the officials, unable to keep the oath completely, became reckless when they had once broken it. In other words, the conscious degradation of perjury (leading

ἐφίενται τῶν κατ' ἀξίαν, ἀφίστανται δὲ καὶ τῶν πράξεων
τῶν καλῶν καὶ τῶν ἐπιτηδευμάτων ὡς ἀνάξιοι ὄντες,
36 *ὁμοίως δὲ καὶ τῶν ἐκτὸς ἀγαθῶν. Οἱ δὲ χαῦνοι ἠλίθιοι*
καὶ ἑαυτοὺς ἀγνοοῦντες, καὶ ταῦτ' ἐπιφανῶς· ὡς γὰρ
ἄξιοι ὄντες τοῖς ἐντίμοις ἐπιχειροῦσιν, εἶτα ἐξελέγχονται·
καὶ ἐσθῆτι κοσμοῦνται καὶ σχήματι καὶ τοῖς τοιούτοις,
καὶ βούλονται τὰ εὐτυχήματα φανερὰ εἶναι αὐτῶν, καὶ
λέγουσι περὶ αὐτῶν, ὡς διὰ τούτων τιμηθησόμενοι.
37 *Ἀντιτίθεται δὲ τῇ μεγαλοψυχίᾳ ἡ μικροψυχία μᾶλλον*
τῆς χαυνότητος· καὶ γὰρ γίγνεται μᾶλλον καὶ χεῖρον
ἐστίν.

We note however that there is probably some ground at the bottom of even undue self-depreciation; and also that such characters have a tendency to sink to their own standard.
36 The Vainglorious man is conspicuous by his ignorance of himself, and seeks by a vulgar display of such external advantages as he does possess to secure for himself that admiration to
37 which his merits do not entitle him. Littlemindedness is more opposed to Highmindedness than Vaingloriousness is. It is a worse error, and also a commoner one.

and Vaingloriousness.

Littlemindedness is the worse extreme.

to *μικροψυχία*, or a low moral estimation of one's-self), extinguished all scruples as to minor offences, and all desire to avoid them, and so the *whole* character settled down to the level of the estimate of itself already formed. We may extend the remark to the moral influence of the estimation of society on the character of individuals. Recovery from some sins is rendered all but hopeless, out of all proportion to their relative guilt, simply by the arbitrary ban of society upon them. The offender in fact acquiesces himself in this estimate of his degradation and soon comes to deserve it. Thus *ἡ τοιαύτη δόξα χείρους ποιεῖ.* This is familiarly expressed in the proverb, 'Give a dog a bad name,' etc.

5. *τοῖς ἐντίμοις*] See note on § 27.

10. *χεῖρον ἐστίν*] Though Aristotle gives no reasons for this statement, we may suggest, (1) Its tendency to make men grow worse (§ 35), and (2) Its outward aspect being the reverse of that of Highmindedness. Both

1 IV. Ἡ μὲν οὖν μεγαλοψυχία περὶ τιμήν ἐστι μεγάλην,
ὥσπερ εἴρηται· ἔοικε δὲ καὶ περὶ ταύτην εἶναι ἀρετή τις,
καθάπερ ἐν τοῖς πρώτοις ἐλέχθη, ἣ δόξειεν ἂν παρα-
πλησίως ἔχειν πρὸς τὴν μεγαλοψυχίαν ὥσπερ καὶ ἡ
ἐλευθεριότης πρὸς τὴν μεγαλοπρέπειαν. Ἄμφω γὰρ
αὗται τοῦ μὲν μεγάλου ἀφεστᾶσι, περὶ δὲ τὰ μέτρια καὶ
2 τὰ μικρὰ διατιθέασιν ἡμᾶς ὡς δεῖ. Ὥσπερ δ' ἐν λήψει

CHAP. IV.—*On Ambition.*

The proper objects of Ambition and its relation to High-mindedness.

1 We may now descend to the level of ordinary life, and
describe another Virtue which, with its related Vices, has for
2 its object Honour on a moderate scale, just as we before dis-

these reasons were given in ch. i. for preferring Prodigality to Sordidness.

Further, χαυνότης and μικροψυχία must be carefully distinguished from ἀλαζόνεια and εἰρώνεια which are discussed in ch. vii. *Inter alia*, note that while μικροψυχία is here said to be worse than χαυνότης, Aristotle regards εἰρώνεια as a less evil than ἀλαζόνεια. See vii. 17. Hence too we must not confuse μικροψυχία with Humility, though it is true that the character of Highmindedness as described in this chapter shows that Humility would find no place as a Virtue in Aristotle's system.

γίγνεται μᾶλλον] The deficiency of moral aspiration is much more common than vaingloriousness. The dignity of our moral nature, the worth (ἀξία) that belongs to man as man, and the motive for moral action supplied by such a reflection, is totally unrecognised by the majority of mankind. [See further a Supplementary Note, too long to be introduced here, on the character of the μεγαλόψυχος, p. 234.]

CHAP. IV.—In this Chapter habits are discussed differing from those in the last chapter in degree rather than in kind; just as Liberality was related to, and yet differed from, Munificence. We must recollect that the *real* subject-matter to which High-mindedness refers was explained to be 'Self-Esteem in relation to merits' (last ch. § 3); but that *practically* it might be viewed as concerned with the pursuit of honour on a grand scale (§ 10). In this chapter Aristotle takes the latter point of view at once as his starting-point, with the proviso that only honour on a moderate and ordinary scale is now in consideration.

3. ἐν τοῖς πρώτοις] Referring (as in § 4 below) to II. vii. 8.

καὶ δόσει χρημάτων μεσότης ἐστὶ καὶ ὑπερβολή τε καὶ
ἔλλειψις, οὕτω καὶ ἐν τιμῆς ὀρέξει τὸ μᾶλλον ἢ δεῖ καὶ
3 ἧττον, καὶ τὸ ὅθεν δεῖ καὶ ὡς δεῖ. Τόν τε γὰρ φιλότι-
μον ψέγομεν ὡς καὶ μᾶλλον ἢ δεῖ, καὶ ὅθεν οὐ δεῖ, τῆς
τιμῆς ἐφιέμενον, τόν τε ἀφιλότιμον, ὡς οὐδ᾽ ἐπὶ τοῖς
4 καλοῖς προαιρούμενον τιμᾶσθαι. Ἔστι δ᾽ ὅτε τὸν φι-
λότιμον ἐπαινοῦμεν ὡς ἀνδρώδη καὶ φιλόκαλον, τὸν δὲ
ἀφιλότιμον ὡς μέτριον καὶ σώφρονα, ὥσπερ καὶ ἐν τοῖς
πρώτοις εἴπομεν. Δῆλον δ᾽ ὅτι πλεοναχῶς τοῦ φιλο-
τοιούτου λεγομένου, οὐκ ἐπὶ τὸ αὐτὸ ἀεὶ φέρομεν τὸν
φιλότιμον, ἀλλ᾽ ἐπαινοῦντες μέν, ἐπὶ τὸ μᾶλλον ἢ οἱ
πολλοί, ψέγοντες δ᾽ ἐπὶ τὸ μᾶλλον ἢ δεῖ. Ἀνωνύμου
δ᾽ οὔσης τῆς μεσότητος, ὡς ἐρήμης ἔοικεν ἀμφισβητεῖν
τὰ ἄκρα· ἐν οἷς δ᾽ ἔστιν ὑπερβολὴ καὶ ἔλλειψις, καὶ τὸ
5 μέσον. Ὀρέγονται δὲ τιμῆς καὶ μᾶλλον ἢ δεῖ, καὶ
ἧττον, ἔστι δ᾽ ὅτε καὶ ὡς δεῖ· ἐπαινεῖται γοῦν ἡ ἕξις

tinguished the Liberality of moderate means from the Munifi-
3 cence appropriate to vast wealth. The term 'Ambition,' by
which this habit is sometimes described, is not definitely re-
stricted to it, being sometimes employed also to denote an
4 excessive pursuit of Honour. 'Ambitious' and 'Unambi-
5 tious' may either of them be terms of praise or of blame. The
point to notice however is that there *is* a right and a wrong

The phraseology in reference to this Virtue is unsettled but its existence is no less certain.

6. It so happens that in our words 'ambition,' 'ambitious,' 'unambitious,' we have terms of similar ambiguity. As Aristotle says in the text, 'ambitious' is sometimes equivalent to 'manly and of noble spirit' (*ἀνδρώδη καὶ φιλόκαλον*), and yet 'unambitious' is likewise a term of praise reserved for 'men of moderation and self-control' (*μέτριον καὶ σώφρονα*). When we praise an 'ambitious' spirit we do so from its favourable contrast with the complacent indifference to 'rise above themselves' found in the majority of men, when we blame it we do so in reference to the standard of propriety, which it transgresses in its excessive eagerness for honour. Cf. *σώφρων* as used in the last Ch. § 4.

αὕτη, μεσότης οὖσα περὶ τιμὴν ἀνώνυμος. Φαίνεται δὲ πρὸς μὲν τὴν φιλοτιμίαν ἀφιλοτιμία, πρὸς δὲ τὴν ἀφιλοτιμίαν φιλοτιμία, πρὸς ἀμφότερα δὲ ἀμφότερά πως.
6 Ἔοικε δὲ τοῦτ' εἶναι καὶ περὶ τὰς ἄλλας ἀρετάς. Ἀντικεῖσθαι δ' ἐνταῦθ' οἱ ἄκροι φαίνονται διὰ τὸ μὴ ὠνομάσθαι τὸν μέσον.

1 V. Πραότης δ' ἐστὶ μὲν μεσότης περὶ ὀργάς, ἀνωνύμου δ' ὄντος τοῦ μέσου, σχεδὸν δὲ καὶ τῶν ἄκρων, ἐπὶ τὸν μέσον τὴν πραότητα φέρομεν, πρὸς τὴν ἔλλειψιν ἀπο-
2 κλίνουσαν, ἀνώνυμον οὖσαν. Ἡ δ' ὑπερβολὴ ὀργιλότης τις λέγοιτ' ἄν. Τὸ μὲν γὰρ πάθος ἐστὶν ὀργή, τὰ δ'

(and the latter in both directions) *in fact*, though our phraseo-
6 logy may not sufficiently indicate it; and this defect of language is the sole cause that we have apparently in this case the opposition of two extreme habits *inter se*, without a settled mean state in contrast with both of them.

CHAP. V.—*On the regulation of the Temper.*

No settled phraseology exists in regard to this Virtue.

1 Due moderation in the regulation of the Temper may be termed Meekness. There is no one term in settled use to describe this virtue, nor indeed the related vices. We may perhaps employ the term 'Meekness,' though it suggests rather a
2 deficiency in this respect. The excess we may describe as a

CHAP. V.—See what was said in the note on the Catalogue of Virtues, at the end of B. II. on the position occupied in the list by πραότης, as being intermediate between the *personal* virtues that precede and the *social* virtues which follow it.

10. ὀργιλότης τις] 'Passionateness' and 'impassionateness' seem to express the ideas required, and their somewhat uncouth character reproduces that of the Greek originals for which Aristotle apologizes by adding τις here and in § 5.

11. τὸ μὲν πάθος ἐστὶν ὀργή] It will be remembered that all Virtue and Vice are held by Aristotle to consist in the moderate, excessive, or defective indulgence of some feeling in

3 ἐμποιοῦντα πολλὰ καὶ διαφέροντα. Ὁ μὲν οὖν ἐφ' οἷς
δεῖ, καὶ οἷς δεῖ, ὀργιζόμενος, ἔτι δὲ καὶ ὡς δεῖ, καὶ ὅτε,
καὶ ὅσον χρόνον, ἐπαινεῖται· πρᾶος δὴ οὗτος ἂν εἴη,
εἴπερ ἡ πραότης ἐπαινεῖται. Βούλεται γὰρ ὁ πρᾶος
ἀτάραχος εἶναι, καὶ μὴ ἄγεσθαι ὑπὸ τοῦ πάθους, ἀλλ'
ὡς ἂν ὁ λόγος τάξῃ, οὕτω καὶ ἐπὶ τούτοις καὶ ἐπὶ τοσοῦ-
4 τον χρόνον χαλεπαίνειν. Ἁμαρτάνειν δὲ δοκεῖ μᾶλλον
ἐπὶ τὴν ἔλλειψιν· οὐ γὰρ τιμωρητικὸς ὁ πρᾶος, ἀλλὰ
5 μᾶλλον συγγνωμονικός. Ἡ δ' ἔλλειψις, εἴτ' ἀοργησία
τίς ἐστιν, εἴθ' ὅ τι δή ποτε, ψέγεται. Οἱ γὰρ μὴ ὀργιζό-
μενοι ἐφ' οἷς δεῖ ἠλίθιοι δοκοῦσιν εἶναι, καὶ οἱ μὴ ὡς δεῖ,
6 μηδ' ὅτε, μηδ' οἷς δεῖ· δοκεῖ γὰρ οὐκ αἰσθάνεσθαι οὐδὲ
λυπεῖσθαι, μὴ ὀργιζόμενός τε οὐκ εἶναι ἀμυντικός. Τὸ δὲ
προπηλακιζόμενον ἀνέχεσθαι καὶ τοὺς οἰκείους περιορᾶν

sort of Passionateness, Anger being the feeling in itself morally
3 indifferent in which the excess or defect takes place. We
shall then apply the term 'Meek' to a man who, though he
is roused to anger on right occasions and in due measure,
is naturally of a tranquil disposition, and never allows his
4 anger to get the better of his reason. His leaning is towards
a deficiency in the feeling of anger, and forgiveness of injuries
5 comes more naturally to him than revenge. That deficiency,
impassionateness (if we may venture so to call it), is a fault.
6 It leads to a neglect of self-defence, and a submission to insult

General characteristics however may be given of Meekness, which tends towards defect rather than excess in Anger. The defect itself is a sort of impassionateness.

itself morally indifferent, neither good nor bad. See note on II. vii. 2. That feeling is in this case Anger. We are accustomed to give a bad sense to 'Anger,' and to describe the nobler forms of the passion by 'Indignation.' That 'Anger' had not always this restricted sense in English may be seen from such passages as 'Be ye angry and sin not,' and S. Mark. iii. 5, where 'anger' is attributed to our Lord.

1. ἐφ' οἷς] 'on right occasions' (ἐπὶ with dative as usual expressing the conditions of the action).

2. οἷς δεῖ] 'with right persons' (dative of reference).

7 ἀνδραποδῶδες. Ἡ δ' ὑπερβολὴ κατὰ πάντα μὲν γίνεται· καὶ γὰρ οἷς οὐ δεῖ, καὶ ἐφ' οἷς οὐ δεῖ, καὶ μᾶλλον ἢ δεῖ, καὶ θᾶττον, καὶ πλείω χρόνον· οὐ μὴν ἅπαντά γε τῷ αὐτῷ ὑπάρχει. Οὐ γὰρ ἂν δύναιτ' εἶναι· τὸ γὰρ κακὸν καὶ ἑαυτὸ ἀπόλλυσι, κἂν ὁλόκληρον ᾖ, ἀφόρητον γίνεται.
8 Οἱ μὲν οὖν ὀργίλοι ταχέως μὲν ὀργίζονται, καὶ οἷς οὐ δεῖ, καὶ ἐφ' οἷς οὐ δεῖ, καὶ μᾶλλον ἢ δεῖ, παύονται δὲ ταχέως· ὃ καὶ βέλτιστον ἔχουσιν. Συμβαίνει δ' αὐτοῖς τοῦτο, ὅτι οὐ κατέχουσι τὴν ὀργὴν ἀλλ' ἀνταποδιδόασιν ᾗ φανεροί εἰσι διὰ τὴν ὀξύτητα, εἶτ' ἀποπαύονται.
9 Ὑπερβολῇ δ' εἰσὶν οἱ ἀκρόχολοι ὀξεῖς καὶ πρὸς πᾶν ὀργί-
10 λοι καὶ ἐπὶ παντί· ὅθεν καὶ τοὔνομα. Οἱ δὲ πικροὶ δυσ-

directed against one's-self or one's friends, which is slavish.
The excess falls under four types (§§ 7—11): 7 The vice of excess is exhibited in every variety of detail, *e.g.* in the objects, the occasions, the degree, the amount of provocation, the endurance of the feeling, etc. Errors in all these respects would scarcely be united in one instance, and if so, would be intolerable. Hence we have several types of the
The passionate. 8 excess in question. (1) The *passionate*, who are soon angry, without due cause, and in too violent a degree, but soon come round. Their passion, being utterly unrestrained, speedily ex-
The quick-tempered. 9 hausts its force. (2) The *quick-tempered*, who are angry in a moment and at anything and everything—hence their name.
The sulky. 10 (3) The *sulky*, who are hard to appease; and their anger,

5. ὁλόκληρον] see note above on i. 38.

6. The four classes described in §§ 8—11 have naturally many points in common. Their characteristic features seem to be respectively, (1) Violence and ungovernableness of temper (ὀργίλοι)—(2) Extreme irritability and touchiness (ἀκρόχολοι),—(3) A sulky and irreconcilable temper (πικροί)—(4) General ill-nature and revengefulness (χαλεποί).

8. ὃ καὶ βέλτιστον ἔχουσιν] 'and that is the best point about them.'

10. ᾗ φανεροί εἰσι] 'in a way that one may see,' *i.e.* 'openly;' as opposed to διὰ τὸ μὴ ἐπιφανὲς in § 10.

11. ὑπερβολῇ . . . ὀξεῖς] 'The quick-tempered are also excessive in their irritability:' taking ὑπερβολῇ as qualifying ὀξεῖς.

διάλυτοι, καὶ πολὺν χρόνον ὀργίζονται· κατέχουσι γὰρ
τὸν θυμόν. Παῦλα δὲ γίνεται, ὅταν ἀνταποδιδῷ· ἡ γὰρ
τιμωρία παύει τῆς ὀργῆς, ἡδονὴν ἀντὶ τῆς λύπης ἐμποι-
οῦσα. Τούτου δὲ μὴ γινομένου τὸ βάρος ἔχουσιν· διὰ
γὰρ τὸ μὴ ἐπιφανὲς εἶναι οὐδὲ συμπείθει αὐτοὺς οὐδείς,
ἐν αὑτῷ δὲ πέψαι τὴν ὀργὴν χρόνου δεῖ. Εἰσὶ δ' οἱ
τοιοῦτοι ἑαυτοῖς ὀχληρότατοι καὶ τοῖς μάλιστα φίλοις.
11 Χαλεποὺς δὲ λέγομεν τοὺς ἐφ' οἷς τε μὴ δεῖ χαλεπαί-
νοντας, καὶ μᾶλλον ἢ δεῖ, καὶ πλείω χρόνον, καὶ μὴ διαλ-
12 λαττομένους ἄνευ τιμωρίας ἢ κολάσεως. Τῇ πραότητι
δὲ μᾶλλον τὴν ὑπερβολὴν ἀντιτίθεμεν· καὶ γὰρ μᾶλλον
γίνεται· ἀνθρωπικώτερον γὰρ τὸ τιμωρεῖσθαι. Καὶ
13 πρὸς τὸ συμβιοῦν οἱ χαλεποὶ χείρους. Ὁ δὲ καὶ ἐν τοῖς

being suppressed, lasts long, and is only removed by revenge.
Its concealment prevents any attempts on the part of others
to appease it, and makes its subjects a curse to themselves as
11 well as to their best friends. (4) The *ill-tempered*, whose
anger is generally ill-directed, unrestrained in degree and
12 duration, and seldom to be appeased without revenge. Excess
is worse than Defect in the case of anger. It is more common,
13 and it is also more practically inconvenient. It is impossible

The ill-tempered

Excess is the worse extreme.

Precise practical rules are impossible

5. τὸ μὴ ἐπιφανὲς] Compare what Tacitus says of Mucianus (*Hist.* iii. 53, fin.), 'callide *eoque* implacabilius.'

6. πέψαι] literally 'to digest' ἐν αὑτῷ, *i.e.* without the external aid of 'smoothing down' (συμπείθειν) mentioned in the previous line.

8. χαλεποὶ] literally 'harsh and hard to deal with,' nearly what we mean by 'a thoroughly nasty temper.' It will be noticed by referring to § 8, that the point in which χαλεποὶ are distinguished from ὀργίλοι, is that the former retain anger πλείω χρόνον.

10. τιμωρίας ἢ κολάσεως] For the distinction see note on III. v. 7. There is no emphasis however on the distinction here, the former only being really applicable.

13. οἱ χαλεποὶ is here used as a generic term for all the four different forms of excess just described.

ὁ δὲ καὶ κ.τ.λ.] See II. ix. 7,

πρότερον εἴρηται, καὶ ἐκ τῶν λεγομένων δῆλον· οὐ γὰρ ῥᾴδιον διορίσαι τὸ πῶς καὶ τίσι καὶ ἐπὶ ποίοις καὶ πόσον χρόνον ὀργιστέον, καὶ τὸ μέχρι τίνος ὀρθῶς ποιεῖ τις ἢ ἁμαρτάνει. Ὁ μὲν γὰρ μικρὸν παρεκβαίνων οὐ ψέγεται, οὔτ' ἐπὶ τὸ μᾶλλον οὔτ' ἐπὶ τὸ ἧττον· ἐνίοτε γὰρ τοὺς ἐλλείποντας ἐπαινοῦμεν καὶ πράους φαμέν, καὶ τοὺς χαλεπαίνοντας ἀνδρώδεις ὡς δυναμένους ἄρχειν. Ὁ δὴ πόσον καὶ πῶς παρεκβαίνων ψεκτός, οὐ ῥᾴδιον τῷ λόγῳ ἀποδοῦναι· ἐν γὰρ τοῖς καθ' ἕκαστα καὶ τῇ αἰσ-
14 θήσει ἡ κρίσις. Ἀλλὰ τό γε τοσοῦτον δῆλον, ὅτι ἡ μὲν μέση ἕξις ἐπαινετή, καθ' ἣν οἷς δεῖ ὀργιζόμεθα καὶ ἐφ' οἷς δεῖ, καὶ ὡς δεῖ, καὶ πάντα τὰ τοιαῦτα, αἱ δ' ὑπερβολαὶ καὶ ἐλλείψεις ψεκταί, καὶ ἐπὶ μικρὸν μὲν γινόμεναι ἠρέμα, ἐπὶ πλέον δὲ μᾶλλον, ἐπὶ πολὺ δὲ σφόδρα. Δῆλον οὖν ὅτι τῆς μέσης ἕξεως ἀνθεκτέον. Αἱ μὲν οὖν περὶ τὴν ὀργὴν ἕξεις εἰρήσθωσαν.

to lay down precise rules as to the right objects, degree, duration, etc., of anger. Small errors on either side are not serious, and indeed often gain our approbation on account of
14 the element of good which may be traced in them. That there however *is* a virtue to be cultivated and that there *are* vices to be avoided in the regulation of temper is abundantly clear. The practical details must be left to individual feeling and judgment.

where nearly the same words occur. ἐκ τῶν λεγομένων, 'from what we are now saying.'

8. τῷ λόγῳ] see note II. ix. 7, 8.

9. αἰσθήσει] 'individual feeling.' Questions of casuistry such as these cannot be determined by scientific rules. So much depends upon the infinite variety of circumstances bearing upon any given action, and even granting all such circumstances could be taken into accurate account, so much still depends on the physical and moral constitution of the agent, that individual feeling (αἰσθήσει) or, as a modern writer might say, 'each man's conscience,' must in the last resort decide such points.

1 VI. Ἐν δὲ ταῖς ὁμιλίαις καὶ τῷ συζῆν καὶ λόγων καὶ
πραγμάτων κοινωνεῖν οἱ μὲν ἄρεσκοι δοκοῦσιν εἶναι, οἱ
πάντα πρὸς ἡδονὴν ἐπαινοῦντες καὶ οὐθὲν ἀντιτείνοντες,
2 ἀλλ' οἰόμενοι δεῖν ἄλυποι τοῖς ἐντυγχάνουσιν εἶναι· οἱ δ'
ἐξ ἐναντίας τούτοις πρὸς πάντα ἀντιτείνοντες καὶ τοῦ
λυπεῖν οὐδ' ὁτιοῦν φροντίζοντες δύσκολοι καὶ δυσέριδες
3 καλοῦνται. Ὅτι μὲν οὖν αἱ εἰρημέναι ἕξεις ψεκταί εἰσιν,
οὐκ ἄδηλον, καὶ ὅτι ἡ μέση τούτων ἐπαινετή, καθ' ἣν
ἀποδέξεται ἃ δεῖ καὶ ὡς δεῖ, ὁμοίως δὲ καὶ δυσχερανεῖ.
4 Ὄνομα δ' οὐκ ἀποδέδοται αὐτῇ τι, ἔοικε δὲ μάλιστα
φιλίᾳ· τοιοῦτος γάρ ἐστιν ὁ κατὰ τὴν μέσην ἕξιν οἷον
βουλόμεθα λέγειν τὸν ἐπιεικῆ φίλον, τὸ στέργειν προσ-

CHAP. VI.—*On Friendliness, or Amiability.*

Phraseology and general nature of the habit explained (§§ 1–5).

1 In their conduct and deportment in society some men, whom
we may perhaps describe as 'obsequious,' shrink under any
circumstances from making things unpleasant; they would
rather sacrifice a principle than say or do anything disagree-
2 able. Others again seem to enjoy running counter to every
one and every thing, and care not how much pain they cause.
3 These we may call 'cross-grained and quarrelsome.' In an
intermediate position are those whose approbation and dis-
approbation are regulated upon principle, who love to give
pleasure, though they do not shrink from inflicting pain when
4 it is needful: characters whom we may describe as 'friendly,'

CHAP. VI.—We now come to the group of Virtues, three in number, which relate to our conduct in and towards society. The order of the Catalogue in II. vii. is departed from. There it was ἀλήθεια — εὐτραπελία — φιλία. Here it is φιλία—ἀλήθεια—εὐτραπελία. The order is not of much importance, but it seems unnatural to separate εὐτραπελία and φιλία (both dealing with τὸ ἡδὺ), by interposing between them ἀλήθεια (dealing with τὸ ἀληθὲς). This would appear from Aristotle's own summary in viii. 12, below.

9. ἀποδέξεται] 'to approve.' See note on I. iii. 4.

11. τοιοῦτος γάρ ἐστιν κ.τ.λ.]

5 λαβόντα. Διαφέρει δὲ τῆς φιλίας, ὅτι ἄνευ πάθους ἐστὶ
καὶ τοῦ στέργειν οἷς ὁμιλεῖ· οὐ γὰρ τῷ φιλεῖν ἢ ἐχθαί-
ρειν ἀποδέχεται ἕκαστα ὡς δεῖ, ἀλλὰ τῷ τοιοῦτος εἶναι.
Ὁμοίως γὰρ πρὸς ἀγνῶτας καὶ γνωρίμους καὶ συνήθεις
καὶ ἀσυνήθεις αὐτὸ ποιήσει, πλὴν καὶ ἐν ἑκάστοις ὡς
ἁρμόζει· οὐ γὰρ ὁμοίως προσήκει συνήθων καὶ ὀθνείων
6 φροντίζειν, οὐδ' αὖ λυπεῖν. Καθόλου μὲν οὖν εἴρηται
ὅτι ὡς δεῖ ὁμιλήσει, ἀναφέρων δὲ πρὸς τὸ καλὸν καὶ τὸ
συμφέρον στοχάσεται τοῦ μὴ λυπεῖν ἢ συνηδύνειν.
7 Ἔοικε μὲν γὰρ περὶ ἡδονὰς καὶ λύπας εἶναι τὰς ἐν ταῖς

5 and their disposition as 'friendliness.' That disposition differs
from 'friendship,' because it has not its root in affection, but
in a *natural inclination* to give pleasure and avoid giving
pain: and moreover because it is not limited to particular
persons, but is felt towards all in due measure and proportion.
6 This natural tendency to please is controlled however by
7 several considerations, such as the following:—(1) Can it be

For he that holds the mean position is just such a man as we should wish to call 'a good friend,' if the element of affection were superadded. Friendliness + Affection = Friendship. In Greek, however, there are no two words exactly corresponding to this distinction between 'friendliness' and 'friendship,' and so φιλία has to be employed for both.

3. τῷ τοιοῦτος εἶναι] 'because it is his nature to do so.' He makes himself generally pleasant and agreeable (or if necessary the reverse), not because he likes (or dislikes) you, but because it comes naturally to him under certain circumstances, and it makes no difference whether he knows you personally or not, except so far as acquaintanceship introduces some element of feeling (see § 8 below, and cf. § vii. of next Chapter, τῷ τὴν ἕξιν τοιοῦτος εἶναι). See also Bacon's Essay on 'Good Nature' throughout, and especially 'Neither is there only a habit of goodness directed by right reason (cf. ἕξις . . . κατὰ τὸν ὀρθὸν λόγον), but there is in some men, *even in Nature, a disposition towards it:* as on the other side there is a Natural Malignity. The lighter sort of malignity turneth to a crossness or frowardness' (cf. δύσερις καὶ δύσκολος).

9. συνηδύνειν] 'to contribute

ὁμιλίαις γινομένας, τούτων δ' ὅσας μὲν αὐτῷ ἐστὶ μὴ καλὸν ἢ βλαβερὸν συνηδύνειν, δυσχερανεῖ, καὶ προαιρήσεται λυπεῖν. Κἂν τῷ ποιοῦντι δ' ἀσχημοσύνην φέρῃ, καὶ ταύτην μὴ μικρὰν, ἢ βλάβην, ἡ δ' ἐναντίωσις μικρὰν
8 λύπην, οὐκ ἀποδέξεται, ἀλλὰ δυσχερανεῖ. Διαφερόντως δ' ὁμιλήσει τοῖς ἐν ἀξιώμασι καὶ τοῖς τυχοῦσι, καὶ μᾶλλον ἢ ἧττον γνωρίμοις, ὁμοίως δὲ καὶ κατὰ τὰς ἄλλας διαφορὰς, ἑκάστοις ἀπονέμων τὸ πρέπον, καὶ καθ' αὑτὸ

exercised with propriety and with advantage? *e.g.* it is better to give pain than to sacrifice a principle, as we have said; nor again should we hesitate to stand in a man's way to save him at the cost of small present annoyance from bringing
8 great future disgrace or injury upon himself. (2) Regard must be had to the social position of those with whom we are associating, our degree of acquaintance with them, and so on.

Friendliness may be described as the desire to please subject to due consideration of circumstances, results, etc.

to pleasure'; to 'rejoice with them that do rejoice.'

1. τούτων δ' ὅσας] this must refer to ἡδονὰς only and not to λυπάς. 'Such pleasures as he cannot conscientiously join in he will frown upon.' He will not only not 'do such things, but he will have no pleasure in those that do them.' Cf. viii. 8, ἃ γὰρ ὑπομένει ἀκούων, ταῦτα καὶ ποιεῖν δοκεῖ.

Notice the combination of natural kindliness of disposition with a stern and uncompromising hatred of moral wrong. There is nothing weak and effeminate about this natural friendliness (φιλία). It is in the best sense of the word a manly feeling. Moreover, the combination spoken of is quite true to human nature. The 'Apostle of Love' was also one of the 'Sons of Thunder,' and some of the most vehement denunciations in Scripture occur in his writings. Even persecution (to take an extreme case) has been conscientiously sanctioned and practised by men otherwise conspicuous for their kindliness and benevolence of nature. Witness M. Aurelius, S. Louis of France, etc.

2. The student will notice the usual distinction between μὴ καλὸν, 'morally wrong,' and βλαβερὸν 'materially harmful,' corresponding to the distinction between καλὸν and συμφέρον in the preceding section.

5. διαφερόντως δ' ὁμιλήσει] Cf. iii. 26.

μὲν αἱρούμενος τὸ συνηδύνειν, λυπεῖν δ' εὐλαβούμενος,
τοῖς δ' ἀποβαίνουσιν, ἐὰν ᾖ μείζω, συνεπόμενος, λέγω δὲ
τῷ καλῷ καὶ τῷ συμφέροντι. Καὶ ἡδονῆς δ' ἕνεκα τῆς εἰσ-
9 αὖθις μεγάλης μικρὰ λυπήσει. Ὁ μὲν οὖν μέσος τοιοῦ-
τός ἐστιν, οὐκ ὠνόμασται δέ, τοῦ δὲ συνηδύνοντος ὁ μὲν
τοῦ ἡδὺς εἶναι στοχαζόμενος μὴ δι' ἄλλο τι ἄρεσκος, ὁ
δ' ὅπως ὠφέλειά τις αὐτῷ γίγνηται εἰς χρήματα καὶ ὅσα
διὰ χρημάτων, κόλαξ· ὁ δὲ πᾶσι δυσχεραίνων εἴρηται

(3) Ulterior consequences must always be taken into consideration. Great subsequent pleasure or profit may some-
9 times be secured by slight momentary pain. The Excess has two types, distinguished by their motives. If it be merely an exaggerated and disinterested desire to please, we call it 'Obsequiousness.' If it be adopted from motives of self-interest, we term it 'Flattery.' The Defect has been sufficiently characterized already. Owing to the want of a definite

The Excess and Defect. Of the former there are two types, Obsequiousness and Flattery.

2. τοῖς δ' ἀποβαίνουσιν κ.τ.λ.] 'but regulating his conduct by the consequences if they be on a larger scale,' as compared, that is, with the present circumstances (see Analysis).

3. ἡδονῆς . . . τῆς εἰσαῦθις μεγάλης] 'for the sake of a pleasure that will presently be a considerable one.'

6. ἄρεσκος] The ἄρεσκος is what we should call an *insincere* or *unreal* man: one who professes to take the greatest interest in you, and uses the most friendly and even affectionate language, when he really cares nothing about you. Theophrastus graphically describes him as 'a man who when he enters a house at once asks to see the babies; the moment he sees them he declares that they are the very image of their father, and kisses and fondles them, though he cares nothing about them.'

8. κόλαξ] The ancient 'Parasite' and the Mediæval Courtier would be typical instances. *e.g.* Polonius and Osric in *Hamlet*, Act III. Sc. ii. (l. 393), and Act V. Sc. ii. (l. 98, etc.). It is recorded that one of the courtiers of Philip of Macedon wore a shade over his left eye and walked lame, because the king had lost the sight of his left eye and been wounded in the leg. The modern servility of 'the Alexandra limp' shows that the race is not extinct.

ὅτι δύσκολος καὶ δύσερις. Ἀντικεῖσθαι δὲ φαίνεται τὰ ἄκρα ἑαυτοῖς διὰ τὸ ἀνώνυμον εἶναι τὸ μέσον.

1 VII. Περὶ τὰ αὐτὰ δὲ σχεδόν ἐστι καὶ ἡ τῆς ἀλαζονείας μεσότης· ἀνώνυμος δὲ καὶ αὐτή. Οὐ χεῖρον δὲ καὶ τὰς τοιαύτας ἐπελθεῖν· μᾶλλόν τε γὰρ ἂν εἰδείημεν τὰ περὶ τὸ ἦθος, καθ' ἕκαστον διελθόντες, καὶ μεσότητας εἶναι τὰς ἀρετὰς πιστεύσαιμεν ἄν, ἐπὶ πάντων οὕτως ἔχον συνιδόντες. Ἐν δὴ τῷ συζῆν οἱ μὲν πρὸς ἡδονὴν καὶ λύπην ὁμιλοῦντες εἴρηνται, περὶ δὲ τῶν ἀληθευόντων τε καὶ ψευδομένων εἴπωμεν ὁμοίως ἐν λόγοις καὶ πράξεσι

and recognised name for the mean state, the excess and defect sometimes appear to be opposed to one another immediately.

CHAP. VII.—*On Straightforwardness or Truthfulness.*

1 Turning now to the behaviour of men in regard to the pre-

General explanation of the Habits in question and their phraseology (§§ 1–6).

1. Ἀντικεῖσθαι δὲ φαίνεται κ.τ.λ.] So it was also in the case of φιλοτιμία, iv. 6.

CHAP. VII.*—We next proceed to consider the virtue of Truthfulness or Straightforwardness in words and actions considered out of any relation to the pleasure or pain caused to others.

The excess and defect here must not be confused with χαυνότης and μικροψυχία in ch. iii. See further note on iii. 37 and also that on μεγαλόψυχος, p. 235.

4. ἀνώνυμος κ.τ.λ.] otherwise Aristotle would hardly have had recourse to the strange description ἀλαζονείας μεσότης, 'moderation in respect of boastfulness.' In II. vii. 12 ἀλήθεια and ἀληθής τις were suggested (the 'τις' showing some doubtfulness about the application of the word). ἀλήθεια, however, is 'truth' rather than 'truthfulness.' ἀληθινὸς, *i.e.* 'genuine,' 'real,' would more nearly express what we want in the adjectival form at any rate, but there is no abstract substantive to correspond.

Οὐ χεῖρον κ.τ.λ.] This is because the habits described are none the less real and definite, though language may not supply words to mark their distinctions. (See note on II. vii. 2.)

* See *Supplementary Notes on this Chapter*, passim.

2 καὶ τῷ προσποιήματι. Δοκεῖ δὴ ὁ μὲν ἀλαζὼν προσποι-
ητικὸς τῶν ἐνδόξων εἶναι καὶ μὴ ὑπαρχόντων καὶ μειζό-
3 νων ἢ ὑπάρχει, ὁ δὲ εἴρων ἀνάπαλιν ἀρνεῖσθαι τὰ ὑπάρ-
4 χοντα ἢ ἐλάττω ποιεῖν, ὁ δὲ μέσος αὐθέκαστός τις ὢν
ἀληθευτικὸς καὶ τῷ βίῳ καὶ τῷ λόγῳ, τὰ ὑπάρχοντα
ὁμολογῶν εἶναι περὶ αὑτόν, καὶ οὔτε μείζω οὔτε ἐλάττω.
5 Ἔστι δὲ τούτων ἕκαστα καὶ ἕνεκά τινος ποιεῖν καὶ μηθε-
νός. Ἕκαστος δ' οἷός ἐστι, τοιαῦτα λέγει καὶ πράττει

2 tensions which they make in society, we observe that the
Braggart lays claim to qualities which he does not possess at
3 all, or possesses in a degree below his claims; the Dissembler
4 disclaims or depreciates his own merits; the Truthful man, with
a genuineness that embraces his whole life and conversation,
5 represents himself just as he is, neither more nor less. The
Simulation or Dissimulation thus described may be practised
with or without a special motive; but, generally speaking,
men's words, acts, and lives are a true reflex of their character and disposition, unless there be some special motive for

1. προσποίημα] 'pretensions.'

3. εἴρων is a very difficult word to translate. As ἀλαζὼν is one who boastfully lays claim to qualities that do not belong to him, so εἴρων is the reverse of this, and εἰρώνεια therefore is a conscious and intentional concealment or disclaiming of good qualities that really belong to one. 'Irony' is too wide, it *may* take this form among others. 'False Modesty' and 'Reserve' are too unconscious and often unintentional. 'Dissembler' and 'Dissimulation' are too closely allied with deceit, at least in modern English, though it does not seem that they were always used with this bad connotation: *e.g.* in Bacon's Essay on 'Simulation and Dissimulation.' Perhaps on the whole either 'Dissimulation' or 'Self-Depreciation' come nearest to what we want: but the word in Greek itself is used in different senses, as we see from § 14-16 of this Chapter.

7. This distinction is further discussed in § 10, etc. With some persons the habits of bragging or of self-depreciation are so ingrained that they are exhibited even when it is impossible to imagine a motive, and where detection seems inevitable, and, as Aristotle proceeds to remark, except there be a definite motive such conduct is a true index of a character corresponding.

6 καὶ οὕτω ζῇ, ἐὰν μή τινος ἕνεκα πράττῃ. Καθ' αὑτὸ δὲ
τὸ μὲν ψεῦδος φαῦλον καὶ ψεκτόν, τὸ δ' ἀληθὲς καλὸν
καὶ ἐπαινετόν. Οὕτω δὲ καὶ ὁ μὲν ἀληθευτικὸς μέσος
ὢν ἐπαινετός, οἱ δὲ ψευδόμενοι ἀμφότεροι μὲν ψεκτοί,
μᾶλλον δ' ὁ ἀλαζών. Περὶ ἑκατέρου δ' εἴπωμεν, πρότε-
7 ρον δὲ περὶ τοῦ ἀληθευτικοῦ. Οὐ γὰρ περὶ τοῦ ἐν ταῖς
ὁμολογίαις ἀληθεύοντος λέγομεν, οὐδ' ὅσα εἰς ἀδικίαν ἢ
δικαιοσύνην συντείνει (ἄλλης γὰρ ἂν εἴη ταῦτ' ἀρετῆς),
ἀλλ' ἐν οἷς μηθενὸς τοιούτου διαφέροντος καὶ ἐν λόγῳ
8 καὶ ἐν βίῳ ἀληθεύει τῷ τὴν ἕξιν τοιοῦτος εἶναι. Δόξειε
δ' ἂν ὁ τοιοῦτος ἐπιεικὴς εἶναι. Ὁ γὰρ φιλαλήθης, καὶ
ἐν οἷς μὴ διαφέρει ἀληθεύων, ἀληθεύσει καὶ ἐν οἷς δια-
φέρει ἔτι μᾶλλον· ὡς γὰρ αἰσχρὸν τὸ ψεῦδος εὐλαβή-
σεται, ὅ γε καὶ καθ' αὑτὸ ηὐλαβεῖτο· ὁ δὲ τοιοῦτος
9 ἐπαινετός. Ἐπὶ τὸ ἔλαττον δὲ μᾶλλον τοῦ ἀληθοῦς
ἀποκλίνει. ἐμμελέστερον γὰρ φαίνεται διὰ τὸ ἐπαχθεῖς
10 τὰς ὑπερβολὰς εἶναι. Ὁ δὲ μείζω τῶν ὑπαρχόντων

6 the contrary. And seeing that any falsehood is in itself
reprehensible, we have no hesitation in according praise to
Truthfulness and censure both to Boastfulness and Dissimula-
tion, but especially to the former. Now to speak of each
7 character in order. The Truthful man is not only truthful in
his dealings, or where his interest is involved, but all his life
and conversation are truthful, from the natural love which he
8 has of truth in itself: and similarly he shuns falsehood even
in matters indifferent, and therefore much more in all other
9 cases. This habit is evidently in itself a virtue. If however
such a man should err, it will be on the side of depreciating,
10 rather than exaggerating, his own merits. Boastfulness has
several types. (α) It may be without a definite motive,

'Truthfulness' pervades the whole character in which it is found (§§ 7—10).

The Excess, Boastfulness, under various types (§§ 10—13).

13. ὡς αἰσχρὸν is in contrast with καθ' αὑτό. Falsehood under circumstances involving disgrace, contrasted with falsehood *per se*.

προσποιούμενος μηθενὸς ἕνεκα φαύλῳ μὲν ἔοικεν (οὐ γὰρ ἂν ἔχαιρε τῷ ψεύδει), μάταιος δὲ φαίνεται μᾶλλον ἢ
11 κακός. Εἰ δ' ἕνεκά τινος, ὁ μὲν δόξης ἢ τιμῆς οὐ λίαν ψεκτὸς, ὡς ὁ ἀλαζὼν, ὁ δὲ ἀργυρίου, ἢ ὅσα εἰς ἀργύ-
12 ριον, ἀσχημονέστερος. Οὐκ ἐν τῇ δυνάμει δ' ἐστὶν ὁ

coming naturally as it were to a man. In that case it is
11 rather foolish than actually vicious. (β) It may be assumed with a view to secure honour, or with a view to make gain;
12 the latter being the worse form. And observe that Boastfulness is a moral state, the character of which is determined mainly by its motive or purpose. For the force of

1. φαύλῳ μὲν ἔοικε] 'is a bad man in some sense.' This is in natural contrast with the statement in § 8, δόξειε δ' ἂν κ.τ.λ.

4. ὡς ὁ ἀλαζὼν] As the ἀλαζὼν is the character whose different types Aristotle is now distinguishing, it seems out of place to give as an example of *one* of them 'ὁ ἀλαζών.' Two other readings are proposed (α) ὡς ἀλαζὼν (omitting ὁ), *i.e.* 'he is not very much to be blamed, for a braggart' (=considering that he is a braggart): (β) ὁ ἀλαζὼν (omitting ὡς), *i.e.* 'He who does it for the sake of honour is not very much to be blamed—he who boasts, I mean.' Thus the words supply the place of the participle προσποιούμενος which must be understood with ὁ, and if the sentence were written in full would follow τιμῆς. It is most probable however that the words ὡς ὁ ἀλαζὼν represent a marginal gloss that has crept into the text.

5. Οὐκ ἐν τῇ δυνάμει κ.τ.λ.] Boastfulness as a reprehensible habit consists not so much in the mere capacity (δύναμις) or propensity to boast. That may arise in a manner from natural constitution (τῷ τοιόσδε εἶναι—with which compare a similar statement as regards Friendliness, vi. 5, τῷ τοιοῦτος εἶναι κ.τ.λ.), or from force of habit (κατὰ τὴν ἕξιν—with which again compare τῷ τὴν ἕξιν τοιοῦτος εἶναι in § 7 above). The moral depravity of Boastfulness depends rather upon the motives for which it is adopted (προαίρεσις), the distinction between some of which motives has just been pointed out. The distinction is in fact the same as that which discriminates ἄρεσκος and κόλαξ in the last Chapter.

The remark is introduced in the text to show that the classification just made of boasters according to their motive indicates a real moral difference.

ἀλαζὼν, ἀλλ' ἐν τῇ προαιρέσει· κατὰ τὴν ἕξιν γὰρ καὶ
τῷ τοιόσδε εἶναι ἀλαζών ἐστιν, ὥσπερ καὶ ψεύστης ὁ
μὲν τῷ ψεύδει αὐτῷ χαίρων, ὁ δὲ δόξης ὀρεγόμενος ἢ
13 κέρδους. Οἱ μὲν οὖν δόξης χάριν ἀλαζονευόμενοι τὰ
τοιαῦτα προσποιοῦνται ἐφ' οἷς ἔπαινος ἢ εὐδαιμονισμὸς,
οἱ δὲ κέρδους, ὧν καὶ ἀπόλαυσίς ἐστι τοῖς πέλας καὶ ἃ
διαλαθεῖν ἔστι μὴ ὄντα, οἷον μάντιν σοφὸν ἢ ἰατρόν.
Διὰ τοῦτο οἱ πλεῖστοι προσποιοῦνται τὰ τοιαῦτα καὶ
14 ἀλαζονεύονται· ἔστι γὰρ ἐν αὐτοῖς τὰ εἰρημένα. Οἱ δ'
εἴρωνες ἐπὶ τὸ ἔλαττον λέγοντες χαριέστεροι μὲν τὰ
ἤθη φαίνονται· οὐ γὰρ κέρδους ἕνεκα δοκοῦσι λέγειν,
ἀλλὰ φεύγοντες τὸ ὀγκηρόν· μάλιστα δὲ καὶ οὗτοι τὰ
15 ἔνδοξα ἀπαρνοῦνται, οἷον καὶ Σωκράτης ἐποίει. Οἱ δὲ

habit or natural disposition may make a man boastful, just as some men have a natural propensity for lying, and others adopt it for a special purpose. In the case of Boastfulness the special purpose is the main point by which we judge the
13 habit. To return to the two last-mentioned types of Boastfulness. The manner in which they are displayed varies with the difference of motive. If the motive be honour, pretension is made to qualities which are praised or envied by men. If it be gain, pretension is made to qualities that are useful, and the absence of which is not likely to be detected; *e.g.* quackery
14 and fortune-telling. This is the commoner type. The Dissemblers, on the other hand, disclaim their own merits, and this in moderation is not altogether unattractive, as in the
15 case of Socrates. The same habit in an extreme form is very

The Defect, Dissimulation, falls under the two types of Self-Depreciation and Affectation

7. *οἷον μάντιν σοφὸν κ.τ.λ.*] *e.g.*, weather-prophets, fortune-tellers, quack-doctors, etc.

12. *φεύγοντες τὸ ὀγκηρόν*] 'wishing to avoid (the appearance of) giving themselves airs.' *ὀγκηρὸς* means literally 'bulky' or 'swollen,' and thence 'pompous' (L. and S.).

13. The *εἰρωνεία* of Socrates is well known. It consisted in a profession of ignorance, doubt, and a desire to be instructed, by which unwary opponents were

καὶ τὰ μικρὰ καὶ τὰ φανερὰ προσποιούμενοι βαυκοπανοῦργοι λέγονται καὶ εὐκαταφρόνητοί εἰσιν. Καὶ ἐνίοτε ἀλαζονεία φαίνεται, οἷον ἡ τῶν Λακώνων ἐσθής· καὶ
16 γὰρ ἡ ὑπερβολὴ καὶ ἡ λίαν ἔλλειψις ἀλαζονικόν. Οἱ δὲ μετρίως χρώμενοι τῇ εἰρωνείᾳ καὶ περὶ τὰ μὴ λίαν ἐμποδὼν καὶ φανερὰ εἰρωνευόμενοι χαρίεντες φαίνονται.
17 Ἀντικεῖσθαι δ' ὁ ἀλαζὼν φαίνεται τῷ ἀληθευτικῷ· χείρων γάρ.

1 VIII. Οὔσης δὲ καὶ ἀναπαύσεως ἐν τῷ βίῳ, καὶ ἐν ταύτῃ διαγωγῆς μετὰ παιδιᾶς, δοκεῖ καὶ ἐνταῦθα εἶναι ὁμιλία τις ἐμμελής, καὶ οἷα δεῖ λέγειν καὶ ὥς, ὁμοίως δὲ

contemptible, and is often nothing but Boastfulness in dis-
16 guise, in short 'the pride that apes humility.' In moderation
17 however it is not (as we said) offensive, and in any case is preferable to the other extreme of Boastfulness.

CHAP. VIII.—*On Geniality.*

Explanation of terms.

1 Some part of life being necessarily spent in recreation, there must be in that part also a propriety of conduct, and this will apply, though in different degrees, both to speakers

lured on to discomfiture in argument.

1. προσποιούμενοι] This clause stands in contrast with τὰ ἔνδοξα ἀπαρνοῦνται, and therefore we may understand some such words as μὴ δύνασθαι to complete the sense. 'Those who disclaim small merits, and such as they obviously possess.'

Thus we have two types of εἰρωνεία distinguished:—(1) the more favourable type of 'Self-Depreciation,' of which Socrates is an instance, and which is exhibited also by the μεγαλόψυχος (see iv. 28, note); and (2) the more unfavourable type of 'affectation,' which often is a mere disguise of 'Boastfulness.'

βαυκοπανοῦργοι] 'affected knaves.' βαῦκος = 'prudish or affected.'

11. ὁμιλία τις ἐμμελής] 'a graceful way of conducting oneself in society.'

καὶ ἀκούειν. Διοίσει δὲ καὶ τὸ ἐν τοιούτοις λέγειν ἢ
2 τοιούτων ἀκούειν. Δῆλον δ' ὡς καὶ περὶ ταῦτ' ἔστιν
3 ὑπερβολή τε καὶ ἔλλειψις τοῦ μέσου. Οἱ μὲν οὖν τῷ
γελοίῳ ὑπερβάλλοντες βωμολόχοι δοκοῦσιν εἶναι καὶ
φορτικοί, γλιχόμενοι πάντως τοῦ γελοίου, καὶ μᾶλλον
στοχαζόμενοι τοῦ γέλωτα ποιῆσαι ἢ τοῦ λέγειν εὐσχήμονα καὶ μὴ λυπεῖν τὸν σκωπτόμενον· οἱ δὲ μήτ' αὐτοὶ
ἂν εἰπόντες μηθὲν γελοῖον τοῖς τε λέγουσι δυσχεραίνοντες ἄγριοι καὶ σκληροὶ δοκοῦσιν εἶναι. Οἱ δ' ἐμμελῶς
παίζοντες εὐτράπελοι προσαγορεύονται, οἷον εὔτροποι·
τοῦ γὰρ ἤθους αἱ τοιαῦται δοκοῦσι κινήσεις εἶναι, ὥσπερ δὲ τὰ σώματα ἐκ τῶν κινήσεων κρίνεται, οὕτω καὶ
4 τὰ ἤθη. Ἐπιπολάζοντος δὲ τοῦ γελοίου, καὶ τῶν πλείστων χαιρόντων τῇ παιδιᾷ καὶ τῷ σκώπτειν μᾶλλον ἢ
δεῖ, καὶ οἱ βωμολόχοι εὐτράπελοι προσαγορεύονται ὡς
χαρίεντες. Ὅτι δὲ διαφέρουσι, καὶ οὐ μικρόν, ἐκ τῶν
5 εἰρημένων δῆλον. Τῇ μέσῃ δ' ἕξει οἰκεῖον καὶ ἡ ἐπι-

2 and listeners in such scenes: and here too the law of the
3 mean holds good. In the one extreme we have the Buffoon, who can never resist a laugh however ill-timed, however painful to the feelings of others. In the other we have the Boor, who neither jokes himself, nor tolerates it in others. The mean state (1) is characterized by quickness and versatility
4 of Wit, though, as nothing is easier than to raise a laugh, the
5 Buffoon often gets credit for such versatility. (2) Tact again

Characteristics of the Mean state are (1) Versatility and readiness of wit. (2) Tact in the choice of subjects of ridicule.

1. διοίσει κ.τ.λ.] The same difference in fact as exists in other cases between the doer of an act and one who is only an accessory.

10. Observe the play on words between εὐτράπελοι and εὔτροποι, both having the same derivation, but the former having gained a metaphorical sense like 'versatile,' while the latter retains its literal meaning. The notion is that they are called 'quick-witted' because their wits move quickly.

13. ἐπιπολάζοντος] See note on I. iv. 4.

δεξιότης ἐστίν· τοῦ δ' ἐπιδεξίου ἐστὶ τοιαῦτα λέγειν καὶ
ἀκούειν οἷα τῷ ἐπιεικεῖ καὶ ἐλευθερίῳ ἁρμόττει· ἔστι γάρ
τινα πρέποντα τῷ τοιούτῳ λέγειν ἐν παιδιᾶς μέρει καὶ
ἀκούειν, καὶ ἡ τοῦ ἐλευθερίου παιδιὰ διαφέρει τῆς τοῦ
ἀνδραποδώδους, καὶ αὖ τοῦ πεπαιδευμένου καὶ ἀπαιδεύ-
6 του. Ἴδοι δ' ἄν τις καὶ ἐκ τῶν κωμῳδιῶν τῶν παλαιῶν
καὶ τῶν καινῶν· τοῖς μὲν γὰρ ἦν γελοῖον ἡ αἰσχρολογία,
τοῖς δὲ μᾶλλον ἡ ὑπόνοια· διαφέρει δ' οὐ μικρὸν ταῦτα
7 πρὸς εὐσχημοσύνην. Πότερον οὖν τὸν εὖ σκώπτοντα
ὁριστέον τῷ λέγειν ἃ πρέπει ἐλευθερίῳ, ἢ τῷ μὴ λυπεῖν
τὸν ἀκούοντα, ἢ καὶ τέρπειν; ἢ καὶ τό γε τοιοῦτον ἀόρι-
8 στον; ἄλλο γὰρ ἄλλῳ μισητόν τε καὶ ἡδύ. Τοιαῦτα δὲ
καὶ ἀκούσεται· ἃ γὰρ ὑπομένει ἀκούων, ταῦτα καὶ ποιεῖν
9 δοκεῖ. Οὐ δὴ πᾶν ποιήσει· τὸ γὰρ σκῶμμα λοιδόρημά τι

is another characteristic, which insures that its possessor, whether speaking or listening, shall never forget what it is becoming for a gentleman and a man of refinement, even in
6 the way of recreation, to speak or to listen to. As an obvious instance of the application of such 'tact,' we note what a difference there is between coarseness and innuendo.
7 Whether then he draws the line at what is becoming to a gentleman, or at what will give pleasure, or at least no pain,
8 to his hearers, is perhaps not easy to define. But in any case he will not willingly listen to anything which he would shrink
9 from saying himself. For though law does not restrain ridi-

2. *ἐλευθέριος* here means 'a gentleman,' just as conversely *ἀνδραποδώδης* means 'a low and vulgar man.'

7. *αἰσχρολογία*] 'outspoken obscenity,' *ὑπόνοια* 'innuendo.' The difference would be well illustrated by the contrast between Rabelais and Sterne, or between the coarseness of Aristophanes and the 'intrigue' of a modern French play.

9. *εὐσχημοσύνην*] 'decency.'

13. *ποιεῖν . . . ποιήσει*] in the sense of *σκώπτειν* or *λέγειν*. As there are certain jokes which he would not himself make, so he will also refuse to listen to them.

ἐστὶν, οἱ δὲ νομοθέται ἔνια λοιδορεῖν κωλύουσιν· ἔδει δ' ἴσως καὶ σκώπτειν. Ὁ δὴ χαρίεις καὶ ἐλευθέριος οὕτως
10 ἕξει, οἷον νόμος ὢν ἑαυτῷ. Τοιοῦτος μὲν οὖν ὁ μέσος ἐστὶν, εἴτ' ἐπιδέξιος εἴτ' εὐτράπελος λέγεται· ὁ δὲ βωμολόχος ἥττων ἐστὶ τοῦ γελοίου, καὶ οὔτε ἑαυτοῦ οὔτε τῶν ἄλλων ἀπεχόμενος, εἰ γέλωτα ποιήσει, καὶ τοιαῦτα λέγων ὧν οὐθεν ἂν εἴποι ὁ χαρίεις, ἔνια δ' οὐδ' ἂν ἀκούσαι. Ὁ δ' ἄγριος εἰς τὰς τοιαύτας ὁμιλίας ἀχρεῖος· οὐθὲν γὰρ
11 συμβαλλόμενος πᾶσι δυσχεραίνει. Δοκεῖ δὲ ἡ ἀνάπαυ-
12 σις καὶ ἡ παιδιὰ ἐν τῷ βίῳ εἶναι ἀναγκαῖον. Τρεῖς οὖν αἱ εἰρημέναι ἐν τῷ βίῳ μεσότητες, εἰσὶ δὲ πᾶσαι περὶ

cule as it does personal abuse, yet a true gentleman is a law
10 to himself in such matters. The Buffoon however can never resist a joke. No consideration for persons or regard for proprieties ever restrains him. The Boor on the other hand is quite useless in social intercourse. He contributes nothing
11 to it himself, and acts as a continual damper: and yet some rest and recreation is a real necessity in life.

The Excess is Buffoonery.

The Defect, Boorishness.

12 This concludes our account of the three Social Virtues.

2. σκώπτειν] Understand 'ἔνια κωλύειν' from the preceding.

οὕτως] *i.e.* as if actually restrained by law.

4. εἴτ' ἐπιδέξιος εἴτ' εὐτράπελος λέγεται] There being no settled name for this Virtue, Aristotle hesitates by which of its two principal characteristics (see §§ 3—5) he shall describe it.

7. Observe the emphatic contrast between οὐθὲν and ἔνια, because there are *some* things which a man of refinement (χαριεὶς) would not say himself, which however he would not think it necessary to protest against if he heard them (see § 1 διοίσει δὲ κ.τ.λ.)

8. ἄγριος corresponds with ἀγροῖκος in the Catalogue of II. vii. It describes a man who is deficient in humour and the sense of the ludicrous, and one who acts as a sort of kill-joy in convivial society. In the former aspect he resembles Sydney Smith's Scotchman who needed a surgical operation to get a joke into his head; and in the latter he recalls Thackeray's description of the 'usual English expression of suppressed agony and intense gloom.'

λόγων τινῶν καὶ πράξεων κοινωνίαν. Διαφέρουσι δ' ὅτι ἡ μὲν περὶ ἀλήθειάν ἐστιν, αἱ δὲ περὶ τὸ ἡδύ. Τῶν δὲ περὶ τὴν ἡδονὴν ἡ μὲν ἐν ταῖς παιδιαῖς, ἡ δ' ἐν ταῖς κατὰ τὸν ἄλλον βίον ὁμιλίαις.

1 IX. Περὶ δὲ αἰδοῦς ὥς τινος ἀρετῆς οὐ προσήκει λέγειν·
2 πάθει γὰρ μᾶλλον ἔοικεν ἢ ἕξει. Ὁρίζεται γοῦν φόβος
τις ἀδοξίας, ἀποτελεῖται δὲ τῷ περὶ τὰ δεινὰ φόβῳ
παραπλήσιον· ἐρυθραίνονται γὰρ οἱ αἰσχυνόμενοι, οἱ δὲ
τὸν θάνατον φοβούμενοι ὠχριῶσιν. Σωματικὰ δὴ φαί-
νεταί πως εἶναι ἀμφότερα, ὅπερ δοκεῖ πάθους μᾶλλον ἢ
3 ἕξεως εἶναι. Οὐ πάσῃ δ' ἡλικίᾳ τὸ πάθος ἁρμόζει, ἀλλὰ
τῇ νέᾳ· οἰόμεθα γὰρ δεῖν τοὺς τηλικούτους αἰδήμονας
εἶναι διὰ τὸ πάθει ζῶντας πολλὰ ἁμαρτάνειν, ὑπὸ τῆς
αἰδοῦς δὲ κωλύεσθαι. Καὶ ἐπαινοῦμεν τῶν μὲν νέων

CHAP. IX.—*On the quasi-virtue, 'Sense of Shame.'*

The 'Sense of Shame' is not properly a Virtue for several reasons.

1 Shame cannot strictly be called a Virtue, for (1) it is an
2 occasional feeling rather than a permanent state. It may be
defined as 'a fear of disgrace,' and its outward marks resemble
those of fear. Shame makes us blush, Fear makes us pale,
3 and these are similar physical and transient effects. (2) It

CHAP. IX.—The subject of this concluding Chapter is the Sense of Shame. The Chapter is evidently fragmentary, for we hear nothing of the Excess of the feeling, the embodiment of which was described as ὁ καταπλήξ in II. vii. 14. In fact the discussion ends abruptly at the words ἀλλά τις μικτή in § 8, after which a few words have been added to connect this Book with the Books that follow, which are thought to be not Aristotle's, or at any rate not to belong to this treatise.

6. πάθει μᾶλλον ἢ ἕξει] If so, not properly a Virtue. See II. v.

φόβος τις ἀδοξίας] αἰδὼς has a variety of meanings in Homer, but in all cases it is 'a sentiment which has ultimate reference to the standard of public opinion' (Gladstone, *Juv. Mundi.* p. 384). In *Odyss.* ii.

τοὺς αἰδήμονας, πρεσβύτερον δ' οὐδεὶς ἂν ἐπαινέσειεν
ὅτι αἰσχυντηλός· οὐθὲν γὰρ οἰόμεθα δεῖν αὐτὸν πράτ-
4 τειν ἐφ' οἷς ἐστὶν αἰσχύνη. Οὐδὲ γὰρ ἐπιεικοῦς ἐστὶν
ἡ αἰσχύνη, εἴπερ γίγνεται ἐπὶ τοῖς φαύλοις· οὐ γὰρ
5 πρακτέον τὰ τοιαῦτα. Εἰ δ' ἐστὶ τὰ μὲν κατ' ἀλήθειαν
αἰσχρὰ, τὰ δὲ κατὰ δόξαν, οὐθὲν διαφέρει· οὐδέτερα
γὰρ πρακτέα, ὥστ' οὐκ αἰσχυντέον. Φαύλου δὲ καὶ τὸ
6 εἶναι τοιοῦτον οἷον πράττειν τι τῶν αἰσχρῶν. Τὸ δ'
οὕτως ἔχειν ὥστ' εἰ πράξειέ τι τῶν τοιούτων αἰσχύνεσ-
θαι, καὶ διὰ τοῦτ' οἴεσθαι ἐπιεικῆ εἶναι, ἄτοπον· ἐπὶ
τοῖς ἑκουσίοις γὰρ ἡ αἰδὼς, ἑκὼν δὲ ὁ ἐπιεικὴς οὐδέποτε
7 πράξει τὰ φαῦλα. Εἴη δ' ἂν ἡ αἰδὼς ἐξ ὑποθέσεως
ἐπιεικές· εἰ γὰρ πράξαι, αἰσχύνοιτ' ἄν· οὐκ ἔστι δὲ
τοῦτο περὶ τὰς ἀρετάς. Εἰ δ' ἡ ἀναισχυντία φαῦλον
καὶ τὸ μὴ αἰδεῖσθαι τὰ αἰσχρὰ πράττειν, οὐθὲν μᾶλλον

is not even a becoming feeling, except in youth: in mature
4 age we certainly should not praise it. (3) It has no place in
good men as such, because it is felt only when wrong has
5 been done. If it be urged that some of the occasions for
shame are only conventionally wrong, we reply that a good
6 man will avoid even these. If it be said that a good man
ought to retain the capacity for feeling shame in case he
should do wrong, we reply that as all wrong-doing to which
shame is appropriate is voluntary, such occasions will not
7 arise. Thus shame would be only virtuous provisionally; pro-
vided, that is, that wrong has been done. Hence it is not
strictly a Virtue. We need not however therefore hesitate

Shamelessness however is certainly a Vice.

64-5, both *αἰδὼς* and *νέμεσις* are appealed to as distinct motives against wrong-doing.

12. *ἐξ ὑποθέσεως*] 'subject to a condition,' the condition being that *if* wrong has been done shame will be a virtuous feeling, not otherwise. No virtue properly so called is subject to such a limitation as this. Aristotle is ready to admit that 'the man that blushes is not quite a brute,'

8 τὸ τοιαῦτα πράττοντα αἰσχύνεσθαι ἐπιεικές. Οὐκ ἔστι δ' οὐδ' ἡ ἐγκράτεια ἀρετή, ἀλλά τις μικτή· δειχθήσεται δὲ περὶ αὐτῆς ἐν τοῖς ὕστερον. Νῦν δὲ περὶ δικαιοσύνης εἴπωμεν.

8 to call Shamelessness a Vice. We do not describe even Continence as a Virtue, because of the mixture of bad desires which it necessarily implies. But of this hereafter. We now proceed to discuss Justice.

though he will not regard him as virtuous on the strength of this. To do so would be to encourage 'doing evil that good may come,' or 'continuing in sin that grace may abound.'

2. *οὐδ' ἡ ἐγκράτεια*] For an explanation of *ἐγκράτεια* see note on I. iii. 7. The point here is that as not even *ἐγκράτεια* is called a Virtue because it implies strong bad *desires*, though they are successfully combated, *a fortiori* Shame cannot be called a virtue, which presupposes actual wrong-*doing*.

3. *ἐν τοῖς ὕστερον*] viz. in B. VII.

νῦν δὲ περὶ δικαιοσύνης] Thus not only is the subject of *αἰδὼς* unfinished, but that of *νέμεσις* and *ἐπιχαιρεκακία*, of which we had so confused an account in II. vii. 15, is not even alluded to.

NOTE ON CHAPTER III.

THE CHARACTER OF THE μεγαλόψυχος.

Several questions arise in reference to this important character, some of which are inserted here to avoid making the notes too bulky. We have in this chapter Aristotle's conception of a perfect and ideal character (see especially § 16), combining the full social and moral conditions of *καλοκἀγαθία*.

The definition from which the whole discussion starts is that the Virtue of *μεγαλοψυχία* consists in '*a well-grounded self-esteem*' (ὁ μεγάλων αὑτὸν ἀξιῶν ἄξιος ὤν, § 3), and hence the whole character is, according to our modern ideas, somewhat disfigured by self-consciousness. It may be worth while to state some of the principal objections which are commonly made against it.

(1) The pervading *selfishness* of the character. He has no thought for others (§ 29): even his Benevolence is referred to himself and resolved into a desire for superiority (§ 24). (Compare Hobbes's celebrated theory that Benevolence is simply the love of power and the desire to exercise it.) His courage is based upon a somewhat selfish calculation likewise (§ 23). His love of Truth is similarly qualified (§ 28): so also is his forgiveness of injuries (§ 30).

(2) The conspicuous *pride* of his character, and the total absence, not to say of humility (on which see note § 37), but even of modesty (§§ 18, 22, 28).

(3) That such a man would be practically an offensive, unamiable, unsociable character (§§ 27, 29, 31).

Such are some of the criticisms commonly made on the character before us. We may feel sure however, after making all allowance for the difference between the ancient Greek and the modern Christian point of view, that a character so palpably defective and repulsive could never have appeared to Aristotle, not to say admirable, but ideally perfect. Hence, without attempting a defence of all its details, it may be worth while to endeavour to arrive at a somewhat more sympathetic view of this ideal character.

1. The first point would seem to be, as we have already hinted, that it *is* an *ideal* character. It implies the combination of all the virtues in such perfection as never is actually found (τὸ ἐν ἑκάστῃ ἀρετῇ μέγα, § 14). Just as Plato and others have con-

structed ideal States, so Aristotle has here delineated an ideal Man. In both cases alike some allowance must be made for the difference between theory and fact in a world where things, as they are, are not ideal. Within certain limits we may say, '*tant pis pour les faits.*'

2. Aristotle had a strong sense of the dignity of Human Nature; of the grandeur and worth of Man as Man, in contrast with all the rest of animate and inanimate creation. He felt something of what a modern writer has called 'the Enthusiasm of Humanity.' (See further, *Ecce Homo*, 3d ed. p. 162, etc.) This seems to be the key to his conception of the μεγαλόψυχος. The μεγαλόψυχος is one who is deeply conscious of the dignity of his Human Nature, and penetrated by this consciousness is elevated thereby to live a life in all respects worthy of such an ideal. 'He becomes a law unto himself' (ὥσπερ νόμος ὢν ἑαυτῷ, as we read in viii. 10). Doubtless this intense self-reliance of the μεγαλόψυχος appears from our modern Christian point of view an inadequate foundation on which to build the whole structure of the moral character. But it may well be asked whether, apart from revelation, any nobler or more effective stimulus to Virtue can be suggested than the feeling that any other conduct is unworthy of the dignity of human nature. We may also remember that S. Paul appeals in a very similar manner to the feeling that sin is unworthy of, and inconsistent with, our Christian profession and renewed nature, and argues that we should therefore scorn to commit it. A well-known saying of Goethe's recognises the value of this self-estimate: 'If you would improve a man, it is best to begin by persuading him that he is already what you would have him to be.'

In contrast with the character we have described, the χαῦνος is one who unworthily lays claim to such a dignity. He desires 'the loaves and fishes' of virtue and worth. So long as he can secure the honour and glory accorded to merit, he is more or less indifferent to the grounds on which he obtains it (§ 36), since it is obvious that it can be obtained from men on secondary and morally indifferent grounds (see §§ 19, 20). The μικρόψυχος on the other hand is one who has no noble aspirations at all. He is quite content with low and grovelling aims, and has therefore no chance of moral elevation. Hence Aristotle declares Littlemindedness to be a worse type of character than Vaingloriousness. The Vainglorious man does not shrink from grand and difficult tasks, he rather courts them, and his unbounded self-confidence may sometimes even carry him through (*e.g.* Cleon at Sphacteria, if we accept the estimate of him in Thucydides and Aristophanes).

At any rate he will probably be elevated by actual contact with them, even as Dante says, when he has met the great Poets, 'che di *vederli* in me stesso m'esalto.' Compare also Tennyson, *Queen Mary*, Act II. Sc. ii.:

> Yet thoroughly to believe in one's own self,
> So one's own self be thorough, were to do
> Great things, my lord.

But the Littleminded or Pusillanimous man can never rise to any great effort; and this is precisely the character which Dante brands in the well-known line, 'Che fece per *viltate* il gran rifiuto' (*Inf.* iii. 60).

We may account thus for the strong denunciation of the χλιαροὶ in Rev. iii. 15, 16, and for the supreme contempt of Dante, in *Inf.* iii. 36-51, for those 'Che visser senza infamia e senza lodo.' In *Rhet.* I. ix. 11 *μεγαλοψυχία* is described as *ἀρετὴ μεγάλων ποιητικὴ εὐεργετημάτων, μικροψυχία δὲ τοὐναντίον*. Compare also La Rochefoucauld (*Max.* 41), 'Ceux qui s'appliquent trop aux petites choses deviennent ordinairement incapables des grandes.'

Two further points call for a few words of explanation:

(1) The distinction between *χαυνότης* and *ἀλαζονεία*.

(2) The apparent and real repugnance between Highmindedness and Humility.

(1) (*a*) It must be remembered that *ἀλαζονεία* is the Excess in relation to one of the three *Social* Virtues (viz. *ἀλήθεια*) *i.e.* it has reference to a man's bearing in and towards society. (See note on Catalogue of Virtues at the end of Bk. II.) *Χαυνότης* has no such reference necessarily. We see from its position in the Catalogue that it is more of a personal Vice, even though its exercise must be more or less public. It relates rather to a moral *state or condition* of character, whereas *ἀλαζονεία*, though based upon this, relates especially to an *outward manifestation* of character. Hence Aristotle says, in IV. vii. 12, the moral estimate of *ἀλαζονεία* depends much more on the purpose for which it is practised than on the mere fact of the tendency to, or capacity for, such conduct existing in the person himself.

(*β*) Another distinction would seem to be this. The *ἀλαζὼν* lays claim to the possession of anything which can be the subject of admiration (*προσποιητικὸς τῶν ἐνδόξων*, IV. vii. 2), especially personal qualities, such as strength, cleverness, skill, etc. etc., and (as we judge from the opposition to *ἀληθευτικὸς*, and also from the *consciousness* involved in the Vice of Defect, *εἰρωνεία*), generally speaking, he is a *conscious* deceiver: his Boastfulness has its root in a vice of Untruthfulness. He knows that he is an impostor. The *χαῦνος*, on the other hand, is most frequently himself deceived. His Vaingloriousness springs from the root of personal Vanity, by which he is so blinded in his estimate of things, so 'clouded with his own conceit,' that he regards all occasions merely as opportunities for self-display; and this of course especially applies to great occasions—these being a preliminary condition of *χαυνότης*, *μεγαλοψυχία* and *μικροψυχία*.

It should be further observed that Aristotle attributes *frequent* *εἰρωνεία* to the *μεγαλόψυχος* (IV. iii. 28), which plainly shows that *εἰρωνεία* is widely different from *μικροψυχία*.

2. It has sometimes been argued (*e.g.* by Aquinas and others) that *μεγαλοψυχία* is not inconsistent with Christian Humility. Without going so far as this, we ought at any rate to take into consideration the following points:

(*α*) *μικροψυχία* must on no account be confounded with Humility, which has nothing in common with it, as has been already sufficiently explained. See note on IV. iii. 37.

(*β*) The modern popular notion of Humility is a very false one, in two ways especially:—

(i) Humility is generally thought to consist in a conscious (not to say, often insincere) self-depreciation. In that sense it somewhat resembles *εἰρωνεία* both in its better and worse phases (see note on IV. vii. 15). Now the Humility of true greatness is a *just* estimate of its power, not a depreciatory one. If it be consciously depreciatory, it is simply the 'pride of modesty' (see IV. vii. 15). It only appears depreciatory to those who are lost in admiration of a standard above their own reach or aspirations. When Sir Isaac Newton said that in his highest efforts he felt as if he were only a child picking up pebbles on the shore of the boundless ocean of knowledge, that was a humble and yet a just estimate of the powers of human genius, though to an ordinary man it might seem unduly depreciatory. The Greeks, on the other hand, not having yet learnt how limited are man's powers in the universe, could not understand how a low estimate of unusual powers could still be a just one.

(ii) The popular notions of Conceit and Humility are simply a high or a low self-estimate, without any regard to the relation between the estimate and the merits: just as Liberality and the reverse are often popularly judged by the amount spent, without regard to the relation which it bears to the means of the giver.

At the same time, looking at several expressions in the chapter under consideration, we must admit that the modern notion of Humility as a Virtue was foreign, and perhaps necessarily so, to the Greek mind. As we have said, a low estimate, which is also a genuine and sincere one, of human power and human virtue, can come only from the consciousness of defeat and failure; and it would be as much out of place amidst the first daring flights and as yet unbaffled efforts of the Greek mind, as melancholy would be in the sanguine years of childhood, which have not yet been sobered by disappointment.[1]

At the same time some sort of recognition of a feeling akin to humility occurs in the commendation allowed to the better type of *εἰρωνεία* in IV. vii. 14.

It is interesting to contrast with this picture what has not inaptly been described as S. Paul's delineation of an ideal character in 1 Cor. xiii., especially vv. 4, 5, and 7. Also the total divergence of the ancient and modern conceptions of a perfect character is curiously illustrated by the following statement of a recent moralist, whether we accept it or not:—'Were the perfect man to exist, he himself would be the last to know it; for the highest stage in advancement is the lowest descent in humility' (Archer Butler).

It may be worth while to compare with Aristotle's ideal sketch an actual instance of a character embodying many of the traits here depicted. Lord Macaulay in his Life of Pitt, p. 181 (*Biographies*, edition 1867), observes that Pitt may be considered as in many respects a noble embodiment of Aristotle's conception of the *μεγαλόψυχος*. We may compare the following traits or incidents with the portraiture in this chapter:

'No person could hear Pitt without perceiving him to be a man of high, intrepid, and commanding spirit, proudly conscious of his own rectitude and of his own intellectual superiority, incapable of the low vices of fear and envy, but too prone to feel and show disdain (§§ 18, 22). Pride pervaded the whole man, . . . was marked by the way in which he walked, in which he sate, in which he stood, and above all, in which he bowed (§ 34). Several men of note (§§ 26, 28) who had been partial to Pitt . . . were so much irritated by the contempt with which he treated them that they complained in print of their wrongs. . . . His ambition had no mixture of low cupidity. There was something noble in the cynical disdain with which the mighty minister scattered riches and titles to right and left among those who valued them, while he spurned them out of his own way' (§§ 18 fin., 33, etc.). At the age of twenty-two he was offered 'one of the easiest and most highly paid places in the service of the Crown. The offer was at once declined, for the young statesman had resolved to accept no post which did not entitle him

[1] Compare the grounds on which Arist. (*Rhet.* II. xii. 11) states that the young are *μεγαλόψυχοι*,—*οὔτε γὰρ ὑπὸ τοῦ βίου οὔπω τεταπείνωνται ἀλλὰ τῶν ἀναγκαίων ἄπειροί εἰσιν*, and the old are *μικρόψυχοι* for the converse reason (II. xiii. 5). Also Mansel (*Gnostics*, pp. 22-24) notes the little attention paid in Greek Philosophies to the problem of Evil, and accounts for the fact somewhat similarly.

to a seat in the Cabinet, and announced that resolution in the House of Commons,' and that at a time when the Cabinet was usually restricted to about seven members, and even Burke was not included in it (εἰς τὰ ἔντιμα μὴ ἰέναι ἢ οὗ πρωτεύουσιν ἄλλοι, §§ 27, 33).

Lastly, it should be noted (and this perhaps increases our difficulty in taking an appreciative view of Aristotle's sketch in this chapter), that now-a-days the habit of mind indicated by μεγαλοψυχία is far less common than formerly, and even in comparatively recent times, and that anything approaching to self-assertion is viewed with increasing repugnance. Mr. Mill in his Essay on Liberty protests against the English dislike for eccentricity or conspicuousness of any kind, and deplores the tendency to a dull and dead level of mediocrity which society at present fosters. But be the cause what it may, the fact is undeniable. What would be thought now-a-days of such a title-page to a book, once so common, as 'A most learned and edifying discourse by . . .'? The late Lord Dalling writes, 'One of the absurdities of the English character of the present day, is that no one has an estimate of his intrinsic value.' Yet it may well be doubted whether any great reform, religious or political, has been effected, or any deep impression left in the world's history or literature, by any one who did not display the self-confidence and even self-assertion of Aristotle's μεγαλόψυχος in a considerable, and often, to our modern notion, a somewhat distasteful degree. There is no more remarkable instance of this than that of Dante. This spirit breathes throughout the whole of his Divine Poem. He promises immortal fame to those who are named by him in it: to be mentioned there, even for censure, is no small argument of distinction: he fears lest a timid statement of truth, though perhaps increasing his present fame, should injure it with those 'who shall call these days ancient': he boldly ranks himself among the six great poets of the world; and so on in innumerable other passages. Nor was this bold self-reliance limited to mere flights of poetry. Boccaccio relates that when appointed to go from Florence on an embassy to Boniface VIII., Dante hesitated, and assigned as his reason, 'If I go, who remains? and if I remain, who goes?' So in the *Convito* (I. x.) he does not shrink from saying, 'fidandomi di me più che d'un altro.' Whatever may have been thought of this self-reliance at the time, the verdict of posterity has fully justified it; and may we not apply the reflection of Aristotle in a similar case, and ask, If this be so, πῶς οὐκ ἄτοπον εἰ ὅτ' ἔστιν . . . μὴ ἀληθεύσεται κατ' αὐτοῦ τὸ ὑπαρχον; (I. x. 7.) 'There was a time' (says Dean Church) when great men dared to claim their greatness . . . in the consciousness of a strong and noble purpose and of strength to fulfil it.' To take an instance of a more recent date, Wordsworth, in his Preface to his own Poems, undeterred by the storm of unpopularity and ridicule by which he was then assailed, confidently asserts the immortality of his work, and this, writes Professor Shairp, 'is not vanity, but the calm confidence of a man who feels the rock under his feet, and who knows that he is in harmony with the everlasting truth of things.' Merely to suggest other cases, without entering into details, the same self-reliance is conspicuous in men so different as Mohammed, Savonarola (Milman's *Essays*, p. 9), Angelo Politiano (Roscoe's *Life of Lorenzo de' Medici*, p. 92, etc.), and in almost all 'self-made men,' as they are styled in modern times. Certain it is that whether society likes or dislikes the habit, the μεγαλόψυχοι, and often even the χαῦνοι, are those who chiefly advance themselves, and arrive at distinction, more or less lasting: so true to life is the reflection of Goethe—

> Und wenn ihr euch nur selbst vertraut,
> Vertrauen euch die andern Seelen;

and again—

> So bald du dir vertraust, so bald weisst du zu leben.

APPENDIX.

BOOK X. CHAPTERS VI—IX.

Aristotle now reverts to the subject of Happiness, the various questions arising out of the Definition in I. vii. having been disposed of. In two respects especially the following discussion differs from that in B. I. (1) The object now is not so much to give a formal Definition of Happiness, as to prove its general character to be contemplative (*θεωρητική*). (2) Happiness is here considered in the abstract and in its highest ideal development, as it is found in the life of the gods, and no longer under the practical limitations by which it is modified in the life of man (vii. 8). Thus in B. I. we were frequently reminded that it was not ideal Happiness and ideal Virtue but human Happiness and human Virtue that we were in search of. (See especially I. vi. 13 and xiii. 5, 6.) Now however it is argued that human Happiness is not the highest form of Happiness (viii. 1—3, etc.). Hence while Happiness is still affirmed to consist in an active state of Excellence (*ἐν ταῖς κατ' ἀρετὴν ἐνεργείαις*, vi. 8), yet, since Excellence (*ἀρετή*) may be either Moral or Intellectual, it is proved (ch. vii. and viii.) that the latter is superior to the former on various grounds, and especially because Moral Excellence (implying, as it does, imperfection and the liability to evil) cannot be attributed to the gods (viii. 7). Consequently the Happiness of the gods, which is naturally the highest and most perfect, must depend on Intellectual activity. Hence we conclude generally that the perfection of Happiness consists in Intellectual activity (*θεωρία*—for which see Glossary, p. xli.). Practically none but the best of men, and these only imperfectly, can ever approach to such perfection of Happiness. Most men can never rise above that which constitutes peculiarly *human* Happiness (εὐδαιμονία ἀνθρωπινὴ, I. xiii. 5), viz. the Excellence not of the higher portion (τὸ λόγον ἔχον) of the Soul, but of the subordinate part (τὸ ἐπιθυμητικόν).

Let this distinction then be borne in mind in reading these Supplementary Chapters. Aristotle has shown in the previous Books that man's Happiness in this world consists in the due regulation of his actions and passions under the control of Reason. His purpose now is to show that the most perfect Happiness consists in the full development and activity of Reason itself, unfettered by the necessity of exercising any such control over the lower nature. In a word, if we might venture on such a modernism, we might say that hitherto he has discussed the Happiness of earth; now he is describing the Happiness of heaven. (See *Supplementary Notes.*)

VI. *Εἰρημένων δὲ τῶν περὶ τὰς ἀρετάς τε καὶ φιλίας καὶ ἡδονάς, λοιπὸν περὶ εὐδαιμονίας τύπῳ διελθεῖν, ἐπειδὴ*

CHAP. VI.—*Happiness does not consist in Amusement, but in Active Excellence.*

Happiness is a condition which is (1) active,

1, 2 We have before proved (1) that Happiness is not a passive but an active condition; and (2) that it is a condition which

CHAP. VI.—The following is a brief outline of the argument in the next three Chapters. (Ch. vi.) Happiness having been already shown (I. vii.) to be something sought for its own sake, and it being conceivable that either Amusement or active Virtue might be alleged as answering to that description, ch. vi. is devoted to proving that not Amusement, but Active Virtue, constitutes Happiness. (Ch. vii.) This Active Virtue, or rather Excellence, being either Moral or Intellectual, Happiness is is shown to belong to the latter. (Ch. viii.) Several reasons are given for thus asserting the superiority of Intellectual over Moral Excellence; and the Chapter concludes with some remarks of practical detail.

1. ἀρετὰς, viz. Books II—VI. φιλίας, Books VIII. and IX. ἡδονὰς, Appendix to Book VII.

τέλος αὐτὴν τίθεμεν τῶν ἀνθρωπίνων. Ἀναλαβοῦσι δὴ
2 τὰ προειρημένα συντομώτερος ἂν εἴη ὁ λόγος. Εἴπομεν δ' ὅτι οὐκ ἔστιν ἕξις· καὶ γὰρ τῷ καθεύδοντι διὰ βίου ὑπάρχοι ἄν, φυτῶν ζῶντι βίον, καὶ τῷ δυστυχοῦντι τὰ μέγιστα. Εἰ δὴ ταῦτα μὴ ἀρέσκει, ἀλλὰ μᾶλλον εἰς ἐνέργειάν τινα θετέον, καθάπερ ἐν τοῖς πρότερον εἴρηται, τῶν δ' ἐνεργειῶν αἱ μέν εἰσιν ἀναγκαῖαι καὶ δι' ἕτερα αἱρεταί, αἱ δὲ καθ' αὑτάς, δῆλον ὅτι τὴν εὐδαιμονίαν τῶν καθ' αὑτὰς αἱρετῶν τινὰ θετέον καὶ οὐ τῶν δι' ἄλλο· οὐδενὸς
3 γὰρ ἐνδεὴς ἡ εὐδαιμονία ἀλλ' αὐτάρκης. Καθ' αὑτὰς δ' εἰσὶν αἱρεταὶ ἀφ' ὧν μηδὲν ἐπιζητεῖται παρὰ τὴν ἐνέργειαν. Τοιαῦται δ' εἶναι δοκοῦσιν αἱ κατ' ἀρετὴν πράξεις· τὰ γὰρ καλὰ καὶ σπουδαῖα πράττειν τῶν δι' αὑτὰ αἱρετῶν. Καὶ τῶν παιδιῶν δὲ αἱ ἡδεῖαι· οὐ γὰρ δι' ἕτερα αὐτὰς αἱ-

is complete in itself, and is sought for its own sake only. (2) Desired for its own sake.
3 Now it might be thought that both Virtuous Actions and Amusements fulfil these conditions:—the former for obvious reasons; the latter, partly because their *results* are not neces- Such are—(i) Active Virtue; (ii) Amusements.

2. εἴπομεν ὅτι οὐκ ἕξις] viz. in I. viii. 9. He adds here the consideration introduced by καὶ γάρ, viz., that if Happiness were a mere state or condition (ἕξις) it would not be inconsistent with a life of lethargy, and even of misery. The same argument was used in I. v. 6, to prove that Virtue (which is a ἕξις, and therefore may be inactive) is not identical with Happiness.

6. ἐν τοῖς πρότερον] Especially in the Definition of Happiness in I. vii.

7. ἀναγκαῖαι has the same meaning as βίαιος (according to the usual explanation) in I. v. 8 (note). Actions chosen only as means to obtain a further result (δι' ἕτερα αἱρεταὶ) are 'necessary' or 'compulsory,' if we wish to secure that result.

10. αὐτάρκης] If any further result is sought by an action, that action is not αὐτάρκης. Consequently if Happiness were not sought for its own sake it would not be αὐτάρκης, as it was shown to be in I. vii. 6, etc.

14. τῶν παιδιῶν αἱ ἡδεῖαι] 'those amusements from which we derive pleasure.' Conceivably some recreations may be prac-

ροῦνται· βλάπτονται γὰρ ἀπ' αὐτῶν μᾶλλον ἢ ὠφελοῦνται, ἀμελοῦντες τῶν σωμάτων καὶ τῆς κτήσεως. Καταφεύγουσι δ' ἐπὶ τὰς τοιαύτας διαγωγὰς τῶν εὐδαιμονιζομένων οἱ πολλοί, διὸ παρὰ τοῖς τυράννοις εὐδοκιμοῦσιν οἱ ἐν ταῖς τοιαύταις διαγωγαῖς εὐτράπελοι· ὧν γὰρ ἐφίενται, ἐν τούτοις παρέχουσι σφᾶς αὐτοὺς ἡδεῖς· δέονται
4 δὲ τοιούτων. Δοκεῖ μὲν οὖν εὐδαιμονικὰ ταῦτα εἶναι διὰ τὸ τοὺς ἐν δυναστείαις ἐν τούτοις ἀποσχολάζειν, οὐδὲν δὲ ἴσως σημεῖον οἱ τοιοῦτοί εἰσιν· οὐ γὰρ ἐν τῷ δυναστεύειν ἡ ἀρετὴ οὐδ' ὁ νοῦς, ἀφ' ὧν αἱ σπουδαῖαι ἐνέργειαι· οὐδ' εἰ ἄγευστοι οὗτοι ὄντες ἡδονῆς εἰλικρινοῦς καὶ ἐλευθερίου ἐπὶ τὰς σωματικὰς καταφεύγουσιν, διὰ τοῦτο ταύ-

But Happiness cannot consist in Amusement, because—(a) Those who say so are incompetent judges, knowing no higher pleasure than Amusement.

sarily, or even usually, beneficial; and partly because princes and their associates, whose happiness the world envies, devote their lives to amusement. Our first object then must be to
4 show that Happiness cannot consist in Amusement. (a) First, those who, as we have said, find their happiness in Amusement have no experience of any higher pleasure. They are no more fit to judge therefore what pleasures are the highest than children are, who for the very same reason prefer Amuse-

tised merely as a duty, *e.g.* because necessary to health, as when they are prescribed to an overworked student by physicians, in which case there is an ulterior result in view and the remarks which follow would not apply. (See *Supplementary Note.*)

3. τῶν εὐδαιμονιζομένων οἱ πολλοὶ] 'The majority of those who are commonly reputed happy.' This was noticed also in I. v. 3.

5. οἱ ἐν ταῖς κ.τ.λ.] 'Those who are skilful in such pastimes,' *i.e.* those who have the art of ministering to their amusement, *e.g.* courtiers, poets, musicians, court-fools, or worse characters.

5, 6. To ἐφίενται and δέονται the nominative is οἱ τύραννοι. To παρέχουσι the nominative is οἱ εὐτράπελοι.

10. σπουδαῖαι ἐνέργειαι] 'active states of excellence,' which may be either Moral or Intellectual (as we have often seen before). ἀρετὴ is here named as the source of the former, νοῦς as that of the latter, condition of activity.

τας οἰητέον αἱρετωτέρας εἶναι· καὶ γὰρ οἱ παῖδες τὰ παρ'
5 αὑτοῖς τιμώμενα κράτιστα οἴονται εἶναι. Εὔλογον δὴ, ὥσπερ παισὶ καὶ ἀνδράσιν ἕτερα φαίνεται τίμια, οὕτω καὶ φαύλοις καὶ ἐπιεικέσιν. Καθάπερ οὖν πολλάκις εἴρηται, καὶ τίμια καὶ ἡδέα ἐστὶ τὰ τῷ σπουδαίῳ τοιαῦτα ὄντα· ἑκάστῳ δὴ ἡ κατὰ τὴν οἰκείαν ἕξιν αἱρετωτάτη ἐν-
6 έργεια, καὶ τῷ σπουδαίῳ δὲ ἡ κατὰ τὴν ἀρετήν. Οὐκ ἐν παιδιᾷ ἄρα ἡ εὐδαιμονία· καὶ γὰρ ἄτοπον τὸ τέλος εἶναι παιδιὰν, καὶ πραγματεύεσθαι καὶ κακοπαθεῖν τὸν βίον ἅπαντα τοῦ παίζειν χάριν. Ἅπαντα γὰρ ὡς εἰπεῖν ἑτέρου ἕνεκα αἱρούμεθα πλὴν τῆς εὐδαιμονίας· τέλος γὰρ αὕτη. Σπουδάζειν δὲ καὶ πονεῖν παιδιᾶς χάριν ἠλίθιον φαίνεται καὶ λίαν παιδικόν· παίζειν δ' ὅπως σπουδάζῃ, κατ' Ἀνάχαρσιν, ὀρθῶς ἔχειν δοκεῖ· ἀναπαύσει γὰρ ἔοικεν ἡ παιδιὰ, ἀδυνατοῦντες δὲ συνεχῶς πονεῖν ἀναπαύσεως δέονται.

ment to anything else. And as there is a difference between the objects held in esteem by childhood and manhood, so there is naturally a difference between the objects held in esteem by
5 good and bad men. The decision of good men (to whom, as often before, we appeal) is, that Happiness depends not on Amusement, but on Virtuous Action, and therefore we con-
6 clude that it does so depend. (β) Besides, is it not absurd to say that we labour and toil all life long for the sake of Amusement, as would be the case if Amusement were Happiness (or the Chief Good)? It is far more rational to regard Amusement as existing for the sake of work (relaxation being sometimes necessary) than work as existing for the sake of Amuse-

(β) Amusement is with a view to work, not work with a view to Amusement

4. πολλάκις εἴρηται] *e.g.* I. viii. 13, and passages quoted in note there.

10. Ἅπαντα γὰρ κ.τ.λ.] Since we may say that Happiness only is desired for its own sake, and *everything* else ultimately for the sake of Happiness, it will follow that if Happiness and Amusement are identical, *everything* we do is with a view to Amusement, which seems a *reductio ad absurdum*.

Οὐ δὴ τέλος ἡ ἀνάπαυσις· γίνεται γὰρ ἕνεκα τῆς ἐνερ-
7 γείας. Δοκεῖ δ' ὁ εὐδαίμων βίος κατ' ἀρετὴν εἶναι· οὗτος
δὲ μετὰ σπουδῆς, ἀλλ' οὐκ ἐν παιδιᾷ. Βελτίω τε λέγομεν τὰ σπουδαῖα τῶν γελοίων καὶ τῶν μετὰ παιδιᾶς, καὶ τοῦ βελτίονος ἀεὶ καὶ μορίου καὶ ἀνθρώπου σπουδαιοτέραν τὴν ἐνέργειαν· ἡ δὲ τοῦ βελτίονος κρείττων καὶ εὐδαιμο-
8 νικωτέρα ἤδη. Ἀπολαύσειέ τ' ἂν τῶν σωματικῶν ἡδονῶν

ment: and if so Amusement ceases to be itself a final end.

(γ) Amusement has no necessary connexion with what is most noble in man.

7 (γ) Again Happiness has been shown to be dependent on Virtue. Now Virtue is a matter not of Amusement but of Earnestness, and every one admits that what is earnest is better than what is amusing, and if it be better, its practice must be nobler and more likely to lead to Happiness. This applies not only to our better, as distinguished from our lower, nature, but also to the better natures among men as dis-
8 tinguished from the inferior. It is clear however that if Happiness should consist in Amusement, the lowest of man-

1. οὐ δὴ τέλος ἡ ἀνάπαυσις] Thus Amusement is in fact after all not even an end desired for its own sake. Recreation is needed for the sake of work, and (as Aristotle says elsewhere) the busier we are the more we need amusement.

ἕνεκα τῆς ἐνεργείας] 'in order that we may be able to work.'

3. μετὰ σπουδῆς = σπουδαῖος, in its literal sense, *i.e.* 'serious,' or 'earnest'; see note on I. viii. 13. Compare Archbp. Whately:—'Happiness is no laughing matter, gay spirits and love of amusement (παιδιὰ) are commonly spoken of as if a proof of Happiness, whereas the reverse is very often, perhaps generally, the case.' They are in fact rather an indication of the absence of repose either of Body or Mind, for which, as Aristotle has just pointed out, Amusement acts as a sort of compensation. This does not apply to the case of children, to whom παιδιὰ is natural, as is admirably expressed by the etymology of the word. Compare also Addison in the *Spectator* (No. 381): 'I have always preferred Cheerfulness to Mirth. The latter I consider as an *act*, the former a *habit*, of the mind. Mirth is short and transient, Cheerfulness fixed and permanent.' (Cf. note on βίος τέλειος, I. vii. 16.)

7. ἤδη here almost = *ipso facto*.

ὁ τυχὼν καὶ ἀνδράποδον οὐχ ἧττον τοῦ ἀρίστου· εὐδαιμονίας δ' οὐδεὶς ἀνδραπόδῳ μεταδίδωσιν, εἰ μὴ καὶ βίου· οὐ γὰρ ἐν ταῖς τοιαύταις διαγωγαῖς ἡ εὐδαιμονία, ἀλλ' ἐν ταῖς κατ' ἀρετὴν ἐνεργείαις, καθάπερ καὶ πρότερον εἴρηται.

1 VII. *Εἰ δ' ἐστὶν ἡ εὐδαιμονία κατ' ἀρετὴν ἐνέργεια, εὔλογον κατὰ τὴν κρατίστην· αὕτη δ' ἂν εἴη τοῦ ἀρίστου.*

kind would be (to say the least) equally capable of it with the noblest, and this is obviously absurd, and inconsistent with what has already been proved. Hence we conclude as before that active Virtue and that alone can form the groundwork of Happiness.

CHAP. VII.—*Pre-eminence of Intellectual over Moral Excellence.*

1 Happiness, being dependent on Virtue or Excellence, is naturally dependent on the highest form of Excellence, viz.

Intellectual Excellence is the highest type of Excellence, for—

2. *εἰ μὴ καὶ βίου*] *Ζωὴ* is mere animal life, in which all, slaves and free, have an equal share. *Βίος* is life viewed in relation to its duties, occupations, and pursuits, and nearly=(as Grant translates) 'career.' This latter, according to Aristotle's notion, a slave could not have. He is merely a passive, though living, instrument in his master's hands. Compare 'A slave is a living machine, a machine is an inanimate slave' (VIII. xi. 6.) 'A slave is a part of his master, he is like a living portion of his body, though separated from the rest' (*Pol.* I. vi.).

Such passages enable us to see how Aristotle denied to a slave any independent career (*βίος*) and consequently any share in Happiness, as defined by his theory. Similarly, it will be remembered, in I. ix. 9, 10, he pronounces children and the lower animals to be incapable of Happiness (see note there). Recollect also that Aristotle maintained that man was formed by nature to be a member of a community (*φύσει πολιτικὸς ἄνθρωπος*), and therefore life severed from the community (as that of a slave was) was necessarily imperfect, and consequently could not be happy (see note on I. vii. 6, *fin.*).

Εἴτε δὴ νοῦς τοῦτο, εἴτε ἄλλο τι, ὃ δὴ κατὰ φύσιν δοκεῖ ἄρχειν καὶ ἡγεῖσθαι καὶ ἔννοιαν ἔχειν περὶ καλῶν καὶ θείων, εἴτε θεῖον ὂν καὶ αὐτὸ, εἴτε τῶν ἐν ἡμῖν τὸ θειότατον, ἡ τούτου ἐνέργεια κατὰ τὴν οἰκείαν ἀρετὴν εἴη ἂν ἡ τελεία εὐδαιμονία. Ὅτι δ' ἐστὶ θεωρητικὴ, εἴρηται.

2 Ὁμολογούμενον δὲ τοῦτ' ἂν δόξειεν εἶναι καὶ τοῖς πρότερον καὶ τῷ ἀληθεῖ. Κρατίστη τε γὰρ αὕτη ἐστὶν ἡ ἐνέργεια· καὶ γὰρ ὁ νοῦς τῶν ἐν ἡμῖν, καὶ τῶν γνωστῶν, περὶ

Excellence of the noblest part of our nature in its highest
developement, whether we call it Intellect or whatever else it
2 be which is most divine in man. Hence to prove that the
highest Happiness consists in Intellectual activity we have the
following arguments:—(*a*) Intellect is the *noblest* part of our

(*a*) It is the excellence of the noblest part of man (κρατίστη).

4. κατὰ τὴν οἰκείαν ἀρετὴν] As Aristotle said in I. vii. 14, *fin.* ἕκαστον εὖ κατὰ τὴν οἰκείαν ἀρετὴν ἀποτελεῖται.

5. θεωρητικὴ] The student must endeavour to form a clear conception of what Aristotle means by θεωρία, θεωρητικὴ, θεωρεῖν, etc., before proceeding further. No one word in English adequately represents the idea. See Glossary under θεωρία, p. xli.

εἴρηται] The nominative is ἡ τούτου (τοῦ νοῦ) ἐνέργεια. The reference is very doubtful. Possibly, speaking from memory, Aristotle may be referring to B. VI., where the functions of νοῦς and of Intellectual Excellence generally are described.

6. καὶ τοῖς πρότερον perhaps refers to I. v. 7, where βίος θεωρητικὸς is mentioned as one of the chief types of life to which Happiness has been held to belong. Though Aristotle does not there assert that this is true, and in fact expressly reserves the consideration of the question, yet as he proves in that chapter that Happiness cannot belong to any of the other types of life enumerated, it may by implication be assigned to this type, viz. βίος θεωρητικός. At any rate it is only said that the statement in the text is 'consistent with' (ὁμολογούμενον) what was said before.

8. νοῦς has been explained in B. VI. to be the faculty by which we are capable of seeing intuitively the truth of Axioms or General Principles. These are the principles from which all demonstrative proof starts, and they are the foundations upon which all scientific knowledge rests. Thus νοῦς is the highest of our intellectual faculties, because it deals with the highest

3 ἃ ὁ νοῦς. Ἔτι δὲ συνεχεστάτη· θεωρεῖν τε γὰρ δυνάμεθα συνεχῶς μᾶλλον ἢ πράττειν ὁτιοῦν, οἰόμεθά τε δεῖν ἡδονὴν παραμεμῖχθαι τῇ εὐδαιμονίᾳ, ἡδίστη δὲ τῶν κατ' ἀρετὴν ἐνεργειῶν ἡ κατὰ τὴν σοφίαν ὁμολογουμένως ἐστίν· δοκεῖ γοῦν ἡ φιλοσοφία θαυμαστὰς ἡδονὰς ἔχειν καθαριότητι καὶ τῷ βεβαίῳ, εὔλογον δὲ τοῖς εἰδόσι τῶν

3 nature, and its objects are also the noblest. (β) Intellectual activity is able to be more *continuous* than any other form of activity. (γ) *Pleasure* is confessedly an ingredient of Happiness, and the palm among pleasures, for purity and perma-

(β) It is most continuous in its activity (συνεχεστάτη).

(γ) It has the purest and most lasting pleasure (ἡδίστη).

and most important of all truths. Moreover it does not *discover* or prove them, but it *recognizes* them, it *sees into* them (θεωρεῖ). Hence the statement made above (see the note on εἴρηται, § 1) that the operation of νοῦς is θεωρητική.

1, 2. θεωρεῖν and πράττειν are emphatic and in contrast.

3. παραμεμῖχθαι] It was explained in I. viii. 10—14 in what sense Aristotle considers pleasure to be an ingredient in Happiness.

ἡδίστη δὲ κ.τ.λ.] Observe the contrast between σοφία and φιλοσοφία. The pleasures of philosophy, or the *pursuit* of Truth, are commonly thought (δοκεῖ) to be of a very high order: confessedly, therefore, the pleasure of the *possession* of Truth (σοφία) must be higher still; for possession (as he proceeds) must be better than pursuit; fruition better than aspiration. Φιλόσοφος was a title first assumed by Pythagoras as being a more modest one than σοφός. He would not call himself 'a wise man,' but a 'lover of wisdom.'

6. εὔλογον τοῖς εἰδόσι κ.τ.λ.] 'It is reasonable to suppose that those who have attained knowledge pass their time more pleasantly than those who are still seeking it.' This, however, is a point much disputed, and the balance of general opinion is perhaps the other way. The saying of Lessing is well known: 'Did the Almighty, holding in his right hand, Truth, and in his left, Search after Truth, offer me the choice, I should prefer in all humility, but without hesitation, Search after Truth.' Pascal (*Pensées*, I. ix. 34) compares the pleasures of the acquisition and the pursuit of knowledge to the pleasures of having won a game, and of actually playing the game. Similarly Butler, (*Sermons*, xv.), 'Whoever will in the least attend to the thing will see that it is the gain-

4 ζητούντων ἡδίω τὴν διαγωγὴν εἶναι. Ἥ τε λεγομένη
αὐτάρκεια περὶ τὴν θεωρητικὴν μάλιστ' ἂν εἴη· τῶν μὲν
γὰρ πρὸς τὸ ζῆν ἀναγκαίων καὶ σοφὸς καὶ δίκαιος καὶ οἱ
λοιποὶ δέονται, τοῖς δὲ τοιούτοις ἱκανῶς κεχορηγημένων
ὁ μὲν δίκαιος δεῖται πρὸς οὓς δικαιοπραγήσει καὶ μεθ' ὧν,
ὁμοίως δὲ καὶ ὁ σώφρων καὶ ὁ ἀνδρεῖος καὶ τῶν ἄλλων
ἕκαστος, ὁ δὲ σοφὸς καὶ καθ' αὑτὸν ὢν δύναται θεωρεῖν,
καὶ ὅσῳ ἂν σοφώτερος ᾖ, μᾶλλον· βέλτιον δ' ἴσως συν-
5 εργοὺς ἔχων, ἀλλ' ὅμως αὐταρκέστατος. Δόξαι τ' ἂν

nence, is allowed to belong to the pleasure of the *pursuit of knowledge*. Still greater then must be the pleasure of the con-
4 scious *possession of knowledge*. (δ) Intellectual activity is most *self-sufficient* and independent of external appliances.
5 (ε) This is the only sort of activity which can be truly said to

(δ) It is most independent of circumstances (αὐταρκεστάτη).

ing, not the having of it (knowledge), which is the entertainment of the mind.' Shakespeare again,—

> 'All things that are,
> Are with more pleasure chased than enjoyed.'

Superior as the pleasures of knowledge are, it may perhaps be true of them as of lower pleasures, that 'pleasure unattained is like the hare we hold in chase, . . . pleasure attained is the same hare hanging up in the sportsman's larder, disregarded, despised, dead' (Horace Smith). Or, once more, in the familiar words of Pope,

> 'Man never is, but always to be, blest.'

It should, however, be remembered that Aristotle uses the words 'possession of knowledge' here in reference to his own doctrine of θεωρία, *i.e.* an *active* fruition not a *passive* possession of it. See this fully explained in the Glossary under θεωρία.

3. σοφὸς is taken as the type of διανοητικὴ ἀρετή, δίκαιος καὶ οἱ λοιποὶ represent ἠθικὴ ἀρετή.

4. κεχορηγημένων] See note on I. viii. 15, ἀχορήγητον ὄντα.

6. The cases of σώφρων and ἀνδρεῖος are further explained in § 4 of next chapter.

7. σοφὸς is not 'wise' in the popular sense, but one who has attained σοφία in the technical sense of the last section, one who has reached the goal of philosophy. The full fruition of σοφία is that θεωρία already explained.

9. In §§ 5-8 Aristotle in the last place argues the superiority of intellectual activity to all

αὐτὴ μόνη δι' αὑτὴν ἀγαπᾶσθαι· οὐδὲν γὰρ ἀπ' αὐτῆς γίνεται παρὰ τὸ θεωρῆσαι, ἀπὸ δὲ τῶν πρακτῶν ἢ πλεῖον
6 ἢ ἔλαττον περιποιούμεθα παρὰ τὴν πρᾶξιν. Δοκεῖ τε ἡ εὐδαιμονία ἐν τῇ σχολῇ εἶναι· ἀσχολούμεθα γὰρ ἵνα σχολάζωμεν, καὶ πολεμοῦμεν ἵν' εἰρήνην ἄγωμεν. Τῶν μὲν οὖν πρακτικῶν ἀρετῶν ἐν τοῖς πολιτικοῖς ἢ ἐν τοῖς πολεμικοῖς ἡ ἐνέργεια· αἱ δὲ περὶ ταῦτα πράξεις δοκοῦσιν ἄσχολοι εἶναι, αἱ μὲν πολεμικαὶ καὶ παντελῶς· οὐδεὶς γὰρ αἱρεῖται τὸ πολεμεῖν τοῦ πολεμεῖν ἕνεκα, οὐδὲ παρασκευάζει πόλεμον· δόξαι γὰρ ἂν παντελῶς μιαιφόνος τις εἶναι, εἰ τοὺς φίλους πολεμίους ποιοῖτο, ἵνα μάχαι καὶ φόνοι γίγνοιντο. Ἔστι δὲ καὶ ἡ τοῦ πολιτικοῦ ἄσχολος, καὶ παρ' αὐτὸ τὸ πολιτεύεσθαι περιποιουμένη

be desired entirely for its own sake: the only sort of activity in
6 which we can repose, and this rest or repose is an essential characteristic of Happiness. Take the most striking developements of practical (as distinguished from intellectual) activity, viz. War and Statesmanship. War is utterly inconsistent with repose, and it is inconceivable that it should be desirable *per se:* it can only be so for its results. To Statesmanship the same remarks apply. It excludes the idea of repose, and its pursuit always implies the ulterior aim of securing for one's-

(ε) It is the only form of activity in which we can absolutely repose (σχολαστική)

other activity, because in it, and in it alone, we can absolutely repose and be satisfied (ἐν τῇ σχολῇ ἐστίν). That this cannot be said of any kind of *action* is proved by taking what are considered the noblest types of action (see beginning of § 7), viz. War and Statesmanship. They are essentially ἄσχολοι (l. 8). We cannot rest in *them*. *A fortiori* we cannot do so in any inferior type of practical activity.

4. ἐν τῇ σχολῇ] Happiness implies repose. This idea is well expressed by Wordsworth:

> Craving peace,
> The central feeling of all happiness,
> Not as a refuge from distress or pain,
> A breathing time, vacation, or a truce,
> But for its absolute self; a life of peace,
> Stability without regret or fear,
> That hath been, is, and shall be evermore.

12. ἡ τοῦ πολιτικοῦ] Understand from the preceding sentence either πρᾶξις or ἐνέργεια.

δυναστείας καὶ τιμὰς ἢ τήν γε εὐδαιμονίαν αὑτῷ καὶ τοῖς πολίταις, ἑτέραν οὖσαν τῆς πολιτικῆς, ἣν καὶ ζητοῦμεν
7 δῆλον ὡς ἑτέραν οὖσαν. Εἰ δὴ τῶν μὲν κατὰ τὰς ἀρετὰς πράξεων αἱ πολιτικαὶ καὶ πολεμικαὶ κάλλει καὶ μεγέθει προέχουσιν, αὗται δ' ἄσχολοι καὶ τέλους τινὸς ἐφίενται καὶ οὐ δι' αὑτὰς αἱρεταί εἰσιν, ἡ δὲ τοῦ νοῦ ἐνέργεια σπουδῇ τε διαφέρειν δοκεῖ θεωρητικὴ οὖσα, καὶ παρ' αὑτὴν οὐδενὸς ἐφίεσθαι τέλους, ἔχειν τε ἡδονὴν οἰκείαν (αὕτη δὲ συναύξει τὴν ἐνέργειαν), καὶ τὸ αὔταρκες δὴ καὶ σχολαστικὸν καὶ ἄτρυτον ὡς ἀνθρώπῳ, καὶ ὅσα ἄλλα τῷ μακαρίῳ ἀπονέμεται, κατὰ ταύτην τὴν ἐνέργειαν φαίνεται ὄντα. Ἡ τελεία δὴ εὐδαιμονία αὕτη ἂν εἴη ἀν-

self or one's country power, honour, or in short Happiness. Happiness then, if an ulterior aim of political life, cannot be
7 identified with it. Intellectual activity then unites all the qualities now enumerated, and, if it be life-long, is the perfect

1. *γε* draws attention to *τὴν εὐδαιμονίαν*. If Happiness itself is an ulterior end of the Statesman's activity, we have the clearest proof that it is not identical with it.

2. *ἑτέραν οὖσαν τῆς πολιτικῆς*] explained by *παρ' αὐτὸ τὸ πολιτεύεσθαι* in I. 13, p. 249. The prosperity which is secured by Statesmanship is obviously something different from the practice of Statesmanship itself: even as peace, the object of war, is different from war. In *θεωρία* or intellectual activity there is no such result separate from the activity itself.

3. § 7 is a recapitulation. *Εἰ δὴ* must be understood with each clause up to that which commences with *καὶ τὸ αὔταρκες δή*, which is the apodosis of the sentence.

7. *σπουδῇ*] 'earnestness,' or 'intensity.'

9. *αὕτη συναύξει τὴν ἐνέργειαν*] 'This (*i.e.* the pleasure of it) helps to intensify the activity itself.'

10. *σχολαστικὸν*] 'capability of affording repose,' in reference to § 6; *ἄτρυτον* (from *τρύω*, to wear) 'freedom from weariness.' See § 3 (*init.*) and last chapter § 6 (*fin.*). *ὡς ἀνθρώπῳ*, 'so far as is possible for man.' Compare the limitation at the end of I. x. *μακαρίους δ' ἀνθρώπους*, 'happy as men.'

θρώπου, λαβοῦσα μῆκος βίου τέλειον· οὐδὲν γὰρ ἀτελές
8 ἐστι τῶν τῆς εὐδαιμονίας. Ὁ δὲ τοιοῦτος ἂν εἴη βίος
κρείττων ἢ κατ᾽ ἄνθρωπον· οὐ γὰρ ᾗ ἄνθρωπός ἐστιν οὔ-
τω βιώσεται, ἀλλ᾽ ᾗ θεῖόν τι ἐν αὐτῷ ὑπάρχει· ὅσῳ δὲ
διαφέρει τοῦτο τοῦ συνθέτου, τοσούτῳ καὶ ἡ ἐνέργεια
τῆς κατὰ τὴν ἄλλην ἀρετήν. Εἰ δὴ θεῖον ὁ νοῦς πρὸς
τὸν ἄνθρωπον, καὶ ὁ κατὰ τοῦτον βίος θεῖος πρὸς τὸν
ἀνθρώπινον βίον. Οὐ χρὴ δὲ κατὰ τοὺς παραινοῦντας
ἀνθρώπινα φρονεῖν ἄνθρωπον ὄντα οὐδὲ θνητὰ τὸν θνη-
τόν, ἀλλ᾽ ἐφ᾽ ὅσον ἐνδέχεται ἀθανατίζειν, καὶ πάντα
ποιεῖν πρὸς τὸ ζῆν κατὰ τὸ κράτιστον τῶν ἐν αὑτῷ· εἰ
γὰρ καὶ τῷ ὄγκῳ μικρόν ἐστι, δυνάμει καὶ τιμιότητι πολὺ
9 μᾶλλον πάντων ὑπερέχει. Δόξειε δ᾽ ἂν καὶ εἶναι ἕκασ-

Such a life is divine rather than human.

8 ideal of Happiness. True, such a life is beyond man's reach.
It is as much beyond such Happiness as he can attain to, as
pure Intellect is beyond our composite and imperfect human
nature. Still we must strive after that perfection which we
can never hope fully to reach, for the life of the Intellect is
the life of that which is not only most divine in man, but
9 which also constitutes each man's true and proper self. From

Still it is most truly human.

1. μῆκος βίου τέλειον] See note on I. vii. 16.

5. τοῦ συνθέτου] 'the whole compound nature of man,'—including not only the divine element of intellect, but the animal body, with its passions, appetites, etc. See next chapter § 3, where this argument is more fully worked out.

8. A favourite maxim of Greek writers: among others Cf. Eur. *Alc.* 799: ὄντας δὲ θνητοὺς θνητὰ καὶ φρονεῖν χρεών.

10. ἀθανατίζειν] 'to act the immortal.' The termination -ίζω often has the force of acting or imitating, without becoming, what the root of the verb implies, *e.g.* Μηδίζω, 'to take the side of the Medes'; Φιλιππίζω, 'to join Philip's party'; σοφίζω, 'to set up to be σοφός.'

12. τῷ ὄγκῳ μικρὸν] literally 'small in its bulk.' This need not necessarily imply that Aristotle believed the intellect (νοῦς) to have 'bulk' at all, *i.e.* to be material, any more than Horace's 'divinæ *particula* auræ.' It is a popular way of speaking.

13. εἶναι ἕκαστος] *i.e.* 'to be

τος τοῦτο, εἴπερ τὸ κύριον καὶ ἄμεινον· ἄτοπον οὖν γίνοιτ' ἄν, εἰ μὴ τὸν αὐτοῦ βίον αἱροῖτο ἀλλά τινος ἄλλου. Τὸ λεχθέν τε πρότερον ἁρμόσει καὶ νῦν· τὸ γὰρ οἰκεῖον ἑκάστῳ τῇ φύσει κράτιστον καὶ ἥδιστόν ἐστιν ἑκάστῳ. Καὶ τῷ ἀνθρώπῳ δὴ ὁ κατὰ τὸν νοῦν βίος, εἴπερ τοῦτο μάλιστα ἄνθρωπος. Οὗτος ἄρα καὶ εὐδαιμονέστατος.

1 VIII. Δευτέρως δ' ὁ κατὰ τὴν ἄλλην ἀρετήν· αἱ γὰρ κατ' αὐτὴν ἐνέργειαι ἀνθρωπικαί· δίκαια γὰρ καὶ ἀνδρεῖα καὶ ἄλλα τὰ κατὰ τὰς ἀρετὰς πρὸς ἀλλήλους πράττομεν ἐν συναλλάγμασι καὶ χρείαις καὶ πράξεσι παντοίαις ἔν τε τοῖς πάθεσι διατηροῦντες τὸ πρέπον ἑκάστῳ. Ταῦτα δ' εἶναι φαίνεται πάντα ἀνθρωπικά.
2 Ἔνια δὲ καὶ συμβαίνειν ἀπὸ τοῦ σώματος δοκεῖ, καὶ πολλὰ συνῳκειῶσθαι

this point of view no other life could be so truly natural to man, nor, by consequence, so truly happy.

CHAP. VIII.—*Secondary position of Moral Excellence.*

Conversely, we may show that Moral Excellence holds a secondary place, for—(i) It is essentially human, and never can be more than this.

1 Thus far we have shown how Intellectual Excellence holds the first place. We can also bring positive arguments to prove that Moral Excellence as compared with it holds a secondary place in regard to Happiness. (i) First, it is *essentially human*, and bound up with all the imperfections of man's composite nature. In proof of this—(α) Justice, Courage, and other Moral Virtues in detail, have for the sphere of their action the circumstances of ordinary human
2 life. (β) Some Moral Virtues would have no meaning apart

each man's self,' 'to constitute personality.' Not a man's features, or his body, or his appetites, or his passions, but his intellect, is his proper self, which distinguishes him from all other men, and all other beings whatsoever. τουτο μαλιστα ἄνθρωπος in l. 5 has the same meaning.

2. τινος ἄλλου is neuter, 'of something else.'

3. τὸ λεχθὲν πρότερον] viz. I. ix. 5.

7. Δευτέρως δὲ . . . ἀρετὴν] Understand βίος εὐδαίμων ἐστίν.

13. πολλὰ συνῳκειῶσθαι τοῖς πάθεσι] 'has many points of connexion with the feelings,'

3 τοῖς πάθεσιν ἡ τοῦ ἤθους ἀρετή. Συνέζευκται δὲ καὶ ἡ φρόνησις τῇ τοῦ ἤθους ἀρετῇ, καὶ αὕτη τῇ φρονήσει, εἴπερ αἱ μὲν τῆς φρονήσεως ἀρχαὶ κατὰ τὰς ἠθικάς εἰσιν ἀρετάς, τὸ δ' ὀρθὸν τῶν ἠθικῶν κατὰ τὴν φρόνησιν. Συνηρτημέναι δ' αὗται καὶ τοῖς πάθεσι περὶ τὸ σύνθετον ἂν εἶεν· αἱ δὲ τοῦ συνθέτου ἀρεταὶ ἀνθρωπικαί. Καὶ ὁ βίος δὴ ὁ κατ' αὐτὰς καὶ ἡ εὐδαιμονία. Ἡ δὲ τοῦ νοῦ

3 from the existence of a body and bodily appetites. (γ) Practical Wisdom, though a sort of crown to all the Moral Virtues, is, together with them, concerned with our passions, and therefore with the imperfections of our composite nature. Hence we conclude that any Happiness depending on Moral Excel-

and therefore with our bodily nature.

2. *φρόνησις* here as elsewhere is opposed to *σοφία*, as practical wisdom is opposed to speculative or theoretical. See note on II. vi. 15.

In B. VI. it has been shown that there can be no virtue without this practical wisdom (*φρόνησις*), which is the guiding principle or intellectual side of all the Moral Virtues, and conversely that the possession of this practical wisdom implies the possession of all the Moral Virtues in detail, for, if practical, it must proceed to action. Hence the intimate connexion now asserted in the text between *φρόνησις* and *ἠθικαὶ ἀρεταί*, and of both together with the passions and appetites of our nature, which it is their whole aim to regulate. The purpose of the argument is to show the inferiority of practical wisdom (*φρόνησις*), whose activity is *ἠθικὴ ἀρετή*, to intellectual wisdom (*σοφία*), whose activity is *θεωρία*. *Φρόνησις* being (in the sense explained) the crown of all Moral Excellences, as *σοφία* is of all Intellectual, the two classes are fitly contrasted under their highest types. Hence *καὶ ἡ φρόνησις*, '*even* practical wisdom.'

5. *συνηρτημέναι*] literally, 'And these are linked also with the feelings around our composite nature.' Practical wisdom, and with it all Moral Excellence, are bound up with the affections (see II. iii. 3, etc. etc.), and therefore imply the imperfections of the lower part of our composite human nature, and thus never can be more than human.

7. *ἡ εὐδαιμονία*] understand *ἡ κατ' αὐτάς*.

ἡ δὲ τοῦ νοῦ] sc. *εὐδαιμονία*. *κεχωρισμένη* sc. *τῶν παθέων* from the preceding sentence, *κεχωρισμένη* being opposed to *συνηρτημέναι*.

κεχωρισμένη· τοσοῦτον γὰρ περὶ αὐτῆς εἰρήσθω· διακρι-
4 *βῶσαι γὰρ μεῖζον τοῦ προκειμένου ἐστίν. Δόξειε δ' ἂν*
καὶ τῆς ἐκτὸς χορηγίας ἐπὶ μικρὸν ἢ ἐπ' ἔλαττον δεῖσθαι τῆς ἠθικῆς· τῶν μὲν γὰρ ἀναγκαίων ἀμφοῖν χρεία καὶ ἐξ ἴσου ἔστω, εἰ καὶ μᾶλλον διαπονεῖ περὶ τὸ σῶμα ὁ πολιτικός, καὶ ὅσα τοιαῦτα· μικρὸν γὰρ ἄν τι διαφέροι· πρὸς δὲ τὰς ἐνεργείας πολὺ διοίσει. Τῷ μὲν γὰρ ἐλευθερίῳ δεήσει χρημάτων πρὸς τὸ πράττειν τὰ ἐλευθέρια, καὶ τῷ δικαίῳ δὴ εἰς τὰς ἀνταποδόσεις (αἱ γὰρ βουλήσεις ἄδηλοι, προσποιοῦνται δὲ καὶ οἱ μὴ δίκαιοι βούλεσθαι δικαιοπραγεῖν), τῷ ἀνδρείῳ δὲ δυνάμεως, εἴπερ ἐπιτελεῖ τι τῶν κατὰ τὴν ἀρετήν, καὶ τῷ σώφρονι ἐξουσίας·
5 *πῶς γὰρ δῆλος ἔσται ἢ οὗτος ἢ τῶν ἄλλων τις; ἀμφισ-*
βητεῖται δὲ πότερον κυριώτερον τῆς ἀρετῆς ἡ προαίρεσις

lence can never be more than merely human Happiness.

(ii) It is more or less dependent on external circumstances.

4 ii. While under no circumstances can the body and its welfare be wholly neglected, yet Moral, as compared with Intellectual, Excellence has much greater need of external circumstances, regarding at any rate the active exercise of each. Moral Virtue cannot be practised, nor Moral Character mani-
5 fested, without favourable circumstances; and the more ex-

2. This is the converse aspect of the argument in § 4 of the last ch.

7. *πρὸς δὲ τὰς ἐνεργείας*] 'for their respective activities, there will be a great difference,' viz. for those of Moral and Intellectual Excellence.

11. *δυνάμεως*] 'power' or 'strength,' *e.g.* a cripple or paralytic could not display active courage (*ἐπιτελεῖν τὰ κατὰ τὴν ἀρετήν*).

12. *ἐξουσία*] 'opportunity' or 'license to indulge.' There would be no outward difference between the teetotaller and the drunkard if there were nothing but water to be had.

14. *ἀμφισβητεῖται δὲ πότερον κ.τ.λ.*] The importance of intention (*προαίρεσις*) was insisted on in III. ii. 1, *μᾶλλον τὰ ἤθη κρίνειν τῶν πράξεων*. '(Intention) is a greater test of character than actions are.' So also in II. iv. 3, where the conditions necessary to a virtuous act were enumerated; and among them is a deliberate resolution arising from pure motives, etc.

ἢ αἱ πράξεις, ὡς ἐν ἀμφοῖν οὔσης. Τὸ δὴ τέλειον δῆλον
ὡς ἐν ἀμφοῖν ἂν εἴη. Πρὸς δὲ τὰς πράξεις πολλῶν δεῖ-
ται καὶ ὅσῳ ἂν μείζους ὦσι καὶ καλλίους, πλειόνων.
6 Τῷ δὲ θεωροῦντι οὐδενὸς τῶν τοιούτων πρός γε τὴν
ἐνέργειαν χρεία, ἀλλ' ὡς εἰπεῖν καὶ ἐμπόδιά ἐστι πρός
γε τὴν θεωρίαν· ᾗ δ' ἄνθρωπός ἐστι καὶ πλείοσι συζῇ,
αἱρεῖται τὰ κατ' ἀρετὴν πράττειν· δεήσεται οὖν τῶν
7 τοιούτων πρὸς τὸ ἀνθρωπεύεσθαι. Ἡ δὲ τελεία εὐδαι-
μονία ὅτι θεωρητική τις ἐστὶν ἐνέργεια, καὶ ἐντεῦθεν ἂν
φανείη. Τοὺς θεοὺς γὰρ μάλιστα ὑπειλήφαμεν μακα-
ρίους καὶ εὐδαίμονας εἶναι· πράξεις δὲ ποίας ἀπονεῖμαι
χρεὼν αὐτοῖς; πότερα τὰς δικαίας; ἢ γελοῖοι φανοῦν-

cellent the Virtue, the more numerous are the circumstances
6 required for its full development. All such circumstances
are to Contemplation only hindrances, even when they cannot
7 be dispensed with. iii. Finally, only Intellectual Excellence
can be attributed to the gods: for—(α) There are no circum-
stances under which they could exercise some of the Moral

(iii) It cannot be attributed to the gods.

4. Observe the limiting and emphasizing force of γε here and in l. 6.

6. ᾗ δ' ἄνθρωπος κ.τ.λ.] In actual human life intellectual activity cannot rightly be severed from moral practice. So that the philosopher, like others, stands in need of these external appliances for the exercise of Virtue. He does not however need them *as a philosopher*, but as a man among men, nor with a view to his peculiar work, intellectual activity. On the contrary, though otherwise necessary, to it they are only impediments.

8. ἀνθρωπεύειν 'to be a man,' ἀνθρωπεύεσθαι 'to act one's part as a man.' The same difference exists between the active and middle of many similar words, *e.g.* δουλεύω, πρεσβεύω, πολιτεύω, etc. So in III. vi. 12 ἀνδρίζεσθαι 'to play the man.'

9. ἐντεῦθεν] The outline of the argument is—All activity must be either πρακτική, or ποιητική, or θεωρητική. The two former cannot be assigned to the gods who are supremely happy, and yet they live, and live actively too. Hence their activity must be θεωρητική, an intellectual or contemplative activity.

ται συναλλάττοντες καὶ παρακαταθήκας ἀποδιδόντες καὶ ὅσα τοιαῦτα; ἀλλὰ τὰς ἀνδρείους, ὑπομένοντας τὰ φοβερὰ καὶ κινδυνεύοντας, ὅτι καλόν; ἢ τὰς ἐλευθερίους; τίνι δὲ δώσουσιν; ἄτοπον δ' εἰ καὶ ἔσται αὐτοῖς νόμισμα ἤ τι τοιοῦτον. Αἱ δὲ σώφρονες τί ἂν εἶεν; ἢ φορτικὸς ὁ ἔπαινος, ὅτι οὐκ ἔχουσι φαύλας ἐπιθυμίας; διεξιοῦσι δὲ πάντα φαίνοιτ' ἂν τὰ περὶ τὰς πράξεις μικρὰ καὶ ἀνάξια θεῶν. Ἀλλὰ μὴν ζῆν τε πάντες ὑπειλήφασιν αὐτοὺς καὶ ἐνεργεῖν ἄρα· οὐ γὰρ δὴ καθεύδειν ὥσπερ

Virtues: (β) They have none of those moral imperfections which others presuppose: (γ) If moral activity, and *a fortiori* productive activity, be excluded, there is only intellectual activity left. Therefore the activity of the gods, whose life is essentially a most blessed one, is contemplative or intellectual.

5. φορτικὸς] 'gross,' or 'degrading'; see note on I. v. 1.

6. διεξιοῦσι δὲ πάντα κ.τ.λ.] Of the precise sense in which these Virtues are exercised in our experience the statement in the text is obviously true, Virtue being, as has been said, 'goodness in a state of warfare.' Whether there may not be a higher sense and a different sphere of action in which analogous Moral Virtues may be attributed to the Deity is another question, which the argument here leaves untouched. After all it is to some extent a question depending (1) on the precise meaning of the Greek words δίκαιος, σώφρων, etc., as was the case in reference to ἔπαινος being inapplicable to the gods—see I. xii. 3. Also (2) still more on the Greek conception of the Divine nature, for which see Glossary *s.v.* θεὸς and φύσις. We may well compare Butler's argument, Anal. i. c. v. (p. 97, Angus's edition). 'Nor is our ignorance what will be the employments of that happy community, nor our consequent ignorance what particular scope or occasion there will be for the exercise of veracity, justice, and charity amongst the members of it with regard to each other any proof that there will be no sphere of exercise for those virtues. Much less, if that were possible, is our ignorance any proof that there will be no occasion for that frame of mind or character which is formed by the practice of those particular virtues and which is a result of it,' etc

τὸν Ἐνδυμίωνα. Τῷ δὴ ζῶντι τοῦ πράττειν ἀφαιρουμένου, ἔτι δὲ μᾶλλον τοῦ ποιεῖν, τί λείπεται πλὴν θεωρία; ὥστε ἡ τοῦ θεοῦ ἐνέργεια, μακαριότητι διαφέρουσα, θεωρητικὴ ἂν εἴη. Καὶ τῶν ἀνθρωπίνων δὴ ἡ ταύτῃ
8 συγγενεστάτη εὐδαιμονικωτάτη. Σημεῖον δὲ καὶ τὸ μὴ μετέχειν τὰ λοιπὰ ζῶα εὐδαιμονίας, τῆς τοιαύτης ἐνεργείας ἐστερημένα τελείως. Τοῖς μὲν γὰρ θεοῖς ἅπας ὁ βίος μακάριος, τοῖς δ' ἀνθρώποις, ἐφ' ὅσον ὁμοίωμά τι τῆς τοιαύτης ἐνεργείας ὑπάρχει· τῶν δ' ἄλλων ζώων οὐδὲν εὐδαιμονεῖ, ἐπειδὴ οὐδαμῇ κοινωνεῖ θεωρίας. Ἐφ' ὅσον δὴ διατείνει ἡ θεωρία, καὶ ἡ εὐδαιμονία, καὶ οἷς μᾶλλον ὑπάρχει το θεωρεῖν, καὶ εὐδαιμονεῖν, οὐ κατὰ συμβεβηκος ἀλλὰ κατα τὴν θεωρίαν· αὐτὴ γὰρ καθ' αὑτὴν τιμία. Ὥστ' εἴη ἂν ἡ εὐδαιμονία θεωρία τις.

Hence we infer that as men approach to this ideal their
8 Happiness is highest. Indeed we find a complete scale of corresponding degrees between Happiness and the capacity for intellectual activity. In the lower animals both are totally absent. In the gods, both are present in perfection. Among men, both exist imperfectly, but in exact proportion to each other: and we affirm that this correspondence is not accidental, but that it implies an essential connexion between

1. *τοῦ πράττειν* 'moral action,' *τοῦ ποιεῖν* 'productive, or creative, action.' (See Glossary *s.v.* *πρᾶξις, ποίησις.*) The former has been excluded by the arguments in § 7. As to the latter, it is clear from this passage as well as many others that Aristotle did not believe in God as a Creator in our sense of the word. He would consider such work as unworthy of him (*φορτικὸν*), inconsistent with the perfection of His nature and mode of existence. See further Glossary *s.v.* *θεὸς—φύσις.*

10. *οὐδὲν εὐδαιμονεῖ*] See note on I. ix. 9.

The argument of § 8 closely resembles the process of Modern Induction called by Bacon 'The Scale of Degrees,' 'Tabula graduum,' or by Mill, 'The Method of Concomitant Variations.'

13. *αὐτὴ γὰρ*] 'For this in itself (*i.e.* *θεωρία*) is essentially ad-

9 Δεήσει δὲ καὶ τῆς ἐκτὸς εὐημερίας ἀνθρώπῳ ὄντι· οὐ
γὰρ αὐτάρκης ἡ φύσις πρὸς τὸ θεωρεῖν, ἀλλὰ δεῖ καὶ τὸ
σῶμα ὑγιαίνειν καὶ τροφὴν καὶ τὴν λοιπὴν θεραπείαν
ὑπάρχειν. Οὐ μὴν οἰητέον γε πολλῶν καὶ μεγάλων δεή-
σεσθαι τὸν εὐδαιμονήσοντα, εἰ μὴ ἐνδέχεται ἄνευ τῶν
ἐκτὸς ἀγαθῶν μακάριον εἶναι· οὐ γὰρ ἐν τῇ ὑπερβολῇ τὸ
αὔταρκες οὐδ' ἡ πρᾶξις, δυνατὸν δὲ καὶ μὴ ἄρχοντα γῆς
10 καὶ θαλάττης πράττειν τὰ καλά· καὶ γὰρ ἀπὸ μετρίων
δύναιτ' ἄν τις πράττειν κατὰ τὴν ἀρετήν. Τοῦτο δ' ἔστιν
ἰδεῖν ἐναργῶς· οἱ γὰρ ἰδιῶται τῶν δυναστῶν οὐχ ἧττον
δοκοῦσι τὰ ἐπιεικῆ πράττειν, ἀλλὰ καὶ μᾶλλον. Ἱκα-
νὸν δὲ τοσαῦθ' ὑπάρχειν, ἔσται γὰρ ὁ βίος εὐδαίμων τοῦ
11 κατὰ τὴν ἀρετὴν ἐνεργοῦντος. Καὶ Σόλων δὲ τοὺς εὐδαί-
μονας ἴσως ἀπεφαίνετο καλῶς, εἰπὼν μετρίως τοῖς ἐκτὸς
κεχορηγημένους, πεπραγότας δὲ τὰ κάλλισθ', ὡς ᾤετο,

Happiness and Intellectual activity. And therefore again we assert that the highest Happiness is Intellectual.

Human Happiness cannot dispense with a moderate degree of external prosperity.

9 To descend once more to practical details. For man this continuous activity of Intellect only is a practical impossibility. He cannot be independent of some amount of external advan-
10 tages. That that amount, however, is not excessive, but mode-
11 rate, theory, experience, and the teaching of the wisest among

mirable,' a characteristic proved to belong to Happiness also in I. xii.

§§ 9-13. The concluding Sections recur to some practical questions connected with the conclusion now reached: the relation of Happiness to external circumstances; the concurrence of Aristotle's theory with those of previous philosophers, and, what is still more important, with facts; the superiority of Happiness as now defined, owing to the good-will of heaven favouring that life which is 'likest God's.'

3. τὴν λοιπὴν θεραπείαν = 'the other care that the body needs,' besides the securing of mere health and sustenance. μὴν in the next sentence is corrective. We must not take this 'θεραπεία' to include too much.

6. ὑπερβολῇ] Understand τῶν ἐκτὸς ἀγαθῶν.

καὶ βεβιωκότας σωφρόνως· ἐνδέχεται γὰρ μέτρια κεκτημένους πράττειν ἃ δεῖ. Ἔοικε δὲ καὶ Ἀναξαγόρας οὐ πλούσιον οὐδὲ δυνάστην ὑπολαβεῖν τὸν εὐδαίμονα, εἰπὼν ὅτι οὐκ ἂν θαυμάσειεν εἴ τις ἄτοπος φανείη τοῖς πολλοῖς· οὗτοι γὰρ κρίνουσι τοῖς ἐκτὸς, τούτων αἰσθανόμενοι μό-
12 νον. Συμφωνεῖν δὴ τοῖς λόγοις ἐοίκασιν αἱ τῶν σοφῶν
δόξαι. Πίστιν μὲν οὖν καὶ τὰ τοιαῦτα ἔχει τινά, τὸ δ' ἀληθὲς ἐν τοῖς πρακτοῖς ἐκ τῶν ἔργων καὶ τοῦ βίου κρίνεται· ἐν τούτοις γὰρ τὸ κύριον. Σκοπεῖν δὴ τὰ προειρημένα χρὴ ἐπὶ τὰ ἔργα καὶ τὸν βίον ἐπιφέροντας, καὶ συνᾳδόντων μὲν τοῖς ἔργοις ἀποδεκτέον, διαφωνούντων δὲ
13 λόγους ὑποληπτέον. Ὁ δὲ κατὰ νοῦν ἐνεργῶν καὶ τοῦ-
τον θεραπεύων καὶ διακείμενος ἄριστα καὶ θεοφιλέστατος ἔοικεν εἶναι· εἰ γάρ τις ἐπιμέλεια τῶν ἀνθρωπίνων ὑπὸ θεῶν γίνεται, ὥσπερ δοκεῖ, καὶ εἴη ἂν εὔλογον χαίρειν τε

12 men, combine to show. Still whatever weight we may assign to the authority of the wise, the last appeal must be to facts, and to the practical experience of life. To this tribunal we would refer all that has been asserted in the course of this
13 treatise. One more practical consideration we subjoin. If, as is generally believed, the gods regard the affairs of men, they will naturally love and favour those who are most like

Those whom the gods love best, viz. the wise, are naturally the happiest

2. Ἀναξαγόρας οὐ πλούσιον] Anaxagoras of Clazomenæ, in Ionia, resigned all his property to his relations and gave himself up to philosophical study for some thirty years at Athens.

6. τοῖς λόγοις = our definitions or theories.

7. μὲν οὖν, as usual, fixes a strong emphasis on the preceding word, and thus marks a contrast between πίστιν and τὸ ἀληθές. 'Some *ground for belief* may be afforded by such a *consensus*, but the test of *actual truth* is to be derived in practical subjects from facts and from life.' Cf. Shakespeare, *Henry V.* Act. I. Sc. i.:

> So that the art and practic part of life
> Must be the mistress to this theoric.

12. λόγους ὑποληπτέον] 'we must take them to be mere theories.'

αὐτοὺς τῷ ἀρίστῳ καὶ τῷ συγγενεστάτῳ (τοῦτο δ' ἂν εἴη ὁ νοῦς) καὶ τοὺς ἀγαπῶντας μάλιστα τοῦτο καὶ τιμῶντας ἀντευποιεῖν ὡς τῶν φίλων αὐτοῖς ἐπιμελουμένους καὶ ὀρθῶς τε καὶ καλῶς πράττοντας. Ὅτι δὲ πάντα ταῦτα τῷ σοφῷ μάλισθ' ὑπάρχει, οὐκ ἄδηλον. Θεοφιλέστατος ἄρα. Τὸν αὐτὸν δ' εἰκὸς καὶ εὐδαιμονέστατον· ὥστε κἂν οὕτως εἴη ὁ σοφὸς μάλιστ' εὐδαίμων.

1 IX. Ἆρ' οὖν εἰ περὶ τούτων καὶ τῶν ἀρετῶν, ἔτι δὲ καὶ φιλίας καὶ ἡδονῆς ἱκανῶς εἴρηται τοῖς τύποις, τέλος ἔχειν οἰητέον τὴν προαίρεσιν, ἢ καθάπερ λέγεται, οὐκ ἔστιν ἐν τοῖς πρακτοῖς τέλος τὸ θεωρῆσαι ἕκαστα καὶ γνῶναι, ἀλ-

themselves. Such are those in whom Intellect and Wisdom are most developed. And all will admit that the greatest Happiness will be found in those whom the gods love best. Therefore from this practical point of view also, the highest Happiness is linked with Wisdom or Intellectual Activity.

CHAP. IX.—*Conclusion of the Treatise on Ethics, and transition to the Complementary Science of Politics.*

In conclusion we must apply our theories to practice.

1 This sketch of Virtue and subjects akin to it might now be concluded, except that no theory on such matters can be con-

CHAP. IX.—This Chapter forms a general conclusion to the whole treatise. When we turn from theory to practice, Ethics must look for some authority to enforce its injunctions on those who will not hear. Failing the intervention of the State, Parental authority must take its place. In either case a scientific study of Politics or of the principles of Statesmanship is a necessary sequel to that of Ethics, if theory is to be carried on to practice at all. In the absence of any accessible means for such a study Aristotle proposes to write a treatise on the subject himself, and the concluding words of the Book lead us at once to the commencement of his treatise on Politics.

10. *οὐκ ἔστιν ἐν τοῖς πρακτοῖς κ.τ.λ.*] Compare I. iii. 6, *τὸ τέλος οὐ γνῶσις ἀλλὰ πρᾶξις*: also II. ii. 1, and many other passages.

2 λὰ μᾶλλον τὸ πράττειν αὐτά; οὐδὲ δὴ περὶ ἀρετῆς ἱκανὸν τὸ εἰδέναι, ἀλλ' ἔχειν καὶ χρῆσθαι πειρατέον, ἢ εἴ
3 πως ἄλλως ἀγαθοὶ γινόμεθα. Εἰ μὲν οὖν ἦσαν οἱ λόγοι αὐτάρκεις πρὸς τὸ ποιῆσαι ἐπιεικεῖς, πολλοὺς ἂν μισθοὺς καὶ μεγάλους δικαίως ἔφερον κατὰ τὸν Θέογνιν, καὶ ἔδει ἂν τούτους πορίσασθαι· νῦν δὲ φαίνονται προτρέψασθαι μὲν καὶ παρορμῆσαι τῶν νέων τοὺς ἐλευθερίους ἰσχύειν, ἦθός τ' εὐγενὲς καὶ ὡς ἀληθῶς φιλόκαλον ποιῆσαι ἂν κατοκώχιμον ἐκ τῆς ἀρετῆς, τοὺς δὲ πολλοὺς ἀδυνατεῖν πρὸς
4 καλοκαγαθίαν προτρέψασθαι· οὐ γὰρ πεφύκασιν αἰδοῖ πειθαρχεῖν ἀλλὰ φόβῳ, οὐδ' ἀπέχεσθαι τῶν φαύλων διὰ τὸ αἰσχρὸν ἀλλὰ διὰ τὰς τιμωρίας· πάθει γὰρ ζῶντες τὰς οἰκείας ἡδονὰς διώκουσι καὶ δι' ὧν αὗται ἔσονται, φεύγουσι δὲ τὰς ἀντικειμένας λύπας, τοῦ δὲ καλοῦ καὶ ὡς ἀληθῶς ἡδέος οὐδ' ἔννοιαν ἔχουσιν, ἄγευστοι ὄντες.
5 Τοὺς δὴ τοιούτους τίς ἂν λόγος μεταρρυθμίσαι; οὐ γὰρ οἷόν τε ἢ οὐ ῥᾴδιον τὰ ἐκ παλαιοῦ τοῖς ἤθεσι κατειλημ-

2 sidered complete until it is connected with practice. Mere
3 theories of Virtue can never make men good, unless they are previously disposed to goodness. On the majority of man-
4 kind such theories have no effect whatever. With them we must appeal not to shame but to the fear of punishment: pleasure is all they seek, pain the only thing they avoid: these therefore are the only feelings through which we can
5 influence them. Virtue is in truth hard enough to attain to, even when all circumstances are favourable; if they are otherwise, the voice of the teacher is powerless.

Moral theories have no influence except on those already fitted to receive them.

2. ἢ εἴ πως ἄλλως] 'or by any other means that there may be'—other, that is, than ἔχειν καὶ χρῆσθαι.

5. Theognis made this remark in reference to the dignity of the physician's calling, if only the gods should have enabled him to heal the minds and characters of men as well as their bodies.

8. κατοκώχιμον (κατέχω) = 'capable of being influenced or restrained by.'

17. τοῖς ἤθεσι κατειλημμένα]

μένα λόγῳ μεταστῆσαι. Ἀγαπητὸν δ᾽ ἴσως ἐστὶν εἰ πάντων ὑπαρχόντων δι᾽ ὧν ἐπιεικεῖς δοκοῦμεν γίνεσθαι,
6 μεταλάβοιμεν τῆς ἀρετῆς. Γίνεσθαι δ᾽ ἀγαθοὺς οἴονται, οἱ μὲν φύσει, οἱ δ᾽ ἔθει, οἱ δὲ διδαχῇ. Τὸ μὲν οὖν τῆς φύσεως δῆλον ὡς οὐκ ἐφ᾽ ἡμῖν ὑπάρχει, ἀλλὰ διά τινας θείας αἰτίας τοῖς ὡς ἀληθῶς εὐτυχέσιν ὑπάρχει· ὁ δὲ λόγος καὶ ἡ διδαχὴ μισεῖν,' οὐκ ἐν ἅπασιν ἰσχύῃ, ἀλλὰ δέῃ προδιειργάσθαι τοῖς ἔθεσι τὴν τοῦ ἀκροατοῦ ψυχὴν πρὸς τὸ καλῶς χαίρειν καὶ μισεῖν, ὥσπερ γῆν τὴν θρέψουσαν τὸ σπέρμα.
7 Οὐ γὰρ ἂν ἀκούσειε λόγου ἀποτρέποντος οὐδ᾽ αὖ συνείη ὁ κατὰ πάθος ζῶν· τὸν δ᾽ οὕτως

The acquisition of Virtue depends on Disposition, Training, Teaching.

6 Now there are three courses, as it is commonly held, by which men arrive at Virtue. (1) Natural disposition; (2) Moral training; (3) Intellectual teaching. The first is clearly beyond our control. As to the last, its influence varies in different cases, and depends on the hearer's mind having been previously prepared,
7 like soil for the seed. Passion when supreme will not hear, and indeed cannot understand, any argument but that of force.

'firmly fixed in the character.' For a similar statement cf. II. iii. 8, χαλεπὸν ἀποτρίψασθαι πάθος ἐγκεχρωσμένον τῷ βίῳ. Also compare the expression συνειλημμένα μετὰ τῆς φαυλότητος in II. vi. 18.

4. φύσει . . . ἔθει . . . διδαχῇ] We might compare the various causes suggested in I. ix. for the acquisition of Happiness: πότερόν ἐστι μαθητὸν (= διδάχῃ), ἢ ἐθιστὸν ἢ ἄλλως πως ἀσκητὸν (= ἔθει), ἢ κατά τινα θείαν μοῖραν ἢ καὶ διὰ τύχην (= φύσει).

6. τοῖς ὡς ἀληθῶς εὐτυχέσιν] 'those who are in the truest sense fortunate.' Compare III. v. 17, τὸ εὖ καὶ τὸ καλῶς τοῦτο πεφυκέναι ἡ τελεία καὶ ἀληθινὴ ἂν εἴη εὐφυΐα.

7. ἡ διδαχὴ] Aristotle is perhaps led to lay stress on the inadequacy of mere intellectual teaching in Morals, on account of the undue prominence given to it by Plato, who held all Virtue to be (1) intellectual, (2) διδακτόν. The words μή ποτ᾽ οὐ introduce the statement in a suggestive form, and almost = 'perhaps,' or 'it would seem that.'

8. προδιειργάσθαι] διεργάζομαι is similarly used by Theophrastus for the 'tilling' of land.

11. οὐδ᾽ αὖ συνείη] 'he could

ἔχοντα πῶς οἷόν τε μεταπεῖσαι; ὅλως τ' οὐ δοκεῖ λόγῳ
8 ὑπείκειν τὸ πάθος ἀλλὰ βίᾳ. Δεῖ δὴ τὸ ἦθος προϋπάρχειν πως οἰκεῖον τῆς ἀρετῆς, στέργον τὸ καλὸν καὶ δυσχεραῖνον τὸ αἰσχρόν. Ἐκ νέου δ' ἀγωγῆς ὀρθῆς τυχεῖν πρὸς ἀρετὴν χαλεπὸν μὴ ὑπὸ τοιούτοις τραφέντα νόμοις· τὸ γὰρ σωφρόνως καὶ καρτερικῶς ζῆν οὐχ ἡδὺ τοῖς πολλοῖς, ἄλλως τε καὶ νέοις. Διὸ νόμοις δεῖ τετάχθαι τὴν τροφὴν καὶ τὰ ἐπιτηδεύματα· οὐκ
9 ἔσται γὰρ λυπηρὰ συνήθη γινόμενα. Οὐχ ἱκανὸν δ' ἴσως νέους ὄντας τροφῆς καὶ ἐπιμελείας τυχεῖν ὀρθῆς, ἀλλ' ἐπειδὴ καὶ ἀνδρωθέντας δεῖ ἐπιτηδεύειν αὐτὰ καὶ ἐθίζεσθαι, καὶ περὶ ταῦτα δεοίμεθ' ἂν νόμων, καὶ ὅλως δὴ περὶ πάντα τὸν βίον· οἱ γὰρ πολλοὶ ἀνάγκῃ μᾶλλον
10 ἢ λόγῳ πειθαρχοῦσι καὶ ζημίαις ἢ τῷ καλῷ. Διόπερ οἴονταί τινες τοὺς νομοθετοῦντας δεῖν μὲν παρακαλεῖν ἐπὶ τὴν ἀρετὴν καὶ προτρέπεσθαι τοῦ καλοῦ χάριν, ὡς

8 The second of the courses above named therefore alone remains: Moral training is our necessary starting-point in the formation of childhood so in; such training moreover must begin in childhood, and it can only be secured by the authority of Law; for it must always be a painful process till we become
9 accustomed to it, and especially so in youth. Moreover the majority of men (who yield only to force and to the fear of punishment) need to have their conduct and occupations thus regulated for them not in youth only but all through life.
10 Hence it has been thought to be the duty of a legislator to

We must begin with Moral training, and that must be enforced by external authority.

not even understand.' See note on I. iv. 6 (διὸ δεῖ τοῖς ἔθεσιν ἦχθαι κ.τ.λ.), and cf. οὐδ' ἔννοιαν ἔχουσιν, ἄγευστοι ὄντες, in § 4 of this Chapter.

13. περὶ πάντα τὸν βίον] For, as Aristotle says in I. iii. 7, διαφέρει δ' οὐθὲν νέος τὴν ἡλικίαν ἢ τὸ ἦθος νεαρός· οὐ γὰρ παρὰ τὸν χρόνον ἡ ἔλλειψις.

14. διόπερ οἴονταί τινες κ.τ.λ.] Ancient and modern views of legislation are in marked contrast in this respect. See note on I. xiii. 3, and cf. V. xi. 1, ὁ νόμος ἃ μὴ κελεύει ἀπαγο-

ὑπακουσομένων τῶν ἐπιεικῶς τοῖς ἔθεσι προηγμένων, ἀπειθοῦσι δὲ καὶ ἀφυεστέροις οὖσι κολάσεις τε καὶ τιμωρίας ἐπιτιθέναι, τοὺς δ' ἀνιάτους ὅλως ἐξορίζειν· τὸν μὲν γὰρ ἐπιεικῆ καὶ πρὸς τὸ καλὸν ζῶντα τῷ λόγῳ πειθαρχήσειν, τὸν δὲ φαῦλον ἡδονῆς ὀρεγόμενον λύπῃ κολάζεσθαι ὥσπερ ὑποζύγιον. Διὸ καί φασι δεῖν τοιαύτας γίνεσθαι τὰς λύπας αἳ μάλιστ' ἐναντιοῦνται ταῖς ἀγαπωμέναις ἡδοναῖς.
11 Εἰ δ' οὖν, καθάπερ εἴρηται, τὸν ἐσόμενον ἀγαθὸν τραφῆναι καλῶς δεῖ καὶ ἐθισθῆναι, εἶθ' οὕτως ἐν ἐπιτηδεύμασιν ἐπιεικέσι ζῆν καὶ μήτ' ἄκοντα μήθ' ἑκόντα πράττειν τὰ φαῦλα, ταῦτα δὲ γίγνοιτ' ἂν βιουμένοις κατά τινα νοῦν
12 καὶ τάξιν ὀρθήν, ἔχουσαν ἰσχύν. Ἡ μὲν οὖν πατρικὴ πρόσταξις οὐκ ἔχει τὸ ἰσχυρὸν οὐδὲ τὸ ἀναγκαῖον, οὐδὲ δὴ ὅλως ἡ ἑνὸς ἀνδρός, μὴ βασιλέως ὄντος ἤ τινος τοιούτου· ὁ δὲ νόμος ἀναγκαστικὴν ἔχει δύναμιν, λόγος ὢν

appeal to the nobler instincts of those in whom nature or good training has implanted such instincts, but to compel obedience from all others by pains and penalties, and, speaking generally, by inflicting such pains as are most opposed to the
11 offending pleasures. All this implies a guiding Intellect, with power to enforce its decrees. Where then is this to be
12 found? Parental authority, and indeed that of any single individual, except he be an absolute monarch, lacks that

Parental authority cannot adequately enforce it.

ρεύει, i.e. 'quod lex non jubet vetat.'

2. κολάσεις τε καὶ τιμωρίας] For this distinction see note on III. v. 7.

7. αἳ μάλιστ' ἐναντιοῦνται κ.τ.λ.] Compare the argument in II. iii. 4, αἱ δὲ ἰατρεῖαι διὰ τῶν ἐναντίων πεφύκασι γίνεσθαι.

11. ταῦτα δὲ γίγνοιτ' ἂν] δὲ marks the apodosis or conclusion of the sentence.

15. λόγος ὢν κ.τ.λ.] 'being a declaration proceeding as it were from wisdom and intelligence.' *i.e.* Law expresses in an impersonal form the conclusions of human wisdom. As expressing such conclusions, it commands our obedience, as doing so impersonally and in the abstract, it does not excite our resentment. Aristotle in the *Politics* describes Law as νοῦς ἄνευ ὀρέξεως.

ἀπό τινος φρονήσεως καὶ νοῦ. Καὶ τῶν μὲν ἀνθρώπων ἐχθαίρουσι τοὺς ἐναντιουμένους ταῖς ὁρμαῖς, κἂν ὀρθῶς αὐτὸ δρῶσιν· ὁ δὲ νόμος οὐκ ἔστιν ἐπαχθὴς τάττων τὸ
13 ἐπιεικές. Ἐν μόνῃ δὲ τῇ Λακεδαιμονίων πόλει μετ᾽ ὀλίγων ὁ νομοθέτης ἐπιμέλειαν δοκεῖ πεποιῆσθαι τροφῆς τε καὶ ἐπιτηδευμάτων· ἐν δὲ ταῖς πλείσταις τῶν πόλεων ἐξημέληται περὶ τῶν τοιούτων, καὶ ζῇ ἕκαστος ὡς βούλε-
14 ται, κυκλωπικῶς θεμιστεύων παίδων ἠδ᾽ ἀλόχου. Κράτιστον μὲν οὖν τὸ γίγνεσθαι κοινὴν ἐπιμέλειαν καὶ ὀρθὴν καὶ δρᾶν αὐτὸ δύνασθαι· κοινῇ δ᾽ ἐξαμελουμένων ἑκάστῳ δόξειεν ἂν προσήκειν τοῖς σφετέροις τέκνοις καὶ φίλοις εἰς ἀρετὴν συμβάλλεσθαι, ἢ προαιρεῖσθαί γε. Μάλιστα δ᾽ ἂν τοῦτο δύνασθαι δόξειεν ἐκ τῶν εἰρημένων νομοθετικὸς γενόμενος· αἱ μὲν γὰρ κοιναὶ ἐπιμέλειαι δῆλον ὅτι διὰ νόμων γίγνονται, ἐπιεικεῖς δ᾽ αἱ διὰ τῶν σπουδαίων. Γεγραμμένων δ᾽ ἢ ἀγράφων, οὐδὲν ἂν δόξειε διαφέρειν, οὐδὲ δι᾽ ὧν εἷς ἢ πολλοὶ παιδευθήσονται, ὥσπερ οὐδ᾽

power. Law however possesses it, and its interference is not
13 resented as that of a fellow-man would be. Practically how-
14 ever Law seldom even attempts such an aim; and, failing that, the duty devolves upon each individual in his own sphere. It is clear however that he will best perform it by becoming acquainted with the principles of Legislation, seeing

The State could do so but seldom attempts it. Individuals must therefore do the best they can, and they must

4. Λακεδαιμονίων] See note on I. xiii. 3.

8. κυκλωπικῶς θεμιστεύων] In allusion to the often-quoted patriarchal society of the Cyclops described by Homer, *Od.* ix. 114-5:

θεμιστεύει δὲ ἕκαστος παίδων ἠδ᾽ ἀλόχων, οὐδ᾽ ἀλλήλων ἀλέγουσιν.

10. δρᾶν αὐτὸ δύνασθαι] 'that there be power to carry it out.' This is explained by ἔχουσαν ἰσχὺν in § 11 above.

13. νομοθετικὸς γενόμενος] Legislation is naturally the highest branch of πολιτική. See § 20, *fin.* of this chapter. At the very outset (in I. ii. 8) Aristotle described Ethics as πολιτική τις, and this concluding chapter brings out the connexion still more forcibly.

ἐπὶ μουσικῆς καὶ γυμναστικῆς καὶ τῶν ἄλλων ἐπιτηδευμάτων. Ὥσπερ γὰρ ἐν ταῖς πόλεσιν ἐνισχύει τὰ νόμιμα καὶ τὰ ἔθη, οὕτω καὶ ἐν οἰκίαις οἱ πατρικοὶ λόγοι καὶ τὰ ἔθη, καὶ ἔτι μᾶλλον διὰ τὴν συγγένειαν καὶ τὰς εὐεργεσίας· προϋπάρχουσι γὰρ στέργοντες καὶ εὐπειθεῖς τῇ
15 φύσει. Ἔτι δὲ καὶ διαφέρουσιν αἱ καθ' ἕκαστον παιδεῖαι τῶν κοινῶν, ὥσπερ ἐπὶ ἰατρικῆς· καθόλου μὲν γὰρ τῷ πυρέττοντι συμφέρει ἡσυχία καὶ ἀσιτία, τινὶ δ' ἴσως οὔ, ὅ τε πυκτικὸς ἴσως οὐ πᾶσι τὴν αὐτὴν μάχην περιτίθησιν. Ἐξακριβοῦσθαι δὴ δόξειεν ἂν μᾶλλον τὸ καθ' ἕκαστον ἰδίας τῆς ἐπιμελείας γινομένης· μᾶλλον γὰρ τοῦ προσφόρου τυγχάνει ἕκαστος. Ἀλλ' ἐπιμεληθείη μὲν ἂν ἄριστα καθ' ἓν καὶ ἰατρὸς καὶ γυμναστὴς καὶ πᾶς ἄλλος ὁ τὸ καθόλου εἰδώς, ὅτι πᾶσιν ἢ τοῖς τοιοῖσδε· τοῦ κοι-
16 νοῦ γὰρ αἱ ἐπιστῆμαι λέγονταί τε καὶ εἰσίν. Οὐ μὴν ἀλλὰ καὶ ἑνός τινος οὐδὲν ἴσως κωλύει καλῶς ἐπιμεληθῆναι καὶ ἀνεπιστήμονα ὄντα, τεθεαμένον δ' ἀκριβῶς τὰ συμβαίνοντα ἐφ' ἑκάστῳ δι' ἐμπειρίαν, καθάπερ καὶ ἰατροὶ ἔνιοι δοκοῦσιν ἑαυτῶν ἄριστοι εἶναι, ἑτέρῳ οὐδὲν

act on the same principles as those which should guide State legislation.

that the moral training of society—the main object of all good legislation—and that of individuals must be guided by the same principles, and also that parental authority is to the family what laws are to the State. The former has indeed the advantage of resting upon natural affection and mutual

The special advantages sometimes claimed for private instruction do not supersede the use of such general knowledge.

15 good-will; and this home-training has the further merit that it can adapt its treatment better to the special circumstances of individuals, and that it can enter into minuter details. But even so it is best dealt with by those who have studied the problem in its general form; just as the scientific physician sur-
16 passes the empiric, although the latter may occasionally effect

9. *οὐ τὴν αὐτὴν μάχην περιτίθησι*] 'does not impart the same style of fighting.' *Περιτιθέναι* is similarly used in the sense of 'conferring' or 'imparting,' with *κράτος, τιμήν, ἐλευθερίαν*, etc.

ἂν δυνάμενοι ἐπαρκέσαι. Οὐδὲν δ' ἧττον ἴσως τῷ γε βουλομένῳ τεχνικῷ γενέσθαι καὶ θεωρητικῷ ἐπὶ τὸ καθόλου βαδιστέον εἶναι δόξειεν ἄν, κἀκεῖνο γνωριστέον ὡς ἐνδέ-
17 χεται· εἴρηται γὰρ ὅτι περὶ τοῦθ' αἱ ἐπιστῆμαι. Τάχα δὲ καὶ τῷ βουλομένῳ δι' ἐπιμελείας βελτίους ποιεῖν, εἴτε πολλοὺς εἴτ' ὀλίγους, νομοθετικῷ πειρατέον γενέσθαι, εἰ διὰ νόμων ἀγαθοὶ γενοίμεθ' ἄν. Ὅντινα γὰρ οὖν καὶ τὸν προτεθέντα διαθεῖναι καλῶς οὐκ ἔστι τοῦ τυχόντος, ἀλλ' εἴπερ τινός, τοῦ εἰδότος, ὥσπερ ἐπ' ἰατρικῆς καὶ τῶν
18 λοιπῶν ὧν ἔστιν ἐπιμέλειά τις καὶ φρόνησις. Ἆρ' οὖν μετὰ τοῦτο ἐπισκεπτέον πόθεν ἢ πῶς νομοθετικὸς γένοιτ' ἄν τις; ἢ καθάπερ ἐπὶ τῶν ἄλλων, παρὰ τῶν πολιτικῶν; μόριον γὰρ ἐδόκει τῆς πολιτικῆς εἶναι. Ἢ οὐχ ὅμοιον φαίνεται ἐπὶ τῆς πολιτικῆς καὶ τῶν λοιπῶν ἐπιστημῶν τε καὶ δυνάμεων; ἐν μὲν γὰρ τοῖς ἄλλοις οἱ αὐτοὶ φαίνονται

17 startling cures. On the same principle then we maintain that the best educator in private life is he who understands the
18 general principles of legislation. Next we ask—How is such knowledge to be acquired? At first we should be inclined to answer—From Statesmen: but strange to say in Politics theory and practice are dissevered. Those profess to teach who do not practise, viz. the Sophists: others practise but do

These principles cannot be learn at present either from Statesmen, who are empirics,

7. τὸν προτεθέντα] 'any given case that may be put before you.' This is the great point of difference between scientific and empiric knowledge. The latter may chance to achieve great success in one or two single cases (see § 16 *init.*), the former alone can deal with *any* case.

10. ἐπιμέλεια] 'attention' or 'practice.' See I. ix. 4, διά τινος μαθήσεως καὶ ἐπιμελείας. Φρόνησις also is specially *practical* wisdom. See note on II. vi. 15 and B. VI. c. v. throughout.

13. ἐδόκει] The nominative apparently is νομοθεσία understood from νομοθετικὸς, and the reference is probably (as Grant suggests) to I. ii. 7, or it may be to VI. viii. 2.

14. ἐπιστημῶν καὶ δυνάμεων] See note on I. i. 4.

τάς τε δυνάμεις παραδιδόντες καὶ ἐνεργοῦντες ἀπ' αὐτῶν, οἷον ἰατροὶ καὶ γραφεῖς· τὰ δὲ πολιτικὰ ἐπαγγέλλονται μὲν διδάσκειν οἱ σοφισταί, πράττει δ' αὐτῶν οὐδείς, ἀλλ' οἱ πολιτευόμενοι, οἳ δόξαιεν ἂν δυνάμει τινὶ τοῦτο πράττειν καὶ ἐμπειρίᾳ μᾶλλον ἢ διανοίᾳ· οὔτε γὰρ γράφοντες, οὔτε λέγοντες περὶ τῶν τοιούτων φαίνονται (καίτοι κάλλιον ἦν ἴσως ἢ λόγους δικανικούς τε καὶ δημηγορικούς), οὐδ' αὖ πολιτικοὺς πεποιηκότες τοὺς σφετέρους
19 υἱεῖς ἤ τινας ἄλλους τῶν φίλων. Εὔλογον δ' ἦν, εἴπερ ἐδύναντο· οὔτε γὰρ ταῖς πόλεσιν ἄμεινον οὐδὲν κατέλιπον ἄν, οὔθ' αὑτοῖς ὑπάρξαι προέλοιντ' ἂν μᾶλλον τῆς τοιαύτης δυνάμεως, οὐδὲ δὴ τοῖς φιλτάτοις. Οὐ μὴν μικρόν γε ἔοικεν ἡ ἐμπειρία συμβάλλεσθαι· οὐδὲ γὰρ ἐγίγνοντ' ἂν διὰ τῆς πολιτικῆς συνηθείας πολιτικοί· διὸ τοῖς ἐφιεμένοις περὶ πολιτικῆς εἰδέναι προσδεῖν ἔοικεν
20 ἐμπειρίας. Τῶν δὲ σοφιστῶν οἱ ἐπαγγελλόμενοι λίαν

not profess to teach, viz. Statesmen. As to the latter, they seem to act by a sort of instinct and from experience rather than on fixed principles; they never write or speculate upon Politics; they cannot even train their children and their
19 friends in their own profession, as they doubtless would if they could. Still we would not depreciate the value of experience, which is an essential condition of the knowledge of
20 Statesmanship. As to the former (viz. the Sophists), they

or from professed teachers (the Sophists), who are charlatans.

4. After οἱ πολιτευόμενοι understand πράττουσιν.

6. καίτοι κάλλιον κ.τ.λ.] Not improbably a sneer at the statesman and orator Demosthenes, all of whose writings are oratorical and not political.

12. οὐ μὴν μικρόν γε κ.τ.λ.] This is to correct the apparent depreciation of the value of experience involved in the above censure of practical statesmen.

14. πολιτικῆς συνηθείας] 'familiarity with political life.' The fact that this, apart from a body of fixed and conscious principles (l. 4), makes men statesmen, is a proof of the importance of practical experience.

15. προσδεῖν] On the force of this compound see note on I. x. 9.

φαίνονται πόρρω εἶναι τοῦ διδάξαι· ὅλως γὰρ οὐδὲ
ποῖόν τί ἐστιν ἢ περὶ ποῖα ἴσασιν· οὐ γὰρ ἂν τὴν
αὐτὴν τῇ ῥητορικῇ οὐδὲ χείρω ἐτίθεσαν, οὐδ' ἂν ᾤοντο
ῥᾴδιον εἶναι τὸ νομοθετῆσαι συναγαγόντι τοὺς εὐδοκι-
μοῦντας τῶν νόμων· ἐκλέξασθαι γὰρ εἶναι τοὺς ἀρί-
στους, ὥσπερ οὐδὲ τὴν ἐκλογὴν οὖσαν συνέσεως καὶ
τὸ κρῖναι ὀρθῶς μέγιστον, ὥσπερ ἐν τοῖς κατὰ μουσι-
κήν· οἱ γὰρ ἔμπειροι περὶ ἕκαστα κρίνουσιν ὀρθῶς τὰ
ἔργα, καὶ δι' ὧν ἢ πῶς ἐπιτελεῖται συνιᾶσιν, καὶ ποῖα
ποίοις συνᾴδει· τοῖς δ' ἀπείροις ἀγαπητὸν τὸ μὴ διαλαν-
θάνειν εἰ εὖ ἢ κακῶς πεποίηται τὸ ἔργον, ὥσπερ ἐπὶ
γραφικῆς. Οἱ δὲ νόμοι τῆς πολιτικῆς ἔργοις ἐοίκασιν·
πῶς οὖν ἐκ τούτων νομοθετικὸς γένοιτ' ἂν τις, ἢ τοὺς
21 ἀρίστους κρίναι; οὐ γὰρ φαίνονται οὐδ' ἰατρικοὶ ἐκ τῶν

know nothing about the subject they profess to teach: else they would not confuse it with, or even rank it below, the Art of Rhetoric, nor absurdly fancy that a mere selection of the best laws from various systems constitutes Statesmanship, forgetting that the whole pith of the matter lies in the principle on which the selection is made. Experience and practice alone, in this as in other arts, can qualify a man to form any but a very rough judgment of results, and still more of the
21 means which lead to them. The mere study of collections of

6. ὥσπερ οὐδὲ τὴν ἐκλογὴν κ.τ.λ.] In what is called a system of 'Eclecticism,' the real system is the principle on which the selection is made. The fact that the selected details form parts of other systems is a secondary and accidental consideration.

10. τοῖς δ' ἀπείροις κ.τ.λ.] The practical *results* of a system when at work is a matter that any one living under it can form some opinion about. The *means* best adapted to secure any given results, their compatibility with other conditions (δι' ὧν . . . συνᾴδει), and so forth, can only be estimated by those who have special training and experience. From the latter consideration Bacon says that popularity is a positive objection against any system of a philosophical character, and from the former he makes an exception in favour of 'Politics and Theology.'

συγγραμμάτων γίνεσθαι. Καίτοι πειρῶνταί γε λέγειν οὐ μόνον τὰ θεραπεύματα, ἀλλὰ καὶ ὡς ἰαθεῖεν ἂν καὶ ὡς δεῖ θεραπεύειν ἑκάστους, διελόμενοι τὰς ἕξεις. Ταῦτα δὲ τοῖς μὲν ἐμπείροις ὠφέλιμα εἶναι δοκεῖ, τοῖς δ' ἀνεπιστήμοσιν ἀχρεῖα. Ἴσως οὖν καὶ τῶν νόμων καὶ τῶν πολιτειῶν αἱ συναγωγαὶ τοῖς μὲν δυναμένοις θεωρῆσαι καὶ κρῖναι τί καλῶς ἢ τοὐναντίον καὶ ποῖα ποίοις ἁρμόττει, εὔχρηστ' ἂν εἴη· τοῖς δ' ἄνευ ἕξεως τὰ τοιαῦτα διεξιοῦσι τὸ μὲν κρίνειν καλῶς οὐκ ἂν ὑπάρχοι, εἰ μὴ ἄρα αὐτόματον, εὐσυνετώτεροι δ' εἰς ταῦτα τάχ' ἂν γένοιντο.

22 Παραλιπόντων οὖν τῶν προτέρων ἀνερεύνητον τὸ περὶ
τῆς νομοθεσίας, αὐτοὺς ἐπισκέψασθαι μᾶλλον βέλτιον
ἴσως, καὶ ὅλως δὴ περὶ πολιτείας, ὅπως εἰς δύναμιν ἡ
23 περὶ τὰ ἀνθρώπινα φιλοσοφία τελειωθῇ. Πρῶτον μὲν

laws can never make a man a Statesman. The most we can say is that such a study may be useful to those who have already gained something of the Statesman's mind.

Hence we propose to investigate the subject of Politics for ourselves.

22 The field then is still open: a fresh and independent in-
vestigation of the true principles of Statesmanship is called
for to complete the subject of the Science of Human Life.
We propose therefore to undertake such an investigation,
23 availing ourselves of the labours of our predecessors in that

1. *συγγραμμάτων*] 'treatises,'—not, as it is sometimes translated, 'prescriptions'—as is clear from what follows.

10. *εὐσυνετώτεροι*] 'more intelligent.' Though the study of medical treatises, or of collections of laws, can never make men physicians or statesmen, it may make them more intelligent and 'appreciative' in such subjects respectively.

15. *ἡ περὶ τὰ ἀνθρώπινα φιλοσοφία*] This term was considered by Aristotle to include Ethics, Economics, and Politics—three practical Sciences dealing with the life and conduct of man in reference to himself, to his family, and to society respectively. The subject of Economics, though not mentioned here, occupies the first Book of the so-called 'Politics' of Aristotle.

οὖν εἴ τι κατὰ μέρος εἴρηται καλῶς ὑπὸ τῶν προγενεστέρων πειραθῶμεν ἐπελθεῖν, εἶτα ἐκ τῶν συνηγμένων πολιτειῶν θεωρῆσαι τὰ ποῖα σώζει καὶ φθείρει τὰς πόλεις καὶ τὰ ποῖα ἑκάστας τῶν πολιτειῶν, καὶ διὰ τίνας αἰτίας αἱ μὲν καλῶς, αἱ δὲ τοὐναντίον πολιτεύονται· θεωρηθέντων γὰρ τούτων τάχ᾽ ἂν μᾶλλον συνίδοιμεν καὶ ποία πολιτεία ἀρίστη, καὶ πῶς ἑκάστη ταχθεῖσα, καὶ τίσι νόμοις καὶ ἔθεσι χρωμένη. Λέγωμεν οὖν ἀρξάμενοι.

field, as well as of the experience supplied by constitutions that have already existed. Hence we may perhaps gather what is the most perfect form of government, and also what laws and customs are best suited to each particular form.

2. *συνηγμένων πολιτειῶν*] 'collections of constitutions;' in reference to such *συναγωγαὶ* as are mentioned above in § 21; or else, as some suppose, in reference to a collection framed by Aristotle himself. Fragments said to belong to such a work still exist.

SUPPLEMENTARY NOTES AND ILLUSTRATIONS.

P. 1, I. i. 1. μέθοδος] See further Mansel's note on Aristotle's use of this word in Aldrich's *Logic*, Ch. vi. '*De Methodo.*' Its use in the text may be illustrated by *Poet.* xix. 1, ἐν τοῖς περὶ τῆς ῥητορικῆς κείσθω· τοῦτο γὰρ ἴδιον μᾶλλον ἐκείνης τῆς μεθόδου.

P. 9, I. iii. 7. διαφέρει δ' οὐθὲν, κ.τ.λ.] Compare *Ant. and Cleop.* Act I. Sc. iv.—

> 'As we rate boys, who, being mature in knowledge,
> Pawn their experience to their present pleasure,
> And so rebel to judgment.'

Also see further the discussion on the etymology of ἀκολασία, in III. xii. 5-8.

ἀκρατέσιν] The following extracts will illustrate, from a modern point of view, the difference between ἐγκρατὴς and σώφρων: 'He who refrains from gratifying a wish on some ground of *reason* (ἐγκρατὴς), at the same time feels the wish as strongly as if he gratified it. The object seems to him desirable; he cannot think of it without wishing for it. . . . On the other hand, when a *stronger passion* controls the weaker (σώφρων), the weaker altogether ceases to be felt. For example, let us suppose a bribe offered to two such men to betray their country. Neither will take the bribe. But the former may feel his fingers itch as he handles the gold. . . . The other will have no such feelings; the gold will not make his fingers itch with desire, but, perhaps, rather seem to scorch them. . . . The difference between the two men is briefly this, that the one has his anarchic or lower desires under control, the other feels no such desires; the one, so far as he is virtuous, is incapable of crime; the other, so far as he is virtuous, is incapable of temptation. . . . Or again, while a *virtuous* man is one who controls and coerces the anarchic passions within him, so as to conform his actions to law (ἐγκρατής), a *holy* man is one in whom a passionate enthusiasm absorbs and annuls the anarchic passions altogether, so that *no internal struggle takes place* (σώφρων), and the lawful action is that which presents itself first, and seems the one most natural and most easy to be done.'—(*Ecce Homo*, pp. 148-150.)

Hence in IV. ix. 8 Aristotle denies that ἐγκράτεια is, strictly speaking, a Virtue, but only ἀρετή τις μικτή.

The distinction given in the Notes between ἀκόλαστος and ἀκρατὴς may be further illustrated by the statement in VII. viii. 1, ὁ μὲν ἀκόλαστος οὐ μεταμελητικός . . . ὁ δὲ ἀκρατὴς μεταμελητικὸς πᾶς. Also ἀκολασία is described as συνεχὴς πονηρία like consumption, etc., ἀκρασία as οὐ συνεχὴς like epilepsy, etc.

P. 12, I. iv. 4. ἐπιπολαζούσας] The former of the two explanations given in the Notes seems preferable, viz., that which is 'obvious,' or 'on the surface,' = Latin '*in promptu esse*.' This suits the two other places where the expression occurs in the *Ethics*, viz., I. v. 4, IV. viii. 4. Also the phrase ἐπιπολῆς εἶναι occurs in *Rhet.*, etc., in the sense of 'to be obvious.'

—— 5. What is stated in the note on γνωρίμων . . . διττῶς is not only true of 'a being of more perfect knowledge,' but also of ourselves in the higher and more advanced stages of our knowledge. As Grote says, 'Even facts are then employed, directed, modified, by an acquired intellectual capital, and by the permanent machinery of universal significant terms in which that capital is invested.' Compare the distinction in the text with that drawn by Pope, *Essay on Man*, iv. 361-2, between Human and Divine *Love*:—

'God loves from whole to parts: but human soul
Must rise from individual to the whole.'

P. 13, I. iv. 6. As a further illustration of the necessity of personal experience for the appreciation of Moral facts or ideas, add John vii. 17, 'If a man *will do* (θέλῃ ποιεῖν) his will he shall *know* of the doctrine.'

P. 15, I. iv. 7. Ὧι δὲ μηδέτερον, *i.e.* neither the ὅτι nor the διότι. The lines from Hesiod which follow are embodied by Livy (xxii. 29), in a speech of Minucius when acknowledging his bad treatment of Fabius.

P. 16, I. v. 3. βοσκημάτων βίον προαιρούμενοι] Compare *Hamlet*, Act IV. Sc. iv.—

'What is a man,
If his chief good and market of his time
Be but to sleep and feed?—a beast, no more.'

P 17, I. vi. 5. θέσιν διαφυλάττων] Perhaps it would be more correct to give θέσις *h.l.* the more technical sense of a 'paradox,' which is assigned to it by the Definition in *Topics*, I. ii., θέσις ἐστὶν ὑπόληψις παράδοξος τῶν γνωρίμων τινὸς κατὰ φιλοσοφίαν.

—— 7. ἐγκυκλίοις] Cf. *Pol.* I. vii. 2, where ἐγκύκλια διακονήματα are the ordinary daily duties of slaves.

P. 37, I. vii. 20. The explanation of 'ἀρχαὶ derived from experience' given in the notes, is different from that adopted in the earlier edition, and, I believe, more correct. Under any circumstances, ἐπαγωγὴ *h.l.* is not to be confused with the logical process of Induction, which (1) itself starts from ἀρχαί, and does not give them; and (2) is a process to which θεωροῦνται (denoting immediate apprehension) would not apply. Ἀρχὴ here is simply 'what one starts with,' not necessarily (as in I. iv. 5) 'a general principle' (see Glossary, *s.v.* ἀρχή). It *may* be 'a general principle,' as in Mathematics, which a reference to (sometimes) a single fact of experience is sufficient to establish without further or formal proof. Such a reference to experience would be ἐπαγωγὴ in the sense of this passage. Or it *may* be a simple fact, as the facts of observation in Physics and other *a posteriori* sciences, where again no further proof is required, *e.g.* 'This body falls with a definite accelerating velocity;' or as in Morals (so this passage asserts), *e.g.* 'This action is right,' or 'This approves itself to me,' or *vice versa*.

P. 37, I. vii. 21. Μετιέναι δὲ κ.τ.λ.] Observe the generality and vagueness of this word (lit. 'to go after'), as also of θεωρεῖν ('viewed' or 'perceived'), and of ἄλλαι δ' ἄλλως. Aristotle's object here is not to enter upon the thorny subject of the nature of the evidence on which ἀρχαὶ rest, but only to insist on the *negative* point, that at any rate there is never *demonstrative* proof or a direct establishment of the διότι. Grote (*Fragments*, p. 131) translates, 'We ought in all our investigations to look after the ἀρχὴ in the way which the special nature of the subject requires, and be very careful to define it well.'

P. 42, I. viii. 12. It may be worth while to quote at length the passage in *Ecce Homo* referred to in the note:—'Those who think that we should not make pleasure our chief object, yet commonly maintain that he who lives best will actually attain the greatest amount and the best kind of pleasure. . . . The practical objection to Epicureanism is not so much that it makes pleasure the *summum bonum*, as that it recommends us to keep this *summum bonum* always in view. For it is far from being universally true that to get a thing you must aim at it. There are some things which can only be gained by renouncing them. . . . Now a practical survey of life seems to show that pleasure in its largest sense—a true and deep enjoyment of life—is also not to be gained artificially. . . .' So Mill, *Autobiography*, p. 142: 'Those only are happy (I thought) who have their minds fixed on some object other than their own happiness. . . . Aiming at something else, they find happiness by the way. . . . Ask yourself whether you are happy and you cease to be so.' [The same is true of *bodily* health, etc.]

P. 54, I. x. 11. τὰς τύχας οἴσει . . . τετράγωνος] Cf. Dante, *Par.* xvii. 24, 'Ben tetragono ai colpi di ventura.'

—— 12. διαλάμπει τὸ καλὸν] Cf. a similar metaphor in Shakespeare's *Taming of the Shrew*, Act IV. Sc. iii.—

> 'And as the sun breaks through the darkest clouds,
> So honour peereth in the meanest habit.'

P. 58, I. xi. 4. προϋπάρχειν . . . ἢ πράττεσθαι] This corresponds with the distinction in Hor. *A. P.* 179, 'Aut agitur res in scenis aut acta refertur.' Compare the use of προϋπάρχειν in IV. ii. 14, also in *Rhet.* I. ii. 2. Aristotle describes unartificial proofs as being ὅσα μὴ δι' ἡμῶν πεπόρισται ἀλλὰ προϋπῆρχεν. In the *Poetics* Aristotle several times refers to incidents which are ἔξω τῆς τραγῳδίας, or ἔξω τοῦ δράματος (cf. esp. the phrase ὅσα πρὸ τοῦ γέγονεν, in xv. 7), and gives precepts for the management of such incidents, which rest on the fact noticed in this passage, viz., that they make a less distinct impression upon us; *e.g.* in reference to such incidents, a *deus ex machina* is less objectionable (xv. 7): improbability generally is more admissible, *e.g.* the circumstances connected with the murder of Laius and the marriage of Jocasta by Œdipus (xv. 7; cf. xiv. 6).

—— 5. συλλογιστέον] Owing to the almost invariably technical use of this word in Aristotle for a logical conclusion or inference, this passage is frequently translated, 'we must conclude.' This does not however suit the general context, or the combination of particles δὴ καί. It should be rather, 'we must take into our calculation then this difference also,' viz., the difference resulting from our being present to, or absent from, the scene of action, as well as the difference in weight among troubles themselves, even when we *are* present. On this latter difference cf. x. 12. This sense of συλλογίζεσθαι occurs in Hdt. ii. 148, and in a passage still more closely parallel in Dem. *de Fals. Leg.* p. 356, ἐπειδὰν τοὺς καιροὺς συλλογίσηταί τις ἐφ' ὧν ἐγράφη, καὶ τὰς ὑποσχέσεις, κ.τ.λ.

P. 59, I. xii. 1. Thus these three classes of Goods correspond to those in vii. 4, δυνάμεις being good as means; τίμια good always *per se* as ends; ἐπαινετὰ good *per se* as ends, and also good as means. In § 2, τὸ ποιόν τι εἶναι refers to the former condition of ἐπαινετά, and τὸ πρός τι πῶς ἔχειν to the latter.

P. 62, I. xiii. 8. ἐξωτερικὸς] Besides the explanations of this word given in the note two others deserve notice—(1) It has been thought to mean simply any discourse or treatise *other than* that in hand. (2) Grote (*Aristotle*, i. 69) maintains the view that it means *outside* the regular method of Philosophy; *i.e.* discussion conducted in the method of Dialectic (in the technical Aristotelian sense). With the explanation given in the note compare that of ἐγκύκλιοι λόγοι in v. 7.

P. 69, I. xiii. 20. It should be particularly noted that φρόνησις, in spite of its constant connexion with Moral Virtue (συνέζευκται ἡ φρόνησις τῇ τοῦ ἤθους ἀρετῇ καὶ αὕτη τῇ φρονήσει, X. viii. 3), is itself an intellectual quality. Dante (*Conv.* iv. 17) thinks it necessary to bring Aristotle's authority against the opinion 'held by many' that it was a Moral Virtue. In proof of this (besides the distinct statement in the text)—(1) It is discussed by Aristotle in B. VI. among the διανοητικαὶ ἀρεταί; (2) In X. viii. θεωρία is shown to be superior to ἐνέργειαι κατ' ἀρετὴν on the ground of its superiority to the kindred intellectual excellence of φρόνησις which is allied to *them*; (3) φρόνησις is described in *Rhet.* I. ix. 13 as ἀρετὴ διανοίας καθ' ἣν εὖ βουλεύεσθαι δύνανται περὶ ἀγαθῶν καὶ κακῶν τῶν εἰρημένων εἰς εὐδαιμονίαν.

P. 77, II. ii. 6. ὁμοίως δὲ καὶ τὰ ποτά, κ.τ.λ.] Compare *Merchant of Venice*, Act. I. Sc. ii., 'They are as sick that surfeit with too much as they that starve with nothing. It is no mean happiness, therefore, to be seated in the mean.'

P. 79, II. iii. 2. ὡς ὁ Πλάτων φησίν] Probably in reference to *Laws*, B. II.

P. 84, II. iv. 3. Add to the note on ταῦτα δέ, κ.τ.λ.—The 'motive' which led to the execution of some of Michelagnolo's great works was (if we may believe tradition) mean and spiteful, but this, if true, does not affect our estimate of their artistic merit; nor do we think less of Benvenuto Cellini's Perseus because he consoles himself, on failing to kill an enemy, with the reflection, that, if God would permit him to complete that work, he would thereby crush his hated rivals more effectually than if he killed them with the sword.

Again, as to the condition βεβαίως καὶ ἀμετακινήτως. If an artist wishes to destroy his work, being dissatisfied with it, and regrets having executed it, neither does this affect its artistic worth. In fact, artists are frequently bad judges of the relative merits of their own works (cf. Plato, *Phædo*, p. 274, *fin.*), and poets (among others notably Wordsworth) have frequently altered for the worse some of their finest passages. The artistic merit of such works or passages remains the same notwithstanding.

P. 94, II. vi. 15. Illustrate further the necessity for adding the qualification ὡς ἂν ὁ φρόνιμος ὁρίσειεν (as explained in the Notes), by the reflection of Pope, *Essay on Man*, II. 169, etc.:—

'Let pow'r or knowledge, gold or glory, please,
Or (oft more strong than all) the love of ease;

Thro' life 'tis followed, ev'n at life's expence:
The merchant's toil, the sage's indolence;
The monk's humility, the hero's pride;
All, all alike, find reason on their side.'

Also by La Rochefoucauld (quoted by Pattison, *l.c.*), 'Il n'y a pas de violente passion qui n'ait sa raison pour s'autoriser.' Again, the 'so-called dictates of conscience and reason are sometimes only passions in the form of a syllogism' (Ugo Foscolo). In B. VII. c. iii. Aristotle explains at length how Reason may help a man to go wrong *selon les règles*.

P. 95, II. vi. 17, etc. The refutation of the misconceptions of Aristotle's theory contained in these sections affords an answer also to another objection sometimes brought against it, that it makes the difference between Virtue and Vice to be *quantitative* only, and not *qualitative*; a question of *degree* merely, and not of *kind*; so that Virtue is a little more or less of Vice, and Vice a little more or less of Virtue; or, as it has also been put, that 'Virtue is only Vice a little exaggerated or a little controlled.' Take the following illustration:—Excess or defect of temperature will (so to speak) destroy Water by converting it either into Steam or Ice; a moderate degree (though within considerable limits) will preserve it in the form of Water: but Water is not a little more Ice or a little less Steam. The difference, though *quantitative* in respect of temperature, is *qualitative* in respect of the resulting material. So Virtue differs from Vice *qualitatively*, and is not Vice increased or Vice diminished, though in respect of the πάθη and πράξεις, with which they deal, the difference may be mainly, or even wholly, *quantitative*.

P. 97, II. vii. This proof of the Definition of Virtue (as explained in the Notes) is a good instance of 'Inductio per Enumerationem Simplicem,' or (as it is sometimes called) 'Perfect Induction': since if the Catalogue of Virtues is complete, all the possible cases to which the Conclusion can refer have been examined in the Premisses. By the same method, any general proposition relating to a *limited and ascertainable* number of cases may be established, as, *e.g.*, 'all the Popes (until the present) have reigned less than twenty-five years.'

P. 99, II. vii. 3. Ἐλλείποντες δὲ] In VII. ix. 5 it is stated that ἀκρασία and ἐγκράτεια, like ἀκολασία and σωφροσύνη, are defective in a third related term, and for a similar reason.

P. 101, II. vii. 8. ἐπιδικάζονται] A legal term, relating to a double claim for some disputed object. Similarly, in IV. iv. 4, ὡς ἐρήμης ἔοικεν ἀμφισβητεῖν τὰ ἄκρα. Still it is clear that if there is Excess and Defect there *must be* a Mean, else how could the transition occur from the one to the other of these extremes? If the balance has turned, there must have been a point when it was even. This is admirably put by Pope (*Essay on Man*, ii. 207, etc.), when, speaking of 'extremes,' he says—

> 'Tho' each by turns the other's bound invade,
> As in some well-wrought picture light and shade,
> And oft so mix, the diff'rence is too nice,
> Where ends the virtue or begins the vice.
> Fools! who from hence into the notion fall,
> That vice or virtue there is none at all.'

P. 104, II. vii. 15. *ὁ δὲ ἐπιχαιρέκακος, κ.τ.λ.*] It should be noted that Aristotle corrects himself on this point in *Rhet.* II. ix. 5, Ὁ γὰρ αὐτός ἐστιν ἐπιχαιρέκακος καὶ φθονερός. In fact, they are (to borrow his illustration in c. xiii.) like the convex and concave sides of a circumference, τῷ λόγῳ δύο ἀχώριστα πεφυκότα. The true defect of the feeling of νέμεσις would be a sort of moral indifference, such as is typified in the popular (though perverted) conception of 'a Gallio.' Also we might illustrate the feeling implied in νέμεσις by Ps. lxxiii. 3, etc., 'I was grieved at the wicked; I do also see the ungodly in such prosperity.' In the present day the recognition of the virtuous side of Resentment (νέμεσις), as well as that of Anger, Self-Esteem, and perhaps Ambition, has rather fallen into the background. (See further, note p. 238.) The following passage from Dr. Abbott's most suggestive *Bible Lessons* (p. 175), on the Virtue of Resentment, is worth quoting:—'Anger is indifferent, being sometimes right and sometimes wrong; vindictiveness gives a selfish character to anger, and is always wrong. But there is an anger that is always right, such as one feels at the sight of cruelty, injustice, and oppression, a moral recoil of sentiment from evil.' After pointing out the etymological significance of Resentment as 'recoil of sentiment,' he proceeds, 'Resentment then is a Virtue, and a man who feels no resentment at the sight of injustice is destitute of a true sense of sin. There is almost as great a deficiency of resentment in the world as there is an excess of vindictiveness.'

It may be worth while to compare the νέμεσις of Aristotle with Resentment as depicted by Bishop Butler, and to contrast both with Anger in its legitimate manifestation by the πρᾶος, as in *Eth.* IV. c. v.

Νέμεσις, both in *Eth.* and *Rhet.*, is emphatically connected with the undeserved *prosperity* of the wicked, rather than with the mere *fact* of their turpitude. See esp. *Rhet.* II. ix. 1, 7. Hence (1) it 'marches with' Envy; (2) it is in some sense the converse to Pity, which is aroused by undeserved *adversity* (*Rhet.* II. ix. 1).

Resentment is (according to Butler) of two kinds, 'Sudden Anger,' and 'Settled Resentment.' The latter is Resentment proper, and in that aspect it is aroused 'not by natural but moral evil,' not by suffering, pain, or loss, but by injury; 'it is never occasioned by harm as distinct from injury.' So again, 'its natural object is one who has been in a *moral* sense injurious to oneself or others.'

Anger, on the other hand, (1) may be aroused (as Butler says) by mere harm as distinct from injury;' [though no doubt the 'harm' is often spontaneously assumed to be also 'injury.' Cf. *Eth.* V. viii. 10, ἐπὶ φαινομένῃ ἀδικίᾳ ἡ ὀργή ἐστιν, also VII. vi. 1, ὁ μὲν γὰρ λόγος ἢ ἡ φαντασία, ὅτι ὕβρις ἢ ὀλιγωρία, ἐδήλωσεν· ὁ δὲ [θυμὸς] ὥσπερ συλλογισάμενος ὅτι δεῖ τῷ τοιούτῳ πολεμεῖν χαλεπαίνει δὴ εὐθύς]; (2) it is more of a *personal* feeling [Aristotle's *Rhet.* II. ii. 1, ἔστω ἡ ὀργὴ ὄρεξις μετὰ λύπης τιμωρίας φαινομένης διὰ φαινομένην ὀλιγωρίαν τῶν εἰς αὐτὸν ἢ εἰς αὐτοῦ τινα μὴ προσηκόντως. So, *ib.* II. iv. 30, Ὀργὴ ἐστιν ἐκ τῶν πρὸς ἑαυτόν. Compare Butler, Sermon viii. p. 437, ed. Angus]; (3) 'its reason and end (says Butler) is to prevent and resist sudden force, violence, and opposition, considered merely as such.' Similarly, Aristotle (*Eth.* IV. v. 6) notes that in its absence a man is not ἀμυντικός.

In *Rhet.* II. iv. 31, etc., Aristotle describes the feeling of μῖσος, in contrast with ὀργή, in terms which bring it into close resemblance to Butler's Resentment, *e.g.* ὀργὴ περὶ τὰ καθ' ἕκαστα, . . . τὸ δὲ μῖσος καὶ πρὸς τὰ γένη· τὸν γὰρ κλέπτην μισεῖ καὶ τὸν συκοφάντην ἅπας· καὶ τὸ μὲν ἰατὸν χρόνῳ (cf. *Eth.* IV. v. 8, etc.) τὸ δ' ἀνίατον—καὶ τὸ μὲν λύπης ἔφεσις, τὸ δὲ κακοῦ—Ὁ μὲν ὀργιζόμενος λυπεῖται· ὁ δὲ μισῶν οὔ, κ.τ.λ.

P. 106, II. viii. 2. ἀνδρεῖος . . . πρὸς τὸν θρασὺν δειλός] As, for instance, Fabius in the estimate of Minucius: 'Pro cunctatore segnem, pro cauto timidum, affingens vicina virtutibus vitia, compellabat' (Livy, xxii. 12 *fin.*)

P. 107, II. viii. 7. Speaking generally, we may say that the Excess is better when the Virtue mostly relates to the *encouragement* of the Feeling with which it is concerned, and the Defect when the Virtue mostly relates to its *repression*.

P. 110, II. ix. 4. We might illustrate εὐκατάφοροι *h.l.* by an expression applied in Athenæus to Chæremon, that he was ἐπικατάφορος ἐπὶ τὰ ἄνθη, *i.e.* 'fond of dwelling on descriptions of flowers.'

P. 111, II. ix. 8. ὁ μὲν μικρὸν, κ.τ.λ.] Hence it follows that the Virtuous mean is not like a straight line without breadth, but a moderately wide path, not to be too closely defined, although after all—

'Sunt certi denique fines
Quos ultra citraque nequit consistere rectum.'

P. 113. It has been suggested that the same *social* principle probably underlies Dante's classification of vices, in respect of their moral turpitude. (There is of course no such gradation intended in Aristotle's classification here.) 'Dante's moral standard is wholly social. The worst crime is fraud, because it strikes at the root of society by undermining confidence [cf. *Inf.* xi. 55]. . . . Next in the scale of evil is violence, less dangerous, because avowed and open. The most venial of the sins of Hell is incontinence, which chiefly concerns the individual alone' (Symonds' *Introduction*, p. 120).

III. i. 11. In VII. ix. 4 Aristotle gives an instance of *καλὴ ἡδονή* overpowering a resolution to act in the case of the Neoptolemus of Sophocles, who was unable to abide by the determination which he had formed to deceive Philoctetes, *καίτοι δι' ἡδονὴν οὐκ ἐνέμεινεν, ἀλλὰ καλήν.* Cf. VII. ii. 7, where the paradoxical phrase *σπουδαία τις ἀκρασία* is suggested for this case.

P. 119, III. i. 13. Hence in the case mentioned by Jeremy Taylor, 'He that threw a stone at a dog, and hit his cruel stepmother, said that though he meant it otherwise, yet the stone was not quite lost,' the act would not be involuntary, not being *ἐπίλυπον καὶ ἐν μεταμελείᾳ.* Somewhat similar would be Aristotle's condemnation of Pompey's morality in *Ant. and Cleop.* Act II. Sc. vii., when he will not consent beforehand to a scheme of treachery, but regrets that it had not been carried out without his being consulted:—

'Repent that e'er thy tongue
Hath so betrayed thine act; being done unknown,
I should have found it afterwards well done,
But must condemn it now.'

P. 120, III. i. 14. *οὐ δοκεῖ δι' ἄγνοιαν πράττειν . . . ἀλλ' ἀγνοῶν*] *δι' ἄγνοιαν πράττειν* is applied to an act *caused* by ignorance; *ἀγνοῶν πράττειν* to an act which is merely *accompanied* by ignorance.

P. 121, III. i. 17. *ὥσπερ Αἰσχύλος τὰ μυστικὰ*] Æschylus is said to have been accused of divulging some portions of the Eleusinian Mysteries in one of his plays, and to have defended himself on the ground that never having been himself initiated, he must have done it, if at all, unconsciously.

P. 122, III. i. 20. The conception of an Involuntary act is more definite and positive than that of a Voluntary act. Hence Involuntary is investigated first (as in Book V. Injustice is discussed before Justice, cf. V. i. 8), and this Definition of 'Voluntary' simply *excludes* the two conditions which have been shown to constitute Involuntariness, viz., *βία* and *ἡ καθ' ἕκαστα ἄγνοια*. The words *οὗ ἡ ἀρχὴ ἐν αὐτῷ* refer to the former, and *εἰδότι τὰ καθ' ἕκαστα ἐν οἷς ἡ πρᾶξις* to the latter. In V. viii. 6, 7, Involuntary acts *βίᾳ* are described as *ἀτυχήματα*, those *δι' ἄγνοιαν* as *ἁμαρτήματα*.

The supplementary §§ 21, etc., contain an argument similar to that in §§ 11, etc. : as it was there shown that the *violence* of pleasure is not such as to constitute the involuntariness of *compulsion*, so it is contended here that the *blindness* of passion or desire does not constitute the involuntariness of *ignorance*.

P. 123, III. i. 25. *ἀκούσια λυπηρὰ*] This is true in all cases, for *ἀκούσια βίᾳ* are of course *λυπηρὰ* at the moment (*κατὰ τὸν καιρὸν*, § 6), and *ἀκούσια δι' ἄγνοιαν* are *ἐπίλυπα* (§ 13) as soon as we discover what we have done.

—— 27. *φευκτά μὲν*] The converse of the argument from *δεῖ* in § 24. In that case we ought to *do* something; in this case we ought to *avoid* something.

Ἄτοπον δή, κ.τ.λ.] The reason for this assertion seems to be that so many of our actions proceed rather from unreasoning impulse than conscious and deliberate purpose, that we should have to relegate too large a proportion of our lives to the sphere of involuntary action on the supposition in question. The opponent's contention would prove too much, as in § 22. *Τὰ ἄλογα πάθη* refer to *θυμὸς* and *ἐπιθυμία*; cf. *Rhet.* I. x. 8, *ἄλογοι δὲ ὀρέξεις, ὀργὴ καὶ ἐπιθυμία*.

P. 124, III. ii. 3. Compare I. xiii. 18, *τὸ δὲ ἐπιθυμητικὸν καὶ ὅλως ὀρεκτικὸν*, which shows that *ἐπιθυμία* falls under *ὄρεξις* as its genus.

P. 125, III. ii. 6. It is difficult to find a precise equivalent for *θυμὸς*, but we can gather its meaning (1) from Plato's use of *θυμὸς* or *τὸ θυμοειδὲς* as the element of Spirit, or Will, or Resolution, or whatever it may be called, which gives practical effect to the abstract decisions of Reason, in its conflict with the *ἐπιθυμίαι*, and causes the man's action to follow *it* rather than *them*; (2) From Aristotle's use of the word elsewhere, *e.g.* the description of the Spurious Courage of *θυμὸς* (High Spirit or Impetuosity) in III. viii. 10, etc.; also the opposition of impulsive to deliberate action, *τὰ ἐκ θυμοῦ . . . τὰ ἐκ προνοίας*, *Eth.* V. viii. 9; also from its occasional interchange with *ὀργή*, *e.g. Rhet.* I. x. 8, etc.,

Eth. III. i. 24, V. viii. 9; also from the greater evil of ἀκρασία τοῦ θυμοῦ as compared with ἀκρασία τῶν ἐπιθυμιῶν, *Eth.* VII. vi. (cf. II. iii. 10, χαλεπώτερον ἡδονῇ μάχεσθαι ἢ θυμῷ). Hence I have ventured, though with much hesitation, to translate it *h.l.* 'Spirit,' in the sense of an impulsive and resolute, but unreflecting, source of action. St. Hilaire, though translating the word by 'colère' in i. 27, paraphrases it in this chapter 'la passion que le cœur inspire.'

P. 131, III. iii. 11-13. θέμενοι τέλος τι . . . ἀφιστανται] Shakespeare has described the process similarly in 2 *Henry IV.* Act I. Sc. iii.—

'When we mean to build,
We first survey the plot, then draw the model;
And when we see the figure of the house,
Then must we take the cost of the erection;
Which if we find outweighs ability,
What do we then, but draw anew the model
In fewer offices; or, at least, desist
To build at all?'

P. 136, III. iv. 4. In technical language, the σπουδαῖος is related to τἀληθὲς as the *causa cognoscendi*, not the *causa essendi*. Such a relation is similar to that claimed by the Vatican Council towards Papal Infallibility, as *declaring*, but not *constituting*, the Popes infallible.

P. 137, III. v. 1. As a further illustration of Plato's theory of the involuntary error of Vice, we might say that he regards a vicious choice as like that of a man who should take poison mistaking it for wholesome medicine. *At the time* he takes what he thinks is good for him, though it is in reality bad. He does not however choose it as such, and so he commits not a 'crime,' but a 'blunder,' which, in Plato's estimate at any rate, was better. Aristotle, in V. ix. 6, adopts language very similar to that of Plato, when he says οὔτε γὰρ βούλεται οὐθεὶς ὃ μὴ οἴεται εἶναι σπουδαῖον. So also in *Rhet.* I. x. 8.

P. 138, III. v. 4. οὐδεὶς ἑκὼν πονηρὸς, κ.τ.λ.] It should be noted that πονηρὸς has the double sense of 'wretched' and 'wicked' (compare 'cattivo' in Italian),—language, in this and many other words, reflecting the natural tendency to connect physical and moral imperfections. The former sense was doubtless intended by the unknown author of the line quoted in the text, as the antithesis with μάκαρ would show.

P. 139, III. v. 7-15. The general argument of these sections is that legislators never punish except for what is voluntary, and they are so careful about this as to follow up to their sources vicious acts, which might seem *prima facie* involuntary, and if they can trace them, however remotely, to an *avoidable* cause, they treat them as voluntary, and punish accordingly. So fully, therefore, do *mankind generally* hold the voluntariness of Vice, that we are treated as responsible not only for our immediate actions, but also for all the demonstrable and inevitable results of our actions, however little we may have contemplated those results. If we fire a train of gunpowder, we are responsible for the damage done at the other end, though it may be far beyond our reach.

P. 143, III. v. 17. ὃ παρ' ἑτέρου . . . εὐφυΐα] Compare *Poet.* c. xxii. § 9, μόνον γὰρ τοῦτο [τὸ μεταφορικὸν εἶναι] οὔτε παρ' ἄλλου ἔστι λαβεῖν, εὐφυΐας τε σημεῖόν ἐστιν.

P. 147, III. vi. 10. ὑπόγυια ὄντα] Lambinus translates, 'iis impendentibus atque instantibus quæ mortem afferunt.' The following illustrations are in favour of the interpretation 'handy,' or 'close at hand,' rather than 'sudden.' In *Pol.* VII. (VI.) viii. 3, Commerce is said to be ὑπογυιότατον πρὸς αὐτάρκειαν, the readiest or most handy means for securing independence. And *Rhet.* II. iii. 12, κεχρονικότες, καὶ μὴ ὑπόγυιοι τῇ ὀργῇ ὄντες· παύει γὰρ ὀργὴν ὁ χρόνος, where ὑπόγυιος means 'while they are still close at hand to the feeling of anger': 'quum non recentes ab ira sumus' (Muretus). [Compare τῷ παθεῖν ὅτι ἐγγυτάτω κείμενον, *Thuc.* III. xxxviii. 1.]

Twice in the *Rhet.* (I. i. 7, II. xxii. 11) the adverbial phrase ἐξ ὑπογυίου occurs = 'suddenly,' 'on the spur of the moment.' It seems probable that Aristotle would have employed it here if that had been the sense intended. His meaning seems rather to be that courage is exercised not only when death actually occurs, but also in dangers like those of war, when it appears imminent or close at hand, even if it be ultimately escaped. Thus a prisoner may be actually led out ὡς ἐπὶ θάνατον, or βάσανον, and even if he were released unhurt, might have displayed courage as genuine as if he had actually died. The passage will thus be very similar to that in *Rhet.* II. v. 2, where, after defining those things which are, strictly speaking, φοβερά, Aristotle adds, καὶ τὰ σημεῖα τῶν τοιούτων φοβερά· ἐγγὺς γὰρ φαίνεται τὸ φοβερόν· τοῦτο γάρ ἐστι κίνδυνος, φοβεροῦ πλησιασμός.

P. 148, III. vii. 1, 2. Compare *Macbeth,* Act I. Sc. vii.—

> 'I dare do all that may become a man;
> Who dares do more is none.'

P. 150, III. vii. 7, 8. Observe the two characteristics of the θρασὺς here indicated—(1) his excess of confidence (§ 7); (2) his desire to *display* his courage; he wishes 'to appear unto men' to be brave (§ 8). So also the βάναυσος in IV. ii. 20. With the words ἐν οἷς οὖν δύνανται μιμεῖται compare *Merchant of Venice*, Act III. Sc. ii.—

'There is no vice so simple but assumes
Some mark of virtue on his outward parts.
How many cowards, whose hearts are all as false
As stairs of sand, wear yet upon their chins
The beards of Hercules and frowning Mars,
Who inward searched, have livers white as milk;
And these assume but valour's excrement
To render them redoubted.'

P. 150, III. vii. 9. θρασύδειλοι] Another instance of this character on its comic side may be found in Sir Andrew Aguecheek in *Twelfth Night*. See especially Act III. Sc. iv., and his disposition as described in Act I. Sc. iii.—'He is a great quarreler, but that he hath the gift of a coward to allay the gust he hath in quarreling,' etc.

P. 151, III. vii. 13. Very similarly Sir T. Browne, *Rel. Med.* i. 44, writes,—'It is a brave act of valour to contemn death; but where life is more terrible than death, it is then the truest valour to dare to live.' We might compare with the opinion of Hadrian, quoted in the Notes, a well-known order of the day of Napoleon, in which he declared any Frenchman who committed suicide to be a deserter from the army. So in *Ethics* V. xi. 2, 3 the Suicide is described as τὴν πόλιν ἀδικῶν. In Hamlet's celebrated Soliloquy (Act III. Sc. i.) the question of Suicide is argued on grounds similar to those in the text, but with the different result that the possible future ills after death leave the balance in the cowardly calculation *against* suicide. Compare Claudio's conclusion in *Measure for Measure*, Act III. Sc. i.—'Ay, but to die,' etc.

P. 152, III. viii. 2. Shakespeare represents Ulysses as plying Achilles with a similar argument—*Troilus and Cressida*, Act III. Sc. iii.—

'But it must grieve young Pyrrhus now at home,
When fame shall in our islands sound her trump,
And all the Greekish girls shall tripping sing,—
"Great Hector's sister did Achilles win,
But our great Ajax bravely beat down him."'

(So a few lines below)—

'*Ach.* Shall Ajax fight with Hector?
Patr. Ay, and perhaps receive much honour by him.
Ach. I see my reputation is at stake.'

P. 153, III. viii. 5. Tacitus (*Hist.* iii. 18) notices the converse effect of *facility of retreat* in diminishing the courage of soldiers: 'Et propinqua Cremonensium mœnia, quanto plus spei ad effugium, tanto minorem ad resistendum animum, dabant.'

—— 6. κενὰ τοῦ πολέμου] Another illustration of this might be found in the strange and dazzling costumes adopted by the Samnites, in B.C. 308, to strike terror into the Romans. The Dictator Papirius Cursor forewarned his troops of the unreality of such a display, 'horridum militem esse debere . . . illa prædam verius quam arma esse,' etc.—(Livy ix. 40.)

P. 156, III. viii. 11. θυμοῦ ἐξελαυνόμενα . . προορῶντα] Compare Shakespeare, *Ant. and Cleop.* Act III. Sc. xiii.—

> 'To be furious
> Is to be frighted out of fear; and in that mood,
> The dove will peck the estridge; and I see still,
> A diminution in our captain's brain
> Restores his heart.'

—— 12. φυσικωτάτη, κ.τ.λ.] In reference to the comparative amount of the elements of θυμὸς and προαίρεσις in Courage, Professor Mahaffy (*Rambles in Greece*, p. 146) remarks that the ordinary Greek Courage involved more θυμὸς than accords with our notions, but that these again seem to allow more of that element than Aristotle's ideal of Courage. [See Introduction, p. xxxvi, etc., and note on ix. 4.] Greek generals, instead of advising coolness, specially incite to rage, ὀργῇ προσμίξωμεν, etc., as if a man not in this state would be sure to estimate the danger and run away.

P. 158, III. viii. 16. ἀξίωμα] In *Pol.* II. v. 25, οἱ μηδὲν ἀξίωμα κεκτημένοι ['peu jaloux de leur dignité' (St. Hilaire)] are opposed to θυμοειδεῖς καὶ πολεμικοὶ ἄνδρες. See *inf.* p. 234 *fin.*, on the advantage gained by even the χαῦνος in this respect.

P. 161, III. ix. 6. ἕτοιμοι γὰρ οὗτοι κ.τ.λ.] Like the 'Luculli miles in Horace *Ep.* II. ii. 26-40.

P. 162, III. x. 3. φιλομύθους καὶ διηγητικούς, κ.τ.λ.] This seems to be precisely the type of character assigned to the Athenians in Acts xvii. 21, 'who spend their time in nothing else but to hear and tell some new thing.'

P. 169, III. xii. 3. δόξειε δ' ἄν, κ.τ.λ.] The former of the cases mentioned in the note would, in fact, be exactly that of Falstaff in his well-known soliloquy on Honour, 1 *Henry IV.* Act v. Sc. 1; or again in Sc. 3 (*fin.*), 'Give me life: which if I can save, so; if not, honour comes unlooked for, and there's an end.'

P. 171, III. xii. 6. The absence of κόλασις, indicated by the word ἀκόλαστος, is expressed by the Latin 'improbus.' Compare with this passage I. iii. 7, where those who live κατὰ πάθος are described as children in character.

P. 182, IV. i. 30-32. A good illustration of this better type of ἄσωτος will be found in Timon of Athens, as depicted by Shakespeare in the first two Acts of the play. Compare especially with § 31 *fin.* Timon's reflection in Act II. Sc. ii.—

> 'No villainous bounty yet hath pass'd my heart;
> Unwisely, not ignobly, have I given.'

Dante also recognises two somewhat similar classes of Prodigals, whose moral turpitude he considers to be so different that he places those corresponding to Aristotle's better type (§ 31) in the fourth circle of Hell, but the latter in the seventh circle, ranking them, in fact, with the Suicides. Cf. δοκεῖ δ' ἀπώλειά τις αὐτοῦ εἶναι καὶ ἡ τῆς οὐσίας φθορὰ, ὡς τοῦ ζῆν διὰ τούτων ὄντος (§ 5). He also connects the Vice of the former with ἀκρασία, that of the latter with κακία (*Inf.* xi. 70, etc.)

P. 188, IV. ii. Μεγαλοπρέπεια. I am inclined now, on the whole, to prefer the translation 'Magnificence' for μεγαλοπρέπεια. That word is not, it is true, in our usage limited to the expenditure of money; but, on the other hand, it is not so restricted to the notion of mere amount as Munificence would seem to be. It is important to observe that the *conspicuousness* and *grandeur* of the expenditure and its occasion is the essential point of difference between μεγαλοπρέπεια and ἐλευθεριότης. Naturally, greatness of amount is an almost necessary accompaniment of such conditions. Still it is only *one* form of the grandeur implied in μεγαλοπρέπεια. Cf. οἷον μέγεθος (§ 10); also, διαφέρει τὸ ἐν τῷ ἔργῳ μέγα τοῦ ἐν τῷ δαπανήματι (§ 18). We see also in both the Excess and Defect that *display* and *showiness* are an essential element in this group of habits. The βάναυσος thinks *most* of the display, and that in reference to himself chiefly (§ 20). The μεγαλοπρεπὴς thinks worthily and adequately of the display, and not exclusively in reference to himself. (Contrast ἐμμελῶς in § 5 with λαμπρύνεται παρὰ μέλος in § 20. See also πῶς κάλλιστον καὶ πρεπωδέστατον, § 9, etc. etc.) The μικροπρεπὴς does not rise to a grand occasion at all. He is 'paltry' rather than merely 'sordid.' Note that he too is described as τὰ μέγιστα ἀναλώσας sometimes (which could scarcely be said of the 'Sordid' man), but that he wishes to make a display and keep his money too; and so ἐν μικρῷ τὸ καλὸν ἀπολεῖ (§ 21). He lacks that almost 'scientific instinct' (see §§ 5, 10) by

we may sometimes translate ψυχή 'soul,' sometimes 'mind,' sometimes perhaps 'vital principle.' It must always be borne in mind that the object of translation is not 'verbum verbo reddere,' but to convey to a modern hearer as far as possible the same ideas and impressions as the original would have produced in a contemporary.

ii. It would be an error to regard this work in the light of a modern treatise carefully written and revised by its author, put forth as the formal result of his labours in one special field of knowledge, and intended by him to occupy a definite position among his collected works. So far is this from being the case that the Nicomachean Ethics as they have come to us are generally thought to consist of fragments of two or more distinct treatises which were never intended to form parts of one whole. And more than this, they have sometimes been regarded as merely notes of different courses of oral lectures, taken down by one or more pupils, perhaps, and perhaps not, revised by Aristotle himself. We find (1) promises of subsequent discussion unfulfilled, or announced arrangements departed from[1]; (2) inconsistent theories or statements in different Books[2]; (3) confusion in the grouping of arguments or in the statement of single arguments[3]; (4) sometimes a series of arguments appears in a sort of skeleton form, as if they were merely heads or memoranda[4]; (5) sometimes arguments in support of a point from which the discussion has passed on, seem to be added like after-thoughts, just

[1] See II. vii. 16.

[2] This applies chiefly to other Books than I.-IV.

[3] As perhaps in I. viii. 10 etc., I. ix. 4.

[4] See II. iii., v.; III. ii.

P. 205, IV. iii. 25. τὰ μὲν ἡδέως ἀκούει τὰ δ' ἀηδῶς] Compare Shakespeare, *Ant. and Cleop.* Act III. Sc. i.—

> 'I have done enough : a lower place, note well,
> May make too great an act : for learn this, Silius,
> Better to leave undone, than by our deed
> Acquire too high a fame, when him we serve 's away.
> . . . .
> Who does i' the wars more than his captain can
> Becomes his captain's captain : and ambition,
> The soldier's virtue, rather makes choice of loss,
> Than gain, which darkens him.
> I could do more to do Antonius good,
> But 'twould offend him.'

διὸ καὶ τὴν Θέτιν] Mr. Monro of Oriel College has kindly sent me the following note on this passage:—

'The reference to the prayer of Thetis is, I think, correct. Aristotle is probably repeating an observation made by one of the earlier *grammatici*, the point being this:—In *Iliad* i. 394-407 Achilles advises Thetis to remind Jove of a great service she had done him, and which he tells at length. In the regular Homeric style the same story would be repeated in the prayer of Thetis, vv. 503-510, in place of which we only have the general form εἴποτε δή σε, κ.τ.λ. Thetis does not *relate* her services—οὐ λέγει τὰς εὐεργεσίας. This is just the sort of point which an ancient critic would notice, and I have no doubt that it had been noticed before Aristotle's time.'

Similarly in *Twelfth Night* (Act III. Sc. iv.) Antonio οὐ λέγει τὰς εὐεργεσίας to Sebastian, though compelled to hint at them—

> 'Is't possible that my deserts to you
> Can lack persuasion? Do not tempt my misery,
> Lest that it make me so unsound a man
> As to upbraid you with those kindnesses
> That I have done for you.'

P. 206, IV. iii. 27. ἀργὸν καὶ μελλητὴν, ἀλλ' ἢ ὅπου τιμὴ, κ.τ.λ.] Compare *Hamlet*, Act IV. Sc. iv.—

> 'Rightly to be great,
> Is not to stir without great argument,
> But greatly to find quarrel in a straw,
> When honour 's at the stake.'

—— 29. Καὶ πρὸς ἄλλον, κ.τ.λ.] Contrast this with the description of the ἄρεσκος in vi. 1. 9. He lives altogether πρὸς ἄλλον, and that, *ἄνευ πάθους καὶ τοῦ στέργειν οἷς ὁμιλεῖ* (*ib.* § 5). But if the *μεγαλόψυχος* does in any degree conform his words or actions to suit another, it will be for the sake of a friend.

P. 206, IV. iii. 30. *οὐδὲ μνησίκακος*] Compare *Coriolanus*, Act v. Sc. iii.—

> 'Thinkst thou it honourable for a noble man
> Still to remember wrongs?'

P. 207, *ib.* 31. *οὐδ' αὖ ἀνθρωπολόγος*] Contrast the *χαῦνος*, § 36 (*fin.*), *λέγουσι περὶ αὑτῶν*. Wordsworth's well-known four sonnets on 'Personal Talk' may also be referred to in illustration.

οὐδ' αὖ ἐπαινετικὸς] Compare what Thackeray says of Addison, 'He did not praise, because he measured his compeers by a higher standard than most people have.' Pope describes the same trait in Addison, 'Alike reserved to blame or to commend,' but with a cynical imputation. —(*Prologue to Satires*, l. 205.)

δι' ὕβριν] Compare the account of *ὕβρις*, given in *Rhet.* II. ii. 5, as being *τὸ βλάπτειν καὶ λυπεῖν ἐφ' οἷς αἰσχύνη ἐστὶ τῷ πάσχοντι, μὴ ἵνα τι γίγνηται αὐτῷ ἄλλο . . οἱ γὰρ ἀντιποιοῦντες οὐχ ὑβρίζουσιν ἀλλὰ τιμωροῦνται.* So (*ib.* § 4) *ἐπηρεασμὸς* (as resulting from *καταφρόνησις*) is *οὐχ ἵνα τι αὐτῷ, ἀλλ' ἵνα μὴ ἐκείνῳ.* The grotesque and sometimes coarsely comic treatment of his subject adopted by Dante in that part of Hell called Malebolge (where various types of fraud are punished) is an indication of his utter contempt for sinners of that class. He is *κακολόγος δι' ὕβριν*.

—— 33. *μᾶλλον τὰ καλὰ καὶ ἄκαρπα*] A constant demand for *utility* Aristotle would apparently regard as a mark of rank 'Philistinism.' Cf. *Pol.* V. (VIII.) iii. 12, *τὸ ζητεῖν πανταχοῦ τὸ χρήσιμον ἥκιστα ἁρμόττει τοῖς μεγαλοψύχοις καὶ ἐλευθέροις.*

—— 34. *κίνησις βραδεῖα . . . καὶ λέξις σ άσιμος*] So Malvolio in *Twelfth Night*, Act III. Sc. iv., proposes to assume 'a sad face, a reverend carriage, a slow tongue, in the habit of some sir of note.'

P. 208, IV. iii. 35. *ἑαυτὸν ἀποστερεῖ, κ.τ.λ.*] Compare Shakespeare, *Merchant of Venice*, Act II. Sc. vii.—

> 'And yet to be afeard of my deserving
> Were but a weak disabling of myself.'

Or again, *Henry V.* Act II. Sc. iv.—

> 'Self-love, my liege, is not so vile a sin
> As self-neglecting.'

So Dante on the demoralising effects of 'viltate' (μικροψυχία), *Inf.* ii. 45, etc. (Cary's translation),—

> 'Which oft
> So overcasts a man, that he recoils
> From noblest resolution, like a beast
> At some false semblance in the twilight gloom.'

And La Rochefoucauld similarly of 'faiblesse:'—'La faiblesse est le seul défaut que l'on ne saurait corriger' (*Max.* 130). 'La faiblesse est plus opposée à la vertu que le vice' (*Max.* 445).

P. 208, IV. iii. 35. ὠρέγετο γὰρ, κ.τ.λ.] The more so perhaps as Aristotle (*Rhet.* II. xiii. 9) states that a too great regard for self is a mark of μικροψυχία—μικροψυχία γάρ τις καὶ αὕτη [sc. ἡ λίαν φιλαυτία].

P. 213, IV. v. 3. With this definition of πραότης compare Dante's conception of it as being 'not so much unresisting gentleness to evil as the righteous indignation which repels it *without any feeling of personal irritation.*'—(M. F. Rossetti.) [See Supplementary Note on IV. iii. 31.] So in the *Convito* (iv. 17) he gives as a description of the πραότης of Aristotle, 'The Virtue which moderates our anger and our too great patience against our external ills.' If we look only at the former aspect of it (see § 6, *fin.*), the πρᾶος might degenerate to Hamlet's description (Act II. Sc. ii.), and become

> 'Pigeon-livered and lack gall,
> To make oppression bitter.'

Further, Dante punishes this vice of defect (Accidia) in the same Circle with the vice of Excess (Iracundia). These habits are distinguished from νέμεσις with its related vices, in that the former involve the notion of *personal* injury (including that of friends, ὁ γὰρ φίλος ἕτερος αὐτός); also that they include what Bishop Butler calls 'harm' as well as injury. See also Supplementary Note on II. vii. 15.

P. 214, IV. v. 8. παύονται δὲ ταχέως] Cf. Shakespeare, *Henry VIII.* Act I. Sc. i.—

> 'Anger is like
> A full-hot horse, who being allowed his way
> Self-mettle tires him.'

ἢ φανεροί εἰσι] Cf. VII. vi. 3, ὁ θυμώδης οὐκ ἐπίβουλος, . . . ἀλλὰ φανερός.

—— 8, 9] The first two classes here mentioned resemble the 'passionate' and the 'peevish' of Bishop Butler's eighth Sermon (p. 440, ed. Angus):—'As to the abuses of Anger, which, it is to be observed, may be in all different degrees (ἡ ὑπερβολὴ κατὰ πάντα μὲν γίνεται, § 7), the first which occurs is what is commonly called passion. . . . This distemper of the mind seizes men upon the least occasion in the world, and perpetually without any reason at all, and by means of it they are plainly every day, every waking hour of their lives, in danger of running into the most extravagant outrages (§ 8). Of a less boisterous but not of a less innocent kind is peevishness (cf. *οἱ ἀκρόχολοι ὀξεῖς*), which I mention with real pity for the unhappy creatures who . . . are obliged to be in the way of it (cf. *τοῖς μάλιστα φίλοις*, § 10). That which, in a more feeble temper, is peevishness, and languidly discharges itself upon everything which comes in its way (*πρὸς πᾶν ὀργίλοι καὶ ἐπὶ παντί*), the same principle in a temper of greater force and stronger passions becomes rage and fury.'

P. 217, IV. vi. 2. *δύσκολος*] Equivalent to *difficilis* in Horace's description of Old Age, *A. P.* 173. Conversely, Dante mentions 'Affability' (by which word he translates Aristotle's *φιλία*) as one of the four Virtues peculiarly appropriate to Old Age (*Conv.* iv. 27).

P. 220, IV. vi. 8, *fin.* With this characteristic of *φιλία* compare 'Let the righteous rather smite me *friendly*, and reprove me' (Ps. cxli. 5). Also Shakespeare, *Two Gentlemen of Verona*, Act III. Sc. i.—

> 'Thus for my duty's sake, I rather choose
> To cross my friend in his intended drift,
> Than, by concealing it, heap on your head
> A pack of sorrows,' etc.

IV. vi. 9. (As another illustration of the habits of the *κόλαξ*)—Swift in his Journal to Stella writes: 'Did I ever tell you that the Lord Treasurer hears ill with the left ear, just as I do? I dare not tell him that I am so, for fear he should think that I counterfeited to make my court.' A striking, though exaggerated, illustration of the Churl (*ὁ πᾶσι δυσχεραίνων*) may be found in Apemantus (*Timon of Athens*), who stands in vivid contrast with the herd of *κόλακες* who surround Timon in his prosperity.

P. 222, IV. vii. 5. *ἐὰν μή τινος ἕνεκα πράττῃ*] Some special motive may intervene as a disturbing force, and then the resulting act may not be a true index of general character, of what the man is *ἐν βίῳ τελείῳ*. *e.g.* one who is *δύσερις καὶ δύσκολος* by nature, may occasionally be transformed by self-interest into a *κόλαξ*.

P. 223, IV. vii. 7. *Οὐ γὰρ περὶ τοῦ ἐν ταῖς ὁμολογίαις, κ.τ.λ.*] Hence one 'who sweareth to his neighbour and disappointeth him not, though it were to his own hindrance,' would be classed as *δίκαιος* rather than *ἀληθής*.

ἐν οἷς . . . ἀληθεύει] There is an abrupt change of construction here from ἀλλὰ περὶ τοῦ ἐν οἷς μηθὲν διαφέρει . . . ἀληθεύοντος, which the former clause would have led us to expect.

P. 223, IV. vii. 8. ἔτι μᾶλλον] The mercenary, interested, or malicious lie is worse than the lie simple, just as κόλαξ is worse than ἄρεσκος, or the ἀλαζὼν ἀργυρίου ἕνεκα of § 11 is worse than the ἀλαζὼν of § 10. In the former case there would be falsehood and injustice as well.

—— 11. The parenthetical use of ὁ ἀλαζὼν, if that reading be adopted, is exactly parallel to that of ὁ ἐγκρατὴς in VII. ix. 2.

—— 12. οὐκ ἐν τῇ δυνάμει, κ.τ.λ.] The interpretation given in the Notes is confirmed by the use of the same phrase in *Rhet.* I. i. 14, to distinguish the Sophist from the Dialectician; the essence of the former being the *conscious* use of a fallacious argument against an opponent not likely to detect it (*argumentum ad ignorantiam*). The *motive*, or 'particular condition of the Will' (Grant), is the important point. Compare also the statement in VII. x. 2, that φρόνησις differs from δεινότης (mere cleverness or shrewdness), κατὰ τὴν προαίρεσιν. So in V. ii. 4, Aristotle observes that one who commits adultery τοῦ κερδαίνειν ἕνεκα, would not be called ἀκόλαστος, but ἄδικος or πλεονέκτης. The difference of purpose (προαίρεσις) in that case, as in the case in the text, quite alters the moral character of the act. Cf. VIII. xiii. 11, and see Glossary.

P. 225, IV. vii. 13. ἐν αὐτοῖς τὰ εἰρημένα] ἐν αὐτοῖς refers to τὰ τοιαῦτα, and τὰ εἰρημένα are the qualities of being profitable, and of being easily assumed without detection.

—— 14. μάλιστα δὲ καὶ οὗτοι] The καὶ is explained by a reference to § 2, where τὰ ἔνδοξα were stated to be the sphere of ἀλαζονεία also.

P. 226, IV. vii. 15. καὶ ἡ λίαν ἔλλειψις ἀλαζονικὸν] Repudiating for oneself μικρὰ καὶ φανερὰ at once suggests, and is of course intended to suggest, a '*par exemple!*' on the part of others, and so amounts to 'fishing for compliments.' Dickens has familiarised us with types of this character in Pecksniff and Uriah Heep. In fact, this baser type of εἰρωνεία approaches most nearly in Aristotle's catalogue to the modern vice of Hypocrisy, and only needs the condition of being exercised in a moral or religious sphere to make it identical with it. The following illustrations may be added:—When Diogenes, treading on Plato's carpet, is said to have exclaimed, 'I am treading on Plato's vanity,' the latter replied, 'Yes, and with a different vanity of your own.' So S. Augustine, 'Vainglory often glories most vainly of the very contempt of vainglory.' Congreve has indicated a more harmless type of the same disposition—

'Careless she is with artful care,
Affecting to seem unaffected.'

La Rochefoucauld attributes to human nature generally this characteristic of βαυκοπανουργία—'On ne se blâme que pour être loué' (*Max.* 33).

P. 227, IV. viii. 3. εὔτροποι] This quickness of intellectual movement in the εὐτράπελος stands in contrast with the afterthought-wit so happily described in the French phrase, 'l'esprit de l'escalier;' and it is similar in kind to the power of employing metaphor (τὸ γὰρ εὖ μεταφέρειν τὸ τὸ ὅμοιον θεωρεῖν ἐστίν), stated by Aristotle (*Poet.* xxii. § 9) to be a mark of genius.

P. 228, IV. viii. 6. τῶν καινῶν] This expression (as in the *Poetics*) does not refer to what is technically known as the 'New,' but the 'Middle' Comedy. The 'New' had not yet arisen. (See Donaldson, *Theatre of the Greeks*, sixth ed., pp. 63, etc.)

πρὸς εὐσχημοσύνην] It does not, however, therefore follow that the latter method has the advantage from the point of view of morality. It is quite possible to maintain the reverse. Speaking of Shakespeare's occasional αἰσχρολογία, Coleridge writes:—'It may sometimes be gross, but I boldly say that he is always moral and modest. (?) In our day, decency of manners (εὐσχημοσύνη) is preserved at the expense of morality of heart, and delicacies for vice are allowed (ὑπόνοια), whilst grossness against it is hypocritically, or at least morbidly, condemned.'

—— 7. τὸν εὖ σκώπτοντα] Compare with this expression the definition of εὐτραπελία in *Rhet.* II. xii. 16, as πεπαιδευμένη ὕβρις.

P. 229, IV. viii. 9. ἔδει δ' ἴσως καὶ σκώπτειν] Juvenal (iii. 153) regards liability to ridicule as the hardest part of the lot of poverty; and La Rochefoucauld remarks, 'Le ridicule déshonore plus que le déshonneur' (*Max.* 326).

—— 10. πᾶσι δυσχεραίνει] Compare *Merchant of Venice*, Act I. Sc. i.—

> 'And other of such vinegar aspect
> That they'll not show their teeth in way of smile,
> Though Nestor swear the jest be laughable.'

P. 240 (Introductory Note to Book x.) The same distinction, derived doubtless from Aristotle, between the Active and the Contemplative Life, constantly reappears in Mediæval writers. With Dante especially it is a favourite subject. He symbolises the antithesis in the *Commedia* by Leah and Rachel, and also (in a somewhat different aspect) by Matilda and Beatrice, and in the *Convito* by Martha and Mary. The following passage especially may be quoted in illustration,—'In truth it should be known that we can have in this life two kinds of Happiness, according as we follow two different good and excellent paths which lead us thither;

the one is the Active Life and the other the Contemplative. The latter (though by the Active we arrive, as has been said, at true Happiness) leads us to the highest Happiness and Felicity [compare *εὐδαίμων* and *μακάριος* in I. x. 14], as the Philosopher proves in the tenth Book of the Ethics.'—*Convito*, iv. 17.

P. 243, X. vi. 3. *τῶν παιδιῶν αἱ ἡδεῖαι*] Such recreations as are suggested in the Note would fall under the head of *συμφέροντα* rather than *ἡδέα* (see II. iii. 7). A higher class still might deserve the title of *καλὰ* (see VII. iv. 5), and such the *σπουδαῖος* would take pleasure in (§ 5), since he, like all men, needs *ἀνάπαυσις* (§ 6). To such Aristotle would rather apply the term *διαγωγή* [cf. *Pol.* V. (VIII.) v. 10, *τὴν διαγωγὴν ὁμολογουμένως δεῖ μὴ μόνον ἔχειν τὸ καλὸν ἀλλὰ καὶ τὴν ἡδονήν*], and he would consider Music as fulfilling such a condition. The whole passage in *Pol.* V. (VIII.) v. 10-13, should be compared where Aristotle again explains why *παιδιὰ* is often thought to be *τέλος*, and why it is not really so.

P. 246, X. vi. 6. *οὐ δὴ τέλος ἡ ἀνάπαυσις*] Cf. *Pol.* V. (VIII.) v. 10, *ἡ γὰρ παιδιὰ χάριν ἀναπαύσεώς ἐστι . . . [ἡ δ' ἀνάπαυσις] τῆς διὰ τῶν πόνων λύπης ἰατρεία τίς ἐστιν.*

P. 253, X. vii. 8. Οὐ *χρὴ κατὰ, κ.τ.λ.*] This standard of Happiness, though superhuman (*κρείττων ἢ κατ' ἄνθρωπον*), is still human, in the same way that the Christian standard of moral perfection is a true standard to set before men, even though the highest human efforts can never be otherwise than an asymptote in reference to it.

P. 255, X. viii. 3. *συνέζευκται δὲ καὶ ἡ φρόνησις, κ.τ.λ.*] Hence the *ἀκρατὴς* cannot be *φρόνιμος*, though he may be *δεινὸς*, see VII. x. 1. Also in VI. xiii. 6 we read, *οὐχ οἷόν τε ἀγαθὸν εἶναι κυρίως ἄνευ φρονήσεως, οὐδὲ φρόνιμον ἄνευ τῆς ἠθικῆς ἀρετῆς*, and in VII. ii. 5, *πρακτικός γε ὁ φρόνιμος.*

P. 256, X. viii. 4. *αἱ γὰρ βουλήσεις ἄδηλοι, κ.τ.λ.*] Compare *Measure for Measure*, Act I. Sc. i.—

> 'For if our virtues
> Did not go forth of us, 'twere all alike
> As if we had them not.'

—— 5. The dispute as to the relative importance of intention or act, 'will' or 'deed,' in Morals, twice referred to by Aristotle, may remind us of the later theological controversy respecting the rival claims of Faith and Works.

P. 261, X. viii. 11. *κρίνουσι τοῖς ἐκτὸς τούτων αἰσθανόμενοι μόνον*] Compare *Merchant of Venice*, Act II. Sc. ix.—

> 'What many men desire! that "many" may be meant
> By the fool multitude, that choose by show,
> Not learning more than the fond eye doth teach;
> Which pries not to the interior.'

—— 13. *εἰ γάρ τις ἐπιμέλεια, κ.τ.λ.*] Compare Addison, *Cato*, Act V. Sc. i.—

> 'If there 's a power above us
> (And that there is all nature cries aloud
> Through all her works), he must delight in virtue,
> And that which he delights in must be happy.'

The following scheme will show at a glance the connection of Ch. vi.-viii.

- *ἐνέργειαι*
  - desired for their results. Happiness *not* this, c. vi. § 2.
  - desired for themselves.
    - *παιδιά.* Happiness *not* this, c. vi. §§ 3-8.
    - *ἐνέργειαι κατ' ἀρετήν.*
      - *ἠθικήν.* Happiness *not* this, c. viii.
      - *θεωρητικήν.* Happiness *is* this, c. vii.

[*The occasion of a Fourth Edition being called for induces me to add a few more 'Supplementary Notes and Illustrations,' some of which, it is hoped, may be interesting to more advanced students than those for whom the footnotes generally are intended.*]

P. 38, B. I. viii. 1. In illustration of this use of ὑπάρχοντα, compare *Poet.* xxii. 2, where 'a riddle' is defined, τὸ λέγοντα ὑπάρχοντα ἀδύνατα συνάψαι, *i.e.* 'while describing *actual facts* to make an impossible combination.'

P. 66, B. I. xiii. 15. ἀλλή τις φύσις τῆς ψυχῆς] A good account of Aristotle's theory of the three 'φύσεις τῆς ψυχῆς' in contrast with the view of Plato of three souls in one body (see Dante, *Purg.* iv. 5, 6), will be found in Grote's Aristotle, II. pp. 191-6, 221, etc. The varieties of soul are not mutually exclusive species of the same genus, but successive types of development, the higher types possessing all the properties of the lower, *plus* others of their own.

Pp. 104, 281-2. αἰδὼς and νέμεσις] We might add to the illustrations above given the Homeric conception of αἰδὼς and νέμεσις. 'If a man breaks θέμις in any way, he feels that others will disapprove. This feeling is called αἰδώς. Hence αἰδὼς has as many shades of meaning as there are ways in which θέμις can be broken:—"sense of honour," "shame," "reverence," etc. And the feeling with which he himself regards a breach of θέμις by another person is called νέμεσις,—"righteous indignation."' (Jebb's Introduction to Homer, p. 55.)

Pp. 119, 283, III. i. 13. Add the following illustration from Cic. *Phil.* II. xii. § 29: 'Quid refert utrum voluerim fieri, an gaudeam factum?'

P. 146, III. vi. 5. οὐδ' εἰ θαρρεῖ μέλλων μαστιγοῦσθαι ἀνδρεῖος] This is well illustrated by the following remarks of Fuller (*Holy War*, v. c. 2) in reference to many of the Templars having succumbed to torture. 'It is to be commended to one's consideration whether slavish and servile souls will not better bear torment than generous spirits, who are for the enduring of honourable danger and speedy death, but not provided for torment, which they are not acquainted with, neither is it the proper object of valour.' Comp. *inf.* c. ix. § 6.

P. 151, III. vii. 12. Add to the illustrations in the note the graphic contrast drawn by Livy (vii. 10) between the Gaul and Torquatus before engaging in single combat. He says of the latter, 'pectus animorum iraeque tacitae plenum, omnem ferociam in discrimen ipsum certaminis distulerat.' Conversely, Tacitus ascribes both to the Gauls and Britons the habit censured by Aristotle in the text: 'in deposcendis periculis eadem audacia, et ubi advenere, in detractandis eadem formido.' (*Agricola*, c. xi.)

Pp. 152-3, III. viii. 2, 3. In the following passage Dante recognises this form of courage due to αἰδὼς:

> But shame soon interposed her threat, who makes
> The servant bold in presence of his lord.
>
> *Inf.* xvii. 89, 90. (Cary's *Translation.*)

P. 176, IV. i. 11. τῶν ἀπ' ἀρετῆς] We may compare with this periphrasis the following expressions in the Epistle to the Romans: οἱ ἐξ ἐριθείας (ii. 8), οἱ ἐκ περιτομῆς (iv. 12), οἱ ἐκ νόμου (iv. 14).

Pp. 205, 291, IV. iii. 25. Compare further Tac. *Ann.* v. 18 (*fin.*): 'Nam beneficia eo usque laeta sunt dum videntur exsolvi posse: ubi multum antevenere, pro gratia odium redditur': which is thus commented on by Oldbuck in Scott's *Antiquary*: 'from this a wise man may take a caution not to oblige any man beyond the degree in which he may expect to be requited, lest he should make his debtor a bankrupt in gratitude.' In *Germ.* xxi. (*fin.*) Tacitus mentions as a proof of the generosity of the German barbarians, 'nec data imputant, nec acceptis obligantur.'

P. 206, IV. iii. 28. εἴρωνα δὲ πρὸς τοὺς πολλοὺς] Most MSS. read εἰρωνεία (*auct.* Grant) which certainly avoids the great difficulty of finding any construction for the accusative εἴρωνα.

P. 214, IV. v. 8. ἀνταποδιδόασιν κ.τ.λ.] Thus Cleon (*ap.* Thucyd. III. xxxviii. 1) remarks that summary vengeance is always most effective and satisfactory; and conversely (in illustration of § 10) Tacitus says of Domitian (*Agricola*, c. 42) that he was 'praeceps in iram, et *quo obscurior eo irrevocabilior.*'